THE MARRIAGE OF
LIKENESS

THE
MARRIAGE OF
LIKENESS

SAME-SEX UNIONS
IN PRE-MODERN EUROPE

John Boswell

HarperCollinsPublishers

HarperCollins*Publishers*
77–85 Fulham Palace Road,
Hammersmith, London W6 8JB

Published by HarperCollins*Publishers* 1995
1   3   5   7   9   8   6   4   2

First published in the USA by
Villard Books, a division of Random House, Inc., 1994

Copyright © John Boswell 1994

John Boswell asserts the moral right to
be identified as the author of this work

A catalogue record for this book is
available from the British Library

ISBN 0 00 255508 5

Set in Goudy

Printed in Great Britain by
HarperCollinsManufacturing Glasgow

This book is dedicated
with gratitude and affection to
James Meehan,
without whom
it would not have been completed.
And with sadness to
Mac and David,
and all the others
who did not live
to see it finished.

PREFACE

*T*HIS BOOK HAS TAKEN much longer to write than I expected it would when I began it twelve years ago. It was undertaken as the result of a notice about a ceremony of same-sex union sent to me by a correspondent who prefers not to be named. I thank him heartily now without disclosing his identity. In the meantime, many professional obligations (being chair of several departments, including the largest one, at the university where I teach), completing another book that already languished on my desk,[1] the deaths of many close friends from AIDS, and several major computer disasters have all steadily impeded my progress and prevented completion of the book I had intended to finish at least five years ago.

The unnamed correspondent brought to my attention a version of the ceremony published in Jacques Goar's *Euchologion*,[2] for which there was no adequate bibliographical help or manuscript identification. To track down manuscript versions, I began at the western end of Europe (the British Library) and worked my way east, summer by summer, library by library. It took me several years to come across manuscript versions of the ceremony (I found none in the British Library), and the first ones I encountered could have been viewed as ceremonies solemnizing special friendships.[3] At first I felt discouraged by this, and decided that Goar had misinterpreted or misrepresented Italian documents he had seen; it was not until years later that I

---

[1] *The Kindness of Strangers: The Abandonment of Children in Western Europe from Late Antiquity to the Renaissance* (New York, 1988).
[2] See discussion of this ersatz version on p. 185, n. 124.
[3] These are the Paris manuscripts, so identified in the list of manuscripts on pp. 372–74. Two of them are published in the Appendix of Documents (Nos. 2 and 3) and translated in the Appendix of Translations as Nos. 5 and 8.

discovered he had in fact done so, but in a direction opposite to the one I had first suspected.

The next summer when I got to Italy I discovered many versions of the ceremony that were obviously the same-sex equivalent of a medieval heterosexual marriage ceremony (though not necessarily a precise equivalent of its modern descendants). Only then did it occur to me how remarkable it was that there should *not* have been a ceremony solemnizing or hallowing friendship in the religion of the teacher who described friendship as the highest love.[4] In retrospect, and considering how much distortion and censorship of the ceremony I have discovered, I wonder if the Paris versions represent simplified (or even bowdlerized) medieval versions of the ceremony of union. In any event, I publish them here so that readers can judge for themselves.

Over the years, I have often spoken publicly about the ceremony and its ramifications. I now doubt that this was a wise decision, but at the time I felt an obligation to share information about the discovery. At least one of these addresses was published; several were videotaped and sold or distributed without my authorization. This is particularly unfortunate because over the decade I have been assembling the material, my opinions on various aspects of it have evolved and changed, as is inevitably the case in any long scholarly project. Many people may have been misled in minor ways by what I said at earlier stages of my research, since these informal presentations on work in progress were widely disseminated and quoted.

Possibly as a result of these developments, a number of critics have offered critiques of or disagreements with a work that did not yet exist. Such comments are to informed criticism and disagreement what the modern American vulgarism "preboarding" is to boarding a plane. No one could possibly have known what would be said in this study, even by paying close attention to lectures or videotapes of the work as it developed.

Over the dozen years I have worked on the project I have amassed an enormous debt to many individuals, only a few of whom I will remember to thank. First and foremost, I am forever indebted to James Meehan, whose timely intervention rescued the project at

---

[4] Discussed on p. 194.

many junctures where, without his cheerful and unstinting assistance, I would have abandoned it. This help involved not only his laboriously transferring the contents of disks from one operating system to another during several computer disasters, but even making long trips to photograph manuscripts I needed to consult but could not see myself. In an equally practical way Elizabeth Archibald provided assistance of the most direct kind while I was conducting research in Italy, Jerone Hart offered practical support of crucial kinds in the United States, and John S. Morgan has faithfully contributed for years to the research expenses for the project. For pointers, bits of information, or advice about how to translate I am grateful to Geoffrey Block, Marie Boroff, Paul Bushkovitch, David Cohen, Ljerka Debush, Katherine Dittmar, Harvey Goldblatt, Jeri Guthrie, Peter Hawkins, Thomas Head, Michael Jones, Diana Kleiner, Matthew Kuefler, E. Litsas, Harry Magoulias, Kathryn Miller, Bruce O'Brien, Dennis O'Neal, Jaroslav Pelikan, Zlatko Plese, Alexander Schenker, and, above all, to Ralph Hexter, on whom I have always relied as my most attentive and helpful critic, and who has rendered timely and generous assistance at every stage of the writing. In the end, of course, responsibility for everything said in the pages that follow is mine alone.

CONTENTS

Appendices

LIST OF ABBREVIATIONS

[ ]: Indicates that the work in question has traditionally been attributed to the name in brackets, but is now thought to have been composed by someone else (e.g., [Lucian,] *Affairs of the Heart* refers to a work once thought to have been written by Lucian, but no longer).

AB: *Analecta Bollandiana* (Brussels, 1882–).

ANRW: *Aufstieg und Niedergang der römischen Welt*, ed. H. Temporini (Berlin and New York, 1972–).

B.C.E.: Before Christian Era (in earlier writings, B.C.).

CCSL: *Corpus Christianorum . . . series latina* (Turnhout, 1953–).

C.E.: Christian Era (in earlier writings, A.D.).

CIL: *Corpus inscriptionum latinarum* (Berlin, 1863–).

CSEL: *Corpus scriptorum ecclesiasticorum latinorum . . .* (Vienna, 1866–).

CSTH: John Boswell, *Christianity, Social Tolerance, and Homosexuality: Gay People in Western Europe from the Beginning of the Christian Era to the Fourteenth Century* (Chicago, 1980).

Dmitrievskij: Alexei Dmitrievskij, Описание литургическихъ рукописей [*Opisanie Liturgicheskix Rukopisei*], 2: Εὐχολόγια (Kiev, 1901).

EL: *Ephemerides Liturgicae* (Rome, 1887–).

Jastrow: Marcus Jastrow, ספר מלים (*A Dictionary of the Targumim, the Talmud Babli and Yerushalmi, and the Midrashic Literature*) (Brooklyn, 1903).

JPS Tanakh: *Tanakh—The Holy Scriptures: The New Jewish Publication Society Translation according to the Traditional Hebrew Text* (New York, 5748/1988).

KJV: King James or Authorized Version of the Bible (1611).

LCL: *Loeb Classical Library* (Cambridge, Mass., and London).

Lampe: *A Patristic Greek Lexicon*, ed. G. W. H. Lampe (Oxford, 1961).

LSJ: A Greek-English Dictionary, eds. H. G. Liddell, R. Scott, H. S. Jones, and R. McKenzie, 9th ed., with Supplement (Oxford, 1968).

LXX: Septuagint (Greek version of the Jewish Scripture); many books not contained in Protestant versions occur in the LXX and are retained in modern Roman Catholic translations, which rely on the LXX; where the numberings (of books or verses) differ, the KJV numbers are given first and LXX variants provided in square brackets.

Mansi: Mansi, J. D., and P. Labbeå, *Sacrorum conciliorum nova et amplissima collectio* (Florence, 1759–1927).

Matrimonio: Il Matrimonio nella società altomedievale (Settimane di studio del centro italiano di studi sull'alto medioevo, xxiv, 22–28, aprile 1976) (Spoleto, 1977).

MGH: Monumenta Germaniae historica (Hanover, 1826–).

    Epp.: Epistolae

    Legum: Leges

    SS: Scriptores.

    SSRRGG: Scriptores rerum germanicarum in usum scholarum.

    SSRRLL: Scriptores rerum langobardarum.

    SSRRMM: Scriptores rerum merovingicarum.

OCD: The Oxford Classical Dictionary, 2nd ed., eds. N. G. L. Hammond and H. H. Scullard (Oxford, 1970).

OCS: Old Church Slavonic.

ODB: The Oxford Dictionary of Byzantium, ed. Alexander Kazhdan et al. (New York, 1991).

OED: The Oxford English Dictionary (Oxford, 1971).

OLD: The Oxford Latin Dictionary, ed. P. G. W. Glare (Oxford, 1982).

PG: Patrologiae cursus completus. Series graeca, ed. J. P. Migne (Paris, 1857–76).

PL: Patrologiae cursus completus. Series latina, ed. J. P. Migne (Paris, 1841–64).

PO: Patrologia Orientalis (Paris, 1904–).

PWRE: Paulys Realencyclopädie der classischen Altertumswissenschaft, ed. G. Wissowa (Stuttgart, 1894–1963).

RP: Rhalles, G. A., and M. Potles, Σύνταγμα τῶν θείων καὶ ἦερῶν κανόνων. 6 vols. (Athens, 1852–59).

Williams: Williams, Craig, "Homosexuality and the Roman Man: A Study in the Cultural Construction of Sexuality," Ph.D. Dissertation, Yale University, 1992. Note: there is also a Williams cited in Chapters 2, 5, and

6 (Gordon Williams, "Some Aspects of Roman Marriage Ceremonies and Ideals," *Journal of Roman Studies* 48 [1958] 16–29). The two should not be confused. The latter is usually cited with title as well.

Zepos: J. and P. Zepos, eds., *Jus Graeco-Romanum* (Athens, 1931).

1: *Novellae et aureae bullae imperatorum post Justinianum,* ed. C. E. Zachariae von Lingenthal.

4: *Practica ex Actis Eustathii Romani* [Πεῖρα Εὐσταθίου τοῦ Ῥωμαίου], ed. C. E. Zachariae von Lingenthal.

INTRODUCTION

*T*HREE PECULIAR FEATURES of the psychological landscape of the modern West particularly influence any modern reader's understanding and perception of romantic love and coupling patterns (for either or both genders) in ancient societies. The first is the virtual obsession of modern industrial culture with this subject. To an observer of the modern West's cultural monuments it would probably seem that romantic love was the *primary interest* of industrial society in the nineteenth and twentieth centuries. An overwhelming proportion of popular literature, popular art, and popular music have as their central focus the seeking out, celebration of, or lament over romantic love, which is surprising and noteworthy considering that the vast majority of the population to which these cultural messages are directed is either already married or too old or young to be involved in such pursuits. Those immersed in this "sea of love"[1] tend to take it for granted; even many scholars of the subject fail to notice how remarkable is the degree of its prominence in the cultures in which they grew up. Very few premodern or nonindustrialized contemporary cultures would agree with the contention—uncontroversial in the West—that "the purpose of a man is to love a woman, and the purpose of a woman is to love a man."[2] Most human beings in most times and places would find this a very meager measure of human value.

In other cultures and in premodern Western societies other subjects have formed the primary material of public culture: celebration of heroic figures or events; reflections on the seasons; observations on

---

[1] From a No. 1 American song of 1959, "Sea of Love," recorded by Lou Phillips.
[2] Also from a No. 1 American song, "The Game of Love," recorded by Wayne Fontana in 1965.

the success, failure, or precariousness of agricultural cycles; histories of families (in which romantic love plays a small role, if any); explorations or elaborations of religious or political traditions. Of the West itself, it would probably be fair to say that philosophical, military, and religious literature make up the vast majority of what survives from nearly all societies except Augustan Rome, twelfth- and thirteenth-century Europe, and the last two centuries. So few writers take note of this oddity that there are no theories to explain it, but it must be clearly recognized as a profound disjunction between our society and most others—including nearly all those assessed in this study.

A second peculiarity is the almost universal expectation that romantic love and marriage are inextricable, causally interrelated, and largely coterminous. In very few human societies do similar assumptions prevail, and this pairing was not common even in earlier European cultures, as will be seen presently. The distortion occasioned by the deliberate and emphatic coupling in the popular imagination of romantic love and marriage is much greater than may be immediately apparent: it is not simply an error to suppose that in most other societies people married for love; it is a serious misprision to imagine that they would have even *accepted* a correlation between the two. Although the medieval dictum that "to love one's wife with one's emotions is adultery"[3] represents an ascetic extreme (and not a description of ordinary experience), it does reflect, accurately, an understanding of the meaning and purpose of marriage profoundly different from its modern counterparts.

Nor was the *longue durée* of Judeo-Christian matrimonial tradition anywhere near consistent.[4] In the twentieth century, many Christians who would rabidly insist on this or that aspect of "moral matrimony" (e.g., procreative purpose in the view of the Roman Catholic hierarchy—but probably not the average Catholic layperson; sexual fidelity for most Protestants) casually accept the fact that Solomon was "married" to seven hundred women while he also maintained three hundred concubines.[5] Although they would doubtless not approve if one

---

[3] For sources of this, see pp. 118ff.

[4] On matrimony and its variations in the Bible, see Claire Gottlieb, "Varieties of Marriage in the Bible: [sic] and their Analogues in the Ancient World" (Ph.D. diss., New York University, 1989).

[5] For the meaning of "concubine," see Chapter 2, p. 30. On Solomon's marital arrangements,

of their contemporaries engaged in such behavior, they have little trouble applying the term "marriage" to such relationships. Aside from the moral questions this episode raises,[6] it throws the deeper meaning of "marriage" in a historical context into lively uncertainty. What did it *mean* to be one of seven hundred women "married" to Solomon, who also had three hundred concubines? How much of a commitment could there have been on either side? Indeed, how often could the one thousand women who belonged[7] to the king through marriage or concubinage even have had casual intercourse (social or sexual) with him?

For most of its history Roman Catholicism has insisted through the writings of its theologians that procreative purpose is the sole legitimation of sexual union between husband and wife, even though many prominent figures in Judeo-Christian history were regarded by their contemporaries (and the church) as married when their marriage was obviously not procreative: e.g., Elkanah and Hannah, Zacharias and Elizabeth—both of which were (and are) regarded as legitimately married couples even when they had no children at all[8]—as well as Joseph and Mary, whose marriage the same theologians have insisted was never consummated at all.[9] Ordinary marriages in imitation of this, in which the couple did not engage in sexual relations but were still regarded as a married couple, were widely known in Roman Catholic Europe. (This topic is discussed further in Chapter 4.)

In premodern Europe marriage usually began as a property arrangement, was in its middle mostly about raising children, and ended about love. Few couples in fact married "for love," but many grew to love each other in time as they jointly managed their household, reared their offspring, and shared life's experiences. Nearly all surviv-

---

see 1 Kings 11:3, where these numbers are given explicitly. The text itself seems to disapprove, since the chapter begins "But king Solomon loved many strange women . . ."

6. These are attenuated perhaps by the fact that the prohibition of polygamy presumably postdated this; but the prohibition was never divinely revealed either to Jews or Christians, which also might raise a variety of questions, but never seems to.

7. Although this usage appears somewhat sexist, it seems to me to reflect accurately the historical reality, which was also sexist.

8. For the first, see 1 Sam. 1. Elkanah also had two wives: this aspect of the general problem of matrimony is addressed above, and in Chapters 3 and 4. For the second pair, see Luke 1.

9. Although controversial in the early church, once the formula "ever-virgin Mary" had been incorporated in the Greek and Roman liturgies in the early Middle Ages, this doctrine enjoyed wide support. It is not accepted by Protestants.

ing epitaphs to spouses evince profound affection.[10] By contrast, in most of the modern West, marriage *begins* about love, in its middle is still mostly about raising children (if there are children), and ends—often[11]—about property, by which point love is absent or a distant memory.

Even in modern cultures with vast and standardized legal establishments, the technical definition of "marriage" is difficult to formulate, and at the time of this writing there are hundreds of legal battles under adjudication about whether given heterosexual couples are actually "married" or not.[12] Laws of the fifty states comprising a single country with a single federal tax system vary widely about such matters as common-law marriage (i.e., recognized but not formally established relationships),[13] grounds for divorce, parental rights over children, and the nature and disposition of community property. This results from the fact that although "marriage" seems to the unreflective to be a tightly defined and specific phenomenon, its actual parameters and ramifications become surprisingly vague under close scrutiny. Moreover, what a society recognizes as "marriage" depends only partly on a precise definition. Roman Catholics, Protestants, Jews, and nonreligious lawyers all have quite specific and different definitions of what constitutes a "marriage," but in most large American cities each of these groups is generally willing, de facto, to recognize the validity of the others' marriages. This is also true of unions that do not match any group's definition, if the parties regard themselves as "married," even though all the groupings have very different

---

10. Of course, this is to some extent a self-selected sample, since someone who felt little affection for a spouse would not be likely to erect any sort of monument.

11. More than 50 percent of heterosexual marriages in America end in divorce at the time of this writing (December 1992).

12. Mostly legal battles over what is currently designated "palimony"—i.e., the expectation on the part of one party that a relationship would have legal or financial consequences comparable to matrimony. Faithful Roman Catholics, although technically ineligible for divorce, can seek an annulment—a declaration that there never *was* a marriage—from the church.

13. Twelve of fifty states (and the District of Columbia) recognize common-law marriage, according to Graham Douthwaite, *Unmarried Couples and the Law* (Indianapolis, 1979), 11 (with listings by name beginning p. 274), although the "states are not uniformly agreed as to the nature of the conduct and the formalities which can result in the status of common-law spouses." Cf. Weyrauch, "Informal and Formal Marriage," *University of Chicago Law Review* 88, 91 (1960), p. 28: "A valid definition of common law marriage without infinite qualifications can hardly be found." A much higher percent of states recognized such marriages in 1922, when Otto Koegel published his *Common Law Marriage and Its Development in the United States* (Washington, D.C., 1922), 164–66.

ideas about the aims, rationale, definition, requirements, theoretical effects, and appropriate ceremonies for marriage.

Even aside from technical requirements or exact definitions, precision is impossible about so common a matter as the marriage ceremony itself, about which most people—aside from those who professionally officiate—have relatively little knowledge. "Walking down the aisle together" is a common figure for marriage in literature, song, and everyday speech, although in the vast majority of wedding ceremonies the bride and groom do not actually walk down the aisle together, but meet at the altar.[14]

In addition to the first two peculiarities of modern attitudes toward love (the "sea of love," and the presumption that romantic love and heterosexual matrimony are inseparably linked), a third psychological feature of the modern West complicating both the writing and reading of this study is the salient horror of homosexuality characteristic of the West since the fourteenth century. Although most societies have sexual taboos, and many of them apply to certain forms of same-sex behavior (or even to all same-sex erotic activity), few, if any, other major cultures have made homosexuality—either as a general classification of acts according to gender or as an "orientation"—the primary and singular moral taboo it has long been in Western society: "the sin that cannot be named," "the unmentionable vice," "the love that dare not speak its name." Those who have never had occasion to question this extraordinary prejudice, especially if they personally entertain reservations about homosexual acts, may have difficulty apprehending how remarkable this degree of revulsion actually is. Murder, matricide, child molesting, incest, cannibalism, genocide, even deicide are *mentionable*: why are a few disapproved sexual acts that injure no one so much more horrible than these? Because they are worse? In fact, no moral system of general application in the West would actually categorize homosexual relations between consenting adults as worse than child molesting (which is now commonly discussed) or genocide (which is almost a preoccupation in the West since World War II).

It is actually the affective, taboo aspect of the subject that has

---

[14.] It is possible that the expression refers to their walking down the aisle together *after* the ceremony, but most references in popular culture do not seem to suggest this.

rendered it unmentionable until recently rather than its intrinsic moral gravity. Many citizens of cultures in which the taboo operates never fully grasp this, and entertain a vague horror of the acts in question—a horror necessarily unexamined, since its object could not, until the last few decades, be named or discussed. This inarticulate horror did render the acts viscerally, and therefore *functionally*, the worst of all sins. But even following the most ascetic traditional Roman Catholic morality to the letter,[15] homosexual sodomy would be on the same moral grounds as heterosexual sodomy, about which there has been comparatively little concern in Western society—not that it has been approved, but there have been no witch hunts to hound out of society those who enjoy it, no widespread efforts to detect who might be engaging in it privately, no social conflict about whether those who indulge in it should be eligible for the military, or teaching positions, or the clergy. One might wonder why behavior that is the predominant erotic interest of a very small percentage of the population (less than 10 percent was Kinsey's estimate; many more recent estimates are lower) should occupy so large a proportion of moral fulmination, scholarly writing, and public debate (enormously more than 10 percent).

Although no satisfactory explanation for this preoccupation has ever been advanced,[16] its reality can hardly be doubted by residents of the societies in which it obtains, and its severely distorting influence must be taken into account in attempting to form a clear picture of the sexual attitudes of earlier stages of Western civilization. One clear example of the pervasive effect of the prejudice is the revulsion in Germanic and Anglo-Saxon cultures at any form of male-male intimacy or affection. Even many areas (the Slavic countries, for in-

15. Since the revulsion came to the United States from Europe, I assume that it is to Roman Catholic Europe that one must look for explanation of the moral repugnance associated with the subject. Although I have studied the matter, I have never fully understood why American Protestants, who otherwise reject "procreative purpose" as a litmus test for moral sexual acts, should retain such a vivid horror of homosexuality. Whether or not it is condemned in the New Testament is now a subject of lively debate, but was not always. On the other hand, American Protestants usually cite the Old Testament, in which it is condemned along with many behaviors easily tolerated by modern Christians (eating pork and shellfish, sleeping on mountains, touching women during menstruation).

16. The idea that there is a "natural" horror of homosexuality will not stand close scrutiny either philosophically—see CSTH, pp. 8–17—or empirically, since there are so many societies that accept or even idealize homosexual behavior of various sorts: see David Greenberg, *The Construction of Homosexuality* (Chicago, 1988).

stance, such as the former Soviet Union, where homosexual acts were punished with prison terms from 1960 to 1993) that maintain severe legal sanctions against same-gender sexuality nonetheless find public displays of affection between men ordinary and untroubling. Although such gestures may not be indicative of homosexual interest, in the United States or England or Germany they would be taken as such and would inspire horror or disgust or be considered immoral. (Figures 1 and 2 illustrate this point.)

The question that will immediately leap to the mind of a resident of the modern West about the same-sex liturgical unions described in the following chapters, for example, is "were they homosexual?" The apparently urgent, morally paramount distinction suggested by this question—between all heterosexual acts and relationships and all homosexual acts and relationships—was largely unknown to the societies in which the unions first took place, making the question anachronistic and to some extent unanswerable (if not beside the point), and even where the difference was noticed and commented on, it was much less important to premodern Europeans than many other moral and practical distinctions regarding human couplings. It was adultery that troubled most medieval Christians (particularly in the Mediterranean), not the gender of the party with whom it was committed.

In this regard, epistemology is even more complicated than politics, though the two are usually intertwined. When a concept of a "gay marriage" is introduced, most residents of the modern West can either locate a place in their conceptual framework where a gay counterpart of heterosexual marriage would be located, more or less symmetrical to it, or, especially if they entertain grave reservations about either homosexuality (Christian fundamentalists) or heterosexual marriage (many contemporary nonreligious persons, both gay and straight), they feel that such a juxtaposition is inherently unlikely or improper. Marriage is (for better or worse, depending on their point of view) *essentially* a heterosexual phenomenon. ("Heterosexual" is thus a suppressed parameter of their definition of marriage.) Although most residents of modern democracies would deny a specifically procreative formulation of the purpose of marriage, many would agree with the presupposition (factually wrong even in premodern Europe) that marriage is quintessentially a union of male and female.

Thus, to those who fall on one side of the epistemological divide, it is relatively easy to recognize and absorb ideas about a ceremony of same-sex union, because they have a place to locate the information. But for those on the other side, it is extremely difficult to do so, somewhat like being asked to contemplate the existence of a square circle. For the latter group, it may be helpful to recognize that same-sex unions in the Western tradition are by no means a bizarre aberration. Many cultures other than Western ones have recognized and institutionalized same-sex unions—Japanese warriors in early modern times,[17] Chinese men and women under the Yüan and Ming dynasties,[18] Native Americans from a number of tribes (mostly before white domination),[19] many African tribes well into the twentieth century,[20] and residents (both male and female) of the Middle East,[21] South-East Asia,[22] Russia,[23] other parts of Asia,[24] and South America.[25] Of course, the fact that people elsewhere have recognized same-sex unions does not in itself demonstrate that the Western tradition ever did so, but it should help to counter the visceral disinclination even to consider such a possibility.

This problem is further complicated by the fact that the vast majority of heterosexual people experience intense love relations—both erotic and nonerotic—with the opposite gender but, consciously at least, have only nonerotic feelings for their own gender. It is easy for them to imagine that gay people mistake nonerotic same-sex feelings

[17.] See, e.g., Paul Schalow, *The Great Mirror of Male Love* (Stanford, 1990), esp. pp. 27ff.

[18.] Bret Hinsch, *Passions of the Cut Sleeve* (Berkeley, 1990), 127–33, 177–78, 194.

[19.] Walter Williams, *The Spirit and the Flesh: Sexual Diversity in American Indian Culture* (Boston, 1986), esp. pp. 94–95, and Will Roscoe's beautiful and moving account of We'wha, a Zuni *berdache*, in *The Zuni Man-Woman* (Albuquerque, 1991).

[20.] Edward Evans-Pritchard, *The Azande: History and Political Institutions* (Oxford, 1971), 199–200; "Sexual Inversion among the Azande," *American Anthropologist* 72 (1970), 1429–30, 1432; Henri Junod, *The Life of a South African Tribe* (London, 1927), 1:492–94.

[21.] Harold Dickson, *The Arab of the Desert: A Glimpse into Badawin Life in Kuwait and Sau'di Arabia* (London, 1951), 229; Georg Steindorff, *Durch die libysche Wüste zur Amonsoase* (Bielefeld, 1904), 19; Mahmud Mohammad 'Abd Allah, "Siwan Customs," *Harvard African Studies* 1 (1917), 1–28, p. 20.

[22.] John W. Layard, *Stone Men of Malekula* (London, 1942), 487–88, 490; Ralph Linton, "Marquesan Culture," in Abram Kardiner, *The Individual and His Society: The Psychodynamics of Primitive Social Organization* (New York, 1839), 174.

[23.] Louis Luzbetak, *Marriage and the Family in Caucasia: A Contribution to the Study of North Caucasian Ethnology and Customary Law* (Vienna, 1951), 84.

[24.] Waldemar Jochelson, *The Koryak* (Leiden, 1905–8), 32, 754.

[25.] See, e.g., Pero de Magalhães de Gandavo, *História da Província Santa Cruz* (São Paolo, 1964).

for erotic ones, since the latter seem inherently unlikely to them, and they can easily identify with intense nonerotic feelings for their own sex. In fact, however, most gay people parallel heterosexuals in this regard, and experience a range of feelings, both erotic and nonerotic, for their own gender. This means that while simple friendship is always a possible interpretation of any particular same-sex relationship, heterosexuals will be more inclined to assume this as the most likely interpretation, while gay people will only consider it one of two distinct possibilities.

Normally the task of a historian is to piece together an account of what happened from the available sources, offer some analysis of the causes and effects involved, and present his or her findings in the most accessible form to readers or students. In a case like the present one, for the reasons adduced above, this task is enormously more complicated, because many readers, rather than being eager for the information to be thus gathered and relayed, will be inclined to resist it. Practicing the normal skills of the historian in such circumstances becomes extremely difficult, perhaps counterproductive—rather like attempting to perfect the breast stroke against a riptide. It has been a struggle for the writer not to overcompensate by weighting arguments in favor of what will seem intuitively unlikely to most readers; it has been his aim simply to present the largest possible amount of evidence for the most reasonable inferences. Speculation has been kept to a minimum, although many questions remain unanswered by the sources.

Attentive readers will note that in the following chapters there is much more information about men than about women. This discrepancy is unavoidable. The vast majority of premodern historical sources were written by men, for men, about men; women figure in them either as property or as objects of sexual desire. Women who chose to form and maintain permanent unions with other women fell in neither of these categories. In a previous study I defended a comparable inequity with the statement that "no one could offset the overwhelming disproportion of data regarding male and female sexuality without deliberate distortion,"[26] thinking no one could possibly argue for falsification of the historical record even for a worthy cause. None-

[26] *CSTH*, p. xvii.

theless, a feminist acquaintance published a very harsh review of that work,[27] pillorying me for not having produced more materials relating to women.

This situation is exacerbated by a problem afflicting all efforts to widen the scope of mainstream history to include minorities of various sorts: if groups previously ignored by the historical profession are separated into particular chapters, studies, or courses, their "marginalization" is increased rather than diminished, and they are seen not as a significant part of the history of the whole but as a side-stream running along the main current. On the other hand, if no effort is made to compensate for centuries of neglect of some groups and focus on the ruling male elite, a realistic view of human history will never emerge. To remedy that problem, I have in this study opted, as I do in my classroom, to make a point of examining and commenting on female correlates of male-recorded and male-centered phenomena as part of general history.

It is difficult to account for the fact that although many, many sources indicate that women also formed permanent same-sex unions, all of the surviving ceremonies invoke male archetypes. This is probably a subset of the general domination of women by men in Western society, as evidenced in the fact that in most Christian communions the father still "gives the bride away," although notions of women as the property of fathers or husbands have long since disappeared. Since the parties entering into matrimony officially marry each other, it is entirely possible that women were content to devise their own forms and promises, as they might do today.

The general inattention of male churchmen to female homoeroticism may even have been advantageous for women.[28] Most male writers probably did not regard lesbianism as worth worrying about. In a curious medieval Irish tale about an unmarried woman who asked the king to determine who was the father of her child, it was finally determined that she had been inseminated through sex with another woman who had herself previously had sex with her own husband. The king's perspicacity in thinking of this answer was regarded as

[27] It seems to me more courteous to mention neither the acquaintance's name nor that of the journal.

[28] From a broader perspective, see Melvin Goldstein, "Some Tolerant Attitudes toward Female Homosexuality throughout History," *Journal of Psychohistory* 9, 4 (Spring, 1982), 437–60.

praiseworthy, but the story registered no shock or horror at the idea of the two women having sex, simply concern to locate the biological father.[29] Such preoccupation with women as bearers and conduits of bloodlines rather than as beings with their own erotic lives and needs is typical of premodern European sources.

There is, unfortunately, little written on female homoeroticism in Europe in antiquity or during the Middle Ages.[30] For the most part, what has been written is cited in the pages that follow—accounts of lesbianism (sometimes involving permanent unions) in late ancient Rome, and pairs of lesbians involved in lasting relationships in high medieval religious orders.[31] The disproportion reverses itself from the late Middle Ages on, as male writers who were more and more disturbed by the possibility of male homosexuality found it less threatening to describe lesbian relationships (assuming, probably, that they were not actually sexual). Readers of this book may note that

---

[29.] Translated and discussed in David Greene, "The 'Act of Truth' in a Middle-Irish Story," *Saga och Sed [Annales academiae regiae Gustavi Adolphi]* 1976, pp. 30–37.

[30.] An exception is Bernadette Brooten, "Paul's Views on the Nature of Women and Female Homoeroticism," *Immaculate and Powerful: The Female in Sacred Image and Social Reality*, ed. C. W. Atkinson, C. H. Buchanan, M. R. Miles (Boston, 1985), 61–87. See also the Summer, 1992, issue of the *Medieval Feminist Newsletter*, E. Ann Matter, "My Sister, My Spouse: Woman-Identified Women in Medieval Christianity," *Journal of Feminist Studies in Religion* (1986), reprinted in *Weaving the Visions: New Patterns in Feminist Spirituality*, eds. Judith Plaskow and Carol P. Christ (San Francisco, 1989), pp. 51–62.

[31.] *CSTH*, pp. 220–21, now also translated *Medieval Latin Poems of Male Love and Friendship*, trans. Thomas Stehling (New York, 1984), Nos. 112, 113. Two examples of lesbianism that did not fit well into subsequent chapters are worth adducing here: in the second half of the twelfth century, Bishop Étienne de Fougères of Rennes divided women into three groups: the *riche dame*, the lesbian, and the perfect wife (Étienne de Fougères, *Le Livre des manières* [Geneva, 1979]; the lesbian section begins on p. 97, vv. 276ss. They were discussed by Jeri Guthrie, "Maternity Effaced: Coquette, Lesbian and *Noble Dame* in *Le Livre des manières*," an unpublished paper delivered to the Medieval Association of the Pacific. I am grateful to her for providing me a copy). Two of the three were introduced as negative examples: only the perfect wife escaped censure. His discussion of lesbianism began with confusing but typical conflations of animal behavior and homosexuality (see *CSTH*, pp. 137–43, 152–56, 201–2, 308–9, 389–90), which had previously been directed at males, but under the intensifying hostility of the period came also to be visited on women.

At the end of the twelfth century a monk saw in a vision the poor souls suffering for homosexual behavior in purgatory. To his surprise, a great number of women ("the lesser sex" [. . . . *minorem sexum* . . . , p. 325]) were there—something that had been "to that time" unsuspected by him, although, as he acknowledged, he ought to have realized from the New Testament that women as well as men were affected by this "crime," "which can not decently be named either by a Christian or by any non-believer or pagan" ("Vision of the Monk of Eynsham," in *Eynsham Cartulary*, ed. H. E. Salter [Oxford, 1908] 2:257–371, pp. 323–30). He uses the phrase *innaturalem prostitutionem* for this form of homosexuality (p. 325); it is unclear whether "prostitution" is simply a convenient derogation or he actually understood Rom. 1:26 to refer to prostitution.

although in earlier chapters female same-sex unions are rarely introduced, in the chapter on early modern and modern observations anthropologists often chose female examples of homosexuality (though more objective accounts of the period suggest male homosexual relationships were actually more numerous).

The project has been further complicated by the fact that, although composing the pages that follow has required mastery of many different specialties (other than arcane languages), many readers may not be interested in the technical niceties of liturgical development or the details of moral and civil laws regarding marital status. The text has been aimed, therefore, at readers with no particular expertise in any of the specialties that have undergirded the research; all technical materials have been relegated to notes, which will be of value to specialists but can generally be skipped by other readers. Some whole chapters may be too specific for those with limited interest in the history of nuptial liturgy: the material in Chapter 6, for example, has been deliberately set apart as a separate discussion, of interest to those specifically concerned about liturgical niceties but perhaps not fascinating for the general reader. Those who find it uninteresting may well skip it without losing the thread of the study.

THE MARRIAGE OF
LIKENESS

1

"What's in a Name?"

THE VOCABULARY
of
LOVE AND MARRIAGE

NLY A NAÏVE and ill-informed optimism assumes that any word or expression in one language can be accurately rendered in another; in fact, this is not the case, and is one reason why experts in certain subjects must learn the languages in which the texts they analyze were actually written. Translators must tread an excruciatingly fine line: "helping" readers too much—by providing too much or too little specificity—can in fact be deceiving them.

It will be obvious to thoughtful readers that a considerable problem in conducting an investigation of this kind is presented by the inevitable difficulty of assessing—through the alembic of written sources a thousand or more years old—the emotions, feelings, and desires involved in human emotional relationships. Most English speakers will feel they can recognize, intuitively, distinctions among feelings that might be characterized loosely as "erotic," "friendly," "fraternal," or "parental." In actual fact, however, such feelings are often confused both by the subject who experiences them and the person to whom they are directed, resulting in not only romantic disappointment and misunderstandings between friends but also guilty feelings about incestuous desire or a failure to recognize abusive relationships between parents and children.

Most such feelings—although profound, urgent, and ubiquitous—

3

are difficult to specify, not only because language is a frail medium for powerful and overwhelming emotions but also because the feelings themselves are often jumbled, shifting, and imprecise, to such an extent that many languages fail to make distinctions that English speakers consider essential: many ancient and modern tongues, for example, fail to distinguish in any neat way between "friend" and "lover." For classical Greek, for example, it is conventional (especially in societies marked by extreme antipathy to homosexual feelings and behavior) to render ἕταιρος as companion and ἑταῖρα as "courtesan," or "lover," although the basic meanings of the two words are the same, and there is every reason to believe (especially about classical Athens) that there was little distinction in the nature of the relationships in the two cases. Likewise in Syriac and other Semitic languages there are few distinctions among terms for "love" or "like."[1]

While a combination of love and hate may be a rare extreme, feelings of love are almost always combined with other emotions—jealousy, pride, anger, resentment, desire, and so on—so that a single term like "love" is inadequate to express them. Humans are, moreover, rarely sure about precisely what their feelings are in a given case; this ambivalence is the subject of much popular culture in the West, along with the realistic theme that even the most powerful and apparently stable emotions are given to sudden and unpredictable change.

One way of distinguishing in modern English feelings basic to this study is to differentiate between "loving" and being "in love." They are not mutually exclusive categories; on the contrary, with some simplification one might posit that the latter is a subset of the former, but its distinctiveness is important in the modern West. While it would be appropriate, for example, to "love" almost any other human (many ethical systems, indeed, adduce loving all other human beings as an obligation of moral life), the range of persons one might decently be "in love with" is highly circumscribed—by age, gender, availability, and relationship (both blood and legal). One should "love" but not be "in love with" one's siblings, for example, whereas

---

[1] Syriac r-h-m, for example, can refer to "desire" in a physical sense or "to love" one's neighbor as oneself; the noun can name a "lover" or a trusted friend. Arabic ḥabīb (حبيب) has a comparable range of meanings. Both are approximated in modern French aimer, which might be used for a friend, for culinary preference, or for the love of one's life. Even in English one might say "I *love* a certain performer," though the same person might have difficulty saying "I *love* you" to a potential romantic partner.

either "love" or "being in love" is possible with most classmates of the apposite gender in high school. "Loving" one's students is admirable; being "in love" with them suspect or reprehensible, even criminal in some circumstances. One presumes that young children "love," but are not capable of being "in love."

Many people are unsure about "love" and "in love" even in their own relationships, and a gradual transition from being "in love" to "loving" is probably characteristic of most long-term marriages, without the participants' being able to pinpoint a time when the shift took place. Nonetheless, we think of "being in love" as the necessary precondition of matrimonial satisfaction. Being "in love" involves passion and usually, but not always, sexual interest. (Some humans have very little sexual interest, but still appear to fall "in love" with other people.) "Love" might or might not include passion and sexuality; in the vast majority of its incarnations (e.g., among family members) it does not, and in many situations erotic interest would be thought to detract from or corrupt "love."

In this study the English term "love" is used to include "being in love," but *is not its lexical equivalent*. "Eros," "erotic," "romance," "romantic," "passion," and "passionate" are correlates of being "in love," and as such a distinct subset of "love" as a general phenomenon. Where the sources are sufficiently clear and precise to allow it, I have distinguished "love" from being "in love" in my analysis and translations, but very often premodern writers were either unwilling or unable to draw such distinctions, and in many cases even if they intended to do so the differentiation they encoded can no longer be deciphered with confidence. English usage in this area, even if clearly articulated, probably could not be mapped precisely onto Greek or Latin vocabularies of love and eroticism, which were reflective of (and engendered by) very different personal experiences, social structures, and worldviews.

The idea that Greek-speakers of the ancient world, for example, made nice distinctions among the several Greek words that express "love"—a notion widely popularized among the English-reading public by C. S. Lewis[2]—is a misprision. In fact, the three most common

---

In *The Allegory of Love* (Oxford, 1936) and *The Four Loves* (New York, 1960); this idea is perpetuated in Alan Soble, *Eros, Agape and Philia: Readings in the Philosophy of Love* (New York, 1989). Benjamin Warfield had argued previously in "The Terminology of Love in the

Greek expressions for "love" (each a verb and a noun: ἐρᾶν-ἔρως, φιλεῖν-φιλία, ἀγαπᾶν-ἀγάπη)³ were largely interchangeable,⁴ although each carried with it a slightly different congeries of associations. Ἔρως was associated chiefly with passionate love, being "in love," and its English derivatives "eros"/"erotic" provide a good approximation of its meaning (though there is no associated verb in

New Testament" (*The Princeton Theological Review* 16 [1918] pp. 1–45, 153–203) that ἀγαπᾶν and ἀγάπη predominate in the New Testament because they had become the most common words for "love" in spoken Greek at the time. P. Spicq, in *Agapè dans le Nouveau Testament: Analyse des Textes* (Paris, 1958), insisted instead that these two had been deliberately selected by Christian writers from the available range of Greek words because they had connotations of rational, evaluative love rather than mere feeling or passion. Spicq's work includes an exhaustive bibliography of the subject and detailed word counts, but a far more thorough and judicious survey was undertaken by Robert Joly (*Le vocabulaire chrétien de l'amour est-il original?* Φιλεῖν et Ἀγαπᾶν *dans le grec antique* [Brussels, 1968]), who concluded that constantly shifting lexical preference for the various words evinces no pattern or thought, and that they are by and large semantically equivalent in most Greek texts. See also Anders Nygren, *Agape and Eros* (Chicago, 1953).

3. A fourth expression related to "love" as a concept in classical Greek (στέργειν-στοργή) had a more specific connotation, being used chiefly in relation to feelings associated with ascendant or descendant biological relation. Christians added χάρις to their vocabulary of love, but in secular Greek this had been related to sexual favors (χαρίζειν meant specifically to gratify a partner sexually), not "love," and in Christian Greek it had little to do with human sentiment. For its erstwhile sexual use see in particular Yvon Garlan and Olivier Masson, "Les Acclamations pédérastiques de Kalami (Thasos)," *Bulletin de Correspondance Héllénique* 106 (1982) 1: *Études*, 3–21, p. 17.

4. Many Greek authors employ them interchangeably: Polybius uses both φιλεῖν and ἀγαπᾶν to mean "like" (as in "likes to do . . ."); Herodotus generally puts φιλεῖν in this same sense, but also adduces it twice for "to love" and four times for "to kiss"; Plutarch writes φιλεῖν and ἀγαπᾶν with approximately equal frequency for "like/love," but φιλεῖν appears just as often in his works meaning "kiss," whereas in four or five instances of the word in Philostratus it means "kiss." Magical papyri show φιλεῖν where Attic authors would probably have ἐρᾶν. Φιλεῖν and ἐρᾶν appear indistinguishable in Achilles Tatius (e.g., at 1.9, 6.20, 77.6 in relation to distinctly sexual passion). In Xenophon of Ephesus' romance *Ephesiaca* φιλεῖν and ἐρᾶν both characterize the erotic feelings of Habrocomes for Anthia, and the former also names the loyalty of a female slave to Anthia (2.3.5, 2.4.1). Plutarch applies ἐρᾶν to the earth's thirst for rain (*Erotikos* 770A) and to love between brothers (ἐρῶντες ἀλλήλων καὶ φιλοῦντες ἀδελφοί, Περὶ φιλαδελφίας 480B). The relative fungibility of the terms is particularly clear when they are used in lists to describe the same affection in the same sentence: e.g., Dio Cassius 80[79].15.4 ἐκεῖνον...συντόνῳ καὶ δευσοποιῷ ἔρωτι ἠγάπα, ὥστε...μᾶλλον αὐτὸν φιλῆσαι...[of a homosexual relationship]; Ἐράσθην, ἐφίλουν, ἔτυχον, κατέπραξ᾿, ἀγαπῶμαι *Greek Anthology* 5.51 (probably "I fell in love, I kissed, I was lucky, I acted, I am loved," although ἐφίλουν might be just another expression for "love"). Cf. 12.5: τοὺς λευκοὺς ἀγαπῶ, φιλέω δ᾿ ἅμα τοὺς μελιχρώδεις; and 9.401: ἡ φύσις...φιλίης θεσμοὺς ἀγαπῶσα. In *Lucius or the Ass*, attributed (wrongly?) to Lucian (trans. M. D. Macleod [London, 1967] LCL, Lucian, vol. 8), the relationship of Achilles to Patroclus is characterized by both ἀγαπᾶν and φιλία, but the author makes clear that he understands this to have been a distinctly physical relationship (sec. 54). (He says, for example, that their φιλία was mediated by pleasure—τῆς ἐκείνων φιλίας μεσῖτις ἡδονή; while this is open to a variety of interpretations, given the context it seems clear that it was sexual pleasure between them.)

English). Φιλία was the general term for friendship, usually considered (then and now) distinguishable from "eros," but the related verb φιλεῖν was the single most common word for "love" in every sense, and was regularly employed for everything from "liking" a comrade to passionately "kissing" a lover.[5] Ἀγαπᾶν was used both for divine and chaste human love, and for specifically physical relationships, often between members of the same sex.[6] Plato himself referred to the archetypal Attic lovers Harmodius and Aristogiton, claimed to have founded the Athenian democracy, by using within a single sentence both ἔρως and φιλία for the same relationship.[7]

Ἀγαπᾶν was similarly broad in application,[8] but less frequent in occurrence until the Jewish and Christian scriptures established it as the verb of preference to describe any love within the bounds of moral life.[9] Ἐρᾶν is used very rarely (only three times) for "love" (usually אהב in Hebrew) in the vast Greek translation of the Jewish scriptures known as the Septuagint, and φιλεῖν only slightly more often,[10] while ἀγαπᾶν occurs constantly, obviously representing the

---

5. Dio Cassius (80[79].16.1) even says that the athlete Zoticus was "loved" (ἐφιλήθη) by the emperor Elagabalus for the size of his private parts. Φιλέω is used for the kiss Judas uses to betray Jesus, e.g., in Matt. 26:48.

6. As noted above (n. 4), in [Lucian's] Lucius or the Ass §54, the love between Achilles and Patroclus was said specifically to have been physical, although ἤγαπα (from ἀγαπᾶν) was used to describe how Achilles felt about Patroclus.

7. ὁ γὰρ Ἀριστογείτονος ἔρως καὶ ἡ Ἁρμοδίου φιλία βέβαιος γενομένη...Symposium 182D. W. R. M. Lamb in the LCL translation of the Symposium (p. 113) rendered this very literally as "Aristogeiton's love and Harmodius's friendship."

8. Xenophon, for instance, deliberately conflates ἐρᾶν with φιλεῖν in his Symposium, 8.18: ἐρῶντες τῆς φιλίας (cf. 8.3, where ἔρως unites husband and wife). A similar conflation occurs in Athenaeus (13.563), who uses φιλῶν for the feelings of a lover enjoying the physical appearance of a youth. Lucian, in the Toxaris, uses φιλεῖν and ἀγαπᾶν more or less randomly, as if there were little or no difference between them.

9. On the reasons for this shift, see authors cited in n. 1, above. It is not true, as some exegetes pretend, that ἀγαπᾶν is simply the verb used for God's love or human love directed to God. God's affections are also expressed by φιλεῖν, as in John 16:27, and ἀγαπᾶν is used both of heterosexual passion (Hos. 3:1, and five times of husbands loving their wives in Ephesians and Colossians) and for the decidedly human sentiments of David and Jonathan (1 Kings 18:1). This is consonant with ordinary Greek lexical custom, in which ἀγαπᾶν often denoted sexual passion (e.g., Athenaeus 13.579, Lucian Toxaris 25).

10. For example, in the apocryphal 1 Esd. 4:24–25, a man's wife is referred to as his ἐρωμένη, and immediately after this the text asserts that a man loves his wife more than his parents, using the verb ἀγαπᾷ for this conjugal feeling, presumably because it can apply to both kinds of affection, whereas ἐρᾶν in reference to parents would be unusual. The other occurrences of ἐρᾶν are Esther 2:17 and Prov. 4:6. The noun ἐραστής ("lover") occurs seventeen to nineteen times, depending on the manuscript tradition consulted. (The textual history of the LXX is complex.)

general term for "love" of whatever sort.[11] Ἐρᾶν does not occur at all in the New Testament—a particularly striking absence, since ἐρᾶν and its derivatives are among the most common subjects of Greek literature of the period. Instead, φιλεῖν (25 times) and ἀγαπᾶν (136 times) are used exclusively as the verbs for a wide variety of emotions, feelings, and desires that would be translated into English as "like" or "love"—reflecting, as Joly has shown, ordinary contemporary usage.[12] Greek Christian culture did alter the connotations of the words χάρις and χαρίζειν, which had been hitherto associated with sexual favors, and attached them to concepts of selfless, disinterested love instead of the giving or receiving of sexual pleasure, their erstwhile associations.[13]

Apart from these small changes, the traditional range of connotations of the various words for "love" persisted among Greek-speakers throughout the Middle Ages and into early modern times. Ἐρᾶν remained uncommon in a culture consciously de-emphasizing human eroticism,[14] but the other words retained a wide popularity and range of associations. Despite the moving and classic formulation of selfless love as ἀγάπη in 1 Cor. 13–14, Christians applied the term to everything from ordinary human desire[15] to illicit sexual passion,[16] and

[11] Στέργειν, another common Greek word, is used only once, in conjunction with φίλος: Στέρξον φίλον καὶ πιστώθητι μετ' αὐτοῦ (Ecclesi. 27:17).

[12] See note 2.

[13] Nearly ubiquitous in the New Testament, it occurs in every book except Matthew, Mark, and the first and third epistles of John, with a wide range of meanings, mostly related to God's favor or kindness.

[14] Very occasionally it was used as a way to analogize loftier forms of love: e.g., St. John Chrysostom (Contra eos qui subintroductas habent virgines 1 [PG 47:495–97]) employs ἐραστής of sexual passion between male and female; it occurs again in reference to God in Quod regulares feminae viris cohabitare non debeant (9 [and passim] [PG 47:531–32]), but clearly implying passion, suggesting that instead of a human lover virgins should accept God in this capacity, since ultimately He is more passionate and His love more enduring. Clearly, the traditional sense of ἐραστής underlies this usage.

[15] Anna Comnena uses ἀγαπᾶν for the "desire" of the soldiery that Alexis should ascend the imperial throne: τὴν αὐτοῦ ἀνάρρησιν καὶ ἠγάπων καὶ ἐπηύχοντο (2.4.8).

[16] For the former see the New Testament, Epistles, passim; in the case of the latter Christians were following standard antique usage: see, e.g., [Lucian,] Lucius or the Ass, in which Achilles is said (§54) to have "loved" Patroclus—in an explicitly sexual sense—and ἤγαπα is employed for this. For later instances, see Nomocanon XIV titulorum, in I. B. Pitra, Iuris ecclesiastici graecorum historia et monumenta 2 (Rome, 1868) 8.14, p. 529: Μὴ ἐχέτωσαν αἱ διακόνισσαι συνόντας αὐταῖς τινας ἐν τάξει δῆθεν ἀδελφῶν ἢ συγγενῶν ἢ τῶν καλουμένων ἀγαπητῶν, ἀλλ ' ἢ καθ' ἑαυτὰς οἰκείτωσαν, ἢ τοῖς ἀληθέσιν αὐτῶν ἀδελφοῖς, ἢ θείοις ἢ γονεῦσιν ἢ παισίν ("Deaconesses shall not live with anyone in the way of a 'brother' or 'relative' or someone called a 'dear friend,' but must either live by

φιλεῖν functioned simultaneously as the identifier of noble friendship and a passionate kiss.[17]

Latin, which became the principal medium of Christian culture, had fewer terms than Greek for human feelings, and generally divided love into (1) *amor-amare*, the broadest category; (2) *dilectio-diligere*, personal inclination for a person or thing; and (3) (especially among Christians) *c[h]aritas*, moral love, loosely corresponding to ἀγάπη.[18] Like its Greek counterpart, it was equally likely to be applied to the sexual passion of husband and wife or to a chaste friendship between celibates pursuing religious virginity.[19]

Comparable barriers baffle discussion and historical analysis of "marriage." It is nearly impossible to formulate in a precise and generally acceptable way what is meant by "marriage," either by modern speakers or in ancient texts. "There can be no single answer to the question, what does marriage mean; each culture must seek its own answer."[20]

It is particularly difficult, perhaps impossible, to map onto the grid of premodern heterosexual relationships what modern speakers understand by "marriage."—i.e., to say that this or that premodern arrangement is the equivalent of modern marriage. This is partly because there is, in fact, little unanimity about what constitutes marriage in modern societies, as the welter of legal cases over the issue eloquently

---

themselves or with their real brothers or uncles or parents or children"; ca. 580, citing as authority Nicea Canon 3, Basil to Gregory, Code 1.3.9, Novels 1.2).

[17.] Many English words are traces of the former (e.g., "philanthropy") and a few (e.g., "philander") of the latter; for medieval use of φιλεῖν as "kiss," see, e.g., *Ecloga Legum in Epitome Expositarum* ['Εκολγῆ νόμων τῶν ἐν ἐπιτόμῳ ἐκτεθειμένων] in Zepos 4:26, pp. 1–585, 21:11, p. 405: 'Εὰν ἐφίλησεν ὁ μνηστὴρ τὴν μνηστὴν ἐν τῷ τῆς μνηστείας καιρῷ . . . φιλεῖν is often used of the kiss that sealed betrothal among Christians (e.g., Sinai 973, fol. 58v). Even in late antiquity φιλία might be used of homosexual passion: see above, pp. 5–6.

[18.] Used in place of ἀγάπη, for example, in the Latin rendering of 1 Cor. 13–14, but not for most of the many instances of ἀγαπᾶν in the Greek Old Testament. On the other hand, in most of the Middle Ages it was the general term for "love," including that between husband and wife. Formulas for divorce generally specify the absence of *caritas* between spouses as legitimate cause: see, e.g., *MGH Legum 5.1: Formulae*, ed. Karl Zeumer (Hannover, 1886), "Marculfi formularium" 2:30, p. 94 (*Dum et inter illo et coniuge sua illa non caritas secundum Deum, sed discordia regnat . . .* ; cf. Cyrille Vogel, "Les rites de la célébration du mariage: Leur signification dans la formation du lien durant le haut Moyen Age," in *Matrimonio*, p. 457).

[19.] E.g., in pseudo-Cyprian, *De singularitate clericorum* 32 (CSEL 3.3, p. 207), where it is deliberately applied to both in juxtaposition: *Grande miraculum, ut uirginum caritas uirgines faciat uelut coniuges credi et coniugum caritas coniuges faciat uelut uirgines aestimari.*

[20.] Ellen Kandoian, "Cohabitation, Common Law Marriage, and the Possibility of a Shared Moral Life," *Georgetown Law Journal* 75, 6 (August, 1987) 1829–73, p. 1861.

demonstrates. Even the two parties involved in a long-standing relationship often disagree—vehemently—about whether it was a "marriage" or not. It is idle to appeal to definitions or dictionaries: even the courts find these inadequate for solving the problem. Since even within a legalistic and culturally homogeneous society such as the United States in the twentieth century great controversy can surround both particular cases and problems of defining the general parameters of the concept (e.g., is the gender of the partners essential to its definition? should "common-law" marriage have statutory force in a given jurisdiction, or in any jurisdictions?), it is only to be expected that in less unified, less literate societies there should be even greater variation and uncertainty.

It is my understanding that most modern speakers of English understand the term "marriage" to refer to what the partners expect to be a permanent and exclusive union between two people,[21] which would produce legitimate children *if they chose to have children*, and which creates mutual rights and responsibilities, legal, economic, and moral, although these vary by couple and jurisdiction. (Certainly a union that entailed *no* change in rights or responsibilities for either party would not be considered a marriage by most people.)

Such a relationship is both more and less than any variety of heterosexual coupling in the ancient world, most of which were property arrangements—except those of concubine and lover; few were based on emotional or affective considerations or hopes (again, excepting concubine and lover).

In this study, "marriage," "matrimony," "nuptial," "conjugal," and comparable terms have been applied to premodern couplings according to the definition that would have applied *at the time*—insofar as it can be assessed—rather than in their familiar modern meanings. A few exceptions to this, involving a deliberate comparison of ancient and medieval patterns with modern categories, are clearly identified. Because my aim has been in large measure to *determine* whether forms of premodern same-sex couplings constituted "marriages," and since there is no *historical* reason to suppose they could not—much as per-

---

[21.] Expectation is the crucial element: about half of marriages in the United States are in fact not permanent, and more than half of all spouses commit adultery. Neither of these aspects would induce most observers to conclude that the marriages affected by divorce or infidelity were not actually marriages; they simply failed to meet popular and personal ideals.

sonal distaste or prejudice might predispose some individuals to believe the contrary—I have on the one hand employed the most general phraseology I could ("union," "coupling," etc.) and on the other not shrunk from applying "marriage" or related terms when it has seemed the most accurate description.

Greek terminology regarding marriage was so fluid that it is nearly impossible to infer the precise nature of a relationship from words alone. Γάμος (or frequently the plural γάμοι)[22] was the most common legal term for a wedding, and by extension for marriage, but, as Redfield observes, "*Gamos* is the name, in its primary significance, not of a ceremony but of the sexual act itself.[23] . . . Civil marriage, which is a ἱερὸς γάμος,[24] is placed in contrast with the μεθημερινοὶ γάμοι contracted with prostitutes and with the Πανὸς γάμος, . . . marriage which takes place in the wild and is associated with masturbation, bestiality, and rape."[25]

A further complication in analyzing the sources is presented by the fact that the common words for "husband" and "wife" were simply the nouns for "man" and "woman" (cf. English, "I now pronounce you *man* and wife"). While context leaves little room for doubt in many cases that a legal spouse is meant, in many others it is unclear whether the writer means a woman's "man" or her "husband" (or a man's "woman" or "wife"). The difference might be considerable. A noted instance of this, deliberately exploiting the ambiguity, occurs in the New Testament in John 4:18, when Jesus says to the Samaritan woman He meets at a well that she has had five ἄνδρας ("men," though without the following qualification one might translate it as "husbands"), and the one she has at the moment is not her ἀνήρ ("man" or "husband"), to which she responds, "Sir, I perceive that thou art a prophet."[26]

---

22. E.g., Theodoret of Cyrus, *Graecarum affectionum curatio* 8 (PG 83:1032); Xenophon of Ephesus, *Ephesiaca* 1.8.1, 2.7.1, 3.7.2; [Lucian,] *Lucius or the Ass* §36: τῶν καλῶν γάμων. I have been unable to detect any pattern in the use of singular vs. plural.

23. Although he does not list them, many instances of the use of γαμεῖν meaning simply "to have sexual intercourse with" could be cited from classical Greek writings: see, e.g., *LSJ*, s.v. γαμέω, 1.2.

24. E.g., in Plato, *Republic* 5,458e; *Laws* 8, 841b.

25. James Redfield, "Notes on the Greek Wedding," *Arethusa* 15 (1982), 181–201, p. 188, drawing for the third type on P. Borgeaud, "Du paysage à l'érotique, Musique," in *Recherches sur le Dieu Pan* [Rome, 1979] 2.2, pp. 115–135.

26. Of course Jesus could hardly have uttered this to the Samaritan woman in Greek, and we cannot be sure what the equivalent Aramaic would have been. As it reached the Christian

Latin usage offers comparable opportunities for confusion, using words for "wedding"—especially *nuptiae*—both as a general designation for "marriage" and for sexual interactions that were certainly not matrimonial. The common expressions for "husband" and "wife" were "man" (*vir*) and "woman" (*mulier*),[27] creating the same potential muddle as their Greek equivalents.[28] But Romans did have technical, exact terms for both "marriage" (*matrimonium*) and "spouse" (*uxor, coniux*).[29] The advantages of this exactitude for the translator are offset, however, by the problem of overprecision in the expressions for "to marry," which are divided into a phrase for the male (*duco*) and another for the female (*nubere*), both meaning simply "to marry," but reflecting gender in the way that "actor" and "actress" do in English.[30] (Greek sometimes made this distinction by using the active voice of γαμέω for the male and the passive for the female.)

At the intersection of ancient texts and modern historical and moral analysis there are thus at least three notable roadblocks in the way of investigators of "marriage":

1. The meaning (in modern terms) may be clear enough, but the task of translating complicated by phrasing that cannot be repro-

---

community in Greek and Latin, it seems to imply that although He was reluctant to condemn or judge her, all of her sexual relationships had been too casual to qualify as "marriage" in His view. For an analysis of this passage from a very contemporary point of view, see J. Eugene Botha, *Jesus and the Samaritan Woman: A Speech Act Reading of John 4:1–42* (New York, 1991).

27. In Aeneid 4:192, Vergil writes that Dido joins herself to Aeneas "as her man/husband" (*cui se pulchra viro dignetur iungere Dido*), although his readers realize the magnitude of her misapprehension if she believes Aeneas is or will be her "husband"; *viro* is, ironically, accurate here only in its sense of "man."

28. Thus the Latin rendering of John 4:18 is able to exploit the ambiguity of the Greek: *quinque enim viros habuisti, et nunc quem habes non est tuus vir.*

29. Not without exception: Apuleius, *Metamorphoses* 1.7, uses *uxor* in relation to a long-standing but completely unofficial relationship; an oracle tells "what day will make marriage bonds strong" (*qui dies copulas nuptiarum affirmet*). *Nuptias* is used throughout very loosely, as in 7.21, where it describes the ass's tendency to jump on any "marriageable girl" or "attractive lad" (*seu virgo nubilis seu tener puellus . . . aversa Venere invitat ad nuptias*); effeminate priests say that their leader has bought an ass to be his "husband" (*maritum*) 8.26; *matrimonium* is used for a relationship between the ass and a strange woman in arena (10.29; the same event is *nuptiis* at 10.34). All of this semantic fluidity and imprecision is reflected in the Greek version—γαμεῖν, e.g., is used for casual sexual relations (e.g., §32).

30. As opposed, for example, to the distinction in English between "doctor" and "nurse," which do not simply reflect gender. For other Latin terms related to but not denoting matrimony see pp. 40–41 and 104.

duced exactly in English. In Luke 20:35, for example, the Greek utilizes a distinction between male and female roles in marriage that can be conveyed in few modern languages.[31] Premodern translations reflected the phrasing of the original—"The children of this world marry, and are given in marriage: But they which shall be accounted worthy to obtain that world, . . . neither marry, nor are given in marriage" (KJV).[32] The significance of this is probably lost on contemporary readers. Newer versions sometimes repeat the KJV's wording,[33] sometimes come up with an entirely novel understanding,[34] and occasionally arrive at a concise and accurate way to render the idea in contemporary speech: "The children of this world take wives and husbands, but those who are judged worthy of a place in the other world . . . do not marry . . .".[35]

In the ecclesiastical Greek of the medieval church, the most common term for heterosexual marriage was "crowning," because the wearing of nuptial crowns was the most dramatic symbolic act in marriage ceremonies (although not a part of all Eastern heterosexual rites: see pp. 206–08). But it would be confusing, if not precisely "wrong," to translate Greek verbs and nouns derived from στεφαν– as "crown," since English readers associate "crown" primarily with anointing or installing royalty. In some cases it is best to render it literally as "crown" with explanation; in others, it is clearer and more helpful to render it as

[31.] οἱ υἱοὶ τοῦ αἰῶνος τούτου γαμοῦσιν καὶ γαμίσκονται, οἱ δὲ καταξιωθέντες τοῦ αἰῶνος ἐκείνοι...οὔτε γαμοῦσιν οὔτε γαμίζονται. The Vulgate gives *Filii huius saeculi nubunt et traduntur ad nuptias, illi vero, qui digni habebuntur saeculo illo . . . neque nubent neque ducent uxores*. . . .

[32.] Cf. Rheims-Douai: "The children of this world marry, and are given in marriage; But they that shall be accounted worthy of that world, . . . shall neither be married, nor take wives." This is a good literal translation, but confusing even to someone who can read the Greek. What distinction did the translators intend between "be married" and "take wives"?

[33.] E.g., New Revised Standard Version: "Those who belong to this age marry and are given in marriage; but those who are considered worthy of a place in that age . . . neither marry nor are given in marriage."

[34.] E.g., New American Bible: "The children of this age marry and remarry; but those who are deemed worthy to attain to the coming age . . . neither marry nor are given in marriage." I can see no justification for "remarry" here: although it is difficult to convey the sense of the Greek, there is no doubt about what it *means*.

[35.] English version of the Jerusalem Bible. Other translations of this version (e.g., the original French, the Castilian, the German, etc.) are equally effective. Cf. Revised English Bible: "The men and women of this world marry; but those who have been judged worthy of a place in the other world . . . do not marry."

"to marry," which is, in fact, what it connoted to Greek speakers.[36]

2. The meaning may be clear but rely on terminology that is ambiguous, and the translator must decide whether (and if so, how) to present the linguistic ambiguity: the case of the woman at the well and her "men" is a good case in point, and a brief examination of various English renderings will demonstrate to the reader how difficult a task it is.

3. The meaning itself may be uncertain, and the translator must guess how to present the lack of clarity in the text: an example of this, also from the New Testament, is 1 Cor. 7:36–38, about a man "and his virgin,"[37] as confusing in the Greek as it is in most English translations. It has most often been understood as a statement about a father wondering whether to marry off his daughter,[38] but recent exegesis has concluded that it may refer to an engaged couple, which is entirely different.[39]

On the other hand, the normal word in the Gospels for "to be engaged" was μνηστεύομαι—the word used of Mary in both Matthew (1:18: μνηστευθείσης τῆς μητρὸς αὐτοῦ Μαρίας τῷ Ἰωσήφ) and Luke (1:27: παρθένον ἐμνηστευμένην ἀνδρί, and 2:5: τῇ ἐμνηστευμένῃ). As husband and wife, the Gospels generally refer to them simply as man (e.g., Matt. 1:19: Ἰωσὴφ δὲ ὁ

---

36. A less delicate but equally apt parallel is presented by the modern French *baiser:* to be discussed below. The Greek word for take or celebrate "Communion"—εὐχαριστεῖν—is an apposite liturgical parallel. The word in Greek literally means "to give thanks," and is related to the modern Greek for "thank you," but to Westerners "thanksgiving" is not an appropriate or helpful translation of "Communion."

37. εἰ δέ τις ἀσχημονεῖν ἐπὶ παρθένον αὐτοῦ νομίζει, ἐὰν ᾖ ὑπέρακμος, καὶ οὕτως ὀφείλει γίνεσθαι, ὃ θέλει ποιείτω· οὐχ ἁμαρτάνει· γαμείτωσαν. In the Vulgate: *Si quis autem turpem se videri existimat super virgine sua, quod sit superadulta, et ita oportet fieri; quod vult faciat; non peccat, si nubat.*

38. E.g., Chrysostom, *De Virg.* 78 [PG 48:590]; Basil, *De Virg.* 56 [PG 30:784]; Augustine, *Quaest. in Hept.* 4.57 [CSEL 28:361]; see modern discussion in Pierre de Labriolle, "Le 'mariage spirituel' dans l'antiquité chrétienne," *Revue historique* 137, 2 (1921), 204–25, esp. p. 207.

39. The New American Bible comments, "The passage is difficult to interpret, because it is unclear whether Paul is thinking of a father and his unmarried daughter (or slave), or a couple engaged in a betrothal or spiritual marriage." The Revised English Bible offers two translations which cover both possibilities; the New Revised Standard assumes that it deals with a betrothed couple, as does The New Jerusalem Bible. The KJV takes perhaps the safest approach, by simply translating very literally: "But if any man think that he behaveth himself uncomely toward his virgin, if she pass the flower of her age and need so require, let him do what he will, he sinneth not: let them marry." This is exactly what the Greek says, but offers a modern English reader very little clue about what is actually being discussed.

ἀνὴρ αὐτῆς) and woman (Matt. 1:20: Μαριὰμ τὴν γυναῖκά σου).

Engagement actually offers a particularly useful example of the problematic interaction of custom, law, and language, since in premodern Europe betrothal was understood not simply as the period of preparation for marriage, but the time between a binding promise to marry (sometimes arranged at birth) and the actual marriage (during which time the couple might or might not live together, depending on local custom). One of two Italian expressions for "to become engaged"[40] is *dare promessa di matrimonio;* for the "betrothed" parties the general term is *promessi sposi.* Modern Italian for "betrothal" is *fidanzamento* (from "trust," or "confidence," like English "betrothal"), but the engaged are more commonly referred to as *promessi sposi*— "promised spouses"—a clear indication of the public expectations attached to "engagement." By contrast, betrothal is such a small part of English marital custom that foreign words are borrowed for its key players—like French *fiancé*—as if there were no English terms.

Even greater potential for error is posed by terms for nonmarital but long-standing relationships. Modern English has no standard term for same-sex partners in a permanent, committed relationship, so it is virtually impossible to translate ancient terms for this (of which there were many) accurately into contemporary English. "Spouse" is confusing and objectionable to many (both gay[41] and straight, though for very different reasons); "partner" works better, but is rather vague, since the same term could apply to a long-term relationship based purely on legal or financial interest. Nonetheless, I have relied heavily on it in translating ancient and medieval terms for same-sex partners: the ambiguity is often present in the original as well.

Probably the most common word in contemporary English is "lover," but it is quite misleading because it is also frequently applied to relationships of the majority, which are entirely different, and con-

40. The other is *fidanzare.*
41. Problems relating to use of the word "gay" are not addressed in this study, although they have been amply addressed elsewhere in the modern literature on gender preference. "Same-sex" is sufficiently clear to make evident what is under discussion in most of this text, and I have thought it best not to complicate further an already long and taxing analysis by addressing as well the problem of whether or not "gay people" lived in premodern Europe. I do not, however, recant my many published opinions on this subject.

taminate the word's use in relation to homosexual couplings. A heterosexual "lover" is generally *not* the equivalent of a spouse: it is either someone to whom a heterosexual is *not* married (or not *yet* married) or a love interest *in addition to* a spouse, seen on the side and usually clandestinely (a "paramour"). These associations are not apposite to "lover" as applied to same-sex couples, for whom the word almost always designates the primary and exclusive focus of erotic life, usually intended to remain so permanently. Using "lover" for same-sex partners implicitly suggests that *all* same-sex unions are illicit relationships, comparable to what passes between a heterosexually married male and his mistress rather than to the man's union with his wife. Since this is precisely what is under investigation here, it would be a poor analytical procedure to prejudge it with semantic careless-ness.[42]

Heterosexual and homosexual relationships are not, of course, necessarily symmetrical (although it may be worth noting that all heterosexual relationships are not similar, either). This was doubtless even more true of the ancient world, because subordination was almost inevitably a part of ancient relationships between men and women (probably the reason that "brother" was used to distinguish same-sex unions from both standard heterosexual unions and some familiar patterns of homosexual relationships, such as ἐραστής–παῖς couplings: see the following remarks on "brother").

"Concubine" is similarly problematic. To a modern English reader its connotations are largely derisive, suggesting (like "lover") an essentially illicit relationship. But in most premodern cultures, including a large portion of those at issue here, concubinage was a legal and moral relationship, clearly defined and with specific and well-articulated boundaries in relation to marital unions, with which it might overlap or coexist. On the other hand, there seems to be no alternative to this term, firmly established as it is in English usage, and

---

42. By contrast, an effort to *remove* a homosexual interpretation would be appropriate in the case of the British working-class expression "mate," which denotes a friend, with distinctly non-erotic connotations; the same word in the mouth of an American speaker would unambiguously designate a partner in a heterosexual relationship assumed to be erotic. To translate the British expression into French as *conjoint*, or the American word as *camarade* would be quite wrong, although those are the correct words if applied to the proper context. Similarly, the Latin *vir* might be said "literally" to mean "man," but it is often used for "husband," and rendering it "literally" as "man" in such cases would distort the meaning, suggesting a *less specific* relationship than the Latin writer intended.

readers will simply have to be on guard against assuming that a "concubine" is inherently incompatible with "a spouse" or is a violation of a marital understanding or contract. In modern America concubinage would certainly pose an impediment to marriage—morally, legally, and emotionally—but it is not in relation to *modern* marriage that premodern concubinage should be understood, and in most premodern cultures a "concubine" occupied a legitimate (if inferior) position, not an illicit one.

By far the most significant problem in the whole catalogue of semantic slippage related to love and sexuality is the use of sibling designations for romantic partners, of either gender. The historical background for this is sketched out in chapters following, period by period. This seems the appropriate juncture to address the larger issue of the proper translation of such terms into English. "Brother" and "brotherhood" have often had sexual or romantic overtones in modern English during the last two centuries.[43] Walt Whitman used "brother" in ostensibly homoerotic contexts (e.g., "Calamus," No. 5), although he consistently denied any homosexual aspect to his poetry (see the discussion in Jonathan Katz, *Gay American History: Lesbians and Gay Men in the U.S.A.* [New York, 1976], pp. 337–40). The song "Daniel" by rock star Elton John, known to be gay,[44] uses "brother" as a term of endearment in a same-sex relationship (with Bernie Taupin), but John himself insists that the two were just friends. On the other hand, Matt Groening, when asked whether his cartoon characters Akbar and Jeff are properly interpreted as gay, answers, ". . . they are either brothers or lovers or possibly both. [Whispering] But they're gay."[45] Moreover, "brother" is commonly used in contemporary personal ads for sexual partners, apparently in senses closely related to the imperial Latin usage of the word for "brother."[46]

[43.] See, for example, discussion and references passim in Georges Michel Sarotte, *Comme un frère, comme un amant: l'homosexualité masculine dans le roman et le théâtre américains de Herman Melville à James Baldwin* (Paris, 1976) [English trans. Richard Miller, *Like a Brother, Like a Lover: Male Homosexuality in the American Novel and Theater from Herman Melville to James Baldwin* {New York, 1978}].

[44.] After denying it for many years, presumably to spare his mother, John admitted frankly to being gay in "The Rebirth of Elton John," an interview by Philip Norman in *Rolling Stone* (March 19, 1992), 42–49, 110.

[45.] Doug Sadownick, "Groening Against the Grain," *The Advocate* 571 (February 26, 1991) 30–35, p. 31.

[46.] A random sampling: "Early 50's, new to scene, looking for totally masculine kid brother, son or junior partner type. . . ." *Honcho* (January 1985), p. 87. "YOUNGER BROTHER. Pro-

Sibling referents are, to be sure, more often understood to imply the opposite of erotic interaction in modern English culture ("he treated me like a brother"), and for this reason it would predetermine, for most readers, interpretation of the nature of the relationships described in premodern sources to render such words in their simplest, "most literal" sense as "sister" or "brother," especially in unfamiliar contexts, where the reader will have difficulty correcting for the misdirection[47] (as opposed, e.g., to "sister/brother" in the Song of Songs, where the erotic context is unmistakable and, in the twentieth century, largely uncontroversial).[48]

There are comparable problems with the English verb "fraternize." In English it carries a double freight: it can mean simply "socialize" (usually only with *equals*) or it can refer specifically to emotional or sexual intimacy, as in prohibitions of commissioned officers "fraternizing" with noncommissioned personnel. (The point of the prohibition is obviously to maintain status distinction, since "fraternize" suggests a relation of equality.) To use the ostensible French equivalent, *fraterniser*, in the intimate sense would be grossly misleading, since it carries the connotations only of the first English sense, i.e., to consort with someone on a basis of equality (hence, the *fraternité* of the Revolution).

Perhaps the closest parallel to this is the problem of rendering the modern French *baiser* into English. Most English speakers will have

---

fessional GWM, 36. . . . wishes to meet younger brother under 26 for friendship and possible relationship. . . ." *Metroline: News for the Gay Community* 13, 16 (August 24, 1990) p. 65. "Little Bro[ther] W[an]t[e]d. . . ." *The Advocate* 559 (September 11, 1990), Classifieds p. 5. "BIG BROTHER . . . Big brother type seeks friendship, relationship with cute "boyish" looking guy 18–25. . . ." *Frontiers: The Gay Newsmagazine* 9, 9 (August 31, 1990), p. C–12. "BIG-BRO[THER]/DAD WANTED . . ." in *Frontiers: The Gay Newsmagazine* 9, 9 (August 31, 1990), p. C–14. "LITTLE BRO[THER] W[A]NT[E]D. . . ." *Frontiers: The Gay Newsmagazine* 9, 9 (August 31, 1990), p. C–18. "2 hot lovers, early 30's, . . . seek younger brother for hot, safe fun. . . ." *Frontiers: The Gay Newsmagazine* 9, 9 (August 31, 1990), p. C–20. "WANTS LITTLE BROTHER. Masc. GWM 34, 5'9", 170 lbs., brown hair, beard. . . . Seeking a submissive younger guy 18–26" *Metroline: News for the Gay Community* 14, 13 (July 12, 1991) p. 50.

47. Although there are certainly instances of its being used in a plainly nonerotic sense, even among those familiar with the Song of Songs. For example, one of the seven traditional Jewish wedding blessings is "brotherhood" (אחוה), which probably does not suggest any erotic involvement, although the word used for "friendship" (רעות) in the same context could refer to a friend, associate, neighbor, lover, or paramour, according to Jastrow, c. 1475.

48. But it was very problematic in premodern Europe: see commentary on pp. 128–131. Volkov translates *pobratimstvo* as "fraternisation," and Frček renders the Greek as *"fraternité adoptive."* Both are misleading on many fronts.

been taught in French classes that it means "to kiss," which it certainly does, but in everyday street language in French-speaking nations today it has also taken on the meaning "to fuck," with *embrasser* (formerly, "to hug") substituted for "to kiss." For reasons of Anglo-Saxon reticence and propriety, this cannot be taught to most students in British or American schools, but the conscientious scholar certainly should not translate *baiser* "literally" as "kiss" where it actually means (even more "literally") "fuck."

The nearest English parallel to this particular semantic confusion is probably the expression "to sleep with." Should it be rendered as "to sleep with" in a language where "to sleep with" does not mean to have sex?[49] One might argue that this is the "most literal" interpretation, but if the culture does not recognize "to sleep with" as meaning *specifically* to have intercourse, even if some readers understand the expression to suggest *metaphorically* that the two people had intercourse, others can reasonably deny that this is what is intended. If the translator wishes to do an honest service he will therefore have to render it as "to have sex," even though the original writer could be said to have deliberately chosen the blander "to sleep with" over something more direct like "to have sex." If the result of a "literal translation" is that readers misunderstand what happened, it is a mistranslation, no matter how "accurately" one might claim the words correspond to the original.

The nouns most commonly translated from Greek (ἀδελφός), Latin (*frater*), or Slavic (брат-) as "brother" are similar. The ceremony discussed on p. 182 and translated on pp. 291–94 is titled and uses phrases that could be translated "become brothers," or "make brotherhood" (e.g., ἀδελφοποιία, братотворения),[50] and one approach would be to render them this way, "literally." But if, as seems inescapably clear (see Ch. 7), the meanings of the nouns to contemporaries were "lover," and "form an erotic union," respectively, then "brother" and "make brothers" are seriously misleading and inaccurate translations for English readers, who will relate such concepts

---

49. Although, for example, in modern French *se coucher avec* ("to lie down/go to bed with") does have this sense, *dormir avec* (the most "literal" counterpart of "sleep with") does not. Similarly, in Spanish, *acostarse con*, the equivalent of *se coucher avec*, connotes sexual activity *in addition to* its "literal" meaning, but *dormir con* usually does not.

50. The творит from which the second part of this term is derived generally has connotations in the Bible of doing *good* (e.g., in John 4:34, 5:29, 6:28).

more to feelings of goodwill and fraternal concern than to intimacy or romantic attachment. In biblical, Egyptian, or imperial Roman culture, "brotherly love" might be either erotic or not; to modern readers it is emphatically and unambiguously not; therefore, translations must retain an ambiguity not conveyed by the most "obvious" or "literal" equivalent. Within many of these very ceremonies "brother" is used as the general term of address for all Christians, but clearly the point of the rite is not simply "brotherhood" in this sense.[51]

"Brother" is used in the Jewish Scriptures (1) to designate a physical brother or cousin or nephew[52]; (2) as a term of endearment for a spouse (Tobit) or a lover (the Song of Songs, in which, if they are spouses, that is not the main issue)[53]; (3) to convey a sense of alliance or loyalty.[54] In the New Testament it becomes the standard term of endearment of Christians for one another, and this usage persists in homiletic and epistolary Greek and Latin, but probably does not reflect everyday usage, in which the first two senses of the word are doubtless much more common.

The English words themselves are somewhat bewildering. For example, "brotherhood" and "brother" seem to be closely related, but their lexical applications are quite disparate. "Brotherhood" is rarely used to describe the quality of being a "brother" in the most obvious sense of "brother." One does not normally speak of having "brother-

---

[51.] In medieval Slavic usage братотворения and related terms were the most common words for the rite and the relationship it established. By early modern times the rite was called побратимство and the parties so united побра~имы, which seems to introduce new subtleties. The prefix по- can connote in modern Russian a time limitation (as in побегать, "to run for a while," or поспать, "to sleep for a while"); in this sense, побратимство could be understood to mean "temporary brotherhood." But по- also connotes intensification or repetition (as in повторять, "to repeat"), and degree of affection (as in подруга, "girl friend," from друг, an ordinary friend) or mutuality (подобно, "similar to," and помощник, "assistant"). In these senses there is no direct English equivalent, but this form is late.

[52.] For the last, see Gen. 29:15, where Laban says to Jacob, who is unambiguously his nephew, "Because thou art my brother" (אָחִי)("Ότι γὰρ ἀδελφός μου εἶ).

[53.] But note that the Greek word in the Song is ἀδελφιδ– , which had usually meant niece/nephew in classical Greek. In most Slavic translations брат- or a derivative is employed in Tobit *both* as a marital term of endearment and for relatives (usually cousins).

[54.] 1 [LXX:3] Kings 20 [LXX 20]:32–33: as a gesture of conciliation the king of Israel refers to Ben-hadad, king of Syria, as "my brother" (ἀδελφός μού ἐστιν), which his listeners ("used to paying close attention to what he says") pick up, and say, "'Αδελφός σου υἱὸς Αδερ." In 1 Macc. 12, the high priest Jonathan (successor of Judas Maccabeus as leader of the Jews) refers to the Spartans in a letter to them as the "brothers" of the Jews (τοῖς ἀδελφοῖς) and speaks of the "friendship" (φιλία 12:10) and "brotherhood" (ἀδελφότης at both 12:10 and 12:17) they share.

hood" with natal siblings; terms like "relationship" are employed for that. "Brotherhood" is used almost exclusively to describe relationships between persons not actually born of the same parents—confraternities, unions, relations of good will, ethnic relationship, and so on. (It is the defining term among blacks to distinguish who is inside and who outside the black community—a "brother" is in. Strikingly, white groups, like the Masons or the Ku Klux Klan, also use "brother" in this way.) It is, moreover, a much more gendered term in English than in any ancient language: "brotherly love" evokes male bonding, even in a family setting, whereas φιλαδελφία or *caritas fraterna* are more inclusive, and might suggest sisterly as well as brotherly affection. (Among other reasons, there is no specifically female way to express this abstraction in Greek or Latin, so the same term must convey both.)[55]

It is not surprising that the abstraction has substantial metaphorical use, but it is rather odd that its most immediate and basic meaning is wanting completely in everyday speech. English speakers feel they know what "brotherhood" means because they know what a "brother" is, but in fact two biological brothers are not related, in normal English, by "brotherhood," although the members of a fraternity or a labor union or the French republic are.

In other words, most of the familiar meanings of "brotherhood" are not extensions of its biological sense, which has fallen out of regular use, but represent oblique transfers of unarticulated, deeply felt notions of what is good in sibling relations. This is not simply a function of the abstract ending "-hood": many closely related terms employing the same suffix serve double functions, both to define physical relation and to characterize metaphorical extensions of it—e.g., "fatherhood," "motherhood," "manhood." One can speak of the "fatherhood" of God, for example, and also ask a friend how he is enjoying "fatherhood" in the biological sense. But if a man wished to say that he loved someone else because the latter was his brother, he would not say that he particularly relished this "brotherhood": he would have to use a circumlocution like "because we are brothers." This seems to be because "brother," unlike many other terms of biological relation,

---

[55] Neither the ἀδελφ– in φιλαδελφία nor the *fratern-* is specifically male: the former could be short for ἀδελφή; Latin had no equivalent of *fraternus* derived from *soror*.

carries in most societies a freight of metaphorical meaning that out-weighs and partially obscures its biological significance.

For all these reasons, translating εὐχὴ εἰς ἀδελφοποιία or молитва на братротворение as "prayer for brotherhood" would be completely misleading. It would suggest the sort of benediction that might in modern times be asked upon a fraternal organization of many persons, whereas, no matter what one understands to have been the precise nature of the relation, the ancient ceremony unmistakably commemorated and established something personal and specific be-tween *two persons only*—a couple of some sort—and was not an invo-cation of the much more general type of human relationship denoted by English "brotherhood," which can and most often does comprise more than two. (The normal Greek word for "brotherly love" in this larger sense was φιλαδελφία—from which the American city Phila-delphia takes its name; it does occur in some of the ceremonies [e.g., in the ceremony translated in Appendix of Translations, No. 3], al-though *not* to describe the union of the two people: it is used instead to describe the relationship of the apostles, a model for all permanent Christian unions, including heterosexual matrimony.)

Moreover, in premodern Europe, as has been noted, although a countererotic sense of "brother" was known,[56] it coexisted with dis-tinctly erotic meanings of the same word, creating an ambiguity in the texts that was entirely conscious. The presence or absence of legal connection, eroticism, even simple affection, was irrelevant to the use of "brother" in most premodern contexts. "Brotherly" relations ranged from the overtly sexual (Petronius Arbiter, Tobias, or Song of Songs in the Jewish Scriptures) to the completely impersonal: monas-tics were, by and large, prohibited from maintaining "personal friend-ships" with other monastics, even though they were all "brothers," and so referred to each other. What is common to all of these uses of sibling reference is a notion of equality: one would not normally speak of God being "brother" to man, or of the abbot as "brother" to monks, or of the bishop as "brother" to his flock. Instead, one would use terms of paternity: God is father to humans, the abbot father to monks, the bishop shepherd to his flock. And in relationships where authority is the hallmark, sibling metaphors are comparatively rare:

56. See pp. 67–71.

describing marriages in sibling terms went almost entirely out of favor by the High Middle Ages. Instead, terms of possession or domination were applied to the husband, and of subjection or possessedness to the wife.

When one considers the various ways in which premodern Christians used sibling terminology—for other Christians, for monastics, for chaste spouses, for all the peoples of the world—it becomes clear that the only aspect of the relationship between persons called "brothers" contained in the term itself is a general notion of equality. Christians insist that all the people of the world are "brothers," with one Father, to suggest an equality of human beings, a notion popular among all the highly developed religions of the early empire, and maintained in the face of widespread slavery and oppressive totalitarian political structures.[57] To a certain extent "fraternal" imagery was employed as a substitute for and challenge to hierarchy and government. For monastics, the "brothers" of the community were all equals in a chosen family under the "abbot," a word derived from the Aramaic term for "father." Christians were "brothers," both as the children of God and as equals under the paternal care of priests (from πρεσβύτεροι, "elders") and bishops (ἐπίσκοποι, "overseers"). Husbands and wives were to treat each other with mutual respect and love, even if the husband enjoyed a certain privileged position in the *structure* of church and state.

A further confusion inherent in comparing the modern concept of "brother" to older ones is economic: in modern societies, "brother" is largely an immaterial relationship. Societies are no longer organized chiefly by family ties; brothers are largely independent of each other, legally, financially, and emotionally. They almost always live in separate households as adults, sometimes very far apart, and are not likely to be important to each other except to the extent they *choose* to be, by virtue of affective ties or sentiment. In premodern societies, wealth was not distributed by salary, but was held by families. Hence, brothers were economically dependent on each other, and held legal responsibility for each other in a variety of ways, or were jointly dependent on a father who supported and controlled them. They

[57.] Although, ironically, it was Christianity that popularized the very notion that "order" is inherently "holy" in the term "hierarchy" (from Greek, ἱερός, "holy," and ἀρχή, "order").

rarely lived far apart, and commonly occupied the same household, if not the same house.

Hence, "to become brothers" suggests to a modern reader entering into one of several types of affective or organizational relationships known in modern, industrial societies, a bond created almost exclusively by blood relationship rather than affinity of taste or shared experience (e.g., buddies) or eroticism (the primary occasion of permanent bonding in modern societies). But in preindustrial societies "to become brothers" implied much more, and was not just one of many affective relationships. It meant becoming a joint socioeconomic unit, recognized by and important to both society and the economy, with material and juridical consequences. In this sense it was much more closely related to modern marriage, in which the two parties form a new household unit of mutual responsibility, whether or not the emotional or sexual context of the union persists or is satisfying.

Indeed, the countererotic sense of "brother" was largely unknown in the premodern Christian world, because *all* relationships were expected to be chaste in the sense of subordinating desire to responsibility. Even husbands and wives were expected to have chaste relationships, and sibling analogies were quite common for Christian marriage. "Chastity" in this context did not imply the *absence* of sexuality, but simply its proper use. All Christian men and women were "brothers" and "sisters" in Christ, and they could certainly marry and have sex. Even within marriage, the metaphor of sibling relationship did not necessarily imply an absence of sexuality, although it could sometimes do so. More commonly, it suggested that the relationship was not *based primarily* on sexual attraction, but on respect and prudent affection, comparable to sibling relationships; the sexual aspect of the union was to be kept in its proper place. In the West, the latter might have been understood to be for procreation only, although it is doubtful that the average Christian couple felt this way, no matter how vehemently learned theologians insisted on the point. Most ordinary Christians in their hearts may well have shared the official view of the East: that any use of sexuality *within marriage* was chaste. This would enable them to read the biblical Tobit and Song of Songs without surprise at the apparent juxtaposition of sibling relationship and intense eroticism.

To retain this rich multiplicity of connotations—sexual, asexual; transcending and incorporating sex—I have employed the most neutral terms I could devise in translating the original concepts, such as "union" for ἀδελφότης (which could be rendered "brotherhood"), or "be united" instead of "become siblings," which would be overtly and distinctly misleading to most English speakers, since it would evoke notions of adoption.

Those inclined to reject the erotic or romantic component of the relationships in question could hardly be misled by this: whatever *sort* of union it is, it is unquestionably a union, and those involved are certainly being "united," whether through collateral adoption, spiritual friendship, or same-sex relationship. This approach seems to me the only honest methodology, and to have the least distorting effect on the translations, since it retains the ambiguity present in the original texts. I have provided, in notes, sample translations in one instance (Appendix of Translations, No. 5, n. 84) resolving the ambiguity in both directions: in one set, "brother" and related words have been used in English; in the second set, words suggesting "homosexual marriage" have been used to translate Greek terms that may have connoted this to contemporaries.

A further translation difficulty is presented by the rubric designating the ceremonies discussed and published herein, identified in the original manuscripts with a variety of designations, most commonly Greek terms such as ἀδελφοποιία or ἀδελφοποιήσις or Slavic братотвор– (with several endings, depending on the time and place of the manuscript's composition). Goar rendered the Greek terms in Latin as *spiritualis fraternitas*; Frček translated the Old Church Slavonic as *"fraternité adoptive,"*[58] although no word occurring in or relating to the ceremony in any version in any language justifies introducing the concept "adoptive."

In light of what has been already discussed about the difficulties of conveying to English readers the multiple valences, both erotic and nonerotic, of sibling reference, it should be obvious that such translations are likely to be grossly misleading. Because of the efforts of Goar and other writers to disguise the nature of the same-sex union, one

---

58. Other scholars writing in French use *fraternisation*; this is arguable in French, but wrong in English: the English equivalent has a standard, distinctly different meaning, discussed above.

must add to this problem the uncertainties introduced by the vagaries of both ancient and contemporary words related to "spirit." Goar labeled the ceremony he published "Office for spiritual brotherhood."[59] Since the word for "spiritual" does not occur in a single manuscript title for the ceremony,[60] one must wonder what inspired him to do so,[61] and many have followed his lead in assuming that the ceremony involved the establishment of some sort of religious tie. Reasons to question this have already been discussed.

In the New Testament the Greek word πνευματικός could refer to the life of the mind or soul as opposed to that of the body, the spirit of God (in any of the three persons of the Trinity), the law given by God, anyone inspired by this law,[62] or heavenly or nonworldly things.[63] It was frequently used of the human spirit, as in Matt. 26:41

---

59. Ἀκολουθία εἰς ἀδελφοποιίαν πνευματικήν (Officium ad spiritualem fraternitatem ineundam). André Jacob, "Les euchologes du fonds Barberini grec de la Bibliothèque Vaticane," Didaskalia IV (1974), 131–222, possibly inspired by Goar (whom he cites for comparison with texts he discusses), also titled the ceremony "Officium ad fraternitatem spiritualem ineundam" (e.g., for Barb. grec 293, fols. 51v–55r, where the actual rubric is simply Εὐχὴ εἰς ἀδελφοποίησιν; Barb.grec 329, fols. 116–18, where the title of the ceremony is really <Τάξις εἰς> τὸ ποιῆσαι ἀδελφούς; Barb. grec 345, fols. 64r–65v, where the title is Τάξις εἰς τὸ ποιῆσαι ἀδελφούς). These transparent efforts to disguise the nature of the ceremony are too obvious to complicate discussion of it. See also p. 192, n. 143.

60. A sampling of actual Greek titles includes Εὐχὴ εἰς ἀδελφοποιῆσιν, the earliest rubric and the most common until the eleventh century, Ἀκολουθία εἰς ἀδελφοποίησιν, which began to appear in that century, Τάξις εἰς τὸ ποιῆσαι ἀδελφούς, which was common from the next century on, Τάξεις καὶ ἀκολουθία (or Ἀκολουθία καὶ τάξις) εἰς ἀδελφοποίησιν, which appeared a hundred years later, and Τάξις γεναμένοι [sic] εἰς ἀδελφωποῖαν, known from a few late medieval manuscripts. The Slavic rubrics also omitted any word for "spiritual": the earliest of these had мол<итва> [prayer] на братосьтворение, but it later became чинь [office] братотворенїю.

61. Given the content of his long notes on the ceremony (discussed on p. 267), it is not too hard to surmise.

62. In this case it is strikingly contrasted (e.g., in 1 Cor. 2:14–15) with ψυχικός, which one might have supposed meant more or less the same thing, but in early Christian parlance it did not, because the preeminent meaning of πμεῦμα had to do with the divine. Jerome was able to utilize the Latin animalis to render this word in his translation of the New Testament, which worked well: anima was Latin for "soul," and for most of Christian history animals, lacking judgment and divine inspiration, were considered a negative example. The triumph of Scholasticism reversed this, inculcating the idea that the animal kingdom constituted a sort of "mirror" of God's plan for the universe. This idea was, surprisingly, retained by Protestantism while most other medieval theological innovations were rejected. If animals constitute any sort of "mirror" it is a "fun house" type, filled with distortions and startling twists: many animal parents devour their children, kill each other over food, and mate indiscriminately. None have marriage or any other liturgical ceremonies, none can read or are known to have received divine revelation.

63. Headings from the Greek-English Lexicon of the New Testament and Other Early Christian Literature, by Walter Bauer, William Arndt, and F. W. Gingrich (Chicago, 1979), s.v. πνευματικός, q.v. for specific examples.

("the spirit is willing but the flesh is weak"), where it is perfectly obvious that both spirit and flesh are human.[64] In later Greek it could mean "of the breathing," "spirited," "fierce," "of the soul" (as opposed to the body), "supernatural," or "spiritual" in perhaps the most common English sense (see following).[65] But it still very commonly applied to humans, as in the liturgical saying "And with thy spirit."[66]

In any event, if Goar and his followers thought that inserting the word "spiritual" would obviate any comparison to heterosexual matrimony they were quite mistaken. "Spirit" or "spiritual" occurs in most Christian liturgies of any sort, and "spiritual" was part of heterosexual matrimonial rhetoric from its earliest days.[67] How could a blessing performed in a church not be "spiritual" in some important sense?[68] The blessing of the married couple—even when it had become a full office with sacramental implications—was often called a "spiritual blessing."[69]

The Modern French spirituel can mean "witty," in a distinctly worldly sense; "soulful" (e.g., expressing emotion); or "spiritual" in the English sense just mentioned.[70] The English is also varied: most commonly it means "religious," "pious" ("he was a deeply spiritual person"), but it can also mean simply "supernatural" in a clearly nontheistic context ("a spiritualist"), and "of the heart" ("there was a spiritual bond between us"). Only the third of these is unmistakably related to the ceremony. "Soul mates" would be a much more realistic translation than "spiritual brotherhood."

---

64. Cf. 1 Cor. 7:34.

65. These are the headings in Lampe, s.v. πνευματικός.

66. E.g., εἰρήνη πᾶσιν. καὶ τῷ πνεύματι σου.

67. See, e.g., Tertullian, De virgin.veland 11.9 (CSEL 76:96, ll. 43–45): Si autem ad desponsationem velantur, quia et corpore et spiritu masculo mixtae sunt per osculum et dexteras . . . Note that "veiling," a kiss, and the joining of right hands are all parts of the ceremony of same-sex union, as are references to "spirit," however it is understood.

68. Ἡ πνευματικὴ συγγενεία was "spiritual relationship," but not in a modern sense: it simply referred to godrelationships created by sponsoring a child at baptism, and would subsist between people mechanically without their ever even having met each other (e.g., the brother of one's sponsor was one's "spiritual uncle," etc.). There were whole treatises on such relationships by Pediasimos, Chomiatenos et al.

69. For example, Sinai 973 (C.E. 1153) (Dmitrievskij VIII, p. 101): Αὐτὸς καὶ νῦν εὐλόγησον τὸν γάμον τοῦτον εὐλογίαν πνευματικήν, καὶ ἕνωσον καὶ διαφύλαξον τοὺς δούλους σου ἐν εἰρήνῃ καὶ ὁμονοίᾳ, καὶ δὸς αὐτοῖς τὸν στέφανον τῆς ἀφθαρσίας; in Dmitrievskij LXIV Holy Sepulcher (Constantinople) 8 (182) (fifteenth century), p. 461 (of couple being betrothed): ἵνα, κατὰ σάρκα καὶ κατὰ πνεύματα καὶ κατὰ ψυχὴν ἑνωθέντες τῷ φόβῳ σου.

70. Spiritual in French refers to Afro-American Christian hymns.

2

"For Family and Country"

HETEROSEXUAL MATRIMONY

in

THE GRECO-ROMAN WORLD

"This is what it means to be married: to have sons one can introduce to the family and the neighbors, and to have daughters of one's own to give to husbands. For we have courtesans [ἑταίρας] for pleasure, concubines [παλλακάς] to attend to our daily bodily needs, and wives to bear children legitimately and to be faithful wards of our homes."[1]

"For is there anything better than a wife who is chaste [σώφρων], domestic, a good house-keeper [οἰκόνομος], a rearer of children; one to gladden you in health, to tend [θεραπεῦσαι] you in sickness, to be your partner [παραμυθήσασθαι] in good fortune, to console you in misfortune; to restrain the mad passion of youth [τοῦ τε νέου τὴν ἐμμανῆ φύσιν] and to temper the unseasonable harshness of old age? And is it not a delight to

---

[1]. Demosthenes, *Against Neaera* 122, quoted by Athenaeus, 13.573b. (Athenaeus then adds tales about young people in love who refuse to marry sensibly, suggesting considerable variation in ancient attitudes. The editor of the *LCL* Athenaeus [vol. 6, p. 95, n. e] notes the minor inaccuracy of the quotation [παλλακείας for Demosthenes' θεραπείας] but does not provide the exact citation in Demosthenes.)

acknowledge [ἀνελέσθαι] a child who shows the endowments of both parents?"[2]

Because the majority of evidence about erotic relationships[3] in premodern Europe pertains to heterosexual relations, it seems most appropriate to present a sketch of these as general context and to juxtapose the fewer homosexual examples against them.[4] This is a heuristic approach, simply proceeding from a larger sample of cases to a smaller one, and not intended to suggest that homosexual relationships were imitative of heterosexual counterparts. The two are obviously conceptually related, and were in some cases similar, but not, as will be seen, in all.

In the cities of the Mediterranean basin during classical antiquity —i.e., from about 400 B.C.E. to around 400 C.E.—heterosexual couplings generally took four forms: use, concubinage, marriage, and romance.

Women were used sexually by men who controlled or possessed them: neither the mores of pagan culture nor the precepts of most ancient religions hindered a man's sexual access to women under his power. Such women might be slaves, former slaves (i.e., freedwomen), household servants, captives taken in war, clients, or others who came under a man's political or economic domination in some way. "If you're not in love with your music-girl, please send her to me for ten talents," Alexander wrote to an acquaintance.[5] Often such relationships were long-standing. It was common, for example, for sterile women to lend their own maids to their husbands to produce an heir.[6] The reverse of this—sexual use of male dependents by female

---

[2.] Cassius Dio, 56.3.3–4 (*LCL, Dio's Roman History* 7, trans. Earnest Cary [London, 1924]).

[3.] Although any sexual interaction between two persons might be considered an erotic "relationship," I use the word here in its widely recognized meaning of a long-standing relation, or "coupling." Simple prostitution (as opposed to the more complex and sophisticated variety practiced by courtesans), casual sexual encounters, rape, and other common forms of sexual intercourse have been omitted from this discussion, not because they were insignificant in premodern Europe, but because they do not fall within this understanding of the word "relationship."

[4.] The disproportion is startlingly less in the ancient world than it would be for modern industrial nations. Much evidence might, indeed, leave the observer with the impression that in antiquity sexual activity was about 50 percent homosexual: see *CSTH*, pp. 3–90.

[5.] Plutarch, *Erotikos* 760C. Later (768A–B) Plutarch notes that slave women reject the advances of masters if they are themselves in love with someone else.

[6.] This creates a very complicated set of relationships in Jacob's household, recounted in Gen.

masters or owners—probably took place occasionally, but was risky for the woman, and there is little evidence of it.[7]

Relationships of this sort obviously entailed few or no obligations on the male's part, either in terms of conferring status or property on his partner or in terms of commitment to longevity.

The term "concubine" is derived from the Latin verb "to lie with,"[8] and denotes a social inferior (but *not* usually a *possessed* person) maintained in a long-standing relationship for the sexual fulfillment of a male. (It was very rare for women to have male concubines; if they used subordinate females for this it has left no record.) Sometimes some commitment was involved in relations of this sort. Concubines might live in the household or be maintained in a separate home, usually though not always depending on whether there was also a wife. The closest modern equivalent is usually designated a "kept woman," although greater independence of means for women in the modern West has rendered such arrangements rare. In premodern Europe, concubinage was certainly more respectable (for both parties) than prostitution,[9] and there might even be an official concubine, recognized by the family, community, or the state in the case of a monarch. Such relationships differed from marriage in that they would not normally involve property or status or dynastic rights

---

29, 30. This kind of relationship is usually more private and difficult to detect in public documentation, but the problem is alluded to in various ethical and legal discussions.

[7.] There was much Roman legislation about women of higher status having sexual relations with slaves or unfree dependents; its import varied by century, but it is fair to say that it was nearly always to the disadvantage of the woman and often harshly punitive. See, for example, *Code* 5.4.3 and *Digest* 23.2.61.1. In literature, although it makes a titillating episode in many works of fiction, such interest on the part of mistresses almost always results in an unhappy turn of events (e.g., in Xenophon of Eph. 2.2–10, 3.12). Both the Hebrew Bible (Gen. 39:7–20) and the Qur'an (12:23–34) recount an incident in which the wife of Joseph's master, Potiphar, tries to force him to have sex with her and he is thrown into prison as the consequence of refusing; he becomes an archetype of masculine beauty in Islamic culture and she a symbol of evil among Jews, Christians, and Muslims. (Interesting is the Talmud's transformation of this heterosexual incident into a homosexual one [Sotah 13b and commentary by Rashi], imputing sexual interest in Joseph to Potiphar himself—as if the peculiar enormity of homosexuality alone could explain the circumstances.)

[8.] *Concumbere*, whence *concubinus*; Latin speakers also used *pellex/paelex* and *amica*. Greek used either a literal translation, παρακοιμώμενος, or πάλλαξ (or παλλακή), from which Latin borrowed *pellex*. Cf. Hebrew פִּילֶגֶשׁ, also probably borrowed from the Greek. For brief observations on the origin of these words, see Saul Levin, "Hebrew (pi[y]léḡeš), Greek παλλακή, Latin *paelex*: the Origin of Intermarriage among the Early Indo-Europeans and Semites," *General Linguistics* 23.3 (1983), 191–97.

[9.] "Nor is adultery committed by someone by virtue of having a concubine; for since concubinage is recognized by law, its punishment cannot be legal," *Digest* 25.7.3.1.

for the concubine, or at least not those of a wife: they were an *alternative* to marriage or in addition to it. Typically, a concubine did not fulfill some requirements for a marriage partner (i.e., proper family, social class, or economic status), but would meet sexual or emotional needs in a more personal and respectable way than a mere slave used for sexual release (or a prostitute). "In contrast to marriage, which was a social institution by which families of the same standing entered into an alliance to perpetuate themselves, concubinage was a personal union, an affair of love, at least on the part of the man."[10]

Concubines were usually free, in theory at least, to terminate the relationship at will, but were often actually dependent economically on wealthy men. Relationships of this sort appear to have lasted for months, or years at most, in antique cities, although it is not inconceivable that some were permanent.[11] Usually men married concubines if they intended to remain with them forever, although St. Augustine dismissed his, after fifteen years and a child, *instead of* marrying her.[12] In polygamous societies concubinage was usually permanent, as noted below.

Marriage, the only respectable sexual relationship for women in antiquity, took two forms.[13] Polygamy was widespread among some Mediterranean peoples for rich males.[14] According to the Bible, Solomon, the wisest of the patriarchs,[15] had seven hundred wives and three hundred concubines.[16] Polygamous marriage was understood to

---

10. Jean-Louis Flandrin, *Families in Former Times: Kinship, Household and Sexuality*, trans. Richard Southern (Cambridge, 1979), 181.

11. St. Augustine's relationship with a concubine lasted fifteen years, and was the sole serious erotic commitment of his life, although he did regard a particular friend as his "alter ego" (described in *Confessions*, 4).

12. This relationship may nonetheless have influenced his view of concubinage, since he was willing to consider a "wife" any woman who intended to be faithful to the man she lived with: *De bono conjugali*, 5.5 (*PL* 40:376–77).

13. For literature on Greek marriage, see n. 25, p. 34 and n. 70, p. 46. Scholarly studies of Roman marriage are more numerous; only a sampling can be mentioned here. See, for example, Astolfi Riccardo, (*La lex Iulia et Pappia* (Milan, 1986), and note 17, below.

14. It was actually polygyny, the form of polygamy involving a single man and several women: see Laura Betzig, "Roman Polygyny," *Ethology and Sociobiology* 13 (1992), 309–49.

15. According to the Aggadah and the Hebrew Bible, Abraham, Isaac, and Jacob were the only "patriarchs," but 4 Macc. 16:25 [LXX] refers to these three by name, adding "and all the patriarchs" (καὶ πάντες οἱ πατριάρχαι), and "The Testaments of the Twelve Patriarchs," now thought to be a Jewish work, gives the last words of Jacob's twelve sons. Both of these instances suggest that in pre-Christian Jewish thought "patriarch" had a broader meaning than it would acquire in Aggadah, as it does now in ordinary English.

16. 1 Kings 11:3. The wives were of royal blood, the concubines not (ibid.). Solomon's relationship with his wives—but not his concubines—is criticized, ibid., 4–14, because they were

be *permanent*, because it was designed for males, who simply got *additional* wives (or concubines) if earlier ones ceased to be satisfying in one way or another (i.e., grew boring, became too old, or failed to produce heirs of the right sex, etc.). Women in such a system usually could not remarry.

The most common type of heterosexual marriage in all Mediterranean societies (and the only legal form at Athens and Rome) was monogamy: a male-female couple.[17] Such unions were often officially possible only for the propertied classes, but the monogamous permanent relationships of the lower classes were apparently understood as analogous. Such couplings were not irrevocable, at least for males: divorce was permitted, usually (but not always) at the man's instigation, in nearly all pre-Christian cultures of the Mediterranean.[18] Romans idealized and praised with the term *univira* (which means, loosely, "one-man woman") women who had only a single husband;[19] the ideal applied both to women who maintained lifelong marriages and to those who declined to remarry after being widowed. No similar term or concept applied to men.

Indeed, the *social institution* of heterosexual marriage (as opposed to the personal experience of it, or its religious significance, etc.) has been in most premodern societies primarily a property arrangement.[20] These societies provided few means of acquiring wealth besides ownership—of land, of persons, or of precious items. People could not

foreign and he allowed them to influence his religious beliefs. On matrimony and its variations in the Bible, see Claire Gottlieb, "Varieties of Marriage in the Bible: [sic] and their Analogues in the Ancient World," (Ph.D. diss., New York University, 1989). Polygamy was less common among the Jews than among their contemporaries in the ancient Mediterranean.

17. The best study of Roman marriage is now Susan Treggiari, *Roman Marriage: Iusti Coniuges from the Time of Cicero to the Time of Ulpian* (Oxford, 1991), which supersedes a large earlier bibliography, conveniently summarized and addressed therein. Suzanne Dixon's briefer treatment in Chapter 3 of *The Roman Family* (Baltimore, 1992) is also useful, and easier to read.

18. Although unable to hazard a guess about the rate of divorce, Treggiari does cite (pp. 435–82) specific statements implying that a long marriage was rare: e.g., *Rara sunt tam diuturna matrimonia, finita morte non divortio in[terrupta]*, from *The So-Called Laudatio Turiae*, ed. Erik Wistrand (Göteburg, 1976), 1:27–28.

19. See, e.g., Gordon Williams, "Some Aspects of Roman Marriage Ceremonies and Ideals," pp. 23–24, who shows that the word *solus* (applied to the husband) was also used to express admiration for the wife in this context.

20. This point was argued well by Treggiari in an early article, "Consent to Roman Marriage: Some Aspects of Law and Reality," *Classical Views* 26 (1982), 34–44, pp. 34–35. She concludes, "Money, political influence, social position, the perpetuation of the family were all bound up with the choice of partner."

simply go to work and draw a salary; and for both families and individuals, maintaining and expanding the base of such wealth was the concern most closely approximating the need to find a job and/or career in modern industrial nations. A young couple would have little means of supporting themselves without drawing on the family's resources, so fixing a dowry or some other transfer of property at the time of marriage was imperative. Moreover, matrimony (note the relationship to "patrimony") entailed either a gain in family worth (through marriage to an equally or more prosperous family) or a loss, if the new spouse had no resources and would merely carve a share out of what the family had. In either case, the children of the union would have a claim on the family's resources, and this made any marriage a legitimate and pressing concern of most of the kin of the prospective bride and groom. It would not be an exaggeration to say that most upper-class marriages before modern times were business deals, arranged with dynastic and property considerations uppermost in mind, and emotional and sexual aspects secondary: "Roman marriage was clearly perceived as a family affair, not an individual decision based on personal attraction.[21] . . . the matter is clearly seen as one for family discussion, since it will have an impact on the family for generations to come."[22]

Nor would it be too gross an oversimplification to assert that making a profitable marriage was the chief *business* of the upper classes, since inheriting and marrying money were the sole legitimate ways to obtain wealth, apart from farming, land-holding, or government office. Commerce, in nearly all its aspects, was déclassé, to the point of actually excluding a person from the ranks of the nobility in many premodern cultures.

Thus, Cicero lists as business matters about which one might seek professional advice finding a husband for a daughter, the purchase of a farm, and tips on agricultural practices.[23] The imperial poet Martial (second half of the first century), whose writings are as suffused with eroticism as any modern fiction, criticized an acquaintance for spend-

---

[21.] Suzanne Dixon, *The Roman Family* (London, 1992), 62. Cf. Wolff, *Written and Unwritten Marriages*, 78–79: "The bride legally was considered as a mere object of the contract that was made by and between her κύριος and her future husband." Wolff was writing of the particular case of Roman Egypt, but the observation is valid on a wider scale.

[22.] Ibid., p. 63.

[23.] *De Oratore* 3.133, noted in Treggiari, p. 35.

ing his wife's dowry on male lovers, and noted that it was the more reprehensible because she was a wife "such as an unworthy husband could scarcely dare pray for." But what made the wife so "worthy" was not any quality associated with romance or erotic satisfaction—she was "rich, noble, learned and chaste": hardly qualities to excite passion, but very desirable attributes from the point of view of the business side of a sensible marriage.[24]

There were, in fact, special ceremonies to arrange the business transactions necessary to marriage: the ἐγγύη in Athenian society,[25] the *sponsalia*[26] in Rome, both corresponding roughly to formal betrothal[27] in medieval and early modern Europe. These preceded what would today be considered the "wedding," but in the eyes of most premodern jurists and families the marriage was contracted—and therefore valid and binding—from the time these financial and legal arrangements were concluded, and failure to proceed with the concluding ceremonies constituted a breach of contract (rather than simply a personal loss).

Some scholars have seen in these customs the residue of more primitive marriage arrangements, such as the outright sale of brides.[28] Such sales—sometimes thinly disguised—also persisted throughout premodern Europe.[29] Other matrimonial customs, such as carrying the bride over the threshold and burning the carriage on

---

[24.] 12.97. In another poem (12.75) Martial confesses that he prefers his own male partners to the most enormous dowry a wife might bring. The *Epigrams* are, of course, satirical, but hardly less informative for that. On the other hand, Plutarch (*Erotikos* 767C–E) sharply criticizes men who value wives solely for their dowries or their ability to produce children, urging that husbands and wives could enjoy genuine friendship (φιλία) with each other (N.B., not romantic love [ἔρως]).

[25.] From a word also used for such purely financial arrangements as setting bail or posting a surety. "The *enguē* is the ceremony whereby title to the woman is transferred. It is a transaction between men, ideally between father-in-law and son-in-law." James Redfield, "Notes on the Greek Wedding," *Arethusa* 15 (1982), 181–201, p. 186.

[26.] From the word for "promise," "contract," "guarantee."

[27.] From a word for "pledge faith." "Betrothal is a social and sometimes also a political pact which creates and cements alliances between families." Judith Evans-Grubbs, "Abduction Marriage in Antiquity: A Law of Constantine (CTh ix.24.1) and Its Social Context," *Journal of Roman Studies* 79 (1989), 59–83, p. 79.

[28.] "It is a well established result of recent researches that the Greek marriage law—like those of other nations, Indo-Germanic as well as non-Indo-Germanic, whose social system was patriarchal—started with the purchase concept of marriage," Wolff, *Written and Unwritten Marriages*, 76. Plutarch sarcastically suggests to those who oppose marriage for love that they should revert to the custom of buying brides in the marketplace: *Erotikos* 753D. Roman brides were pelted with nuts, a custom also applied to newly *purchased* slaves.

[29.] Boccaccio's Griselda, etc.

which she was transported to the groom's home, may be survivals from ceremonial (or genuine) abduction as a mode of marriage.[30] Abduction for marriage was common in some areas of the Mediterranean and figured prominently in myth and history, as noted below.[31]

Lower-class unions were more informal and presumably undertaken chiefly for reasons of emotional attachment, sexual fulfillment, a desire for offspring, or economic support (the last two might coincide), but until relatively late in European history such unions were rarely recognized by the law or accorded much public significance, even though those who knew the couple doubtless regarded them as married. Even among the poorer classes—except for the utterly indigent and servile—property played some role, if a less prominent one than among their wealthy neighbors: the ability of the parents to give either or both parties something would in many cases be crucial to their viability as a couple.

This is what made dowry, dower, morning-gift, and other customary forms of fixing on prospective spouses some form of wealth, modest or great, so central and indispensable to premodern marriage, and so prominent in legal, social, and ceremonial sources regarding premodern marriage. The fact that the vast majority of newlyweds today will earn their own keep through their own labor and a regular salary is the reason dowry has so receded from prominence in contemporary marital considerations: it is now almost entirely sentimental and symbolic, while "earning power" and assets acquired *during the union* have become major sticking points in divorce settlements. (In most earlier communities the husband merely had to return the dowry to divorce his wife, and the wife could claim little beyond this no matter what the circumstances of the split.)

This should not be construed to mean that marriage did not fulfill

---

30. Plutarch speculates on these relationships in *Roman Questions* 27, 271d–e; this is noted and discussed in Redfield, pp. 191–92. As Redfield observes, the expression ἐπαυλία, for the bride's first night in her new home, suggests abduction: it is derived from the verb "to camp out" or "sleep in the open." Cf. Cretan abduction practices, *infra*.

31. P.Oxy. L 3581 records an interesting complaint from a fourth- or fifth-century woman who married the man who abducted her and then sued him for divorce when he cohabited with another woman: see discussion in Roger Bagnall, "Church, State and Divorce in Late Roman Egypt," 41–61, pp. 41–42. So familiar is abduction marriage in the Hellenistic world that in literature older women even abduct younger men they wish to marry, as in Plutarch's Ἐρωτικός, in which a rich young widow abducts a boy she loves, to the shock of the townspeople, although in time they accept the marriage.

very personal needs. It was essential to standing in the community for the propertied classes, afforded intimacy and emotional support, constituted the basis of running a household—also a crucial source of emotional stability—provided the satisfaction of parenting, and entailed pivotal changes in status. For adults of both sexes in the ancient world the difference between being unmarried and married was enormous. It was often the criterion for legal independence from parents for males. For women, who never achieved full independence, it was even more profound: marriage was the initiation rite into adulthood (something her husband had usually gone through in another context).[32] She became adult by virtue of her marriage, and a great deal of the ceremony associated with marriage symbolized the bride's leaving girlhood behind and entering into matron status.[33] A woman who never married would always be a dependent, in many ways a child, whereas a married woman managed a household, and could even do so on her own if left a widow.[34]

A partner's beauty (masculine or feminine), status, and wealth could also be obtained through marriage. Although much ancient evidence suggests that physical attractiveness was an asset for both bride and groom, a marriage simply for love would have been thought incontinent: beauty added to the dowry of the bride or the desirability of the groom, but could rarely be the overriding factor in the choice of a mate, particularly for young people under the influence of powerful dynastic pressures.[35]

---

[32] For elaboration on this see Anne Schwerdtfeger, *Ethnological Sources of the Christian Marriage Ceremony* (Stockholm, 1982), 2:1: "The puberty rite: forerunner of the basic marriage ceremony."

[33] In his excellent article on "Some Aspects of Roman Marriage Ceremonies and Ideals," *Journal of Roman Studies* 48 (1958), 16–29, Gordon Williams rightly highlights three ideals of Roman marriage: a single marriage to one husband (N.B., not to one wife); wifely obedience; the permanence of the marriage bond. Because of the first, it is clear that even the third is primarily an issue for women (i.e., there was no pressure against a male's divorcing his wife or remarrying after her death), suggesting that *matrimony* made more difference in the life of a woman than in that of her husband.

[34] Even in modern Russian the expression for a man's marrying is basically "to get a woman"—Женитьця—while for a woman it is essentially "to come out" (выходить or выйти Замуж За), i.e., to become a member of the larger society, as at Rome. In aristocratic English-speaking circles, especially in the United States, "coming out" is the prelude to courting and marriage, marking the beginning of marriageability for young women from good families. It is presumably from this that gay culture derived its expression "coming out" of the closet.

[35] See the sage discussion of this in Treggiari, *Roman Marriage*, pp. 100–103, and the sage observations on marriage for love in Bradley, *Discovering*, pp. 125–30. The latter concludes

All these relationships were strikingly different from superficially similar modern counterparts. Several—even all—of them were possible for the same man (but not the same woman) at the same time. Especially since marriage was by and large a property and dynastic arrangement, a man might well have a wife for dynastic and economic reasons, plus a concubine and a number of slave women for sex (or love), as Demosthenes and others noted.[36] He might even go to prostitutes on top of all this. This appears to have been a common pattern for prosperous Greek and Roman males, and was not considered immoral or even promiscuous.[37] In Plautus' Menaechmi (1.2), a husband asserts sharply to his wife that his love life is none of her business—an attitude utterly incomprehensible in the context of modern marriage.

The disjunctions between ancient and modern marriage were, however, deeper than the mere possibility of multiple relationships. They also entailed fundamentally different expectations. Since Romans did not look to marriage to fulfill erotic needs, even a devoted and happy marriage did not depend on (or disclose) sexual orientation (as it might in modern societies where people choose marital partners primarily for emotional and sexual fulfillment), nor would it have the same significance for a Roman as it would for an American to be in love with someone other than his spouse. In modern Judeo-Christian cultures, such a situation suggests faithlessness, instability, treachery, even greed—a desire to have erotic pleasure *in addition to*

(p. 129) that "it is not an acceptable inference . . . that the Roman ideal of conjugal love actually created, on a broad scale, marriages that by today's standards could be regarded as emotionally satisfying."

36. In Lucian's *Toxaris* a man complains that enemies have "ravished our concubines and wives" (NB: in that order): ὑβρίζοντες τὰς παλλακίδας καὶ τὰς γυναῖκας (39–40). The thirteenth book of Athenaeus's *Deipnosophists* is entitled Περὶ γυναικῶν, which would ordinarily suggest that it is "about wives," but Athenaeus makes clear in its introduction that it is actually about "women," (περὶ γαμετῶν) and concubines (ἑταιρῶν). (There is considerable material about homosexuality in it as well.)

37. An adult Roman male could commit only a few sexual failings: he would incur contempt as unchaste if his appetite for sex led him to financial or political foolishness or if he took the passive role in a sexual relationship or sold his sexual favors; if he violated the sanctity of someone else's family or marriage (through adultery or child molesting), he would incur scandal and possibly violent retribution. This does not mean that women were satisfied to have their husbands engaging in extramarital sex, and Martial's *Epigrams* are full of witty humor about the complaints of wives in such circumstances. They clearly have little recourse besides complaining: the husbands are violating no law, and not even doing something that will bring disgrace on themselves. Nor would a woman's male relatives likely intervene against a husband unless he brought another freeborn sexual partner into the house, who might constitute a rival to the wife.

the satisfactions of conjugal relations. Since the latter was not demanded or even expected of premodern matrimony, extramarital affairs in the ancient world were simply "the pursuit of happiness": the choices were to be content in marriage probably without erotic fulfillment, or to seek sexual satisfaction in some other context.

For this reason it is difficult, perhaps impossible, to map onto the grid of premodern heterosexual relationships what modern speakers understand by "marriage": nothing in the ancient world quite corresponds to the idea of a permanent, exclusive union of social equals, freely chosen by them to fulfill both their emotional needs and imposing equal obligations of fidelity on both partners. Indeed, the notion of voluntary "partnership" that lends itself to legal debate about contemporary marital arrangements would hardly have applied to matrimony before the late empire: it was, as noted, more like the adoption of the woman into the man's family.[38]

Moreover, *all* of these relationships have in common that the rigidly hierarchical nature of ancient social structures—everyone was bound through dependence or subordination to persons above and below her/him—were imported overtly into the relationships, even into marriage, so that emotional aspects were limited and shaped to a large extent by the social roles of the partners.

Recognizing all this, some scholars have drawn the exaggerated conclusion that love and marriage were wholly unrelated in premodern societies, that marriage was purely arranged and economic, and had no affective aspect. A few have even claimed that people did not "fall in love" in earlier times.[39] This is only a slightly less distorted and uncritical view than the earlier assumption that our ancestors looked to marriage for erotic fulfillment just as modern people do.

---

38. With some exceptions: see below, note 82. Athenian men probably married at age thirty, women at about half that age: see Mark Golden, "Demography and the Exposure of Girls at Athens," *Phoenix* 35, 4 (1981), 316–31, esp. pp. 322–23 and n. 25. For the Roman world, see P. A. Brunt, *Italian Manpower 225 B.C.–A.D. 14* (Oxford, 1971), 137.

39. So, e.g., John d'Emilio and Estelle Freedman, *Intimate Matters: A History of Sexuality in America* (New York, 1988), seem to imply, emphasizing at many points that romantic love only emerges in the West in the nineteenth and twentieth centuries; cf. d'Emilio's own earlier *Sexual Politics, Sexual Communities: the Making of a Homosexual Minority in the United States, 1940–1970* (Chicago, 1983). Keith Hopkins, in his excellent article "Brother-Sister Marriage in Roman Egypt," *Comparative Studies in Society and History* 22, 2 (1980), 303–354, makes the much more reasonable claim that ". . . widespread experience of romantic love has been rare in preindustrial societies and has been connected . . . with women's control over property" (p. 346).

Historians are just now developing a more nuanced and complicated picture, one which suggests that although most people hoped love would *follow* from marriage (N.B., not occasion it), it was not conceptualized as romantic love in a modern sense, but was more like friendly, parental,[40] or sibling relationships. Catullus even wrote to his mistress, Lesbia:

> I once loved you, not simply as the common people love a mistress,
> but as a father loves his sons and sons-in-law.[41]

And if marriage was expected to fulfill sexual needs, this would not be because one chose a partner who matched precisely his or her sexual interest, but because the spouses were considerate of each other's desires, and voluntarily limited the arena of sexuality to marriage. Spouses who were actually "in love" with each other were thought extraordinary and odd before the later empire.[42]

Nonetheless, one does encounter in antiquity, especially under the empire, heterosexual relationships based less on property and status considerations and more closely corresponding to what later ages would call "lovers": i.e., two people involved in a romantic relationship without a predominant coercive element, either legal (as in slavery) or economic (as in concubinage).[43] Neither property nor household considerations were central in such relationships (the parties usually did not occupy the same household, at least at first). They were based on mutual attraction and love between persons whose

---

40. In their ideal form all these relationships, as far as the evidence allows us to infer, involved a male ten to twenty years older than the female, who was somewhere between ten and twenty. This made filial affection seem more natural than it might in modern relationships where there is typically less age difference. There is some evidence that this was the most common pattern in reality as well as a cultural ideal, but it is difficult to be certain, and there was undoubtedly much variation over time and place. Most of the works cited above, nn. 17 and 20., address this question.

41. *Carmina* 72.3.

42. See, e.g., Xenophon, *Symposium* 8.3: "Nicerates, I hear, loves and is loved by his wife" (Νικήρατος, ὡς ἀκούω, ἐρῶν τῆς γυναικὸς ἀντερᾶται). (If exclamation points had been known in antiquity one could well imagine one at the end of this statement.) Plautus refers to "*amatores mariti*" as a special class of person (*Menaechmi* 129). As late as Plutarch (second century C.E.) one finds astonishment at a husband's being "in love" with his wife (*Erotikos* 761E: Ἀδμήτῳ...ἐρῶντι μὲν αὐτῷ τῆς γυναικός; note that this is a treatise on erotic love.)

43. It would be unrealistic to say there was *no* element of coercion.

social and economic statuses were either comparable or irrelevant; they were rarely married to each other, though they might be married to someone else. Such arrangements were for the most part possible only in prosperous, sophisticated societies in which women could maintain themselves in their own households without military protection—i.e., the urban centers of the Mediterranean and southern Europe. They were depicted in popular literature as both exclusive and permanent ("eternal, undying love"), although the evidence suggests they were actually neither.[44]

This notion of "lovers" on terms of relative equality (at least within the relationship) either accompanied or caused a shift among some elements of the population in expectations of marriage. At Athens and in the Roman republic, legal heterosexual matrimony was essentially the transfer of power over a woman, who had been under the control of her father (or brother, or uncle, or some adult male), to that of her new husband (or his father, if the husband was not head of his own household), who then stood in this role as her controller/protector.[45] Romans called this marriage *cum manu*:[46] the basic idea was that all persons in a household were subject to the adult male, the *paterfamilias*; this included his wife, children, servants, clients, and slaves. The word *familia*, from *famulus*, "servant," described this unit, and was significantly different from its modern English derivative, "family," which generally applies only to kin and does not denote ownership or control. (Note, for example, that any member of the *familia* would be considered available to the *paterfamilias* for sexual purposes,[47] whereas in the modern family it is only the wife.)

---

44. This literature survives mostly in Greek from the empire, and includes the Hellenistic novels discussed below, as well as the *Satyricon* (likewise discussed below) and love poetry such as that of Ovid.

45. Gordon Williams points out that the same word, *morigera* ("dutiful," "obliging"), is used in Latin literature to describe filial piety and wifely obedience: "Some Aspects of Roman Marriage Ceremonies and Ideals," pp. 21–22.

46. This phrase, which literally means "with hand," is untranslatable. The "hand" is the symbol of authority or control in premodern Europe: compare the modern expression "to ask for her hand."

47. Apparently including his own children: *percide si vis, filium tuum; nefas non est* ("screw your son, if you wish; it is not wrong") Martial 6:39. On the other hand, daughters would lose their social standing and value if they were not virgins at the time of marriage, so fathers would be highly unlikely to molest them. Whether child molesting was common in the ancient world is extremely difficult to judge: the most common words for "child" in both Greek (παῖς) and Latin (*puer*) also mean "slave," so in many cases when an adult is said to be having sex with someone designated by these terms it could simply be with his slave or

But a different form of marriage became common under the empire. Technically, the new form was *sine manu* "without authority": the wife did not become the property of her husband, or even legally a part of his *familia*, but was conceptualized as an adult person in her own right or as an extension of her former family, now joined to the husband's (i.e., as opposed to her becoming a member of his *familia*). Within the household (though certainly not outside it) there was a semblance of equality. This may not seem an enormous change, and, indeed, it did not make a great difference in the status of women, but it did bring in its train many other subtle changes. In effect, the previous system had been one of collateral adoption,[48] and this was often recognized explicitly—a wife was basically "adopted" by her husband and his family. It was, that is, not so much two families being united as one family taking on a new member. A wife is "called a sister," observed the Roman writer Gellius (second century C.E.), "because she is given birth, as it were, apart, and then separated from the family into which she was born and transferred into another household."[49] It is worth noting that it was during the period when Egyptian marriage most resembled modern egalitarian marriage that the terms "brother" and "sister" were used by husband and wife, to express affection if not as an accurate reflection of biological relationship: "In the course of fifteen hundred years, Egyptian marriage contracts moved from no-fault divorce with significant compensation for the divorced wife, through community of property and reciprocal if unequal moral obligations between husband and wife, to virgin marriage in which the wife was bound to subserve her husband under threat of legal and religious penalties. And it was this last development which became embedded within western culture."[50]

---

servant. Kelley Ditmar of the Yale history department is preparing a study of child molestation in ancient and medieval Europe.

48. Raymond Westbrook in his two-volume study, "Old Babylonian Marriage Law," (Ph.D. diss., Yale, 1982), demonstrates that "marriage should . . . be compared to other forms of status such as adoption rather than to forms of contract" (his description in the Abstract).

49. *Noctes Atticae* 13.10: *Soror, inquit, appellata est, quod quasi seorsum nascitur separaturque ab ea domo in qua nata est et in aliam familiam transgreditur.* This is a fanciful etymology of *soror*, not actually a comment on the nature of marriage, but the description of collateral adoption is no less accurate for that. For corroboration of my inference in relation to the ancient family, see David Herlihy, "Family," *American Historical Review* 96, 1 (February 1991), 1–16, p. 5. "There is ample evidence," Hopkins notes of Roman Egypt, "of husbands calling wives 'sister' and of wives calling husbands 'brother' " (p. 312).

50. Hopkins, p. 342.

The newer type of marriage came closer to symbolizing the joining of two families represented in the person of the husband and wife, and this contributed to notions of marriage as a union of near-equals rather than simply males acquiring females as property. It was not a complete or even a dramatic change (even today in most of Europe and the United States wives take the surname of their husbands, which suggests adoption into his family rather than partnership of two lineages), but it was an important one, picked up by many of the ethical systems of late antiquity, including Christianity.

Three of the most important consequences of this shift were: (1) the woman's consent (rather than simply her parents') was increasingly emphasized as necessary to valid marriage;[51] (2) wives could sue their husbands for divorce; (3) the right of husbands to have sex with any members of the *familia* (or all social inferiors) was restricted in many households.[52]

These trends are eloquently evidenced in the marriage contracts that survive on papyrus from Roman Egypt from the centuries before and after the beginning of the Christian Era. They were drawn up for people who were ethnically and culturally Greek, but lived, like most of the peoples of the Mediterranean at the time, under Roman rule.

In 92 B.C.E., a couple negotiated the following agreement prior to their marriage:

> Philiscus son of Apollonius . . . acknowledges to Apollonia, . . . daughter of Heraclides, . . . having . . . as guardian her brother Apollonius, that he has received from her in copper money 2 talents 4000 drachmae, the dowry for her agreed upon with him. Apollonia shall live with Philiscus, obeying him as a wife should her husband, owning their property in common with

---

[51.] This is a very complex issue. See discussion below, pp. 50ff.

[52.] For the nature of the restrictions, see the limitations imposed in the contract cited just below, where the husband is not to bring any other partners home, but it is not clear that he could not resort to them outside the house. The *Digest* (45.1.121.1) records a case in which a woman had stipulated to her husband-to-be that he would owe her two hundred [denarii?] if he resumed cohabitation with his concubine, which he did. Papinian saw no reason why she could not demand the money, since the contract was *ex bonis moribus*. But note there is no suggestion that his doing so violates the marital understanding itself: it is simply a contract issue.

him. All necessaries and clothing and whatever else is proper for a married woman [ὄσα προσήκει γυναικὶ γαμετῆι][53] Philiscus shall supply to Apollonia, whether he is at home or abroad, in proportion to their means. Philiscus shall not be entitled[54] to bring in another wife[55] besides Apollonia, nor to have a concubine or a male lover,[56] nor to have children by another woman[57] while Apollonia lives, nor to inhabit another house over which Apollonia is not mistress, nor to eject or insult or illtreat her, nor to alienate any of their property to the detriment of Apollonia. If he is proved to be doing any of these things or fails to supply her with necessaries or clothing or other things as stated, Philiscus shall forthwith forfeit to Apollonia the dowry of 2 talents 4000 drachmae of copper. In like manner Apollonia shall not be entitled to spend the night or day away from the house of Philiscus without consulting him,[58] or to consort [συνεῖναι] with another man or to dishonour the common home or to cause Philiscus to be shamed by any act that brings shame upon a husband. If Apollonia chooses of her own will to separate from Philiscus, Philiscus shall repay her the simple[59] dowry within ten days from the date of the demand. If he does not repay as stated, he shall forthwith forfeit to her one and a half times the amount of the dowry which he has received.[60]

[53.] See n. 16 about the difficulties of translating γύνη. Hunt and Edgar render this "a wedded wife."

[54.] Hunt and Edgar render μὴ ἐξέστι "it shall not be lawful," but this is too strong.

[55.] γυναῖκα ἄλλην: a problem for translators, because γύνη means both "woman" and "wife." Although this society did not allow polygamy, "another wife" seems justified by the context (in contrast to a concubine or boyfriend).

[56.] A more literal reading of the Greek (μηδὲ παλλακὴν μηδὲ π[αιδ]ικὸν ἔχειν) than the one provided by Hunt and Edgar, who have "not to keep a concubine or boy." ἔχειν means "to have," not "to keep," and a παιδικά might be an adult. Cf. B. P. Grenfell and A. S. Hunt, eds., *New Classical Fragments and Other Greek and Latin Papyri* (London, 1897).

[57.] ἐξ ἄλλης γυναικός: the same phrase rendered "another wife" above.

[58.] ἄνευ τῆς Φιλίσκου γνώ[μ]ης; Hunt and Edgar give "without Philiscus' consent," which seems too strong. γνώμη means "judgment."

[59.] Hunt and Edgar translate "bare": the idea is that she is entitled to nothing beyond the dowry.

[60.] Abridged and revised (as noted) from A. S. Hunt and C. C. Edgar, *Select Papyri with an English Translation* (London, 1932), vol. 1, no. 2, pp. 4–9. The terms are quite typical, almost formulaic; many similar contracts survive, but because the papyri are still being published it is not possible to give statistics. For further commentary, see Hopkins, "Brother-Sister Marriage," passim.

Although it is more like modern marriage to the extent that it is a contract (both literally and figuratively) between the bride and groom, and does not involve the parents of either,[61] this arrangement nonetheless seems rather businesslike. Sensible, mutually advantageous alliances were the cultural ideal of marriage in most of the ancient world, even under the later empire as unions became more egalitarian and affective.[62] Even in Achilles Tatius' intensely romantic novel *Clitophon and Leucippe* the protagonist's father arranges a sensible marriage for him to a homely woman with a fortune (1.7).

On the other hand, there is a considerable romantic literature from this same milieu in which spouses are depicted as ardent lovers, drawn to each other by beauty or character, uninterested in anyone else despite constant temptations and assaults on their virtue, and faithful to each other to the end of their lives.[63] The idea that love might provoke a marriage is not new, but in most previous Greek and Latin literature its role had been much more one-sided: a male (human or divine) captivated by the beauty of a female took her as his bride (sometimes, as in the *Iliad*, literally *took* her; more commonly he asked her father or guardian for her "hand"). There was some ancient tradition of reciprocity of love between spouses, at least as much as is suggested by the Song of Songs,[64] but this was not a common motif

---

61. The change in Hellenistic Egypt from a contract between the husband and the father of the bride (γάμος ἔγγραφος) to one of consent between the couple (συγχώρησις) could be viewed as a local peculiarity, but the evidence has led the major authorities on the development of marriage to view it as reflecting broader tendencies in the Roman Empire: see, e.g., Wolff, passim, and Korbinian Ritzer, *Formen, Riten und religiösen Brauchtum der Eheschliessung in den christlichen Kirchen des ersten Jahrtausends*. Liturgiewissenschaftliche Quellen und Forschungen, 38 (Münster, 1962), p. 20 (the French translation of this work [*Le mariage dans les églises chrétiennes du Ier au XIe siècle* {Paris, 1970}], often cited by those who prefer not to read the German original, is unreliable and omits much material, especially in the notes).

62. This is ultimately why, Keith Hopkins ("Brother-Sister Marriage") concludes, brother-sister marriage was common in this area—it was sensible and personally satisfactory, although presumably not based on the sort of ἔρως later ages would associate with marriage. Moreover, "if a wife was divorced without fault on her side, she had a contractual right to a substantial part of [the] common property. This was not a matter of law, but of custom and contract," p. 336.

63. Hopkins argues that love plays a substantial role in marriage in Roman Egypt ("the demotic marriage contracts, in which emotion, love for another or hatred for a spouse, was recognized as adequate grounds for a divorce," p. 353).

64. Jacob wants to marry Rachel (rather than Leah) because she is attractive (Gen. 29, 30), although the marriage is also quite practical, but in general the Hebrew Scriptures seem to separate erotic interest—which is often destructive—from marriage, which is either for companionship and mutual support or for children. The Song of Songs constitutes such a singular exception to this—the bride and groom speak of each other in almost entirely erotic tones—that most European commentators found it deeply perplexing.

before the empire.[65] Although in most of the Hellenistic examples it is a theme of escapist fantasy, it is embedded in a deeply conventional literature, and clearly embodies a widespread *wish* that marriage could be based on love and choice, if not a reflection that it actually was.

It is difficult to weigh this tradition against the nearly universal ethical advice of the same environment to contract marriages based on good judgment and to aspire to a friendly, siblinglike, or parental affection toward a spouse.[66] Possibly they cannot be reconciled: they may represent the differing values of several elements in a large and diverse population, or the sort of paradoxical feelings even within individuals that complicate human bondings. Tension between the two models of marriage is quite evident within most of the romance novels themselves, and sometimes forms part of the plot. In *Clitophon and Leucippe*, for example, both of the male protagonists find that parentally arranged matches interfere with erotic passions (one homosexual, one heterosexual). "I am caught on the horns of a dilemma," one laments. "Love and my father are at odds."[67] And while the hero and heroine of Xenophon of Ephesus' romance novel are deeply in love with each other and drawn together by mutual attraction, their parents in fact arrange the marriage, for reasons completely unrelated to their feelings, and without consulting them. A wealthy widow in Plutarch's *Erotikos* abducts the youth she wants to marry because his friends have advised him against the match and she fears he is vacillating. But his parents appear to have favored the union, and it is unlikely she could have succeeded without their support. Although in this fiction love *becomes* the substance of marriage, even in the most idealized literature it is rarely the *occasion* for it.

Of the four types of lasting heterosexual relationships outlined here, only two had specific legal significance, both for reasons of prop-

---

65. In Plutarch's Ἐρωτικός [752C] Plutarch himself protests against a speaker's characterizing (heterosexual) marriage as "loveless union devoid of friendship" (ἀνέραστον καὶ ἄμοιρον φιλίας κοινωνίαν), but later in the same dialogue one of the *advocates* of marriage for love concedes that love makes marriage "stormy and chaotic"—as if most marriages would not be undertaken for love (753D).

66. Lucian's *Toxaris* (ed. and trans. A. M. Harmon in *LCL*, Lucian, vol. 5 [Cambridge, 1936] §§44–54) includes an interesting episode involving a man who falls in love with a woman at first sight while visiting her father and asks to marry her. The father, more typically, is seeking a sensible match, and rejects the man because he is poor. The suitor then enlists his friends to abduct her.

67. ἐν μεθορίῳ κεῖμαι δύο ἐναντίων· ἔρως ἀνταγωνίζεται καὶ πατήρ. Achilles Tatius, *Clitophon and Leucippe*, ed. and trans. S. Gaselee (Cambridge, 1969) 1.11.3, p. 36.

erty: use, which was a man's utilization of his own property, and marriage, which involved allocations of family property that needed legal regulation. Concubinage, although frequently mentioned in Roman law, entailed few legal consequences (either of property or status), and lovers none. On the other hand, both Greek and Roman marriages were conceived to be chiefly practical matters of fact rather than complex interactions of law, theology, and morality, as they were to become later in Europe. Law intruded only to protect property or inheritance rights;[68] the couple's relationship and obligations to each other were supervised (if they were supervised) by the community and family, whose recognition of their union was what made it a reality.

Of the four, moreover, marriage was the only one whose parameters were publicly marked or solemnized. Its acknowledgement was to a large extent what distinguished it, at the practical level, from the other three, all of which were private and largely unmarked by the surrounding society, except in fiction. In cultures that regard marriage chiefly as the process of a male's *obtaining* a woman, through purchase, abduction, or negotiation, the act of sexual intercourse is the primary marker of his ownership, both because it shows that he has taken full possession (both literally and figuratively), and because the bride would after this no longer be desirable to another groom.[69]

In the political and tribal city-states of the ancient Mediterranean consummation was not, however, the most important aspect of a marriage, partly because it was private and largely unverifiable. Instead, the union was first and foremost an alliance of families, and other markers of aspects of the coupling were emphasized in public ritual. Greek marriage was celebrated (usually in winter)[70] with sacrifices to

---

68. As a consequence, there is considerable Roman legislation on legitimate marriage: Roman property law of all sorts is enormous and complex. There is less Greek law of all sorts, and correspondingly less about marriage. Demosthenes' orations against Spudias (41) regarding a marriage portion, and against Neaera (59, quoted at the head of this chapter) about the liceity of a citizen's keeping a foreign concubine are particularly revealing about the interaction of Greek expectations, legal provisions, and practice.

69. It might be compared, somewhat crudely, to breaking an item in a store in industrial nations: "You break it; you own it."

70. The month of Γαμηλιών ("marriage month") corresponded roughly to late January and early February in the modern calendar. The most thoughtful treatments of both Greek and Roman matrimonial celebrations are those of Anne Schwerdtfeger, *Ethnological Sources of the Christian Marriage Ceremony* (Stockholm, 1982) and Ritzer, *Formen, Riten und religiösen Brauchtum*, as noted above, nn. 32 and 61.

the deities of marriage (usually Zeus and Hera, the archetypes of the married couple: see below), a ritual bath for the bride, a wedding feast at the bride's (i.e., her father's) home (during which the couple wore crowns),[71] the transporting of the veiled bride on a cart or carriage from her father's house to her new home (her husband's) by the groom and his best friend, preceded by a crowd of people singing the wedding chant ("Hymen"). This procession was lit by candles or torches. At her new home she was conducted, still veiled, into the "bridal chamber," and the attendants sang the *epithalamium* (song for the wedding chamber) outside as—they assumed—the key act of the marriage ceremony took place: its physical consummation (the act by which the husband took full "possession" of the wife). On the day after the ceremony gifts were presented to the bride.

Such ceremonies give few clues about the ideology of Greek marriage. Most elements of the ceremony relate to transfer of the bride to another household (cart, consummation) or to her emergence into society as an adult woman (banquet, ritual bath, special clothing, hymn). Sacrifices to gods and torches suggest a belief in some mystical or theological aspect to matrimony, but it is hard to be sure what it was. Zeus and Hera were the gods of marriage: they were brother and sister as well as husband and wife, and for this reason as well as others they hardly constituted apt models for human marital bliss. Zeus was noted for constant philandering, and there is very little reflection in Greek literature of any domestic happiness in their relationship. Although Hera was the goddess of marriage, she was not known as a mother,[72] whereas the most notable divine mothers (e.g., Leto and Demeter) were not notably associated with marriage.[73] At its best, marital happiness in the Greek imagination seems to have involved ὁμοφροσύνη—a union of "spirits" or harmony of minds[74]—but not erotic satisfaction, sexual fidelity, or romantic fulfillment.[75]

---

71. Ritzer, p. 16; Ritzer says the groom also gave a banquet at the couple's house (pp. 17–18).
72. She bore the epithet ζυγία in Greek ("of marriage"), whereas in Latin Juno was also called "Lucina" ("giving light," i.e., "of childbirth").
73. Redfield makes this point as well: p. 182.
74. Cf. the opinion of Redfield, p. 197, and his translation of *Odyssey* 6.180–84, ibid., pp. 196–97: "To you may the gods give all those things you desire in your heart:/ A husband, a house, and union of minds may they give you/Which is good. There nothing better or finer than that/When in union of minds and intention there hold a house/A man and woman."
75. Of many illustrations of this one might cite, for example, the legend that Hercules gave his own wife Megara to Ioläus, his (male) lover, before begetting any children by her (i.e., before

Roman marriages usually took place in June. The bride put away on the preceding day the clothing worn by unmarried girls,[76] and for the wedding donned a special tunic and belt,[77] had her hair done in a traditional arrangement,[78] and was covered with a large, flame-colored veil (the *flammeum*). By imperial times, the central symbolic act took place in the bride's house: in the presence of friends, relations, and dependents, the couple expressed their consent to the marriage, the matron of honor (*pronuba*) joined their right hands (*dextrarum junctio*), and they kissed. In much of the Roman world a priest presided over or officially witnessed the ceremony.[79] Then the contract, if there was one,[80] was signed.[81] These elements reflect the tendency of imperial couples to regard marriage as a partnership comparable to a commercial consortium rather than the simple sale of a woman to one man by another.[82]

The remainder of the Roman celebration was more ancient and less reflective of imperial views of marriage. After a religious sacrifice and a wedding banquet, the bride was "taken" (*deducitur*) to the home of her husband in a public procession, where the groom met her and carried her over the threshold. As in Greece, the wedding party

---

consummating the marriage? this is not clear) because he thought she was unlucky (Diodorus Siculus 4.31). The "romance" in this tale clearly subsists only between Hercules and Ioläus; the wife is simply a valued possession. Compare stories of friends in Lucian, and Lantfrid and Cobbo in the early Middle Ages.

76. E.g., the *toga praetexta*.

77. *Tunica recta* and "knot of Hercules."

78. *Sex crines* and *vittae*.

79. See Ritzer, p. 20, and Wolff, p. 39.

80. Even authors who believe in some uniform marital contract (e.g., Ritzer: see following note) admit that under Roman law *nuptiae sine scriptura* (matrimony with no written documentation) counted as legal marriage (Ritzer, p. 20). Cf. Wolff: "Marriage did not require any special form in order to be recognized by the law" (p. 83); "Any serious and exclusive union of a man and a woman . . . was admissible as a real marriage" (ibid., p. 72). This was an ancient understanding: the Laws of the Twelve Tables (6.5) count any woman who lives with a man for an entire year as his legal wife. In time, as noted below, legal marriage was restricted to certain classes and cultural-linguistic groups within the empire.

81. These contracts, written on wax and wood—which perished in the climate of Italy, unlike parchment from Egypt—do not survive, and we have no direct knowledge of their contents. Nonetheless, Ritzer (p. 28) and others assume that later Christian comments about the nature of marriage may be taken as indicative of the provisions of pagan contracts. Christians unquestionably borrowed much of their matrimonial custom and theory from pagan Rome, but also added strikingly original ideas (e.g., mutual sexual fidelity, no divorce), and this inference seems to me reckless and anachronistic.

82. The adaptation of ideas of *societas* and *consortium*—both forms of partnership, originally commercial—to apply to heterosexual matrimony is very lucidly and conveniently addressed by Treggiari, *Roman Marriage*, pp. 249–51.

then sang an *epithalamium* outside the bridal chamber during what they assumed was the consummation of the marriage.

Consummation was not essential to Roman marriage, at least judging by surviving legal provisions.[83] In Roman law consent and "marital affection" (*maritalis affectio*) were the essential components of legal marriage,[84] and if these were present any couple not precluded by legal status or kinship would be legally married as long as they both consented to and intended to persevere in the marriage, whether it had been physically consummated or not.[85] Nor were children integral to Roman ideals of matrimony: on the contrary, much imperial legislation was designed to inspire upper-class couples to have children, which they were obviously not inclined to do on their own. No one took childlessness as undermining the validity or reality of their marriages, simply as a default of civic duty. In his treatise on the purpose of marriage Musonius Rufus insisted that procreation alone could hardly justify it, since one could get children from any sexual union.[86] Matrimony was necessary for κηδεμονία—mutual care.[87] Similarly, in a celebrated formulation of late Roman law, marriage was defined as "a partnership for life."[88]

[83] "Sexual union and consummation of the marriage were no more essential in Roman matrimonial law than a wedding cake is in ours," James Brundage, *Law, Sex, and Christian Society in Medieval Europe* (Chicago, 1987) 36. As will be emphasized in subsequent chapters, laws are not necessarily a reliable indication of ordinary social practice or popular belief, but in this case many comments and reflections in literature suggest that this was the common view as well. For example, in Apuleius, *Metamorphoses* 6.9, when Venus complains about her son's relationship with Psyche, she objects that their marriage was "between persons of different social status, in a country house without witnesses, and without the consent of the father," and asserts that offspring will therefore be illegitimate. Cf. 6.23.

[84] *Digest* 50.17.30: *Nuptias non concubitus, sed consensus facit*; ibid. 24.1.32.13: *Non enim coitus matrimonium facit, sed maritalis affectio*. See also P. E. Corbett, *The Roman Law of Marriage* (Oxford, 1930), 95.

[85] "The legal basis of marriage in classical Roman law was the consent of the participants, and so becoming man and wife was not a process in which any governmental participation was required," Lee, p. 410 n. 31, confirming the earlier view of Corbett.

[86] On the other hand, he also argues that the procreation of children is the *sole* legitimation of intercourse, even within matrimony: ἐν γάμῳ καὶ ἐπὶ γενέσει παίδων, "What Is the Chief End of Marriage?" Cora Lutz, *Musonius Rufus "The Roman Socrates"* (New Haven, 1947), 86.

[87] Ibid., pp. 88–89. Dixon disagrees with this (p. 67: "the purpose of Roman marriage was the production of legitimate citizen children"), but it is difficult to see why she should be trusted over Roman citizens.

[88] *Digest* 23.2.1: *Nuptiae sunt . . . consortium omnis uitae*; cf. the English translation of *The Digest of Justinian*, ed. Alan Watson (Philadelphia, 1985) 2:657; cf. 34.1.16.3. The formulation also occurs in literary expressions (e.g., *Uxor est quae femina viro nuptiis collocata in societatem vitae venit*, Quintilian, *Declamationes minores* 247.2; Augustine uses *naturalem in*

The classical formulation of Roman law on the constitution of marriage avers that "consent, not cohabitation, makes a marriage" (*nuptias non concubitus sed consensus facit*),[89] but the issue is actually rather more complex than this makes it appear. First of all, the consent of *all* the parties to the marriage is at issue—i.e., not simply that of the bride and groom but also of their legal guardians,[90] which makes it less comparable to the modern situation. And, perhaps more important from our perspective, the "consent" of the bride is *assumed* unless she protests officially,[91] which would have been very difficult, and was actually an impediment only if the fiancé could be shown to be "unworthy" or "base" (*indignum moribus vel turpem*)—i.e., the marriage was *not* dependent simply on her desires or preferences.[92]

The divine archetypes of marriage in the Roman religion, Jupiter and Juno, enjoyed no more connubial success or felicity than their Greek equivalents. Instead, their relationship appears in mythology to subsist in Jupiter's philandering and Juno's shrewish complaining about it. *Amor*, or Cupid—passionate or romantic love—was conceptualized in Roman myth as the child of Venus and Vulcan, who were not married.[93] Neither Venus nor her son had any particular relationship to marriage initially, though in later literature a loose association begins to surface.[94] The primary deity of matrimony for Romans was *Concordia*, "harmony," a close parallel to the Greek ὁμοφροσύνη.

---

diverso sexu societatem (*De bono coniugali* 3.3), but probably means sexual intercourse. See further examples in Treggiari, *Roman Marriage*, pp. 249–51.

89. *Digest* 50.17.30 (Ulpian). On the stages of development of this principle, and whether a woman's consent was necessary under the early republic, see Alan Watson, *The Law of Persons in the Later Roman Republic* (Oxford, 1930), 4, 57, and con., Susan Treggiari, "Consent to Roman Marriage: Some Aspects of Law and Reality," *Échos du Monde classique: Classical News and Views*, New Series 1 (1982) 34–44. Treggiari's position seems to me more judicious.

90. *Digest* 23.2.2 (Paulus): "Marriage is not valid unless all consent to it: that is, those who will wed and their guardians" (*nuptiae consistere non possunt, nisi consentiant omnes, id est qui coeunt quorumque in potestate sunt*).

91. *Digest* 23.1.12 (Ulpian): *Sed quae patris voluntati non repugnat, consentire intelligitur.* Cf. Dixon, p. 64: ". . . even express refusal could be discounted, particularly in the case of the bride."

92. Ibid.: *Tunc autem solum dissentiendi a patre licentia filiae conceditur, si indignum moribus vel turpem sponsum ei pater eligat.* Divorce after marriage did not require "grounds" during the classical period of Roman law (i.e., before the fourth century), but it is unlikely that a daughter could divorce her husband without the knowledge and consent of her living male relatives.

93. Although Apuleius (*Metamorphoses* 5:29–30) depicts Venus as regarding both her relationships with Vulcan and with Mars as "marriages."

94. See previous note and next chapter.

One can, indeed, trace a shift in the Roman ideology of marriage: under the republic it was conceptualized chiefly as a transfer of a woman from possession as a child by her father to possession as a wife by her husband. Under the empire this was replaced by an increasingly partnerlike and unitive notion, not excluding ideas of ownership entirely, but emphasizing instead the joining of two adults. Both conceptions idealized marriage as *concordia*—"harmony," "peace"—and frequently illustrated this in art with the linking of right hands: the *dextrarum junctio* that formed a central symbol of the imperial wedding. Jupiter and Juno, the archetypal divine married couple, were also brother and sister, a situation that, if somewhat shocking to modern sensibilities, evoked for Romans the union of persons of the same generation and the same status (having the same parents)—i.e., a more egalitarian relationship than patriarchal husband and possessed wife.[95] It also carried overtones of commercial contract and political treaty, often evoked in art either by portraying political alliances as marriages or by using political symbolism to depict matrimony.

Perhaps the most significant aspect of Roman marriage law, at least from the point of view of societies influenced by it, was that although other issues were emphasized in various times and places in Europe,[96] the overall tendency of European and Mediterranean society was to emphasize consent and marital affection (though somewhat difficult to define) as the primary determinants of valid marriage, a view based squarely on Roman law: "It is not cohabitation, but consent that makes marriage";[97] "Not coitus but marital affection constitutes matrimony."[98] Despite its emphasis on procreation as the *theoretical justification* for marriage, the Christian church by and large adhered to this basic foundation of (pagan) Roman law.[99]

This change and de-emphasis on control over marriageable women

---

[95.] This was not only well known to educated Romans, but emphasized in classics of literature like Vergil's *Aeneid* 1:47: *ego . . . et soror et coniunx*. It is also worth noting that nearly all ancient creation myths postulate incest at the outset. The Jewish Scriptures avoid this in the first generation by depicting Eve as a separate creation, but they are mute about how the second and third generations avoided marrying close relatives. Christians refused to speculate on this.

[96.] In the West most notably issues of dowry formalities and consummation; in the East most notably ceremonial formalities—e.g., the presence of priest.

[97.] *Nuptias non concubitus, sed consensus facit* (50.17.30).

[98.] *Non enim coitus matrimonium facit, sed maritalis affectio* (24.1.32.13).

[99.] See Chapter 4.

made it more difficult to distinguish legitimate marriage from *contubernium* (simple living together of those not entitled to legal marriage) and concubinage (which might be preferred by a Roman male even though he could legally marry). The latter problem had been hitherto addressed by upper-class Romans by keeping very strict control over unmarried citizen women, so that, in fact, the only relationships they were allowed to form would lead to legal marriage. As Roman society became more varied and open, and this strict control was no longer acceptable, the law increasingly gave up distinguishing strictly between *justae nuptiae* and other forms of cohabitation.[100] (Christians would often fail to see any difference: see below.)

[100.] See on this difficulty *Digest* 34.9.16.1 and 34.2.35 pr, 39.5.31 pr. The crucial distinction seems to be intention: *concubina igitur ab uxore solo dilectu separatur* (Paulus, *Sententiae* 2.20.1). Cf. *Digest* 25.7.4, Libro 19 resp.: *Concubinam ex sola animi destinatione aestimari oportet*; and 23.2.65.1: *si in eadem voluntate perseverat*.

"A Friend Inspired by God"

SAME-SEX UNIONS
— *in* —
THE GRECO-ROMAN WORLD

*D*URING THIS SAME PERIOD (i.e., roughly 400 B.C.E. to 400 C.E.) there were, very broadly speaking, also four types of same-sex relationships; these exhibit some parallels to heterosexual unions, but also some peculiarities.[1] In general, the divisions

---

[1] There has been an explosion of scholarship on homosexuality in classical antiquity during the last decade. For the more limited literature to 1980 (when it was still risky to write on this subject), see *CSTH*, esp. p. 4 n. 3, p. 17 n. 25, and p. 61 n. 3. I did not engage K. J. Dover's *Greek Homosexuality* (Cambridge, 1978), which appeared just as *CSTH* did; I am as unpersuaded by some of its specifics as I am in awe of its general good sense. (For example, Dover's inferences about intercrural intercourse from vase paintings are oddly naïve—as if erotic art constituted a reliable indication of actual sexual practice. [Dover has modified some of his views in the "updated" edition of *Greek Homosexuality* "with a new postscript" {Cambridge, 1989}.]) To him may now be added Michel Foucault's superficial but challenging overview of Greek and Roman sexual constructs in his *Histoire de la sexualité*, esp. vols. 2: *L'Usage des plaisirs* (Paris, 1984) and 3: *Le Souci de soi* (Paris, 1984); Paul Veyne, "La famille et l'amour sous le Haut-Empire romain," *Annales E.S.C.* 33 (1978), 3–23, and idem, "L'Homosexualité à Rome," *L'Histoire* 30 (1981), 76–78; J. P. Sullivan, "Martial's Sexual Attitudes," *Philologus. Zeitschrift für klassische Philologie* 123 (1979), 288–302; F. Buffière, *Éros adolescent: La pédérastie dans la Grèce antique* (Paris, 1980); Jan Bremmer, "An Enigmatic Indo-European Rite: Paederasty," *Arethusa* 13.2 (1980), 279–98; Yvon Garlan, Olivier Masson, "Les Acclamations pédérastiques de Kalami (Thasos)," *Bulletin de Correspondance Hellénique* 106 (1982) I: *Études*, 3–21; Gerda Kempter, *Ganymed: Studien zur Typologie, Ikonographie und Ikonologie* (Cologne, 1980); D. S. Barrett, "The Friendship of Achilles and Patroclus," *Classical Bulletin* 57 (1981), 87–93, which includes a thorough review of the literature on homosexuality in Homer; J. N. Adam, *The Latin Sexual Vocabulary* (Baltimore, 1982); David Cohen, "Law, Society and Homosexuality in Classical Athens," *Past and Present* 117 (1987), 3–21. None of these works takes into account the chapter on Roman homosexuality in *CSTH*; for criticism of it see Ramsay MacMullen, "Roman Attitudes to Greek Love," *Historia* 31, 4 (1982), 484–502, and

among the homosexual four are more fluid and less legalistic than among varieties of heterosexual unions. The latter had to be legally distinguished because they often determined the status of offspring and the disposition of property; the former usually did not.

Exploitation of males owned or controlled by other males was widespread; it was both a common act of aggression against defeated foes to rape them,[2] and a very ordinary use of slaves.[3] The Roman poet Martial complains sarcastically to a friend that he must rely on his own hand for sexual release while the friend has a "troop" of

more thoughtful and informed observations in Eva Cantarella, "Etica sessuale e diritto. L'omosessualità maschile a Roma," *Rechsthistorisches Journal* 6 (1987), 277–92, expanded in *Secondo natura: La bisessualità nel mondo antico* (Rome, 1988 [English trans. Cormac O'Cuilleanain, *Bisexuality in the Ancient World* {New Haven, 1992}]), and Danilo Dalla, *"Ubi Venus mutatur": Omosessualità e diritto nel mondo romano* (Milan, 1987); for general agreement (plus some revisions), Saara Lilja, *Homosexuality in Republican and Augustan Rome* (Helsinki, 1982). Robin Scroggs, *The New Testament and Homosexuality* (Philadelphia, 1983), although addressed to religious issues, provides a useful overview of sexual practices and attitudes in the Mediterranean during the first centuries of the Christian Era, as does Carlos Espejo Muriel, *El Deseo negado: Aspectos de la problemática homosexual en la vida monástica (siglos III–VI d.c.)*, (Granada, 1991). I disagree with both of their conclusions; I also find myself in substantial disagreement with Bernard Sergent's very peculiar anthropological approach in *L'Homosexualité dans la mythologie grècque* (Paris, 1984) [English trans. Arthur Goldhammer, *Homosexuality in Greek Myth* (Boston, 1986)], and, to a lesser extent, with Aline Rousselle, *Porneia* (Paris, 1983) [English trans. Felicia Pheasant, *Porneia: On Desire and the Body in Antiquity* (New York, 1988)]. Neither Elaine Pagels' *Adam, Eve, and the Serpent* (New York, 1988) nor Peter Brown's *The Body and Society: Men, Women, and Sexual Renunciation in Early Christianity* (New York, 1988) sheds much light on this topic. For more recent statements of my own views, see "Revolutions, Universals and Sexual Categories," in *Salmagundi* 58–59: *Homosexuality: Sacrilege, Vision, Politics* (Fall 1982–Winter 1983), 89–113, reprinted with revisions in *Hidden from History: Reclaiming the Gay and Lesbian Past*, ed. Martin Duberman, George Chauncey, and Martha Vicinus (New York, 1989), 17–36; "Concepts, Experience and Sexuality," *Sexuality in Greek and Roman Society*, vol. 2 (Spring, 1990) of *Differences: A Journal of Feminist Cultural Studies*, pp. 67–87. The field has been greatly enriched lately by the contributions of John J. Winkler, *The Constraints of Desire: The Anthropology of Sex and Gender in Ancient Greece* (New York, 1990), whose tragic death precluded what might have been a very fruitful dialogue on these subjects. His contribution is also notable in *Before Sexuality: The Construction of Erotic Experience in the Ancient Greek World*, ed. David Halperin, John Winkler, and Froma Zeitlin (Princeton, 1990). A more strident and doctrinaire approach—still valuable for the immense learning in which it is rooted—is presented by David Halperin, *One Hundred Years of Homosexuality and Other Essays on Greek Love* (New York, 1990). Halperin criticizes CSTH harshly and at great length from a constructionist perspective while incorporating many of its findings almost verbatim (e.g., compare his pp. 2–3 with CSTH, pp. 18–21, published ten years before, and not credited). Work on female homoeroticism in either Greek or Roman antiquity remains minimal: for a rare exception, see Judith Hallett, "Female Homoeroticism and the Denial of Roman Reality in Latin Literature," *Yale Journal of Criticism* 3.1 (Fall, 1989), 209–27.

2. Either personal or national foes: Catullus boasts that he will put his penis up the anus and down the throat of rivals in a famous off-color poem ("Paedicabo ego vos et irrumabo," 16).

3. Mark Golden, "Slavery and Homosexuality at Athens," *Phoenix* 38.4 (1984), 308–24, does not actually concentrate on the issue addressed here, but nonetheless provides a useful introduction to both homosexuality and slave culture at Athens.

passive slaves for this purpose that he could lend (2.43). A character in the Hellenistic novel *Affairs of the Heart* claims that it is possible to discern the sexual preference of a friend by noting the gender of his servants.[4] Because such relationships were private and of no legal consequence, they are hard to identify in the records; our main sources of information about them are casual references in fiction, poetry, graffiti, and so forth, all of which suggest that they were extremely common.[5]

Homosexual concubinage was perhaps less common than heterosexual, but by no means rare.[6] From the evidence of Augustan poetry, one could conclude that Roman men of a certain status had a male slave called a *concubinus* whose specific function was to meet their sexual needs before marriage.[7] As part of the wedding festivities he was dismissed (at least from this post), and there was risqué humor about the situation. Juvenal's ninth satire consists of a conversation with a male prostitute who is part of a complex and regular arrangement with a Roman male and his wife. Marriage contracts from Roman Egypt (as noted) often specify as a condition on the part of the wife that the husband may not have concubines of *either gender* in the house.[8]

[4.] Chapter 10, p. 164, in the *LCL* edition, ed. M. D. Macleod (Cambridge, Mass., 1967).

[5.] Plutarch speculates that freeborn Roman youths wore amulets called *bullae* to identify them as free and unavailable for sexual use, as opposed to slave boys who were fair game: *Roman Questions* 288A–B. Martial's *Epigrams* are filled with references to sexual use of slaves, male and female. For a guide to such literature and analysis of it see *CSTH*, Chapter III, and Williams.

[6.] Demosthenes "is said to have taken into his house Cnosion, an adolescent, even though he had a wife, and she, in annoyance, to have slept with Cnosion," Athenaeus, *Deipnosophistae* 13.593. The term παιδικά often refers to a male concubine, as opposed to a "lover" (which would be either ἐραστής or ἐρώμενος). Plutarch relates that Alexander's wife Thebe resented his making her younger brother his παιδικά (*Life of Pelopidas*, 28).

[7.] See *CSTH*, p. 78, and references there, as well as more recent studies cited in note 1 above. The Greek word for this was πρόκοιτος (as in Dio 80 [79].16.3 [the text of the *Epitome* is confusingly numbered in the *LCL* edition: I have given the chapter headings first, the marginal numberings in brackets]). Although some gentlemen might have preferred a female for this purpose, it is worth remembering that there was no effective means of contraception at the time, and while experienced adults might have learned how to avoid procreation, adolescent males probably could not be trusted to do so.

[8.] Seneca the Elder, in his *Controversia* 4, mentions that the orator Haterius uttered some famous remarks in the course of "defending a freedman accused of being his patron's concubine" (*cui obiciebatur quod patroni concubinus fuisset*). It is not clear what the nature of this "objection" would have been, since Roman males were free to use slaves, and probably freedmen, as they wished. Indeed, the remark that became so well known was that "sexual service [*inpudicitia*] is an offense for the freeborn, a necessity for the slave, and a duty for the freed."

By far the most common type of same-sex relationship in premodern Europe (as it is now in the modern West) was that of "lovers"—i.e., two women or two men united by affection, passion, or desire, with no legal or institutional consequences for status, property, household, and so on.

The classical Attic form of such relationships will already be familiar to most readers, both because it figures so prominently in Attic literature and because it has lately been the subject of much scholarly inquiry.[9]

Homosexual "lover" relationships were parallel in some ways to ancient heterosexual "lover" relations, but exhibited a number of notable differences. They were prominent throughout ancient history, not just at a few points, and often constituted the same-sex equivalent of marriage, at least in the sense that they were the most common and typical relationship among the group in question and generally set the tone for other interactions. In fourth-century Athens, they were similar to heterosexual marriage in that an age difference of nearly a generation was the cultural ideal for both homosexual and heterosexual relationships;[10] in that entering into such a relationship constituted a sort of "coming out" as a young adult (like the bride's entering adult society through marriage);[11] and in that the older person played the role of educator and protector, comparable to that of the husband in a heterosexual marriage.[12]

These factors can easily be exaggerated, however; combined with a shallow misreading of "popular literature" (like the picture of love provided by modern rock music), they have produced an arch, stylized, and misleading view of Greek homosexuality in much modern literature on the subject, which generally portrays classical homosexual relations as formal, brief interactions[13] between an older "lover"

---

[9] See n. 1, above.

[10] Aristotle (*Politics* 7.16) says that men should marry at thirty-seven and women at eighteen. Plato recommends that men not marry till twenty-five to thirty (*Laws* 6.773c). Hesiod gives thirty for the husband and seventeen for the wife (*Works and Days* 696–98); Plutarch quotes and approves this (*Erotikos* 753A). Most women in romances and other fiction marry at sixteen or seventeen.

[11] For this see especially Golden, "Slavery and Homosexuality," as cited above.

[12] Note Plutarch's report of the sequestering of Spartan men under thirty (mentioned below), whose lovers or older male relatives went to the market for them, rather like women in a harem.

[13] For an ancient argument to this effect, see Plutarch, *Erotikos* 770B–C.

(the ἐραστής) and a "beloved" (the ἐρώμενος) who is always considerably younger and generally somewhat passive.[14] That this was the cultural myth, at least in fourth-century Athens, is beyond doubt, but it is the business of historians to get beyond cultural façades.[15]

It is probably wrong to imagine that "lover" and "beloved" were clearly defined positions or roles: ancient writers often express uncertainty about who played which part in well-known relationships[16]— or in any relationship[17]—and the same terms are employed in Greek to describe heterosexual relations that are largely unrelated to such stereotypes.[18] A better way for an English speaker to understand the

[14.] The Hellenistic writer Strato obviously mocks this convention with his Epigram 4 (in *Greek Anthology* 12), in which he praises, successively, young men of twelve, thirteen, fourteen, fifteen, sixteen, seventeen, and older, pointing out that those who are beyond seventeen will likely expect some reciprocity in sexual activity (but not suggesting that this is necessarily a bad thing). Cf. 11.248: "Who could be unattractive today if he was attractive yesterday? And if he is attractive today, what could happen to make him unattractive tomorrow?" Even Athenians at the height of the popularity of such stereotypes parodied them: Golden explores this quite thoughtfully in "Age Differences Between *Erastai* and *Eromenoi*," *Phoenix* 38.4 (1984), 321–24, pointing out a vase, for example, on which two boys are graphically depicted having sex. On the other hand, ideals of physical beauty in the whole of the ancient world (as in modern times) tended to focus on the young: thus Psyche brags to her sisters (unwittingly telling the truth) that her husband is a young man just beginning to grow his beard (Apuleius, *Metamorphoses* 5.8); cf. 5.16. On the other hand, Apuleius either perpetuates or parodies the Attic convention when a young man having an adulterous relationship with an older woman is scolded by her husband for "defrauding his lovers" by engaging in sex with married women before it is his time to do so (9.28). The husband then forces his attentions on the youth himself, sarcastically claiming that matrimonial harmony has led him and his wife to enjoy similar tastes (*eadem nobis ambobus placerent*).

[15.] To what extent these patterns influenced women is difficult to say: there is virtually no information about Attic lesbianism. By the time information about lesbians becomes more abundant (e.g., Lucian: see below) Attic social ideals were no longer the rule even for males. Plutarch says specifically of Sparta (*Life of Lycurgus*, 18) that "this sort of love" (i.e., homosexual: οὕτω δὲ τοῦ ἐρᾶν) was so well thought of by them that even the "young girls had love relations [ἐρᾶν] with beautiful and good women [τὰς καλὰς καὶ ἀγαθὰς γυναῖκας]" (a stock phrase to describe desirable male lovers).

[16.] Despite his generally espousing an extremely rigid and formalist view of ancient sexual relationships, Halperin is forced to admit that there was great uncertainty in antiquity about who played what role in the relationship of Achilles and Patroclus (*One Hundred Years*, p. 86).

[17.] E.g., [Lucian,] *Affairs of the Heart*, §48, p. 224.

[18.] Achilles Tatius, for example, uses ἐραστής and ἐρωμεν– (with either masculine or feminine endings) for both homosexual and heterosexual relationships throughout his novel, and explicitly includes in the latter category instances where the woman is a fully mature adult (e.g., at 1.10), exactly the same age as her lover. Leucippe is the ἐρωμένη of Clitophon, at the same time that Clitophon himself is the ἐρώμενος of Melite. Melite is described (7.1) as the ἐρῶσα of Clitophon, although elsewhere their feelings are characterized in more reciprocal terms (7.6: ἀλλήλων ἐρῶντες). In general it seems that ἐρώμενον is used of Clitophon as the "beloved" of Melite because she is more ardent than he (e.g., at 5.22.6, 6.9.1). Lucian describes a man beloved of a woman as ἐρώμενος in the *Toxaris* (16), as does Athenaeus (13.579), and [Lucian's] "The Ass" (§12, 51). Xenophon of Ephesus has Anthia

terms would be to connect them to our habit of saying that someone "admires" someone else in a romantic context; one person is thus the "admirer" and the other the "admired" (though this expression is less common).[19] Although this does suggest some inequality, it does not describe, in any detail, what will happen (or has taken place) between the two, and its use may arise from circumstances as different as one person's being more vocal about his or her feelings than the other or a significant inequality in the interest the two parties have in each other. Being the "admired" does not necessarily mean being un-moved, having no reciprocal feelings, or needing to be persuaded. It may be the result of being shyer, younger, or already attached. Even at their most basic level these terms are often given insufficiently nuanced analytical attention by historians of Greek social life.[20] Since "beloved" is in general a term for the object of one's affections, and since the affections at issue in the vast majority of Greek litera-ture are those of adult males who would admit only an active role, the "beloved" must necessarily appear as either a younger male (though how much younger remains an open question) or a female.[21]

There were, moreover, competing cultural ideals about same-sex couples even in fourth-century Athens. In a very famous portion of one of his best-known works, the *Symposium* (a dialogue on love), Plato characterized same-sex unions very pointedly as permanent, ex-clusive unions of coevals, in the context of a myth specifically de-signed to explain the origins of human eroticism. Humans were all originally double, the speaker explains: double men, double women, or, in some cases, a mixture of male and female ("androgynes"), all

---

refer to Habrocomes as her "husband and beloved" (ἄνδρα, τὸν ἐρώμενον), though they are exactly the same age. Plutarch has (*Erotikos* 761E) Admetus in love with his wife (ἐρῶντι μὲν αὐτῷ τῆς γυναικός) and also the beloved of Hercules (ἐρωμένου δ' αὐτοῦ γενομένου).

19. One of the relatively few classicists to recognize this is DeWitt, who renders ἐρασταί in Demosthenes' *Erotic Essay* (*LCL*, Demosthenes, vol. 7 [Cambridge, 1949]) as "admirer," and notes (p. 45, note b), "The Greek word means 'lover' or 'sweetheart,' applied to men as well as women."

20. This is especially, lamentably true of Winkler and Halperin, as cited above, and to a lesser extent of Dover. Keith DeVries of the University of Pennsylvania is preparing a splendid antidote to this view based on a wider survey of Greek erotic art than has been used by any previous scholar, so well documented and cogently argued that even Halperin had to print a retraction (though he called it an "Addendum") at the end of his *One Hundred Years* (p. 225) after he read the manuscript.

21. As late as Achilles Tatius (second century)—e.g., 6.19—ἐρώμενος is used with the clear meaning of "object of affection," regardless of gender or age (cf. note 18, above).

with two heads, four hands, four feet, and so on. When they were split in half by the gods they spent the rest of their lives seeking their other halves; the parts of the androgyne form heterosexual unions with former halves of the opposite gender; the halves of female beings "have practically no interest in men,"[22] but form unions with women. The halves of the male beings likewise "have no natural inclination for [heterosexual] marriage or parenting,"[23] but when they happen on the right male "are filled with the most wondrous friendship [φιλίᾳ] and intimacy [οἰκειότητι] and love [ἔρωτι], and are unwilling . . . to be apart from each other for a second.[24] And they spend their whole lives together . . ." (*Symposium*, 191–92).

This tale accounts for precisely the range of sexual preference familiar to modern readers: heterosexuals, male homosexuals, and lesbians, all of whom have, according to the myth, permanent and innate sexual preferences. It suggests, moreover, that each group would form *roughly comparable* lifelong, exclusive attachments. (Note that the halves of the beings would be of the same age and social status.) Although other views of homosexual relations can be elicited from literature of the period, this is one of relatively few *analytical explanations* of erotic interest (as opposed to casual observations of custom), and issues from the pen of an extraordinarily thoughtful and articulate observer, himself involved in both a heterosexual union and same-sex attachments. In the same work he cites the eagerness of Achilles to join his lover Patroclus in death as an explicit parallel to a wife's being willing to die for her husband.[25] (Both men were old enough to be famous warriors: if there was an age differential it was not great.)[26] Another speaker in the same dialogue maintains that even in cases of

---

22. οὐ πάνυ αὗται τοῖς ἀνδράσι τὸν νοῦν προσέχουσιν 191E.
23. πρὸς γάμους καὶ παιδοποιίας οὐ προσέχουσι τὸν νοῦν φύσει 192B.
24. Literally: "for the smallest bit of time."
25. *Symposium* 180A, referring to *Iliad* 18.80ff. and 329ff.; cf. also 34. In *Odyssey* 24.77, the poet says that after Achilles' body was cremated, his bones were placed in a golden amphora and mixed with those of Patroclus. At *Iliad* 19.330–32 Achilles says that he intended to entrust his son to Patroclus, although the son is only mentioned one other place in the entire poem; Patroclus was obviously much more important to Achilles than his son. Even Shakespeare recalled their relationship as homoerotic (*Troilus and Cressida*, act 5, scene 1, ll. 17–20). At *Iliad* 23.83 Patroclus, in an apparition, asks that his bones and Achilles' be interred together —something normally reserved in ancient society for married couples or members of the same family; Achilles also wishes it (23.243–44); and they were (as noted above). For the take of [Lucian] on all this, see "The Vocabulary of Love and Marriage," Chapter 1, nn. 4, 6, and 16.
26. But see the uncertain comments on this in Plato, *Symposium* 180.

the archetypal pattern of an older lover and a younger beloved the two "will be together throughout their whole lives and share everything in common."[27] Two other characters in the dialogue (Pausanias and Agathon) "maintained a relationship that sounds"—in the words of K. J. Dover—"rather like a homosexual 'marriage,' "[28] and which was wistfully admired by the speakers in the dialogue as the state to which any male would aspire but only a lucky few would attain.[29] In the *Phaedrus* Plato also presupposed the general equality of the lover and beloved (ὁμοπτέρους ἔρωτος χάριν), and predicted that even couples who indulged in sexual expression of their love rather than maintaining it as a nonphysical friendship[30] would "pass through life as friends, . . . believing that they have given and received the greatest pledges of love (πίστεις τὰς μεγίστας) (256C–D)." Theocritus writes *(Idyl, 29)* to his younger lover of three years that their union should be lifelong, that age should not matter, and that as they both grow older they will become like Achilles and Patroclus.

Zeno was said to have argued that lovers should be kept until the age of twenty-eight—by which time they were scarcely "youths" in either ancient or modern reckonings.[31] Aristotle describes as admirable—but not bizarre or unexpected—a pair of male lovers who spent their whole lives together, maintaining a single household, and arranged to be buried beside each other.[32] In a late classical novel involving a lengthy dispute over whether it is better for men to love other men or women, the proponent of the former, having argued that same-sex loves are the "most stable" of erotic passions, expresses the hope that he will be buried with his lover after they have passed

---

27. 181D: ὡς τὸν βίον ἅπαντα συνεσόμενοι καὶ κοινῇ συμβιωσόμενοι.

28. Kenneth Dover, "Classical Greek Attitudes to Sexual Behavior," *Arethusa* 6.1 (1973), 59–73, p. 72 n. 37. This is seconded by H. A. Shapiro, "Courtship Scenes in Attic Vase-Painting," *American Journal of Archaeology* 85 (1981), 133–43, p. 137, who refers to it as "the best documented Athenian homosexual 'marriage.' "

29. Plato, *Symposium* 193C: "possibly they are among the fortunate few." But this very speech makes clear that their happiness is precisely what any man would hope for: "for thus would our race attain happiness, if each of us should manage to find love and his or her own partner [παιδικά]." Although παιδικά often refers specifically to the passive partner in a homosexual relationship, these comments are explicitly predicated of women and men (καὶ ἀνδρῶν καὶ γυναικῶν), and "partner" seems the only reasonable interpretation.

30. Which he took as inevitable in the *Symposium* [191E], but then discouraged here in the *Phaedrus* and even more strongly in his last work, the *Laws*.

31. Athenaeus 13.563e.

32. Philolaus, a great law giver at Thebes, and Dioclese, an Olympic athlete: *Politics* 2.96–7 (1247A). Their tombs, at Thebes, were a tourist attraction in Aristotle's day.

their lives together.[33] A speaker in the *Ephesiaca* asserted categorically that "true love has no age limit."[34]

Doubtless the most surprising and counterintuitive aspect of Greek same-sex eroticism was not its frequency or duration, but its long and hallowed relationship to democracy and military valor, which modern military officials tend to find improbable or even unbelievable. This association extended from the example of Harmodius and Aristogiton,[35] a pair of lovers who were believed to have founded the Athenian democracy by concerted violence, to Pelopidas and Epaminondas,[36] to Alexander and Bagoas. Of the first two, no less acute a mind than Plato's observed that

> Our own tyrants learned this lesson through bitter experience, when the love[37] between Aristogiton and Harmodius grew so strong that it shattered their power. Wherever, therefore, it has been established that it is shameful to be involved in sexual relationships with men [χαρίζεσθαι ἐρασταῖς], this is due to evil on the part of the legislators, to despotism on the part of the rulers, and to cowardice on the part of the governed.[38]

In the same *Symposium* Phaedrus argued that no one's behavior is better than that of those who are in love, because they would rather behave badly in sight of father or comrade (ἑταῖρος) than in view of those they love. He even advanced the idea that

> if we could somewise contrive to have a city or an army composed of lovers and those they loved,[39] they could not be better citizens of their country than by thus refraining from all that is

[33.] [Lucian,] *Affairs of the Heart*, ed. and trans. M. D. Macleod (London, 1967), §46, 8:220.
[34.] 5.1.12: ἔρως ἀληθινὸς ὅρον ἡλικίας οὐκ ἔχει.
[35.] Note that this name might be the origin of Geiton in the *Satyricon*, discussed below. The Greek prefix ἀριστο– simply means "the best."
[36.] See below in this chapter.
[37.] For Aristogiton the word is ἔρως; for Harmodius it is φιλία, though it was a mutual relationship, thus subtly suggesting that the two are the same phenomenon, viewed from different perspectives: see Chapter 1: "The Vocabulary of Love and Friendship."
[38.] *Symposium* 182; cf. Plutarch *Moralia* 767, where the same story is told. Others doubted it: see, for example, D. S. Barrett, "The Friendship of Achilles and Patroclus," *Classical Bulletin* 57, 6 (April 1981), 87–93.
[39.] Lamb has "lover" and "beloved," but for reasons adduced elsewhere, I question this translation.

base in a mutual rivalry for honor; and such men as these, when fighting side by side, one might almost consider able to make even a little band victorious over all the world. For a man in love would surely choose to have all the rest of the host rather than the one he loves see him forsaking his station or flinging away his arms; sooner than this, he would prefer to die many deaths: while, as for leaving the one he loves in the lurch, or not succoring him in peril, no man is such a craven that the influence of Love [Ἔρως] cannot inspire him with a courage that makes him equal to the bravest born; and without doubt what Homer calls a "fury inspired"[40] by a god in certain heros is the effect produced on lovers by Love's peculiar power. Moreover, only such as are in love will consent to die for others.[41]

Perhaps inspired by this recommendation (although it merely expressed common sense in relation to the social relations of men in antiquity), about twenty years later (378 B.C.E.). Gorgidas did create such a company of three hundred men, composed of pairs of lovers. They were known as the "Sacred Band" (ἱερὸς[42] λόχος) of Thebes, because, as Plutarch later explained, "even Plato calls the lover a friend 'inspired of God.' "[43] Living long after, Plutarch was in a position to know that the troop had played a crucial role in many military engagements (e.g., Tegyra, 375, and Leuctra, 371), and

. . . was never beaten, until the battle of Chaeronea [338 B.C.E.]; and when, after the battle, Philip [of Macedon, who won the battle] was surveying the dead, and stopped at the place where the three hundred were lying, all where they had faced

---

[40.] *Iliad* 10.482, 15.262.

[41.] *Symposium* 179; I have followed for the most part, but in a few places adapted the translation of W. R. M. Lamb for the *LCL* edition of the *Symposium* (Cambridge, 1967), pp. 101–103 (mostly dealing with terms for "love" and "lover," which are at issue in this study). Experts in Greek and the classics will want to check the original, which I do not provide because it is readily available.

[42.] This is the word that Greek-speaking Christians used for both "sacred" and "holy," as evident in the English word "hierarchy" (holy order).

[43.] *Symposium* 179A: ἔνθεον φίλον. Plutarch does not comment on the irony of Plato's recommendation becoming reality, but no historians doubt the general outlines of this account. I have interpreted Plutarch's comments as presupposing monotheism, which seems to me the most cautious view. Many thoughtful Greeks and Romans envisioned a single god, long before the advent of Christianity.

the long spears of his phalanx, with their armor, and mingled one with another [μετ' ἀλλήλων ἀναμεμιγμένους],[44] he was amazed, and on learning that this was the band of lovers,[45] burst into tears and said: "Perish miserably they who think that these men did or suffered aught disgraceful."[46]

Much later (third century of the Christian Era), Athenaeus (13.602) would echo the idea that young men become exceptionally brave under the influence of love for each other, and added that "This was proved, at any rate, by the Sacred Band organized at Thebes."[47]

The idea that same-sex relationships would compromise the masculinity of military personnel and introduce morale problems is so fixed and unquestionable in modern military establishments that this idealization of homosexual relationships in warrior societies may seem preposterous to contemporary readers. Obviously Philip was aware of a contrary prejudice and condemned it vehemently when confronted with the dazzling courage of the Sacred Band. "It is not only," Plutarch noted, "the most warlike peoples, Boeotians, Spartans, Cretans, who are the most susceptible to [this][48] love, but also the greatest heros of old, Meleager, Achilles, Aristomenes, Cimon, Epaminondas. Epaminondas, in fact, loved two young men, Asopichus and Caphisodorus. The latter died with him at Mantineia and is buried close to him . . ."[49] In his "Life of Pelopidas"—a great military hero even among warlike peoples—he adds that "Ioläus, who shared the labors of Hercules and fought by his side, was beloved of him. And Aristotle says that even down to his day [fourth century B.C.E.] the

---

44. The most literal rendering of μετ' ἀλλήλων ἀναμεμιγμένους would involve sexual intercourse, but I have cautiously adhered to the published translation, ackowledging the possibility that the men's bodies were intertwined only in death.

45. Here again I have changed Perrin's arch "lovers" and "beloved," because the English "lovers" allows more possibilities than traditional nineteenth-century translations.

46. "Life of Pelopidas," 18, in *LCL, Plutarch's Lives*, vol. 5, trans. Bernadotte Perrin (London, 1917). I have checked the Greek, but (with the exceptions adduced in previous notes) I admire Perrin's generally elegant translation.

47. Plutarch says the band was organized "by Epameinondas," but this appears to be a mistake: Epameinondas was simply the lover of Pelopidas, one of its most successful commanders.

48. As the rest of the quote makes clear.

49. Plutarch, *Erotikos* 761 C–D. I have slightly altered the English translation of W. C. Helmbold in the *LCL* edition (vol. 9) of Plutarch's *Moralia* (London, 1969), which is old-fashioned and misleading on Greek homosexual relations.

tomb of Ioläus was a place where same-sex lovers[50] plighted mutual faith."[51] Centuries before, Plato had put the same idea in the mouth of Aristophanes, who claimed that males who preferred other males and "delight to lie with them and to be clasped in men's embraces . . . are the finest boys and young men, for they have the most manly nature. . . . Their behavior is due to daring, manliness and virility, since they are quick to welcome their like."[52]

Romans knew these Greek hero couples—part of their cultural heritage—and added to them the *Aeneid*'s Nisus and Euryalus,[53] a pair of soldiers in the army of Aeneas who were greatly devoted to each other. Nisus (who was running third), "remembering the love of Euryalus,"[54] essentially threw a race in favor of Euryalus (Book V), who, moved by this gesture of love, demanded that Nisus nonetheless receive a prize, which Aeneas granted him. Nisus later begged to be killed in Euryalus' place (Book IX), when the latter was in mortal danger, but instead both were slain. Vergil called them blessed—*fortunati ambo* (9:447)—and vowed that their devotion would be remembered as long as his poetry. Hadrian and Antinoüs—the former one of the most effective commanders of the Roman army[55] and the most outstanding of the "five good emperors"[56]—were among the best known and most romantically idealized couples of antiquity.[57] Statuary of Antinoüs survives in great abundance,[58] and games and

---

50. Perrin has "lovers and beloved." "Same-sex lovers" certainly includes "lovers and beloved," but the latter does not necessarily allow for the possibility of the former. How much difference this makes is discussed in n. 45.

51. ἐπὶ τοῦ Ἰόλεω τὰς καταπιστώσεις ποιεῖσθαι τοὺς ἐρωμένους καὶ τοὺς ἐραστάς. Plutarch, "Pelopidas," 18, as cited above. Though I have emended three words, Perrin's English accurately conveys the connubial overtones of the Greek. Cf. discussion of this below.

52. *Symposium* 192A, loosely following the translation of Lamb.

53. The poet generally employs *amicus* to characterize their relationship, which is not clear evidence of its nature, since Cicero would use the term to describe male acquaintances with whom he doubtless had no romantic interest and also, in the feminine, to name a girlfriend or courtesan. A figure named Euryalus also occurs in the *Odyssey* in a context involving athletic contests (8:115ff.).

54. *Aeneid* 5:334: *non tamen Euryali, non ille oblitus amorum.*

55. He was the first emperor since Tiberius (about a century) to retire in peace rather than succumb to assassination or death in battle.

56. Nerva, Trajan, Hadrian, Antoninus Pius, and Marcus Aurelius: all great generals.

57. Unlike many Roman males, Hadrian appears to have been interested exclusively in males: he paid so little attention to his "official" wife that his biographer Spartianus even suspected him of poisoning her (1.7.23; cf. Gibbon, *Decline and Fall of the Roman Empire* [London, 1898] 1:313).

58. Cassius Dio says that Hadrian erected monuments to Antinoüs "throughout the entire world" (69:11).

cities were established in his honor after his untimely death.[59] "The loftiest and most typical development of the Hadrianic period was the creation of the character of Antinoüs"[60]—an attachment which no one at the time believed brought Hadrian's masculine or military character into any question.[61]

In relation to modern attitudes it is worth bearing in mind that most modern armies accept—some even draft—women, which in cultures dominated by the myths of male dominance and universal heterosexuality might certainly be expected to create morale (and moral) difficulties.[62] Greek and Roman military societies would have been shocked and outraged by the very idea, whereas male behavior was generally idealized and male-male relationships were imagined to involve a distillation of the best elements of male character into a lofty mutual love.[63]

Roman same-sex relationships have been less studied, and one is inclined to contrast, mentally at least, the rather idealized and formal lover/beloved relationships imputed to the Greeks with the riotous and promiscuous sexuality that forms such a lurid mythology about the Roman Empire. In fact, in addition to the rather more sensational aspects of Roman sexuality presented—as sensational—by imperial literature, there were also many same-sex couples in the Roman world who lived together permanently, forming unions neither more nor less exclusive than those of the heterosexual couples around them. (Divorce was very common in heterosexual marriages at Rome,[64] as well as nonmarital sexuality, at least for the male, as noted above.)

[59] See discussion in CSTH, pp. 84–86, and more recently, Royston Lambert, Beloved and God: The Story of Hadrian and Antinous (New York, 1984).

[60] Eugenia Strong, La scultura romana da Augusto a Costantino, rev. and trans. G. Gianelli (Florence, 1926), 2:228.

[61] Although the extent of his grief was thought excessive for a man; Spartianus [14.5] comments, Antinoum suum, dum per Nilum navigat, perdidit, quem muliebriter flevit.

[62] At the time of this writing the "Tailhook" convention incident has in fact put the highest ranks of the navy in complete disarray.

[63] This argument is certainly as old as Aristophanes' speech in the Symposium, but becomes a standard part of the many debates about the relative merits of homosexual and heterosexual passion (technically called dubbii) in premodern literature: see, e.g., CSTH, pp. 124–27, 255–65. Whether sexuality was always a part of this lofty love or not varies according to the view a particular writer takes of the purposes and limits of human sexuality. Pausanias in the Symposium, calling same-sex love "Heavenly," and opposite-gender attachment "Vulgar," obviously considered sexuality, if contained in an appropriate courting ritual, acceptable at Athens.

[64] However, neither Treggiari nor Dixon is able to hazard an estimate of the rate.

Cicero mentions casually that Catiline's "lover"—a consul—approached him on Catiline's behalf.[65] Hadrian and Antinoüs were doubtless the most famous romantic couple in imperial Rome of the second century, although there was no legal relationship between them; both were free men united simply by love, and when Antinoüs died tragically Hadrian grieved for him publicly as he would have for a wife.[66]

The *Satyricon* of Petronius Arbiter is an elaborate and lively description of this culture of love relationships (homosexual and heterosexual), as are half a dozen other romance novels of the first few centuries of the Christian Era. The *Satyricon*'s protagonists are a same-sex couple whose erotic difficulties with each other and with other (often heterosexually married) people in their lives constitute the basic plot of the novel. The two men differ only slightly in age (and the difference is insignificant),[67] and they function as social equals, both free males (*iuvenes ingenui*, 107) on their own in the world. Their relationship is the sole stable element in their lives, despite the difficulties attendant on it (which provide dramatic interest). Although Giton is clearly the "passive" partner sexually,[68] he is not less devoted to Encolpius than the latter is to him, and Petronius wittily explodes the stereotype of the uninterested youth in his tale of the boy of Pergamum who, bribed to have sex with an older man, then keeps him awake all night demanding more.[69]

---

65. *Post reditum in senatu* 4: *Alter a me Catilinam, amatorem suum, multis audientibus . . . reposcebat.*
66. See discussion in *CSTH*, p. 85. None of the more recent studies of Roman homosexuality discuss this.
67. Giton may be a play on the ancient Attic hero-lovers Harmodius and Aristogiton, as noted above. Giton is 16 (97). Although he is a former gladiator (9), Encolpius cannot be much older, since he adduces the fact that he is *adhuc iuvenis* as an excuse for his inability to perform with Circe (130). Moreover, women of all ages as well as men are attracted to both Giton and Encolpius throughout the story.
68. Giton is consistently referred to as a *puer*, does the cooking (9), is fought over by male admirers (rather than doing any fighting himself), and discloses that his mother persuaded him not to be a man (81), but all these aspects amount, in the end, to his being what modern speakers would call a "queen"—i.e., an effeminate male—playing the "feminine" role in a relationship with a man. He is certainly not a "boy" in any traditional sense, and is passive only sexually. The two males vying for his favors allow him to choose which will be his "brother" (80). Moreover, Encolpius, though also a former gladiator, has long curls (associated with youth and feminine beauty; 18), and is accused by his best friend of being able to dominate only women and boys (9).
69. The older man finally threatens to call the boy's father, which had previously been the boy's weapon against him (*Satyricon* 85–87). Achilles Tatius (1.10) says that both boys and girls

The protagonists' relationship is referred to as *contubernium* (11), which Petronius may have understood as "cohabitation" or as the form of marriage appropriate when different classes or noncitizens were involved.[70] When Giton is forced to participate in a heterosexual marriage ceremony (26) it is clear that the participants (and the author) regard it as an utter travesty, whereas Encolpius thought that his relationship with Giton was "so long established that it had become a bond of blood."[71] Facing death at sea, Giton and Encolpius make plans to be buried together and bind themselves together with a belt (114).

Although the *Satyricon* betrays profound Greek influence,[72] it is written in Latin, and Latin did not have words comparable to the Greek for "lover/beloved."[73] The word "brother" is used throughout for a long-standing homosexual partner,[74] manifestly as a technical term.[75] In a striking scene, a woman trying to seduce one of the two men says, "You have a 'brother,' I realize: for I was not too shy to inquire. But what is to prevent you from 'adopting' a 'sister,' too?"[76]

---

have psychological reasons to feign indifference to venereal pleasure, but that this should not be taken at face value.

70. Given hints about the social background of the two, it is unlikely that they would have been entitled to legal marriage. Their nationality is less clear: the names "Giton" and "Encolpius" are obscene puns on Greek words: the former can mean "neighbor," but γίτονας also specifically referred to the testicles, and the latter means, essentially, "in the lap."

71. 80: . . . *vetustissimam consuetudinem putabam in sanguinis pignus transisse.* . . .

72. See, e.g., Graham Anderson, *Ancient Fiction: The Novel in the Graeco-Roman World* (London, 1984), Chapter 12.

73. *Amator/amans* and *amatus* could obviously be used, but they lacked the cachet and precise connotations of ἐραστής and ἐρώμενος. Like English "lover," *amator* could be used to describe someone fond of horses or roses or salt cod, whereas ἐραστής would normally be used only for erotic feelings for humans. But see Chapter 1.

74. E.g., at 9, 10, 11, 13, 24, 25, 79, 80, 91, 97, 101, 127, 128, 129, 130, 133. The shepherds Corydon and Amyntas in the *Eclogues* of Calpurnius also call each other *frater*; the subtext is certainly the overtly homoerotic relationships of Theocritus and Vergil.

75. Cf. *Greek Anthology* 4.44, where φράτερ is used instead of ἀδελφός, obviously because the Latin has a technical sense the Greek equivalent might not. For the friendly address at issue in this poem, see, inter alia, Hyginus, *Liber de munitionibus castrorum*, 45, and Fronto, *Ad amicos*, particularly 2.25, where the phrase *domine frater* occurs. *Frater* became a standard form of address among the caesars, not necessarily invoking but clearly analogizing its intense emotional connotations and notions of equality: see, e.g., Ammianus Marcellinus 15.8.12 (*amantissime mihi omnium frater*); cf. Aurelius Victor, *Liber de caesaribus*, ed. Franz Pichlmayr (Leipzig, 1911), p. 100. Cf. Apuleius, *Metamorphoses* 8:7: *illium amicum, coaetaneum, contubernalem, fratrem* . . . (meant to be ironic, but revealing in the choice of synonyms). In Arabic, too, words for "brother" had connotations of friendship and passionate love: see, e.g., E. W. Lane, *Arabic-English Lexicon* (London, 1863), s.v. اخ, and R. Dozy, *Supplément aux dictionnaires arabes* (Beirut, 1981), 1:13.

76. 127: *Habes tu quidem et fratrem, neque enim me piguit inquirere; sed quid prohibet et sororem adoptare?*

This suggests that she recognized the relationship between them as special, as did the people she asked. She acknowledged that it might be a bar to other sexual interactions, and also that it was comparable in some way to heterosexual love relations (hence, she might be "adopted" as his "sister" by analogy). The exchange also implies, since Petronius had a sharp ear for quotidian speech, that the term "brother" was widely understood in the Roman world to denote a permanent partner in a homosexual relationship, an inference justified by ancient literary sources from many cultures,[77] if largely ignored by modern scholarship on ancient sexuality.[78] Catullus, for example, constructed a brilliant pun on *both* the biological and sexual meanings of "brother" and "sister" in his poem about Aufilenus and Aufilena, siblings who were the "brother" and "sister," respectively, of two of

---

77. "Gilgamesh's affection for his friend [Enkidu] is described in terms appropriate for relations both with kin and with objects of sexual desire. Enkidu is often called Gilgamesh's 'brother' (ahu) . . . [and] the word that describes Gilgamesh's anticipated attraction to Enkidu is also used to describe Enkidu's anticipated attraction to the prostitute from Uruk, with whom he mates for six days and seven nights," Halperin, *One Hundred Years*, p. 81; similar observations are offered in Jeffrey Tigay, *The Evolution of the Gilgamesh Epic* (Philadelphia, 1982), 30; Anne Draffkorn Kilmer, "A Note on an Overlooked Word-Play in the Akkadian Gilgamesh," ZIKIR ŠUMIM: *Assyriological Studies Presented to F. R. Kraus on the Occasion of his Seventieth Birthday*, ed. G. van Driel, Th. J. H. Krispijn, M. Stol, and K. R. Veenhof (Leiden, 1982); and George F. Held, "Parallels between the Gilgamesh Epic and Plato's *Symposium*," *Journal of Near Eastern Studies* 42 (1983) 133–41, pp. 136–37. See also Chapter 4. In the *Iliad* Apollo is astonished by Achilles' love for Patroclus because it surpasses in its intensity the love that most men bear toward a brother or a son (24:44–52); Achilles himself acknowledges this at 19:321–27. For a discussion, see Halperin, *One Hundred Years*, p. 84.

78. Lexicographers have generally recognized these sexual senses of *frater* and *soror* as distinct and common meanings (see, e.g., OLD, s.v. *"frater,"* 3b; s.v. *"soror"* 1.d), but other classicists have ignored them almost entirely (with a few exceptions, such as Stempel, p. 32– nimirum amasias suas, quibus ius coniugium non darent, id est, concubinas atque meretrices, quasi honestiore nomine, sorores appellabant; Patlagean, "Rituels," pp. 628–29, following Florence Dupont, *Le plaisir et la loi du "Banquet" de Platon au "Satiricon"* [Paris, 1977] pp. 164–69); and Williams. That *frater* did not essentially mean a biological brother is recognized by Émile Benveniste, *Indo-European Language and Society*, trans. Elizabeth Palmer (London, 1973), pp. 172–73, although Benveniste did not identify its possible homosexual meaning, probably too troubling for him. It is remarkable, for example, that no Latinist has considered the possibility that the "brother" whose death Catullus laments so bitterly (65, 68, 101) was a lover rather than a sibling. There are no independent data confirming that Catullus had a biological sibling, and there are certainly more literary parallels for a lament over a lover or friend "loved like a brother" (e.g., David's for Jonathan: see below, pp. 135–37) than for the loss of a relative (and 68.28–30 seems to suggest a sexual relationship). Catullus' poetry is filled, moreover, with overt homoeroticism (e.g., 15, 16, 21, 25, 30, 38, 48, 50, etc.). Tamassia argues that the Sacred Band was a "military brotherhood" (*fratellanza militare*), but says both that he cannot discuss this further (*più in là . . . non possiamo andare*, p. 8) and that the claim that the band was held together by homosexual attraction *could not* be true (*non può rispondere al vero*, ibid.).

his friends.[79] Martial not only uses *frater* and *soror* with unambiguously sexual meanings (2.4), but even refers to them as "naughty names" (*nomina nequiora*), and purports to be outraged when a male with whom he does *not* have a sexual relationship refers to him as "brother" (10.65).[80] Corydon, a famous same-sex lover of antiquity, is addressed as "brother" by a number of speakers in Calpurnius' *Eclogues*.[81]

"Brother" and "sister" were common terms of endearment for heterosexual spouses in ancient Mediterranean societies—most notably in those cultures that linked marriage with love—and in this sense their use by homosexual couples constitutes a parallel to rather than a deviation from the majority culture.[82] Using words suggesting sibling relationship or affective, intimate, family ties (Latin *affinitas*)—rather than the terms of control related to power and hierarchy—constituted a hallmark of ancient lovers of whatever gender. It evokes a relationship of general equality,[83] of persons in the same generation, in which

---

[79.] Poem No. 100: This is, he wryly observes, "truly sweet brotherly love" (*fraternum vere dulce sodalicium*). It seems possible that Tibullus 3.23 is also paronomastic in a bitterly ironic way, although the most obvious reading is *frater* in a countererotic sense.

[80.] In the *Metamorphoses* of Apuleius (8.7) a man feigning deep affection for someone recently deceased describes him with a very interesting sequence of affectionate designations: *amicum, coaetaneum, contubernalem, fratrem . . .* ("friend, boyhood companion, comrade, brother").

[81.] 1:8 (*frater Corydon*); cf. 4:17, 78, all published in A. Baehrens, *Poetae Latini minores* (Leipzig, 1881).

[82.] "From the middle of the second millennium B.C.E. . . . . it became usual for commoner husbands [sc. in Roman Egypt] to call their wives 'sister,'" although during this period it was *not* common for men actually to marry their sisters (barely six of five hundred known marriages outside the royal family during this period are fraternal): Hopkins, "Brother-Sister Marriage in Roman Egypt," p. 311. Note Oxyrhynchus Papyrus 744 ("Hilarion to his *sister* Alis very many greetings . . ."), of which Hopkins notes, "It is clear that Alis was Hilarion's wife, but the greeting 'sister' is not proof that she was his sister" (p. 317); the letter, written just before the beginning of the Christian Era, was first published in *The Oxyrhynchus Papyri*, 4, ed. Bernard Grenfell and Arthur Hunt (London, 1904), pp. 243–44, and is often reprinted (e.g., in *Select Papyri*, ed. Hunt and Edgar, no. 105, in *Greek Papyri in the British Museum*, ed. F. G. Kenyon [London, 1893], 1.42.1, and in *Roman Civilization: Selected Readings*, ed. M. Reinhold and N. Lewis [New York, 1955], 2:404). All commentators since Grenfell and Hunt have agreed with Hopkins that "sister" is a certain indication here only of marital, not of blood relationship. See also the comments of Kenyon, Letronne, and Peyron to the effect that "sister" was a common term of endearment for Egyptian wives in *Greek Papyri*, p. 31, *ad unam*, and more broadly, H. Thierfelder, *Die Geschwisterehe im hellenistischrömischen Ägypten, Fontes et Commentationes*, 1 (Munster, 1960). One might view this use as merely a subset of the tendency to use "brother" or "sister" for very dear friends: "for certainly when we wish to compliment those who seem to be friends there can be no greater flattery than to call them siblings" (Quintilian[?], *Declamationes* 321).

[83.] Treggiari, *Roman Marriage*, pp. 107–19, explores this thoughtfully, noting how frequently children brought up in the same household later married.

neither party is dependent on or subordinate to the other, without coercion or status differential.[84] This is probably an accurate reflection of the rather looser and more egalitarian love relations under the empire.[85] (Indeed, scholars have argued that in some ancient societies it was common for husbands to adopt their wives legally as sisters.)[86] Sibling relationships were a particularly rich metaphor in a society permeated with the model of the exceptional love and self-sacrifice of Castor and Pollux—frequent figures of Roman art and literature[87]— and likely to be less shocking as archetypes of sexual interaction in a culture whose chief deities (e.g., Jupiter and Juno)[88] were often both

[84] "There is no greater degree of affection than calling someone 'brother'; how could a friendship be more blessed than to imitate brotherhood?" Quintilian (?), *Declamationes* 321. Cf. *Panegyrici Latini*, ed. Emil Baehrens (Leipzig, 1874), Mamertinus 7, pp. 107–8: *Sic uos geritis quasi iuniores ambo, ambo seniores, neuter plus suis moribus fauet: uterque se uult hoc esse, quod frater est.* Greek *Anthology* 7.551 (Agathias Scholasticus) lauds the ὁμο³ροσύνη—a word associated particularly with matrimonial harmony, as noted previously—of two brothers who lived, died, and were buried together. The text gives no indication that they were not biological brothers. For ancient comparisons of "friend" and "brother" status, see Xenophon, *Anabasis*, 7.2.25, Polybius 7.9. Stempel (pp. 8–15) discusses in detail equality as the chief content of *fraternitas* (e.g., p. 8: *Inter reliqua cognationum nomina dulcissimum videbatur nomen fratrum in primis propter aequalitatem et concordiam*). Women friends also used *soror* in addressing each other: see, e.g., Apuleius, *Metamorphoses* 1.12.

[85] Plutarch (second century) wrote a treatise about "brotherly love" (Περὶ φιλαδελφίας), by which he meant, quite literally, the love that *ought* to exist between natal brothers; he lamented that in his day brotherly love was as rare as its opposite (μισαδελφίαν) had been among the ancients (ἐπὶ τῶν παλαιῶν) (Moralia 478C, LCL, 6:248).

[86] This literature is large and contentious. See, e.g., Éduard Cuq, "Les Actes juridiques susiens," *Revue d'Assyriologie et d'archéologie orientale* 28, 2 (1931), 47–71, pp. 51–53; P. Koschaker, "Fratriarchat, Hausgemeinschaft und Mutterrecht in Keischriftrechten," *Zeitschrift für Assyriologie und Verwandte Gebiete* 41 (1933), 1–89; David Freedman, "A New Approach to the Nuzi Sistership Contract," *Journal of the Ancient Near Eastern Society* 2.2 (1970), 77–85; Samuel Sandmel, "The Haggada within Scripture," *Journal of Biblical Literature* 80 (June 1961), 105–22; Samuel Greengus, "Sisterhood Adoption at Nuzi and the 'Wife-Sister' in Genesis," *Hebrew Union College Annual* 46 (1975), 5–31.

[87] Note, e.g., Martial (who nonetheless uses *frater/soror* in a sexual sense) 7.24, Strabo 6.2, Claudian, *De piis fratribus*. Tiberius restored and rededicated the temple of Castor and Pollux out of love for his own brother (Suetonius, *Tiberius* 20). On the other hand, Musonius Rufus explicitly opposes the comparison of intense friendship and biological brotherhood, arguing that the latter is vastly better: Cora Lutz, *Musonius Rufus "The Roman Socrates"* (New Haven, 1947), 100–101.

[88] Apuleius, *Metamorphoses* 6.4, for example, has a character address Juno as "sister and wife of great Jupiter" (*Magni Iovis germana et coniuga*). Such couplings were also known in imperial mystery religions: Isis and Osiris were sibling lovers who produced a holy child, Horus. Their relationship, though both fraternal and erotic, was associated chiefly with passion: see, for example, the demotic love spell invoking "Isis . . . , holding on her shoulders her brother who is her bedfellow," published in Hans Dieter Betz, *The Greek Magical Papyri in Translation, including the Demotic Spells* (Chicago, 1986), 66. Among the Egyptians, whose myths influenced the entire Mediterranean, sibling marriage among the ruling classes was an empirical reality, and widely noted among neighboring peoples. For example, Ptolemy II married his sister Arsinoe, who was officially known thereafter as Arsinoe "Philadelphus"

husband and wife and brother and sister.[89] Although sibling relationships were sometimes invoked in the ancient world as archetypally asexual,[90] the seeming paradox is no more difficult to comprehend than the apparent inconsistency of modern prohibitions against parent-child incest and the common tendency of English speakers to use terms like "momma," "old lady," "daddy," "old man," "baby," and so on, in specifically sexual contexts.[91] Williams observes that Roman males might describe "their wives or sexual partners in terms otherwise used of their male friends, or . . . their relationships with friends by means of words and actions otherwise used of their erotic partners, and this overlap is in turn focused on the word *frater*."[92]

Although writers sometimes infer from the literary stereotypes of fourth-century Athens that all ancient homosexual relationships were temporary and age-related, the evidence suggests, as noted above, that this picture is exaggerated even for Athens, and homosexual relationships in the rest of ancient Europe were certainly far more varied and flexible than this, probably not very different from their heterosexual counterparts. Plutarch, writing in Greek for a Roman audience of the second century,[93] makes this point explicitly: ". . . the lover of

---

("brother-lover"): see Hopkins, "Brother-Sister Marriage in Roman Egypt," p. 311 and n. 26.

[89] See the interesting rhetorical use made of this by Cicero, *De domo sua*, 34.93, where he accuses his opponent of having a comparable relationship with his wife/sister. Cf. *Pro Caelio* 13.32, where he insinuates the same thing more snidely (. . . *mulieris viro—fratrem volui dicere; semper hic erro*). Christians suspected pagans in general of incestuous relations: Tertullian says Stoics sleep with their sisters (*quia per hanc adulescentes tui cum sororibus dormiunt* [CSEL 20:296]), and Irenaeus (*Contra Haereses* 1:3 [PG 7:508–9]) charges the pagans with using a pretense of fraternal affection to cloak incestuous relations: "Others are more modest and at the outset pretend that they are living with 'sisters,' but as time passes they are found out when the 'sister' turns out to be pregnant by the 'brother.'"

[90] Xenophon, for example, says in the *Constitution of Sparta* (2.13) that Lycurgus' strictures against sexual expression in male-male relationships at Sparta meant that men lived with adolescents "like fathers with sons, or brothers with brothers" (ἢ γονεῖς παίδων καὶ ἀδελφοὶ ἀδελφῶν εἰς ἀφροδίσια ἀπέχονται). Alcibiades complained that Socrates exercized such restraint when they passed the night together that it was as if he had slept with his father or elder brother (*Symposium* 219C); [Lucian,] *Affairs of the Heart* repeats this with only the father image (§49, p. 226), but subsequently denies it flatly (§54), asserting that this relationship was unquestionably sexual. *Greek Anthology* 10.20 seems to play on *both* the erotic and countererotic connotations of ἀδελφός.

[91] A similar inconsistency occurs in regard to lesbianism: although its existence was acknowledged in the ancient world, Achilles Tatius uses as an expression for an asexual interlude that it was as if one "woman arose from the bed of another woman" (8.5.3; cf. 5.25.7).

[92] "Homosexuality and the Roman Male," p. 319.

[93] Plutarch was born in Boeotia in central Greece about 45 C.E., came to Rome as a teacher of philosophy, became a consul, and returned to his native Greece to administer Roman government as a procurator. He died in 120 C.E.

beauty will be fairly and equably disposed toward both sexes, instead of supposing that males and females are as different in the matter of love as they are in their clothes."[94] He suggests, further, that the upper age limit for "lovers" and lower limit for "beloveds" would be precisely the same regardless of the genders involved.[95]

In antique romances male lovers usually have permanent, exclusive relationships precluding similar relations with other men, not necessarily excluding a heterosexual marriage; they appear to be unions characterized by general equality, although there is sometimes an age differential, and the idea that one party will be the "lover" and one the "beloved" persists even in the face of social realities militating against it. For example, Klinias, the "lover" of Charicles in Achilles Tatius' *Clitophon and Leucippe*, is twenty-one: not exactly an "older man" except in a purely technical sense. In Xenophon of Ephesus' romance novel, the *Ephesiaca*, two boys about the same age fall in love,[96] but one takes on the role of "lover" and must undertake to rescue the other from the clutches of an older man by abducting him at swordpoint from the latter's home, having had to sell all his belongings and take sail to get there.[97]

There are, in fact, three prominent couples in this novel: Habrocomes and Anthia are (respectively) the hero and heroine whose marriage of love (though arranged) and subsequent misadventures constitute the major plot of the novel. Though they are separated through most of it and constantly tempted or threatened to marry or sleep with other partners (always of the opposite sex), they remain absolutely faithful to each other and are ecstatically reunited at the end of the novel. Their faithful servants Leucon and Rhode,

---

94. *Erotikos* 767B.

95. *Erotikos* 754C.

96. A point is made of their being the same age and both relatively young: 3.2.3. One might argue that the author's bringing this up discloses a cultural presupposition that lovers would ordinarily be of different ages, but the novel itself argues against this (see the following note). Moreover, *cultural suppositions* are less important in the present context than hints of real social life. And, finally, one might consider the parallel to modern expectations: if an older male were alone with a beautiful young woman for some time one might well entertain suspicions that would be less pronounced if the same girl were alone with a friend (of either gender) from school. This is not because older men regularly cohabit with young girls, but because we imagine (correctly or not) that they will be tempted to do so, whereas her own friends are used to her allure and have reason to relate to her in other ways.

97. 3.2.6. Note that the whole story of Hippothoos and Hyperanthes, as noted below, is elaborately parallel to that of Habrocomes and Anthia, who were also about the same age, and also both young (Habrocomes is sixteen when the story begins).

who have suffered through misadventures and separation from their beloved master and mistress, are reunited with them at the end, now prosperous and free, and the two couples remain friends. A third couple consists of two males, Hippothoos and Cleisthenes. The former, an ex-pirate, is a devoted friend of the hero; the great love of his life was a young man named Hyperanthes, who died tragically. Hippothoos settles down at the end of the novel in a permanent romantic relationship with another young man (Cleisthenes) who is both beautiful and of good family (εὖ γεγονότων, 5.9.3—an essential element for a marriage partner). They live as a permanent couple on terms of equality and friendship with Habrocomes and Anthia and Leucon and Rhode.

Habrocomes and Anthia are legally married in a ceremony described in the novel; Leucon and Rhode, being servile, probably are not legally married, but their relationship is treated as comparable to that of their masters, permanent and based on love.[98] The author establishes many parallels between Hippothoos' two homosexual loves and the heterosexual relationships in the novel: his first partner's name is a play on Anthia's name (hers means "beautiful"; his "more than beautiful" or "extremely beautiful"); he and Hippothoos meet at a festival like Habrocomes and Anthia; the young man's parents arrange a relationship with another man based on economic advantage (like most heterosexual marriages), and he and Hippothoos must escape (one might say "elope") to live happily together.[99]

When all the principals in the novel are finally reunited, the author has each couple go to bed together "as they are inclined":[100] Habrocomes with Anthia, Leucon with Rhode, Hippothoos with Cleisthenes. Hippothoos raises a great tomb to his first lover, Hyperanthes, and lives with Cleisthenes in a lasting union of apparent equality, "sharing his goods" (5.9.2, 5.15.4). Although the text has been damaged, it seems to indicate that the legal aspect of this rela-

---

98. At 2.3.6 they are described simply as being "joined together" (συνῆσαν ἀλλήλοις), and their feelings for each other are said to consist in a "unity born of love" (κοινωνήματα ἐξ ἔρωτος).

99. The relationship between Aigiale and his girlfriend (5.1) is even more closely parallel to that of Hippothoos and Hyperanthes.

100. ὅπως ἔτυχον (5.13.6). In another context one might translate this "as fate would have it," or "as circumstances determined," but given the action and theme of the novel it is not credible that the author intended us to believe that the partners in these unions were simply yielding to circumstance.

tionship took the form of adoption.[101] Roman law viewed with utter horror the prospect of a male's marrying an adopted child of the opposite gender,[102] but was much more indulgent when the genders were the same[103] or the adoption was actually undertaken as a form of or prelude to matrimony.[104]

Most ancient writers—in striking opposition to their modern counterparts—generally entertained higher expectations of the fidelity and permanence of homosexual passions than of heterosexual feelings. Plutarch adduces with evident disapproval cases of husbands who allowed their wives to be unfaithful to gain some advantage, and then notes, "By contrast, of all the many [homosexual] lovers there were and have been, do you know of a single one who surrendered his beloved, even to gain honor from Zeus? I do not" (*Erotikos* 760B). The proponent of homosexual passion in the Hellenistic debate *Affairs of the Heart* says that wisdom and experience teach that love between males (ἄρρενας) is the "most stable" (βεβαιοτάτους) of loves.[105] This prejudice was doubtless influenced by the *Symposium* of Plato, in which heterosexual relationships and feelings are characterized as "vulgar,"[106] and their same-sex equivalents as "heavenly."[107] The contrast exercised wide influence on subsequent discussions of love.[108]

101. Dalmeyda prints καὶ τὸν Κλεισθένη πα<ῖδα ποιησάμενος ὁ Ἱπ>πόθοος, which he identifies as an "editorial correction" to a lacuna of some twenty-two letters in the manuscript (p. 77). Since the α is in doubt, but the π is not, it seems more likely that the missing words were πο<ιησάμενος υἱὸν ὁ Ἱπ>πόθοος, a more common phrase for this, not requiring substantially more letters. I would prefer to read πο<ιησάμενος ἀδελφὸν ὁ Ἱπ>πόθοος, but there is apparently insufficient space for this in the (sole) manuscript (described by Dalmeyda, pp. xxxiii–xxxix).

102. Whether one's own adopted child or a sibling adopted by a parent: *Digest* 23.2.44 ("It is considered such an awful thing to marry an adopted daughter or granddaughter, that the prohibition against it remains in force even if the adoption is ended by emancipation") and 45.1.35.2. But contrast the opinion of Gaius (*The Institutes of Gaius*, ed. Francis de Zulueta [Oxford, 1985] 1.61, p. 18), allowing marriage after emancipation, followed by Justinian's *Institutes* 1.10.2.

103. *Digest* 45.1.38.15: . . . *adoptiui patris persona coniungi poterit.*

104. Cf. n. 101, above, and p. 14.

105. 36, p. 206.

106. Πάνδημος, which might also be rendered "general" or "ordinary": I have taken my cue from LSJ, which cites this very discussion as the *locus* for the meaning "vulgar." Cf. the comparable Latin expression in Catullus 72.3: *ut vulgus amicam*.

107. Οὐράνιος. It was clearly possible for homosexual passions to be πάνδημος (e.g., 181E), but it is not clear that heterosexual relationships were ever οὐράνιος.

108. Plutarch (*Erotikos* 764B) says that the Egyptians also had a dichotomy of "heavenly" and "vulgar" love, and Achilles Tatius, an Alexandrian Greek of the second century, refers to the same dichotomy (2.36.2). German and English speakers of the Victorian era derived

Such a lofty evaluation of homosexual unions is related, in both a helpful and difficult way, to the overlap of ancient concepts of homosexual love relationships and male friendship. Ancient writers rarely admit the possibility of friendship involving women—either between two women or between a man and a woman. This was almost certainly because by and large only males were thought to dispose of the moral character and intelligence necessary for friendship (or, according to some, for real love),[109] and because nearly all ancient writers considered friendship to be essentially and inherently a relationship between equals: since women were not equal to men, they could hardly qualify as friends. Although words for "friend" or "friendship" are occasionally used in relation to girlfriends or marriage,[110] analysis of friendship itself almost always and almost everywhere focused on men.[111]

Many ancient descriptions of friendship are, nonetheless, distinctly romantic, and given the most common expectations of marriage (and the actual circumstances surrounding it), it is not surprising that many men looked to other men as the obvious source of emotional intimacy and closeness from an equal.[112] Classical literature of many

---

terms for what would now be called "gay men" from these words (*Uranian, uranisch, Urning,* etc.): see *CSTH*, pp. 42–43, and John Lauritsen, *The Early Homosexual Rights Movement* (n.p., 1974), passim.

[109.] "It is not appropriate for a free man to be in love with slave males: this is merely copulation, like love for women," Plutarch, Ἐρωτικός 751B (*LC*, p. 318). Cf. ibid., 752C: "Decent women cannot, of course, without impropriety either receive or bestow a passionate love" (ἐπεὶ ταῖς γε σώφροσιν οὔτ' ἐρᾶν οὔτ' ἐρᾶσθαι δήπου προσῆκόν ἐστιν). But elsewhere in the same dialogue another speaker observes, "If, then, . . . we have regard for the truth, passion for men and for women are one and the same thing: love" 751F (trans. adapted from Helmbold's).

[110.] *Amica* is common in Latin for a concubine or mistress (too common, in fact, to list occurrences), but no Latin philosophical treatises on friendship consider these relationships. Aristophanes (*Thesm.* 479) does seem to use φίλος to mean a heterosexual lover, but this is relatively rare in Greek. Athenaeus (13.571d) discusses the double meanings "companion/ friend" and "girlfriend/courtesan" of ἑταῖρα, and uses φίλη in reference to courtesans. Cf. n. below.

[111.] Notable exceptions are Aristotle, e.g., in *Nicomachean Ethics* 1161a–b, 1162a, *Rhetoric* 2.1381b; *Xenophon, Hiero* 3.7; and Plutarch, *Erotikos* 769A–C. The first and last specifically posit φιλία as a property of marriage; Xenophon uses the term to embrace the feelings of parents for children, children for parents, wives for husbands, and male companions (ἑταῖροι). On the tendency to collapse distinctions, A. W. H. Adkins notes that "every relationship from sexual passion to guest-friendship, relationships whose differences we should emphasize much more than their resemblances, is denoted by *philotes*" (" 'Friendship' and 'Self-sufficiency' in Homer and Aristotle," *Classical Quarterly* n.s. 13 (1963), 33–45, p. 36.

[112.] Aristotle argued that friendship was *principally* affection between equals (e.g., in *Nicomachean Ethics* 8.1157b and *Politics* 3.1287b), which makes his using it of marriage all

sorts often links friendship with *eros*: in Apuleius' *Metamorphoses* a speaker laments that due to the inactivity of Venus and Cupid (i.e., in the absence of *eros*) "there are no more conjugal pairings, no friendly unions, no love of children"—as if the three were equally dependent on the operations of Venus and Cupid.[113] ". . . The concepts of *concordia*, *unanimitas*, and of the *foedus amoris* are applied not only to friends, but also to brothers and to spouses."[114]

Often friends lived in each other's houses—sometimes permanently.[115] This is not to suggest that all (or even most) ancient friendships between men were in fact erotic, but rather that the distinction between a "friendship" and a "love relationship," so obvious, intuitive, and important to modern readers, would have seemed odd and unproductive to most ancient writers. It would certainly have marred a friendship involving ancient pagans if one party had taken some sexual advantage of the other (even subtly, by exploiting inexperience or youth, for example), but a consensual physical aspect would have been utterly irrelevant to placing the relationship in a meaningful taxonomy. Moreover, most pagan Europeans would have been utterly mystified by the concept "just friends," which presupposes that friendships are less powerful and intense than erotic relationships.[116] "Just friends" would have been a paradox to Aristotle or Cicero: no relationship was more emotional, more intimate, more intense than friendship. Friendship was, moreover, in the view of ancient writers on the subject, primarily a two-person relationship, as opposed to the modern idea that it is desirable to have as many friends as possible. (Ancient writers would consider most such "friends" acquaintances and deny that real friendship was possible with them.) Friendship was also passionate and indissoluble, and much ancient literature idealizes intense, lifelong friendships involv-

---

the more surprising. Roman writers also conflate the elements of friendship with those of other human commitments, e.g., marriage.

113. . . . *Non nuptiae coniugales, non amicitiae sociales, non liberum caritates* . . . 5:28; Cupid was nursing the wound inflicted by Psyche, and Venus was enjoying herself in the ocean.

114. Williams, "Homosexuality," p. 319.

115. See, e.g., Iamblichus, *Life of Pythagoras*, 235 (Damon and Pythias συνέζων...καὶ ἐκοινώνουν ἁπάντων); Cicero, *De amicitia* 1.2 (Sulpicius lived with Quintus Pompeius *coniunctissime et amantissime*), 4.15 (Cicero himself lived with Scipio; cf. also 27.103: *una domus erat, idem victus isque communis*).

116. Conversely, ancient writers mention it as a notable fact when a man happened to be in love with his wife (e.g., Plutarch, *Erotikos* 761E; Lucian, *Toxaris* 61). This seems odd to modern sensibilities.

ing great sacrifice on the part of one or both friends—motifs the modern world tends to associate almost exclusively with romantic love.[117]

Speech patterns aggravate and emphasize the confusion, in both ancient languages and modern ones. In English, for example, although one might say "she is just a friend"—meaning there is no (conscious) erotic element—one could also say "so-and-so is bringing his friend," by which sophisticated hearers would understand the speaker to mean that it is, in fact, a romantic attachment. The crucial information in both cases is encoded in the context surrounding "friend," which is a general term, and simply signifies a close personal relationship. "Just" in the first example means specifically "not erotic," and "his" in the second, where one would expect "a," conveys that it is a special connection, generally taken in the modern West to mean "erotic."[118]

"Friend" is similarly ambiguous in Greek, though almost exclusively in a homosexual context. In the *Phaedrus*, for example, Plato suggests that while the "lover" of a young man is "in love," the beloved feels "friendly,"[119] and mistakes his feelings, which are basically the same as the lover's, for friendship,[120] though in fact he desires to see, to touch, to kiss, to lie with or beside him—feelings not

---

117. Lucian (*Toxaris*, 61) tells a story about a man who saved his best friend from a fire, leaving his own wife and infant to fend for themselves. When rebuked for this he replied that he could easily get another wife and more children—as if they were fungible and of little particular emotional significance—but he could not easily find another friend like the one he rescued. The rebuke suggests that some of his contemporaries would not have so privileged a friendship; the same setup was used by other ancient writers to contrast the uniqueness of siblings with the relative interchangeability of spouses and children (e.g., Plutarch, *Moralia* 481E [Περὶ φιλαδελφίας], or Herodotus 3.119, in which a Persian woman chooses to save her brother instead of her children, saying that she could get more children but not another brother). Other tales of friendly devotion in the *Toxaris* include that of Agathocles, who sold his house to provide his friend Deinias money, and then followed him into exile and remained with him until his death; Euthydicus and Damon, childhood friends who went to Athens to study philosophy together after the former risked his life to save his friend from drowning at sea; and Demetrius of Sunium, who worked as a stevedore by day to bribe the guard at the jail where his friend Antiphilus was wrongly imprisoned, slept outside the bars at night, and finally had himself committed to the jail (through a false confession) to be with his friend. Note a similar story about friends joined by *una fratellanza* in Boccaccio, *Decameron*, Day 10, Story 8 (discussed below, pp. 176–77).

118. The difference in English between "her friend" and "a friend of hers" is considerable, at least in social circles where nonlegal permanent relationships are recognized.

119. 255A: αὐτὸς ("the beloved"), ὧν φύσει φίλος τῷ θεραπεύοντι ("the lover").

120. 255E: καὶ οἴεται οὐκ ἔρωτα ἀλλὰ φιλίαν εἶναι.

characteristic of "friendship" as understood either then or now.[121] This might be taken to indicate that Plato thinks there *is* a distinction, even if some people have difficulty applying it, but he then discloses that in his view the highest goal of the youth is "friendship with his lover"[122]—a deliberate conflation of the two. Plutarch likewise refers to the attachment between lovers as "erotic friendship"[123] —combining the two concepts—and says that a lover is "a friend inspired by God."[124] In his discussion of the nature of love (the Ἐρωτικός)[125] he uses ἐραστής ("lover") and φίλος ("friend") interchangeably, as do a great many ancient writers.[126] Athenaeus has Zeno say that "Eros is the god of friendship and concord."[127] In Latin *amica* almost invariably refers to a sexual partner, creating a vocabulary of rich ambiguity revolving around "friend," "friendship," and "love."[128]

Obviously Plato, Aristotle,[129] Plutarch, Cicero, and other ancient males had and knew friendships that were not erotic, and love relationships that were not friendships. The point is not that the two could not be distinguished, but that there was a substantial overlap, which is not a part of modern conceptualizations of friendship, owing

---

121. Ibid.: ὁρᾶν, ἅπτεσθαι, φιλεῖν, συγκατακεῖσθαι.

122. ἡ παρ' ἐραστοῦ φιλία (256E). In describing one of the most famous same-sex couples of the ancient world—Harmodius and Aristogiton, whose enduring and exclusive love was thought to have brought about the institution of Attic democracy—he uses both ἔρως and φιλία: ὁ γὰρ Ἀριστογείτονος ἔρως καὶ ἡ Ἁρμοδίου φιλία (182C). Although the phrasing could be taken to suggest that the two men had quite different sorts of feelings for each other, it must be remembered that their example is adduced in a discussion of ἔρως.

123. ἐρωτικὴ φιλία: *Life of Pelopidas* 18.2. Cf. *Erotikos* 768E, where he notes that Aphrodite and Eros together produce φιλία.

124. Ἔνθεον φίλον τὸν ἐραστὴν προσεῖπε (*Life of Pelopidas* 18), attributing it to Plato, presumably on the basis of *Symposium* 179, where the Sacred Band is also at issue (or *Phaedrus* virtually passim). On the translation of this as a reflection of monotheism, see n. 43, above.

125. Ed. and trans. W. C. Helmbold in LCL, *Moralia* 9 (Cambridge, 1969) 303–442.

126. Lucian, in the *Toxaris*, for example, which is a dialogue on friendship.

127. 561c: τὸν Ἔρωτα θεὸν εἶναι φιλίας καὶ ὁμονοίας (Book 13 [LCL 6:32]).

128. Catullus plays adroitly on this in 72 and 109 (which F. W. Cornish translates for the LCL, Catullus [Cambridge, 1988] as heterosexual, although the Latin text is ambiguous about the gender of the "friend").

129. Halperin, *One Hundred Years*, p. 131, says that Aristotle "refuses to consider the erotic relationship between man and boy a species of friendship," and then quotes a portion of the *Nicomachean Ethics* (8.3.5) in which Aristotle several times specifically discusses sexual relations as φιλία, and raises the question of whether or not this is genuine friendship. The relationships in question are not necessarily between man and boy, however; the discussion treats the young generally as ἐρωτικοί and having sudden passions, including friendship: φιλοῦσι ταχέως καὶ ταχέως παύονται.

to the pervasive taboo against homosexuality in modern nations. Homosexuality would "defile" a modern friendship in the eyes of the heterosexual majority, or at least transform it into something *other* than friendship. It would only have complicated an ancient one, in the same way that sexuality would complicate a friendship between a man and a woman in the modern West. And just as in modern heterosexual friendships the role of eroticism is often not entirely clear—even to those involved—it was probably often cloudy to the parties in intense same-sex friendships in the ancient world.[130]

A large part of the reason sexuality would complicate an ancient friendship is that the primary and defining characteristic of friendship (as opposed to any other emotional commitment) was its inherent equality: friendships had to take place between equals, or the relationship itself had at least to entail a general equality.[131] Since most ancient concepts of male sexuality presupposed that the "active" or insertive party somehow dominated the "passive" or receptive partner, sex would appear to introduce an element of subordination or inequality into a friendship, and thus complicate it. (This is part of the reason that women, who were always thought to be subordinated in sex through their passivity, were not suitable as "friends.") This popular ideology of sex as involving an older or more powerful or richer male deriving pleasure through insertion from a younger or poorer or dependent male or a female should not be confused with a description of reality, any more than the English insult "fuck you" should be taken to indicate either the likelihood of sex between the speakers involved or the belief that performing the act in question always and everywhere humiliates or demeans the other party. The same inarticulate stereotypes and rhetorical shorthand for sexual power in the ancient world almost certainly yielded in private, then as now, to a more flexible reality, responsive to the complex varieties of individual human desires and passions. While in public, then, there might seem to be a conflict between friendship and sexuality—although, as noted, the two were often deliberately conflated—there is

---

130. The poem, "Marcus amans puerum," often attributed to Claudian (late fourth, early fifth century, but possibly a later imitation) explicitly uses the Latin *amicus* with the sense of "lover": "The day hears 'son'; the night and the bed hear 'friend' " (*"Nate" dies audit, nox et torus audit "amice"*) in *Poetae latini minores*, ed. Emil Baehrens (Leipzig, 1879–83) 3:306.
131. *Sed maximum est in amicitia superiorem parem esse inferiori*, Cicero, *De Amicitia* 19.69.

no reason to believe that a sexual friendship was any rarer or more (or less) difficult then than now.

A fourth type of homosexual relationship known in the ancient world consisted of formal unions—i.e., publicly recognized relationships entailing some change in status for one or both parties, comparable in this sense to heterosexual marriage. Cicero, though notoriously straightlaced, persuaded Curio the Elder to honor the debt his son had incurred on behalf of Antonius, to whom the younger Curio was, in Cicero's words, "united in a stable and permanent marriage, just as if he had given him a matron's *stola*."[132] It is most unlikely that Cicero, in making this comparison, actually regarded the relationship as a "marriage," either morally or legally. His remark is bitterly sarcastic. What is open to speculation is whether he felt that there was some de facto comparability between this sort of same-sex relationship and established heterosexual unions.

Same-sex relationships did sometimes involve utilization of the customs and forms of heterosexual marriage. The poet Martial describes, at the opening of the second century, how

The bearded Callistratus married the rugged Afer
Under the same law by which a woman takes a husband.
Torches were carried before him, a bridal veil covered his face,
Nor was the hymn to you, O god of marriage, omitted.[133]
A dowry was even agreed on. Does this not, Rome, seem
Enough? Do you expect him also to bear a child?[134]

Such unions were not always private. A few years earlier, the emperor Nero (ruled C.E. 54 to 68) "married a man [named Sporus] in a very public ceremony with a dowry and a veil [*flammeum*], with all the solemnities of matrimony, and lived with him as his spouse."[135] A

---

[132] Philippic 2.18.45: *te . . . tamquam stolam dedisset, in matrimonio stabili et certo collocavit.* The *stola* was the distinctive garb of a married Roman woman.

[133] Talasse: see Martial 1.35, 3.93, 12.95, Livy 1.9.12, Catullus 61.127.

[134] Martial 12.42 (misidentified in CSTH, p. 82, as 11.42): *Barbatus rigido nupsit Callistratus Afro/hac qua lege viro nubere virgo solet./praeluxere faces, velarunt flammea vultus,/nec tua defuerunt verba, Talasse, tibi./dos etiam dicta est. nondum tibi, Roma, videtur/hoc satis? expectas numquid ut et pariat?* Cf. 1.24, where a male is said to have "married" the day before, using the word specifically denoting the bride's role at a wedding (*heri nupsit*).

[135] Suetonius, *Nero* 28, related with more detail in Dio Cassius (*Epitome* 62.28; see n. 7, above, for difficulties of this text), who says that there was a marriage contract, and that both the

friend gave the "bride" away, "as required by law."[136] ". . . He took this Sporus with him, carried on a litter and decked out in the finery normally worn by empresses, and often kissed him."[137] The marriage was celebrated separately in Rome and in Greece.[138] On another occasion, the emperor himself "was given in marriage to a freedman, just as Sporus had been given to him, and even imitated the cries and wailings of a virgin being deflowered."[139]

By Juvenal's time, a little later in the century, such ceremonies had become, at least in his disapproving view, absolutely commonplace: " 'I have a ceremony to attend tomorrow morning in the Quirinal valley.' 'What sort of ceremony?' 'Nothing special:[140] a friend is marrying another man[141] and a small group is attending.' "[142]

"Gracchus has given a cornet player (or perhaps he performed on a straight instrument?)[143] a dowry of four hundred sesterces,[144] signed the marriage tablets,[145] said the blessing, held a great banquet, and

---

Romans and the Greeks celebrated the marriage publicly (cf. the speech of C. Julius Vindex at 63.22.4). Cf. Tacitus (*Annals* 15.370), generally a very reliable source, who mentions all the same details: *uni ex illo contaminatorum grege (nomen Pythagoras fuit) in modum sollemnium coniugiorum denupsisset. inditum imperatori flammeum, missi auspices, dos et genialis torus et faces nuptialies.* It is difficult to discount such detail.

136. "ὥσπερ ὁ νόμος ἐκέλευε" Dio 62[63].13. The friend was Tigellinus.

137. Suetonius, *Nero* 28. Dio adds that subjects were expected to address Sporus as "lady," "empress," or "mistress" (62[63].13).

138. So Dio 62.28 and 62[63].13.

139. Suetonius, *Nero* 29. Suetonius gives the freedman's name as Doryphorus, but both Tacitus and Dio give Pythagoras: Tacitus, *Annals* 15.37, Dio 62.28. (Multiple marriages, regardless of gender, were not unusual: all a Roman male had to do to get rid of a wife was repudiate her. But all accounts of this arrangement suppose [solely on the basis of their knowledge of the two ceremonies?] that a *ménage à trois* was involved.)

140. Literally, "Why do you ask?" (*Quid quaeris?*)—clearly indicating that, to Juvenal's disgust, those invited to the ceremony are not in any way fazed by it.

141. The Latin expresses the gender oddity by applying the word *nubere*, which refers specifically to the role played by the bride at a Roman wedding, to the male *amicus*. Cf. Martial 1.24, where the same play on words occurs, and discussion of laws against same-sex marriage below.

142. Juvenal, *Satire* 2:132–35. The original is in verse, but I have shortened it to such an extent that the verse divisions would no longer be of value. Ramsay's translation in the LCL edition is questionable and misses much subtlety.

143. An obscene pun: *fellatio* (either heterosexual or homosexual) was thought filthy by Romans, even those not in any way scandalized by homosexual acts.

144. G. G. Ramsay, the LCL translator, gives "four hundred thousand sesterces" (p. 27) for Juvenal's *quadringentia dedit . . . sestertia dotem.* Four hundred would be a small dowry by the standards of the imperial upper classes, four hundred thousand quite respectable.

145. Dixon believes (pp. 66–67) that these privately recorded the terms of the engagement (in case there was later a divorce), rather than constituting a public record of the marriage. If she is correct, it corresponds roughly to a modern prenuptial agreement rather than a marriage license.

the new 'bride' reclines in his husband's lap. A man who once bore the waving shields [of Mars][146] . . . now dons brocade and a long train and a bridal veil. . . . A man born to nobility and wealth is given in marriage to another man!"[147] Although Juvenal adduces this as an example of the decline of Roman mores (the subject of all his poetry), part of what dismayed him was obviously its casual and accepting reception by his contemporaries.

A woman in Lucian's *Dialogues of the Courtesans* (5.3), about half a century later, describes herself as having been "married" to another woman, who was her "wife," for a "long time" (γεγάμηκα[148] πρόπαλαι ταύτην...καὶ ἔστιν ἐμὴ γυνή), although there are no clues about any legal or ceremonial aspects of the relationship. (The women in this story are characterized as being exclusively interested in other women [5.2].)[149] And a contemporary romance writer included in his novel about love "a digression about Berenice, the daughter of the king of Egypt, and her wild and inordinate passions,[150] and how she slept with Mesopotamia. . . . Berenice married Mesopotamia, and there was war between Garmos and Berenice on account of Mesopotamia."[151]

One might view these unions as "imitative of" heterosexual marriage, but it would be more cautious to see them as modes of "participating in" the majority culture. They present two particularly

---

146. Gracchus was apparently one of the Salii, priests of Mars who carried sacred shields in procession at Rome. He had also been a gladiator: see lines 143ff. and 8.201, 210.

147. Juvenal, *Satire* 2:117–120, 124–25, 129.

148. Note that she employs the Greek for the male's role in a marriage rather than the phrase for a female.

149. By contrast, a character in the Hellenistic novel *Affairs of the Heart*, falsely attributed to Lucian, sarcastically proposes that if male homosexuality is to be accepted, lesbianism (τῆς τριβακῆς ἀσελγείας) might as well be, too—distinctly suggesting that this would be preposterous and unheard of (§28, p. 194).

150. ἀγρίων αὐτῆς καὶ ἐκθέσμων ἐρώτων: cf. Lucian's ἀλλόκοτον (*Dialogues* 5.1). Roman and Greek writers appear to have found lesbianism peculiar, even when they accepted male homosexuality as ordinary.

151. *Iamblichi Babyloniacorum reliquiae*, ed. Elmar Habrich (Leipzig, 1960), 17, p. 58. This is a paraphrase by the ninth-century patriarch Photius; the original has been lost. Most scholars trust Photius' abridgements as generally reliable: see Tomas Hägg, *Photius als Vermittler antiker Literatur: Untersuchungen zur Technik des Referierens und Exzerptierens in der Bibliotheke* (Uppsala, 1975), and Warren Treadgold, *The Nature of the "Bibliotheca" of Photius* (Washington, 1980). For an earlier discussion of this, see *CSTH*, p. 84. Although I believe this was the first time the idea of a real marriage between the two women had been seriously proposed in scholarly literature, none of the many critics of *CSTH* has challenged it.

interesting aspects. Before the empire, it would probably not have occurred to same-sex couples to take part in wedding ceremonies of this sort, because heterosexual marriage was almost entirely a dynastic and property arrangement having to do with descendants and inheritance, with virtually no relation to the sort of emotional ties that inspired same-sex unions. It was only the increasing emphasis on love as cause, effect, or concomitant of matrimony that would have created in the minds of citizens of the empire of the first and second centuries some relation between heterosexual marriages and same-sex unions. In addition, the diminution under the early empire of the dynamic of complete subordination of the bride—the waning of marriage *cum manu*, "with hand," for example, the increasingly egalitarian concepts of matrimonial obligations, mutually binding contracts, and so on—removed one of the difficulties that marriage would have earlier posed for at least one of two males seeking to solemnize their relationship. Under the newer conceptualization neither one need become the property, dependent, or *famulus* of the other: they could form a partnership not unlike that of Egyptian marriage contracts.

The fact that in heterosexual unions the woman was given, by the male who owned or controlled her, into the control or ownership of another male nonetheless posed some problems for any same-sex unions drawing on their symbolism or authority. In the case of two women, which would gain control? Berenice, as a ruler, probably entertained and raised few doubts about this in her fictional world. But what about reality? And in the case of two males, which one would *yield* control—a much more disturbing question in a world where masculine control and privilege formed the basic social foundation. This is presumably what prompts Juvenal's uneasiness about a man "born to wealth and nobility" being *given away* in marriage.[152]

Conflict between gender expectations and same-sex involvement in traditional heterosexual marriage patterns is more evident in the

---

[152.] The issue was further complicated by the fact that one of the chief assets of a bride was her virginity, and it was far from clear to ancient writers whether inexperience in a male was the equivalent of physical virginity in a female. Achilles Tatius in the second century wonders "whether there is any virginity among men" (εἰ τις ἐστὶ καὶ ἐν ἀνδράσι παρθενία, 5.20).

case of Elagabalus,[153] emperor from 218 to 222.[154] Brought to the imperial throne in his early teens through a combination of his alleged relationship to a previous dynasty, the intervention of powerful female relatives, political turmoil at Rome, and rebellious troops, he shocked his subjects with his utter lack of decorum in sexual matters, particularly because he flagrantly took a passive role with other males, behavior thought feminine and inappropriate for any adult male citizen, especially an emperor. He had a long-lasting relationship with an athlete, Hierocles,[155] which his most reliable biographer clearly (but unhappily) regarded as a marriage,[156] to the point not only of characterizing Hierocles as his "husband,"[157] but even of describing the emperor's affairs with other men as "adultery."[158] (On the other hand, this same writer evinces about as much disgust at Elagabalus'

---

153. Actually named Avitus; called Elagabalus (from the Greek ῾Ελεογάβαλος) after the god he worshiped and introduced to Rome. Since most modern historians use this name, I have done so as well. He styled himself "Antoninus" to derive prestige from the Antonines, claiming to be descended from them. Dio refers to him as "the false Antoninus" or Sardanapalus, after a famous ancient voluptuary. Lampridius names his biography "Antoninus Elagabalus."

154. There are two detailed accounts of Elagabalus' reign and personal life: the *Epitome* of Dio, Books 79–80 (ed. and trans. Earnest Cary [London, 1927] 9 in the *LCL* Dio), and the account by Lampridius in the *Scriptores Historiae Augustae* (ed. and trans. David Magie [London, 1924]). The former is generally thought more credible—indeed, Dio says he was an eyewitness to much of what he records (80.1.1)—while the latter is almost universally viewed with suspicion. The accounts are, nonetheless, in substantial agreement. Dio adds much more lurid detail, and Lampridius appears to have confused Zoticus with Hierocles at one point (as noted below). Both authors explicitly acknowledge a deep hostility to Elagabalus, and given his evident sexual excesses it is easy to imagine that they embroidered their accounts to his discredit.

155. Dio 80[79].5, 14, 15, 16. Lampridius (10) says that he "married" Zoticus: "he was given in marriage to him and cohabited with him, to the point of having a maid of honor . . ." (*nupsit et coit, ita ut et pronubam haberet* . . .). But Lampridius appears to have confused Hierocles and Zoticus: at first he describes Zoticus (ibid.) as having great influence at court, whereas Dio says that Zoticus was only in the emperor's palace and good graces for a single night, and then expelled from Italy. Later (15) Lampridius identifies Hierocles as the emperor's favorite, whose dismissal is demanded by the soldiers; Zoticus is not mentioned. Lampridius may simply have confused the names, or have taken as a wedding the fact that Zoticus was brought to the palace crowned with garlands and with burning torches (Dio 80[79].16.3–4: Or perhaps Dio failed to recognize it as such? But it is difficult to imagine that Dio has failed to recognize or suppressed any shocking details, given what he does report). Elagabalus' having a wedding with Hierocles is strongly suggested by Dio's ἐγήματο (80[79].5.5), which corresponds to Lampridius' *nupsit*.

156. Dio, 80[79].5.5, unmistakably includes both heterosexual and homosexual unions under the rubric "marriage" when he says, "Of his marriages, in which he sometimes took the male role and sometimes the female, more will be said . . ." (περὶ μὲν τῶν γάμων αὐτοῦ, ὧν τε ἐγάμει ὧν τε ἐγήματο . . . , καὶ γὰρ ἠνδρίζετο καὶ ἐθηλύνετο . . .).

157. Dio 80[79].14.1 and 4: ὁ δὲ δὴ ἀνὴρ αὐτῆς [sic, meaning Elagabalus] ῾Ιεροκλῆς ἦν. Note that the use of the ordinary Greek for "husband," ἀνήρ ("man"), heightens the paradox.

158. 80[79].15.3: ἐμοίχευον αὐτον.

heterosexual unions—of which there were five, including one to a vestal virgin—as he does toward the homosexual marriage to Hierocles. Doubtless he accurately perceived that the heterosexual ones, though more conventional, were actually less genuine.)[159] Another source says that at this time men who wished to advance in the imperial court either had husbands or pretended they did.[160]

The conflict between the increasingly narrower sexual attitudes of the period and the youthful suzerain's extraordinary (even by imperial standards) licentiousness may have played a role in bringing about his assassination (Dio says that it did). What this reflects about general attitudes would be impossible to say, not only because the details of his erotic excesses remain murky (and were unquestionably exaggerated by contemporary writers for dramatic effect), but also because he exhibited many failings as a ruler that may have played a larger role than his sexual idiosyncrasies in creating the discontent of the soldiers who ended his reign, although his biographers, writing to please his successors, tended to dwell on the latter, which made more colorful reading. The vast majority of emperors of the third century had short, violent reigns, without any element of erotic extravagance: in this regard Elagabalus' end was perhaps the most ordinary aspect of his life.

Nonetheless, the tendency toward more and more ascetic public morality and insistence on traditional sex roles produced in the middle of the following century (342) an extravagantly worded and highly propagandistic law forbidding same-sex weddings—at least those involving traditional gender roles:

When a man marries [a man][161] as if he were a woman,[162] what can he be seeking, where gender has lost its place? where the sin is something that it is unseemly [even] to know? where Venus is transformed into a different form? where love is sought, but does

159. As he says explicitly at 80[79].9.1.
160. Lampridius 11: *qui maritos se habere iactarent*. On Lampridius, see n. 155.
161. The meaning of this phrase is perfectly clear; I have supplied the words in brackets not to strengthen the meaning, but because many MSS include *viro* ("a man") at precisely this point: see the apparatus to Haenel's edition, loc. cit. The word *nubere* is generally used for the action of the bride in a heterosexual wedding; the male's role is most commonly denoted by *ducere*. Martial and other classical writers play on this specific and unambiguous meaning of *nubo*.
162. Literally, "as a woman offering herself to men."

not appear? We order the laws to arise, justice to be armed with an avenging sword, so that those shameless persons guilty of this either now or in future should be subjected to exquisite punishment.[163]

It is obvious from the wording of the law that gender roles and expectations are as much at issue as same-gender sexuality. The word employed for "marry" is *nubere*, the Latin term for the bride's part, the word used in derision by Martial, Juvenal, and the biographers of Nero and Elagabalus to describe a male's playing what was seen as an archetypally female social role: being given away in marriage, surrendered into the power and control of the husband.[164] It may seem oddly severe for the Code to prescribe death for something that was obviously a familiar part of the Roman social landscape, but the era witnessed many dramatic transformations of traditional patterns. At the opening of the century Christianity was illegal; by its close paganism was punishable by death. Not long before the emperors had apparently issued an equally bombastic regulation regarding heterosexual marriage,[165] and the Code also prescribed death for adultery, in a particularly lurid and imaginative way: adulterers were to be sewn into a leather sack and burned alive (11.36.4; this is also the penalty

---

163. Theodosian Code, 9.7.3, rescript of Constantius and Constans: *Cum vir nubit in feminam viris porrecturam, quid cupiat, ubi sexus perdidit locum? ubi scelus est id, quod non proficit scire? ubi Venus mutatur in alteram formam? ubi amor quaeritur, nec videtur? iubemus insurgere leges, armari iura gladio ultore, ut exquisitis poenis subdantur infames, qui sunt vel qui futuri sunt rei.* Dalla, *Ubi Venus Mutatur*, takes his title from this law, but denies that it relates to homosexual marriages (p. 63, n. 2), claiming almost in passing that the phrase *vir nubit in feminam* is purely metaphorical, without explaining what considerations lead him to believe this. He also misdates the rescript as belonging to 390, apparently confusing it with 9.7.6, which may account in part for his misreading it. For earlier discussions of this law, see *CSTH*, pp. 123–24 and literature cited there.

164. Plautus (*Casina*, 1011) also uses *nubere* in this sense, in a servant's suspicions about two men (*novom nuptum cum novo marito*, 859), and when Chalinus says that he has "married" two men (*duobus nupsi*). The use of *nuptum* with *maritum* is obviously evidence of the usage in question; in the second case, since the context is Chalinus' complaint that neither of the men did his duty, *nubere* also clearly denotes the female role in marriage.

165. "In A.D. 295, the emperors Diocletian and Maximian issued a long and bombastic decree against incestuous marriages in which they called upon Roman citizens to celebrate marriages in accord with Roman laws. . . . 'Henceforeward we wish propriety and holiness to be observed by everyone in all marriage-making; they should remember that they are subject to Roman discipline and laws; they should know that only those marriages are lawful which are permitted by Roman law,' " Hopkins, p. 354, citing the *Mosaicarum et romanarum legum collatio*, 6.3–4, in *Fontes iuris romani antejustiniani*, ed. Salvatore Riccobono (Florence, 1940–43), vol. 2. The nature, purpose, and reliability of this work are all in considerable doubt, which is why I qualify Hopkins' reference with "apparently."

for parricide). Not only is there no known instance of such a draco-nian penalty ever being applied (even though Constantine's wife, Fausta, was executed for adultery; many believe this was political), but it was almost certainly abrogated by the *Novellum Majoriani* 9.1, which prescribed exile for adultery and called it a precedent. Even this was probably not actually enforced: only husbands, fathers, broth-ers, paternal uncles, first cousins, and other paternal relatives could accuse a woman of adultery (9.7.2).[166] In short, the code containing the draconian prohibition of same-sex weddings is not a reliable indi-cation of Roman sexual practice even for the century to which it theoretically applied, although knowing *what* it prohibited may pro-vide some clues. The severity of the penalty proposed for men "mar-rying as women" may be an indication of how negatively the compilers of the Code viewed the practice, but it is not likely evi-dence of the actual fate of those involved, any more than the exotic penalty for adultery could, by any stretch of the imagination, be taken to indicate the elimination of adultery among the Roman populace.

Nonetheless, for a variety of reasons, such weddings did become less common as the empire waned. Part of the reason for this was the rise or dissemination of other forms of same-sex union—modes of establishing formal unions more particular to same-sex couples. Some of these doubtless left no record: such relationships were unlikely, after all, to entail major property or inheritance consequences, and there was not much incentive to make a legal record of them. At the opening of the fourth century B.C.E. Xenophon noted that in a num-ber of Greek states, "as in Boeotia,[167] man and boy live together, like married people,"[168] but he provided no details about formal aspects of the relationships, nor is it easy to tell how many states he has in mind. Thebes, which gave rise to the Sacred Band of lovers, was in

---

166. Adultery was apparently an offense only women could commit under this code, and not even all women: "If the mistress of a tavern, that is, the wife of a tavern keeper, should be found in adultery, she can be accused; but if her maid-servant or a woman who gives service in the tavern should be apprehended in adultery, she shall be acquitted in consideration of her mean status" (9.7.1, trans. Pharr).

167. The Greek state immediately to the north of Athens: it is hardly possible that Xenophon was misinformed about social customs there. Plato also adduces Boeotian homosexual rela-tionships as in same ways exemplary: *Symposium* 182B.

168. Translation by E. C. Marchant, *Xenophon: Scripta Minora* (London, 1925), *Constitution of Sparta* 2:12, p. 147. This is the only reasonable way to understand the Greek (ἀνὴρ καὶ παῖς συζυγέντες ὁμιλοῦσιν), although "like married people" is not literally expressed.

Boeotia. The context of the remark is his commendation of Lycurgus for discouraging at Sparta same-sex relationships based solely on physical attraction.[169] By contrast, at Sparta men were permitted to "live with" (συνεῖναι) young males only out of love and a desire to assist in their training and education. This is as opposed, he says, to the "other Greek states, for example Boeotia," where they live as a married couple, or Elea,[170] where same-sex relationships are based on "favors."[171]

It is known that male couples swore oaths and made pledges to each other at the tomb of Ioläus, Hercules' beloved.[172] This may have constituted a formalization of same-sex unions, comparable to a heterosexual wedding, but too little is known about the custom and the content of the "pledges" to be sure. If they swore to remain together for life, and did so, would this constitute a same-sex marriage? According to literature, many ancient Greek same-sex couples, such as Achilles and Patroclus, or Epaminondas and Caphisodorus, were in fact buried together, like husband and wife.[173]

Of three types of formal unions more detail is known.

1. The most reliable geographer and ethnographer of pagan antiquity, Strabo (whose life traversed the beginning of the Christian

---

169. Note the implication that this would require strong legal action: Xenophon adds that "I do not wonder that people find this unbelievable, for in many states the laws do not hinder desire for young men."

170. A Greek settlement in southern Italy: cf. Plato, *Symposium* 182B, as noted above.

171. Presumably the suitor offered the young man he admired gifts, and the young man allowed the suitor "favors" with his person. Χάρις would be used for both the gift and the sexual favor, creating a rich set of suggestive puns (of interesting relationship to later Christian concepts of "grace," also χάρις). This is the pattern suggested in Suetonius, and in much other Greek literature (summarized in David Robinson and Edward Fluck, *A Study of Greek Love-Names, Including a Discussion of Paederasty and a Prosopographia* [Baltimore, 1937]). These complicated differences had already been described in the *Symposium* of Plato, 182B: ". . . it is easy to note the rule [νόμος] with regard to love [τὸν ἔρωτα] in other cities: there it is laid down in simple terms, while ours here is complicated [ποικίλος]. For in Elis and Boeotia and where there is no skill in speech they have simply an ordinance that it is seemly [καλόν] to gratify lovers [χαρίζεσθαι ἐρασταῖς], and no one whether young or old will call it shameful. . . . But in Ionia and many other regions where they live under foreign sway, it is counted a disgrace," trans. W. R. M. Lamb (*LCL* ed. [London, 1967]).

172. Plutarch, *Erotikos* 761E. Cf. *Life of Pelopidas*, 18.4, where he describes what happens at the tomb as καταπιστώσεις ποιεῖσθαι.

173. For Achilles and Patroclus, see pp. 59–60, above, and p. 95, below. For Epaminondas and Caphisodorus, see Plutarch, *Erotikos* 761D. Epaminondas was not heterosexually married. His best friend, Pelopidas, who was married to a woman, was captain of the Sacred Band of Thebes, composed of pairs of male lovers (Plutarch, *Life of Pelopidas*, 18, 20).

Era), described a ceremony of ritual abduction establishing a legal relationship between male lovers in Crete.[174]

They [the Cretans] have peculiar laws[175] regarding love. For they acquire their lovers [κατεργάζονται τοὺς ἐρωμένους] not by persuasion but by abduction. The lover advises friends[176] three or more days beforehand that the abduction is going to take place. If they sequester the youth [παῖς][177] or he avoids the designated road it would be a considerable disgrace, as if they acknowledged that he was unworthy of such a lover. When they encounter each other, if the abductor is the young man's equal or superior in social class and other respects, they pursue and restrain him only a little, in observance of the law, and then willingly relinquish him. If [the abductor] seems unworthy, they take the youth away.

The pursuit is not over until the youth is finally brought to the abductor's quarters.[178] They regard as the most worthy of love young men who are outstanding not in beauty [κάλλει], but in character and attractiveness [κοσμιότητι].[179] After giving the youth a present, he takes him to the country, to any spot he wishes. The witnesses to the abduction accompany them, and after feasting and hunting for a couple of months (for it is not

---

174. Strabo presents these details as part of his description of Crete in his day, but says that he is drawing on the work of Ephorus, who lived several centuries earlier. It is thus impossible to be sure whether to view the abduction as a custom of only the fourth century B.C.E. (Ephorus' day) or as one that persisted into the Christian Era, as Strabo seems to imply. Crete was widely thought to be particularly associated with homosexual passions, even in a Greek-speaking world where such feelings were accepted as ordinary: for example, Aristotle, *Politics* 2.10; Plato, *Laws* 636b–d; Timaeus, frag. 144; Heraclides, *Ponticus*, 508.

175. τὸ νόμιμον: H. L. Jones, the LCL translator (*The Geography of Strabo* [London, 1928]), p. 155, renders this as "They have a peculiar custom," but νόμος is much stronger than "custom": he renders it "law"—which is certainly what it means—further on in the same passage, in regard to gifts and the youth's statement of consent.

176. Jones and other translators and commentators have taken this to refer to the friends of the youth to be abducted, but in light of what follows it seems to me equally possible that it is both these and the lover's own friends, who will accompany them to the country.

177. See n. 198, below.

178. ἀνδρεῖον: one of the public dining halls of Sparta and Crete, in which all males, even if married, dined on prescribed food.

179. This does not seem to make much sense: the text may be corrupt here, or it may simply mean that a *combination* of physical appearance and character was preferable to beauty alone.

permitted to keep the young man away longer than this), they return to the city.

The young man returns bearing as gifts a military outfit and an ox and a chalice (these are specified by law) and other things besides, so many that the friends must contribute to covering the expenses. He sacrifices the ox to Zeus and gives a feast for those who accompanied them, at which he states publicly in regard to his relationship [ὁμιλίας] with his lover whether he is pleased about it or not. The law prescribes this so that if any force was used for the abduction he can at this point seek redress and extricate himself [sc., from the relationship].

It is a disgrace for young men who are good-looking and from good families not to have lovers, as if this were the consequence of their own conduct. Those who have been abducted are called "partners"[180] and enjoy special privileges: at dances and races they are given places of honor, and they are allowed to wear finer clothes than others—what their lovers gave them. Not only that, but even when they are older they wear distinctive clothing, which indicates that they are "special" [κλεινός].[181] For they call the beloved "special," and the lover his "friend."[182] These are their legal arrangements regarding love [τὰ περὶ τοὺς ἔρωτας].[183]

---

180. Or "companions": literally, "those who stand beside" (παρασταθέντες). This expression, which is known only twice in Greek literature (here and in Athenaeus' quotation of it [11.782c]) has somehow befuddled most previous commentators. The comparable παραστάται, "standing [or placed] beside" refers both to soldiers in line and to "comrades." Παρασταθέντες seems to be the equivalent of "live-in," "significant other," or other designations for nonmarital partners who "stand beside" their "other half" in life. Koehl, "The Chieftain Cup," pp. 106–7, suggests that it is derived from the fact that the abducted youth "stood beside" his older lover in the andreion and acted as his cup-bearer, recalling the relationship between Zeus and Ganymede, which also began with an abduction.

181. Or perhaps "illustrious," "outstanding," "distinguished." The word literally means "famous," but this hardly seems appropriate, since Ephorus/Strabo purport to be discussing an ordinary occurrence.

182. φιλήτορα. This might also be translated as "lover," from φιλέω rather than ἐράω; on possible distinctions (or lack thereof) between these words, see Chapter 1.

183. Strabo, Geography 10.4.21. Cf. Athenaeus 11.782c, 11.502b. Athenaeus adds no new information, and may be entirely dependent on Strabo/Ephorus, although in the second passage he credits Hermonax. For modern commentary on this passage see J. Harrison, Themis (Cambridge, 1927), pp. 16–29; H. Jeanmaire, Couroi et Couretes (Lille, 1939), pp. 450–55; R. F. Willetts, Cretan Cults and Festivals (London, 1962), pp. 116–17, 205; Robert Koehl, "The Chieftain Cup and a Minoan Rite of Passage," Journal of Hellenic Studies 106 (1986),

Apart from the abduction aspect, this practice has all the elements of European marriage tradition: witnesses, gifts, religious sacrifice, a public banquet, a chalice, a ritual change of clothing for one partner, a change of status for both,[184] even a honeymoon.[185] The public statement at the banquet prefigures what would eventually become the single most important element of marriage in Roman and Christian law: a declaration of consent to the union. (Cf. the modern formula: "Do you take . . . ?")

The abduction[186] is less remarkable, by the standards of the times, than it seems. The ruler of the gods, Zeus, maintained a permanent relationship with a beautiful Trojan prince, Ganymede, after abducting him and carrying him off to heaven;[187] they were the most famous same-sex couple of the ancient world, familiar to all its educated residents.[188] Zeus even gave Ganymede's father a gift—the equivalent of a dower or "morning gift"

99–110; and Sergent, passim. All of these writers consider the custom an initiation rite of some sort; none considers its relation to marriage.

[184.] P. A. Cartledge, "The Politics of Spartan Pederasty," *Proceedings of the Cambridge Philological Society*, n.s. 27 (1981), 16–36, notes (p. 36, n. 78) that "in Sparta admission to membership of a common mess . . . was a condition of full citizenship," thus emphasizing the ritual coming of age involved in the rite, the aspect that has most attracted the attention of previous commentators (e.g., Sergent, Jeanmaire).

[185.] Nonetheless, few other scholars have made the connection, even though the passage is well-known and has been the subject of considerable discussion in other contexts. See, e.g., Bernard Sergent, *L'Homosexualité dans la mythologie grecque* (Paris, 1984) (English trans. *Homosexuality in Greek Myth*, by Arthur Goldhammer [Boston, 1986]), Part 1 and passim, and bibliography cited there. Sir Richard Burton, in the "Terminal Essay: D. Pederasty," appended to his translation of the *Arabian Nights* (London, 1885; reprinted in *Sexual Heretics: Male Homosexuality in English Literature, 1850–1900*, ed. Brian Reade [New York, 1970], pp. 158–93), p. 184, seems to notice this, and refers to the custom as "marriage ceremonies" (in quotation marks). Mark Golden, "Slavery and Homosexuality," remarks in a note, "At least some Cretans practiced a socially accepted form of homosexual courtship and marriage in the mid-fourth century" (p. 319, n. 49, citing the Ephorus/Strabo passage translated above).

[186.] I carefully avoid the word "rape," which raises other issues. It would only be reasonable to regard it as a rape if the youth so identified it when given the opportunity to do so. Greek distinguishes between "abduction" (ἁρπαγή) as a general phenomenon (which might involve rape, but does not necessarily) and "sexual violence" (ὑβρίζειν), which could occur *in situ* without any abduction. The distinction in Latin between *raptus* and *stuprum* is less clear.

[187.] This story was popular at least as early as Pindar (fifth century B.C.E.), *Olympian Odes*, 1.44, 10.105. Homer had already made it familiar (see note 189), and by Vergil's time (*Aeneid* 5.255) the legend had aquired the dramatic image of an eagle's seizing Ganymede, which would subsequently constitute the standard artistic representation of the incident. (Ovid, *Metamorphoses* 10.155ff, specified that the eagle was in fact Zeus, which was accepted by most later writers and artists.)

[188.] The Latin equivalent of the Greek name "Ganymedes" was "Catamitus," which was used as a generic noun for a passive male homosexual. The English "catamite" is derived from it.

for the bride's family in a heterosexual marriage.[189] The inhabitants of Chalcis honored what they believed to be the very spot of Ganymede's abduction, called the Harpagion ("Place of Abduction").[190] Moreover, as late as Boccaccio (*Decameron*, Day 5, Tale 1) an abduction marriage that takes place seems to find its most natural home in Crete.

Heterosexual abduction marriage was also extremely common in the ancient world[191]—especially in the neighboring state of Sparta, with which Crete shared its constitution and much of its social organization,[192] where it was the *normal* mode of heterosexual marriage. (After her abduction the bride's head was shaved and she was dressed in men's clothing—establishing further curious parallels to the Cretan abduction of young men.)[193] It remained frequent well into modern times,[194] and even under Christian influence men who abducted women were often only constrained to marry them, and not punished in any (other?) way.

189. Homer, *Iliad* 5.265, 20.232: a rare breed of horses; in other versions of the tale it is a golden vine.
190. Athenaeus 13.601F.
191. "It was the law among the Byzantines that if a man abducted a virgin and married her immediately, the marriage itself was the penalty," Achilles Tatius (second century) 2.13.3 (νόμου γὰρ ὄντος Βυζαντίοις, εἴ τις ἁρπάσας παρθένον φθάσας ποιήσει γυναῖκα, γάμον ἔχειν τὴν ζημίαν).
192. Plutarch says (*Life of Lycurgus* 15.3) that "their [heterosexual] marriages were by abduction" (ἐγάμουν δὲ δι' ἁρπαγῆς), which has been taken as accurate by most scholars (e.g., W. K. Lacey, *The Family in Classical Greece* [Ithaca, N.Y., 1968], pp. 197–98; Evans-Grubbs, p. 68; Ian Jenkins, "Is There Life After Marriage? A Study of the Abduction Motif in Vase Paintings of the Athenian Wedding Ceremony," *Bulletin of the Institute of Classical Studies* 30 [1983], 137–45). Note that Plutarch also gives a wry inversion of this in his *Erotikos*, when a mature widow abducts a young man she wants to marry. The word Plutarch uses—ἁρπαγή —is, of course, also the word used by Strabo for the Cretan abduction. (The *Life of Lycurgus* includes much that is dubious: cf. Evans-Grubbs for a more sober assessment.) Plutarch goes on to say that Spartan men did not live with their wives immediately after their marriages, but continued to reside in the ἀνδρεῖα for some time and merely visited them from time to time briefly at night to beget children (ibid.). Given what we know about Spartan social organization, this seems credible. Cf. following note and n. 178.
193. Plutarch, *Life of Lycurgus* 15.3. Athenaeus (13.602E) adds that "among the Spartans it was the law [νόμος] for women before they married to consort with [ὁμιλεῖν] men as if they were youths [ὡς παιδικοῖς]" (presumably an allusion to anal intercourse to prevent conception).
194. See, for example, Judith Evans-Grubbs, "Abduction Marriage in Antiquity: A Law of Constantine (CTh ix.24.1) and Its Social Context," *Journal of Roman Studies* 79 (1989), 59–83, and D. G. Bates, "Normative and Alternative Systems of Marriage among the Yoruk of Southeastern Turkey," *Anthropological Quarterly* 47 (1974), 270–87, esp. p. 272: "Among the Yoruk of Turkey 20% of all marriages take place by means of bride theft or elopement, which can not always be distinguished from bride theft." Many of the instances at issue in such studies were probably "rape."

In a society where women were regarded as property and their sexuality their major asset, by the time an abducted woman was returned most of her value was gone, and the more public attention was focused on the matter the less likely it was she would ever find a husband.[195] And in a moral universe where the abduction of Helen (and of the Sabine women)[196] provided the foundation myths of the greatest contemporary political entities, such an act was as likely to seem heroic as disreputable. The *Erotic Discourses* attributed to Plutarch begin with stories of abduction for love, both heterosexual and homosexual.[197]

It is perhaps also worth noting that Cretan youths were constrained to marry heterosexually as a group, by age cohort, and certainly not for love. They did not even live with their new wives until the latter[198] were old enough to manage the household (implying that at the time of the arranged marriages they were not), but instead the new husbands remained in the barracks (ἀνδρεῖον) with the other males.[199] It is thus most likely that even if an adult male had both a male "partner" and a wife, he would actually *live with* the former rather than the latter, at least until he was relatively old. Plutarch says that at Sparta men under thirty did not go to the marketplace, but had their needs supplied by older male relatives (συγγενῶν) and their lovers (ἐραστῶν,

195. "In the eyes of the law, an abduction that has been allowed to succeed becomes *ipso facto* an elopement," Evans-Grubbs, p. 65. Moreover, as Evans-Grubbs notes, women may sometimes have collaborated in their own abductions: "No doubt, like virtually all marriages in antiquity, the matches had been arranged by the parents of the bride and groom, with little thought for the wishes of the parties involved. By allowing themselves to be 'abducted,' these brides had exercized their choice in the only way they could," p. 71. Legislation was thus directed specifically against both the parents and the abductee in late antiquity: e.g., Theodosian Code 9.24.1, discussed in Evans-Grubbs.

196. Note the importance Plutarch assigns to this (τῶν ἡρπασμένων γυναικῶν) in his *Roman Questions* 101 (287F).

197. Ed. with English trans. by Harold Fowler in the LCL, Plutarch, vol. 10 (Cambridge, 1936). The third story (of five) is unambiguously about rape, and pointedly juxtaposes heterosexual and homosexual instances. See also Lucian, *Toxaris* 44–54, about a Scythian man who abducted a woman whose father would not marry her to him.

198. The Greek for both the males and females being married is παῖς, the same term used for the abducted youth in the same-sex union.

199. Strabo, from Ephorus, 10.4.20. The dowry for the women, like the gifts in the same-sex union, was prescribed by law (half of her brother's portion of the parents' estate). This matches what Plutarch says of Sparta (*Life of Lycurgus*, 15.3–5), which shared many aspects of Crete's constitution.

Life of Lycurgus, 25)—rather like sequestered young women in much of the Mediterranean.

2. Lucian, in the second half of the first century, described a ceremony by which Scythian males (in his day occupying the north shore of the Black Sea and what is now the Crimea) established formal, lifelong relationships with each other.

   A Scythian disputes with a Greek whether his people or the Greeks set greater value on "φιλία." Each adduces five touching instances of extraordinary devotion and attachment between two men (in some cases this involves the sacrifice of wife and children; in most the two appear to have no other relationships). Beyond this, the Scythian alleges that

We consider appropriate to φιλία what you do in regard to marriage [ἐν τοῖς γάμοις]—wooing[200] for a long time and doing everything similar so that we might not fail to obtain the friend, or be rejected. And when a friend has been preferred to all others [προκριθείς], there are contracts for this and the most solemn oath, both to live together [βιώσεσθαι μετ' ἀλλήλων] and to die, if necessary, for each other, which we do. From the point at which we have both cut our fingers and let the blood run into a chalice, dipped the tips of our swords in it, and both drunk from it together, there is nothing that could dissolve what is between us.[201]

It is allowed to enter into such contracts at most three times, since a man who had many such relations [πολύφιλος] would seem to us like a promiscuous and adulterous woman [κοιναῖς...καὶ μοιχευομέναις γυναιξί], and we would not consider that his devotion [φιλία] was as strong if it was divided among many affections [εὐνοίας].

[200.] μνηστευόμενοι, a word used elsewhere in Greek exclusively for heterosexual arrangements leading to marriage, either "wooing," "paying court" (in a romantic sense), or, in a more technical context, "betrothing." Μνηστήρ is a word for "bridegroom"; μνηστεία the word in Christian Greek for a betrothal ceremony.

[201.] Herodotus had described this mode of making a solemn oath among the Scythians about five centuries earlier (4.70). He did not associate it with same-sex unions, either because this was a later development, or because he did not know about that aspect. His corroboration of the mode of solemnizing a great oath is, nonetheless, significant.

Although the words "friend" and "friendship" figure in this description, and it is part of a discussion of φιλία, usually translated as "friendship" (but see pp. 6–7), the concepts φιλία and ἔρως—the latter almost always understood to refer to romantic love—are used interchangeably throughout the dialogue. The relationship between Achilles and Patroclus, which most of the ancient world regarded as erotic,[202] is called φιλία,[203] while that between Orestes and Pylades, who were not usually considered lovers, is labeled ἔρως (7).[204] In the conclusion of the dialogue, the types of love traditionally attributed to Lucian erotic feelings for men (παιδικοὺς ἔρωτας) are explicitly discussed as a subset of φιλία.[205]

In addition to parallels between the same-sex relationship and heterosexual marriage explicitly alleged by the Scythian speaker, it should be noted that use of a drinking chalice was a widespread ritual for heterosexual betrothal in the ancient Mediterranean, attested in the same text (25, 44–45) as well as in many other places.[206]

The exchange of blood is a key component of rituals establishing "artificial kinship"—a broad range of institutions known throughout the world, most of which were not erotic or even emotional (discussed below in more detail). They were often, for

202. Aeschines says (Against Timarchus, 142) that although Homer is discreet about the love between Achilles and Patroclus—for which Aeschines uses both ἔρως and φιλία in this very passage—its intensity was obvious to the "educated" (τοῖς πεπαιδευμένοις) in his audience. See also Aeschylus, Myrmidons fr. 135–36; Plutarch, Erotikos 751C; Philostratus, Epistles 5, 8; [Lucian,] Amores 54; Athenaeus 13.601; and many modern studies, such as W. M. Clarke, "Achilles and Patroclus in Love," Hermes 106 (1978), 381–96; Halperin, "Heroes and their Pals," in One Hundred Years of Homosexuality, 75–87; D. S. Barrett, "The Friendship of Achilles and Patroclus," Classical Bulletin 57.6 (April, 1981), 87–93; Stella Miller, "Eros and the Arms of Achilles," American Journal of Archaeology 90 (1986), 159–70.

203. Earlier writers had also conflated ἔρως and φιλία in regard to this couple: in [Lucian's] Lucius or the Ass §54, the love between them was said to have been specifically physical, although their friendship was "mediated" by pleasure: τῆς ἐκείνων φιλίας μεσῖτης ἡδονή. Cf. Chapter 1, nn. 4, 6, 16.

204. In Affairs of the Heart, §47, they are specifically depicted as ἐρασταί explicitly in the context of sexual relations between men (although the author expresses some uncertainty about who was the ἐραστής and who the ἐρώμενος); the term φιλία is nonetheless applied to their lifelong commitment to each other. See also preceeding note.

205. 51, p. 228.

206. Cf., for example, Athenaeus (slightly later than Lucian) 13.574–76, where he tells one story about such a rite among the Scythians and one from Aristotle about Ionian Massilia, and Plutarch (Erotikos, 768C–D), who associates it with the Galatians.

example, symbolic ratifications of peace, pledges of cooperation between warriors or peoples, or means of forming ties between families or tribes.[207] The mingling of blood in a cup or by pressing incisions together is one of the most consistent features of such customs. But there is absolutely no suggestion of any of these functions in Toxaris' description of the Scythian practice. Words for "brother" or "brotherhood" are not employed anywhere in the text in relation to such unions; there is no indication that any other family or tribal members are involved; and the bond is not presented as political or strategic, or as having any broader social significance than personal emotional attachment. Its significance is manifestly and unmistakably personal and affectional.

It would be fatuous, moreover, to seize on the blood cup as demonstrating a particular relationship to other ceremonies employing similar symbols. Chalices figure prominently in both the Cretan same-sex ritual and in contemporary heterosexual betrothal rituals, and the drinking of someone else's blood (literally or figuratively) is the central act of many Mediterranean ceremonies with many different meanings, including the Christian Eucharist. Usually the use of blood—one's own or someone else's—is a mode of sealing an agreement with particularly visceral solemnity; it is not by itself an indication of the content of the covenant so sealed.[208]

It is true that no sexual component is adduced in relation to the Scythian ceremony, but the numerous references to heterosexual marriage in this dialogue also fail to mention any sexual consequence. Of course, a contemporary might be able to observe, in offspring, evidence of sexuality in heterosexual cases. The absence of such physical evidence in the case of same-sex couples would be an extremely weak argument against physical expression of their love, as it would be in the case of modern gay couples.

A better reason to question the role of sexuality would be the problem of equality adduced previously, which might be espe-

---

207. Tacitus, for example, describes a practice by which kings ratify treaties by commingling and consuming each other's blood (*Annals* 12.47), but it is quite clear that this is a political act, not one involving any personal emotional needs or satisfaction.

208. Achilles Tatius alludes to an association of Scythia and blood in religious rites (8.2), but does not specify their nature.

cially troublesome in societies of warriors, which tend to place great emphasis on masculinity and male roles: would it seem "feminine" and disgraceful for one party (or each in turn) to "submit" to the other sexually? Spartans, Cretans, Romans, and many other military societies of the ancient world—most notably the Sacred Band of Thebes—found ways around this problem (usually by correlating sex roles with age, even if the difference was small). There seems little reason to suppose the Scythians could not have done so as well. Indeed, Philip of Macedon's rejection of imputing any wrongdoing to paired lovers in a military context (quoted above, pp. 62–63) was well-known and widely cited throughout the ancient world.

Two centuries later the last great Roman historian, Ammianus Marcellinus, reported of the barbarian peoples living in the same region (where he had himself been posted as a soldier) that "among them the young men are coupled with adult males in unmentionable sexual unions, and spend the flower of their youth in these unseemly relationships."[209]

3. A third type of formal same-sex union involved the legal practice of "collateral adoption": one man adopted another as his brother, either de facto (as in Petronius et al.) or in some official way. Adopting children was an extremely common practice among Romans, either to have heirs without the bother (and danger, for women) of parenthood, or in some cases simply as a means to bequeath wealth, position, or status to a loved one (often a relative other than a direct descendant).[210] In most such cases men —even bachelors—adopted younger persons as sons or daughters by either of two methods, *adrogatio* or *adoptio*. The advantages for the adoptee are obvious;[211] the disadvantage was that he or she

---

209. . . . *Ut apud eos nefandi concubitus foedere copulentur maribus puberes, aetatis viriditatem in eorum pollutis usibus consumpturi*, 31.9.5. The Latin is clumsy and difficult to translate precisely (Ammianus' native language was Greek), but both *foedus* and *copulare* suggest more than casual sexuality, especially occurring together. Ammianus is generally accepted as a historian of exceptional accuracy. He calls the people in question the Taifali; very little is known about them except that they occupied roughly what had earlier been known as "Scythia," itself a relatively fluid geographical term in the ancient world.

210. For a sketch of adoption in the ancient world, see Boswell, *Kindness of Strangers*, 66 n. 40, 115–16, and bibliography cited there.

211. Both Petronius (passim, but especially 116) and Pliny the Elder (14.1) write bitterly about "legacy-hunting," which had become practically a profession under the empire, when young

became subject to the authority of the adopting *paterfamilias*, which could be awkward or confining.[212]

Under the early empire men began to adopt as *brothers* (rather than as sons) persons who thus became heirs but not children.[213] This could be accomplished simply by a declaration in front of witnesses—no further legal niceties were required. (Note the similarity to Roman heterosexual marriage.) "No one doubts," wrote the jurist Paulus (specifically in the context of fraternal adoption), "that someone can be properly designated an heir thus, 'Let this man be my heir,' as long as the person so designated is present."[214]

---

people would devote their lives to wooing and flattering the elderly wealthy in hopes of being adopted and inheriting their estates.

[212] Roman law is absolutely crammed with the niceties of adoption, including very peculiar circumstances, such as *Digest* 38.6.1.7, in which a man emancipated (i.e., freed from parental control) his son, then adopted him as his grandson, then emancipated him as grandson. The court inquires (but does not decide) whether the biological grandson has been emancipated (i.e., disinherited) along with his father.

[213] This practice should not be confused with other forms of adoption that created "adoptive brotherhood"—as when a father who already had sons adopted another, and he became an "adoptive brother" to his new siblings. Marcus Aurelius and Lucius Verus were called "adoptive brothers" (e.g., by Ammianus Marcellinus 27.6.16) because Hadrian had adopted Antoninus Pius as his son on condition that the latter would then adopt both Marcus Aurelius and Lucius Verus as *his* sons, which he did, making them "brothers." Roman legal texts such as the *Digest* use *frater adoptatus* and *frater adoptivus* to mean both an incidental sibling relationship created by ordinary ascendant/descendant adoption and a genuine sibling adoption employed as a mode of same-sex union.

[214] *Nemo dubitat recte ita heredem nuncupari posse "hic mihi heres esto," cum sit coram, qui ostenditur, Digest* 28.5.59(58). But such an arrangement would be invalidated by a change in "civil status" of the surviving adoptive brother within one hundred days of his "brother's" death: *si post mortem uerbi gratia fratris adoptiui intra centensimum diem adoptiuus frater capite deminutus fuerit, bonorum possessionem accipere non poterit, quae proximitatis nomine fratris defertur* . . . *Digest* 38.8.3. ("Change in civil status" [*capitis deminutio*] refers to loss of freedom [i.e., through enslavement for debt or a crime], loss of citizenship, or loss of family membership.) While this might seem to link *adoptio in fratrem* more closely to family adoptions than to marriage (although, as noted, the two were conceptually similar in any event), *Digest* 38.10.11 specifically links it to marriage. Few previous writers on *adoptio in fratrem* have cited the first passage (Tamassia, p. 51, gives an incorrect reference and then airily dismisses it as irrelevant), and to my knowledge no other scholar has noticed the second (or third), though the second is in fact the sole place in the *Digest* where the phrase *frater adoptivus* occurs. *Adoptiva soror* at 23.2.12.4 could refer to a woman adopted by the interested party's father rather than a female sibling adopted by him; it is not perfectly clear. In general the adjective *adotpivus* in legal texts means "adopting" when applied to parents and "adopted" in reference to children. *Digest* 37.4.3.9 might also be relevant: "If someone's father, but not the son himself, has entered into an adoptive family, does the son have a share in the estate of the adopted family through the father if the father dies?" The answer given is "yes," as "a more humane opinion," but Zizo's case seems significantly different, because he was apparently trying to recover his biological father's estate, not the goods of the adopted brother, although it is difficult to be certain about this.

The adoptee thus acquired a claim on the adopter's property and estate—greater than a biological brother would have, since he would usually be one of several heirs—and the two established thereby a legal relationship, but the adopted brother did not come under the authority or control of the adopter, and would presumably not change his name or status. Given that "adopt a brother" was a specific imperial expression for establishing a relationship with a homosexual lover, and that contemporaries understood Roman heterosexual marriage to be a kind of collateral adoption, with the wife becoming, in essence, a sister, it seems clear enough that such adoptions were understood as a means of establishing in law a same-sex union.[215] "A person who is not a brother," Paul noted, "if he is loved with brotherly affection, is rightly instituted heir with his own name under the designation 'brother.' "[216]

Such relationships drew for archetypes (beyond the obvious fraternal models such as Castor and Pollux) not on the hierarchical model of the Roman family, in which the *paterfamilias* ruled his wife, children, and servants, but rather on Roman commercial law of partnerships, which Ulpian specifically compared to relationships between brothers, since male siblings would enjoy an equality almost unparalleled in the ancient world, being of the same gender, the same status, and the same generation. "Partnership implies," Ulpian noted, "a law of brotherhood."[217] This metaphor derives its force at least partly from the fact that in

---

[215.] This connection is briefly considered by both Everard Otto, *De Jurisprudentia symbolica exercitationum trias* (Utrecht, 1730), 352–64, p. 354, and Christopher August Stempel, *Observationes de adoptione in locum fratris non monstrosa ad L. LVIII § 1 de hered. instit* (Vitemberg, 1748), 33. (This work is erroneously listed in the *National Union Catalogue* and other bibliographical references under the name Crell; Crell simply presided over Stempel's dissertation defense, and his name is therefore listed on the title page; Glück [*Ausführliche Erläuterung der Pandekten* {Erlangen, 1800} 2:349] appears to have been the first person to make this mistake.)

[216.] *Qui frater non est, si fraterna caritate diligitur, recte cum nomine suo sub appellatione fratris heres instituitur, Digest* 28.5.59(58). Juvenal (5.135–40) appears to prefigure this by juxtaposing *amicus/frater* as synonyms (*vos estis fratres*) with his bitter observation that a "sterile wife makes a friend loving and devoted"—meaning that the friend/brother would inherit more if there were no children—but like much of Juvenal this text is densely packed with sarcastic references, and it is difficult to be sure exactly what is meant. Cf. the equally oblique reference in Horace (1.7.54–55): *frater, pater, adde; ut cuique est aetas, ita quemque facetus adopta. CIL* 2.498 (*frater et ser[vus]*) may also allude to this, since it is difficult to imagine other circumstances that would give rise to such a peculiar diad of appellations.

[217.] *Digest* 17.2.63: *societas ius quodammodo fraternitatis in se habeat.*

many premodern societies in which inherited or family wealth was the chief source of economic support, adult brothers often shared financial resources, households, and property: Plutarch speaks of the "many brothers . . . who share a single household [οἰκίᾳ] and table and common properties and slaves."[218] It is striking that during the later empire heterosexual marriage also came to be viewed increasingly as a partnership rather than the acquisition or adoption of a woman by her husband's family, as it had formerly been. Indeed, the *Digest* referred to heterosexual marriage as "a lifetime partnership."[219]

In the second half of the third century a man named Zizonus appealed to the Roman emperors Diocletian and Maximian to reclaim his father's estate, which had been inherited, he believed unfairly, by his father's adopted brother. The suzerains replied in 285 C.E. that since the adopted brother was a *peregrinus* (loosely, a "foreigner"), and Romans could not legally form such relationships with *peregrini*, the union was invalid, and the provincial governor should restore to Zizonus the inheritance that had passed to the adopted brother.[220]

This ruling has spawned a substantial, recondite, and inconclusive scholarly controversy (assessed below).[221] But the most

---

218. "On Brotherly Love," *Moralia* 481 D–E. This is quoted and assessed in the larger context of Roman family structures by Keith Bradley, *Discovering the Roman Family: Studies in Roman Social History* (New York, 1991), 125. Although Bradley's study is generally admirable, he seems to understand *frerèche* as a simple, diachronic phenomenon rather than an abstraction applied to a variety of arrangements in different times and places.

219. *Nuptiae sunt . . . consortium omnis uitae*, as cited above.

220. *Code of Justinian* 6.24.7: Impp. *Diocletianus et Maximianus, A. A. Zizoni. Nec apud peregrinos fratrem sibi quisquam per adoptionem facere poterat. Quum igitur, quod patrem tuum voluisse facere dicis, irritum sit, portionem hereditatis, quam is, adversus quem supplicas, velut adoptatus frater heres institutus tenet, restitui tibi praeses provinciae curae habebit. PP. III. Non. Decemb. Diocletiano II. et Aristobulo Conss.* [285] The passage is much disputed, as noted infra, and some of the controversies bear on its translation. Roughly, it means, "The august Emperors Diocletian and Maximian to Zizone: No one could make someone his brother by adoption among foreigners. Therefore, since you say that what your father wished to do is invalid, the governor of the province will be responsible for restoring to you the portion of the estate inherited by the adopted brother against whom you lay your claim."

221. Probably the first historical assessment of the rescript was that of Everard Otto, *De Jurisprudentia symbolica exercitationum trias* (Utrecht, 1730), 352–64, followed by Christopher August Stempel, *Observationes de adoptione in locum fratris non monstrosa ad L. LVIII § 1 de hered. instit* (Vitemberg, 1748). Most subsequent treatments have taken as their starting points the learned but inconclusive discussion on pp. 254–57 of Karl Georg Bruns and Eduard Sachau in their edition of the *Syrisch-Römisches Rechtsbuch aus dem fünften Jahrhundert* (Leipzig, 1880): e.g., Giovanni Tamassia, *L'Affratellamento* ('ΑΔΕΛΦΟΠΟΙΙΑ) *Studio storico-giuridico* (Torino, 1886), and K. Rhalle, "Περὶ

important question—what is fraternal adoption and what is its function?—has hardly been addressed at all, not because the answer is taken for granted, but because it could not be honestly considered in the moral and intellectual climate of Europe or the United States in the last two centuries.

In the abstract, since fraternal associations are such a familiar and varied part of modern social topography (ranging from monastic orders to labor unions to the Elks), one might imagine many purposes and functions for such a relationship, and since homosexual relationships have been viewed for centuries as bizarre, "unnatural," and immoral aberrations, such an interpretation of this passage would scarcely leap into the minds of investigators. But in their concrete historical context—one in which same-sex passion, commitment, and eroticism were so prominent in so many forms that even modern prejudices have not been able to disguise them—fraternal unions must be seen in more complex terms than as social abstractions. In fact, no modern "fraternal union" involves the actual *adoption* of one person by another, with attendant economic and legal consequences, whereas Roman collateral adoption unquestionably did. Roman law had, moreover, elaborate and detailed provisions for business partnerships (*consortia,* which would establish a relationship of equality in economic terms, or *societates*—see *Digest* 17.2) and for family adoptions.[222] These were well-known and available to anyone who needed to establish an ordinary business or inheritance relationship.[223] The only convincing explanation for col-

---

ἀδελφοποιίας," *Ἐπιστημονικὴ Ἐπετηρίς, Γ (1906–1907)* (Athens, 1909), 293–306. For more modern assessments, see, in addition to the particular studies cited in notes following, Carlo Alfonso Nallino, "Intorno al divieto romano imperiale dell'affratellamento e ad alcuni paralleli arabi," *Studi in onore di Salvatore Riccobono nel XL anno del suo insegnamento* (Palermo, 1936) 3:321–357.

222. Tamassia agrees with Bruns (ut supra) that *l'affratellamento non ha niente di comune coll'adozione* (p. 54). Given the purposes and nature of Roman adoption, it would make much more sense from a practical and legal point of view for someone to adopt his brother as a son than anyone else as his brother. Livy (42.52.5) and Suetonius (*Caligula* 4.3), among others, mention known cases of adoption of a biological brother as a son.

223. Restrictions on the relative ages of adopter and adopted varied in Roman law, and were obviously disregarded in many cases. According to the *Institutes* [1.11.4] there had to be eighteen years difference between the adopted and adopter, and an adopted son older than a father "would outrage nature," because "adoption imitates nature" (ibid.). On the other hand, in the *Digest,* an older collection of Roman jurisprudence, the principle of following "nature" is disregarded (*hi qui generare non possunt, quales sunt spadones, adoptare possunt,*

lateral adoption would seem to be its peculiar personal and emotional value, about which scholars writing in the last century have shown so slight a curiosity as to border on aversion.[224]

The chief areas of dispute have instead been (a) whether the ruling results from some peculiarity of family structure somewhere in the empire;[225] (b) who the *peregrini* were, and why adoption of (or by) them would be invalid;[226] (c) the relationship between

1.7. 2). Cicero complains at length (*De domo sua*, 13–14) about Clodius' adoption by Fronteius, when Clodius was already a senator and Fronteius was a "beardless youth" of twenty—i.e., *younger* than the man he adopted—but the college of pontiffs had clearly allowed this adoption, suggesting that those charged with enforcing the rules did not take them very seriously, at least in Cicero's time. The translator of the *LCL* edition suggests a sexual aspect to this relationship (p. 176, n. b), but this seems imaginary to me: the whole point of the criticism in this section is to impugn the *political* motivations of the adoption. It is patently this to which *vel eo, quo fuit* refers, not to anything sexual. By contrast, Suetonius states flatly that Augustus' adoption by his uncle was prompted by sexual interest (*stupro: Augustus* 68). Augustus himself later adopted Tiberius (Suetonius, *Tiberius* 15) and constrained him to adopt *his* nephew, Germanicus, but there is no imputation of sexuality in these cases.

224. Stempel (e.g., pp. 17, 50) does associate fraternal adoption with emotional ties. Tamassia, pp. 56–57, notes that medieval Byzantine arguments about fraternal adoption not "imitating nature"—because a brother cannot in any case produce a brother (as opposed, i.e., to a father producing a son)—were specious, because this legal tradition was not actually about family adoptions, anyway. Contrast this with the absurd appeal of Charles DuCange, "Des adoptions d'honneur en frère," in idem., ed., Jean de Joinville, *Histoire de St Louis IX*, 2 (Paris, 1668), 260–67, p. 260, to Harmenopoulos' reasoning—more than a thousand years later!—to explain why the *Digest's* rule that a man "loved like a brother" could inherit was not relevant to the rescript of 285.

225. Either a social structure privileging elder brothers, thus requiring testators to "adopt" some other member of the family into this position to leave them an estate (so, for example, Paul Koschaker, "Adoptio in Fratrem," in *Studi in onore di Salvatore Riccobono nel XL anno del suo insegnamento* [Palermo, 1936], 3:361–76), or the practice of fratriarchy, which affected chiefly sisters, for which see n. 86. Koschaker's main evidence for his argument is a similar custom in late medieval Romania, which seems rather strained.

226. Georgios Michaelidos-Nouaros, "Περὶ τῆς ἀδελφοποιΐας ἐν τῇ ἀρχαίᾳ Ἑλλάδι καὶ ἐν τῷ Βυζαντίῳ," *Τόμος Κονσταντίνου Ἀρμενοπούλου ἐπὶ τῇ ἑξακοσιετηρίδι τῆς Ἑξαβίβλου αὐτοῦ (1345–1945)* (Thessalonika, 1952), pp. 251–313, summarizes (p. 280) the main theories about the meaning of *peregrini*: (1) they are persons who are "citizens" only in the technical sense that all inhabitants of the empire were citizens after Caracalla's edict in 212—i.e., not from traditionally Roman families or regions; (2) they are barbarians living under Roman rule; (3) they are Romans forming unions with foreigners. The last is supported by the evidence of Byzantine law (*Basilika* 35.13.17: μηδὲ παρὰ ξένοις τοῖς ἔξω Ῥώμης οἰκοῦσι διὰ θέσεως ἀδελφότης συνιστάσθω· κἄν τις ὡς ἀδελφὸς προσλεφθεὶς κληρονόμος γραφῇ, ἐκπιπτέτω τῆς κληρονομίας, discussed below: see p. 226), but the understanding of medieval Byzantine legists is not necessarily a reliable indication of the intention or understanding of Roman lawmakers. Nallino ("Intorno al Divieto") summarizes various interpretations of these problems: some have argued that all three of the parties (i.e., father, adopted brother, Zizonus) were foreign/noncitizens at the time of the adoption, but subsequently became citizens—hence, the original invalidity and a reason for the emperors' ruling. Others have posited that Zizonus' father and the adopted brother were not of the same status—i.e., that one was a citizen and one was not—and that this made the adoption null. Still others have claimed that all three were citizens, but that

this rescript and laws regarding adoptive brotherhood surviving in Roman provincial compilations;[227] *(d)* whether the practice alluded to in the rescript corresponds to what later ages would call ἀδελφοποιία, *affratellamento*, *Verbrüderung*, побратимство, or "artificial kinship"—all terms for establishing a nonbiological sibling relationship of one sort or another.[228]

The answer to the final question obviously depends on the exact meaning of each of these terms, which are dealt with subsequently in this study. Most previous investigators have assumed without much reflection that the rescript of 285 C.E. refers to an early form of the variety of artificial kinship of interest to them, usually at the price of gross oversimplification.[229] As to the other questions, it would be fair to say that efforts to show that it reveals some peculiarity of family organization in some area of the empire have met with little acceptance,[230] and that a majority of scholars regard it as proof of the existence of collateral adoption, unquestionably legal in some circumstances (if not these).[231]

No answer has emerged to the question of who the *peregrini* were and why such relationships would be invalid with them,[232] but this is actually the least mysterious aspect of the ruling. Part

---

the adoption took place in a foreign country, and was therefore not binding or valid, because citizens do not follow the *ius peregrinorum*. A few have claimed that those involved were not citizens even at the time of the prohibition. Glossators (cited on p. 330) sometimes took *apud peregrinos* to mean *coram peregrinos*—i.e., with *peregrini* officiating, or as witnesses, etc. Cf. n. 242, below.

[227.] All the authors mentioned above assume there is some relation, but their positions vary considerably depending on their view of the Syrian lawcode itself. See below.

[228.] See Chapters 7 and 8, below.

[229.] For example, Rhalle (p. 293–4), Tamassia (p. 63), and Michaelis-Nouarides (p. 299) see it as an unambiguous early form of ἀδελφοποιία, Bruns and Sachau as the primitive *Verbrüderung* (p. 257), and Eduardo de Hinojosa, "La Fraternidad artificial en España," *Revista de archivos, bibliotecas y museos* 3:9, No. 7 (July 1905), 1–18, cites it (p. 3) as the earliest form of *fraternidad artificial*, though he alleges that the latter is nearly always a matter of customary rather than written law.

[230.] Michaelidos-Nouaros, for example, refutes Koschaker quite effectively, especially on p. 278, following the opinions of Otto, Stempel, Rhalle et al., all of whom regarded the union in question as affective rather than institutional. (Rhalle, for example, defines *adoptio in fratrem* —which he explicitly equates with ἀδελφοποιία—as a "practice whereby two or even more people, following various formulae, promise each other complete devotion, love [ἀγάπη], and protection for the rest of their lives" [p. 293].)

[231.] Bruns thinks that the Romans mistook a type of intense, ceremonial friendship as a form of adoption (p. 256), but he does not note the passage about fraternal affection from the *Digest*.

[232.] As noted above, no other scholars have taken cognizance of the *Digest's* stipulations

of the reason it seems perplexing at first is that Romans were not only free to but did in fact *adopt* persons of all sorts: citizens, noncitizens, slaves, children of slaves, freed slaves, infants found on garbage heaps, et al.[233] The whole point of adoption was to confer on the adoptee the adopter's status and position (and fortune): if the adopting party was a citizen, the adopted person became one as well.[234]

Marriage, on the other hand, was restricted for Roman citizens: they could contract valid marriage only with other citizens of comparable social standing or residents of the empire who had specifically been granted *conubium*, the right to enter into legal marriage with Romans.

> *Conubium* is the capacity to marry a wife in Roman law. Roman citizens have *conubium* with Roman citizens, but with Latins and foreigners only if the privilege was granted. There is no *conubium* with slaves.[235]

Conubium was one of two essential privileges entailed by the *ius Latii*—the special legal status of the people who originally formed the Roman state.[236] The children of a union between a Roman and a foreigner who did not enjoy *conubium* would be considered noncitizens, and therefore at a considerable legal disadvantage, even in regard to inheritance.[237] A marital relationship with a noncitizen without *conubium* was either concubinage (if the person was free) or *contubernium* (if a slave),[238] and, though sometimes acknowledged de facto, had inferior legal standing (but not, as Treggiari has shown, without any validity).[239] Soldiers were sometimes granted *conubium cum peregrinis mulieribus*—the right

---

(38.8.3) about invalidating adoptive brotherhood, but the rescript in the Code does not allude to the grounds of *capitis deminutio* cited in the *Digest*.

233. See Boswell, *Kindness of Strangers*, Part I.

234. It could only be legally denied if the father emancipated the adoptee: see *Digest* 50.1.16.

235. *Tituli Ulpiani*, 5.3–5, translated in Treggiari, *Roman Marriage*, p. 43.

236. The other was *commercium*, the right to make legal contracts with Romans without having to appeal to the *praetor peregrinus*, the official in charge of foreigners' affairs at Rome.

237. See Treggiari, *Roman Marriage*, pp. 43–49.

238. From the word for "tavern" (*taverna*), it originally meant simply "living together" and could also be applied to soldiers in barracks or animals in a pen.

239. *Roman Marriage*, pp. 49–51.

to form legal marriages with provincial women—as a reward when discharged from service. This allowed them to legitimize long-standing relationships that would otherwise have had no legal force.[240] The danger of inadvertently contracting even a heterosexual union with someone not recognized as foreign is evident in imperial literature: Seneca wrote, "I promised you my daughter in marriage. Now you have turned out to be a foreigner [*peregrinus*]. I do not have *conubium* with foreigners."[241]

Since a provincial governor is instructed to restore his father's estate to Zizonus, it seems overwhelmingly likely that Diocletian and Maximian regarded the adoptive brotherhood as in this case invalid because one of the two men was a provincial without *conubium*.[242] It could have been either Zizonus' father or the adoptive brother. The fact that Zizonus appealed to the emperors does not show that he was himself a citizen: noncitizens might well appeal to the rulers of the Roman state to obtain redress for the settlement of an estate determined by Roman custom or officials; moreover, all residents of the empire were citizens after Caracalla's edict to that effect in 212 C.E. (This did not mean that all enjoyed *conubium*: rules about ethnically non-Roman citizens marrying Romans varied widely from region to region, and were complicated by the fact that the non-Roman peoples had their own customs and laws, which Roman officials often honored.)[243]

Tamassia argues that because the emperors were in Serbia or Bulgaria at the time their decision was given, Zizonus must have been a native of that region,[244] and he notes that forms of artificial kinship were subsequently very prominent in this area. But

---

240. The privilege was also used negatively as a political tool: when Macedonia was divided into four districts, the *peregrini* residing in them were forbidden both *commercium* and *conubium* with each other as a means of discouraging reunification.

241. *De beneficiis*, 4.35.1: *Promisi tibi in matrimonium filiam; postea peregrinus adparuisti. non est mihi cum externo conubium.* Cf. translation in Treggiari, *Roman Marriage*, p. 47.

242. Cf. the comparable heterosexual incident alluded to in *Digest* 23.2.65.1: *etsi contra mandata contractum sit matrimonium in provincia*, discussed in Treggiari, *Roman Marriage*, p. 51. Although it is linguistically possible that *apud peregrinos* means "in the presence of foreigners," or "among foreigners," it is difficult to relate such a consideration to any known provisions of Roman law dealing with *conubium* or the status of *peregrini*.

243. Writing about an earlier period, Alan Watson conceded, "Which Latin cities [had *conubium*] cannot be determined," *Roman Private Law around 200 B.C.* (Edinburgh, 1971). Cf. Treggiari, *Roman Marriage*, as cited above. The problem only grew more complicated and difficult to judge as the centuries passed.

244. Pp. 47–51.

emperors replied to appeals and suits wherever they were: business did not have to be local to merit imperial attention. And although it is true that forms of "artificial kinship" were subsequently an important aspect of social organization in Serbia and Bulgaria, the first evidence of this occurs almost a millennium later, which hardly seems a conclusive connection. Zizonus is not a Latin name; the only other place in *imperial* literature where a name like it occurs is in the dialogue on Scythian same-sex relationships by Lucian.[245]

Collateral adoption was subsequently declared invalid in some provinces in a handbook of Roman law compiled (in Greek) in the fourth or fifth century and translated into Syriac, Armenian, and Arabic for Roman citizens living in regions of the East where Latin and Greek were not understood. Its precise provisions and their implications for collateral adoption are considered at length below.[246]

Of these forms of same-gender union, the first is the least ambiguous, and the second the most. Once the possibility of a permanent, erotic, same-gender union has been admitted (i.e., as opposed to a view of homosexual relations as inherently transitory, always hierarchical, and/or purely sexual), the Cretan elopement ceremony can hardly be seen as anything else. It is difficult to compare to any modern emotional commitment (since, e.g., one might be a part of it and also enter into a heterosexual marriage, though the latter, in ancient Crete, would *not* correspond to its modern counterpart), but this is true of nearly all personal relationships of the ancient world, very few of which have precise modern equivalents.

The Scythian union is described specifically in terms relating to matrimony, and explicitly establishes a couple, as opposed to some more generalized relationship. That the pair might be "just friends" is a meaningless objection by the standards of the ancient world, since terms and concepts for "friends" and "lovers" were not discrete. It is possible that they were "just friends" in the modern sense, but this

---

245. Beginning in §57; not specifically in relation to such unions. But this occurrence does suggest that Zizonus might have been Scythian, and the union of the type described by Lucian.
246. See pp. 221–27, below, especially p. 221, n. 7.

interpretation requires both a deliberate disregard of portions of the text and a preference for believing that the Scythians had a very peculiar view of friendship, largely unparalleled in ancient Europe, rather than the more economical inference that they honored a form of same-gender union with close parallels in many antique cultures.

Whatever uncertainty might subsist about the third form could hardly be in regard to whether it established a same-gender union, which it unquestionably did, but might rather involve doubts about the exact emotional or sexual content of the relationship. Acknowledgment that it was a functional equivalent of heterosexual marriage would not, however, depend on a precise understanding of this, since the latter also comprised arrangements for a wide variety of personal attachments, ranging from passionate love to business deals and dynastic alliances.

4

"This World Is Passing Away"

VIEWS
of
THE NEW RELIGION

*T*HE TRIUMPH OF CHRISTIANITY over other ancient religions in the fourth century had a less dramatic impact on modes of coupling than its leaders wished and its apologists (and critics)[1] have pretended.[2] Although by the time Europe was largely Christian some aspects of its social infrastructure had been dramatically refashioned, most had not, and many changes in regard to sexual and romantic relationships antedated or bore only an incidental relationship to Christian teaching. For example, during the first centuries of the present era most of European society (whether pagan, Jewish, or Christian) came to expect monogamy and sexual fidelity in marriage for both partners, legislated penalties for violations of this ideal, and began to discourage divorce. These tendencies became evident well before Christianity was a predominant influence, were advocated

---

[1] Jack Goody, for example, in a series of books and articles (e.g., *The Development of the Family and Marriage in Europe* [London, 1983], *Comparative Studies in Kinship* [Stanford, 1969], and *Production and Reproduction* [Cambridge, 1976]) has argued that medieval Christianity transformed European marriage patterns largely in an effort to maximize its own property holdings: for a persuasive critique of this position see Brent Shaw and Richard Saller, "Close-Kin Marriage in Roman Society," *Man: The Journal of the Royal Anthropological Society* n.s. 19 (1984), 432–44.

[2] Although it could certainly be argued that general changes wrought in European society under Christian influence brought in their train more dramatic alterations of matrimonial patterns. For example, Vogel has pointed out that the penitentials and other ecclesiastical sources harshly punished husbands who executed adulterous spouses, although this was explicitly permitted under Greek and Roman law, and was de facto practice in many Germanic cultures even when it was not the written law: see "Discussione," in *Matrimonio* 1:317–18.

by most ancient ethical systems, and had generally been made law by rulers who were not adherents of the Christian religion.[3]

Particularly in matters sexual, it would be a mistake to imagine that the theological program of ascetic Christian theologians was instituted uniformly and *en masse*, like legal or economic changes in the highly structured bureaucracies of the industrial West. Christian practices and attitudes more resembled the rain in Mediterranean cities that fell on the population, ran off, and was redistributed to most people through the artifacts of civilization—in the case of Christian ethics, gradually, through law courts that were over time surrendered to Christian officers and principles.

For the enthusiastic and devout, the most dramatic change in attitudes toward marriage was its profound devaluation. To Christian converts expecting the imminent conclusion of the world, and dramatically transforming their lives in preparation for it, marriage—along with all other human pleasures and satisfactions—seemed trivial, or—worse—a dangerous distraction:

> But this I say, brethren, the time is short: it remaineth, that both they that have wives be as though they had none; and they that weep, as though they wept not; and they that rejoice, as though they rejoiced not; and they that buy, as though they possessed not; and they that use this world, as not abusing it; for the fashion of this world passeth away.[4]

From such a perspective, eroticism was deeply suspect,[5] and passionate, sexual love largely disappeared from Latin *belles lettres*—in which it had hitherto been a major subject—throughout the more than half millennium from about 400 to about 1000 of the Christian Era, as literature fell largely into the hands of ascetic leaders of the new religion. This is not necessarily an indication that the majority of the

---

[3.] The program of moral reform promulgated by Julius and Augustus Caesar at the end of the republic and beginning of the empire was particularly important: on this see the concise overview of L. Raditsa, "Augustus' Legislation Concerning Marriage, Procreation, Love Affairs, and Adultery," ANRW 2.13 (Berlin, 1980), 278–339, or in Treggiari, *Roman Marriage*, pp. 60–80. For a more detailed treatment, see Pál Csillag, *The Augustan Laws on Family Relations* (Budapest, 1976).

[4.] 1 Cor. 7:29–31, specifically in the context of marital advice (most of Chapter 7).

[5.] As late as the opening of the fifth century C.E. the First Council of Toledo had to condemn those who believed human marriage to be "execrable" (Canon 16).

population became less interested in erotic fulfillment than they had been previously; in fact, little is known of the feelings of ordinary people in any premodern society.

The principal and most idiosyncratic personal response of devout Christians to their religion was celibacy,[6] a practice viewed as morally questionable by mainstream Judaism,[7] and as impractical and pointless by the vast majority of pagans.[8] For Christians, in dramatic contrast, it was the premier lifestyle for both women and men, and was pursued both individually and in communities, in deliberate disregard of traditional family and personal considerations focusing on matrimony.[9] For many Christians—especially women—celibacy offered escape from the confinements of ordinary social obligations, and as time passed it also became a route to social power and prestige through the church. Since, as noted above, the point of matrimony had not been primarily emotional or sexual fulfillment, the sacrifice was actually smaller than it seems to modern observers. St. Augustine, whose views of sexuality were to become normative in the Western church, lived with a concubine for fifteen years, had a son by her, and then dismissed her summarily when he had the opportunity to satisfy his ambition by marrying an heiress.[10]

But celibacy was always the response of a dedicated few; even when it was demanded of all ordained clergy—a millennium after the origins of Christianity—large numbers of the parish clergy fell short of

6. I use "celibacy" necessarily in several overlapping senses, because the meaning of the word changed as Europe became Christian. For Romans, *caelebs* meant simply "unmarried"; "virgin" or "chaste" would be applied to persons with no sexual experience. As Christians became convinced that sexuality could not be licit outside marriage, the meanings were conflated, and a man or woman who was celibate was presumed also to be abstaining from sex, though he or she might have engaged in it earlier in life.

7. In rabbinic Judaism, Jews were obligated to reproduce; only marginal movements like the Essenes practiced sexual abstinence.

8. The small number of vestal virgins (classically, six), and the limited term of their obligation to virginity (thirty years, though it had originally been only five) speak eloquently of the difference in pagan attitudes toward celibacy, as does the fact that the virgins were offered by their parents as children rather than choosing this lifestyle freely as adults. For virginity in Greece, see now Giulia Sissa, *Greek Virginity*, trans. Arthur Goldhammer (Boston, 1990). Roman attitudes—at least among the cynical—are aptly encapsulated in Ovid's comment *casta est quam nemo rogavit* ("she is chaste whom no one propositioned," *Amores* 1.8.43).

9. The reasons for this, many of them social rather than religious, are assessed in Peter Brown, *The Body and Society: Men, Women, and Sexual Renunciation in Early Christianity* (New York, 1988).

10. He did not marry her after all: for discussion of these events, see Peter Brown, *Augustine of Hippo: A Biography* (Berkeley, 1970), esp. pp. 39–40, 61–62. This was before Augustine's conversion to Christianity.

the ideal. Monastic communities probably came closer to achieving it, supported as their members were by a shared liturgical and communal life.

The vast majority of Christians continued throughout the Christian Era to form heterosexual marriages. As an institution, Christianity remained overwhelmingly ambivalent about most forms of heterosexual marriage during the first millennium of its existence. This is hardly surprising for a religion whose founder was supposed to have had no biological father, whose parents were not married at the time of His conception, who was believed to have had no siblings,[11] who Himself never married, and whose followers—in direct opposition to those of Judaism and most pagan religions—considered celibacy the most virtuous lifestyle. Jesus had suggested that the "dead" (i.e., those still involved in the sublunary world) bury their own dead (Matt. 8:22); presumably the church felt they should also regulate and celebrate matrimony.

Heterosexual marriage was regarded as a compromise with the material world—a world Christians struggled, with varying degrees of commitment and success, to abandon—and its celebration and regulation were left almost entirely to the habits, customs, and peoples of that world. Obviously, fervent Christians, who had blessings said over their fields and meals and births and deaths and houses, might well have asked a priest to bless their nuptial ceremonies and celebrations, but in the West the church made very little effort to regulate marriage before the tenth century, and only declared it a sacrament and required ecclesiastical involvement in 1215.

Although a thousand years after its inception Christianity would begin to emphasize the biological family as the central unit of Christian society (including, by a somewhat strained analogy, the Holy Family), for half of its existence it was most notable for its insistence on the preferability of lifestyles other than family units—priestly celibacy, voluntary virginity (even for the married), monastic community life.

[11.] From the medieval perspective of both East and West, Mary was the "ever-virgin" Mother of God—i.e., she had no children after Jesus. The "brethren" mentioned in the New Testament were argued to have been Jesus' cousins, a claim consistent with kin nomenclature of Hellenistic Judaism, but obviously tendentious on the part of those who advanced it. See below, pp. 121–22.

The ascetic leaders of the Christian community, despite their diffidence on this subject, nonetheless found it necessary to articulate positions on all forms of heterosexual union known in the ancient world, since these did pose moral difficulties for Christians; many of these relations continued to dominate the interpersonal landscape of Europe for centuries. Not surprisingly, given their attitudes toward the sublunary world, most of their opinions were not innovations or deeply imbricated in Christian philosophy. Many involved a more consistent application of long-standing taboos or moral positions. For example, disapproval of polygamy became even more pronounced in late antique and medieval Europe, and it was as a result *officially* unknown.

Nonetheless, divorce and remarriage, concubinage, and even prostitution remained common in Roman Catholic Europe throughout the Middle Ages (discussed in Chapter 5).

Procreative purpose provided an early and influential rationale for controlling sexuality both inside and outside marriage. Christianity was hardly unique in promulgating the idea that the *purpose*—both biological and moral—of human sexuality was procreation, a position it inherited from Hellenistic Judaism, Stoic thought, Alexandrian Neo-Platonism, and Roman popular prejudice.[12] But Christianity insisted on this point more consistently and vehemently than any other ethical tradition, and once the new religion's power was established this was erroneously incorporated into many European philosophies and legal structures as a *Christian* principle.[13] It probably drew its heightened intensity among Christian peoples from a fervent, almost obsessive Christian emphasis on the afterlife as the primary focus and

---

12. For a brief recent treatment of this idea in pagan Roman thought, not without flaws, see Bradley, *Discovering*, esp. pp. 127–30. Griffin even shows that the striking warning to Christian husbands by Jerome that too much or too intense a love for one's own spouse constituted "adultery" can be traced to Seneca: Jasper Griffin, *Latin Poets and Roman Life* (London, 1985), p. 119, n. 29; also noted in Bradley, p. 146, n. 17.

13. The rejection of this stance in favor of a more nuanced and inclusive view of human sexuality by most of modern Christianity—including Protestant denominations and many Roman Catholics—has been so complete that it may, in fact, be difficult for readers at the close of the twentieth century to imagine how procreative purpose ever came to dominate Christian moral principles, especially since it is so completely absent from the New Testament that it could be seen as *opposed* to apostolic teachings. Honest modern biblical analysis, not pursuing any other agenda, is generally struck by Jesus' disregard for the family (as in Matt. 8:22, Mark 3:33–34, Luke 8:21 and especially 14:26). This was noted in the Middle Ages and adduced as part of the justification for idealization of celibacy.

measure of all earthly value and action—a preoccupation that may now seem counterintuitive even to Christians, living in more worldly and materialistic frames of reference.

This dim view of human eroticism was strengthened and corroborated by two legal traditions fundamental to Christian thought: Roman civil law and rabbinic teaching. Precisely during the centuries of most intense Christian theological development, Roman legists and officials undertook a campaign to encourage reproduction among the upper classes, who were failing to replace themselves. This public campaign involved moral exhortation, civic penalties for the childless, and legal rewards for fecund couples. Such measures pervaded society, and doubtless influenced—even if subconsciously—educated Christian leaders such as Ambrose, Jerome, and Augustine (although the last specifically repudiated procreation as the sole justification for matrimony, insisting that couples who refrained from carnal relations and produced no children were nonetheless properly married).[14] Such a program might have been viewed askance as pagan, but it was legitimized to a considerable extent in the eyes of Jewish converts to Christianity (a majority of the early church) by a parallel insistence on procreation in rabbinic Judaism.[15] For non-Jewish converts Roman ideas may have predominated at first: the most basic aspects of Roman marriage were not cohabitation or even sex or children, but *honor matrimonii* and *maritalis affectio*, but after St. Augustine, Christian thinking was largely stuck with his tripartite formulation for marriage: *fides*, *proles*, *sacramentum*—faithfulness, offspring, and a solemn vow.[16] "Offspring" could have been problematic for followers of Jesus, whose father had no children and who had none himself, but some-

---

[14.] See, e.g., *De bono conjugali* 3.3: . . . *quod mihi non videtur propter solam filiorum procreationem, sed propter ipsam etiam naturalem in diverso sexu societatem. Nunc vero in bono licet annoso conjugio . . . viget tamen ordo charitatis inter maritum et uxorem* (PL 40:375, CSEL 41:192–93).

[15.] For a brief overview of this theme in the Mishnah and Talmud, see Judith Hauptman, "Maternal Dissent: Women and Procreation in the Mishna," *Tikkun: A Bimonthly Jewish Critique of Politics, Culture and Society* 6.6 (Nov.–Dec.) 1991, 81–83. A more thorough and detailed treatment of the role of women in rabbinic Jewish writing is provided in Judith Romney Wegner, *Chattel or Person? The Status of Women in the Mishnah* (New York, 1988). But compare *Genesis Rabbah* 17:7: "It once happened that a pious man was married to a pious woman, and they did not produce children. Said they, 'We are of no use to the Holy One, blessed be He,' whereupon they arose and divorced each other" (trans. H. Freedman and M. Simon in *Midrash Rabbah, 1: Genesis* [London, 1983], pp. 213–14). The husband came to a bad end—suggesting that divorcing for fertility may not be a good idea.

[16.] For example, in *De bono conjugali* ("On the good of marriage") 4:4, 7:6–7, 29:32 (PL 40,

how it was not, perhaps simply because a majority of Christians experienced a normal human desire to bear offspring and welcomed any justification of it.[17]

Both of these lent substantial support to a widespread philosophical effort to make sense of the meaning of sexuality in early Christian Europe without appealing to dynastic, economic, tribal, or national values, all of which were viewed with suspicion or overtly condemned by Christian teaching. What was the point of those troubling feelings and needs that drove so many people to sexual relations, licit or illicit? How could they be explained by Christians who believed in a benevolent and all-wise deity (as opposed to the pagan gods, who were themselves prey to passion and lust)? They were implanted, early theologians theorized, for the preservation of the species, and often misused by humans who "perverted" them for sexual satisfaction rather than propagation of the species.[18]

Of several, the most distinct advantage of this position was its utter simplicity: because it was so easily reduced to a single idea, one so free of the real complications and gray edges of human sexuality, it could be propagated more effectively than any more complex and nuanced view of the diversity and variegation of human sexual needs and experience. Not that intellectual cogency was likely to have been the primary reason for its success: the number of Christians who could have repeated this rationalization for ascetic sexuality was probably not much greater than those who could accurately rehearse the theological niceties of the Trinity, but it was an appealing explanation (a kind of "how it came about" story) that *corroborated* prevailing social attitudes and legal structures in favor of more restricted sexuality. It gained ground rapidly and encountered little opposition.[19]

A second advantage—one easily overlooked in a culture like ours

---

CSEL 41:227), and in *De Genesi ad litteram* 7.12 (CSEL 28:275–76). This was still being cited in papal encyclicals in the twentieth century (e.g., "Casti connubii" of 1930, sec. 543).

17. Augustine himself had some reservations about the importance of *proles:* see n. 22.

18. Thus discounting one of the two explanations provided for heterosexual coupling in Genesis, that Eve was to preclude Adam's being "alone" (2:18).

19. Who could argue that sexuality is not closely linked to the survival of the species? It remained for modern Catholic theological schools to argue that procreation was only *one* of its biological functions: the cementing of matrimonial unions, etc., constituting others. Protestants by and large ignored the whole issue, emphasizing instead the limitation of sexuality to married couples, as rabbinic Judaism had done.

where "the purpose of a man is to *love* a woman"[20]—was that it inculcated responsibility in a world without any widespread, effective, means of family planning. It encouraged men especially to weigh the long-term burdens and responsibilities of bringing up a child against the few minutes of pleasure afforded by intercourse. Many were thus persuaded to curtail their sexual appetites, either by limiting them with a spouse to occasions on which they *intended* to procreate or by forgoing them altogether with women who would not be suitable mothers for their children.

On the other hand, many elements of patristic thought militated against "procreative purpose," both challenging classical attitudes on the subject (which most Christians largely accepted) and establishing a permanent tension in Christian thought, one that would not be resolved until the Reformation.[21] For example, Christians used the rhetorical image of marriage (a terrestrial and material phenomenon to pagans) to symbolize or describe a variety of spiritual realities. "Its symbolic value was raided by traffickers in allegory who . . . attempted to detach the idea of marriage from the institution, thus leaving [the latter] an empty husk devoid even of self-referentiality."[22] By applying marital imagery to relationships and institutions more important than matrimony in their eyes Christians devalued the latter in favor of the former.

This tendency was already evident in the New Testament, in the famous passage in Ephesians (5:22–33) comparing Christ's relationship with the church to that between husband and wife, as well as in the last book of the New Testament,[23] in which an angel describes "New Jerusalem"—the church—as the "bride" of the "lamb": "Come

---

[20] From the 1965 song "The Game of Love," by Wayne Fontana; discussed in Introduction, p. xix.

[21] And which remains unresolved in Roman Catholic thought: although the church's support in the last couple of decades of the "rhythm method" of family planning might be taken as an unmistakable acknowledgement that not all sexual acts within marriage need to be procreative to be moral, this has yet to be promulgated as official doctrine, and the focus of moral discussion has shifted to the extent to which modes of family planning do or do not imitate natural *processes*, an arena completely lacking in premodern discussions of the topic.

[22] Dyan Elliott, *Spiritual Marriage: Sexual Abstinence in Medieval Wedlock* (Princeton, 1993), p. 39.

[23] Called the "Apocalypse" by Roman Catholics and the Orthodox, "the Revelation of St. John" by Protestants. Although the dating of all books of the New Testament is contentious and uncertain, if the Apocalypse was written, as it purports to be, by the disciple John, it must be quite early. Most authorities ascribe it at least to the second half of the first century.

hither, I will shew thee the bride, the Lamb's wife."[24] St. Paul, writing to the Christian community of Corinth (2 Cor. 11:2) had noted, "I am jealous over you with godly jealousy: for I have espoused you to one husband, that I may present you as a chaste virgin to Christ."[25]

This image—the "marriage" of Christ to the church or its people—was widely invoked, written about, and depicted in art.[26] The problems raised by the metaphor (e.g., that Christ was celibate, that celibacy was a higher calling than marriage, that in the allusion to the figure in the Apocalypse quoted above there is a hint of bestiality) were rarely explored or even discussed. On the contrary, St. Paulinus of Nola, a bishop, referred to this as "the great sacrament, in which the church married Christ,"[27] and it was adduced not only in theological writings but also at earthly weddings[28] and in other social contexts. It was even known on what day this marriage took place—Epiphany.[29]

One part of this spiritualization of matrimony arose from Christian males—fathers, brothers, spiritual advisers et al.—who believed that women were better off "saving themselves" for Christ (though the New Testament strongly implies that marriage will be unknown in the afterlife).[30] Paulinus of Nola described his daughter, Eunomia, as "a

---

24. 21:9: δεῦρο, δείξω σοι τὴν νύμφην τὴν γυναῖκα τοῦ ἀρνίου (veni, et ostendam tibi sponsam, uxorem Agni). Note the use of γυναῖκα for "wife" in the original Greek, replaced by the more specific Latin uxor in Jerome's translation.

25. Cf. the very similar remarks about religious women in John Chrysostom, Περὶ τοῦ τὰς κανονικὰς μὴ συνοικεῖν ἀνδράσιν (Quod regulares feminae viris cohabitare non debeant) PG 47:518–32, col. 523.

26. See, e.g., Ernst Kantorowicz, "On the Golden Marriage Belt and the Marriage Rings of the Dumbarton Oaks Collection," Dumbarton Oaks Papers 14 (1960), 3–17, esp. pp. 12–14.

27. Grande sacramentum, quo nubit ecclesia Christo, Carmen 25:167. Note that sacramentum does not yet have the theological implications it would in time acquire. By the fifteenth century a sacramental element had been added to this rhetoric, as in the Council of Florence's decree "Pro Armenis" (. . . sacramentum matrimonii, quod est signum coniunctionis Christi et Ecclesiae . . .).

28. Even in the Roman Catholic marriage ceremony of the twentieth century there is a prayer asking that the union of the man and woman be "an image of the covenant between you [God] and your people," and the observation that such union "is a sign of the marriage between Christ and the church." See Kenneth Stevenson, Nuptial Blessing: A Study of Christian Marriage Rites (New York, 1983), p. 248.

29. Hieronymus Frank, "Hodie caelesti sponso iuncta est Ecclesia: Ein Beitrag zur Geschichte und Idee des Epiphaniefestes," Vom christlichen Mysterium: Gesammelte Arbeiten zum Gedächtnis von Odo Casel O.S.B., eds. Anton Mayer, Johannes Quasten, B. Neunheuser (Düsseldorf, 1951), 192–226.

30. Although Jesus says in Mark 10:9 that what God has joined together (συνέζευξεν) no man may put asunder, implying that marriage is permanent, he also says in three Gospels (Matt. 22:30, Mark 12:25, Luke 20:35) that in heaven people will not marry (οὔτε γαμοῦσιν οὔτε

maiden already promised to eternal marriage in heaven."[31] St. John Chrysostom, who set the tone of Christian sexual ethics for the East as Augustine did for the West, took seriously the improbable idea that virgins would be introduced into the bridal chamber of Christ in heaven.[32] The tendency was accentuated by the imaginations of virgins themselves who were convinced they would, in time, become in some sense the brides of Christ. Febronia, for example, claimed,

> I have a marriage chamber in heaven, not made with hands, and a wedding feast that will never come to an end has been prepared for me. I have as my dowry the entire kingdom of heaven, and my Bridegroom is immortal, incorruptible, and unchangeable. I shall enjoy him in eternal life. I will not even entertain the idea of living with a mortal husband who is subject to corruption.[33]

First prominent in patristic times, such ideas became more pronounced in social and theological circles as communities of religious women arose: all nuns were said to be "married to" Christ and priests "married to" the church, producing a rather promiscuous image, though this was rarely acknowledged by premodern Roman Catholics.[34] As late as the thirteenth century, even in civil law, the idea of

---

γαμίζονται), suggesting that matrimony is a purely earthly arrangement. For the difficult language of marriage in these comments see Chapter 1, "The Vocabulary of Love and Marriage."

[31] *Et simul Eunomia aeternis iam pacta uirago/in caelo thalamis*, Carmen 21:66–67 (CSEL 30:160). In the early medieval life of St. Pelagia (surviving in the much later retelling by Symeon Metaphrastes), God is described as the "bridegroom" (νύμφιος) (PG 116:916–17).

[32] See, e.g., *Quod regulares feminae viris cohabitare non debeant*, 2 (PG 47.516), discussed in Elizabeth A. Clark, "John Chrysostom and the *Subintroductae*," *Church History* 46 (1977), pp. 178–79. Clark confuses the issue of spiritual marriage in general with that of the *subintroductae*, a related but distinct phenomenon discussed below.

[33] The "Life of Febronia" dates from the late sixth/early seventh century, and is edited in P. Bedjan, *Acta Martyrum et sanctorum* (Leipzig, 1890–97) (7 vols.) 5:573–615; this quotation is on p. 595. The text is translated in S. P. Brock and S. A. Harvey, *Holy Women of the Syrian Orient* (Berkeley, Calif. 1987), this passage on p. 165. Cf. the (fifth–sixth century?) "Martyrdom of Martha," Bedjan 2:236–38, trans. Brock, pp. 70–71; and the fifth–sixth century "Martyrdom of Tarbo," Bedjan 2:256–57, trans. Brock, pp. 74–75.

[34] I have addressed these metaphors in terms of the surprise they might induce in modern readers attuned to literal narrative and single-layer metaphor, particularly in their reading of Scripture. To medieval authors, accustomed and devoted to multilayered hermeneutics, the layers of analogy would not necessarily have created moral difficulty, because they need not be viewed as concurrent historical truths. Nonetheless, the metaphor was further complicated, eventually, by the belief that Christ and His mother were the King and Queen of

Christian women being "married" to Christ was casually cited as argument against interreligious matrimony: "For if Christians who commit adultery with married women deserve death on that account, much more do Jews who have sexual intercourse with Christian women, who are spiritually the wives of our Lord Jesus Christ because of the faith and the baptism which they receive in his name."[35]

Ordinary human marriage was also spiritualized among early Christians,[36] partly owing to the force of this rhetoric,[37] but also because of two other factors: general pressure for celibacy, and the inheritance of Roman law and custom, according to which it was consent and "marital affection" that constituted the essence of marriage, not cohabitation. Ambrose insisted "that marriage consisted in the mutual agreement of the couple, not in their carnal copulation."[38] Doubtless this development was related in some way to the belief[39] that Mary the Mother of Jesus had remained perpetually virgin, and that *the archetypal* human couple had therefore never consummated their conjugal relationship. Although controversial among early Christians, Ambrose argued so forcefully for this view that his pupil Augustine

---

heaven—an odd pairing, since He was married to the church, and since kings and queens (and most rulers) were ordinarily a conjugal couple expected to produce heirs for the throne. Furthermore, Christ was conceptualized from the early Middle Ages on as the *pronubus* (roughly, "best man") for *all* Christian marriages.

35. *Siete Partidas*, VII.24.

36. On this subject see de Pierre Labriolle, "Le 'mariage spirituel' dans l'antiquité chrétienne," *Revue historique* 137, 2 (1921), 204–25; Peter Brown, *The Body and Society*, 96, 101, 403–4; Jo Ann McNamara, "Chaste Marriage and Clerical Celibacy," *Sexual Practices and the Medieval Church*, eds. Vern Bullough and James Brundage (Buffalo, N.Y. 1982), 22–33; and Dyan Elliott, *Spiritual Marriage in the Middle Ages*. Brown and (occasionally) Elliott refer to this as "continent marriage," McNamara as "chaste marriage." These are misnomers: for a married couple to confine their sexual activity to their partners, for purely procreative purpose, would make the marriage "continent" or "chaste," no matter how much sexual activity was involved. Réginald Grégoire refers to such unions as "mystical marriages": "Il matrimonio mistico" in *Matrimonio* 2:701–94, but any "mystics" might view marriage as "mystical." "Spiritual" is also slightly misleading, because any relationship founded on Christian principles might be said to be "spiritual," but I have been unable to coin a more satisfactory and cogent designation.

37. Buttressed by the New Testament: "The time is short and those who have wives should live as if they had not . . ." 1 Cor. 7:29–31.

38. McNamara, "Chaste Marriage," p. 28, citing *De institutione virginis* [McNamara gives the title as *De institutione virginibus*, apparently conflating it with the preceding treatise, *De virginibus*], 42 (*PL* 16:331). For the Roman origins of this view, see pp. 49ff. For its later application, see John Noonan, "Marital Affection in the Canonists," *Studia Gratiana* 12 (1967), 482–9.

39. Though as cause or effect is hard to say: Ambrose, a Roman aristocrat, doubtless formulated his arguments about Mary's perpetual virginity (see following) with the Roman law of marriage in mind.

adopted it, and it ultimately prevailed in both the Western and Eastern traditions.[40]

Since Augustine had posited three essential components of Christian matrimony, one of which was offspring, as noted above, one might well wonder how a Christian marriage could be legitimate if it lacked offspring, the second of these. (Of course, Joseph and Mary did have a child whom Joseph adopted, emotionally if not legally, so this might not have been a problem in their particular case.)[41] As if in answer to this, Augustine articulated the interesting position that marriage established an "order of love" (*ordo caritatis*) between partners, and that a decision to refrain from bodily contact would only render this basis for union "firmer, . . . more loving, and more harmonious."[42] A "spouse" (*sponsus, sponsa* in Latin) is "so called," he added, "from the faithfulness of the first promise [*desponsationis*] to marry, and need not have or have ever intended to sleep with the partner. . . . Nor is the name of 'spouse' lost in a case where there was not and will not be any carnal relationship."[43] Likewise, St. Isidore warned that a married couple should not have sexual relations *unless they desired offspring*, although presumably they would remain married whether or not they had children.[44]

Influenced by such opinions and the belief that sexual abstinence was the highest Christian calling, many Christians in many times and places forswore sexual relations altogether, even with their spouses. These are often referred to as "spiritual" marriages, alluding, presumably, to the union of the spirits of the spouses rather than of their bodies. ". . . There was hardly a church province in ancient Christianity in which spiritual marriages were unknown."[45] Augustine's

---

[40] For discussion of the motivations for and precise nature of these arguments, see Brown, *The Body*, pp. 353–55. Jerome also maintained this view: *Adversus Helvidium*, 3–17, 21 (*PL* 23:194–212).

[41] Augustine notes this specifically: *De nuptiis et concupiscientia* 1.11.12 (CSEL 42:224–6).

[42] *Immo firmius erit, quo magis ea pacta secum inierunt, quae carius concordiusque seruanda sunt, non uoluptariis corporum nexibus sed uoluntariis affectibus animorum.* From *De nuptiis et concupiscientia* 1.11.12 (CSEL 42:224). Elsewhere (e.g., *Sermon* 41.21) he contrasted what he called *caritas coniugalis* with marriage based on *libido* (desire): *quasi uxorem libido faciat et non caritas coniugalis.* Note the striking contrast with Chrysostom.

[43] *Coniux uocatur ex prima desponsationis fide, quam concubitu nec cognouerat nec fuerat cogniturus; nec perierat nec mendax manserat coniugis appellatio, ubi nec fuerat nec futura erat carnis ulla commixtio.* Augustine, *De nuptiis*, as above. Both Brown, *The Body and Society*, Chapter 19, esp. pp. 403–404, and McNamara, esp. p. 28, discuss Augustinian views.

[44] *De conjugatis* 5, discussed in Stevenson, *Nuptial Blessing*, p. 53.

[45] Roland Seboldt, "Spiritual Marriage in the Early Church: A Suggested Interpretation of

contemporary St. Pulcheria (d. 453), the eldest daughter of the emperor Arcadius, was proclaimed empress of the Eastern empire when her brother Theodosius II died in 450. She married Marcian, a general, on condition that her vow of perpetual virginity be respected, which it was. Nonetheless, he was proclaimed Augustus and they are shown on imperial coinage as husband and wife.[46] Several Christian splinter groups made asexual marriage a requirement for their members.[47] The English St. Etheldreda insisted on the preservation of her virginity as a condition for two marriages (Bede, Ecclesiastical History, 4, 19).[48] In agreement with Augustine, but arguably in contradistinction to the preceding tradition of the East, the fifty-third canon of the sixth synod (the Third Council of Constantinople, 680–681) held that "the spirit of unity is superior to the joining of bodies."[49] In the twelfth century, at the height of canonistic deliberation about ordinary human marriage and its requirements, Hugh of St. Victor could still argue that the ideals of Christian marriage were most fully realized when the marriage was never physically consummated: only then

---

1 Cor. 7:36–38," Concordia Theological Monthly 30 (1959), 176–84, p. 184; cf. Hans Achelis, Vigines Subintroductae: Ein Beitrag zum VII Kapitel des I Korintherbriefs (Leipzig, 1902), p. 59. Although it is a minor aspect of his study, Stevenson cites hilarious examples of marriages arranged by parents turning out to be "spiritual" (e.g., p. 25).

46. For Marcianus on coinage, see PWRE 14:2 (Stuttgart, 1930), cols. 1514–29, s.v. "Marcianus," no. 34.

47. For example, the Enkratites, discussed in Elliott, and the Abelians, who adopted their partners as children: see Franz Oehler, Corpus Haeresiologici 1 (Berlin, 1856) Praedestinati, Book 1, Chapter 87, p. 265: Mas ergo et femina, sub continentiae professione simul habitantes puerum et puellam sibi adoptabant, in eiusdem coniunctionis pacto successores futuros . . . But to identify a fourth-century stele as Enkratite (Anatolian Studies Presented to Sir William Mitchell Ramsay [London, 1923], p. 81) simply because of the word ἀδελφή seems rather stretched.

48. Other spiritual marriages included that of Scolastica and Iniuriosius mentioned in Gregory of Tours, Historia Francorum 1:47 (MGH SSRRMM 1, 1 [1884], ed. W. Arndt pp. 54–55; cf. Liber in gloria confessorum 31 (ibid. 1, 2 [1885], p. 767; and Monigundius in Liber Vitae Patrum 19, "De b. Monegunde," 1 (ed. B. Krusch in MGH SSRRMM 1,2 [1885] p. 736) [both are discussed in Grégoire, cited above]; Edward the Confessor of England and his wife, mentioned in McNamara, "Chaste Marriage," p. 31, citing William of Malmesbury, Gesta regum Anglorum 2, Chapter 197; and Henry II of Germany and his wife Cunegonde, ibid., citing Vita Sanctae Cunegundis from MGH SS 4:105. For another list of such cases, see Grégoire, pp. 769–70.

49. μείζων ἐστιν ἡ κατὰ πνεῦμα οἰκειότης τῆς τῶν σωμάτων συναφείας. This became an article of Greek canon law, and was cited, for example, by Blastares in the fourteenth century (RP 6:138). This tradition persisted among new converts into the High Middle Ages: St. Magnus of Norway married a woman from a good Scottish family, but lived with her for ten years without physical contact (Orkeyinga Saga, Chapter 45), and St. John of Orkney married twice but never had contact with either wife (Jon's Saga, Chapter 17).

did it properly symbolize the spiritual union between God and the soul.[50]

A second Christian innovation relating to marriage was the fraternalization of the Christian community.[51] As opposed to the Jewish Scriptures,[52] the New Testament deliberately used sibling referents to express fraternal relationships based on affection or common cause rather than blood or heritage: *all human beings* were idealized as the sibling children of God the Father, as opposed to the children of Israel—the tribal unit understood by the Jews to have been first given the covenant with Yahveh.[53] Therefore, "brother," "sister," and "beloved," used by or about Christians, were terms with little specific import beyond the fact that those so designated were human beings (or, in some cases, fellow Christians).[54]

Nothing is as precious to God as love [ἀγάπη], on account of which he became human and "obedient even unto death" [Phil. 2:8]. And it was for this reason that the first calling of his apostles included two brothers,[55] the all-wise Savior indicating thus

---

[50.] See John Bugge, *Virginitas: An Essay in the History of a Medieval Ideal* (The Hague, 1975), p. 86.

[51.] This might be an outgrowth of ecumenical Judaism, but for the most part mainstream Judaism espoused a dramatically different view: God might be the father of all humans, but the family of Jews, descended from Abraham, occupied a special place in His affections, and therefore its members had particular duties to each other. This view grew stronger in the diaspora, largely eclipsing any countertendency before modern times.

[52.] Although sibling terms in the Hebrew Scriptures do involve some ambiguities, this is usually resolved in English translations by use of the word "brethren" (e.g., at Gen. 13.8, 19.7). Sometimes Christians deliberately transformed the sense of passages in the Hebrew Scriptures, as when Serge and Bacchus used "brethren" or "brothers" in Psalm 133 with quite a different meaning (see following note).

[53.] *At quanto dignius fratres et dicuntur et habentur qui unum patrem deum agnoverunt, qui unum spiritum biberint sanctitatis* ("How much more worthily are they called and regarded as 'brothers' who recognize one Father—God—and who drink one spirit of holiness"), Tertullian, *Apologeticum* 39, ed. Franz Oehler (Leipzig, 1854), p. 130. Note that the psalmist's praise of "brethren who dwell together in unity" (Hebrew/KJV 133.1; LXX/Vulgate 132.1) probably applied originally to relatives, but was transformed under Christian influence into a comment on affectionate intimacy: cf. Chapter 5, and discussion of Tobias.

[54.] At least as old as Acts 6:3. This usage is similar to, but broader than, the use of "brother" in African-American communities. Nonetheless, it poses problems in regard to "brothers" who misbehave: see 1 Cor. 5:11, and discussion in Origen, *Commentarium in Mattheum* 13.30 (PG 13:1174–81).

[55.] Presumably James and John, the sons of Zebedee (Matt. 10:2, 26:37, Mark 1:19, 3:17, 10:35, Luke 5:10, John 21:2), although Jesus also called Simon and Andrew (Matt. 4:18–22 and Mark 1:16–20). Simon and Andrew lived together (Mark 1:29). Note that there was never any attempt on the part of Catholic exegesis to demonstrate that these pairs were *not* biological brothers, as there was in the case of Jesus' own "brethren."

at the outset that he wished all his disciples to be united in a brotherly way [ἀδελφικῶς]. We therefore should regard nothing as more important than love [ἀγάπη], which binds everything together and preserves it in harmony [ὁμονοίᾳ].[56]

Though "brothers" of Jesus are referred to several times in the New Testament,[57] Catholic tradition ultimately argued that they were "relatives" of a more distant sort—e.g., cousins—and this strengthened the notion that the Greek for "brother," ἀδελφός, should be understood in a broader sense than mere biological accident.[58] Jesus Himself referred, by contrast, to His *disciples* as His "brothers" (Matt. 28:10 and John 20:17), and specifically asserted that His family consisted of anyone who performed the will of God (e.g., at Mark 3:35, Matt. 12:50).[59]

Since all Christians were thus "brothers" or "sisters" of Christ and each other, this usage evoked a confusing and complicated resonance about marriage, which was actually prohibited to siblings under both Jewish and Roman law. The fact that Romans, in spite of this, had often conceptualized wives as sisters (see Chapter 3, n. 88), and that

56. Isidore of Pelusium, *Epistolarum libri quinque* 1.10 (PG 78.185). The use of ὁμονοία—a word traditionally used for connubial harmony—is also evidence of the spiritualization of marital imagery. Cf. the strikingly similar passage in Origen, *Contra haereses* 7.29 (PG 16.3.3326): καὶ ἡ μὲν φιλία εἰρήνη τίς ἐστι καὶ ὁμόνοια καὶ στοργὴ ἕνα τέλειον κατηρτισμένον εἶναι προαιρουμένη τὸν κόσμον.

57. E.g., at Matt. 12:46, Acts 1:14, Gal. 1:19. St. James was called in the Middle Ages ἀδελφόθεος: διὰ τὸ ὁμότροφον, οὐχὶ κατὰ φύσιν, ἀλλὰ κατὰ χάριν (e.g., by Epiphanius, in PG 42:709).

58. In the mid-third century, Origen (*Contra Celsum* 1, PG 11:748) argued that James was called the "brother of Jesus" "not because of blood relationship or common upbringing, but because of custom [ἦθος] and speech [τὸν λόγον]." About a century later St. Epiphanius made a more elaborate argument along similar lines (but allowing for the possibility of common upbringing [διὰ τὸ ὁμότροφον] PG 42:709; cf. 46:648 and 117:1040), and François Halkin, *Inédits byzantins d'Ochrida, Candie et Moscou* [Brussels, 1963] *Subsidia Hagiographica XXXVIII*, p. 8. Such arguments became standard positions in the Roman Catholic tradition. Thomas Aquinas summarized the nearly unanimous view of previous exegetes and theologians when he asserted that Jesus' "brothers" "were so called, not because of biology, as if they were born of the same mother, but on the basis of relationship, since they were his relatives" (*fratres domini dicti sunt, non secundum naturam, quasi ab eadem matre nati: sed secundum cognationem, quasi consanguinei eius existentes* [*Summa theologica* 3.28.3 ad 5]). Moreover, in the manuscript tradition of Matt. 5:47 some versions replace ἀδελφούς with φίλους, suggesting that the two were thought roughly equivalent by early Christian copyists.

59. But at the cross Jesus seemed to assign the disciple John to a special relationship with his mother: John 19:26–27. This may have been because Jesus and John were already "brothers" in some sense, making Mary John's "mother," but the nature of this relationship remains unclear.

"sister" and "beloved" were both used to characterize relationships of which some members of the hierarchy disapproved (see below), greatly complicated this pervasive metaphor as applied to marriage.

Like the spiritualization of marriage, this conflation may have originated in the New Testament. Paul seems to introduce it in 1 Cor. 9:5, where in the original Greek, he relates "sister" and "wife"[60] in a way that has confused Christian translators ever since.[61] Literally, he asks, "have we not the right to take on our trips a wife [?][62] a sister?"[63] Perhaps he meant to suggest that if he had a wife, he would treat her as a sister, as other important early Christians had done. As it often did, the King James Version retained the original ambiguity, offering its readers an accurate, if unintelligible, text: "Have we not power to lead about a sister, a wife, as well as other apostles, and as the brethren of the Lord, and Çephas?" Other English translations have either resolved the ambiguity of "sister/wife" in favor of the second, or further confused the matter by introducing the concept "believing wife," or "Christian wife." Some gloss the phrase by indicating that the Greek might be rendered "a sister as wife."[64] None suggest that "wife as sister" is more appropriate in historical context, although many factors might induce one to believe it, chief among them the archetypes proffered by the Jewish Scriptures.

Until the advent of the printing press the average Christian did not have access to the exact text of most of the Bible, but the learned elite were much influenced by it, and in turn passed on their testimony—at least in broad outline—to the masses. The content of the Jewish Scriptures, to which Christians had to pay grudging respect as claimants to the fulfillment of its prophecies, was multivalent on human marriage. Of many prooftexts that could be appealed to, three in particular seem to have captured the imagination of Christians casting about for scriptural precedents about human marriage: the marriages of the patriarchs, from whom Christ was descended; the

---

60. μὴ οὐκ ἔχομεν ἐξουσίαν ἀδελφὴν γυναῖκα περιάγειν; Jerome renders this: *Numquid non habemus potestatem mulierem sororem circumducendi . . . ?*

61. It seemed clearer to Jerome, who commented on it in *Adversus Jovinianum,* 1.26 (PL 23:245–46).

62. There is nothing missing in the Greek, but it is difficult to be sure whether the English, to make sense, should not have "as" or "who is" here. See following discussion.

63. Or, possibly, "have we not the right to take on our trips a sister as a wife?" This would seem to make less sense, but see below on the συνεισάκτοι.

64. E.g., both the Revised Standard Version and the New Revised Standard Version.

example of Tobit, which inspired both Jewish and Christian wedding blessings;[65] and the Song of Songs, by far the best known text of human love before the Renaissance.

Adam and Eve were understood as a married couple and the parents of legitimate children (otherwise all humans would be illegitimate), but no ceremony or liturgical blessing was known to have united them, nor was any fulfillment of religious law involved in their union.[66] Indeed, "there does not appear to be any conceptual word for the institution of marriage in the [Hebrew] Bible."[67] The next most obvious and influential archetypes of matrimony were Abraham and Sarah, from whom sprang the Jewish people. Sarah was Abraham's half-sister, but Christians nonetheless drew on their example even as the idea of the Christian people—the new, nonbiological Israel—replaced the "posterity of Abraham" as the definition of God's "chosen people." On the other hand, heightened moral fastidiousness about "consanguinity" rendered the blood relationship between Sarah and Abraham troubling, even when it was invoked.

The problem of relationship also lurked in the background of another famous patriarchal marriage, sometimes nevertheless invoked in matrimonial liturgies among Christians. Jacob married two daughters of Laban, his uncle (Gen. 29, 30)—i.e., his first cousins.[68] Love and passion were not absent from this account: Jacob wanted to marry Rachel, the younger, because she was "beautiful and well-favored" (KJV), but Laban tricked him by introducing Leah, the elder, whom he was anxious to marry off, to the bridal chamber on the wedding night. According to the biblical account, this sealed the marriage. But once he had seen his eldest married, Laban allowed Jacob to marry Rachel as well. The episode well exemplifies the complex web of dynastic considerations and personal feelings in which much premodern matrimony was imbricated—even in its consequences:

---

65. For example, Visigothic heterosexual marriage rituals ended with the prayer from Tobit, according to Stevenson, *Nuptial Blessing*, p. 51.

66. For the peculiar language relating to Eve as "helpmate," see n. 219, below. On matrimony and its variations in the Bible, see Claire Gottlieb, "Varieties of Marriage in the Bible: [sic] and Their Analogues in the Ancient World," Ph.D. diss., New York University, 1989. By "Bible" Gottlieb means only the Hebrew Scriptures, which limits the discussion substantially.

67. Gottlieb, p. 1. Since Gottlieb excludes discussion of the New Testament, this statement is of limited validity.

68. This marriage was of the type called Erēbu, discussed in Gottlieb, Chapter 7.

Leah had six children, and constantly hoped that her many children would endear her to Jacob, though she knew he preferred Rachel. By contrast, Rachel was barren, and though unambiguously Jacob's favorite, she was profoundly troubled by her infertility. She had her handmaid sleep with Jacob to produce a child, which she then regarded as hers, but later she conceived on her own. Meanwhile, Leah "bought" a night with Jacob with mandrakes (caught by one of her sons, 30:16).

This episode in the life of one of the major patriarchs of the Hebrew Scriptures, although rarely invoked as an example to be followed, left its imprint on the consciousness of most who read the Bible, at least partly because it reflected in many ways the reality of ancient marriage patterns. Jacob got one wife because he wanted her, another for family reasons. Both were his cousins, and both loved him, although neither was permitted to choose a marriage partner. Both of them gave him their maids "to wife"[69] in order to produce more heirs, which clearly was how a woman cemented a marriage, in their minds, at least, and suggests a rather loose notion of "marriage." They fought over Jacob, and money was used even within the relationship (as when Leah "bought" Jacob for a night). It was, of course, not a typical relationship, since they were sisters and his cousins—after the Levitical law it was forbidden to marry two sisters—but it was archetypal, in a number of ways, even though later marriage ceremonies were more likely to cite Abraham and Sarah as matrimonial models.

One of the most dramatic models for marriage, for both Jews and Christians, was the story of Tobit,[70] about a deeply religious and upright Jew of the tribe of Naphtali, who lived in Nineveh and practiced good works (providing burial for other Jews and the poor) until he became blind and was financially strapped himself. He then sent his son Tobias off to collect a debt from a relative, Raguel,[71] in Ecbatana.

---

[69] לאשה, 30:4; LXX: καὶ ἔδωκεν αὐτῷ Βαλλαν τὴν παιδίσκην αὐτῆς αὐτῷ γυναῖκα.

[70] Τωβιτ in the LXX for the father and Τωβιας for the son. Both are Tobias in the Vulgate (for which I have used the critical edition of the Vulgate by the Benedictines of St. Jerome's abbey in Rome, vol. 8 [Rome, 1950]). English renderings use either or both (usually one for the father and the other for the son). The date of the text is uncertain, and it survives fully only in two Greek recensions and the Vulgate version, which differs from both. Fragments from Qumran testify to its antiquity and Semitic origin but are incomplete and do not establish a date. The Book of Tobit is not included in either the Jewish Masoretic text or Protestant Bibles, but was quite important to both Jews and Christians in the Middle Ages.

[71] Raguhel in the Vulgate; probably Reuel in the Hebrew original.

Raguel's only daughter, Sarah, though very beautiful, had already been married seven times, and each time an evil demon had slain her groom on their wedding night. As a kindness to both Tobit and Raguel, God sent the angel Raphael, in disguise, to act as guide for Tobias. Raphael warned Tobias about the misfortune attendant on Sarah's previous weddings and prepared him to circumvent the demon.

Because of their kinship,[72] Tobias asked for Sarah's hand in marriage and ultimately overcame Raguel's resistance to marrying his ostensibly lethal daughter to a relative. On the first night, Tobias warned Sarah that they "must not be joined together like heathens that know not God," and then they both prayed and pronounced blessings of God. The wedding was celebrated for fourteen nights—double the usual time—and Sarah and Tobias refrained from copulation for the first three of them.[73] According to the Vulgate, this marriage also involved a written document.[74] (This document was not mentioned in Greek recensions, but was certainly a normal feature of medieval Jewish weddings.)[75]

In the oldest surviving version of the blessings spoken by Tobias and Sarah (that of the Septuagint), they were:

> Lord God of our fathers, may the heavens and the earth, and the sea, and the fountains, and the rivers, and all thy creatures that are in them, bless thee.
> Thou madest Adam of the slime of the earth, and gavest him Eve for a helper.[76]
> From this came the seed of mankind. Thou saidest, "It is not

---

72. The LXX offers two versions of this: according to BA 6:19 Tobias heard about his kinswoman and "loved her" (ἐφίλησεν αὐτήν); the S version elaborates that "when he heard she was his sistèr [αὐτῷ ἀδελφή] from his father's tribe" (σπέρματος), he "loved her passionately" (λίαν ἠγάπησεν αὐτήν); in place of this phrase the BA version has "his soul was joined fiercely to her" (καὶ ἡ ψυχὴ αὐτοῦ ἐκολλήθη αὐτῇ σφόδρα). S substitutes ἡ καρδία for ἡ ψυχή and omits σφόδρα.

73. See, e.g., 8:4.

74. 7:16 in the Vulgate version only: see following remarks.

75. Possibly interjected by the Latin translation in recognition of practices among medieval Jews.

76. 8:6: βοηθόν in the LXX; adiutorium in the Vulgate (8:8). Both words are normally used for military assistance or rescue, often of God, as in the Psalms.

good that the man should be alone; I will make him an help-meet for him, like unto him."[77]

And now, Lord, thou knowest, that not for fleshly lust[78] do I take my sister[79] to wife, but only for the love of posterity,[80] in which thy name may be blessed for ever and ever.[81]

The third paragraph, omitted in the Vulgate (and therefore unknown in the West), combines in an interesting way the values of posterity and companionship that underlay many ancient views of matrimony.

A second influential characteristic of the story of Tobias is the conflation seen elsewhere in the ancient Mediterranean of the positions of spouse and sibling. In the Greek versions, the father Tobit (BA recension: 5:21; S recension: 5:22), the son Tobias (8:4), and the kinsman Raguel (7:15) all refer to their spouses as "sister." In one Greek version Tobias even falls in love with Sarah *because* she is his "sister."[82] Indeed, Raguel acknowledges the marriage of his son-in-law-to-be and his daughter by saying to Tobias, "From this moment on thou art her brother, and she is thy sister."[83]

Although it was ultimately excluded from the Hebrew (Masoretic) text of the Jewish Scriptures, and failed to be included in the Protestant Old Testament, the colorful story of Tobias, with its happy ending (when they returned home the wise Raphael instructed Tobias to administer a salve that restored his father's sight) and exotic hints of magic, captivated the imaginations of both Jews and Christians of the Middle Ages, and influenced views and celebrations of marriage in at least two important ways. The blessings recited by Tobias and Sarah came to form the basis of the "Seven Blessings" that were fundamen-

---

77. This verse does not occur in the Vulgate or in the Rheims-Douai translation made from it. The S recension in the LXX omits the last two words, which are also missing from its source, Gen. 2:18, but became part of Christian prayers inspired by this blessing.

78. LXX (8.7): οὐ διὰ πορνείαν; Vulgate (8:9): *non luxorie causa.*

79. Actually, his cousin, not his sister: see following discussion.

80. Following the Vulgate recension, which has *sed sola posteritatis dilectione* (8.8); LXX has "love of truth": ἀλλ' ἐπ' ἀληθείας (8.7).

81. Rheims-Douai translation (of the Vulgate version, which is slightly different from the LXX).

82. Actually, his cousin; S version, 6:19: καὶ ὅτε ἤκουσεν Τωβιας . . . ὅτι ἔστιν αὐτῷ ἀδελφὴ ἐκ τοῦ σπέρματος τοῦ οἴκου τοῦ πατρὸς αὐτοῦ.

83. My own translation from the LXX, taking both BA and S readings of 7:12. "Brotherhood" is even mentioned as one of the happy creations of God in the Talmudic version of the Seven Blessings, along with "joy and gladness, bridegroom and bride, rejoicing, song, mirth and delight, love, peace, and friendship" (*Kethuboth* 8a, trans. p. 32).

tal to Jewish marriage in the Middle Ages,[84] and remain so today.[85] (They also seem to have inspired a number of Christian wedding prayers.)[86] The Book of Tobit was referred to, commented on, or otherwise mentioned by almost all Christian authors who wrote biblical exegesis (e.g., Ambrose, Augustine—in eight of his works, Cyprian, Jerome, Origen, Athanasius, Didymus, Cedrenus, Zonaras, Nicephorus Callistus, Lucifer Calaritanus, Chromatius of Aquileia, Maximus of Turin, Victricius of Rouen, Prudentius, Cassiodorus, Eusebius, Caesar of Arles, Bede, Commodianus, Leo the Great, Gregory the Great, Abelard, Rupert of Deutz, Hildegard, Rather of Verona, and Agobard of Lyons).

No doubt the most discussed book of the Jewish Scriptures among Christians—and the only scriptural source to treat human passion—the Song of Songs (in Hebrew this phrase means "the greatest of songs") further inculcated the idea that siblings might be acceptable —even ideal—romantic partners. The text, though interpreted throughout Jewish and Christian history to symbolize a variety of relationships (e.g., God and Israel, Christ and the church, God and the individual soul, and so on) is, at its most accessible level, about human passion and desire, and the two enamored speakers refer to each other many times as "brother" and "sister," although their sexual interest is quite obvious. Since in patristic and medieval Christendom they were also clearly "bride" and "groom" or "husband" and "wife" (in Christian thought the only humans between whom sexual interest was licit and morally acceptable),[87] their fraternal apostrophe consid-

---

[84.] They are given in the Babylonian Talmud (a compilation of the Early Middle Ages) as essential to Jewish matrimony at *Kethuboth* ("*Marriage Documents*") 7b–8b.

[85.] See, for example, *The Authorized Daily Prayer-Book*, ed. Joseph Hertz (New York, 1946), p. 1013, and Kenneth Stevenson, *Nuptial Blessing: A Study of Christian Marriage Rites* (New York, 1983), p. 245, where it is reprinted from Hertz.

[86.] Pope Nicholas I in the ninth century cited the blessing of Tobit as basic to marriage: *Siquidem et Thobias, antequam coniugem convenisset, oratione cum ea dominum orasse discribitur . . .* cited in Laiou, p. 201. Tobit, spelled in a variety of ways, appears in a number of the heterosexual marriage ceremonies translated in Appendix 1.

[87.] At least since the time of Origen (d. 253–54), who began his extensive commentary on what he referred to as the "Canticum Canticorum" by explaining that it was "an epithalamium, that is, a wedding song . . . written by Solomon" (*Commentarium in Canticum Canticorum*, Prologue, in *Origenes Werke*, vol. 8: *Homilien zu Samuel I, Zum Hohelied und zu den Propheten Kommentar zum Hohelied in Rufins und Hieronymus' Übersetzungen*, ed. W. A. Baehrens [Leipzig, 1925], in *Die Griechischen Christlichen Schriftsteller*, 30). Most versions of the Vulgate identified the speakers as *sponsus* and *sponsa*; many English translations followed, identifying them as "bridegroom" and "bride." The text has long been known in German as "Hohelied" ("wedding song") (Luther called it "Hohes Lied Salomonis").

erably strengthened the conflation of sibling relationship with romantic pairing implied by patriarchal practice, the Book of Tobit, and Hellenistic custom.

> Thou hast ravished my heart, my sister, my spouse[88]
> How fair is thy love, my sister, my spouse (4:10)
> A garden inclosed is my sister, my spouse (4:12).

It is true that in this work—undoubtedly familiar to all literate Christians throughout premodern European history[89]—"sister" and "brother" are used in both erotic and nonerotic contexts: the "bridegroom"[90] uses "sister" in a clearly erotic way, coupled directly with "spouse";[91] but at the end (8:8) the same word is used in what seems a description of a familial relationship: "We have a little sister [אחות, ἀδελφή] and she hath no breasts. . . ." Similarly, the female speaker says (8:1), "O that thou wert as my brother, that sucked the breasts of my mother! when I should find thee without, I would kiss thee; yea, I should not be despised."[92] In this context it is a curious idea that if the beloved male, who *has* been called "brother" by her throughout, could be designated or thought a *biological* brother she could kiss him openly without scandal, although in fact her interest in him is not "brotherly"— in this sense—at all. One wonders how this relates to the male speaker's calling her "sister" with no pretense of fraternal affection.[93]

---

88. Song of Songs 4:9: in Hebrew, אחתי כלה; in Greek, ἀδελφή μου νύμφη; in the Vulgate, *soror mea, sponsa;* all unambiguous conflations of sister and bride.

89. See, for example, E. Ann Matter, *The Voice of My Beloved: The Song of Songs in Western Medieval Christianity* (Philadelphia, 1990).

90. It is not obvious from the text that the lovers are betrothed; hence, the quotation marks I use around "bridegroom." The Middle Ages certainly understood the two figures in this way (cf. n. 87, above).

91. See, e.g., n. 88, above.

92. The Hebrew, the LXX, and the Vulgate all have basically, "Who will designate you as my brother?"

93. The Hebrew used in the Song for "love," or "beloved," is דוד (sometimes "uncle" in Hebrew), or דודי, rendered in the LXX as ἀδελφιδός (also occasionally "uncle" in Greek; but ἀδελφιδός is used to render Hebrew אח [e.g., at 8:1], so there can be little doubt about its meaning); in the Vulgate דוד is *dilectus* ("beloved") (e.g., at 1:13, 16; 2:3, 8, 9, 10, 16, 17; 4:16; 5:2, 4, 5, 6, 8, 9, 10, 16; 6:1, 2, 3; 7:10, 11, 12, 14; 8:5, 14; 5:1). In Isa. 5:1 דוד is rendered ἠγαπημένῳ (*dilectus* in the Vulgate), but the plural, דדים, is rendered ἀδελφοί ("brothers") at Song of Songs 5:1, *carissimi* in the Vulgate.

Although many sheep and plants have died to provide parchment and paper for an avalanche of speculation on the meaning of this song (since ancient times attributed to Solomon), there has actually been surprisingly little discussion of the meaning of "brother" and "sister" in this famous erotic context. The oldest Jewish commentary effectively dismisses recourse to "brotherly love" as explanation by pointing out that in the Jewish Scriptures brothers are actually more likely to be like Cain and Abel, Ishmael and Isaac, Esau and Jacob—all of whom hated each other—than Moses and Aaron or Joseph and Benjamin, the only notable examples of fraternal devotion.[94] Origen, in his long commentary on the Song, evinces interest only in explaining the metaphorical implications of the bride and groom, not the fraternal address. Of more recent commentary, the Anchor Bible, noting that many English translations fail to translate the terms "presumably to avoid the suggestion of incest," nonetheless explains them thus, "The terms 'brother' and 'sister' are commonplace in many languages with reference to friendly relations without implication of consanguinity, incest, or homosexuality, though by no means limited to purely Platonic relationships."[95] The Jerusalem Bible observes simply that it is an "expression borrowed from Egyptian love poetry."[96] The Interpreter's Bible notes that the address "is exceedingly suggestive of the fertility cult."[97] Both Pope[98] and Fox[99] draw out this same tenuous connection in lengthy studies. But, apart from the ill-informed belief that all Egyptians practiced sibling marriage,[100] there seems little real information in such assertions. Probably the image appealed to all ages because it suggested a relationship of equality, in which

[94] Midrash Rabbah on the Song of Songs 8.1.1; for an English translation see Midrash Rabbah, vol. 9 (London, 1983), trans. Maurice Simon, pp. 302–3. The commentary on 4:10 (see above), the second occurrence of "my sister, my bride" in the text, simply points out that there are ten instances in Scripture where Israel is referred to as God's "bride" (in Simon, pp. 212–13). The conjunction with "sister" apparently did not seem odd enough to the sages to require comment.

[95] Vol. 7C: Marvin Pope, The Song of Songs: A New Translation with Introduction and Commentary (Garden City, N.Y., 1977), p. 480. The negative reference to homosexuality must be based on ignorance of Latin usage, and is perhaps a partisan (i.e., homophobic) defense of the relationship between David and Jonathan, discussed below, which would, in the eyes of many, have been disreputable if tinged with "the love that dare not speak its name."

[96] Note to Song of Songs, 4:9.

[97] Vol. 5 (Nashville, 1982), p. 123.

[98] As above, n. 95.

[99] Michael Fox, The Song of Songs and the Ancient Egyptian Love Songs (Madison, Wisc., 1985).

[100] The reality was much more complicated: see Chapter 3.

neither party owned or dominated the other, comparable to a relationship between a brother and a sister—something few real-life marriages emulated but some ethical writers and many women idealized.[101]

In addition, it may have exercised subliminal fascination because it invited Jews or Christians of either gender to participate in the feelings of the other one, reflecting as it does the desires of both the bride and groom.[102]

"Spiritual marriage" was in many ways a surprising success, given that pagans would have found it utterly inexplicable, although it must be remembered that as a "topos" of sanctity it was no doubt sometimes attributed to couples for whom there was no real evidence of it, but simply a general confidence (especially on the part of their hagiographers) that they must have aspired to a loftier calling than connubial satisfaction. Moreover, spiritual marriage allowed women forced into unwanted marriages and men who married only for dynastic reasons a respectable way to eschew sexual obligations. The men who, like Virro's employer (see Chapter 3, p. 55), had once hired male prostitutes both for their own satisfaction and to produce an heir, could now adopt "spiritual marriage" as consolation (and explanation) for their childlessness. Still, it would not be realistic to rule out genuine religious conviction as a motivation, especially in an age when many Christians cheerfully accepted (in some cases even courted) death for their beliefs.

Fraternalization was a more qualified success, since "brother" and "sister" had been terms in the ancient world for commitment in a milieu (probably including the Song of Songs) about which Christian ascetics had misgivings. Although in the early church sibling referents among Christians had connotations of sexual restraint,[103] these grad-

---

101. See, for example, Lactantius' *Divine Institutes* 5.15 (*nec alia causa est cui nobis inuicem fratrum nomen inpertiamus, nisi quia pares esse nos credimus*).

102. A related point is made by Ann Astell, *The Song of Songs in the Middle Ages* (Ithaca, N.Y., 1992). A more codicological approach to the same text is provided in Matter, as cited above, n. 89.

103. In the late apostolic text *The Shepherd of Hermas* (*Similitudines* 9.11) beautiful maidens surround a man who is trying to keep his distance from them and importune him—indeed, more or less force him—to sleep with them on their tunics, but insist that he will be sleeping with them "as a brother and not as a husband" (κομηθήσῃ ὡς ἀδελφός, καὶ οὐχ ὡς ἀνήρ). (Note that it would also be possible to translate ἀνήρ as "man": hence, he should sleep with them as a "brother and not as a man.") As late as the end of the fourth century—hundreds of years later—St. John Chrysostom would use "sibling" to describe biological

ually dissipated under the influence of the Scriptures (discussed previously) and the pressure of everyday Latin usage: Romans were suspicious of Christians' easy familiarity, and having forgotten or repressed the earlier usage of their own language did not find the analogy of siblings reassuring.[104]

Even notably ascetic Christians like Tertullian, with patriarchal examples, Tobit, and the Song of Songs to appeal to, applied fraternal terminology to ordinary marital relations:

> How shall we manage to relate the joy of that marriage which the church counsels and which a marriage gift and blessing mark, [and] though angels take no notice, the father approves? For on earth children do not marry rightly and legally without their parents' consent.
>
> What a union of two believers, of a single hope, a single prayer, a single discipline, a single service! Brother and sister,[105] both servants, with no distinction of spirit or flesh, and truly two [persons] in one flesh. And where there is one flesh, there also is one spirit: they pray together, they turn together,[106] they undertake fasts together, teaching each other, exhorting each other, sustaining each other. In the church of God they are always

---

relations, of whom no suspicions were in his view reasonable: Πρὸς τοὺς ἔχοντας παρθένους συνεισάκτους (Adversus eos qui apud se habent subintroductas virgines [on some pages of this edition Contra eos . . .]), in PG 47:495–514, especially 508: ἂν δὲ ἀδελφοὶ οἱ συνοικοῦντες ὦσιν, ἀντιδώσουσιν ἀλλήλοις τὴν ὑπηρεσίαν ταύτην. Cf. the somewhat later St. Basil, Liber de virginitate (PG 30:740b).

104. Minucius Felix cites critics of Christianity as claiming that "they recognize each other by secret signs and marks; they fall in love almost before they are acquainted; everywhere they introduce a kind of religious lust, a promiscuous 'brotherhood' and 'sisterhood' [ac se promisce appellant fratres et sorores]" Octavius 9, trans. G. H. Rendall (in LCL, Tertullian and Minucius Felix [Cambridge, Mass., 1953]), p. 337; also cited and discussed in Brown, The Body, Chapter 7 ("A Promiscuous Brotherhood and Sisterhood"). Pagans might have been judging Christians by their own behavior: Tertullian claimed that pagan adolescents slept with their sisters: adulescentes tui cum sororibus dormiunt (De ieiunio adversus psychicos 17 [CSEL 20:296], and Irenaeus of Lyons wisecracked that pagans pretended to live together as brother and sister, but that over the course of time the sister became pregnant by the brother (ἐγκύμονος τῆς ἀδελφῆς ὑπὸ τοῦ ἀδελφοῦ γενηθείσης, Contra haereses 1.3 [PG 7:508–9]).

105. Literally, "both brothers" (ambo fratres), but as the case is probably a heterosexual marriage, this seems a somewhat misleading translation into English. The Latin fratres covers both "brothers" and "sisters," though sorores could be used if the writer particularly wished to distinguish gender. The phrase ambo fratres is strongly reminiscent (though not a quotation of) Vergil's fortunati ambo (Aeneid 9:446), about a male couple (both soldiers), Nisus and Euryalus. See above, p. 64.

106. . . . simul uolutantur . . .

together, together at divine service, together in suffering, in persecution, in refreshment. Neither hides the other, neither avoids
the other, neither is a burden to the other.[107]

. . . They sing together psalms and hymns, and provoke
each other over who best sings to the Lord.

. . . The faithful should not be allowed to marry otherwise,
and if they were permitted, it would not be expedient [for them
to do so].[108]

Augustine, too, observed that a Christian might live with a spouse "in
concord," fulfilling his or her sexual desires, or in "fraternal union"
[fraternam societatem] with no physical relationship.[109]

On the other hand, ideals of "spiritual marriage" and fraternization
overlapped in a very troubling way in the case of religious women
kept in the houses of clergymen under the claim that the relationship
was purely spiritual: the couple functioned, those involved asserted, as
husband and wife only in the sense that he protected her and she kept
house for him, but nothing carnal transpired between them. This was
a device in the early church (before the rise of female monastic communities) of caring for single women devoted to the church, who
probably could not have lived alone unless they were wealthy widows,
and of accommodating the peculiar practice of celibacy on the part
of the clergy in a world organized by household. The women in
such relationships were known at first by the term "cohabiters"
(συνείσακτοι) and ultimately by various other expressions (e.g.,
subintroductae, agapetae, and sorores).[110] The first ecumenical council

---

107. Compare the American pop song: "He Ain't Heavy, He's My Brother."
108. Ad uxorem 2.8.6–9, in CCSL, 1:393–94. See also n. 53, above.
109. Potest igitur christianus cum coniuge concorditer uiuere siue indigentiam carnalem cum ea supplens
. . . siue fraternam societatem sine ulla corporum commixtione, habens uxorem tamquam non
habens, quod est in coniugio christianorum excellentissimum atque sublime. From De sermone
Domini in monte, Libros duos, 1:15, 42 in CCSL 35:46.
110. For the first, see Vulgate Gal. 2:4, where subintroductos falsos fratres is used to translate the
Greek παρεισάκτους ψευδαδέλφους (though παρεισάγω does not have the connota-
tions of secrecy that συνεισάγω does, ψευδαδέλφους ["false brothers"] may have suggested
the connection); for the second, see Antoine Guillaumont, "Le Nom des 'agapètes,'"
Vigiliae Christianae 23 (1969), 30–37; Dictionnaire de théologie catholique 1 (Paris, 1935), s.v.
"Agapètes"; Hans Achelis, "Agapetae," Encyclopedia of Religion and Ethics, ed. James Hasting
(New York, 1926), 1:177. For the last, see following. Note that Chrysostom (Περὶ τοῦ τὰς
κανονικὰς μὴ συνοικεῖν ἀνδράσιν [Quod regulares feminae viris cohabitare non debeant] PG
47:518–32, p. 519) explicitly points out that those he castigates cannot call the women they
live with mothers, sisters, wives, or any sort of relative (οὐδὲ ἄλλο τι συγγενείας

of the Christian church, called to deal with the Arian heresy in 325, found it necessary to address this problem, decreeing in its third canon that

> this great synod has forbidden categorically any bishop, priest, deacon, or any other member of the clergy to maintain in his residence any woman (συνείσακτον) other than his mother, his sister (ἀδελφή), or his aunt, or other women who are above suspicion.[111]

In addition to the bishops at the council, many theologians entertained grave reservations about this practice and how truly "spiritual" it could be, including the contemporary Eusebius, who may have coined the somewhat awkward term συνεισάκτοι,[112] although it was first widely disseminated by the canons of Nicea, and St. John Chrysostom, the greatest patristic authority in the East, who penned two separate treatises against the practice.[113]

In time the conflation of "sister" and "spouse" came also to affect such arrangements, and the women were called both "beloveds" and "sisters." Though the point of the latter was probably a pun on *both* the chaste, charitable sense in which all Christians addressed each other as siblings, and the erotic, marital sense—since these arrangements were sometimes viewed as "spiritual marriages"—the phrase

---

ὄνομα . . .). Palladius in his life of Chrysostom says that the latter wrote against what Palladius terms ἀδελφοζωίας, τὸ δ'ἀληθὲς, κατὰ τῆς ἀσχήμου κακοζωίας περὶ τῶν καλουμένων συνεισάκτων (*De vita S. Joannis Chrysostomi* [PG 47:20]), using ἀδελφός in a distinctly negative sense.

111. Text in E. J. Jonkers, *Acta et Symbola conciliorum quae seculo quarto habita sunt* (Leiden, 1954), p. 40; English translation in H. J. Schroeder, *Disciplinary Decrees of the General Councils* (St. Louis, 1937), p. 21, with commentary.

112. In his *Historia Ecclesiastica* (7.30.12–14), written a year before the Council of Nicea. In the Latin translation of these canons by Atticus of Constantinople (A.D. 419) it is rendered *subintroducta*: PL 84:221A. A Latin version also occurred in many subsequent canonical collections; for example, the *Decretum* of Gratian, which specifically cites Nicea: *Interdixit per omnia sancta sinodus, non episcopo, non presbitero, non diacono, non subdiacono, non alicui omnino, qui in clero est, licere subintroductam mulierem habere, nisi forte aut matrem, aut sororem, aut amitam, aut etiam eas idoneas personas, que fugiant suspiciones,* 1.32.16 [attributed in the text to "Dionysius," although that is questionable], cited as well in many previous collections of canons (e.g., Regino of Prüm, Burchard of Worms, Ivo of Chartres [*Decretum* and *Panormia*]).

113. Πρὸς τοὺς ἔχοντας παρθένους συνεισάκτους and Περὶ τοῦ τὰς κανονικὰς μὴ συνοικεῖν ἀνδράσιν, both in PG 47, as noted above. Both were composed at the end of the fourth century.

"sister" in this context suggested distinct disapproval, implying that the conjugal implications of the word were not absent.[114] Both the Theodosian Code of 438, for example, and Justinian's Code about a century later included an imperial ruling of 420 to the effect that

> It is not seemly that a man who lives a commendable life of ascetic discipline in this world should be tarnished by association with a so-called "sister." If any person, therefore, enjoys any rank in the priesthood, or the honor of the clergy, he should know that consorting with unrelated women is forbidden . . .[115]

The clergy might have living with them only mothers, daughters, and legitimate sisters (expressed by *germana*, a different word, with different connotations from *soror*).[116] These rulings were repeated, at least in the Greek-speaking church, throughout the Middle Ages.[117]

Doubtless more influential on ordinary Christians than either the Scripture (which only a tiny minority could read) or arrangements involving religious women and clerics were the examples provided by "paired saints," whose images were prominently displayed in the art adorning places of worship and recast in popular fable and literature throughout the Christian world. Possibly the oldest such example was that of David and Jonathan in 1 and 2 Samuel in the Jewish Scripture. Although not saints, and born into a society that took a very

---

114. Justinian's Novel 133.3 strikes a similar note, forbidding any women to enter male religious communities, even if they were "called" siblings: *nec si quis forte frater esse dicatur, aut soror . . .*

115. None of the other key words for συνεισάκτοι occur in this Latin text: *Eum, qui probabilem saeculo disciplinam agit, decolorari consortio sororiae appellationis non decet. Quicunque igitur cuiuscumque gradus sacerdotio fulciuntur vel clericatus honore censentur, extranearum sibi mulierum interdicta consortia cognoscant*, 16.2.44. More or less the same passage is also quoted in the Code of Justinian, 1.3.19. Justinian's Code also includes (Novel 123.29) a decree that bishops may not have any female at all (presumably including a relative) living with them, but allows other clergy to have *matrem, et filiam et sororem* (given in the Greek version as μητρός, καὶ θυγατρός, καὶ ἀδελφῆς . . .), suggesting that *soror* did not yet have unsavory connotations at the time of its codification.

116. Not the ordinary word for "sister," which was *soror*; the latter had apparently been rendered suspicious in this context by the disapproving phrase *consortio sororiae appellationis*. Jerome deliberately used *germanas* in discussing 1 Cor. 9:4–5 to obviate any sexual connotations: *Adversus Jovinianum*, 1.26 (PL 23:246).

117. So, for example, the fourteenth-century canonist Blastares (*Syntagma* 3.19 [RP 6:194]) cites *Ancyra* 19 as prohibiting clerics from having "virgin women" living with them "as siblings": παρθένους γυναῖκας κωλύει συνεργχεσθαί τισιν ὡς ἀδελφοῖς.

dim view of same-gender erotic intimacy, David and Jonathan probably appealed to early Christian residents of the Mediterranean as fulfilling the same human longings to which stories of same-gender
fidelity and devotion had been directed in the ancient world (see
Chapter 3, pp. 61ff.)—and because they were both valiant warriors.

The Mishnah—compiled in patristic times—cited them as *the* archetype of lasting love (Aboth 5:16), in contrast to a well-known
heterosexual passion, which it characterized as transitory.

> If love (אהבה) depends on some material cause[118] and the cause
> goes away, the love goes away, too; but if it does not depend on
> a thing, it will never go away. What love depended on some-
> thing? The love (אהבה) of Amnon and Tamar. What love was
> not dependent on something? The love (אהבה) of David and
> Jonathan.

The story of Amnon and Tamar occurs in 2 Samuel (13), in which
David and Jonathan also figure: the comparison is striking, and the
same Hebrew word for "love" is used throughout the Mishnaic passage.[119] Amnon lusted after Tamar, his half-sister (they call each
other "brother" and "sister"), and tricked her into coming to his
house, where he raped her. Afterward he was disgusted and threw her
out. She pointed out to him that rejecting her afterward was even
worse than raping her in the first place. The king, she added, would
have given her to him in marriage.[120] This makes it clear that the
difference between David and Jonathan and Amnon and Tamar lay in
Amnon's having *only* physical desire for her: it is not a question of

---

118. דבר :בדבר is usually "word," but it can also mean "matter," "thing," or "something."
119. This word (אהב) is also the operative word for "love" in the Song of Songs, where it is
decidedly sexual, and is used even in the books containing the story of David and Jonathan
for the love of a husband for a wife (1 Sam. 1:5 [Elkanah for Hanna], cf. Eccl.: 9.9); and for
heterosexual love leading to marriage (1 Sam. 18.28), and it occurs in the following book for
promiscuous sexual desire (1[3 in LXX] Kings 11:1). It is normally used in the Hebrew
Scriptures for affectionate feelings that develop between husband and wife, and for passion
in illicit relationships (e.g., it is the word that forms "lovers" in many places: Jer. 22:20,
Ezek. 16:33, Hos. 2:5[7], etc.). Within 1 Sam. it is used both for the love Michal, Saul's
daughter, has for David (18:20) and for the love of David and Jonathan (18:1). But it is also
used elsewhere in the Jewish Scriptures to describe love of father for son (Gen. 22:2),
enjoyment of food (Gen. 27:4), and loving one's neighbor as one's self (Lev. 19:18, 34).
120. In those days marriage to a half-sister was apparently allowed to Jews, a possible anachro-
nism, since it had been prohibited in Lev. 18:9, 20:17, and Deut. 27:22.

love with or *without* desire. Nor does it seem likely that Jewish sages simply could not conceive of sexual passion between males: see Appendix 3 on the Jews.

By contrast, according to 1 Samuel 18:1, "it came to pass . . . that the soul of Jonathan was knit with[121] the soul of David, and Jonathan loved him as his own soul."[122] The two made a "covenant" together—the text (1 Sam. 18:3) employs the word (ברית) used for a marriage covenant elsewhere in Hebrew Scripture[123]—and David and Jonathan lived together in Saul's house (1 Sam. 18:2), even though Jonathan had children (mentioned in 2 Samuel). David was still unmarried. He later took Jonathan's surviving heir into his household to eat at his table, which he said he did "for Jonathan's sake" (2 Sam. 9:1ff.). After Jonathan was killed, David lamented publicly, "I am distressed for thee, my brother Jonathan: very pleasant hast thou been unto me: thy love to me was wonderful, passing the love of women."[124] Note that he referred to him as having been not "like a" brother or "more than" a brother, but "my brother,"[125] although the two were not in fact siblings.

Although they were mother- and daughter-in-law, and there is

---

121. In Hebrew this is expressed by the normal word for "bind" (as in, e.g., to form a conspiracy or to fasten [נפש יהונתן נקשרה בנפש דוד]), but in Greek it is rendered as συνεδεθη (*sic:* no accents in apparatus), using συνδέομαι, which becomes significant later in the context of same-gender union.

122. Cf. 20:17: "And Jonathan caused David to swear again, because he loved him: for he loved him as he loved his own soul." The phrase to love someone "as one's own soul" (18:1 and 3) has no parallel anywhere else in the Jewish Scriptures (Hebrew [18:1]: ויאהבו יהונתן כנפשו; Greek [18:3]: και δαυιδ διαθηκην εν τω αγαπαν αυτον κατα την ψυχην αυτου [*sic:* no accents in apparatus]; Latin: *diligebat enim eum quasi animam suam*).

123. E.g., at Prov. 2:17 and Mal. 2:14. In Greek it is διαθήκη, also used for the "covenant" of both Old and New Testaments, and perhaps suggesting that this relationship, like Christian marriage, might be triangular, involving God. In Latin it is *foedus*, which is also a common word for a marriage contract. Tamassia takes this as evidence that David and Jonathan had established a "ritual brotherhood" between them (p. 34), but his characterization of "ritual brotherhood" is too broad to be taken seriously.

124. 2 Sam. 1:26. Note that this much-quoted lament also contains the familiar saying, "How are the mighty fallen . . . !"

125. 2 Sam. 1:26: אחי; ἄδελφέ μου Ιωναθαν; *frater mi Ionatha*. "As in the Gilgamesh epic, so in the Books of Samuel the relationship between the friends is constructed as both fraternal and conjugal," Halperin, *100 Years*, p. 83. The Vulgate version, perhaps recoiling from the intensity of the relationship between two males, inserts the wholly inauthentic line: *Sicut mater unicum amat filium suum, Ita ego te diligebam* ("As a mother loves her only child, so I loved you"), unintentionally echoing a wounded Catullus, who remonstrated to his Lesbia that he loved her (*dilexi*) as a father his children (72:3: *dilexi tum te . . . pater ut gnatos diligit et generos . . .*).

little scriptural indication of romantic interest between them,[126] Ruth and Naomi became—at least to readers of the King James Version of the Bible—archetypes of love, owing to Ruth's euphonious and unforgettable lines to her mother-in-law:

> Intreat me not to leave thee, or to return from following after thee: for wither thou goest, I will go; and where thou lodgest, I will lodge: thy people shall be my people, and thy God my God.[127]

This line is much less memorable and dramatic in the original Hebrew, or in any other translation,[128] than it is in Jacobean English, and there is little in the Book of Ruth to suggest that anything other than loyalty bound Ruth to Naomi (who had, in fact, suggested that Ruth depart, along with her other daughters-in-law; but Ruth refused to do so). On the other hand, even Boaz (who fancied Naomi) was moved by the exceptional devotion Ruth showed to her mother-in-law.[129]

Certainly the most controversial same-sex couple in the Christian tradition comprised Jesus and John, the "beloved disciple." The relationship between them was often depicted in subsequent art and literature as intimate, if not erotic.[130] John refers to himself six times as "the disciple whom Christ loved,"[131] causing one to wonder whether in John's view Jesus did not "love" the other apostles. At the very least, he must have meant that Jesus had a *special affection* for him,

---

126. The Hebrew word for "cleave unto" (דבק), the same word used in Gen. 2:24 of husband and wife, is used to describe their attachment (Ruth 1:14). The Vulgate Proverbs (18:24) takes this same word as "friendly": *Vir amabilis ad societatem/Magis amicus erit quam frater*. The line is omitted in the LXX version of Proverbs. The original Hebrew reads, "There are companions (רעים) to keep one company, and there is a friend (אהב) more devoted (דבק) than a brother" (JPS, Tanakh).

127. Ruth 1:16.

128. Although it is rather attractive in the Vulgate: *Ne adverseris mihi ut relinquam te et abeam: quocumque enim perrexeris, pergam, et ubi morata fueris, et ego pariter morabor. Populus tuus populus meus, et Deus tuus Deus meus.*

129. Ruth 2:11. On medieval interpretation of this story, see Gérard de Martel, *Répertoire des textes latins relatifs au Livre de Ruth (VIIe–XVe s.)* (Dordrecht, 1990).

130. Not that the distinction is always so clear. See illustrations 17–19, and the discussion of Aelred of Rievaulx in *CSTH*, pp. 221–26. The only sustained (though not widely accepted) scholarly argument about the sexuality of Jesus is that of Morton Smith, *Clement of Alexandria and a Secret Gospel of Mark* (Cambridge, Mass., 1973).

131. John 13:23, 19:26, 21:7, 20: ὃν ἠγάπα (Vulgate, *quem diligebat*); 20:2: ὃν ἐφίλει (Vulgate, *quem amabat*). On the implications of these verbs, see Chapter 1.

which is corroborated by the fact that while dying on the cross, Jesus made John the guardian of his mother, a situation reminiscent of what would happen if one half of a married couple died before the other. (It also suggests, by implication, that Jesus and John were "brothers"—since they came to share a mother—in some mode beyond the "brotherhood" of all the apostles and Christians.)

On the other hand, the New Testament is far too reticent about all personal feelings to resolve this highly charged controversy fully, and doubtless the evangelists (apart from John himself) thought it best to leave Jesus' personal attachments out of the story. Jerome argued that Jesus loved John the most because he was youthful and virginal—doubtless intending to remove any suspicions of sexuality, but not entirely succeeding, given that younger, unmarried men were expected to provoke desire among older men in the premodern population of the Mediterranean.[132]

The earliest postbiblical paired saints were Perpetua and Felicitas, a Christian noblewoman and a female slave martyred for their beliefs by Roman authorities at Carthage in the early third century (probably 203).[133] Although they were part of a group that included four slain male converts, the two women particularly inspired the imagination of subsequent centuries. The precise nature of the relationship between them is not clear.[134] Each had an infant child, and in the case of Perpetua, a Roman of good family (twenty-two at the time of her martyrdom), this meant that she was married, but a young woman's marriage in second- or third-century Rome did not necessarily indicate anything about the direction of her affections.[135]

[132.] *Adversus Jovinianum* 1:26 (PL 23:247). Jesus called several sets of biological brothers, and a point is made of their calling *as brothers*, although they are never subsequently cited in the context of same-sex union.

[133.] Most scholars now believe that the Latin account of their martyrdom was written before the Greek, even if many more manuscripts of the Greek survive. Possibly one should imagine some combination of both: the continuator mentions (sec. 13) that Perpetua spoke Greek, suggesting that at least her own words were written in Greek (ἤρξατο ἡ Περπετούα Ἑλληνιστὶ μετ' αὐτῶν ὁμιλεῖν/*coepit Perpetua Graece cum illis loqui*). Both have been most recently edited by Cornelius van Beek, *Passio sanctarum Perpetuae et Felicitatis* (Nijmegen, 1936). Note that the Latin *passio* in this context refers to suffering, not a romance between the two women. In Greek it is **ΜΑΡΤΥΡΙΟΝ ΤΗΣ ΑΓΙΑΣ ΠΕΡΠΕΤΟΥΑΣ**. An English translation ("Passion of SS. Perpetua and Felicitas") is available both in Edward Charles Owen, *Some Authentic Acts of the Early Martyrs* (London, 1933), 74–92, and in Herbert Musurillo, *The Acts of the Christian Martyrs* (Oxford, 1972).

[134.] For example, did they occupy the same household?

[135.] See Chapter 2.

This uncertainty is heightened by the fact that neither husband is *ever* mentioned in the official account of their martyrdom:[136] in Felicitas' case this might have been because she was a slave and the marriage of slaves was not legal, but Perpetua was a noble matron, and when her father tried to dissuade her from martyrdom, he adduced his own heartbreak, the fact that her infant son—whom she was still nursing[137]—would have to live on without her, and the pain it would cause her two brothers (sec. 5). One might certainly have expected a tender scene with her husband—possibly even his commanding her under wifely obedience to desist.[138]

The paired femaleness of the two martyrs seems to be what appealed most to Christians, since their fellow male martyrs,[139] who also suffered beheading for their faith, were less often commemorated in later centuries.[140] Though all were killed in the end and kissed each other before dying,[141] Perpetua and Felicity alone refused to don the pagan costumes laid out for them to amuse the crowd (sec. 18), and were themselves first attacked by a mad cow—maintaining the theme of femaleness from beginning to end, as their biographer carefully noted.[142] In other ways, however, they clearly transcended gen-

---

136. Although it is difficult to be sure of the date of either surviving account, internal evidence suggests that at least part of one version was written by Perpetua herself, and the narrator contrasts ancient miracles with "modern ones" (sec. 1: τὰ καινὰ παραδείγματα/*nova documenta*), suggesting that the events he recounts are quite recent.

137. But one of the miracles associated with her death was that when her father finally refused to send her son to nurse with her in prison, he immediately lost his need for her milk, and she did not feel discomfort at having too much milk.

138. Even the procurator enjoins Perpetua (sec. 6) to pity her father and son: he does not mention her husband. But Perpetua herself is addressed in the account, even by her father, with the deferential title *domina* ("mistress"). And she is called the "bride of Christ" as if the only husband who mattered was in heaven: sec. 18 (ὡς ματρῶνα Χριστοῦ/*ut matrona Christi*): although *sponsa*/νύμφη are more common nouns for the "bride" of Christ, it would hardly have been appropriate to apply either word to a woman with a child. The use of ματρῶνα here might be a reason to suspect that the Greek translation was made from the Latin, but Greek in the Roman Empire adopted many Latin terms with legal implications, and *matrona* might simply be one of these. For example, imperial Greek for "freedman" was λιβερτίνος, used in Acts (6:9).

139. Revocatus, Saturninus, Secundulus.

140. Interest in paired females might be pornographic; most modern depiction of lesbianism—either photographic or literary—is aimed at the prurience of heterosexual males.

141. πρῶτον κατεφίλησαν ἀλλήλους ἵνα τὸ μυστήριον διὰ τῶν οἰκείων τῆς πίστεως τελειώσωσιν/*ante iam osculati inuicem, ut martyrium per solemnia pacis consummarent* (sec. 21).

142. The text notes (sec. 20), τὸ θῆλυ αὐτῶν παραζηλῶν διὰ τοῦ θηρίου/*sexui earum etiam de bestia aemulatus*. Note that in both cases motherhood was also prominent: Felicity would not have been martyred (slaying pregnant women was against imperial law) had she not given birth to her child—a daughter—before the day appointed for the martyrdoms.

der, portending other paired saints in centuries to come: Perpetua became a male in her own vision,[143] and both were lauded at the end as the "most manly" of "soldiers."[144]

About half a century later, but in a far more remote venue, St. Polyeuct and Nearchos, Roman soldiers of Greek ancestry in the Armenian city of Melitene, were described in their fourth-century biography[145] as "brothers, not by birth, but by affection."[146] They enjoyed "the closest possible friendship, being both comrades and fellow-soldiers."[147] Metaphrastes added that they "were bound to each other by a friendship which was much stronger than blood or relationship, from which passionate union their souls were tightly

---

143. Sec. 10: καὶ ἐγενήθην ἄρρην/et facta sum masculus.

144. ἀνδριώτατοι . . . στρατιῶται ἐκλεκτοί. This does not appear in the Latin conclusion, which has simply, O fortissimi . . . martyres. . . . Virosissimi would be a more literal translation.

145. Many versions of the story of Polyeuct and Nearchos survive in many manuscripts, and a long debate has failed to resolve questions of priority. B. Aubé published an early Greek and Latin text ('ΑΘΛΗΣΙΣ ΤΟΥ 'ΑΓΙΟΥ ΚΑΙ 'ΕΝΔΟΞΟΥ ΜΑΡΤΥΡΟΣ ΤΟΥ ΧΡΙΣΤΟΥ ΠΟΛΥΕΥΚΤΟΥ/Certamen sancti et gloriosi martyris Christi Polyeucti) in Polyeucte dans l'Histoire (Paris, 1882), app. 1, pp. 73–104. He regarded the Greek as dating from the second half of the fourth century. A summary (presumably of the Greek) called "The Martyrdom [Μαρτύριον] of St. Polyeuct" was made in the tenth century by Metaphrastes (PG 114:417–29). An Armenian version of the biography was published in Vark Ev Vgayaranutink Srpots (Venice, 1874), vol. 2, pp. 239–54. F. C. Conybeare translated this into English in The Apology and Acts of Apollonius and Other Monuments of Early Christianity (New York, 1894). He believed the Armenian had been translated from the Greek, but Arthur Vööbus (A History of Asceticism, p. 137 n. 69) regarded the Armenian version as "archaic" and valuable evidence that the Greek text antedated the Latin. He avoided expressing an opinion about whether the Armenian or Greek was first. Aubé believed that the Greek he published antedated the Armenian, followed by the Latin he printed (app. 2, pp. 105–14), then by Metaphrastes' reworking, then by the Latin given in the Acta sanctorum (for February 13, in Feb., vol. 2, cc. 651–652; also in Aubé, pp. 115–16). An unquestionably later version—a summary of the earlier life used liturgically (i.e., read out on the feast of St. Polyeuct)—appears in Part VI of the Synaxarion of Ter Israel, compiled in the thirteenth century from an earlier fifth-century version and published in Armenian as Haïsmavourk, ed. G. Bayan, in PO, vols. 6, pp. 185–360; 21, pp. 1–880; 27, pp. xl–276; 28, pp. 409–776; 30, pp. 1–270, and quoted here from 19 (Paris, 1926), pp. 5–150. I have noted in the following discussion the relatively few places where the Armenian synaxarion version differs from the Greek, because of the ambiguity about the relationship between the earlier Armenian and the Greek, which I have mostly relied on.

146. ἀδελφοὶ μὲν, οὐ κατὰ γένος, ἀλλὰ κατὰ προαίρεσιν ἐτύγχανον. The Armenian synaxarion says they were "companions to each other, and loved each other like brothers."

147. φιλίαν γνησιώτατοι, ὄντες ἑταῖροί τε καὶ συστρατιῶται, Aubé, p. 80. Aubé corrects the text, which seems lucid enough to me, to read φιλίαν γνησιώτατοι ὄντες [φίλοι], ἑταῖροι τε καὶ συστρατιῶται, admitting in a note (2) that the manuscript provides the reading I have adopted. The liturgical Armenian version (p. 10/904) says that they were "companions to each other (ankeiakiy° mimeany), and loved each other (siréin vmimeans) like brothers (e¬,°ar°)." Note that siréin is the ordinary Armenian verb for any sort of love (like French aimer), and is derived from the noun for "heart" (sira).

bound together, each believing that he lived and breathed wholly in the other's body."[148]

Nearchos was a Christian; Polyeuct was not. When Polyeuct's father-in-law, a Roman official, undertook to enforce a general persecution, he first tried to use his daughter and grandchildren to dissuade Polyeuct from siding with the Christians, but Polyeuct was unmoved. "Neither wife nor children nor terrestrial wealth nor military honor nor human rank" would persuade him to worship pagan gods, which he recognized as worthless.[149] When Nearchos learned that soldiers who sacrificed to pagan gods were to be promoted, while Christians who refused would be beheaded, he became distressed about the separation this would occasion between them, since in his view only he would enter paradise. For a time he refused to disclose to Polyeuct what was troubling him, although Polyeuct saw that he was depressed. Finally, threatening to take it as an indication of diminished friendship, Polyeuct persuaded him to reveal what was on his mind. After Nearchos explained that he was disconsolate because of their impending separation,

> the blessed Polyeuct, not yet understanding the meaning of the separation, leapt up and wrapped himself around [περιπλακείς] Nearchos, begging and pleading with him to know what was to be the cause of the imminent division.
>
> The blessed Polyeuct, joined to [συνημμένος] Nearchos by boundless love,[150] was prepared, he said, to subordinate every-

---

148. οὕτω δὲ φιλίᾳ πρὸς ἀλλήλους συνδεδεμένοι, ὡς πολλῷ πλέον αἵματός τε καὶ συγγενείας, ἐκ τῆς κατὰ πόθον ἀκριβοῦς ὁμονοίας συνηρμόσθαι αὐτῶν τὰς ψυχάς, ἑκατερόν τε ἐν ἑκατέρου σώματι ζῆν ὅλως ἢ καὶ ἀναπνεῖν οἴεσθαι (417). Note that many of these words—e.g., συνδεδεμένοι, ὁμονοίας, συνηρμόσθαι—are associated with marriage in Greek writing. Metaphrastes also uses the Greek word ὁμόψυχον ("one of soul") to describe the friends (e.g., at 420).

149. Οὐ γυνὴ τοῦτον, οὐ παῖδες, οὐ κτημάτων περιουσία, οὐ στρατιωτικὸς κόσμος, οὐκ ἀνθρωπίνη δόξα, Aubé, p. 75.

150. Although in many contexts "friendship" seems an adequate translation of φιλία (see Chapter 1: "The Vocabulary of Love and Marriage," esp. pp. 6ff.), in this instance "boundless friendship" seems a bit wan, and "intense friendship," although possible in English, is a misleading translation of ἀμέτρῳ φιλίᾳ. Since ἀμέτρῳ means "without bounds" and φιλία unquestionably means "love" in many instances, "boundless love," a common English phrase, seems the best way to render ἀμέτρῳ φιλίᾳ here and, in consequence, φιλία elsewhere in the story. The Latin recension has, Beatus vero Polyeuctus immensa Nearcho devinctus amicitia, Aubé, p. 86.

thing to his absolute love [εἰλικρινοῦς φιλίας][151] for Nearchos —injury, death or anything else, to such an extent that he would not even spare his children for the sake of Nearchos, since he counted them, too, as less important than his love for the latter.[152]

. . . "Even if we were to be separated by death, no one would be able to diminish the devotion [φιλίας][153] and love [ἀγάπης] we have for each other."

Nearchos replied, "But this, dearest [φίλτατε], is precisely what weighs on my soul. There is something worse than the death of humans: the separation that I fear might take place.[154] . . . For I had feared that I would lose you from my love [φιλίας] and that we would lose our unity of soul [συνειδήσεως]."[155]

. . . Polyeuct then roused within himself the organ of his soul, and reaching for Nearchos with his bodily eyes, took his hand and asked, "Is this then what you feared, Nearchos, and was this your suspicion about us from the beginning? . . . Did you realize this about the bodily part of our love?"[156]

At this juncture Polyeuct announced that he also believed in Christ, whom he had seen in a vision as a "youth" [νεανίσκος],[157] and, though not yet baptized, he courted martyrdom at the hands of the Roman authorities, in this case his father-in-law, Felix, who adduced his daughter—Polyeuct's wife —as a deterrent to martyrdom. To this, Polyeuct replied, "Of what wife or children would I now boast?"[158] Nor did he yield to the entreaties of his wife (Paulina) herself.

But he never forgot his love for Nearchos, because they were one soul and disposition [διάθεσις] in two bodies. And as

---

151. See preceding note on translation of φιλία as "love."

152. Aubé, pp. 84–85. In Conybeare's somewhat misleading translation of the Armenian, p. 132, this is rendered, "Nay, had I even a child, I would not spare him, if I could indulge my love of Nearchus." But this is rhetorical excess: the Armenian, like the Greek and Latin, had already stated that Polyeuct had children.

153. Here, because it is contrasted with ἀγάπη, "friendship" seems a better translation.

154. Aubé, pp. 83–84.

155. Aubé, p. 89.

156. Ἔοικας οὖν τὰ μὲν σωματικὰ τῆς φιλίας ἡμῶν ἐγνωκέναι; Aubé, p. 89.

157. A word with strong connotations of erotic desire. The Armenian liturgy (p. 11/905) has *eritasard*, which might also mean "adolescent."

158. Ποίαν ἐγὼ νῦν γυναῖκα, ἢ τέκνα φαντάζομαι; Aubé, p. 98.

Polyeuct gazed on Nearchos he said, "Brother Nearchos, remember our secret pledge."[159] These last words he left behind for Nearchos as a seal of salvation.[160]

Although this story survived in many Greek and Latin manuscripts throughout the Middle Ages,[161] and a church was dedicated to St. Polyeuct in Constantinople in the sixth century,[162] Polyeuct and Nearchos were less influential as archetypes of paired saints than either Perpetua and Felicitas (although the memory of Perpetua is spe-

159. St. Polyeuct became the patron of sworn oaths between brothers, at least in the West: see Gregory of Tours, *Historia Francorum* 7.6 (MGH SSRRMM I, ed. W. Arndt [1885] 293–94), and *Miraculorum Liber I: In Gloria Martyrum*, 103 (PL 71: 793; MGH SSRRMM I:555–57), and for modern commentary, Paul Guérin, *Petits Bollandistes: Vies des Saints de l'ancien et du nouveau Testament* (Paris, 1876), 2:487: *les hommes y faisaient leurs serments les plus solennels. Nos rois de la première race confirmaient leurs traités par le nom du saint martyr Polyeucte.* The Armenian version has (p. 12/906), "Do not forget, my brother Nearchos [*edbarim Néarxos*], our secret pact [*ganigeli gowian*]."

160. . . . τῆς Νεάρχου φιλίας οὐκ ἐπελανθάνετο· ἐπειδήπερ ἐν δύο σώματι μία ψυχὴ καὶ διάθεσις καθιστάναι ἐνομίζετο. Προβλεψάμενος τῷ Νεάρχῳ, ἔφη πρὸς αὐτόν· Ἀδελφὲ Νέαρχε, μνημόνευε τῶν ἀπορρήτων ἡμῶν συνθηκῶν. Ταύτην οὖν τὴν τελευταίαν φωνὴν, ὥσπερ σφραγίδα σωτηρίας τῷ Νεάρχῳ καταλιπὼν ὁ μακάριος Πολύευκτος. Aubé, pp. 102–3. These words are steeped in the Septuagint: for example, "our secret pledge" uses συνθηκή, which is quite closely related to the διαθήκη employed to describe the "covenant" between David and Jonathan. The "seal" (σφραγίδα) occurs most prominently in the erotically charged Song of Songs 8:6: Θές με ὡς σφραγίδα ἐπὶ τὴν καρδίαν σου, ὡς σφραγῖδα ἐπὶ τὸν βραχίονά σου· ὅτι κραταιὰ ὡς θάνατος ἀγάπη (KJV: "Set me as a seal upon thine heart, as a seal upon thine arm: for love is strong as death").

161. See, e.g., remarks by the Bollandists, who identified more than twenty manuscripts, mostly in Western collections: AB 16 [1897], p. 306 [eleventh century]; AB 21 [1902], p. 15 [eleventh century]; AB 17 [1898], p. 51; AB 23 [1904], pp. 427, 431; AB 24 [1905], p. 186, [eleventh–twelfth century], p. 202 [twelfth century], p. 227 [eleventh–twelfth century], p. 228 [eleventh–twelfth century], p. 230 [fourteenth century], p. 439 [Aubé's text]; AB 26 [1907], pp. 82, 85; AB 28 [1909], p. 368 [twelfth century]; AB 29 [1910], p. 346; AB 41 [1923] p. 157; AB 44 [1926], pp. 22, 47 [sixteenth century]; AB 47 [1929], pp. 14–15, 20; AB 57 [1939], pp. 234, 323; AB 55 [1937], p. 73; AB 68 [1950], p. 30; AB 75 [1957], pp. 68, 69–70; AB 79 [1961], p. 155; AB 80 [1962], p. 11 [ninth and sixteenth centuries], p. 202 [sixth century]; AB 86 [1968], p. 375 [eleventh century]; AB 88 [1970], pp. 7, 8, nn. 2, 11; AB 90 [1972], p. 106 [eighth to ninth century]; AB 94 [1976], p. 365 [fifteenth century]; AB 94 [1976], p. 365 [fifteenth century]; AB 95 [1977], p. 110, p. 386.

162. A church had already been dedicated to Polyeuct in the later fourth century by Juliana, the daughter of Valentinian: see AB 31 [1912], p. 238, and Alban Butler, *The Lives of the Fathers, Martyrs, and Other Principal Saints* 2 (Dublin, 1871), p. 129. This structure is described in the *Greek Anthology* (LCL ed. by Paton) 1:10. Cf. Martin Harrison, *A Temple for Byzantium: The Discovery and Excavation of Anicia Juliana's Palace-Church in Istanbul* (Austin, Tex., 1989). See also Cyril Mango and Ihor Sevčenko, "Remains of the Church of St. Polyeuktos at Constantinople," *Dumbarton Oaks Papers* 15 (1961), 243–47, and R. Martin Harrison and Nezih Firatli, "Excavations at Saraçhane in Istanbul: Fourth Preliminary Report," *Dumbarton Oaks Papers* 21 (1967), 273–78. For art commemorating Polyeuct, see двѣсторонние таблетки из собора цв. софии в новгороде (Moscow, 1983), and *The Treasury of San Marco Venice*, ed. David Buckton (Milan, 1984).

cifically invoked in the Greek version of the martyrdom of Polyeuct)[163] or Serge and Bacchus. Nonetheless, many themes in the account are familiar. Spouses and children are equally devoid of moment for the saint and her/his biographer in the life of Polyeuct as they had been in that of Perpetua and Felicitas, although it is clear that Polyeuct did have a wife. (It is not clear whether Nearchos did or not.) Polyeuct and Nearchos are literally soldiers, which Perpetua and Felicitas had been only metaphorically.

The love between Polyeuct and Nearchos is the driving force behind the tale as well as its most moving component, even though at the outset it involved a pagan and a Christian. Moreover, this aspect of the story overrides considerations of orthodoxy: Polyeuct dies convinced that he will enter heaven and there be perpetually joined to Nearchos (but apparently not to his wife), even though at the time it was a questionable doctrine whether the unbaptized could be saved or not. (In time, "baptism of blood" would become well-enough established to have rendered Polyeuct's confidence theologically justified.)[164]

Although the point of the story was manifestly to appeal to Christians as a reminder of those who embraced martyrdom as Christians in the face of Roman persecution, it may have evoked particular enjoyment from those sensitive to romantic relationships (or special friendships) with a party of the same gender, particularly since both men were soldiers, and there was a widespread and ancient Hellenistic connection between homoeroticism and the military.[165] In Metaphrastes' version, Polyeuct is specifically said to have embraced death for love of Nearchos,[166] although in the earlier redactions it appears to have been Polyeuct's own inspiration. Certainly Polyeuct's vision of Christ as a "youth"—using a word common in other Greek sources for a young man in his prime as a sexual object—might sug-

---

[163.] Along with Thekla: Aubé, p. 77.

[164.] Indeed, in the Armenian synaxarion Polyeuct's vision of Christ as a "youth" includes the latter's instructions to undergo "baptism of blood" (p. 11/905).

[165.] Important for each of the "paired saint" couples discussed in this chapter, but also for many others, such as the Theodores discussed subsequently, or Philoromus, a Roman official martyred with Phileas, the bishop of Thmuis, commemorated in the Armenian synaxarion along with Polyeuct (p. 10/904).

[166.] καὶ τὸν δι' αὐτοῦ θάνατον προθύμως ὑπέρχῃ. This is confirmed both in the "archaic" Armenian hagiography and in the liturgical office for Polyeuct, where Christ is described as *eritasard* (p. 10/904).

gest, at least subliminally, a homoerotic ambience of the story, although this would depend to a large extent on the hearer's openness to this possibility.[167] One could interpret the story as evoking a pagan notion of friendship, from which sexuality was thought to be absent. Certainly Christians might have found reason to idealize a friendship that transcended the erotic, but whatever the protagonists and writers imagined they were encoding, Christians particularly susceptible to such feelings may have interpreted them more erotically.[168]

This is further suggested by the fact that both Corneille in the seventeenth century and Cammarano[169] in the nineteenth composed plays about Polyeuct in which romantic heterosexual love was the most prominent theme, although, writing in a later age, they felt it necessary to transform the ardent same-sex relationship between Polyeuct and Nearchos into a heterosexual triangle involving Polyeuct, the Roman Severus, and Polyeuct's wife, Paulina.[170] This situation is utterly wanting in the early texts, although erotic/romantic feelings do seem to be present between Polyeuct and Nearchos.[171]

By far the most influential set of paired saints was Serge and

---

167. Aubé, p. 102; the liturgical Armenian has *eritasard*, as noted above (n. 166); the earliest Latin version (Aubé) has *juvenem*. Metaphrastes repeats this part of the story (425), adding two other Greek words (ὁρᾶν, ὁμιλοῦντα) associated with desire for males (e.g., in Plato): νεανίσκον τινὰ λέγων ὁρᾶν προσιόντα μοι καὶ ὁμιλοῦντα.

168. Even Castor and Pollux remained a staple of Christian literature, clearly giving witness to the sustained popularity of same-sex pairings: see, e.g., Pio Franchi de Cavalieri, "I SS. Gervasio e Protasio sono una imitazione di Castore e Polluce?" *Nuovo Bullettino di Archeologia Cristiana* 9 (1903), pp. 109–26; K. Lübeck, "Der heilige Phokas von Sinope," in *Historisches Jahrbuch* 30 (1909), pp. 743–61; and AB 23 (1904), pp. 427–32.

169. Librettist for Donizetti (d. 1848), who composed *Poliuto*, which drew on the plot devised by Corneille, involving a love triangle among Polyeuct, his wife Paulina, and the Roman Severus. Polyeuct is a Christian throughout the opera, and Nearchos is reduced to a very minor role.

170. This five-act play has been edited frequently, e.g. by E. G. W. Brounholtz (Cambridge, 1907), and translated by John Cairncross (Harmondsworth, 1980). An intermediate version of the story, in which the love between the two men does dominate and control their actions but the love of a woman is also involved, is told in Boccaccio, *Decameron*, Day 10, Story 8. On Corneille's play, see Leo Spitzer, "Erhellung des 'Polyeucte' durch das Alexiuslied," *Archivum Romanicum* 16 (1932), 473–500.

171. Although the medieval Greek poem printed by Pitra (*Analecta Sacra: Spicilegio Solesmensi* [Paris, 1876], vol. 1, no. 50, pp. 594–95) does relate at its outset that Polyeuct "ignored" the entreaties of his wife (ὁ ἀθλητὴς νυνὶ Πολύευκτος κολακείαις γυναικὸς μὴ ὑποκύψας), and Nearchos is not mentioned at all. It is unlikely, however, that either Corneille or Cammarano was relying on this text, since both do mention Nearchos, though in a subordinate role.

Bacchus.[172] [173] They were Roman soldiers of high standing in the late third/early fourth century who enjoyed such close friendship with the emperor[174] that they were able to have a friend appointed as a provincial governor. They were also Christians, united in their love for each other in a way that recalls the description by Tertullian of a Christian heterosexual married couple (see pp. 132–33, above).

It was then that Serge and Bacchus, like stars shining joyously over the earth, radiating the light of . . . faith in . . . Jesus Christ, began to grace the palace.

Being as one in their love for Christ, they were also undivided from each other in the army of the world, united

[172.] No ancient hagiography of Serge and Bacchus has ever been translated into English; most modern accounts find it necessary to mention them, but deliberately gloss over their intense relationship (see, e.g., Paul Allard, *La Persécution de Dioclétien et le Triomphe de l'Église* [Paris, 1890], pp. 112–14). A complete English translation of the oldest Greek biography is provided here for the first time in Appendix 5. Its date is uncertain. The Bollandists declined to speculate on a century of composition, but Enzo Lodi, in his more recent *Enchiridion Euchologium Fontium Liturgicorum* (*Bibliothecae Ephemerides Liturgicae*. Subsidia, 15 [Rome, 1979], pp. 227–30) assigns it to the early fourth century. Lodi does not, regrettably, specify the rationale for his datings, but since in this instance he merely cites the Bollandist edition of the "Antiquior," one might infer that he placed credence in the traditional date of their martyrdom (October 7, 309). Serge was clearly widely venerated by the sixth century (as noted just following; cf. Gregory of Tours, who mentions Serge in his *Historia Francorum* 7:31). Metaphrastes clearly paraphrased the "Antiquior" in the tenth century, suggesting that it was already in wide circulation before then, as does a homily (No. 57 in *PO* 4 [Paris, 1908]) of Severus of Antioch, which recounts nearly all the details of their lives and was written in the early sixth century. Severus also relates that in his day the sanctuary of Serge had become a great pilgrimage center, and was renamed Sergiopolis (ibid., pp. 92–93). (For an account of a visit to this city in the early twentieth century, see H. Spanner and S. Guyer, *Rusafa die Wallfahrtsstadt des Heiligen Sergios* [Berlin, 1926]). More than a century earlier, Theodoret of Cyrus (d. ca. 457) had related that in his day the festival of Serge was well-known and important (*Graecarum affectionum curatio* 8; *PG* 83:1033). Visual depictions of Serge and Bacchus date to the fourth century (see, e.g., O. M. Dalton, *Byzantine Art and Archeology* [Oxford, 1911], pp. 283, 316–17, 394, 572), and the "Hymn to Serge and Bacchus," translated on pp. 285–88, is from the sixth century, implying that they were already familiar liturgical figures (cf. a sixth-century icon reproduced in André Grabar, *L'Art byzantin* [Paris, 1938], No. 60). See discussion of the Syriac version, below. They are also invoked in the earliest "Same-Sex Union Ceremony," which occurs in an eighth-century manuscript but represents a much older tradition. There is thus much reason to suppose that one of the versions now known—or a similar text—dates from a century or so of their death. This does not make particular details reliable, but does offer some indication of the early popularity of their influence as "paired saints."

[173.] The *ODB* spells the name Bakchos (e.g., 3:1879, s.v. "Sergios and Bakchos"), but this seems to me precious and counterintuitive; it is exactly the same Greek name (e.g., of a popular deity) usually given in English as Bacchus. Many secondary authorities retain the Greek spelling for Sergios (as in the case above), but since there is an English name Serge, it seems more appropriate to give this as an English equivalent.

[174.] Given as Maximian, but there are historical reasons to doubt this.

[συδεσμούμενοι][175] not in the way of nature, but in the manner of faith, always singing and saying, "Behold, how good and how pleasant it is for brothers [ἀδελφούς] to abide in oneness!"[176]

In time, in fact, they provoked the envy of those less favored. The worst their enemies could think of as a denunciation was that they were Christians, which did provoke the wrath of the emperor. He ordered them to sacrifice to his idols. They refused.

> Immediately [the emperor] ordered their belts cut off, their tunics and all other military garb removed, the gold torcs taken from around their necks, and women's clothing placed on them; thus they were to be paraded through the middle of the city to the palace, bearing heavy chains around their necks.

This was a classic mode of embarrassing males in a society obsessed with warrior masculinity (it had been used in pagan times on Hercules himself); it had nothing to do with Serge and Bacchus being a "pair." However, it failed utterly to embarrass them, since they expected, as Christians,[177] to put on the clothing of "new people," and they recognized that their personal union as males rendered traditional considerations of gender less applicable:

> As brides you have decked us with women's gowns and joined us together for you . . .[178]

---

175. See discussion of this term, below.

176. My translation of Ps. 133:1 (LXX 132:1). The KJV has, "Behold, how good and how pleasant it is for brethren [ἀδελφούς] to dwell together in unity!" The Hebrew is גם־יחד הנה מה־טוב ומה־נעים שבת אחים. For the Greek, doubtless quoted by Serge and Bacchus, see below (n. 188).

177. It could have had something to do with their being Christian: it violates Deut. 22:5, but in the Syriac homily Serge and Bacchus defend themselves on this charge, though somewhat dubiously, arguing that since women can glorify God in such clothing there is no reason they might not (cf. p. 155).

178. Or: "joined us to you." This phrase is extremely difficult to translate: ἁρμοσάμενος, "joined together," usually refers to giving in marriage, a sense which can hardly be wanting here, considering the preceding context and the fact that this is the usage both of the LXX (Prov. 19:14) and the New Testament (2 Cor. 11:2). To whom are Serge and Bacchus given in marriage? Either "to each other" or "to you [i.e., to God]" are possible grammatical constructions of the ἑαυτά that follows. The occurrence just after of εἰς σέ seems to militate against reading ἑαυτῷ as meaning the same thing; such a pleonasm would be not be consistent with

However, the parading of Serge and Bacchus through the streets of the city does recall the penalty for homosexual acts described by Procopius (*Secret History,* 11), Malalas, and Theophanes.[179] This penalty was later than the supposed date (309) of the saints' martyrdom, but it might have antedated the actual composition of their lives. On the other hand, no sexual crime is said in the biography to have been at issue: on the contrary, after a considerable theological argument about the advantages of monotheism over paganism, the infuriated emperor appointed their accusers to their positions in the army and sent Serge and Bacchus off to the remote province to which he had appointed their friend as governor. He wrote a letter saying that if they repented they were to be pardoned and returned to their ranks. "But if they will not be persuaded and persist in their unholy religion, subject them to the severest penalties of the law and remove from them hope of long life with the penalty of the sword. Farewell." On their way, "the two chanted psalms together and prayed as if with one mouth" (again a reminiscence of Tertullian on the heterosexually married).[180]

Bacchus was then flogged to death, leaving his executioners exhausted by the effort. Serge, to whom Antiochus specifically owed his position, was returned to jail.

The Duke, frustrated by his defeat, ordered that [Bacchus'] remains not be buried, but thrown out and exposed as meat to the dogs, beasts, and birds outside the camp. Then he rose and left. When the body was tossed some distance from the camp, a crowd of animals gathered around it. The birds flying above

---

the author's style. On the other hand, in s. 2 ἀλληλῶν is used to express "each other." In 2 Cor. 11:2 it is to Christ that Paul has given the church; but here it is Christ who is giving the bride. Either interpretation is striking, given the genders involved. The Latin gives, *conjunge nos tibi per confessionem* ("join us to you through confession"). This may be a softening of the image, but not necessarily, especially if the writer intended to evoke associations of *conjunx, conjuga.* On the general issue of androgyny in the early church, see Wayne Meeks, "The Image of the Androgyne: Some Uses of a Symbol in Earliest Christianity," *History of Religions* 13.13 (February 1974), 165–208.

179. The best edition of this is that of de Boor (Leipzig, 1883–85), p. 177. All of this is discussed in *CSTH,* pp. 171–74, and also in Evelyne Patlagean, "Byzance et le blason pénal du corps," in *Du Châtiment dans la cité: Supplices corporels et peine de mort dans le monde antique. Table ronde organisée par l'École française de Rome avec le concours du Centre national de la recherche scientifique (Rome 9–11, novembre 1982)* (Rome, 1984), 405–26, on pp. 411–12 (without reference to *CSTH,* although it had appeared four years before).

180. See above, pp. 132–33 and 147. See further in Metaphrastes (n. 202, below).

would not allow the bloodthirsty beasts to touch it, and kept guard throughout the night.

Meanwhile the blessed Serge, deeply depressed and heartsick over the loss of Bacchus, wept and cried out, "No longer, brother[181] and fellow soldier, will we chant together, 'Behold, how good and how pleasant it is for brothers to abide in oneness!'[182] You have been unyoked from me [ἀπεζεύχθης] and gone up to heaven, leaving me alone on earth, now single [μεμονωμένον], without comfort."

(20) After he uttered these things, the same night the blessed Bacchus suddenly appeared to him with a face as radiant as an angel's, wearing an officer's uniform, and spoke to him. "Why do you grieve and mourn, brother? If I have been taken from you in body, I am still with you in the bond[183] of union, chanting and reciting, 'I will run the way of thy commandments, when thou shalt enlarge my heart.'

Hurry then, yourself, brother, through beautiful and perfect confession[184] to pursue and obtain me, when you have finished the course. For the crown of justice for me is to be with you."[185]

The next day Serge was forced to run nearly ten miles in shoes into which nails had been driven through the soles, pointing into the feet. Antiochus rode along beside him in a chariot. During the night, an angel healed his feet, which Antiochus claimed was sorcery when he saw the next day that Serge had no difficulty walking. He forced Serge to run another nine miles in the same cruel shoes, and when this did not dissuade him, he ordered his execution. For his executioners, Serge prayed,

---

181. On the significance of this term, ἀδελφός, see p. 19ff.
182. Ps. 132[M:133]:1.
183. Συνδέσμῳ: see n. 178, above.
184. ὁμολογίας: also "living together," or "togetherness."
185. Σὺν σοὶ γὰρ ἀπόκειταί μοι ὁ τῆς δικαιοσύνης στέφανος. This is only slightly transformed in the Latin version: Quid contristaris aut quid anxiaris, frater? Etsi de corpore abscessi a te, sed confessionis vinculo tecum sum psallens et dicens, Viam mandatorum tuorum cucurri, cum dilataris cor meum. Et tu ergo, Frater, festina, ut per bonam et integram confessionem pervenias ad me, cursum consummans et fidem custodiens. Tecum enim mihi reposita est justitia et corona.

. . . When you lay death upon them, accept their repentance, Lord, and do not remember the sin of ignorance which they have perpetrated against us[186] for your sake.

A great crowd of men, women and children followed to see the blessed one meet his end. Seeing the beauty blooming[187] in his face, and the grandeur and nobility of his youth, they wept bitterly over him and bemoaned him. The beasts of the region left their lairs and gathered together with the people, doing no injury to the humans, and bewailed with inarticulate sounds the passing of the holy martyr.

Bacchus' promise that if Serge followed the Lord he would get as his reward not the beatific vision, not the joy of paradise, not even the crown of martyrdom, but Bacchus himself, was remarkable by the standards of the early church, privileging human affection in a way unparalleled during the first thousand years of Christianity. Moreover, Serge and Bacchus were not biological brothers—and no one ever claimed they were—so the appellation "brother" must be understood as reflective either of ancient usage in erotic subcultures or as reflecting biblical usage (particularly in Greek versions). Either way, it would have distinctly erotic connotations.

Although it is not unambiguous, there are hints in the text that Serge and Bacchus maintained a single household: "*their* household servants" accompanied them when they were dismissed from the emperor's service.[188] "Their" in this sentence has precisely the same ambiguity in Greek as in English: it could refer to the servants of both households or to servants of a single household maintained by Serge and Bacchus. It would not be unusual even for close friends without legal spouses in the ancient world to share a home. (Though Roman

---

186. Presumably "us" refers to Serge and Bacchus, since Serge does not use the plural as a convention of speech.

187. Reading ἐπανθοῦν with MSS 3, 4, 5, 6. The editor prefers the ἐπαρθοῦν of 1 and 2, but this seems to me an inferior reading.

188. See translation in Appendix 5, "The Passion of SS. Serge and Bacchus," sec. 12. On the other hand, the Psalm they quote is not a similar indication, because the Hebrew (quoted at n. 176) uses the word שבת for "dwell together." שבת, which could also mean "rest" ("Sabbath" comes from it), does not normally connote cohabitation. But the Greek, which Serge and Bacchus doubtless quoted, does admit this interpretation: Ἰδοὺ δὴ τί καλὸν ἢ τί τερπνὸν/ἀλλ' ἢ τὸ κατοικεῖν ἀδελφοὺς ἐπὶ τὸ αὐτό. The use of *contubernalis* in the Latin (see n. 204) also suggests a shared home to those who read Latin versions of their biographies (e.g., that published in the *Acta sanctorum*).

soldiers had traditionally been barred from marrying during the term of their service, by this time—the early fourth century—this rule had been relaxed, but no spouses of Serge and Bacchus are ever mentioned in any of the considerable literature, both hagiographical and liturgical, relating to them.)

Moreover, the various words used for "bond" and "union" in the account are striking. For example, σύνδεσμος is not only the strongest of the possible words for "union," or "uniting," but combines a fascinating range of associations, all certainly familiar to the author of the Greek life of Serge and Bacchus. The most direct of these would be New Testament phrases, many quoted or echoed in the text, especially Col. 3:14 ("love, which is the bond of perfection" [ἀγάπην, ὅ ἐστιν σύνδεσμος τῆς τελειότητος]) and Eph. 4:3 ("to keep the unity of the spirit in the bond of peace"). Less clear but even more startling is the use of the same word in [LXX] 1 Kings 14:24,[189] where it has been taken since the time of Jerome[190] to refer to homosexuality ("And there were also sodomites in the land: and they did according to all the abominations of the nations . . .").[191] This is likely a misprision of the Hebrew,[192] but could hardly have been unknown to or missed by the author of the life, if it seemed obvious to Jerome.[193] Its homosexual implication was, moreover, strengthened under Christian influence by the New Testament phrase "bonds of iniquity,"[194] which employed the same Greek word for "bond." Following classical

---

[189.] καὶ σύνδεσμος ἐγενήθη ἐν τῇ γῇ, καὶ ἐποίησαν ἀπὸ πάντων τῶν βδελυγμάτων τῶν ἐθνῶν.

[190.] Vulgate: *sed et effeminati fuerunt in terra, feceruntque omnes abominationes gentium.*

[191.] In the King James, from which I have quoted, this occurs in 1 Kings. In New Testament times σύνδεσμος occurs as part of the stock phrase.

[192.] See Boswell, *CSTH*, p. 99.

[193.] Other biblical passages seem less relevant: in 1 [LXX 3] Kings 6:10 it is simply a unit of measure; in 2 [LXX 4] Kings 11:14 and 12:20, and Jer. 11:9 it refers to treason; in Job 41:7, Dan. 5:6, and Col. 2:19 it stands for body parts or joints. In Dan. 5:12 it means "doubts" or "problems," and in Isa. 58:6 and 9 and in Acts 8:23 it is applied to the "bonds" of wickedness. This range of meanings makes it clear that there was no single denotation associated with it.

[194.] The phrase "the bonds of iniquity" (σύνδεσμος ἀδικίας) (e.g., in Acts 8:23, quoting Isa. 58:6) was common not only in New Testament writing and the Epistle of Barnabas 3:3,5 (which makes part of the oldest surviving Bible codex) but also in a great deal of patristic writing (whether this is related to the occurrence in Kings is hard to say). See, e.g., Athanasius, *Homilia in illud: Ite in castellum* (ed. H. Nordberg, *Athanasiana* [Helsinki, 1962]), 5.1; *Disputatio contra Arium* (PG 28:485: λύειν μὲν πάντα σύνδεσμον ἀδικίας); Basil, *De jejunio* (PG 31:164, 181); Clement of Alexandria (*Paedagogus*, ed. H. I. Marrou, M. Harl et al. in *Sources Chrétiennes* 70, 108, 158 [Paris, 1960–70] 3.12.90).

usage,[195] late antique and patristic writers used σύνδεσμος to describe particularly intimate unions of many sorts,[196] ranging from the union of the Trinity[197] to the marriage of husband and wife.[198]

Serge and Bacchus came to represent to subsequent generations of Christians the quintessential "paired" military saints: they were usually referred to and often pictorially depicted together (sometimes rubbing halos together and with their horses' noses touching),[199] and they became the preeminent "couple" invoked in the ceremony of

---

195. E.g., that of Thucydides and Aristotle (Metaphysica 1045b: οἱ δὲ σύνθεσιν ἢ σύνδεσμον ψυχῆς σώματι τὸ ζῆν . . . ἢ συνουσία ἢ σύνθεσις ψυχῆς καὶ ὑγιείας; De interpretatione 17a: οἱ δ' ἄλλοι πάντες συνδέσμῳ εἷς; Rhetorica 1413b: ὁ γὰρ σύνδεσμος ἕν ποιεῖ τὰ πολλά).

196. Ranging from grammatical agreement—e.g., Ammonius (fifth century C.E.) In Aristotelis analyticorum priorum librum i commentarium (Berlin, 1899), p. 67; The Greek Anthology 11.139 (πτώσεις, συνδέσμους, σχήματα, συζυγίας) and 11:321 (συνδέσμων λυγρῶν)—to the union of body and soul (E.g., Alexander Aphrodisiensis [second–third century C.E.]: σύνδεσμος ἢ συνουσία ἢ σύνθεσις ψυχῆς καὶ ὑγιείας; De corporis hominis natura, ed. J. L. Ideler in Physici et medici Graeci minores, 1 [Berlin, 1841] 7.4–8.3: ἡ τοῦ αἵματος φύσις σύνδεσμος ἐστι τῆς ψυχῆς καὶ τοῦ σώματος; Athanasius, Quaestiones ad Antiochum ducem [PG 28:681: ἡ τοῦ αἵματος φύσις σύνδεσμος ἐστι τῆς ψυχῆς καὶ τοῦ σώματος; Chrysostom, In epistulam I ad Corinthios [PG 61:345 {καὶ γὰρ πολὺς ὁ σύνδεσμος τῆς ψυχῆς πρὸς τὸ σῶμα}])—to sharing a household: e.g., Asclepius the Philosopher (sixth century), In Aristotelis metaphysicorum libros A–Z commentaria, ed. M. Hayduck (Berlin, 1888), p. 387: οὔτε δὲ τῶν συνδέσμῳ ἕν, ὥσπερ ὁ οἶκος.

197. E.g., Epiphanius of Cyprus, Ancoratus 4, 7, Panarion 31, 37; Eusebius, De ecclesiastica theologia 2.17.

198. This usage was especially common and influential: see, e.g., Asterius (fourth–fifth century) Homiliae 1–14 (ed. C. Datema [Leiden, 1970]), 5: τὸν ἀρραγῆ τῶν γάμων σύνδεσμον ("the indissoluble bond of matrimony"); Chrysostom, In Genesim (PG 53:299 [σύνδεσμον ἀγάπης ἀνδρὸς καὶ γυναικός], 300—N.B., using ἀγάπη, another key word in the same-sex union tradition ['Ακουέτωσαν ἄνδρες καὶ γυναῖκες, καὶ μιμείσθωσαν τούτων τὴν ὁμόνοιαν, τῆς ἀγάπης τὸν σύνδεσμον], 350 ["to safeguard the indissoluble bond of matrimony": καὶ τῆς συζυγίας τὸν σύνδεσμον ἀρραγῆ διαφυλάττειν], 53:352 and 360 ["Where there is harmony and peace and union of love between wife and husband" {Ὅταν γὰρ ὁμόνοια ᾖ καὶ εἰρήνη καὶ σύνδεσμος ἀγάπης μετὰ γυναικὸς καὶ ἀνδρός}]); Interpretatio in Danielem prophetam (PG 56:195 [σύνδεσμός ἐστι καὶ τοῦτο τοῦ γάμου, ὥστε πρὸς τὰ σώματα ἐπτόηντο οἱ ἄνθρωποι, . . . ὥστε τὸν τοῦ γάμου σύνδεσμον ἀρραγῆ μένειν]). Athanasius (fourth century) also uses σύνδεσμος with ὁμονοίας and εἰρήνης for the unity of the church, thus conflating marital and ecclesiastical imagery according to ancient tradition (e.g., in Epistula ad Afros episcopos [PG 26:1045: τὸν σύνδεσμον τῆς εἰρήνης]), as did St. Basil (Homiliae super Psalmos, PG 29:384: οὕτως ἂν εἴη καὶ ὁ τῆς ἀγάπης καὶ τῆς εἰρήνης σύνδεσμος, συμφυίαν τινὰ καὶ ἕνωσιν τῶν πνευματικῶν ὀστέων; cf. PG 31:660, 1008). Libanius (a fourth-century pagan) adapts this image to friendship: φιλίας δὲ σύνδεσμος ἀργαγῆς τὰς τῶν βασιλέων συνέχει ψυχάς (Orationes, ed. R. Foerster [Leipzig, 1903–8], p. 152).

199. Although during their martyrdom neither was permitted to ride a horse. See illustration no. 8. A monastery was dedicated to them in Euphratesia: see Vööbus, History of Asceticism, p. 238 (cf. 228 for another community founded in Mesopotamia); "Already the earliest inscription which we possess of monasticism . . . reveals the cult of Sergius . . . [and] It should be noted that this saint was also the favorite among the monks" Vööbus, ibid., p. 351 (cf. p. 65).

same-sex union discussed below.[200] Severus of Antioch said in the early sixth century that he had to mention Bacchus with Serge because "we should not separate in speech those who were joined in life."[201] In what is by far the most common version of their lives,[202] Serge is referred to as the "sweet companion[203] and lover" (ὁ γλυκύς ἑταῖρος καὶ ἐραστής) of Bacchus.[204]

All three of these "pairs" were regularly commemorated in the liturgical cycles of the church.[205] The feast day of Perpetua and Felicitas is celebrated officially on March 7, but in the early church their names were incorporated into the canon of the Mass and remembered at every divine service.[206] St. Polyeuct's feast is celebrated on January

---

200. They also became the special saints of the Byzantine army: see Antoine Poidebard and René Mouterde, "A Propos de Saint Serge," AB 67 (1949), 109–16, especially pp. 114–15; they were usually depicted as soldiers, even when painted for monastic communities: e.g., at the Monastery of St. Catherine in the thirteenth century by an Italian artist (in The Icon, ed. Kurt Weitzmann, Gaiané Alibegašvili et al. [New York, 1982], p. 232). The same authors observe (p. 113), La fréquence des noms de Sergios, Sergis, Sergonas, chez les chrétiens de Syrie et d'Arabie, est un signe non équivoque de la vénération dont ils entouraient le martyr. . . . Dans le matériel recueilli en vue des Inscriptions grècques et latines de la Syrie on trouve en 37 localités des personnages portant son nom.

201. As cited above, n. 172.

202. That of Metaphrastes in the tenth century, printed in Acta sanctorum, October 7, 871–83. About seventeen of the MS versions of the Bibliothèque Nationale contain Metaphrastes, as against three containing the Antiquior; in the Vatican there are seven of Metaphrastes and only one of the Antiquior. The Latin version (given in the Acta) departs significantly from the Greek text at many points.

203. This word evokes the ancient notion of "companion-in-arms": see below on the military aspects of the cult of paired saints.

204. E.g., in Acta sanctorum, 7 October, p. 879. The earlier Latin version, which is not identical, does not contain this phrase but has Serge refer to Bacchus as frater meus et contubernalis (p. 867). Contubernalis is exquisitely ambiguous, since it could refer to persons cohabiting romantically (e.g., slaves in a long-standing union, which for class reasons would not have been recognized in Roman law) or to soldiers sharing a tent (which seems appropriate for Serge and Bacchus, "comrades in arms," but since they lived in a city and directed a school, they most likely did not do so). Cf. p. 104. Ἐρασταί would not be unusual for "lovers" of God or something else, but the singular usually means "lover" in its modern sense.

205. Only a small amount of work has been done on the meaning of "paired saints"—e.g., H. Delehaye, The Legends of the Saints, trans. V. M. Crawford (Notre Dame, 1961), and idem, Les Légendes grècques des saints militaires (Paris, 1909), but during the Middle Ages there was a surprising profusion of paired saints (see, for example, British Library Additional MS 28025 [fourteenth century], which includes joint feasts not only of Serge and Bacchus, but also of Marcellus and Apuleius, Cyprian and Justinus, Cosmas and Damian, Dionysius and Eleutherius). Cosmas and Damian (physicians who were biological brothers, and who were invoked as a pair in the canon of the Mass) are the only familiar pair in this grouping.

206. Along with John, Stephen, Matthias, Barnabas, Ignatius, Alexander, Marcellinus, Peter, Agatha, Lucy, Agnes, Cecilia, and Anastasia. None of the others were paired, either textually or in the popular imagination.

9 in the Armenian church (probably since the fifth century), using an Armenian summary of his life.[207]

The feast of SS. Serge and Bacchus is October 7 in the West, and they have been commemorated more widely than most other saints.[208] They were even more popular in the East: "These two, but particularly Saint Sergios . . . became the most popular of saints among the Christians of Arabia and Syria."[209] Severus, bishop of Antioch from 512–18, though a Monophysite, composed a beautiful homily in Syriac in honor of the two saints, recounting most of the details preserved in their Greek biography: Serge and Bacchus were, respectively, first and second in the emperor's service. Severus even gives the same number of miles as the Greek versions that Serge was forced to run in boots with nails. On the other hand, he expands some details: they not only loved each other but actually resembled each other in size, appearance, greatness, and youth of body and soul.[210] In response to the emperor's forcing them to wear women's clothes their reply was that since wearing female attire does not prevent many women from honoring God, it should hardly impede them.[211]

In the Arabic tradition Bacchus and Serge had separate feasts on October 1[212] and October 7,[213] but each one was mentioned as the

[207.] The feast of Polyeuct is found on pp. 10–13 of the collection of Ter Israel, mentioned above at n. 145.

[208.] They are mentioned, for example, in the popular *Speculum historiale* of Vincent of Beauvais (Graz, 1965), xii.lxxvi, p. 480; at least by the High Middle Ages, there was a cardinal deacon of SS. Serge and Bacchus (see, e.g., discussion in Helene Tillmann, *Pope Innocent III*, trans. Walter Sax [Amsterdam, 1980] in *Europe in the Middle Ages: Selected Studies* 12); cf. *Bibliotheca Hagiographica latina* (Brussels, 1900–1901), vols. K–Z, p. 1102. Long before, Procopius had mentioned (*Anecdota* 4.21.1) a father and son named Bacchus and Serge. For churches dedicated to them, see Antoine Poidebard and René Mouterde, "A propos de Saint Serge"; J. W. Crowfoot, *Churches at Bosra and Samaria, Supplementary Paper 4*, p. 3; Howard Crosby Butler, *Early Churches in Syria, Fourth to Seventh Centuries*, ed. and completed by E. Baldwin Smith (Princeton, 1929; rptd. Amsterdam, 1969), pp. 47, 249–50. See also *Vies des saints et des bienheureux par les . . . bénédictins de Paris*, ed. J. Baudot et al. (Paris, 1935–59), 10:191–97, esp. nn. 2–3 under "Bibl."; François Halkin, *Études d'épigraphie grecque et d'hagiographie byzantine* (London, 1973), pp. 99, 101, 102, 104–5, 107, 119, 120, 308; V:84, 88; VI:334, 336; IV:308; Cyril Mango, "The Church of Saints Sergius and Bacchus at Constantinople," *Jahrbuch der österreichischen Byzantinistik* 21 (1972), 189–93; idem, "The Church of Sts. Sergius and Bacchus Once Again," ibid., 68 (1975), 385–92.

[209.] Butler, as above, p. 47.

[210.] Of course these are all obvious generalities of Greek erotic writing, and it is easy to imagine that Severus simply added them as a rhetorical flourish.

[211.] Ter Israel, pp. 87–88.

[212.] René Basset, "Le Synaxaire Arabe Jacobite," *PO* 1 (Paris, 1907), pp. 316–17.

[213.] Basset, ibid., pp. 327–28.

"partner"[214] of the other (between the two accounts, most of the details of the Greek life are provided),[215] and a third feast commemorated the dedication of their joint church in Roṣafah (الرصافة), the place where Serge died.[216]

To a certain extent, all of these saints (and others who would follow in later centuries) benefited from the ancient Mediterranean admiration of the masculine, of the military (which was then exclusively masculine), and of masculine companionship. All three of the early "paired saints" discussed above had some military, hypermasculine connection, even if only ascribed to them (as in the case of Perpetua and Felicitas, who were called in their Greek life "the most manly").[217] The idea that early Christianity was incompatible with military ethos is a widespread misprision.[218] Not only was the Old Testament (as Christians called it) filled with accounts of military conquest on the part of "God's people,"[219] often led by God Himself, but even the New Testament has more terms drawn from military experience than from any other single aspect of life (the Greek for "sword" alone occurs twenty-seven times).[220] Even angels were depicted as constituting an "army."[221] Although Christ had predicted that those who lived by the sword (μάχαιρα) would die by it,[222] He also stated that He Himself had come not to bring peace but the sword (μάχαιρα).[223] Moreover, this military ethos of Christianity persisted throughout its history: not only was Constantine idealized

---

214. رفيق, a word strikingly like the Greek ἑταῖρος in that it might refer (in the feminine: رفيقة) to a courtesan, girlfriend, mistress, sweetheart, paramour, or companion, or (in the masculine) to a companion of the same gender, often without any sexual implication.

215. The striking promise from Bacchus that Serge would receive him as a reward is omitted, but the Arabic synaxarion does introduce at the point of this vision the word اخوه ("his brother"), which had not hitherto been used of Serge and Bacchus, leaving the impression that the original compiler did have either the Greek text or a document on which the latter was based.

216. Basset, "Synaxaire," PO 3 (Paris, 1909), pp. 310–11.

217. See also the mention (above, n. 143) of Perpetua's dream of herself as a male.

218. Probably owing to a misunderstanding of ancient prohibitions of Christians serving in the Roman army, which was seen as an instrument of pagan oppression. Although it was later controversial for clergy to wage war, many did so, and it was rarely considered wrong for the laity to fight. Crusading was, indeed, an archetypally Christian activity.

219. Even Eve is characterized as βοηθός (N.B. masculine) in Gen. 2:18, quoted in Tob. 8:6. This term usually refers to material aid, most often military, in Greek. (The Hebrew is עזר.) The Latin translation was adiutorium, most commonly used for God Himself.

220. I.e., μάχαιρα. στρατεία, στρατεύεσθαι, στράτευμα, στρατηγός, στρατία, στρατιώτης, στρατολογεῖν—all associated with the military—also occur frequently.

221. E.g., Luke 2:13 (the Nativity), Acts 7:42.

222. Matt. 26:51.

223. Matt. 10:34.

by later centuries for "conquering" (militarily) in the name of Christ,[224] but monastic orders themselves imitated military discipline, severity, and barracks in their organization. (Even tonsure was something of a soldier's haircut.) Military orders of the High and later Middle Ages, like the Templars and Hospitallers, were in fact designed as orders of fighting men, and orders of early modern Europe like the Jesuits were both inspired and dominated by a military ethos. Ignatius Loyola was a converted soldier and organized the Society of Jesus as if it were an army of recruits with military discipline. Both Benedictine and Cluniac monasticism had been more paternal and royalist than the Jesuits in terms of organization, but Benedict himself had suffused his rule—the most common basis of monasticism in the West—with military thought and language,[225] often using the Latin terms *militare* and *militia:* "our hearts and bodies must be prepared to do battle [*militanda*] in holy obedience of his commands" (*Prologue*, pp. 96–97); "whoever renounces his own desires should take up the mighty and shining weapons [*arma*] of obedience to fight [*militaturus*] for the Lord Christ the king" (1:3); "we are all one in Christ and we all do equal service in the army [*aequalem servitutis militiam baiulamus*] under one Lord" (2:52–53); "behold the law under which you seek to do battle [*militare*]" (58:22); "in every place it is one Lord who is served, one king for whom battle is waged [*militatur*]" (61:25–26). (In modern English the body of Christians on earth is often referred to as "the church militant.")

In a Roman world in which order (both political and social) was maintained by the army, this was understandable: God was ultimately the source of order. Even in the Middle Ages strength of arm and skill with weapons tended to determine social and political reality, so it is hardly surprising that God was envisioned as the head of a great army, many of his soldiers being military saints.[226] Latin Christianity

---

[224.] Before the Battle of the Milvian Bridge (which was actually political), he supposedly saw a cross in the sky with the saying "In this you shall conquer" (probably τουτῳ νικᾷ, but thought by the West to have been *in hoc signo vinces*).

[225.] This point is brilliantly explored by Christine Mohrmann in her introduction to the rule: *Sancti Benedicti Regula monachorum,* ed. Philbert Schmitz (Maredsous, 1955), pp. 30–33. All subsequent references to the rule are to the chapters and line numbers in this edition.

[226.] Moreover, feudalism—the predominant mode of social organization in the Middle Ages—was based on loyalty and trust between rungs of a hierarchy, and this seemed to most of those imbricated in the structure to be consistent with Christian admiration of those

even appropriated *virtus* (literally, "maleness") as the basic unit of moral value.[227] Similar associations persist even in a more peaceful age, as evidenced by such very popular modern hymns as "Soldiers of Christ, Arise" (1749), "Onward Christian Soldiers" (composed in 1864), "Go Forward, Christian Soldier" (1861), and "Stand Up, Stand Up for Jesus, Ye Soldiers of the Cross" (1859), all rooted in such ancient literary expressions of Christian military sentiment as Prudentius' *Psychomachia* ("Spiritual Battle" [fourth century]) and Venantius Fortunatus' "Vexilla Regis" (sixth century). Delehaye (see n. 231), for example, explains the popularity of military saints simply by the fact that Christianity first spread among soldiers, something that has become much less certain since his day. But he also noted that military saints clearly fall into two groups: those who are venerated singly, and those in pairs or groups. In the second group are SS. Probus; Tarachus; Andronicus; Juventin and Maximin; and Serge and Bacchus.[228]

In all three of the cases discussed here in detail there was some social inequity that might have been essential to same-sex pairings. Felicitas, for example, was a slave, while Perpetua was a Roman noblewoman; Polyeuct was of grander social standing than Nearchos; Serge was higher in rank than Bacchus and more influential. Two of the three stories involved gender cross-dressing, though not voluntarily.

There is not much of a conceptual distance between the Sacred

---

qualities. Saints often inflicted violent punishment on sinners: see Thomas Head, *Hagiography and the Cult of the Saints* (Cambridge, England, 1990), pp. 172–81; Henri Platelle, "Crime et châtiment divin aux XIe et XIIe siècles d'après la littérature hagiographique du Midi du France," in *La réligion populaire en Languedoc du XIIIe à la moitié du XIVe siècle* (Toulouse, 1976) (*Cahiers de Fanjeaux* 11), 49–59. On the sacralization of feudalism itself, see Jean Flori, *L'idéologie du glaive: la préhistoire de la chevalerie* (Geneva, 1983), and *L'essor de la chevalerie* (Geneva, 1986). The involvement of the clergy in battles in the Middle Ages is generally recognized, but has not been thoroughly analyzed. A comprehensive modern study should appear soon from the pen of Andrew Duggan. In the meantime readers might wish to consult Friedrich Prinz, *Klerus und Krieg in früheren Mittelalter* (Stuttgart, 1971), passim.

227. Although it is rarely recognized as the basic meaning of this noun, this has much to do with the profoundly patriarchal nature of Christian society in Europe. Treggiari does see this, and translates *virtus* as "manliness" even in Isidore's description of what a man should be looking for in a wife (*Roman Marriage: Iusti Coniuges from the Time of Cicero to the Time of Ulpian* [Oxford, 1991], p. 86), but I disagree with her in this instance, where *virtus* must have the conventional Christian meaning of "virtue."

228. He did not list Nearchos and Polyeuct.

Band of Thebes (discussed in Chapter 3, pp. 62–63) and the *holy* pairs among the military martyrs of late antiquity, though it is a connection no previous writer has noted.[229] Nor is it surprising that among early Christians, led by ascetic prelates and theologians to view heterosexual couplings as based purely on terrestrial considerations (property or libido or a desire for posterity), Christian saints who directed their affections toward their own gender (or who could be interpreted to have so directed them), in relationships that could only be based on love, should be idealized and lionized by subsequent centuries as following in the hallowed tradition either of the Sacred Band or of David and Jonathan (or both).[230]

Indeed, so great was the hunger for paired military saints that later ages would frequently invent them. "The number of saints of the Greek church who, according to their Acts, were engaged in military service and whom artists represented with a shield, a buckler, and a lance, is relatively large."[231] Among these were the two Theodores— the General and the Footsoldier—nearly always depicted as a pair (at least one—presumably the General—on horseback), often with arms around each other.[232] The legend began with Theodore the Footsoldier, probably in the fifth century (his story was attributed to Gregory of Nyssa).[233] He was thought to have been martyred in the early fourth century.[234] At least as early as the ninth century he was credited with slaying a dragon. But by the ninth century a second

---

[229] This is less surprising in light of the fact that most of the scholarly work on the saints was effected during the nineteenth century by members of religious orders (like Delehaye: see below, n. 231).

[230] There are many studies of the transfer of ancient learning, myth, and culture from the ancient world to the Christian world. For a rare counterexample, see Ralph Hexter, "The Metamorphosis of Sodom: the Ps-Cyprian 'De Sodoma' as an Ovidian Episode," *Traditio: Studies in Ancient and Medieval History, Thought and Religion* 44 (1988), 1–35.

[231] Hippolyte Delehaye, *Les Légendes grecques des saints militaires* (Paris, 1909), p. 1.

[232] George and Demetrius were also coupled in later art, although no connection between them occurred in literature. Nikolas Oikonomidès, "Le dédoublement de S. Théodore et les villes d'Euchaïta et d'Euchaneia," *AB* 104.1–2 (1986), 327–35, p. 329, believes that the oldest real life of the conscript is ninth century.

[233] Theodore the Conscript was born in the Orient, but came to Greece one winter with the Roman army. This was the time of the persecution of Maximian (cf. Serge and Bacchus). After he set fire to the temple of the mother of the gods at Amaseia, he was burned.

[234] For the development of the legends of the two Theodores, see Delehaye (above, n. 231), pp. 10–42, and, more recently, François Halkin, *Inédits byzantins d'Ochrida, Candie et Moscou* [Subsidia hagiographica, 38] (Brussels, 1963), 6: "Passion de Santi Théodore le Stratélate," pp. 71–85; and Oikonomidès, "Le dédoublement," as cited above. It is also worth considering Henry Maguire, "Disembodiment and Corporality in Byzantine Images of the Saints," *Iconography at the Crossroads: Papers from the Colloquium Sponsored by the Index of*

Theodore had also been invented to form a pair: this was Theodore the General, the details of whose life were clearly modeled on those of the original Theodore.[235] The Byzantines looked to the soldier martyrs for strength to help them through life, and the images of these saints had to look the part. Manuel Philes, a fourteenth-century poet, describing an icon of the two saints Theodore in their armor, said that Hercules himself would not be a match for them.[236] The two Theodores were often depicted in art as embracing each other tenderly, and were invoked in ceremonies of same-sex union as archetypes of male-male love (e.g., in the Appendix of Translations, no. 14). Indeed, they were paired with SS. Serge and Bacchus in a set of Kievan icons dating from before the twelfth century,[237] suggesting that even at this early date artists saw a connection between the two pairs, although the only real connection is that both were understood to be couples.

Sometimes the desire for coupled saints extended beyond military partners: although there is virtually no information about them in the Gospels,[238] the apostles Philip and Bartholomew were widely coupled in the popular imagination among Christians of later centuries (see, e.g., Appendix of Translations, nos. 3, 4, 6, 8, 9, 10, 11, 13, 14, 15). Byzantine legend from the fifth and sixth centuries even depicted their martyrdom together in the city of Hierapolis (in

---

Christian Art, Princeton University, 23–24 March 1990, ed. Brendan Cassidy (Princeton, 1993).

[235.] For these see Halkin, as cited in previous note. Cf. Kazhdan in *ODB* 2047: "His developed biography . . . was modeled on that of Teron." Cf. B. E. Scholz, "Die paarweisesymmetrische Darstellung des Hl. Georg und des Hl. Theodor Stratelates zu Pferde in der Kunst von Byzanz und Georgien im 10.–13 Jahrhundert," *Jahrbuch der Österreichischen Byzantinistik* 32.5 (1982), 243–53; Nikolas Oikonomidès, "Le dédoublement" (as above). De Lacy O'Leary, *The Saints of Egypt* (London, 1937), pp. 262–66, opined that the division was effected in Egypt by the Copts, since one of the accounts was "more closely conforming to the Greek narrative, the other very much altered by the interpolation of Egyptian folklore."

[236.] Henry Maguire, "Disembodiment and Corporality in Byzantine Images of the Saints," p. 4, in *Iconography at the Crossroads,* ed. Brendan Cassidy (as above, n. 234), 1–9. Note that Hercules was also associated with a male lover (discussed above, p. 88). Cf. Alexander Kazhdan and Henry Maguire, "Byzantine Hagiographical Texts as Sources on Art," *Dumbarton Oaks Papers* 45 (1991), 1–22, esp. plates 12–16.

[237.] The panel is now in the Muzeij Cerkovno Archeologichnyj, but was lent to the Courtauld on exhibit, at which time a photograph was published in *Connoisseur* 91 (1933), p. 184, fig. 1. The dating is provided in the legend accompanying the photo.

[238.] Bartholomew is only mentioned in Matt. 10:3, Mark 3:18, Luke 6:14, and in Acts 1:13. His name is coupled with that of Philip in Matthew and Luke, but perhaps only accidentally. Philip is mentioned in Matt. 10:2–4, Mark 3:14–19, Luke 6:13–16, and in John 1:44.

present-day Syria), although there is no historical evidence of this.[239] This may have been simply because their names were so often listed together.[240]

Improbable as it may seem to those reared in the industrial nations of the modern West, which tend to regard homosexuality as a vice so wicked that it cannot even be *named* in polite company, residents of the nations emerging from pagan antiquity into the Christian Middle Ages had many reasons to contemn heterosexual arrangements, viewed as a terrestrial convenience or advantage, and at the same time to admire same-sex passion and unions—the residual cult of the masculine and masculine attachments to the many examples of military martyrs joined at death by their devotion both to God and to each other. All of this makes it less surprising that when the Christian church finally devised ceremonies of commitment, some of them should have been for same-gender couples.

[239]. For sources of Philip's life, see J. E. Ménard, *L'Évangile selon Philippe* (Paris, 1967), and *The Gospel of Philip*, trans. R. M. Wilson (London, 1962), and *Acta apostolorum apocrypha*, ed. M. Bonnet, 2.2 (Leipzig, 1903). For Bartholomew, see *Bibliotheca hagiographica Graeca*, ed. F. Halkin, 4 (Brussels, 1969), 227–232, and M. van Esbroeck, "The Rise of Saint Bartholomew's Cult in Armenia," *Medieval Armenian Culture* (Chico, Calif., 1984), 161–78.
[240]. E.g., in the New Testament (as cited above), and following it in Clement of Alexandria, Basil, Eusebius, John Chrysostom.

5

"What God Has Joined Together"

THE DEVELOPMENT
of
NUPTIAL OFFICES

Before the year 1000, and more precisely before the intrusion of the pseudo-Isidorian decretals in canonical collections in the eleventh century, [ecclesiastical] blessing of a marriage contracted by the laity was considered a *favor*. Under certain circumstances the church refused this favor without forbidding the marriage . . . or declaring it null.[1]

Perhaps because Roman weddings had never lost their public and religious character, the church saw no reason to interfere. As late as the twelfth century, canonists saw the church ceremony as no more than a corollary to the public wedding, allowing therefore a considerable flexibility of ritual forms and regional diversity.[2]

The primary reason pagans had valued heterosexual matrimony had little meaning for Christians. It was not for sexual fulfillment, since

---

[1.] Cyrille Vogel, "Les rites de la célébration du mariage: Leur signification dans la formation du lien durant le haut Moyen Âge," in *Matrimonio*, 397–465, p. 426. Cf. Anne Schwerdtfeger, *Ethnological Sources of the Christian Marriage Ceremony* (Stockholm, 1982), 111: "It is risky to speak of 'Christian marriage' at this period, since there was no real distinction between the Christian and non-Christian ceremonies. It would be more correct to speak of 'marriage among Christians' for several centuries into the Christian era."

[2.] Esther Cohen and Elliott Horowitz, "In Search of the Sacred: Jews, Christians and Rituals of Marriage in the Later Middle Ages," *Journal of Medieval and Renaissance Studies* 20 (1990), 225–48, p. 231.

that could have been obtained by pagans from slaves, prostitutes, or paramours,[3] and would have seemed irrelevant or even disreputable to devout Christians. Even concerns about inheritance and biological posterity were too materialistic for the latter, and at the level of national or religious imperative, baptism effectively sidestepped the issue of "birth" that had been so important to Jews and aristocratic Romans[4] by incorporating into the Christian community adults of any background. This process perpetuated the ambiguous status of blood relationship and kinship in the New Testament.[5] Although Jews were the "posterity of Abraham," and could make liturgical appeal to their "forefathers" in the most literal sense, for Christians God, as the Father of humankind, and the "Fathers of the church" were both related to them in a more vibrant and spiritual way. Indeed, the New Testament felt obligated to assert, against the many Christians who doubted the legitimacy—and sanctity—of matrimony, that "Marriage is honourable in all, and the [marriage] bed undefiled,"[6] although "honourable" (τίμιος) was not exactly high praise.

Sporadic blessings and local offices of marriage no doubt existed in the early Middle Ages—although the question has spawned lively controversy[7]—but did not coalesce for centuries into a coherent or

---

[3.] See comments by Musonius Rufus on this in Chapter 2; cf. Xenophon, *Memorabilia* 2.2.4: "of course people do not beget children on account of sexual interest [ἀφροδισίων ἕνεκα], because the streets are full of people for that. We select for wives those who will bear us the best children, and then marry them to produce children [τεχνοποιούμεθα]."

[4.] Nonetheless, a provincial summary of Roman law unquestionably influenced by Christians says that "all the . . . laws were constituted regarding every matter so that a man could leave his goods as an inheritance to his children" (Arthur Vööbus, *The Syro-Roman Lawbook: The Syriac Text of the Recently Discovered Manuscripts Accompanied by a Facsimile Edition and Furnished with an Introduction and Translation* [Papers of the Estonian Theological Society in Exile, 39], [Stockholm, 1983] p. 60 §157). (The actual text of this work, though Vööbus planned to publish it, never appeared in print.) In the Theodosian Code—also an amalgam of Roman legal principles and Christian belief—the many concerns about remarriage are obviously inspired mostly by concern about the inheritance of children and the possibility that heirs of the first marriage will be disadvantaged by a second: 3.13.3, 4.6.3, 3.17.4, 8.13.1, 8.13.4, 2.21.2, 3.8.2, 3.8.3, 3.9.1, 5.1.8, and Novella Theodosiani 14.1. This concern is acknowledged frankly by John Chrysostom in *De virginibus* XXXVII.3.

[5.] For Jesus' use of "brother," see pp. 121–22.

[6.] Heb. 13:4: Τίμιος ὁ γάμος ἐν πᾶσιν καὶ ἡ κοίτη ἀμίαντος/*Honorabile conubium in omnibus et torus immaculatus*. Note that this comment *follows* the command to "let brotherly love continue" (ἡ φιλαδελφία μενέτω [particularly striking in the Vulgate {*Caritas fraternitatis maneat in vobis*}, because *caritas* is later used for conjugal affection, even in marriage rites]).

[7.] The best study of this topic is still Korbinian Ritzer, *Formen, Riten und religiösen Brauchtum der Eheschliessung in den christlichen Kirchen des ersten Jahrtausends. Liturgiewissenschaftliche Quellen und Forschungen*, 38 (Münster, 1962). There is a French translation (*Le mariage dans les Églises chrétiennes du Ier au XIe siècle* [Paris, 1970]), which is more commonly cited, and updated the

obligatory liturgical tradition in eastern or western Europe. Indeed, the most learned authority on the subject argued forcefully that for its *first thousand years* Christianity required nuptial blessings only for priests; for the laity, an ecclesiastical ceremony was an honor, only permitted to those being married to their own (free) class for the first time.[8] Stevenson disagreed with Ritzer's (better documented) conclusion that there were no standard nuptial liturgies before the eighth or ninth centuries, but the frequent references to the *blessing* of marriage he cited from the early Middle Ages do not indicate liturgies *required* for this purpose: Tertullian, Cyril of Alexandria, and other patristic writers were simply referring to the blessing of the bride.[9] (There was also blessing of fields and of households among early Christians: this did not mean that they *had* to be blessed or were regarded as "sacraments.") In Chrysostom's day whatever form this blessing took occurred on the *eve* of the wedding ceremony; the marriage followed on the next day, in classical *pagan* style.[10]

Uncontrolled and largely undefined until the time of Augustus,

German in a few particulars, but abbreviated many of the notes. Also useful are Kenneth Stevenson, *Nuptial Blessing: A Study of Christian Marriage Rites* (New York, 1983) (hereinafter cited as Stevenson). See also Polycarpus Radó, *Enchiridion liturgicum complectens theologiae sacramentalis et dogmata et leges iuxta novum codicem rubricarum*, II (Rome, 1966), and, for a later age, Jean-Baptiste Molin and Protais Mutembe, *Le rituel du mariage en France du XIIe au XVIe siècle* (Paris, 1973), and Pietro Dacquino, *Storia del Matrimonio cristiano alla luce della bibbia* (Turin, 1984). Worth consulting also are Gaetano Passarelli, "Stato della ricerca sul formulario dei riti matrimoniali," *Studi bizantini e neogreci* (Galatina, 1983), 241–47, and Schwerdtfeger, as cited in n. 1. On the general issue of matrimony in the Middle Ages, see, for the East, E. Herman, "De Benedictione Nuptiali quid statuerit ius byzantinum sive ecclesiasticum sive civile," *Orientalia Christiana Periodica* 4 (1938), 169–234, and for the West, David Herlihy, *Medieval Households* (Cambridge, Mass., 1985), and, less successfully, Georges Dumézil, *Mariages indo-européens* (Paris, 1979); Jack Goody, *The Development of the Family and Marriage in Europe* (Cambridge, England, 1983); Christopher Brooke, *The Medieval Idea of Marriage* (Oxford, 1989); Frances and Joseph Gies, *Marriage and the Family in the Middle Ages* (New York, 1987); Georges Duby, *Medieval Marriage*, trans. E. Forster (Baltimore, 1978), and *Le Chevalier, la Femme et le Prêtre* (Paris, 1981); and Madeleine Jeay, "De l'autel au berceau. Rites et fonctions du mariage dans la culture populaire au moyen âge," in *La culture populaire au moyen âge*, ed. Pierre Boglioni (Montréal, 1979), 41–52.

8. Ritzer, p. 170. Consider also the ruling of Pope Leo the Great, Epistle 167.4 (*PL* 54:1205): *Igitur cuiuslibet loci clericus, si filiam suam viro habenti concubinam in matrimonium dederit, non ita accipiendum est quasi eam coniugato dederit, nisi forte illa mulier et ingenua facta et dotata legitime et publicis nuptiis honesta videatur.* Note that this refers to the case of a priest's marrying his daughter to a man who has a concubine already, and that this must have been frequent enough to elicit a papal ruling.

9. These cases are misleadingly adduced as examples of liturgical ceremonies for marriage in Stevenson, p. 14ff, 24–25. Matrimonial ceremonies were still referred to as the blessing of the bride in England in the eleventh century, according to Stevenson himself, *Nuptial Blessing*, p. 67.

10. Ritzer, pp. 81–82.

Roman marriage was nonetheless a parent to both public church and private rites, the former in principle and the latter in practice. But because most medieval societies had come to see themselves as "Christian" by the early Middle Ages, most social institutions like marriage were also assumed to be in some sense "Christian," even if in fact they were largely or entirely pagan in origin. Augustine considered nuptial blessings to be for the bride alone, to mark her change of status—i.e., not to establish the couple or even to cement their union.[11]

The teaching of the Roman church was ultimately, in part by default of a general ecclesiastical practice, that the couple married each other: the church at most witnessed and blessed (as it blessed everything from fields to swords).[12] Substantial scholarly debate has failed to clarify how early there was a heterosexual Christian marriage "service," and the very uncertainty and lack of evidence underlying this controversy is eloquent testimony to the low priority the early church assigned to the precise form of Christian celebration of matrimony, as is the insistence in the fourth and fifth centuries that priests be married in church—suggesting that laypeople normally were not, and that even priests might forgo it if there were not a canonical requirement. (Priests in most areas even of Western Europe could licitly marry until the reform movement of the eleventh century outlawed this.) This does not mean that no nuptial liturgies survive from this period, simply that they were not regular, and that their performance (or nonperformance) did not affect the legitimacy of the union. The Leonine sacramentary (attributed to Pope Leo, 440–61 C.E.) called the observance *Velatio nuptialis* ("veiling of the bride"), clearly perpetuating pagan Roman notions of marriage, and the ceremony consisted of a blessing of those involved, the exchange of gifts required for marriage, a long blessing for the *bride alone*, prayers about the union of the couple and their procreation of children, and the prayer *Pater mundi conditor* ("God, Founder of

---

[11.] Stevenson cites Tertullian's description of a "Christian" ceremony, which actually amounts to traditional Roman betrothal and nuptial customs (e.g., the *velatio*), followed by a Eucharist, and he cites contemporary evidence from "the Acts of Thomas" suggesting a wedding at home with a blessing pronounced by a family member (pp. 17–19).

[12.] This no doubt explains Ambrosiaster's blessing, wrongly interpreted by Stevenson (pp. 26–27) as constituting a liturgy.

the world").[13] The Leonine sacramentary was absorbed and sup-planted in the following centuries by the Gelasian and Gregorian sacramentaries,[14] rendering this early witness of matrimonial custom somewhat moot.[15]

The Gelasian sacramentary (seventh or eighth century),[16] by con-trast, did name its connubial rite *Actio nuptialis*, and referred within it to marriage as the "yoke of concord, the chain of peace"; it also included a blessing connected with offspring and freedom from the snares of the enemy, and Communion, suggesting an ecclesiastical context.[17] Nonetheless, according to Pierre Toubert, even in Carolin-gian times marriage was not regarded as a sacrament—not only not in the well-defined Tridentine sense, but *really* not considered a sacra-ment.[18] The Carolingian bishop and theologian Hincmar of Reims appears to have been the first to combine consent with consumma-tion as defining marriage,[19] but "not until the twelfth century did the church develop a systematic canon law of marriage and a system of courts able to enforce it."[20]

Gratian's picking up on this and insisting that consummation *and* consent were necessary for marriage raised, among many other diffi-culties, the problem of Joseph and Mary, who never consummated their relationship according to Catholic doctrine. The solution to

---

13. Published by Charles Feltoe: *Sacramentarium Leonianum* (Cambridge, England, 1896), 140–42; discussed in Stevenson, p. 35ff.

14. Although they were clearly influenced by it. Antoine Chavasse, *Le Sacramentaire Gélasien (Vaticanus Reginensis 316). Sacramentaire presbytéral en usage dans les titres romains au VIIe siècle* (Strassburg, 1958) deals with this in some detail. He also dates the sacramentary as seventh century, and carefully compares its contents with that of other early liturgical books (e.g., for marriage ceremonies, see pp. 483–88, although this same material is han-dled more adroitly and briefly by Stevenson, Chapter 2.1 ["The Roman Sacramen-taries"]).

15. There is a brief and lucid discussion of this in Edward Burbidge, *Liturgies and Offices of the Church* (New York, 1886), Chapter 3.

16. The Gelasian was probably promulgated in Gaul, but clearly had Roman origins: see, e.g., Chavasse's discussion of this, pp. i–xxxxiii, and Stevenson's summary, pp. 37–40.

17. Published in H. A. Wilson, *Liber sacramentorum Romanae Ecclesiae* (Oxford, 1894), 265–68. It is translated as Document No. 2 in the Appendix of Translations. The Communion was probably not simply the common cup so widespread in early Eastern ceremonies, but ordinary eucharistic Communion, since the Latin *communicare* is used to describe it.

18. *Même selon l'esprit du temps et la conception que nos auteurs avaient des sacraments comme signes visibles de la grâce opérante, le mariage ne peut être pris en telle acception. Nous en avons mille preuves*, pp. 269–70 in "La théorie du mariage chez les moralistes carolingiens," in *Matrimonio* 1:233–82.

19. Brundage, p. 136.

20. Herlihy, *Medieval Households*, p. 10.

this, according to Peter Lombard and other canonists, was that marriage actually depended on *verbum de presenti* ("present consent"),[21] but this in turn raised further problems. Some canonists finally gave up in disgust before the dilemma—e.g., the Italian Vacarius reverted to the primitive notion that the *traditio* (handing over) of a woman constituted the key point of marriage—but by and large Lombard's notion of consensual marriage prevailed.[22]

In the East the doctrine was a little clearer. Ecclesiastics, civic officials, and laypeople all regarded the priest's role as formative: that is, a legitimate Christian marriage required the offices of a priest.[23] This was probably due less to a deep-seated difference between East and West in the theology of marriage than to a more profound difference between the two halves of the Roman world in regard to the role of the church in quotidian activities. The Eastern hierarchy, supported by the Eastern emperors, generally took a more active role in worldly matters than did most Western ecclesiastics, and it is hardly surprising that this involved the institution of marriage, a public and social event. "The relationship between husband and wife and their legal posterity is not part of the law of nature, but of the state," opined an eleventh-century manual of Byzantine law.[24] On the other hand, neither a church ceremony nor a written document was required if the marriage was publicly announced to friends, or in cases of

---

21. This is the solution favored by St. Thomas Aquinas, *Summa Theologica*, Supplement Q.42–45.

22. This is thoroughly discussed in Brundage, pp. 260–78. It was an innovation of Gratian to insist not only that the consent of the couple and consummation made the marriage, but that the consent of the parents was secondary, perhaps optional. This meant that a couple could be married alone, without anyone else attending, even against the wishes of their parents (like Romeo and Juliet). This was also Aquinas' position. On the reality, as opposed to the theory, of marriage, see Robert Palmer, "Contexts of Marriage in Medieval England: Evidence from the King's Court circa 1300," *Speculum* 59,1 (January, 1984), 42–67.

23. Justinian required middle- and upper-class couples to go to a church to be married, although the point of this was probably to prepare documents, not because church officials actually married the couple: see discussion in Alvian Smirensky, "The Evolution of the Present Rite of Matrimony and Parallel Canonical Developments," *St. Vladimir's Seminary Quarterly* 8.1 (1964), 38–47. See also Ritzer, pp. 77–79, 88–89 (where he suggests that the Armenian community constituted an exception, though he admits on p. 85 that there was not a set liturgy). The *Epanagoge*, a ninth-century collection of post-Roman Byzantine law, recognized marriage as occurring via a church blessing, crowning, or contract (Tit. 16 §1, discussed in Ritzer, p. 113). At the end of the same century Leo the Wise (Novel 89 [PG 107:602–3]) declared marriage without ecclesiastical benediction null.

24. ὅτι ἡ τοῦ ἀνδρὸς καὶ τῆς γυναικὸς συγγένεια καὶ διαδοχὴ οὐ φυσικοῦ νόμου ἐστίν, ἀλλὰ τοῦ πολιτικοῦ, Zepos 4: 1–260, 52.4, p. 235.

common-law marriage where a couple lived together and enjoyed carnal relations.[25] In the eighth century the *Eclogues* acknowledged marriage without any written document if either (a) blessed in a church or (b) announced to friends; they also recognized the common-law marriage of a man with a woman with whom he lived openly and had intercourse.[26] "Marriage," they added, "is established by mutual [literally, "exchanged"] agreement; the addition of a dowry is not essential."[27] Dowry had in the East been very much a matter of social rank in any event: laws specified the rank above which a dowry was essential for marriage.[28]

In both Latin- and Greek-speaking Europe the lack of celerity in developing an official Christian liturgy doubtless reflected the persistent ambivalence Christians—especially ascetic leaders—felt about the mostly worldly purposes of matrimony. In the East, prominent churchmen such as Chrysostom viewed matrimony not as the mode God chose to people the world, but simply as a control for human weakness: "marriage is the remedy for concupiscence."[29] In the West, even a church blessing did not remove the putative impurity of human carnality: couples were generally instructed to refrain from consummation for at least three nights after the ceremony,[30] and in some areas the couple, being impure even after observing this injunction, could not enter a church for up to thirty days after the ceremony.[31]

---

25. Ἀγράφως συνίσταται γάμος ἀδόλῳ συναινέσει τῶν συναλλασσόντων προσώπων καὶ τῶν τούτων γονέων, εἴτε ἐν ἐκκλησίᾳ τοῦτο δι' εὐλογίας ἢ καὶ ἐπὶ φίλων γνωρισθῇ. *Eclogues* 2.6; cf. Justinian, Novel 74.4.2.

26. Discussed in Angeliki Laiou, "*Consensus facit nuptias—et non:* Pope Nicholas I's *Responsa* to the Bulgarians as a Source for Byzantine Marriage Customs," *Rechtshistorisches Journal* 4 (1985), 189–201.

27. Γάμον μὲν οὖν διάθεσις ἀμοιβαία ποιεῖ, τῆς τῶν προικῴων γε οὐκ ἐπιδεομένη προσθήκης, *Eclogues* 22.3. In the Arabic translation of the *Eclogues* effected in the fourteenth century for Arabic-speaking Christians (*Die arabische Ecloga: Das vierte Buch der Kanones der Könige aus der Sammlung des Makarios*, ed. Stefan Leder [Frankfurt, 1985]) this had been altered (§1.2) to require that the dowry be written (كتب), that two priests be present, and that the ceremony be performed with a cross, a ring, and a crown. In §2 (not in the Greek of the *Eclogues*) this is ostensibly contradicted by the ruling (§2) that among Christians—as opposed to the case among "most people" (اكثر الناس)—it is *not* payment of a dowry that constitutes marriage, but the presence of witnesses, the priest's blessing of the couple, and his giving them Communion on the day of their wedding (cf.§ 3[2]).

28. Laiou, pp. 194–95.

29. Γάμος δὲ πορνείας ἀναιρετικὸν φάρμακου (*In illud, propter fornicationes uxorem,* 2 [PG 51:210]).

30. Generally called the "nights of Tobias": see Ritzer, pp. 192–93, 211–12.

31. Caesarius of Arles, Sermon 44.5 (CCSL 103:198); noted by Ritzer as a "Gallican usage," pp. 212, 260; cf. Brundage p. 92, Stevenson, p. 58, and Molin and Mutembe, cited above, n. 7,

The "beloved apostle," John, had offered the assessment of those who accepted the message of Jesus—unmarried Himself and of exceptional biological heritage—that they were "born, not of blood, nor of the will of the flesh, nor of the will of man. . . ."[32] "The Christian endowment of marriage with sacrality acted not in conjunction with its carnal aspects, but rather as a neutralizer of the sin inherent in them."[33] (See below on the ambivalence betrayed in early marriage rituals themselves.)

This does not indicate, of course, that humans in Christian societies did not marry—simply that they tended to follow ancient ethnic customs, some of which matched Roman law, and hence became church law, which generally looked to Roman jurisprudence for its models—while others did not. The *Lex Romana Burgundionum* (law for Romans living under Burgundian rule), for example, stated that "consent makes marriage [*nuptias*]," although it also demanded that a "nuptial gift" be "solemnly acknowledged to avoid any suspicion about the legitimacy of the children."[34] The laws of the Burgundians themselves (i.e., as opposed to those of the Romans living under their rule: see, e.g., sections 66, 69, 86) required payment to the bride's family, which, according to Hans Wolff,[35] amounted to bride-purchase. The Germanic custom of *Morgengabe* (*morgengifu* among the Anglo-Saxons), the payment of a sum *in addition to the bride-price* on the morning after the wedding, was obviously a residuum of paying for the woman's virginity, which could not be sold until the husband had verified that it existed. This custom was dissociated from its origins in the High Middle Ages, and became merely a part of regular prenuptial property arrangements. Diane Hughes notes that "in the Early Middle Ages, consummation [N.B. not consent, which would have

---

pp. 291–92. Cf. "The Penitential of Theodore" (C.E. 668–90), 12:1, suggesting that this custom was not limited to Gaul (translated in John McNeill and Helena Gamer, *Medieval Handbooks of Penance: A translation of the principal libri poenitentiales and selections from related documents* [New York, 1938], p. 208).

32. John 1:13.

33. Cohen and Horowitz, "Rituals of Marriage," p. 237.

34. §37:. . . *consensus perficit nuptias: Quod si pares fuerint honestate personae, consensus perficit nuptias, sic tamen ut nuptialis donatio solenniter celebretur; aliter filii exinde nati legitimorum locum obtinere non poterint.* Discussed in some detail in Hans Julius Wolff, "Written and Unwritten Marriages in Hellenistic and Postclassical Roman Law," *Philological Monographs* 9, published by the American Philological Association (Haverford, 1939), 89.

35. P. 90.

been enough at Rome] made a marriage and *Morgengabe* was its sign."[36]

The difference between Romans paying a dowry and Germans offering a bride-price probably has less to do with the supply of women than with conceptions of the nature of marriage: for Romans until sometime around the third century C.E. it was the *transfer* of a woman from one family to another. Later it was a question of establishing a relationship *between* families. For Germans it was simply the purchase of a wife. If no Roman families were involved—e.g., in the case of slaves or foreigners—a permanent union was simply a *contubernium*, living together, in the eyes of Romans.[37] For Germans, legitimate marriage was possible for just about anyone. Throughout the early Middle Ages (until the great canonical reforms of the twelfth century, which finally defined marriage more carefully) "Betrothal was a contract of alienation, concluded like commercial contracts, between the groom and the clan or tutor of the bride, by means of which she was sold into marriage."[38]

There was also abduction marriage in early medieval Europe, as there had been in Greece: it was called *Friedelehe*. The husband abducted the bride-to-be from her family. The church tried to discourage it, but in general if families could reach a property agreement afterward the marriage would be allowed to stand. (Once a daughter had been deflowered, she could hardly be sold to anyone else.)[39] This tolerance also fit well with a common principle of marriage—*publica vox et fama*, i.e., common knowledge of the marriage or witnesses.[40]

[36] Diane Hughes, "From Brideprice to Dowry in Mediterranean Europe," *Journal of Family History* 3 (1978), 262–296.

[37] As in the case of Serge and Bacchus, noted above, pp. 146ff.

[38] *Die Verlobung war der Veräusserungsvertrag, in der Form des Realkontrakts abgeschlossen zwischen dem Bräutigam und der Sippe und dem Vormund der Braut, durch den diese in die Ehe verkauft wurde.* H. Brunner and Cl. Frh. von Schwerin, *Grundzüge der deutschen Rechtsgeshichte* (Munich, 1930), 222. For English examples of purchasing a bride, and its legality, see the seventh-century Laws of Ine, especially §31, in *The Laws of the Earliest English Kings* (Cambridge, England, 1922), 46, and cf. the Laws of Aethelbert, ibid., no. 31.

[39] Decameron, Day 5, Tale 1, tells of an abduction marriage, after which the couple goes to Crete, where they are joyously welcomed. But a real historical case from the end of the fourteenth century involved a forty-year-old widow, who must have voluntarily married her abductor afterward: *Recueil des documents concernant le Poitou contenus dans les régistres de la chancellerie de France*, ed. Paul Guérin (Poitiers, 1893), 6:1390–1403 (in *Archives historiques du Poitou*, 24).

[40] Discussed in Frances and Joseph Gies, *Marriage and the Family in the Middle Ages* (New York, 1989), 244.

Concubinage also survived, and was even grudgingly accepted by Christian society.[41] This was at least partly because until the twelfth century marriage was not connected, in law, theology, or the popular imagination, with erotic or romantic fulfillment. Indeed, marriage *should not* be based on sexual attraction according to the church: in a famous dictum mistakenly attributed to Jerome[42] and often cited in later ages, any man who loved another man's wife at all or his own wife with his emotions was an adulterer. Up to the twelfth century Christians were expected to have affectionate feelings or sibling or parental devotion (depending on respective ages)[43] to their spouses. It was only in the twelfth century, for reasons amply rehearsed elsewhere,[44] that the idea of "love and marriage" going together like "a

[41.] Frequent instances of concubinage are mentioned even in Irish saints' lives: see David Herlihy, *Medieval Households* (Cambridge, Mass., 1985), 38–40.

[42.] Who may have repeated (*Against Jovinian* 1:49), but did not invent it: see above, p. 113, n. 14.

[43.] In Florence in the early fifteenth century—the first period from which extensive records survive—the average father was forty and the average mother twenty-six, suggesting at least a generation of age difference between most husbands and wives: see David Herlihy, "The Generation in Medieval History," *Viator* 5 (1974), 347–64. The frequent topos of the son unwittingly marrying his mother (e.g., in the Gregorius legend) suggests that generational difference might operate in the other direction as well.

[44.] Those interested in this subject should consult Roger Boase, *The Origin and Meaning of Courtly Love: A Critical Study of European Scholarship* (Manchester, England, 1977); idem, *The Troubadour Revival: A Study of Social Change and Traditionalism in Late Medieval Spain* (London, 1978); *The Expansion and Transformation of Courtly Literature*, ed. Nathaniel B. Smith and J. T. Snow (Athens, Ga., 1980); Joan Ferrante, "*Cortes d'Amor* in Medieval Texts," *Speculum* 55, 4 (October 1980), 686–95; Joan Ferrante, George Economou, eds., *In Pursuit of Perfection: Courtly Love in Medieval Literature* (London, 1973); Paul Imbs, "De la fin'amor," *Cahiers de civilisation médiévale* 12 (1969), 265–85; Douglas Kelly, "Courtly Love in Perspective: The Hierarchy of Love in Andreas Capellanus," *Traditio* XXIV (1968), 119–47; Douglas Kelly, *Medieval Imagination: Rhetoric and the Poetry of Courtly Love* (Madison, Wisc., 1978); Henry Kelly, *Love and Marriage in the Age of Chaucer* (Ithaca, N.Y., 1975); Erich Köhler, *Sociologia della "Fin'amor" saggi trobadorici* (Padua, 1976); Moshé Lazar, *Amour courtois et fin'amors dans la littérature du XIIe siècle* (Paris, 1964); Jack Linsay, *The Troubadours and Their World of the Twelfth and Thirteenth Centuries* (London, 1976); Ivos Margoni, *Fin'amors, mezura e cortezia* (Milan, 1965); *The Meaning of Courtly Love*, ed. F. X. Newman (Albany, N.Y., 1968); Bernard O'Donoghue, *The Courtly Love Tradition* (Manchester, 1982); William Paden, "The Troubador's Lady: Her Marital Status and Social Rank," *Studies in Philology* 72 (1975), 28–50; Alan Press, "The Adulterous Nature of Fin'amors," *Forum for Modern Language Studies* 6 (1970), 327–41; Edmund Reiss, "Fin'amors: Its History and Meaning in Medieval Literature," *Medieval and Renaissance Studies* 8 (1974), 74–99; L. T. Topsfield, *Troubadours and Love* (Cambridge, 1975); *Courtly Literature: Culture and Context*, ed. Keith Busby and Erik Kooper (Philadelphia, 1990); John Benton, "Clio and Venus: An Historical View of Medieval Love," in *The Meaning of Courtly Love*, ed. F. X. Newman (Albany, N.Y., 1969); John Chydenius, *Love in the Medieval Tradition* (Helsinki, 1977); Matilda Bruckner, "Fictions of the Female Voice: The Women Troubadours," *Speculum* 67, 4 (October 1992), 865–91.

horse and carriage" began to take hold.[45] Eventually it swept all before it, but not for several centuries. Before that, it is not that there was *no* connection between love and marriage, but that the relation was either coincidental or postpositive—i.e., love was thought to follow marriage, not to occasion it.

Among medieval Christian Europeans divorce remained common,[46] "lover relationships" were common, and concubinage quite common, even in widely Catholic societies like twelfth-century Europe during the most thorough development of canon law regarding matrimony.[47] Divorce and remarriage after the death of a spouse, controversial (especially for women) in the Roman Empire, were officially prohibited by early theologians, although both were still familiar in Christian Europe. Traditional Roman admiration of *univira* status for women[48] interacted with the growing tendency of Hellenistic society to view marriage as a mutual partnership, and this interrelation (discouraging divorce or remarriage for *either* partner) was influential even before Christian theologians articulated an absolute prohibition. On the other hand, Justinian—one of the most theocratic and self-consciously Christian Byzantine emperors—explicitly allowed voluntary divorce, reasoning that "since mutual affection is the basis for marriage, by the same token the contrary should rightly be grounds for dissolving it."[49] (A formal declaration was

---

45. In the high medieval tale of Ille and Galeron a knight who was mutilated in a tournament imagines that his wife will no longer be able to love him: see Anthime Fourrier, *Le Courant réaliste dans le roman courtois en France au Moyen Age*, 1 (Paris, 1960), 275–78. At roughly the same time, a Latin text describes how a knight married a woman, "driven by the intensity of his passion" (*duxit uxorem, ad id amoris uehemencia motus*) in *Analecta Dublinensia: Three Medieval Latin Texts*, ed. Marvin Colker (Cambridge, Mass., 1975), 226.

46. Cyrille Vogel, "Les rites de la célébration du mariage: Leur signification dans la formation du lien durant le haut moyen âge," in *Matrimonio*, pp. 456–63, concludes that divorce was actually quite common, and cites several formulas from the early Middle Ages; cf. also Gies, p. 56, citing Charles Galy, *La Famille à l'époque Mérovingienne, étude faite principalement d'après des récits de Grégoire de Tours* (Paris, 1901), p. 107, which allows remarriage explicitly *or* entry into a monastery. It is, nonetheless, explicitly Christian (. . . *sive ad servitium Dei in monasterio aut copolam matrimonii sociare voluerit, licentiam habeat* . . .); grounds for divorce were loss of *caritas* and presence of *discordia* (see, e.g., MGH *Legum* 5.1 [Hannover, 1886] pp. 94, 248, 478). The Burgundian Code, §34, allowed divorce for a fine, as did the *Fuero* of Sepúlveda of 1076 (*Los fueros de Sepúlveda*, eds. Emilio Sáez, Rafael Gibert, Manuel Alvar, and Atilano González Ruiz-Zorrilla [Segovia, Spain, 1954], 16, pp. 45–51).

47. Pope Leo the Great, as cited above, n. 8, and discussed in Wolff, p. 101 n. 285. Note the circumstance that the man in this case has a concubine and is still considering marriage.

48. See p. 32.

49. *Novellae* 140: *Nam si mutua affectio matrimonia contrahit, merito eadem contraria sententia ex consensu solvit, repudiis missis quae eam declarent.*

required.)[50] The same was true of most Christians in late antiquity: "When Egyptians wanted a divorce, for instance, they did not allow Christian teaching to stand in their way. Though once persuaded by a priest to take back her ne'er-do-well husband, Aurelia Attiaena of Oxyrhynchus eventually had no hesitation about sending him a bill of repudiation, 'according to Imperial law.' "[51]

Because, in fact, the prescriptions of Christian theologians regarding divorce considerably exceeded any scriptural warrant, one might reasonably infer that they followed rather than fashioned the social patterns of antiquity. And divorce persisted in Christian Europe in several forms throughout the Middle Ages, despite vigorous denunciation of it from theological circles. In much of Western Europe Christians obtained overt authorization for divorce from ecclesiastical authorities,[52] and in most times and places wealthy or well-connected Catholics could arrange an annulment: an official declaration that there had never been a valid marriage. Although theologically different from divorce, and theoretically consistent with official prohibitions of it, annulment was *functionally* a divorce that allowed remarriage.

Concubinage, too, remained common, often public. For males, it was seen as a compromise with the terrible power of sexuality, morally better than recourse to prostitutes.[53] For females, it was often imag-

---

[50]. Subsequent imperial enactments withdrew this concession, but it is indicative of how inadequate confessional sympathies can be as guidelines for interpreting ancient social and moral developments. For a more detailed treatment of the changes in Justinian's legislation, see Brundage, pp. 114–17.

[51]. Peter Brown, *The Body and Society*, p. 251.

[52]. See, for example, MGH *Legum* 5.1: *Formulae*, ed. Karl Zeumer (Hannover, 1886), "Marculfi formularium," 2, in which a number of formulas for divorce are printed (e.g., 30, p. 94) for the everyday use of scribes; they were obviously useful and necessary documents. Cf. Vogel, "Les rites de la célébration du mariage," p. 457.

[53]. Surprisingly, perhaps, prostitution was explicitly permitted in nearly all Christian states till the Protestant Reformation, and often a social institution of considerable importance, as it is again in much of Christian Europe, though now regulated. See CSTH, pp. 7, 228, 261–64, and, more recently, Leah Otis, *Prostitution in Medieval Society: The History of an Institution in Languedoc* (Chicago, 1985), and Ruth Karras, "Holy Harlots: Prostitute Saints in Medieval Legend," *Journal of the History of Sexuality* 1 (1990), 3–32, eadem, "The Regulation of Brothels in Later Medieval England," *Signs: Journal of Women in Culture and Society* 14 (1989), 399–433. Soon to appear are Ruth Karras, "Prostitution in Medieval English Culture," in *Sexuality in the Middle Ages and Renaissance*, eds. Jacqueline Murray and Konrad Eisenbichler, and eadem, *Common Women: Prostitution and Sexuality in Medieval England* (forthcoming from Oxford University Press). Most Christian moralists considered it a vice if a man resorted to or a woman became a prostitute, but almost all viewed the institution itself as necessary to society, and few theologians argued that the state could not tolerate the practice because it

ined to be a necessity, *faute de mieux:* St. Augustine (perhaps influenced by his own long experience with a concubine) professed himself willing to regard any woman who intended to be faithful to a man she was *living with* as "married" to him.[54]

Guntram, a Lombard king of early medieval Orléans, had four sons by different concubines.[55] In fourteenth-century Spain, ultimately noted as the home of extremes of orthodoxy and the Spanish Inquisition, the famous law code of Alfonso the Wise specifically allowed legal concubinage, while duly noting that the church prohibited it.[56] It argued that ancient wise men had allowed concubinage (with a single woman) because it is better to sleep with one woman than many (as in recourse to prostitutes).[57] Males and females also regularly cohabited before they were officially married.[58]

There was, however, some effort on the part of theologians (and later, canon lawyers) to persuade the populace that official heterosexual marriage was the sole legitimate erotic relationship between a man and a woman, and that those willing to compromise with fleshly desires (as opposed to pursuing celibacy, by all accounts a more nearly perfect lifestyle) must do so in the context of an exclusive and permanent covenant—though not necessarily a Christian one.

Justinian's toleration of divorce, on the grounds that "mutual consent" *made* marriage, reflected the persistence in Christian thought of traditional (though pagan) Roman views that mutual consent and marital affection (still difficult to define) were the primary constituents of legal matrimony. Thus, in the ninth century Pope Nicholas I, writing to the Bulgarian tsar, cited the fourth-century patristic authority John Chrysostom—not the *Digest*—as teaching that "it is not

---

was immoral, although by the High and later Middle Ages many other activities (e.g., gambling, divorce, homosexual behavior) would be prohibited on precisely such grounds.

54. *De bono conjugali* 5.5 (*PL* 40:376–77; *CSEL* 41.193–94).

55. Paul the Deacon, *History of the Lombards*, MGH SSRRLL (Hannover, 1878; repr. 1988) 3:34; repeated in Primat's thirteenth-century recapitulation: *Les grandes chroniques*, ed. Jules Viard (Paris, 1920), §24.

56. *VII Partidas* 4.14.

57. Many medieval monarchies also allowed prostitution, although it was technically sinful: see *CSTH*, pp. 212, 282; Leah Otis, *Prostitution in Medieval Society* (as above); and Jacques Rossiaud, *Prostituzione nel Medioevo* (Rome, 1986), translated into English by Lydia Cochrane as *Medieval Prostitution* (New York, 1988). Cf. n. 53, above.

58. See, e.g., Gerald of Wales, *Descriptio Kambriae*, ed. James Dimock (London, 1868), 2.6, pp. 213–14.

coitus that makes marriage, but intention."[59] The obvious import of this was that any two consenting adults could contract a marriage, so long as there was no stated impediment such as blood relationship.

What, in Christian eyes, were to be the bases for moral marriage? St. Jerome listed beauty, good character, and honorable parents as the prime characteristics to be sought in a wife, and wealth and health in a husband, but added that "these things rarely come together in a marriage."[60] Clement of Alexandria had specifically considered love (ἔρως) a bad reason for marrying; reason (λογίσμος) a good one.[61] St. Augustine wrote in his *Confessions* that he desired "fame, wealth, and marriage":[62] if the first two were not deliberately connected with the third, the context is at least revealing. Isidore of Seville had pointed to virtue, heritage, physical comeliness, and wisdom as the most desirable qualities in a male; beauty, descent, wealth, and good character in the female,[63] but added that good character was to be preferred to beauty, suggesting that passionate love was not the ultimate desideratum of heterosexual marriage in his mind. At about the same time the Talmud suggested to Jews that whoever chose a wife for purely pecuniary reasons would have unworthy children.[64] Considerably later, in the thirteenth century Caesar of Heisterbach (3.6) listed beauty, wealth, and lineage as valid reasons for marriage. But despite this sort of opinion and Chrysostom's view, in the more ascetic and

[59] . . . . *Iohanne Chrysostomo magno doctore testante, qui ait: "Matrimonium non facit coitus, sed voluntas,"* PL 119:980 and MGH *Epp.* 5 (Hannover, 1925), 569–70; this opinion is cited in the *Decretum* of Ivo of Chartres 8.17, and his *Panormia* 6.117, and, most important, in the *Decretum* of Gratian 2.27.2.1–3 (Friedlander, 1:1063–64). The whole question is well discussed in Jean Gaudemet, "Le Legs du droit roman in matière matrimoniale," in *Matrimonio* 1:139–79; also Laiou, p. 193. On the other hand, Chrysostom also argued that "love and desire" (ἔρωτα καὶ πόθον) were the ultimate constituents of marriage (σουνοίκησις): Δι' οὐδὲν γὰρ ἡ συνοίκησις αὕτη νενομοθέτηται, ἢ δι' ἔρωτα καὶ πόθον (*Adversus eos qui subintroductas habent virgines* 5 [PG 47:502]).

[60] Adv. Jovinianum 1.47: *cum definisset, si pulcra esset, si bene morata, si honestis parentibus, si ipse sanus ac dives, sic sapientem inire aliquando matrimonium, statim intulit: "haec autem raro in nuptiis universa concordant."*

[61] *Stromata* 2.18 (PG 8:1020).

[62] 6:6: *inhiabam honoribus, lucris, coniugio.*

[63] Isidore of Seville, *Etym.* 9.7.28–29: *In eligendo marito quattuor spectari solent: virtus, genus, pulchritudo, sapientia.* . . . *Item in eligenda uxore quattuor res inpellunt hominem ad amorem: pulchritudo, genus, divitiae, mores. Melius tamen si in ea mores quam pulchritudo quaeratur. Nunc autem illae quaeruntur, quas aut divitiae aut forma, non quas probitas morum commendat.* Trans. Treggiari, *Roman Marriage*, p. 86, but I disagree with her "manliness" for *virtus*: although it is a sexist term, it should be rendered as "virtue."

[64] Kiddushin 4.1 (70a).

antisexual West marriage was generally idealized as a form of intense friendship, and almost never as a means of fulfilling erotic needs. "Insofar as all sexual relations were an enslavement of the human will, marital sex could not be completely exonerated. Ideally, it was to be a brief, transitory element in an enduring relationship of love and friendship which existed not because of, but despite sexuality."[65] Aquinas, for example, summarized the theological tradition to his day by calling matrimony the "greatest friendship." "Between a husband and wife," he opined, "the greatest friendship appears to subsist; they are united not only in the carnal act of copulation, which even among animals inspires a certain sweet tenderness, but also in the sharing of all domestic living arrangements."[66]

The ambivalent role of love in marriage was eloquently evoked in medieval literature. "A woman does not inquire first about her lover's beauty or morals," observes William of Blois in his play Alda, which is, ironically, largely about eroticism. "No, her first questions concern the price that he is willing and able to pay."[67] In a popular literary work of the High Middle Ages a ruler is depicted as prohibiting absolutely the choosing of a wife on the basis of her beauty: wealth alone was to be the criterion;[68] but elsewhere in the same work great ambivalence is evident on the same issue.[69] When the protagonist Gisippus in Boccaccio's tale of Titus and Gisippus (Day 10, Story 8) is urged by his family to marry, he is willing for them to arrange it. They

---

65. Cohen and Horowitz, "Rituals of Marriage," p. 239.
66. *Maxima amicitia: inter virum autem et uxorem maxima amicitia esse videtur: adunantur enim non solum in actu carnalis copulae, quae etiam inter bestias quandam suavem societatem facit, sed etiam at totius domesticae conversationis consortium. . . .* From *Summa contra gentiles* 3.123. It is surprising that Aquinas would link friendship with carnal relations, which most of the ancients would not have done; but note that heterosexual marriage was rarely (if ever) discussed in essays on friendship in the ancient world (e.g., Cicero, Aristotle). In the New Testament, wives are discussed as properly being φιλάνδροι (Titus 2:4), a word that connotes friendship (and which the KJV renders as "love their husbands").
67. P. 113 in "Alda," ed. and trans. Marcel Wintzmeiller, in *La "comedie" latine en France au XII siècle*, ed. Gustave Cohen (Paris, 1931), 107–51.
68. *Gesta Romanorum*, ed. Hermann Oesterley (Berlin, 1872), Tale 277, pp. 678–80.
69. In the same work (Tale 75) a woman says she would marry for "riches, power or beauty," and her sister replies that true love cannot be founded on mercenary interest. Tale 77 recounts the case of one beautiful but poor woman and one homely heiress: the men uniformly prefer the beautiful one. In Tale 81 a queen and her champion marry purely for reasons of state, but in time become "attached" to each other; in 121 an old knight marries a young woman for her beauty while a young knight marries an older woman for her wealth. When they meet the young man falls in love with the older man's wife. Although Tale 151 seems to include what would today be called "wife-swapping," the motivation for this is actually land, not lust.

find him a beautiful fifteen-year-old Athenian girl.[70] But his friend[71] Titus falls in love with the bride-to-be, and Gisippus then wants Titus to have her. This is not easy, since arrangements have already been made for Gisippus to marry Sophronia. It is done by Gisippus' celebrating the "nuptials" (chiefly a wedding banquet at home)[72] and then duping Sophronia into sleeping with Titus, who in the darkness places a ring on her hand. Boccaccio (or his storyteller) clearly felt these were the crucial elements of matrimony, though contemporary theologians disagreed.[73]

One marriage here was for practical reasons; one for love. The practical was depicted as normal and conventional; the marriage for love appeared more romantic, more dramatically interesting, and more unusual.[74] The tale, which had been known in Europe for centuries before Boccaccio retold it,[75] was set in the ancient world, but its continued popularity suggests that Europeans found it appealing and satisfying rather than alien and incomprehensible.

70. I use "girl" here advisedly, not as a casually sexist derogation; fifteen is certainly still "girlhood" in modern understandings. On the other hand, when a nobleman tried to marry a four-year-old peasant girl in twelfth-century England, the bishop objected vehemently: see Adam of Eynsham, *Magna vita sancti Hugonis,* ed. and trans. D. L. Douie and H. Farmer (London, 1962), 2:23–24. Poor parents probably sold daughters of this age.

71. Boccaccio characterizes their friendship as *una fratellanza,* but given the heterosexual nature of this story, and of the *Decameron* in general, too much should not be made of this. In the same tale Titus reproaches himself for feeling passion for his friend's fiancée rather than viewing her, as he should, as a "sister" (*sorella*). There is much irony in the work; it is difficult to be sure that this is not all ironic. A further interesting aspect of this story is its resemblance to Lucian's *Toxaris* in its exaggerated claims for friendship: when Gisippus meets Titus in Rome and believes he has snubbed him, he confesses to a murder so he will be put to death. But Titus then, also falsely, confesses to spare Gisippus. (In the end, the real murderer confesses, and both Titus and Gisippus are released.)

72. A "wedding" in 10.10 seems to involve only the public exchange of vows and a feast.

73. On the reality of marriage, as opposed to the theory (for which see Brundage, nearly passim), see Michel Parisse, *Noblesse et chevalerie en Lorraine médiévale: Les familles nobles du XIe au XIIIe siècle* (Nancy, France, 1982), Chapter 6.

74. In the same story Titus tries to rouse himself to act on his love for Sophronia by repeating to himself that "the laws of love are more powerful than any others" (*le leggi d'amore sono di maggior potenzia che alcune altre*). But see n. 71 about irony, and Michael Clanchy, "Law and Love in the Middle Ages," in *Disputes and Settlements: Law and Human Relations in the West* (Cambridge, 1983), 47–68.

75. It occurs in the *Gesta Romanorum,* Tale 171, where it is attributed to Petrus Alfonsi, in whose *Disciplina clericalis* it is in fact the second story. Alfonsi was a Jew from Islamic Spain who converted to Christianity. Petrus Alfonsi wrote in the late eleventh/early twelfth century; it is impossible to date the *Gesta Romanorum,* but they are probably thirteenth-century, and the quotation of Alfonsi makes clear that this story was incorporated after he wrote his. In the *Gesta* version the disparity is similar: the European knight (from Baldac) desperately loved a woman whom his Egyptian friend planned to marry for purely practical reasons (she was an heiress), but the latter yielded to friendship.

Given the persistent misgivings of Western Christianity about heterosexual matrimony and its functions, it is hardly surprising that it should have taken until the Fourth Lateran Council in 1215 for the church to declare it a sacrament or to develop elaborate canonical rules about the mode of performing it.[76] In the East, as has been noted, it had already been a public liturgical function for some time. This is no doubt why the earliest Greek liturgical manuscript— Barberini 336,[77] probably written in the eighth century in Italy, where Greek liturgical offices were common into early modern times[78]—contains four ceremonies for sacramental union: one for heterosexual betrothal,[79] two separate ceremonies (called simply "prayers")[80] for heterosexual marriage (each labelled εὐχὴ εἰς γάμους),[81] and a comparable "prayer" for uniting two men.[82]

---

76. Rules of consanguinity, related to incest taboos in nearly every known society, were already so complicated in the ninth century that when Pope Nicholas I wrote to the Bulgarians in that century about licit marriage from a Roman Catholic viewpoint he quailed before having to explain them and said that their new bishop would do so: discussed in Laiou, p. 199.

77. Housed now in the Vatican library, where it was formerly labeled the Barberinum S. Marci, then Barberini 77, and then Barberini III.55; these designations were often employed in works of the nineteenth century. For a discussion and detailed table of contents, see Anselm Strittmatter, "The 'Barberinum S. Marci' of Jacques Goar: Barberinianus graecus 336," EL 47.7 (1933), 329–67. In "Notes on the Byzantine Synapte," Traditio 10 (1954), 51–108, p. 70 n. 21, Strittmatter declined to be more specific than saying that Barberini 336 was post-729. The text is doubly paginated: one set of page numbers is indicated by hand and another is printed onto the text. I have generally given the printed numbers first, as they are more readable, but I have also cited the handwritten numbers, because other references may do so. For additional bibliography on the text (but not on the ceremony) see Paul Canart and Vittorio Peri, Sussidi bibliografici per i manoscritti greci della biblioteca vaticana: Studi e testi 261 (Vatican City, 1970), 143–44.

78. Italy had been ruled by the Byzantine Empire on and off throughout the early Middle Ages; a huge population of Greek-speaking Catholics remained into the twentieth century.

79. Strittmatter, No. 210, p. 376.

80. See Viscuso, "A Byzantine Theology of Marriage," pp. 245–46, where he asserts that in canonical discussions of matrimony the terms "blessing," "prayer," and "crowning" are used to refer to ecclesiastical rites for this purpose.

81. These three occur sequentially, although their numeration by Strittmatter does not indicate this. The first prayer for heterosexual union is titled εὐχὴ εἰς γάμους. It is numbered 212 by Strittmatter, and can be found on p. 186 (according to the printed numbers; p. 377 handwritten) of the manuscript; the second (called εὐχὴ ἄλλη εἰς γάμους) is numbered 216, on p. 188/381. On this ceremony, see Giuseppe Baldanza, "Il rito del Matrimonio nell'Eucologio Barberini 336. Analisi della sua visione teologica," EL 93, 4–5 (1979), 316–51. Although the manuscript itself has never been published, most of the Greek text of the nuptial rite in the Barberini 336 appears (for purposes of comparison) in Gaetano Passarelli, "La cerimonia dello stefanoma (incoronazione) nei riti matrimoniali bizantini secondo il codice cryptense G.b. VII (X sec.)," EL 93, 4–5 (1979), 389–91. It remains unclear which of the two versions is more ancient, and what the differences between them indicate, although Baldanza attempted to address these issues. Baldanza also translated both versions into modern Italian: p. 320, nn. 21–22, and p. 321, n. 23.

82. Printed page numbers 204v–205v; old numbers 413–15. In later years a version for two

All three forms of union persisted among Greek-speaking and other Christians, who often based the wording and form of union ceremonies on the Barberini (or a common prototype). Each also underwent considerable individual development.[83] The manual itself dates from the eighth century, but the ceremonies it records are unquestionably much older, so it is impossible to be sure at what point any of the four developed. The authority who has studied the heterosexual nuptial prayers in most detail concluded that the second of these two ceremonies dated from the second or third century.[84] Possibly the ceremony of same-sex union is equally old, although it is difficult to be sure. There are many similarities of wording between this second heterosexual union ceremony and the ceremony of same-sex union, suggesting substantial mutual influence or parallel development.[85]

Each of these forms of permanent Christian union has a different name. The first is called μνηστεία, the normal word for engagement, or betrothal, which was considered an irrevocable bond between a male and a female in the Middle Ages, in both East and West.[86] (But the usual word for the ceremony itself was ἀρραβών.) The verb from which μνηστεία is derived—μνηστεύω—conveyed a much broader range of meanings, from "woo" to "espouse" to "entrust," so that although it unquestionably could mean "betrothal,"[87] it was far from the most specific word for such a ceremony, and could in fact have

---

women would be developed. Although ἀδελφο– could be understood to apply to women, there is no reason to believe that this particular ceremony was not for two men.

83. See works cited above, nn. 1 & 7, especially Stevenson, pp. 97–100, for heterosexual ceremonies. For same-sex unions, see discussion following.

84. Giuseppe Baldanza, "Il rito del Matrimonio nell'Eucologio Barberini 336," as cited above. The reasons are given on pp. 329–34; the conclusion on p. 334.

85. Note that this is not a ceremony for a second marriage, which remained controversial in the East well beyond this point: in the canons of Nicephorus at the beginning of the following century, it was stipulated that second marriage be marked only by a wedding banquet for ten friends (Ritzer, p. 106), and as late as the twelfth century in the West, Gratian, who codified the law of the Western church, termed second marriage "honest fornication" (*Decretum* 2.31.1.9, Friedberg 1:1110). (Gratian attributed this opinion to Chrysostom, but the *correctores* were less sure.) On the ancient origins of this prejudice, see Michel Humbert, *Le remariage à Rome: Étude d'histoire juridique et sociale* (Milan, 1972).

86. See, e.g., Schwerdtfeger, pp. 114–21.

87. The normal word for an "engaged" person in the New Testament is derived from this word, but the Gospels never mention a ceremony, and the question of what "betrothed" means and how it relates to several New Testament texts is much disputed: see Chapter 1, "The Vocabulary of Love and Marriage," pp. 14–15.

referred to a variety of other ceremonies, related to marriage or not.[88] Because of its content and the fact that there are elaborate rules in Greek canon law about betrothal, most often (though not invariably) using μνηστεία as the rubric, it seems reasonable to assume that this was a form of heterosexual betrothal. Betrothal was often performed in conjunction with matrimony—sometimes immediately before. Once the betrothal ceremony had been performed publicly in the Greek-speaking Christian world, only the death of one of the two parties could excuse the other from honoring it.

The second and third ceremonies are both labeled "prayer for marriage": εὐχὴ εἰς γάμος. Γάμος was also the most common Greek word (e.g., in civil and canonical law) for heterosexual matrimony, although it was not the usual word for the ceremony that actually created this relationship, which was more often some derivative of στέφανος, "crown." For example, of the forty-five ceremonies of heterosexual matrimony printed in the largest published collection of Greek liturgical documents only ten rely on the word γάμος; the others use στεφάνωμα or its derivatives either alone or in combination with γάμος.[89] Jacob Goar, the Dominican who edited a critical edition of the Greek prayer books (generally called Euchologia)[90] for the first time in 1647, using the liturgical manuals available in Western libraries, picked up on this general rubric and published the ceremony of heterosexual matrimony under the title "Office of Crowning,"[91] although "crowning" hardly meant "marriage" to Western Christians in any language. Greek liturgical influence was so powerful in Italy that in Italian incoronazione was a common word for what would in Latin be called matrimonium or in English a "wedding."

Given what has already been adduced about the veneration of same-sex pairs (especially military saints) in the early church, and a

---

88. On this, see Lampe, s.v. μνηστεύω and ἀρραβών.
89. Stevenson notes that "crowning" was already understood to refer to heterosexual matrimony in the fifth century in Egypt, where Greek was a native language.
90. Εὐχή is Greek for "prayer" of any sort. Euchologies thus contained more than the official "offices" performed in a church or monastery. This is part of the reason Western liturgical books, usually limited to official ecclesiastical usages, were by and large called "sacramentaries."
91. Ἀκολουθία τοῦ στεφανώματος, on p. 314 of the revised and corrected Venice edition of 1730. Similarly, Edmund Martène, De antiquis ecclesiae ritibus libri tres (Venice, 1788), 1:9:16, published (in Latin) his translation from the Greek euchology of "Ordo servari solitus in sponsalibus celebrandis, videlicet in nuptiarum subarrhatione," under the title "Officium coronationis nuptiarum."

corresponding ambivalence about heterosexual matrimony, it is hardly surprising that there should have been a Christian ceremony solemnizing same-sex unions. Even the Barberini heterosexual marriage ceremony somewhat defensively invokes God as the "architect of nature"—a peculiarly nonscriptural phrase[92] obviously intended to justify a Christian blessing on an ordinary biological aspect of human life.[93] It is followed by the prayerful assertion that God is the "lawmaker for marriage" and has deemed it "not prohibited to all,"[94] a considerable demotion from the already lukewarm "honorable" of the New Testament.[95] By contrast, the same-sex union prayers specifically invoked much admired paired male saint couples,[96] including

[92.] The concept of "nature" (φύσις) occurs rarely in the New Testament, in contrast to much Greek writing of the time, in which it was prominent. See comments in CSTH, pp. 109–13. Baldanza (p. 332) agreed that this phrase seems defensive.

[93.] Similar phrases, slightly modified but still defensive, occur in the fifteenth-century Euchologion identified in Dmitrievskij (No. LXIV) as Holy Sepulcher, Istanbul 8 (182).

[94.] ὁ τοῦ παντὸς κόσμου δημιουργὸς Θεός, ὁ τῆς φύσεως εὑ[ε]ρ[γ]έτης, καὶ τοῦ γάμου νομοθέτης, ὁ τοῦτον μὴ βδέλυκτον εἶναι πᾶσι ηὐδόκησας (Barberini 336, p. 188/381). Βδέλυγμα was the word in the Septuagint for sexual acts prohibited to Jews (e.g., at Lev. 18:22 and 20:13). It is striking to find it here considered and rejected as a description of legitimate matrimony.

[95.] But the line from the New Testament was also invoked in heterosexual marriage ceremonies: in a tenth-century ceremony (Gaetano Passarelli, L'Eucologio cryptense Γ.β. VII [sec. X] [Thessalonika, Greece, 1982] [Ἀνάλεκτα βλατάδων, 36], No. 166.10) there is a prayer in the litany that the marriage might be "honorable" and the bed "undefiled" or "pure" (χαρίσηται αὐτοῖς τίμιον τὸν γάμον καὶ τὴν κοίτην ἀμίαντον). Since ἀμίαντος was often used specifically of virgins, and especially of the Blessed Virgin Mary (as in Athanasius [PG 25:109c], Gregory of Nyssa [PG 46:324b]), of worship (James 1:27), or of God Himself (Heb. 7:26 [Christ], Methodius [PG 18.37]), it would be easy to take this to indicate an expectation that the couple would not have sex, but this, though possible, seems unlikely. (It seems more likely an expression of hope about the state of the woman at the time of the marriage: cf. Holy Sepulcher, Istanbul, 8 (182), Dmitrievskij No. LXIV, p. 464: τοὺς παρθενικοὺς γάμους. In Γ.β. VII (Passarelli No. 166.9) the litany includes the prayer that the couple's life together will remain "blameless" and "not condemned" (τοῦ ἄμεμπτον καὶ ἀκατάγνωστον τὴν συμβίωσιν αὐτῶν διαμεῖναι). Often nuptial prayers appealed for protection from the devil (e.g., the Canterbury Benedictional: see Stevenson, p. 65); such prayers were a commonplace in an age when most people believed in a real devil, but in this particular context they probably disclose underlying misgivings about the institution.

[96.] Most of these ceased in time to be invoked as pairs in this context (though they were often commemorated as paired saints): they included Peter and Paul (discussed below), Peter and Andrew, Jacob and John, Philip and Bartholomew, Cosmas and Damian, and Cyrus and John. Note that all were originally invoked as pairs, although some (e.g., Cosmas and Damian) were actually biological brothers, which is doubtless why they passed out of the ceremony as time wore on. For Cyrus and John, see the early medieval life by Sophronius ("Narratio miraculorum SS. Cyri et Joannis sapientium anargyrorum," PG 87, 3:3380–3673), and secondary analysis in R. P. S. Vailhé, "Sophrone le sophiste et sophrone le patriarche," in Revue de l'orient chrétien 7 (1902), 360–85, and Paul Peeters, Orient et Byzance: Le tréfonds oriental de l'hagiographie byzantine (Subsidia hagiographica 20), (Brussels, 1950) esp. 3.7.

saints Serge and Bacchus, well known archetypes of Christian same-sex pairing.

The name of the fourth ceremony of union is the most difficult to translate: εὐχὴ εἰς ἀδελφοποίησις. One translation would be "prayer for making brothers,"[97] but there are many cogent reasons to regard this as a misleading translation, and to consider this set of "prayers" the same-sex equivalent of the others. Some of these reasons have been discussed in earlier chapters: they range from the peculiar history of "sibling" as a term of romantic endearment in biblical literature (e.g., the Song of Songs, the Book of Tobit—always a part of the Greek Old Testament, David's lament for Jonathan), and echoes of such phrases in the terms of romantic affection employed by such famous paired saints as Nearchos and Polyeuct[98] and Serge and Bacchus,[99] to ordinary parlance[100]—all undoubtedly familiar to compilers of the liturgical manual.[101] Others are assessed in Chapter 1, "The Vocabulary of Love and Marriage."

Medieval usage perpetuated this conflation. In Abelard's high medieval Latin reworking of David's lament for Jonathan, David says "*more* than a brother to me, Jonathan" (*plus fratre mihi, Ionatha*).[102] "Brother" and "sister" are used as terms of intimacy between male lovers in two of the best-known poetical collections of the Middle Ages (*The Cambridge Songs*[103] and *Carmina*

[97.] See discussion of this term in Chapter 1, "The Vocabulary of Love and Marriage," p. 19.

[98.] Not invoked in the ceremony.

[99.] Invoked in all examples of the ceremony. On the use of this term by the two, see p. 151.

[100.] Latin literature as exemplified in Petronius, an unusually accurate observer of—indeed, our major source for—quotidian speech, and reflected in the *Greek Anthology* by the transliteration of *frater* into Greek as φράτερ: see Chapter 3, n. 75.

[101.] It is, of course, also an obvious term of affection between men: St. Augustine used it of Alypius, with whom he lived for most of his adult life (*frater cordis mei*: from *Confessions* 9:4). There is no reason to assume that the relationship was erotic, and also no reason to presume that it was not. Although after his conversion to Christianity Augustine appears to have disapproved of homosexual behavior, he might well have conceptualized a long-standing passionate friendship as something else.

[102.] Abelard (d. 1142) was one of the most learned men of his day, and quite noted for his heterosexual exploits. The poem is reprinted in *The Oxford Book of Medieval Latin Verse*, rev. ed. F. J. E. Raby (Oxford, 1959), No. 172, pp. 246–50.

[103.] The collection was made in the eleventh century; the precise date of individual pieces is not known. In the poem "Lantfrid and Cobbo" (first published in Karl Strecker, *Die Cambridger Lieder* [Berlin, 1926], 18–20; reprinted in *The Oxford Book of Medieval Latin Verse*, as cited in previous note, No. 119, pp. 163–66) the two intimate friends are first described as "two in one" (*quasi duo unus esset*, l. 29)—a characteristic description of matrimonial harmony—and are both referred to by the poet as "brother-friend" (*fratri sotio* [sic]) and use the term "brother" to each other, at least as imagined by the poet (*Hortor, frater, maneas . . . frater fratri facias*, ll. 54, 58). This poem and its significance are discussed in *CSTH*, pp. 193–94.

burana),[104] and "brother" and "sister" were used between husbands and wives in a variety of medieval literary sources, including those in which love was assumed to subsist within marriage.[105]

In addition to Barberini 336, there are at least seven other known versions of such a ceremony from before the twelfth century, from the monastery of St. Catherine on Mount Sinai,[106] Paris,[107] Petersburg,[108] and the Greek Basilian monastery of Grottaferrata,[109] south of Rome. During the twelfth century there was a virtual explosion of copies of the ceremony, with at least seventeen surviving (in Old Church Slavonic and Greek) from the monastery of St. Catherine on Mount Sinai,[110] the Vatican,[111]

---

104. A twelfth-century collection found in a thirteenth-century monastic manuscript at Benediktbeuern. "Deus pater, adiuva" is found on folios 52v–53r of the text, but was only rarely published as part of the collection, e.g., by J. A. Schmeller, in his original edition (*Carmina burana: lateine und deutsche Lieder und Gedichte einer Handschrift des XIII Jahrhunderts aus Benediktbeuern*, in *Bibliothek des literarischen Vereins in Stuttgart*, 16 [1847]), and by Alfons Hilka and O. Schumann, *Carmina Burana* (Heidelberg, 1930–70), No. 127. Later editors, perhaps out of reticence, often neglected it, though it is unquestionably a part of the manuscript. Schumann may have overcome this prudery because he had published a separate article on the poem, "Über einige *Carmina Burana*," *Zeitschrift für deutsches Altertum* 45 (1926), 81–99. The poem is also reprinted, with German translation, in the bilingual edition of the Deutscher Taschenbuch Verlag of 1979. Two complete English translations are available: one in *CSTH*, pp. 378–80, with analysis on p. 250, and one in *Medieval Latin Poems of Male Love and Friendship*, trans. Thomas Stehling, No. 7 in the *Garland Library of Medieval Literature* (New York, 1984), No. 117, pp. 127–29 (with Latin text). The quarrel in the poem is obviously between lovers, one of whom plans to join a monastery while the other asserts that both would then be lonely. In the end the one planning to enter monastic life changes his mind, exclaiming, "Dry your tears, brother" (*Parce, frater, fletibus*, l. 60). It is possible that *frater* in this context is a bitterly ironic monastic term, but given the level of sophistication in the poem this seems quite unlikely.

105. E.g., in the fabliau "Estormi," in *The French Fabliau*, B.N. MS 837, ed. and trans. Raymond Eichmann and John DuVal (New York, 1984), ll. 41 and 44; and in the *Gesta romanorum*, ed. Hermann Oesterley (Berlin, 1872), Chapter 18, pp. 311–13.

106. Sinai 957 from the ninth or tenth century, Sinai 958 from the tenth (both published in Dmitrievskij, Nos. I and III respectively), and Sinai 959 from the eleventh century (also in Dmitrievskij No. V).

107. Coislin 213, of the year 1027, also in Dmitrievskij, No. CLXII. These manuscripts were not produced in France, although those housed in the Vatican probably were written in Italy, which had a large Greek-speaking population throughout the Middle Ages.

108. Codex Greek No. 226 of the tenth century, partially published with commentary in André Jacob, «L'Euchologe de Porphyre Uspenski. Cod. Leningr. gr.226 (Xe siècle)» *Le Muséon: Revue d'études orientales* 78:1–2 (1965), 173–214.

109. This monastery houses many remarkable versions of the ceremony. The earliest (from the tenth century) is Γ.β. VII, published in Gaetano Passarelli, *L'Eucologio cryptense Γ.β. VII* (Thessalonika, Greece, 1982), pp. 130–133, translated in Appendix of Translations, No. 3.

110. Four in Greek: 962, 961, 973, and 1036; one in Slavonic from the *Euchologium Sinaiticum*, the most important liturgical document surviving in that language. This version is translated in the Appendix of Translations, No. 6.

111. Barberini 329, 345, 431, and *Vaticani graeci* 1552, 1554, 1811, 1872, and 1875.

Paris,[112] and Grottaferrata.[113] A slightly smaller number is preserved from the thirteenth century, now housed at Grottaferrata,[114] the Vatican,[115] the monastery of St. Catherine on Mount Sinai,[116] Mount Athos,[117] and on the island of Patmos.[118] Fewer still are known from the fourteenth century,[119] a dark and troubled period for Europe and the Mediterranean in general, but in the fifteenth century there was a resurgence, producing about nine manuscript exemplars.[120] Eleven copies are known from the sixteenth century, the last gasp of manuscript production before printing became the standard mode of disseminating texts.[121]

Most of these ceremonies were written in Greek, either in Italy (where the largest number survive) or in Greece or the Levant; three are in Slavic liturgical languages. No examples survive in Latin, although the ceremony was performed in areas like Ireland,[122] where neither Greek nor Slavic would have been familiar. If Latin versions were used, they must have been lost or destroyed (on the latter possibility, see p. 264). Some Sinai manuscripts[123] give unmistakable evidence in marginal translations and commentary that the ceremony was familiar to Arabic-speaking Christians in Arabic, although no complete Arabic versions survive.

In other words, the ceremony occurs in manuscript collections from all over the Christian world—from Italy to the island of Patmos to the monastery of St. Catherine on Mount Sinai—and is found in some of the oldest Greek liturgical manuscripts known. By the time

---

112. Grec 330 and 392, Coislin 214. These manuscripts were, of course, not written in France, but brought to the collection of Greek liturgical documents now housed in the Bibliothèque nationale.
113. Γ.β. I.
114. Γ.β. VI (only the beginning is preserved; the rest is torn out: see p. 264) and Γ.β. III.
115. Barberini 293, 443; Vaticani graeci 1840.
116. Sinai 960, 966, 982, and 971.
117. Lavra St. Athanasios, published in Dmitrievskij No. XX.
118. Patmos 104 and 105, Dmitrievskij Nos. XIV and XVII.
119. A Slavonic version in the Hilferding collection: see p. 374, n. 16; Sinai 981 (No. XXXIX in Dmitrievskij); Lavra St. Athanasios from Mt. Athos (No. XLVII in Dmitrievskij), and Paris grec 324.
120. Four in Greek from Mt. Athos, two Slavic versions (one translated in Appendix of Translations), and three other Greek versions: Istanbul 8(182) and Sinai 972, 977.
121. Seven of these are in Mt. Athos libraries; one is Athens University 94; Istanbul 615(757), Patmos 703, and Sinai 989 comprise the rest. The ceremony was printed for a while: see comments on Goar, below.
122. See Chapter 7, pp. 259–61.
123. 958 (tenth century), 959 (eleventh century), 961 (tenth or eleventh century).

such manuals were being put into print, however, prejudice against any form of same-sex interaction was so pronounced in the West that the Dominican Jacob Goar, the first to publish it, felt obliged to comment, "It should be known that although this ceremony is prohibited in both ecclesiastical and civil law, we have printed it because we found it in many manuscript books."[124] It is far from clear what "civil" laws forbade the ceremony, and ecclesiastical law only prohibited it to monks. Possibly Goar was simply expressing his own repugnance, which would in itself be revealing.

Initially the ceremony of same-sex union was, like the heterosexual ceremony in the Barberini manuscript, merely a set of prayers, but by the time of the flowering of liturgical marriage ceremonies in the twelfth century it had become a full office, involving the burning of candles, the placing of the two parties' hands on the Gospel, the joining of their right hands, the binding of their hands (or covering their heads) with the priest's stole, an introductory litany (like that in Barberini No. 1), crowning, the Lord's Prayer, Communion,[125] a kiss, and sometimes circling around the altar. Some of these features will be unfamiliar to readers not already acquainted with the historical development of matrimonial ritual, and require some explanation here. A few—such as the liturgical use of candles[126] or a kiss in a ceremony of union—do not.

Few of the known manuscripts have previously been published;[127]

---

124. Ἰστέον ὅτι ταύτην τὴν ἀκολουθίαν, εἰ καὶ παρὰ τοῦ ἐκκλεσιαστικοῦ καὶ βασιλικοῦ νόμου ἐκωλύθη ἐπιτελεῖσθαι, ἀλλ᾽ ἡμεῖς ἐτυπώσαμεν, καθὼς καὶ ἐν ἄλλοις πολλοῖς βίβλοις εὑρήκαμεν, Goar (ed. of 1730), p. 706. Goar's version of this ceremony, like most he published, is a conflation of various manuscripts, and is not to be relied on as representing any one version or period.

125. As opposed to the "common cup" of the heterosexual ceremony in Barberini 336, which Ritzer and Stevenson assert is *not* Communion, but a Jewish or pagan remnant. This difference in later same-sex unions is evident from the preceding antiphon "the holy for the holy," which is unequivocally eucharistic, as noted in Meletius Michael Solovey, *The Byzantine Divine Liturgy*, trans. D. E. Wysochansky (Washington, D. C., 1970), 312–13. Note the metamorphosed revival of this ancient Greek saying in the modern Episcopalian pre-Communion antiphon "the gifts of God for the people of God." Ritzer and Stevenson are probably right, but it is worth noting the opinion of Viscuso (cited above, n. 80), pp. 245–46, that Communion is rarely mentioned even in canonical discussions of heterosexual matrimony and must be *inferred*.

126. See Ritzer, p. 143; Ritzer says here, n. 554, that the carrying of candles by the couple at the outset of a heterosexual ceremony is first mentioned in the thirteenth century in Patmos 105, published in Dmitrievskij, p. 169. Stevenson agrees (p. 100). But candles are first used in the ceremony of same-sex union centuries before this, in Grottaferrata Γ.β. II, from the eleventh century, translated in Appendix of Translations, No. 4.

127. When they have been published this is duly noted, even though no previous editors have

a number are translated in the Appendix of Translations, and editions of some are provided in the Appendix of Documents. The precise contents of both heterosexual and same-sex ceremonies are analyzed and compared in the following chapter.

Little is known with certainty about the compiling of liturgical manuals or even the mode of composition of particular prayers and offices they contain. There is much tradition and speculation that various patristic authorities devised this or that part of a given ceremony, but in fact most probably developed through accretion of local practice and eloquent individual clerics. Location in manuscripts is for this and other reasons not necessarily a reliable clue to the nature of a text. In the Leonine sacramentary, for example, the nuptial prayers are placed under the heading "September" observances, follow prayers for consecrating virgins, and are followed in turn by prayers in time of drought—none of which would provide any clue to the meaning or proper context of the ceremony. In the Gelasian sacramentary the heterosexual nuptial ceremony follows a form for Mass in a monastery and various monastic prayers—hardly a likely context for a heterosexual marriage ceremony—and is followed by prayers for legitimate birth and against a woman's sterility, which seem more appropriate.

The ceremony for same-sex union[128] occurs in a wide variety of contexts, ranging from the blessing of seed[129] to a boy's first haircut[130] to adoption of a child,[131] but by far the most common context is marriage, usually in the following order: heterosexual betrothal,

---

recognized the significance of the ceremony: see commentary on pp. 25–27 and 267ff. By contrast, I have tried to rely on versions of heterosexual marriage ceremonies which are published—since there are many of these—both in the Appendix of Translations and in analytical comparison.

[128.] Ἀδελφοποιήσις in some manuscripts; ἀδελφοποιία in others, usually identified prior to the twelfth century by εὐχὴ εἰς, "prayer for," but after that more commonly by rubrics like ἀκολουθία or τάξις, "office" or "liturgy" (sometimes, as in Vatican Barberini Graecus 329 [twelfth century] Τάξις εἰς τὸ ποιῆσαι ἀδελφούς; Barb.Gr. 345 and Barb.Gr. 293 [thirteenth century] also have Τάξις καὶ ἀκολουθία εἰς ἀδελφοποίησιν). I have generally referred to it in English as the "same-sex union ceremony," for reasons discussed in Chapter 1, "The Vocabulary of Love and Marriage."

[129.] The ceremony following the same-sex union office in the twelfth-century Sinai Euchologion in Old Church Slavonic, translated in Appendix of Translations, No. 6. Mt. Athos Coutloumousi 568 (sixteenth or seventeenth century) also has a blessing of seed following the same-sex union ceremony.

[130.] E.g., in the eighth-century Barberini 336, this both precedes and follows ἀδελφοποιία.

[131.] E.g., in Paris Coislin 213 (dated 1027), adoption precedes and cutting the beard follows.

ceremony for a first heterosexual marriage, ceremony for a second heterosexual marriage (a different office, with less emphasis on procreation), office of same-sex union. About 30 percent of the manuscripts consulted for this study have heterosexual marriage either immediately before or immediately after the same-sex union ceremony,[132] roughly twice as often as the next most common adjacent ceremonies (15 percent have cutting a boy's hair right before or after,[133] and 14 percent have adoption before or after).[134]

A particularly striking juxtaposition published by Dmitrievskij gives a prayer for same-sex union immediately following the "office" for heterosexual marriage but labeled "*another* [italics added] prayer for same-sex union."[135] Further on in the manuscript is a separate "prayer for same-sex union," and it is very difficult to be sure whether this is simply the editor's error, a scribal mistake, a creative mixture of heterosexual and same-sex union ceremonies, or the sole occurrence (to my knowledge) of the same-sex union ceremony twice in the same manuscript.

This alone might suggest the best context for the ceremony were it not for the ostensible improbability of such a liturgical commemoration in the eyes of modern readers, to whom homosexual interest seems a singular evil, profoundly at odds with Christian teaching. Of course, Christians in the early and medieval church had profound misgivings about *all* forms of human sexuality, which is why they

---

[132.] This figure is complicated by the fact that a number of euchologia with highly developed same-sex ceremonies do not contain a heterosexual marriage liturgy at all (e.g., the Sinai Euchologion, the Vatican Barberini grec 345). It is impossible to speculate on what the relationship would be if they had included one.

[133.] Note that hair-cutting (usually of the bride) is associated with heterosexual matrimony in many cultures—even in many Greek cities: see James Redfield, "Notes on the Greek Wedding," *Arethusa* 15 (1982), 181–201, pp. 190–91; W. H. D. Rouse, *Greek Votive Offerings* (Cambridge, 1902), 242; and Herodotus 4.33–35, Euripides, *Hip*.1425, Pausanias 1.18. Fixing the bride's hair a special way was also part of the Roman ceremony.

[134.] Of course some liturgical manuals have only one or the other: the Sinai Euchologion, for example, contains the ceremony of same-sex union but not a heterosexual union ceremony of any sort. The litany of the same-sex union ceremony is one of only three full litanies in this entire collection of many liturgical offices, the other two being that for Pentecost and one for vesting a monk. Athos Athanasios 189 (thirteenth century) (Dmitrievskij XX) also has a ceremony for same-sex union but no office for heterosexual betrothal or matrimony.

[135.] Patmos 104, twelfth to thirteenth century, published in Dmitrievskij XIV, pp. 153–57. The heterosexual ceremony is called Ἀκολουθία τοῦ γάμου (a rare heading) and begins on folio 25v (Dmitrievskij p. 155); according to the published text on folio 30v, without any intervening rubric, is Εὐχὴ ἑτέρα εἰς ἀδελφοποίησιν (p. 156). Then on folio 53r Dmitrievskij prints the rubric Εὐχὴ εἰς ἀδελφοποίησιν without comment or explanation.

idealized celibacy—too much to ask of most people in the very different world of the twentieth century, and a rejection of a principal basis of identity and personal satisfaction even in the eyes of most premodern people. For the most part, even the leaders of the church regarded fornication as fornication, whatever the genders involved.[136] This is still the case in much of the Mediterranean, where *all* deviations from exclusive marital monogamy are viewed with the same combination of theoretical disapproval and Christian forbearance (who is perfect, after all?). As a result, a dalliance by a married man is generally viewed as mildly sinful whether it is with another male or a female, whereas in the West an indiscretion with a person of the same gender would provoke horror and a re-evaluation of the whole identity of the perpetrator. Sexuality between persons joined in some sort of ecclesiastical union, however, probably did not seem even mildly sinful, especially to those who had attended the ceremony.

From a historian's point of view, three nonpolemical questions about the ceremony present themselves:

1. Does it solemnize a personal commitment, as opposed to a religious, political, or family union? The answer to this is unequivocally yes, for reasons almost too obvious to elaborate, but probably worth rehearsing for those who have not examined the other offices in the liturgical manuals. Ceremonies for entering monasteries or receiving Holy Orders (i.e., "becoming brothers" in some sense) occur in most of the same manuscripts, are labeled differently, and are obviously quite distinct in wording, purpose, and symbolism. A treaty of political union using fraternal language is translated in the Appendix of Translations, No. 18. Its many and profound differences from the ceremony of same-sex union will be obvious to the reader. The same-sex union ceremony makes no mention—in any of its varieties in any language —of tribal, clan, or family loyalty or union: it is unmistakably a voluntary, emotional union of two persons (always two: never

---

136. This was true in the early Middle Ages even of the West (see, for example, Gildas on fornication [*Presbiter aut diaconus faciens fornicationem naturalem sive sodomitam*] in *Councils and Ecclesiastical Documents relating to Great Britain and Ireland*, eds. Arthur Haddan and William Stubbs [Oxford, 1869] 1:113, canon 1), and is discussed at greater length in the following chapter. Although this is not the conventional wisdom, it has already been demonstrated in *CSTH*, especially Parts II and III.

more). The only other family relationships to which it might be compared are adoption, discussed separately below, and heterosexual marriage, to which it is indeed closely related, no matter how much some readers may be discomforted by this.

2. Is it homosexual? Certainly in the most obvious sense of this word ("of one sex"): the Greek and Slavic languages leave no doubt about both parties being male or female,[137] nor do the ubiquitous references to male couples such as Serge and Bacchus. (There is an example of the ceremony mentioning two women, but no known examples involving different genders, even though in modern times it was transformed into a looser bond of friendship that might include different genders.)

This question further subdivides into two parts: (a) Was the ceremony "homosexual" in an erotic sense? This is hard to answer for societies without a comparable nomenclature or taxonomy. Most premodern societies drew less rigid distinctions among "romance," "eroticism," "friendship," and "sexuality" than do modern cultures. (b) Did it celebrate a relationship between two men or two women that was (or became) sexual? Probably, sometimes, but this is obviously a difficult question to answer about the past, since participants cannot be interrogated. When heterosexual marriages produced children, it is reasonable to assume that they involved sexual intercourse, but in the case of childless heterosexual couples (usually regarded as "married" by their friends, relatives, and neighbors) it is just as difficult to be sure as it is for same-sex pairs.

It is at least worth noting in this regard that a sexual component is not generally what constitutes the definitive test of "marriage," particularly in premodern societies, where few people married for erotic fulfillment. Even in a culture as preoccupied with sex as the modern West, the vast majority of activities of married couples are not sexual. A much greater percent of their time is spent working, shopping, cleaning, maintaining the household, attending parties or entertainment, taking care of children, friends, or relatives than is devoted to sex itself. Most

---

[137.] Heterosexual marriage ceremonies use masculine and feminine generic names (τόνδε καὶ τήνδε or δοῦλον σοῦ καὶ δούλην). Some Slavic versions envision the possibility of two females, but none of the Greek examplars do.

couples have less and less sex as they age; no one considers them any less "married" as a consequence of this. On the contrary, great longevity is generally considered a sign of a happy and stable marriage whether or not the couple have a lively and satisfying sex life, which is not considered anyone else's business now any more than it was in premodern societies.[138]

3. Was it a marriage? The answer to this question depends to a considerable extent on one's conception of marriage, as noted in the Introduction. According to the modern conception—i.e., a permanent emotional union acknowledged in some way by the community—it was unequivocally a marriage. By ancient standards, it would depend to a considerable extent on the time and place of the ceremony, who was asked, and what they regarded as the purpose and technical definition of marriage. If, for example, the procreation of children was deemed essential to marriage by theologians in a given time and place, it is unlikely they would consider that a same-sex union could constitute a "marriage." But the views of ordinary persons, especially those who witnessed the ceremony and knew the participants, might have been quite different. As has been noted, few modern people would define marriage so narrowly, since many couples in industrial nations have no children and no intention of having them[139] but are nonetheless regarded as "married," as are the many couples who adopt children when they are unable to procreate. This was true in the Middle Ages even of those who held that procreation was God's reason for creating legitimate carnal intercourse. A longstanding couple, with or without children, was likely to be viewed by friends and neighbors as "married." Theological statements predicated on consummation and procreation were always controversial, and doubtless stemmed from ecclesiastical efforts to control and regulate matrimony, particularly to prevent divorce when there were children.

It is worth bearing in mind in this context, moreover, that

---

138. On sex among American couples (including same-sex pairs), see particularly Philip Blumstein and Pepper Schwartz, *American Couples* (New York, 1983).

139. At the time of this writing (December 1992) 42 percent of married American couples are childless, even though the birth rate has climbed sharply in recent years as the "baby boom" generation has decided to have children.

meeting theological or canonistic niceties was probably of less concern to a mostly illiterate Christian community than public symbolism and community acknowledgement—living long together and sharing a home might have been the crucial determinants for a male-female pair in their concrete social context (i.e., among neighbors, friends, and relatives), whether or not they had children or took part in a church service. And in the case of the same-sex ceremony, standing together at the altar with their right hands joined (the traditional symbol of marriage), being blessed by the priest, sharing Communion, and holding a banquet for family and friends afterward[140]—all parts of same-sex union in the Middle Ages—most likely signified a marriage in the eyes of most ordinary Christians.[141]

Moreover, the concept of someone innately and exclusively "homosexual" was largely unknown to the postclassical world, and relationships of this sort were not understood in a sense comparable to modern "gay marriage"—i.e., as a parallel *alternative*—although they did in fact bear much similarity both liturgically and in emotional import. That is to say, although such relationships may have been viewed as irrevocable, consuming, and paramount emotional commitments, "marriage" at the time was not regarded primarily as a means of emotional or sexual fulfillment, but simply as a mechanism for enhancing or perpetuating dynastic succession. Same-sex unions were thus neither a threat to nor a replacement of heterosexual marriage.

Given the native and profound disinclination of most people brought up in modern Christian societies to believe that there could have been a Christian ceremony solemnizing same-sex unions, it may be worth making a few additional observations. It is the ceremonies themselves that speak most eloquently to this question, and since eleven examples are translated in the Appendix 1, along with heterosexual ceremonies of comparable periods, readers may judge for them-

---

[140.] This would obviously not figure in the liturgical office (any more than it does today in heterosexual marriages), but there is ancient pictorial evidence: see pp. 209–10.

[141.] Visible liturgies were probably more influential even outside the Christian community, as Cohen and Horowitz (p. 242) sagely note: "There is no question that the members of any given Jewish community were far more familiar with a Christian wedding procession than with papal bulls and theological tractates, and vice versa."

selves about the relationship. Since, however, interpreting the office as a same-sex union is not only highly controversial but even counterintuitive, it is worth dealing with a few other reservations that might present themselves and are best addressed specifically.

The *least controversial* interpretation of the ceremony would be that it involved the establishment of "spiritual fraternity" of the sort that all Christians, at least since New Testament times,[142] had been instructed to feel toward each other and all human beings.[143] There are three general reasons to doubt this interpretation, despite the strong appeal it exerts by not challenging any dearly held convictions or prejudices:

1. It hardly seems likely that a specific church office would be instituted to establish the sort of ἀγάπη Christians were expected to feel toward each other (and all humans) anyway.

2. It would have been a spectacularly inefficient and nonproductive (not to mention counterintuitive) way to spread this universal love to have Christians stand *two* by *two* before altars throughout the Christian world to solemnize it. The ceremony is *always* clearly for two males or two females; never for a group.

3. The ceremony was often prohibited to monks,[144] but not to the laity—a very curious proscription if it involved only the spreading of "spiritual brotherhood" (for which one might expect monastics to have a special gift or calling). Indeed, one has to wonder why, if the ceremony solemnized an ordinary part of

---

142. See, for example, the comments of St. Sophronius (patriarch of Jerusalem C.E. 634–38 [and therefore possibly influenced by the office of ἀδελφοποιία]), which seem to be almost a foretaste of the ceremony itself (in SS. *Apostolos Petrum et Paulum*, PG 87:3360): ἀλλήλοις ἡμᾶς τῷ συνδέσμῳ τῆς ἀγάπης γιγνώσκων τὸ ἄπτωτον. . . . Τὰς ψυχὰς ὑμῶν ἡγνικότες ἐν τῇ ὑπακοῇ τῆς ἀληθείας, φησίν, εἰς φιλαδελφίαν ἀνυπόκριτον ἐκ καρδίας ἀλλήλους ἐκτενῶς ἀγαπήσατε, καὶ ὡς θεοῦ δοῦλοι, πάντας ἡμᾶς τιμήσατε· τὴν ἀδελφότητα ἀγαπᾶτε, ἀδελφοποιεῖν ἀλλήλοις ἡμᾶς εἰδὼς τὴν ἀγάπησιν. Cf. also translation passages Nos. 1 and 4 in Appendix of Translations.

143. This interpretation is indeed suggested by Goar's titling the ceremony Ἀκολουθία εἰς ἀδελφοποιίαν πνευματικήν (*officium ad spiritualem fraternitatem ineundam*). Although the word πνευματικός (or a related form) does occur in a few manuscripts (e.g., Document No. 3 and Translation No. 8, it does not occur in the title of a single manuscript version of the ceremony consulted for this study (see list on pp. 372–74). Moreover, "spiritual," as has been noted (pp. 25–27), was a loaded and difficult term even in regard to heterosexual marriage, which many theologians felt had to be established through consummation.

144. See pp. 240ff.

Christian spirituality, it was ever prohibited to any Christian at all.

Each of these objections would in itself substantially discredit this theory, whose sole recommendation is that it obviates the need to acknowledge something as unexpected and potentially troubling as an ancient Christian ceremony of same-sex union performed in churches by priests. Taken together, despite this advantage, they are absurd, and render such explanations preposterous.

Moreover, the phrase "spiritual brothers" (πμευματικοὶ ἀδελφοί) is the technical term in Greek canon law for something clearly and entirely different from any relationship created by this ceremony: collateral relationships established through baptism.[145] This type of "kinship" was, according to the late medieval Orthodox canon lawyer Matthew Blastares, the most common form of relationship: "The [kind of kinship] created by baptism must be examined for degree only in relation to marriage, for it is the most extensive category of relationship."[146]

One of the more common interpretations among the few historians and liturgists who have acknowledged the ceremony at all is that it was a Christianized form of "blood brotherhood." Such an interpretation seems highly improbable for a number of reasons. In the few cases where "blood brotherhood" is mentioned in the Middle Ages, it is clearly so identified (see pp. 258–60). The ceremony is probably more ancient than the notions of "blood brotherhood" found among later medieval and early modern Europeans. Moreover, none of the ancient archetypes (e.g., Serge and Bacchus, Peter and Paul)[147] invoked in any version of the ceremony were bound to each other by anything resembling "blood brotherhood,"[148] no blood is exchanged or in-

---

[145.] See, e.g., Matthew Blastares in *RP* 6:139.

[146.] Ibid., p. 127, §3.

[147.] It is relatively obvious why these two saints—jointly leaders in the apostolic church and so reflected in the New Testament—should have been venerated jointly, and it is difficult to imagine that eroticism played a role. On the other hand, the Greek iconographic tradition often portrays them embracing, and this may have been assimilated in the popular imagination to the relationship between Serge and Bacchus.

[148.] Two pairs of brothers are known from the Gospels: Peter and Andrew and James and John. They are not invoked in most versions of the ceremony (except Barberini 336), although many other pairs of apostles regularly are (e.g., Peter and Paul, Philip and Bartholomew). In a prayer from a ceremony of fifteenth-century origin, translated in Appendix of Translations No. 13, the analogy of James and John is, in fact, explicitly considered and rejected.

volved in the ceremony (except that of Jesus in the Communion, but His is also present in heterosexual nuptial masses and the Eucharist— making identification with "blood brotherhood" on this basis impossible), and no names for the ceremony in any language suggest this in any way. Most do have the word "brother" in them, but the word for "blood" is never present.[149] Local European customs of "blood brotherhood" were eventually assimilated into the ceremony and began to influence it, but were clearly not its origin, which must have been in the Greek-speaking Christian East.

Might it be simply a commemoration of friendship? This is at least conceivable but rendered problematic by the fact that the common Greek word for "friend"—ubiquitous in the New Testament—does not occur in the ceremony or in any references to it. And why is the office always for two and never for three or four? Even Jesus, in privileging friendly love over all others, seems to have imagined a plurality of friends.[150] Strikingly, John 15:17 and 17:1 are cited in some versions of the ceremony, but not the very verses from John (15:13–14) dealing with friendship, though they are immediately adjacent to the quoted passages. This would be most peculiar and astonishing if the ceremony itself were about friendship of any sort. It would indeed be curious if the religion of a preacher who so privileged friendship turned out *not* to have a ceremony solemnizing it, and a few of the ceremonies (e.g., Coislin 213 [Appendix of Translations No. 5] and Bibliothèque nationale Grec 330 [Appendix of Translations No. 8]) could be interpreted this way. But most could not: they seem clearly modeled on or themselves to have influenced heterosexual nuptial offices.

Could it be fraternal adoption? It could be,[151] but it is worth remembering that most of the documented instances of "adopting a brother" in the ancient world clearly involved homosexual attach-

---

149. The chief words are ἀδελφοποίησις, ἀδελφοποιία in Greek, побратимство or something similar in Slavic languages. The Greek terms are discussed in Chapters 1 and 2. The Slavic terms are discussed on pp. 19ff. Romanian is *infrăţirea*.

150. "Greater love hath no man than this, that a man lay down his life for his friends. Ye are my friends, if ye do whatsoever I command you." John 15:13–14, addressed to his disciples.

151. This is, indeed, the meaning given for ἀδελφοποιία in the brief and misleading entry by Macrides in the *ODB* 1:19–20. But Tamassia, the author of the only book-length study of the subject, categorically rejects this possibility (pp. 2–3), pointing out that both *adrogatio* and *adoptio*—the two legal varieties of adoption in Roman law—involved acquiring *patria potestas* over someone, which was obviously not the case with ἀδελφοποιία.

FIGURE 1. *This Soviet stamp, showing the grateful reception by the peasantry of Russian soldiers returning from World War II, was not shocking to Russians, who entertained less horror of homosexual interaction than did their Western contemporaries. It is possible that the artist was gay, and concocted the scene for his own delight, but that remains uncertain.*

FIGURE 2. *The Russians were still not shocked: a contemporary mural of Leonid Brezhnev of the Soviet Union and Erich Honecker of East Germany greeting each other with a kiss. In the West, many observers would regard this picture as immoral.*

FIGURE 3. *Since Roman times, the primary symbol of matrimony has been the joining of the right hands of the partners, called the* dextrarum junctio *and symbolized here in a Roman wedding ring from the late empire. This also became the principal gesture in same-sex unions.*

FIGURE 4. *The martyrdom of Saints Perpetua and Felicitas in the early third century as represented in the High Middle Ages. Perpetua and Felicitas are on the far right, with one lying in the lap of the other, perhaps symbolizing that they are usually remembered in tandem. From Vatican Greek 1613, folio 366.*

FIGURE 5. *Seventh-century icon of Saints Serge and Bacchus, wearing gold torques traditionally associated with them and joined by Christ depicted in the traditional Roman position of* pronuba/-us *("matron of honor" or "best man," often a deity) overseeing the wedding of a husband and wife. Originally from the monastery of St. Catherine on Mt. Sinai; now housed in the Kiev Museum of Eastern and Western Art.*

FIGURE 6. An eleventh-century illustrated capital in Metaphrastes' lives of the saints. It shows Saints Serge and Bacchus joined in the capital letter, as they had been in life. From Vatican Greek 1679, folio 48 verso.

FIGURE 7 (above) and following: Scenes of the martyrdom of Serge and Bacchus, from an Italian sarcophagus of 1179. On this side of the sarcophagus, Saints Serge and Bacchus are shown (with halos here and throughout) in the center of the scene being blessed by the hand of God. To the left of them are pagans worshiping a deity seated in a temple. On the right they have been called before the emperor Maximian to answer accusations of practicing Christianity, which they admit.

FIGURE 8. In the next scene, Saints Serge and Bacchus are led to the provincial governor Antiochus. They are on foot; the soldiers leading them are on horseback.

FIGURE 9. On the left of the third scene, Saints Serge and Bacchus appear before Antiochus, who owed his position as governor to Saint Serge. In the right half, Bacchus is being beaten to death while Serge's hair is seized by the man who will behead him. In the upper right appears an angel to escort their souls to heaven.

FIGURE 10. Saints Serge and Bacchus appear before Christ in heaven, who blesses the abbot who commissioned the sarcophagus.

FIGURE 11. On the cover of the sarcophagus, Saints Serge and Bacchus appear on horseback, triumphant, carrying palms of victory.

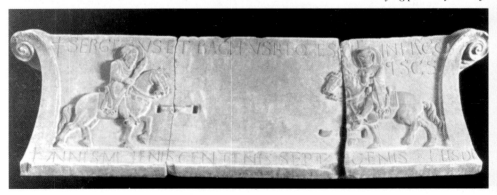

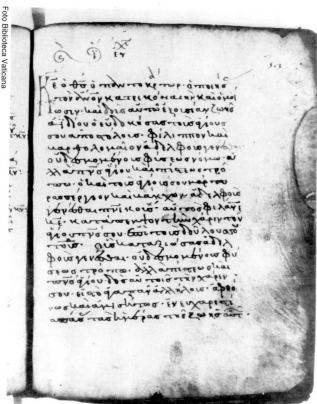

FIGURE 12. Folio 53 recto of Vatican Greek 1811, translated as No. 9 and published as Document No. 4 herein.

FIGURE 13. Medieval depiction of the liturgical union of the Byzantine emperor Basil I and John from the twelfth- or thirteenth-century Skylitzes matritensis. At right, a priest is uniting Basil and John in a church. They stand before an open book on a stand (presumably the Gospel often mentioned in the ceremony itself). At left, John's mother, Danelis, hosts a banquet for the new couple. All the characters are identified by names written above them.

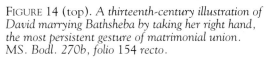

erfabe
dolens
prona
tto plo
rabat 7 dauid 9
fortabat eam 7
duxit eam in u
xorem·

erfabe

FIGURE 14 (top). *A thirteenth-century illustration of David marrying Bathsheba by taking her right hand, the most persistent gesture of matrimonial union. MS. Bodl. 270b, folio 154 recto.*

FIGURE 15 (right). *Medieval (ca. 1300) images of Moses marrying Zipporah.*

FIGURE 16 (below). *A romanticized High Medieval illustration of the martyrdom of Saints Serge and Bacchus, showing the beheading of one while the other looks on in sorrow. It was actually Saint Serge who was beheaded; Bacchus had been beaten to death beforehand. This picture emphasizes their attachment to each other and the pathos of their witnessing each other's martyrdoms.*

FIGURES 17, 18, 19. *A trio of High and Late Medieval sculptural depictions of Christ and Saint John, suggesting that the artists took the relationship between them to be one of affection and intimacy.*

FIGURE 20. *Economics have been a part of heterosexual marriage in most times and places. In India, brothers and cousins of the bride of the maharaja of Kinshangarh bring money as an offering to the groom's family on the morning of the wedding. Older relatives bring bills in larger denominations.*

ments, so this hardly removes the most controversial aspect of the ceremony. Indeed, it makes it worse. In addition, there are both substantive and technical problems. The most obvious substantive problem is the patent difference between adoption, in which one party assumes control over the other, and this ceremony, in which two people are simply joined together, as are the couple in a heterosexual matrimony. Two typical medieval ceremonies of adoption are translated in the Appendix of Translations (nos. 16 and 17) for comparison. A modern adaptation is available in the revised (as of 1979) Book of Common Prayer of the Episcopal Church in America.[152]

A careful reading of the same-sex ceremony dispels any notion of adoption, or even of the creation of a legal *fiction* of brotherhood, since the archetypes invoked, like Peter and Paul or Serge and Bacchus, were not in fact brothers, either biologically or through legal arrangement. It may be doubted whether Peter and Paul were in any sense a couple, but Serge and Bacchus, the most commonly cited archetypes, certainly were, and under the influence of the same cultural predilection that created a pair from the single St. Theodore, it is easy to imagine that Peter and Paul were coupled in the popular imagination. This is really less of an imaginary feat than the creation of a second St. Theodore, though the latter is beyond question. The development of appeal to apostolic concord for *both* heterosexual and same-sex union ceremonies has already been discussed, and it has also been noted that few Christians undertaking heterosexual matrimony would have wished to model their relationships on the couples invoked for them in the apposite rite: Abraham and Sarah, Jacob and Rachel, Joseph and Aseneth, Moses and Zipporah.[153]

Nowhere in the same-sex union ceremony is adoption[154] mentioned or implied. The two parties were being united as Serge and Bacchus had been united; in none of the archetypal examples invoked was there any evidence from history or tradition to suggest adoption.

---

[152] "A Thanksgiving for the Birth or Adoption of a Child," pp. 439–46.

[153] For the first two couples, see above, pp. 124–125. Aseneth (Asenath in modern spelling), the daughter of Potiphar, was given to Joseph as a wife without any evidence of volition on either part. When Moses decided to live with Reuel, Reuel "gave Moses Zipporah his daughter"—again with no indication of desire or consent (Exod. 2:21). Moses later divorced her, though they had produced two children together (Exod. 18:2–4).

[154] Greek: υἱοθεσία; OCS as cited below, n. 156. In Greek παιδοποιία means "the begetting (N.B., not the adopting, although that was common) of children" (see, e.g., Chrysostom, *In illud, propter fornicationes uxorem* 3 [PG 51:213]).

It is, indeed, almost inconceivable that any of the persons invoked actually adopted the other in any formal sense. All were joined by voluntary, personal affection between equals.

"Adoption" was an important theological motif in the New Testament and in patristic writings dependent on it. It is mentioned in the Epistles to Romans,[155] to Galatians,[156] and to Ephesians,[157] all believed in the Middle Ages to have been written by St. Paul. Given the plethora of biblical passages related to heterosexual matrimony employed in its celebration by Christians, it is astonishing that none of the biblical references to adoption would have been incorporated into an office believed to have been its Christian embodiment. A variety of *other* biblical references, however, are found in the ceremony—none of them suggesting any legal or familial relationship. Christians might disagree about the nature of these "unions," with some imagining them to be merely working partnerships, others close personal friendships, and still others Christian same-sex unions (with or without an expressed sexual component), but nothing in the ceremony suggests adoption.

One might say simply that Serge and Bacchus or Peter and Paul were "made brothers," but in what sense? All apostles and all Christians—indeed, all human beings—were brothers, not just in Christian theology, but in everyday Christian thought and language. The ceremony obviously conveyed more than the simplistic tautology that this and that Christian were "brothers." Perhaps a more folkloric term like "blood brother" would come closer to describing its meaning, but the separate difficulties with this concept have already been addressed.

There are, in addition, two technical problems. The first is linguistic: the most common Greek word for the adoption of children was not τεκνοποίησις,[158] which does seem in some ways comparable to ἀδελφοποίησις, but υἱοθεσία, both in Roman law (as written in Greek)[159] and in Scripture, which was doubtless more influential in

---

155. 8:15 (πνεῦμα υἱοθεσίας/*spiritum adoptionis*/духа усыновленія); 8:23; 9:4.
156. 4:5 (υἱοθεσίαν/*adoptionem filiorum*/усыновленіе).
157. 1:5 (υἱοθεσίαν/*adoptionem filiorum*/усыновить).
158. Τεκνοποίησις literally means "making a child," which could be applied either to biological reproduction or to adoption (Xenophon, *Lak. Pol.*, uses τεκνοποιία in this sense). See also n. 160, below.
159. This is the Greek given for "adoption" in *ODB* 1:22, and also occurs in Byzantine law throughout the Middle Ages: see, e.g., nn. 160 and 162, below.

the Middle Ages.[160] By analogy, the ceremony might have been expected to occur under the rubric ἀδελφοθεσία, but it *never* did. It was not until the thirteenth century—almost six centuries after the first occurrence of a fully developed ceremony called ἀδελφοποίησις —that the term τεκνοποίησις began to appear in what seem to have been adoption ceremonies, probably by analogy with the name for the same-sex union ceremony.[161] Goar printed υἱοθεσία as the correct name for the office, but then appended additional prayers from a fourteenth-century Italian manuscript using the term τεκνοποίησις.[162] Only nine of seventeen adoption ceremonies (as opposed to thirty-seven ceremonies of same-gender union) printed by Dmitrievskij from Eastern manuscripts use a form of τεκνοποίησις to name the office: all date from the thirteenth century or later. Even so, titles involving or derived from the more traditional and legally correct υἱοθεσία survived as designations of the practice well into the sixteenth century.

The second technical problem is that adoption was never prohibited under Byzantine law,[163] whereas the ceremony of same-sex union *was* ultimately proscribed, for reasons that remain unclear but probably had to do with the rise of hostility to everything homosexual (discussed in Chapter 7). Moreover, canonists seeking a pretext to outlaw the ceremony of same-gender union frequently remarked on the fact that it was not in fact biologically *possible* to engender a brother, although it was possible to engender a child, and adoption

---

160. Ὑιοθεσία occurs five times in the New Testament; τεκνοποίησις, an alternative word for adoption in later Greek, does not occur at all, and appears to have meant primarily "begetting a child" (its most literal sense) until the fifth century,C.E. *LSJ* cite a few rare instances of its meaning "adoption" as early as the second century before the Christian Era, but Lampe gives as the basic meaning "begetting a child" even for patristic Greek.

161. Barberini 336 does not include an office for adoption.

162. Goar, pp. 561–62: Ἀκολουθία εἰς υἱοθεσίαν (*Officium ad adoptionem*), followed by prayers from a fourteenth-century manuscript from Grottaferrata (called "Falascae" by Goar) which refers to the ceremony as ἀκολουθία εἰς τὸ εὐλογῆσαι τεκνοποιίαν, inspiring Goar to rename the remaining prayers σύνταξις εἰς τεκνοποίησιν (still titled in Latin *adoptionem*, since it is basically the same operation at issue).

163. On the contrary: a church solemnization of adoption was required by civil law at least from the ninth century (Ὥσπερ τὰ τῆς υἱοθετήσεως πράγματα πρὸς τὸ ἀδιάφορον διακείμενα, Zepos 1:156), although ceremonies from this period do not survive. Indeed, the earliest known ceremony (from Sinai 973, [No. VIII, p. 122] printed in Dmitrievskij) is from the middle of the twelfth century (C.E. 1153). It is translated in the Appendix of Translations, No. 16, and bears little resemblance to the same-sex union ceremony, which antedates it by at least six centuries.

should imitate nature, so fraternal adoption was neither possible nor licit. This constituted a questionable and peculiar argument for Christian theologians, both because no ceremony gives evidence of constituting adoption of any sort, as noted, and because, apart from this, Christian thinkers idealized much that was not common or possible in nature, and this objection seems rather farfetched and contrived. "Adoption takes place for inheritance purposes," Blastares claimed, "which is why it was created."[164] Although same-sex unions appear to have had (sometimes controversial) consequences for estates, no evidence apart from occasional condemnations suggests that they were *undertaken* for this reason.

[164.] See discussion of Blastares' opinions, p. 249.

6

"Let Me Not to the Marriage of True Minds Admit Impediments"

COMPARISON OF SAME-SEX
and
HETEROSEXUAL CEREMONIES OF UNION

THE NATURE AND CONTENT OF CEREMONIES OF UNION

The ancient Roman marriage rites were taken over by the Christian Church with very few changes. The auspices of the augurs, of course, were abolished, and the *sacrificium nuptiale*, the nuptial sacrifice of wine or incense, was eventually "converted" and became a nuptial mass. But the legal and ceremonial aspects, namely the reading of the marriage consent from the *tabulae nuptiales* and its signing, the handing over of the dowry, the *dextrarum junctio* or clasping of the right hands, and the cooperation of the deity confirming the legal action and protecting the marriage, *dea pronuba or deus pronubus*—all of these underwent few changes, or changes only with regard to the tutelary deity.[1]

Both the heterosexual and same-sex union formulas appear to have developed chiefly out of commemorations of apostolic peace.[2] Al-

---

[1] Ernst Kantorowicz, "On the Golden Marriage Belt and the Marriage Rings of the Dumbarton Oaks Collection," *Dumbarton Oaks Papers* 14 (1960), 3–17, p. 4. Cf. Anne Schwerdtfeger, *Ethnological Sources of the Christian Marriage Ceremony* (Stockholm, 1982), 123: "The establishment of matrimony as a sacrament did nothing to change the structure, symbols or ritual acts of the ceremony, but rather sublimated them." For studies of the development of Christian nuptial rites, see preceding chapter, note 7.

[2] In addition to the ceremonies edited and translated in this volume, and Goar's composite same-sex union office, 1647 ed., pp. 898–902, 1730 ed., pp. 706–709, note that Origen

199

though the harmony of the apostles might seem an unlikely precedent for unions that are, in the eyes of the twentieth century, expected to provide erotic fulfillment, it must be remembered that in its first millennium devout adherents of the Christian religion did not expect marriage to satisfy emotional or sexual needs. Moreover, "harmony" (at least as expressed in the Latin word *concordia* or Greek ὁμόνοια)[3] was precisely what most people in antiquity sought in marriage, and there is little reason to suppose this changed as antiquity yielded to the Middle Ages.[4] Even the Greek word for "peace" (εἰρήνη), though its derivation is obscure, probably originally had more to do with union[5] than with the absence of conflict.[6] Certainly when Jesus an-

---

equated friendship with peace (*Contra Haereses* 7:29 [PG 16:3:3326]: ἡ φιλία εἰρήνη τίς ἐστι καὶ ὁμόνοια καὶ στοργή ["friendship is a certain peace and concord and affection"]). For the theme of "peace" in heterosexual matrimony, see also Paulinus of Nola (†431) Carmen 25 (*CSEL* 30:238–45, ll. 227–28) (*Ille iugans capita amborum sub pace iugali velat eos dextra quos prece sanctificat*); Ritzer, p. 230, quoting from M. Férotin, *Le Liber Ordinum en usage dans l'église wisigothique et mozarabe d'Espagne du cinquième au onzième siècle*, in *Monumenta Ecclesiae Liturgica*, V (Paris, 1904), MS A; and Richard of St. Victor (in the second half of the twelfth century), *Epître à Severin sur la charité par Ives; Les Quatre degrés de la violente charité: Texte critique avec introduction, traduction et notes*, ed. Gervaise Dumeige (Paris, 1955), 145: *Mutuus namque intimi amoris affectus inter federatos pacis vincula adstringit, et indissolubilem illam perpetuandam que societate gratam et jocundam reddit*. The sixteenth-century heterosexual marriage ceremony recorded in Athanasios 21 (91) from Mt. Athos (Dmitrievskij No. XCIX, p. 759) includes the following invocation: δώρησαι αὐτοῖς πίστιν ἀκαταίσχυντον, ἀγάπην ἀνυπόκριτον, πλησμονὴν σοφίας τὴν εἰς ἀλλήλους ἀγάπην . . . τὸν σύνδεσμον τῆς εἰρήνης ("grant them unabashed faithfulness, sincere love, fullness of wisdom in affection for each other, and . . . the bond of peace"). Even today in the heterosexual marriage ceremony of the current (1977) Episcopal Prayer Book the exchange of peace may be substituted for Communion (p. 436).

3. According to Louis Reekmans ("La «dextrarum junctio»" dans l'iconographie romaine et paléochretienne," *Bulletin de l'Institut Historique Belge de Rome* 31 [1958] 24–95, at p. 81), Greek ὁμόνοια is specifically equivalent, in a matrimonial context, to Latin *concordia*. This is certainly borne out by art, in which the figure of Concordia in the West or ὁμόνοια in the Greek part of the late empire officiated at weddings, presumably replacing some goddess (Hera or a personal *genius*) to act as *pronuba/pronubus*. The idea was that *concordia* both formed and preserved marriage: see Chiara Frugoni, "L'Iconografia del matrimonio e della coppia nel medioevo," *Matrimonio* 2:901–66.

4. The most common biblical word for love of any sort was ἀγάπη, and although it was not usually used in the Scriptures to describe interpersonal passion, its power and precedent were sufficiently influential to preserve it as the preferred term in all sorts of liturgical unions. See Chapter 1, "The Vocabulary of Love and Marriage," pp. 6–9.

5. Especially if ultimately derived, as some have speculated, from the root εἴρω, "to fasten together." Its etymology is unclear: LSJ do not attempt to solve it, but simply refer the reader to the several verbs spelled εἴρω ("say," "connect"). But see J. F. Schleusner, *Novum Lexicon Graeco-Latinum in Novum Testamentum* (Glasgow, 1824), s.v. εἰρήνη: *Proprie* vinculum, *ab* εἴρω necto, *quia pace animi hominum connectuntur et conjunguntur, ad quod etymon allusisse videtur Paul Ephes. IV.3. memorans* συνδεσμὸν τῆς εἰρήνης. . . . The passage in Ephesians does seem to suggest a *connection* between the two meanings, but not that one is the same as the other.

6. In this sense *concordia* is a perfect parallel, as are Semitic nouns for "peace" like שלום and سلم.

nounced that He left His disciples His "peace" (εἰϱήνη, John 14:27) He did not mean the absence of conflict, since He predicted again and again that turmoil and dissension would dog His followers, as it did.[7] Rather, He meant unity and concord *among them.*

One ancient liturgical commemoration of peace, to the extent that it can be reconstructed,[8] reads:

[9] . . . we pray <that> love [ἀγάπην] and brotherly affection [φιλαδελφίαν] be bestowed on us in the bond of peace, and that the desires of our hearts be granted, Thou that alone hast authority, O holy, glorious, honored ruler and Lord, whose name (?),[10] O Thou that dwellest in heaven and lookest down on the lowly,[11] who art seated in heaven and magnified forever. Amen.[12]

This became in time a more common liturgical prayer used in most Greek eucharistic celebrations:

O Almighty God, look down from the heavens upon thy church and all thy whole people and all thy little flock and save us all, Thine unworthy servants, the children of Thy company. Grant unto us thy peace and love [ἀγάπην] and thy help, and send down upon us the gift of thy Holy Spirit, that with pure heart and good conscience[13] we may kiss[14] each other with an holy kiss,[15] not in deceit or hypocrisy,[16] not with the hearts of enmity,[17] but in perfectness and blamelessness, one in spirit, one

---

[7.] Jesus warned as much in Matt. 10:34: "Think not that I am come to send peace on earth: I came not to send peace, but a sword."

[8.] Because it is fragmentary, it is impossible to translate the papyrus fragment exactly.

[9.] Something is missing from the Greek as reconstructed.

[10.] Something is missing from the Greek as reconstructed.

[11.] Ps. 112:5–6.

[12.] Prayer 3 in the Dêr-Balizeh papyrus (*An Early Euchologium: The Dêr-Balizeh Papyrus Enlarged and Reedited,* ed. C. H. Roberts and B. Capelle [Louvain, 1949], 10; and in T. Schermann, *Aegyptische Abendmahlsliturgien* [Paderborn, 1912], 5), which Roberts dates as sixth century. Roberts notes a parallel with the prayer from St. Mark's liturgy, below. This prayer recalls Eph. 4:3 and Col. 3:13–15 in its emphasis on peace, and Eph. 4:2, Rom. 12:9–11, 1 Thess. 4:9, 1 Pet. 1:22, 1 Pet. 2:17, 1 Pet. 3:8, and 2 Pet. 1:7 in its appeal to love (ἀγάπη).

[13.] Cf. 1 Tim. 1:5: "Now the end of the commandment is charity out of a pure heart, and of a good conscience."

[14.] Or "greet": ἀσπασώμεθα.

[15.] Cf. Rom. 16:16: "Salute one another with an holy kiss."

[16.] Cf. 1 Peter 2:1.

[17.] Or "strangers": ἀλλοτρίου.

in the bond of peace and love, one in body and spirit, one in faith, as we were called in one hope thereunto,[18] that we may all come to godly and boundless affection [στοργήν], in Christ Jesus our Lord, with whom Thou art magnified, with Thy most holy, good and life-giving Spirit, now and forever and ever. Amen.[19]

Both the appeal to peace and the invocation of love (expressed by ἀγάπη) become characteristic of ceremonies of union (for either or both genders) in subsequent centuries. All of the heterosexual ceremonies translated in the Appendix of Translations, ranging over a period of eight centuries, include direct or incidental invocations of peace; most other heterosexual liturgies do so as well, as do all of the same-sex ceremonies and most others not translated or published in this volume. Symeon of Thessalonika opined in his fifteenth-century treatise on marriage that "in peace and through peace and concord [ὁμόνοια] they [the husband and wife] are joined together."[20]

Apostolic love (ἀγάπη) and harmony (ὁμόνοια), unlikely as they may seem as conjugal themes, are constants of marital liturgies. Ἀγάπη was not the ordinary Greek word for personal affection (which was usually either φιλία or ἔρως),[21] but it was the liturgical term for love of any sort among Christians, owing at least partly to the fact that it was by far the most common term for "love" of all sorts in the Scriptures, both Jewish and Christian. Heterosexual matrimony was the mystery of love (ἀγάπη) according to John Chrysostom.[22] In a thirteenth-century heterosexual marriage rite from Mount Athos[23] God is beseeched to crown the couple "in love," named by the term ἀγάπη.

---

18. Cf. Eph. 4:3–4: "Endeavoring to keep the unity of the Spirit in the bond of peace. There is one body, and one Spirit, even as ye are called in one hope of your calling." Col. 3:13–15: "Forbearing one another, and forgiving one another, if any man have a quarrel against any: even as Christ forgave you, so also do ye. And above all these things put on charity, which is the bond of perfectness. And let the peace of God rule in your hearts, to the which also ye are called in one body; and be ye thankful [καὶ εὐχάριστοι γίνεσθε]."

19. Published in Brightman, p. 123.

20. Περὶ τοῦ τιμίου νομμοῦ γάμου, 278 (PG 155:508): ἐν εἰρήνῃ καὶ δι' εἰρήνην συνάπτονται καὶ ὁμόνοιαν. Cf. the further blessing "Guard them in peace and concord" (ibid.:509: φυλάξῃ ἐν εἰρήνῃ καὶ ὁμονοίᾳ).

21. See Chapter 1, "The Vocabulary of Love and Marriage," pp. 6ff.

22. In Epistolam ad Colossianos, 4. Hom.12 (PG 62:387).

23. Dmitrievskij No. XX (p. 182).

One of the most common symbols of Christian marriage in the East —crowning—was often coupled in the fourth and fifth centuries with the single most common gesture of marital union anywhere—the joining of right hands (discussed hereafter), and extended to pairs of saints and martyrs as well as to husband and wife.[24] The saints were usually Peter and Paul.[25] This, Reekmans argued, bore a striking resemblance to an Italian sarcophagus depicting a married couple holding hands and being crowned. In such circumstances Christ seems to have taken the place of *concordia* in pagan representations of marriage.[26] It might well be argued that, even granting the nonerotic nature of heterosexual marriage among Christians before the twelfth century, apostles like Peter and Paul or Philip and Bartholomew hardly constituted models for any kind of personal union, since too little was known about their relationships to draw on them for precedent. But it is worth noting that Abraham and Sarah were surely not chosen as heterosexual models because of the particulars of their relationship: should married men have their own Hagar? Should mothers, even stepmothers, be like Sarah in relationship to Ishmael? Rather, they were prominent and cited because of their *position in Judeo-Christian history*, not the actual details of their personal lives.

The prayer for the common cup in heterosexual ceremonies or Communion in same-sex rites usually invoked either the "faith of the apostles"[27] as spreaders of the new covenant or apostolic concord (ὁμόνοια τῶν ἁγίων ἀποστόλων/μαθήτων).[28] The common cup

---

24. For the invocation of martyrs in heterosexual union ceremonies, see, for example, the following texts, all published in Dmitrievskij, and listed here with his item numbers: Sinai 968 (C.E. 1426) (LVI p. 404), Athos Vatoped. 322 (934) (C.E. 1468) (LIX p. 422), Athos Athanas. 88 (fifteenth century) (LXI p. 443), Const. Holy Sepulcher 8 (182) (fifteenth century) (LXIV p. 465), Athos Penteleimon 364 (fifteenth century) (LXXI p. 566), Athos Athanasios 105 (fifteenth century) (LXXIX p. 633), Patmos Ilitari 690 (fifteenth century) (LXXXIII p. 652), Holy Sepulcher (Const.) 615 (757) (1522 C.E.) (XCVI pp. 741–42).

25. Reekmans, "La «dextrarum junctio»," pp. 74–75, catalogued eighteen instances of the crowning of Peter and Paul, and more from the sixth and seventh centuries from Egypt and Italy. See also on crowning: Chiara Frugoni, "L'Iconografia del matrimonio," *Matrimonio* 2:922 (*Cristo incorona i suoi eletti e ripete per gli sposi il gesto già riservato ai santi e ai martiri, a Pietro e Paolo sopratutto*).

26. Reekmans, pp. 75–77.

27. The crowning in heterosexual marriage ceremonies was also performed with appeal to the apostles (στεφάνωσον αὐτούς, Κύριε ὁ Θεὸς ἡμῶν, ὡς ἐστεφάνωσας τὸν χορὸν τῶν ἁγίων σου ἀποστόλων, from the Holy Sepulcher in Istanbul, published in Dmitrievskij, No. LXIV, p. 464).

28. See Daniele Gelsi, "Punti per riflessione sull'ufficio bizantino per la 'incoronazione' degli sposi," *La celebrazione cristiana del matrimonio: simboli e testi. Atti del II congresso internazionale*

was not originally eucharistic,[29] but a survival of the Roman *confarreatio* and other pagan chalice-based matrimonial rituals. It was Christianized by appeal to the faith of the apostles, suggesting that the couple in question, as heads of a Christian household, would play in the spread of the new religion a role comparable to that of the apostles.[30] An Italo-Greek manuscript of the twelfth century even refers to the common cup as "the cup of thy holy disciples."[31] Most representations of Christian marriage from the third to the fifth century are found on gold glass cups, which at least one scholar has argued were Communion cups saved as mementos of the marriage.[32]

The wording of the ceremony of same-sex union is similar in many striking ways to that of medieval Greek heterosexual ceremonies. Most of these similarities and parallels can easily be detected in the translations and documents published in the Appendix of Translations.

The litany that usually begins it is nearly the same as the litany usually recited at the opening of heterosexual marriage ceremonies, and is not simply an ordinary liturgical beginning. Of many substantial litanies provided, for example, in the early (tenth-century) Italian prayer book published as exemplary by Passarelli,[33] numbers 7, 11, 101, 155, 155bis, 162, 250, 256, 266, 276, 286–88, 319, 373, and 379

---

di liturgia. Rome, 27–31 maggio 1985. (Studia Anselmiana, 93. Analecta liturgica, 11) (Rome, 1986), and Baldanza, pp. 348–49. In some versions the example of Cana is invoked, which can also be applied to wine (ibid., p. 349).

[29.] See p. 185, n. 125, above. Of twenty-one heterosexual marriage ceremonies in euchologia studied by Baldanza, "Il rito," only nine had a "common cup," but he considered them mostly noneucharistic (p. 339). Some ceremonies, e.g., the fifteenth-century euchologion Athos Athanasios 105 (Dmitrievskij LXXIX, p. 633), make clear that two cups are at issue in the ceremony—the "common cup" (as described above) *as well as* Communion (ἀπόκεινται δὲ ἐν τῇ ἁγίᾳ τραπέζῃ στέφανα δύο καὶ ποτήριον μετ' οἴνου καὶ ἄρτου, κλάσματα ἓξ μικρὰ πάνυ, εἰ οὔκ εἰσιν ἄξιοι κοινωνῆσαι τῶν ἀχράντων μυστηρίων, εἰ δὲ εἰσὶν ἄξιοι, οὐ χρὴ ποιῆσαι κοινὸν ποτήριον). Cf. also the earlier (thirteenth-century) Patmos 105 (Dmitrievskij XVII, p. 169) in which the priest gives the couple first the "body and blood"— i.e., unmistakably Communion—*and then* the "common cup." Sinai 968 (C.E. 1426) (Dmitrievskij LVI, p. 402) also indicates that on the sacred table (used for performing marriage) there are *two* chalices—one for the "common cup" and the other for Communion. Ritzer found (pp. 99–100) that by the thirteenth century Communion was required for marriage among the Copts.

[30.] Gelsi, p. 298: *Molto interessante è l'idea che la fede degli sposi sia «apostolica», cioè la stessa fede degli apostoli, quali diffusori della nuova alleanza; bevendo alla coppa si beve la fede.*

[31.] Vaticanus Graecus 1863: τὸ ποτήριον τῶν ἁγίων σου μαθητῶν.

[32.] Frugoni, p. 926.

[33.] Gaetano Passarelli, *L'Eucologio cryptense Γ.β. VII (sec. X)* ('Ανάλεκτα βλατάδων, 36) (Thessalonika, 1982).

bear comparison with the normal litany at the beginning of the ceremony of same-sex union, but the one that seems most closely related
is number 166, for the heterosexual marriage ceremony.[34] Most of the
litanies for heterosexual unions in Dmitrievskij's collection also resemble those beginning the ceremony of same-sex union, and are not
similar to other kinds of litanies he printed (e.g., for making a cate-
chumen, p. 78).

Relatively few other services have litanies at all: Dmitrievskij's
thirteenth-century adoption ceremony (No. 105) does not, and in the
Sinai Euchologion only three ceremonies have litanies: same-sex
union, Pentecost, and vesting a monk.[35]

A few further aspects of the wording of the same-sex ceremony
deserve clarification. The phrase "unashamed fidelity" (πίστιν
ἀνεπαίσχυντον) occurs in many of the texts, recalling the New Testament phrase in 2 Tim. 2:15, used there of being a good Christian. It
would be anachronistic to read this biblical phrase either as self-
consciously "liberationist" or as a negative injunction against a sexual
component to the relationship being solemnized.

Similarly, "without offense or scandal" and "to remain unhated
and without scandal" might be read as warnings against a sexual component, but, in fact, emphasis on chaste sexual relations *within* marriage was common in premodern ceremonies, as can be clearly seen in
many heterosexual ceremonies (e.g., those published in the Appendix
of Translations, especially numbers 2, 7, and 12, which span a period
of nearly a millennium). Most of the latter specifically mention "chastity" or invoke God to make one or both parties "chaste." Indeed, a
comparable formula had been common in epitaphs commemorating
heterosexual marriages of long standing in the Greek and Roman
world.[36] In the context of ordinary heterosexual marriage (as opposed

---

[34.] Even to the prayer that the couple's life together will remain "blameless" and "not condemned" (τοῦ ἄεμπτον καὶ ἀκατάγνωστον τὴν συμβίωσιν αὐτῶν διαμεῖναι). On the
other hand, the ceremony of same-sex union in this particular manuscript (translated as No.
3 in Appendix of Translations) does not begin with a litany, as most do.

[35.] In the edition of Jean Frček ("Euchologium Sinaiticum: Texte slave avec sources grecques et
traduction française," *PO* 24 [1933], 611–801, 25 [1943], 490–622) the latter two occur on
pp. 94–95 and 156–57. The heterosexual marriage ceremony seems not to occur at all in this
manuscript, although it does not survive in its entirety.

[36.] Often phrased as "without distinction, without offense, without any disagreement" (*sine
discrimine, sine offensione, sine ulla querela*), used in *CIL* 6:35536, 9810, 27853, and noted by
R. A. Lattimore, "Themes in Greek and Latin Epitaphs," in *Illinois Studies in Language and
Literature*, 28 (1942), 279, and in Suzanne Dixon, *The Roman Family* (Baltimore, 1992), 70.

to the vows of those undertaking a "spiritual marriage"), "chaste" could hardly be reasonably interpreted as meaning "without sex"; it must have meant "faithful," i.e., not cheating on the partner. This is likewise the only reasonable interpretation for comparable phrases in same-sex ceremonies. By contrast, "chastity" itself is never mentioned or appealed to in same-sex unions.

But the most striking parallels have to do with visual symbolism, which was certainly more memorable for the congregation: the sight of a couple standing hand-in-hand at the altar, being joined and blessed by the priest, would last longer in imagination and memory than the precise wording of any ceremony, heard every now and then by congregants but not available in premodern societies with much lower rates of literacy and no printed books.[37] The principal structural similarities between the ceremony of same-sex union and heterosexual nuptial offices were binding with a stole or veil, the imposition of crowns, the holding of a feast after the ceremony for the families and friends, the making of circles around the altar, the use of a cross, occasionally the use of swords, and—virtually always—the joining of right hands.

According to Ritzer (p. 43), the binding of the parties with a stole or veil was a remnant of the Roman *flammeum*, the red veil a Roman bride wore, as did married women when they offered sacrifice. St. Ambrose discussed the placing of a veil over the bride, presumably in Christian marriage, in the fifth century,[38] and St. Paulinus of Nola, his contemporary, in his *Epithalamium* (wedding hymn) described a bishop's placing a veil over both the man and the woman in a heterosexual ceremony.[39] In a tenth-century heterosexual marriage office from Greek-speaking Italy (recorded in Grottaferatta Γ.β. VII),[40] a covering is placed over the couple to be wed, quite like the tying of the right hands in many same-sex union ceremonies (e.g., numbers 3, 4, 12, or 14 in the Appendix of Translations). It is likely, though not certain, that the expression "tie the knot" for

---

[37.] Though premodern texts do not always indicate all the gestures required or expected. For example, not all texts for heterosexual services actually specify the imposition of crowns: their use must often be inferred from the prayer for *removing* them. I have for the most part limited my discussion to gestures actually indicated in the texts.

[38.] Stevenson, p. 27.

[39.] Stevenson, p. 29.

[40.] As published in Passarelli, No. 165.6.

marriage is related to the wedding custom of wrapping right hands in a stole, a part of both heterosexual weddings and same-sex unions.[41]

The veil, as opposed to the binding of hands with the stole, was associated either with virginity—a quality expected of the bride but not always of the husband, since marriages were often dynastic or property arrangements and lineage could be reliably traced only by strict control of motherhood—or with the woman's arrival at a state mature enough to be married. "This veiling signified the adult eligibility of the bride, and had not the implication of marriage vows."[42] In the West, the veil was denied to those who were not virgins (including those contracting a second marriage),[43] at least in the time of Pope Nicholas in the ninth century.[44] But in the Maronite rite, the priest and deacon went to a table on which lay a cross, candles, Gospel, wedding rings, and crowns; the priest then joined the couple's hands and wrapped a stole around them.[45] Aside from the rings (discussed below), these are precisely the symbolic gestures in most same-sex union ceremonies, as indicated in some of the versions translated in the Appendix of Translations. The joining of the hands by the stole was absent from the Tridentine marriage rite, but was reintroduced by Charles Borromeo in his *Liber Ambrosianum*.[46]

Crowns for marriage were already being blessed by the priest in the fourth century,[47] but the earliest heterosexual wedding ceremonies do

---

[41.] See, e.g., discussion of this in Chénon, p. 30. E. Cobham Brewer, *Dictionary of Phrase and Fable* (London, many editions) gives rather unhelpful indications under "Marriage Knot (The)"—suggesting somewhat far-fetched relations to Latin and Hindu customs and ceremonies. But since we know that from the early Middle Ages into early modern times many Europeans tied the *pallium* or something else around their right hands, it seems most sensible to assume that this was the origin of the phrase. According to the *OED*, s.v. "knot," I.11b, "tie the knot" was already current in English by the thirteenth century. Shakespeare used it in *Romeo and Juliet*, iv.ii.24, when Juliet's father wanted the wedding to take place the next day, and said: "I'll have this knot knit up to-morrow evening."

[42.] Schwerdtfeger, p. 116.

[43.] In the time of St. Basil marriages beyond two were considered invalid: see *Collected Letters of St. Basil*, ed. and trans. Roy Deferrari (Cambridge, Mass., 1962 [*LCL*]), 24–26.

[44.] *Verumtamen velamen ilud non suscipit qui ad secundas nuptias migrat* (PL 119:980).

[45.] Stevenson, p. 116

[46.] Stevenson, pp. 172–73. Evidence of the stole in other (published) heterosexual marriage rites is provided in Athos Athanasios 189 (thirteenth century) (Dmitrievskij XX, p. 182), Sinai 968 (c.e. 1426) (Dmitrievskij LVI p. 401), Sinai 977 (c.e. 1516) (Dmitrievskij XCIV pp. 714–16).

[47.] Stevenson, p. 104.

not mention crowning, which was at that time part of the betrothal service.[48] Some Christians opposed the use of crowns in marriage because they were pagan.[49] St. John Chrysostom defended them as a symbol of victory over passion (hardly an encouraging view of marriage from a modern standpoint),[50] but liturgies related them instead to the crowning of martyrs such as Stephen.[51] Crowns had been used to honor the "pure" in the Jewish Scriptures (Wisd. 4:2), in which they were labeled ἀμιάντων ("spotless," "immaculate," like the Virgin Mary).[52] This is particularly striking in relation to Christian ambivalence about heterosexual matrimony because the passage in question begins with the statement that it is "better to have no children yet to have virtue" (Wisd. 4:1), suggesting that when the New Testament speaks of the marriage bed as κοίτη ἀμίαντος,[53] it might in fact have meant a marriage without sex, depending on awareness of the book of Wisdom on the part of New Testament writers. In medieval Germany the crown was used for the bride only if she was a virgin.[54] As late as the fifteenth century Symeon of Thessalonika explained the meaning of the crowns as honoring virginity prior to marriage,[55] but crowning even for a second marriage had been allowed in Constantinople as early as the eighth century.[56]

It is striking that although in the East the priest always performed the ceremony, and crowns were always important, it was in the West that they were most central to the iconography of marriage, and were usually depicted as put on the couple by Christ Himself, acting as the

48. Ibid., p. 99, citing Barb. 336 as an example.
49. Ritzer, p. 43, citing especially Tertullian, De corona.
50. St. John Chrysostom, In Epist. I ad Tim., 2:9 (διὰ τοῦτο στέφανοι ταῖς κεφαλαῖς ἐπιτίθενται, σύμβολον τῆς νίκης, ὅτι ἀήττητοι γενόμενοι, οὕτω προσέρχονται τῇ εὐνῇ ὅτι μὴ κατηγωνίσθησαν ὑπὸ τῆς ἡδονῆς, PG 62:546) and Theodore Studite (PG 99:1092–93); cf. Stevenson, pp. 23–24.
51. Stevenson, p. 101, citing Patmos 104 (thirteenth century).
52. The Book of Wisdom occurs only in the LXX; the Hebrew original (if there was one) does not survive.
53. Heb. 13:4: see discussion and n. 34, above.
54. Wolff, pp. 85–86, with bibliography.
55. παρθενίαν ἄχρι τοῦ γάμου, De matrimonio 276 (PG 155:505). But in Athos Kost. 60 (Dmitrievskij CXXIV p. 855) the crowning is accompanied by an appeal to Stephen's crowning with martyrdom, and the crowning part of the ceremony concludes with Ἅγιοι μάρτυρες, οἱ καλῶς ἀθλήσαντες (p. 856).
56. Ritzer, pp. 146–47: Dieselben setzen wohl die unterschiedslose Krönung der γάμοι und der δίγαμοι als übliche oder wenigstens gedultete Sitte voraus.

pronubus (roughly, "the best man").[57] Just as heterosexual ceremonies during this time rarely mention Communion (whereas most same-sex unions do), same-sex union rites only rarely mention crowning, which may have been too closely associated with female virginity to be regarded as essential when two males were being united. On the other hand, there is little doubt that the custom was associated with the same-sex ceremony. An eleventh-century exemplar does mention the *removal* of the crowns,[58] which necessarily implies their previous imposition, and at least one of the prohibitions of the ceremony to monks (who could not marry in either East or West) specifically refers to the crowns associated with the ceremony,[59] calling them the "crowns of marriage" (στεφανοὺς γάμων).[60]

From ancient times a banquet had been an important part of any European union ceremony, whether to mark the official beginning of

---

[57.] Frugoni, "L'Iconografia del matrimonio," interprets this to mean that in the East it was just a pagan survival, whereas in the West it represented the theological idea of the crowning of saints (passim, but see esp. p. 966). The importance of martyrs in matrimonial language is discussed above.

[58.] Grottaferrata Γ.β. II, translated in Appendix of Translations as No. 4. This was a fairly early and influential version of the ceremony. Strikingly, Stevenson, p. 101, opines that the heterosexual ceremony for removing crowns might be as late as the fifteenth century—another reason (in addition to those given in the commentary on the text) to believe that this prayer was not inadvertently detached from a heterosexual ceremony.

[59.] Harmenopolous, a fourteenth-century jurist, in his commentary on a ruling by the late seventh-century council in Trullo that monks may not dine with women, quotes Peter, the *chartophylax* of the "Great Church" (*Hagia Sophia*), as adding the comment that monks must also not select boys at baptism and make such unions with them ('Ανέδεκτον, φησί, μοναχὸν δέχεσθαι παιδία ἀπὸ τοῦ ἁγίου βαπτίσματος, καὶ κρατεῖν στεφάνους γάμων, καὶ ἀδελφοποιίας ποιεῖν [PG 150:124]). It is striking that this comment occurs in the context of a prohibition of monks having any sort of intercourse (even social) with women. *Chartophylax* means "archivist"; I have been unable to identify this person further, but he must have lived after the council in Trullo (691–692) and before Harmenopolous. On the wider significance of picking up children from the baptismal font in relation to matrimony, see Demetrius Chomatianus in Jean-Baptiste Pitra, *Analecta sacra et classica: spicilegio solesmensi. 6: Juris ecclesiastici Graecorum selecta paralipomena* (Paris, 1891), cols. 642–44, No. clxvi.xii.

[60.] It would be impossible to understand these Greek words any other way. The Latin translation in the *PG* renders them *coronas nuptiales*, as did Goar, although he was so anxious to discount the obvious meaning of the passage (and the ceremony) that he invented and inserted the words *paranymphi more*—"in the fashion of the bridegroom"—right after *coronas nuptiales*, as if this made some sense of the statement. Despite this, he then appended a comment more revealing of the actual intent (and perhaps his own understanding) of the original: "Even today monks of laxer life [διόρθμοι] and just about any layperson, having removed women as a cause of danger, do not refrain from forming these unions" (*Hodie nihilominus Monachi διόρθμοι vitae laxioris, et laici quilibet, eliminatis tamen mulieribus periculi causa, spirituales illas fraternitates inducere non desistunt*). I have omitted *spirituales* from my translation because it is an unusual spelling (normally Goar gives *spiritualis*), and because Goar is known to have inserted this word elsewhere tendentiously: see Chapter 1, "The Vocabulary of Love and Marriage," pp. 25–26.

legal marriage[61] or simply to announce publicly an arrangement of living together more or less permanently (*contubernium*). And from ancient Crete onward it had marked same-sex unions of various sorts. By the end of the Middle Ages a wedding feast was a ubiquitous part of Christian marriage, even when the rituals used for the wedding itself varied widely.[62] It was so important, in fact, that at the opening of the twelfth century priests who blessed second marriages were forbidden to take part in the feast that followed.[63] The feast is rarely mentioned in heterosexual marriage texts or rites of same-sex union, but it is known from a variety of sources. A twelfth-century illustration of such a banquet for two men (recounted in an eleventh-century chronicle) is reproduced in plate 13.

In a modern Greek marriage ceremony after the common cup, the priest takes the couple by the hand and leads them in a circle around the altar three times.[64] The precise origins of this custom are unclear,[65] but it is probably as old as the thirteenth century.[66] It was certainly common by the end of the Middle Ages in both heterosexual and same-sex union rites. Both Slavic and Greek versions of the latter include it, as do many heterosexual ceremonies,[67] and Symeon

---

61. This was true even among the ancient Jews, although then the wedding feast was held at the groom's house (Ritzer, p. 8); the betrothal banquet was hosted by the bride's family (p. 10).

62. Brundage, p. 440. A few nuptial texts (such as Athos Athanasios 189 [thirteenth century] Dmitrievskij XX, p. 184) lack a prayer for removing crowns, but include a prayer for a wedding feast.

63. A. Pavlov, «Каноническіе Отвѣты Никиты, Митрополита Ираклійскаго (XI–XII вѣка) въ ихъ первоначальномъ видѣ и въ позднѣйшей переработкѣ Матѳея властаря (XIV в.)», византійскій временникъ, 2 (1895) 160–76, p. 167; cf. Viscuso, p. 236.

64. Ritzer, p. 144 (*Dann nimmt er beide bei der Hand und führt sie im Kreise herum*), and A. von Maltzew, *Die Sakramente der orthodox-katholischen Kirche des Morgenlandes: Deutsch und slawisch unter Berücksichtigung des griechischen Urtextes* (Berlin, 1898), 274. It is also attested in Athos Athanasios Θ 88 (from the year 1475; Dmitrievskij LXI p. 443); Panteleimon 364 (also fifteenth century; Dmitrievskij LXXI p. 569); Athanasios 21 (sixteenth century; Dmitrievskij XCIX p. 763); cf. Dmitrievskij pp. 465, 814, 831, 906.

65. See Gelsi, pp. 300–4. J. Evenou, "Le Mariage," in A. G. Martimort, ed., *L'Église en prière, III: Les Sacrements* (Paris, 1984), 211, calls this movement *une sorte de danse sacreé du prêtre et des marieés autour de l'Evangile.* A similar triple circle forms part of baptism and the ordination of bishops, priests, and deacons in the Greek church, according to Gelsi, p. 301, who (ibid.) says that it is not mentioned in any document before the fourteenth century. But see preceding note.

66. Maltzew and Stevenson (p. 101) opined that this dated from the fifteenth century, but Ritzer (p. 145 n. 558) noted that it occurred already in the thirteenth-century manuscript Patmos 104, where the priest led the couple three times around the analogion before they sang the troparion of the holy martyrs.

67. Both the Slavic version translated as No. 11 in the Appendix of Translations and the Greek text Athos Coutl. 341 include this gesture. A fifteenth-century heterosexual marriage ceremony from Athos includes both the troparion of the martyrs and leading the newlyweds in a

of Thessalonika described it as an essential part of a wedding in his fifteenth-century study of marriage.[68] Afterward the couple—of whatever gender—sang the hymn referred to as "Holy Martyrs."

Crosses first appear in the same-sex union ceremony in the twelfth century, but do not become a regular feature until the later Middle Ages.[69] They had been part of the Chaldean rite of heterosexual matrimony at least since 676.[70] The use of a cross was basic to Nestorian marriage,[71] and among Copts and Jacobites both a cross and a ring were essential to heterosexual betrothal.[72] Symeon of Thessalonika even called marriage contracts "cross bonds" (σταυρικοὶ . . . δεσμοί).[73] The medieval Maronite heterosexual rite had the priest and deacon go to a table with a cross, candles, Gospel, rings, and crowns; the priest joined their hands and wrapped his stole around them.[74]

Although it is never prescribed in the text, symbolic use of an unsheathed sword was sometimes made in same-sex union ceremonies (e.g., in Ireland), as it was in the Armenian heterosexual marriage rite[75] and in a thirteenth-century Greek heterosexual marriage ceremony preserved in Sinai 966.[76]

The key gesture in union ceremonies of all types was the joining of right hands. This was an ancient Roman gesture[77] (called *dextrarum*

---

circle around the altar singing psalms (Dmitrievskij, p. 443). Other heterosexual services that exhibit this feature are Athos Athanasios 105 (D LXXIX p. 633), Athos Panteleimon 780 (D CXX p. 831), and Athos Kost. 60 (D CXXIV p. 855).

68. PG 155:513, mentioned in Gelsi, p. 301, and in Smirensky, "The Evolution of the Present Rite of Matrimony" (as above, p. 167, n. 23), p. 39.

69. One twelfth-century Greek manuscript does refer to a cross (Sinai 973 from 1153), but it may have been one of those ancillary symbols that was common but rarely prescribed. The cross becomes more prominent in later Slavic versions.

70. Stevenson, p. 118.

71. Ritzer, pp. 90–91.

72. Ibid., pp. 96–97, 99–100.

73. PG 155:505.

74. Stevenson, p. 116.

75. Ibid., p. 109.

76. Printed in Dmitrievskij XXIII p. 214: the couple stand before holy βῆμα; the priest places the crown and the common cup on the table. If the man is a layman, ζώννει αὐτῷ σπαθήν —he is girded with a sword; ἵστησι τὸν μὲν νεώτερον ἐκ δεξιῶν, τὴν δὲ κόρην ἐξ εὐωνύμων, καὶ δίδωσν ηὐτοῖς πρὸς ἕνα κηρόν.

77. See opening quotation. At Athens it was the "essential rite of matrimony" (Émile Chénon, *Recherches historiques sur quelques rites nuptiaux* [Paris, 1912], 26). In Terence's *Andria* a young man considers himself married to a woman who is not a citizen and could not actually be his legal wife; Terence has him recall a moment when, at her mother's deathbed, she put her right hand in his. "[This] represent[ed] the climax of the Roman ceremony, the moment at which the *pronuba* performed the *dextrarum junctio* by laying the bride's right hand in that of

junctio) for formalizing a contract—most often a connubial arrangement. It is also recorded in Tobit (7:13) as the key matrimonial gesture when Raguel espouses his daughter Sarah to Tobit—a text familiar to most of the Middle Ages. It persisted throughout the Middle Ages as the single most critical act in unions of all sorts:[78] by the twelfth century weddings had been transferred in France to the church's door, though in Germany and Italy they were still held at home in later centuries. "Elsewhere the priest took over the function of the bride's father, giving her to her husband and physically joining the couple's hands."[79] The same gesture occurred earlier in a large number of—probably most—same-sex union ceremonies, and is clearly noticeable in four in the Appendix of Translations. It remains today a part of the Eastern Orthodox nuptial ceremony and of those

---

the bridegroom" (Gordon Williams, "Some Aspects of Roman Marriage Ceremonies and Ideals," *Journal of Roman Studies* 48 [1958] 16–29, p. 21).

78. On the *dextrarum junctio* in the ancient world, see Reekmans, "La «dextrarum iunctio» [*sic*]," and Christopher Walter, "The *Dextrarum junctio* of Lepcis Magna in Relationship to the Iconography of Marriage," *Antiquités Africaines* 14 (1979), 271–83, and Glenys Davies, "The Significance of the Handshake Motif in Classical Funerary Art," *American Journal of Archeology* 89 (1985), 627–40. There is general agreement among the three, although Walter shows (pp. 274–75) that the gesture was also sometimes used in other contexts. But he concedes that the primary one was marriage, and notes that even in other uses it drew on metaphors of marital harmony or unity. The most constant associated term in inscriptions (e.g., on coins or military bas-reliefs) is *concordia*, which also occurs on coins where *dextrarum junctio* commemorated imperial marriage, e.g., of Caracalla and Plautilla: *concordia aeternae, concordia felix, propago imperii.* Walter also was not convinced (p. 277) that for Roman times it reflected the actual practice of the marriage rite, as opposed to merely symbolizing marriage in art. He admits that the earliest Byzantine and Germanic sources that survive show the joining of right hands as part of the marriage ceremony, but he did not feel that could be assumed to be a holdover from a Roman practice; in this he followed A. Rossbach, *Römische Hochzeits– und Ehedenkmäler* (Leipzig, 1871), and Reekmans. Davies was largely concerned to show that the *dextrarum junctio* had some other connotations, especially in early Etruscan and Greek art, but ultimately concluded (p. 639) that "the motif appeared sporadically in scenes which allude to marriage from the fifth century B.C.E. onward, and this was to become a major connotation in the latter part of the Imperial period." "The motif then [second century C.E.] took on a new meaning in funerary art, as it was used to illustrate the virtue of *concordia*, a virtue that was particularly required in marriage. As a result the motif became more clearly defined and this [p. 640] definition limited its former rich variety of meaning. With the sarcophagi of the mid- and late Empire the *dextrarum junctio* became associated more strongly with marriage." On this gesture in the Middle Ages, see Chénon, *Recherches historiques*, pp. 25–32.

79. Esther Cohen and Elliott Horowitz, "In Search of the Sacred: Jews, Christians and Rituals of Marriage in the Later Middle Ages," *Journal of Medieval and Renaissance Studies* 20 (1990), 225–49, p. 235. On the very late development of church marriage in Italy (of all places!), see Guido Ruggiero, *The Boundaries of Eros: Sex Crime and Sexuality in Renaissance Venice* (New York, 1985), esp. pp. 26–28, and Christiane Klapisch-Zuber, "Zacharie, ou le père évincé. Les rites nuptiaux toscans entre Giotto et le concile de Trente," *Annales, Économies, Sociétés, Civilisations* 34, 6 (November–December 1979), 1216–43.

of many other Christian groups as well.[80] Reekmans defined the gesture as "the husband and wife exchanging right hands," and added that "one finds it constantly in Roman iconography, both pagan and paleoChristian, until about 600 C.E."[81] Kantorowicz opined that "originally the Roman bridegroom did not clasp hands with his bride, but—in memory, as it were, of the 'Rape of the Sabine Women'— took the bride by the wrist to indicate that she was given in his possession and power and was obliged to obey and serve him."[82]

The *dextrarum junctio* was associated in Roman sculpture with the "cardinal virtues" of the Romans: *concordia, pietas, virtus, clementia*.[83] The prominence of this gesture in heterosexual weddings may have perpetuated in English the expression "to ask for her hand in marriage," although the gesture was originally related to the Roman concept of *manus*—i.e., the control of the woman first by her father and then by her husband—as Kantorowicz noted. Under Christian influence a greater semblance of equality prevailed—the consent of both parties had to be sought genuinely and verified—and since Christian marriage generally had one eye on the virtues and eternal prospects of the couple, the themes of peace, apostolic harmony, and eternal salvation became prominent and were adapted to the joining of hands.

This gesture was then [in the Middle Ages] in use throughout Christendom; one finds it in the marriage rituals of Spain, Italy,

---

[80.] Smirensky, p. 40. It was part of the Orthodox ceremony as Goar printed it. In the contemporary Episcopalian ceremony (Prayer Book of 1977), the rubric has (p. 427), "The Man, facing the woman and taking her right hand in his, says, . . . [prayer]. Then they loose their hands, and the Woman, still facing the man, takes his right hand in hers, and says . . ." Jews also utilized this gesture in marriage ceremonies in the Middle Ages, and still do so today in many Jewish traditions. Cohen and Horowitz disagree with Joseph Gutmann ("Jewish Medieval Marriage Customs in Art: Creativity and Adaptation," in D. Kraemer, ed., *The Jewish Family: Metaphor and Memory* [Oxford, 1989], 54) that the Jewish custom was derived ultimately from the Roman *dextrarum junctio* by way of Christianity, arguing instead that it was part of a "set of common symbols deriving from a shared cultural perception concerning the nature of marriage": "Rituals of Marriage," p. 236. Neither Gutmann nor Cohen/Horowitz appear to note that the gesture occurs in the Book of Tobit, which probably antedates and supercedes any Roman influence on Christianity.

[81.] *La scène des deux époux qui se serrent la main droite; . . . on la retrouvera constamment dans l'iconographie romaine, aussi bien païenne que paléochrétienne, jusqu'aux environs de l'an 600* (pp. 24–25). For patristic instances, see Tertullian, *De orat.* 22 (CSEL 20.196, ll. 12–14) and *De virgin. veland.* 11.9 (CSEL 76.96, ll. 43–45). Cf. Ritzer, p. 21.

[82.] Kantorowicz, "On the Golden Marriage Belt," p. 99.

[83.] Reekmans, p. 41.

Germany, Poland, the low countries, Scandinavia, and England.
. . . In fact, it is one of the most ancient rites of marriage, and
the only one from pagan Rome that survives in Christian practice.[84]

A sarcophagus of the late fourth century depicts a husband and wife
joining their right hands on top of a book, which Reekmans presumed
(p. 73) to be the Gospel used during their wedding ceremony. A bust
of Christ held crowns over their heads. According to Ritzer (p. 43),
the *dextrarum junctio* formed part of Christian heterosexual matrimonial observance from early times. When Theodosius' Christian sister
undertook (virginal) marriage with the general Marcian she had a
coin struck showing her holding right hands with her husband.[85]
Christians used the gesture in the mosaics of Santa Maria Maggiore in
Rome in the late fifth century to illustrate the marriages of Jacob with
Rachel and Moses with Sephora. In the Vatican's illustrated
Octateuch (Vaticanus graecus 746) many marriages are depicted; in
most, the couple is being crowned, but in a few the marriage
is symbolized by the joining of right hands. Scholars have been
uncertain what accounts for the difference.[86] The joining of
right hands was very often associated with crowning, as if the two
necessarily happened simultaneously.[87] Shakespeare[88] defined marriage as

> A contract of eternal bond of love,
> Confirm'd by mutual joindure of your hands.

84. Jean-Baptiste Molin and Protais Mutembe, *Le rituel du mariage en France du XIIe au XVIe siècle*
(Paris, 1974), 88–101, quotation on pp. 88–89. Molin and Mutembe cite Thomas Aquinas as
equating the *dextrarum junctio* with *coniunctio matrimonialis* (p. 89 n. 33), but I have been
unable to locate the citation they provide. Chénon cites a tenth-century Germanic law that
reads, *Conjunctos ipsa illa suis manibus et eiusdem lui a legitimum sibi ad uxorem abendum se tradit*
(p. 27, MGH, *Legum* 4:650). The English heterosexual ceremony of 1549 translated in
Appendix of Translations No. 12 also includes this rubric.
85. E. Stein, *Geschichte des spätromischen Reiches, 1: Vom römischen zum byzantinischen Staate*
(Vienna, 1928), 464–66, and W. Ensslin, "Marcianus," in *PWRE* 14² col. 1515.
86. Walter, for example, pp. 281–82; in the illustrated text of the Chronicle of Skylitzes in
Madrid there are numerous marriage scenes showing crowning, but only one showing *dextrarum junctio*—that of Michael IV (1034–40) and Zoe.
87. See, e.g., A. Rossbach, *Römische Hochzeits– und Ehedenkmäler* (Leipzig, 1871). Cf. also Athos
Panteleimon 162 (1890) (tenth century) (Dmitrievskij IV, p. 41).
88. *Twelfth Night*, V, 1. See other sources (including early modern English ones) cited in Chénon, p. 31 n. 4.

As might be expected, ceremonies of same-sex union were not precisely the same in all particulars as those celebrating heterosexual marriages. No examples mention rings. The role of rings in Christian heterosexual matrimony is hard to trace, partly because they were originally associated with betrothal, and continued to be involved with betrothal ceremonies even when they were commonly employed in marriage itself, and partly because they were not regarded as important even in heterosexual marriage until the thirteenth century—long after the structure of sacramental union had been fully developed for either or both genders.[89] Their significance clearly varied over time: at some points the exchange of rings was a token of future marriage rather than a part of a nuptial rite; at other points (perhaps most commonly) it constituted the bestowing of wealth on the bride—a liturgical symbol for (or replacement of) a property arrangement involving the groom's family and the bride (see, e.g., Appendix of Translations, No. 12). In any event, the rings for men and women were usually of different substances: the bride's was sometimes iron, sometimes brass or silver;[90] the groom's nearly always gold.[91] This difference probably reflected an unfavorable view of women, although it is not explained in the liturgies or contemporary theological writing.[92] By contrast, again and again after the formalities of Christian marriage had been established in the thirteenth century, both theologians and civil statutes declared that rings were not an essential component of (heterosexual) matrimony.[93]

---

[89] Chénon, §§I and III, esp. p. 35; Stevenson, p. 102.

[90] E.g., Athos Vatoped. 322 (934) (c.e. 1468) (D LIX p. 420) prescribes brass for the bride and gold for the groom; in Holy Sepulcher 8 (182), fifteenth century, (D LXIV p. 461) the bride is given silver and the groom gold (by exchange), as is the case in Athos Pantocrator 149, fifteenth century, (D LXV p. 488); in the sixteenth century Athos Kost. 60 (D CXXIV p. 855) prescribes silver for the groom and iron for the bride; they exchange three times.

[91] E.g., Sinai 962, eleventh or twelfth century (D VI p. 73), Sinai 968 (c.e. 1426) (D LVI p. 401); in the betrothal ceremony in Sinai 960, thirteenth century (D XXII p. 193), the iron ring is first put on the man and the gold on the woman; then they exchange three times; but in the marriage ceremony in the same manuscript the priest puts the iron on the male and gold on the female.

[92] This is also indicated by the twelfth-century custom of the woman kneeling to show submission, as recounted in Stevenson, p. 68.

[93] "Matrimony is accomplished not by the giving of a ring but by consent expressed in words" (*Tunc matrimonium inducitur, non tam per anuli dationem quam consensum in verbis expressum*), Geoffrey of Trani (d. 1245), *In titulos Decretalium* (Venice, 1500), fol. 167, cited by Chénon, p. 33, n. 2. Cf. "A ring is not part of the substance of matrimony" (*Anul subarrhatio non est de substantia matrimonii*), cited from a fifteenth-century civil statute from Bologna by Francesco Brandileone, "Die subarrhatio cum anulo. Ein Beitrag zur Geschichte des mittelalterlichen

A formal expression of consent is also missing from the same-sex union ceremonies, but it was uncommon in heterosexual ceremonies until the twelfth century,[94] when it became important for the church, as witness, to verify that all the conditions for canonical marriage were met (largely to forestall the couple suing for annulment later if the marriage did not work out). It was never a required part of the Orthodox heterosexual marriage ceremony, presumably because it was assumed—as it probably was in same-sex unions—that consent had led to the ceremony.[95]

Perhaps the most interesting differences are those involving the biblical passages read in the rituals. For heterosexual marriage these included Gen. 1:26, 1:28, 2:18, 15:15; Prov. 19:14; Ps. 20:4–5, 26:1, 68:28–30, 121:8, 127:1, 5, 128:3–4; Isa. 61:10–11; Matt. 19:1–6 (male and female, become one flesh), 22:2–14 (a wedding feast, but this reading was rare); John 2:1–11 (the wedding feast at Cana), 3:27–29 (the friend of bridegroom); 1 Cor. 6:15–20 (vs. fornication), 7:25–31, 32–35 (commending celibacy!). For the same-sex union ceremony the most common readings were John 15:17, 17:1 and 18–26 (both about love and harmony) and 1 Cor. 13:4–8 (the famous passage about love: still a favorite for union ceremonies of all sorts). The single most common biblical passage for same-sex unions was certainly Psalm 133, which begins, "Behold, how good and how pleasant it is for brethren to dwell together in unity."[96] Although it was probably composed with other meanings in mind, it is easy to see why it suited the context of a celebration of same-sex union.

Strained as the connection might seem to those reluctant to contemplate a nuptial rite for same-sex union, its connection to matrimo-

---

Eheschliessungsrechtes," *Deutsche Zeitschrift für Kirchenrecht*, 3rd ser., 10 (1901), 311–40, p. 338.

94. See Stevenson, p. 68. Although consent had been theoretically important to Roman marriage, no formal ritual for expressing it was ever part of the nuptial rite. In spite of the fact that Christianity also insisted on consent, and was more genuinely concerned about that of the bride, there is very little evidence of it in Christian rituals prior to the end of the Middle Ages, almost none in Greek ceremonies. See Ritzer, pp. 147–49.

95. See Schwerdtfeger, as cited in n. 1, pp. 119–21, and A. Raes, "Le consentement matrimonial dans les rites orientaux," in *EL* 48 (1934), 316. Even in the West there was some confusion about its importance, because sometimes the giving of rings occurred before the expression of consent (confusing the question of what was essential in matrimony) and sometimes after: see Chénon, pp. 45–46.

96. Medieval liturgies used either the LXX or Vulgate version of the Old Testament, in which this is Psalm 132. The LXX has Ἰδοὺ δὴ τί καλὸν ἢ τί τερπνὸν ἀλλ᾽ ἢ τὸ κατοικεῖν ἀδελφοὺς ἐπὶ τὸ αὐτό.

nial union was obviously not so remote to the Middle Ages, since the very same psalm was used in a heterosexual marriage ceremony from the fifteenth century in Bordeaux.[97] The rite also included a cross brought to the door of the church at the beginning of the liturgy and kissed by both husband and wife. The man stood on the right and the woman on the left from the beginning of the service through the entire nuptial Mass. The priest placed what the text called a "pallit" over them (comparable to binding hands with a stole). The couple divided the Host during Communion and sang Psalm 133. The most notable difference between this office and one of the ceremonies of same-sex union (aside from dividing the Host) was that in the heterosexual rite coins, symbolizing the dowry, were blessed during the ritual.[98]

Jean-Baptiste Molin, in his study of medieval marriage symbolism,[99] divides his discussion into ten medieval symbols: (1) the joining of right hands, (2) placing a veil over the spouses, (3) the giving of a ring, (4) the preparing and signing of a nuptial document, (5) the making of a bridal payment, (6) the bestowing of a wedding kiss, (7) the giving of a wedding feast, (8) the rite of the chamber, (9) various minor observations, (10) a verbal expression of consent. Few medieval nuptial liturgies had all ten before the late Middle Ages: Balsamon, a great canonist of the East, opined that in his day (the twelfth century) marriage consisted of a blessing and Communion,[100] both of which are certainly present in most forms of the same-sex union ceremony. Three, five, and ten are at bottom the same thing, according to Schwerdtfeger,[101] and vary mostly by time and place. None of these would be expected where two persons of the same gender formed a permanent union and the families were not involved. The same-sex union ceremony has (1), (2), (6), and (7).

97. Published in E. Allain, "Un *Ordo ad sponsandum* Bordelais du XVe siècle," *Bulletin historique et philologique du Comité des travaux historiques et scientifiques* (1894), 116–24.

98. . . . *petat sacerdos arras, scilicet annulum et xiii arditos* . . . Allain, p. 120, where n. 3 provides many other examples of the blessing of coins in late medieval nuptial ceremonies (Amiens, Limoges, Lyre). *Arditos* were *ardits*, worth three deniers apiece. On the blessing of money as part of some heterosexual rites (it was by no means the rule), see Chénon, pp. 51–64.

99. "Symboles, rites et textes du mariage au moyen âge latin," in *La celebrazione cristiana del matrimonio* (as cited above, n. 28), pp. 107–29.

100. δι' ἱερολογίας καὶ θείας μεταλήψεως τοῦ σώματος καὶ αἵματος τοῦ χριστοῦ, *RP* 4:160.

101. *Ethnological Sources of the Christian Marriage Ceremony* (Stockholm, 1982), 123.

7

THE HISTORY
of
SAME-SEX UNIONS IN MEDIEVAL EUROPE

HE HISTORICAL SETTING OF the ceremony is a bit harder to track than its liturgical context and development. It is, for example, impossible to know whether it represents the Christianization of an ancient same-sex rite—and if so, which one— or a Christian innovation. Since most ancient nuptial and same-sex union rites involved sharing of wine and a feast, it is easy to imagine that these ancient customs were simply arrayed in Christian garb to keep up with the prevailing ethos, just as Roman heterosexual marriage customs were reinvested with Christian meaning and persisted throughout the Middle Ages, or pagan statuary (e.g., of Venus and Cupid) was reconsecrated to Christian use (the Virgin Mary and the baby Jesus).

Saint couples—especially military pairs like Serge and Bacchus or the Theodores—continued to fascinate and preoccupy the Christian public (or at least the males who left literary and artistic records), and provided a Christian voice for the same sentiments that had produced the Roman phenomenon of sexual or institutional "brotherhood." Churches continued to be built for and dedicated to Serge and Bacchus throughout the Eastern end of the Mediterranean all during the early Middle Ages.[1] Many Christians may have understood such

---

[1.] See, e.g., Howard Crosby Butler, *Early Churches in Syria* (cited in Ch. 4, n. 208), 47, 250;

218

couplings simply as expressions of devoted friendship, while those whose own romantic interests were chiefly directed to their own gender doubtless understood them in a more personal way. Both views were probably correct: coupled saints like Peter and Paul may have been overinterpreted as romantic pairs, while Serge and Bacchus were probably correctly so understood. The oldest church in Egypt, widely believed to occupy a spot where the Holy Family lived for some time during their exile in Egypt, is dedicated to St. Serge.[2] Justinian himself, the instigator of laws sharply penalizing homosexual behavior, was believed to have added a structure dedicated to SS. Serge and Bacchus to one already consecrated to SS. Peter and Paul.[3]

Nor should the fact that an area became Christian be interpreted to mean that all of its inhabitants suddenly embraced and followed the most ascetic teachings of the new religion.[4] In many areas of

---

J. W. Crowfoot, *Churches at Bosra and Samaria-Sebaste* (London, 1937), 3; O. M. Dalton, *Byzantine Art and Archeology* (Oxford, 1911), 282–83; the guidebook by Marcus Simaika Pacha, *Guide sommaire du Musée Copte et les principales églises du Caire*, 61–65; Glanville Downey, *Gaza in the Early Sixth Century* (Norman, Okla., 1963), 109–10, 126.

[2.] Called Abu Sarga. It probably dates from the fifth century C.E. See, for example, Jill Kamil, *Coptic Egypt: History and Guide* (Cairo, 1990), and the local manual by Gabriel Bestavros, *St. Sargius Church: The Oldest Church in Egypt*.

[3.] The myths about the reasons for his doing so, dating to the seventeenth century, as well as the notion that the church was in Constantinople, are ably discussed in Cyril Mango, "The Church of Saints Sergius and Bacchus at Constantinople and the Alleged Tradition of Octagonal Palatine Churches," *Jahrbuch der österreichischen Byzantinistik* 21 (1972), 189–93; see also idem, "The Church of Sts. Sergius and Bacchus Once Again," ibid. 68 (1975), 385–92.

[4.] Indeed, the extent of early Christian hostility to same-sex eroticism has been exaggerated by modern Christians, who tend to overlook comparable Christian strictures against divorce or other common aspects of modern life also condemned by the early church, while focusing their energy and moral outrage on this particular social issue. That early Christians had a rather different view was addressed at length in *CSTH*, especially sections II–IV. Although my arguments regarding the exact translation of 1 Cor. 6:9 and 1 Tim. 1:10 have inspired some controversy (see, e.g., J. Wright, "Homosexuals or Prostitutes: The Meaning of ΑΡΣΕΝΟΚΟΙΤΑΙ [1 Cor. 6:9, 1 Tim. 1:10]," *Vigiliae Christianae* 38 [1984], 125–53; and the replies of W. L. Petersen, "Can ΑΡΣΕΝΟΚΟΙΤΑΙ Be Translated by 'Homosexuals'? [1 Cor. 6:9, 1 Tim. 1:10]," ibid. 40 [1986], 187–91; idem, "On the Study of 'Homosexuality' in Patristic Sources," *Studia Patristica* 20 [1989], 283–88; and Robin Scroggs, *The New Testament and Homosexuality: Contextual Background for Contemporary Debate* [Philadelphia, 1983]). Petersen and Scroggs disagree with my proposal for translating the Greek word ἀρσενοκοῖται, but do agree that it is anachronistic to project the term "homosexual" onto an age unaware of the psychological implications of it. I remain unpersuaded by their arguments, partly because the common form of same-sex interaction in the ancient Mediterranean involved commerce. I now realize that a crucial bit of evidence was omitted in Chapter 4 of *CSTH*: an occurrence of the noun ἀρσενοκοῖται in Eusebius, in which there is a connection between it and Sodom. Nonetheless, I remain convinced that it is a fundamental error to imagine that this word connoted "homosexual" or even "homosexual activity" to Paul. It was clearly used in later Greek canon law to mean "anal intercourse," which is not the same thing as homosexuality. For example, in the penitential mistakenly ascribed to John the Faster (d. 595; see

Europe ancient practices persisted for centuries among a populace officially Christian. In Egypt, although Christianity was lively and often quite severe (as exemplified in the Didache, the Apostolic Canons, and the writings of Clement of Alexandria), there was also much variety, as appears in the Gnostic writings and the prominence of dissenting movements in the Egyptian church. Centuries after Christian doctrine had penetrated Egypt and long after the Theodosian Code had made the upper reaches of the Roman state a Roman Catholic theocracy, an Egyptian man wrote down a magical incantation seeking supernatural help to obtain the love of another male.[5] The sixth-century African poet Luxorius, also living in a Christian world, nonetheless wrote a poem about a passively homosexual male who gave his property away to the men with whom he had sex.[6]

N. Suvorov, "Въроятный состав древнъйсшаго исповъднаго и покаяннаго устава въ восточной церкви," Византинийский временникъ 8 [1901] 357–434, 9 [1902] 378–417, pp. 413–14) a canon stipulates, "There is also ἀρσενοκοιτία with females, in which some pitifully blinded men leave the wholesome bread and, unseeing, consume trash; that is to say, leaving the female nature [sc. organ] they [use] the waste vessel of these miserable women who do not want to commit unchastity; many often do this with their own wives, more than with other men" ("Εστι δὲ γυναικεία ἀρσενοκοιτία, εἰς ἣν οἱ ἄνδρες ἐλεεινῶς σκοτούμενοι τὸν καθαρὸν καταλιπόντες ἄρτον, τὸν σκυβαλώδη τυφλώττοντες ἐσθίουσιν· ἤγουν τὴν γυναικείαν ἀφέντες φύσιν, ἐπὶ τὸν ἀφεδρῶνα τὰς ἀθλίας καὶ μὴ βουλομένας πορνεύουσι γυναῖκας· πολλάκις δὲ καὶ τὰς ἰδίας οἱ πολλοὶ πλείω τῶν ἀνδρομανῶν ἀρσενοκοιτῶν ὑποστήσονται· καὶ ἔνθεν ἐν τῇ ἐπιτιμήσει καὶ ἐκεῖθεν ἀνηλεῶς τὴν κόλασιν ἕξουσιν ὑπὲρ πάντας). There are serious problems with this text, which has been erased and pieced back together by Suvorov from other sources. Even so, it makes perfectly clear that ἀρσενοκοιτία could be heterosexual. Moreover, the penances prescribed (p. 414) for this activity were twice those for homosexual activity. It is almost certain, moreover, that neither St. Paul nor his readers had any concept of "homosexuality" as a sexual identity, and, given this fact, one could hardly expect a sophisticated or accurate taxonomy of sexual behavior in writings ascribed to him. One thinks of the Marquis of Queensberry's famous mistake in denouncing Oscar Wilde (whom he called a "Somdomite"); doubtless he had no idea what Wilde actually did in bed. Biblical translators since CSTH have often either recognized its proposed interpretation of these words (e.g., the New International Version and the New Jerusalem Bible) or at least acknowledged that the modern word "homosexual" is an inaccurate rendering of ἀρσενοκοῖται (e.g., The New American Bible). The general argument of CSTH—that Christian opposition to homosexuality in particular (as opposed to ascetic derogation of all nonprocreative sexuality) developed late and incidentally, along with hostility to other minorities (such as Jews)—has met with little opposition over the intervening decade, except for the cranky critique of R. W. Southern, Saint Anselm: A Portrait in a Landscape (Cambridge, 1990), 148–52, ably rebutted by R. I. Moore, "Anti-Semitism and the Birth of Europe," Christianity and Judaism, ed. Diana Wood (Studies in Church History 29) (Oxford, 1993) 33–57, p. 55 n. 60. For a useful collection of European documents relating to homosexuality (but no helpful analysis), see Brigitte Spreitzer, Die Stumme Sünde: Homosexualität im Mittelalter (Göppingen, 1988).

5. Paul Smither, "A Coptic Love-Charm," Journal of Egyptian Archaeology 25 (1939), 173–74.

6. Poem 35 in Luxorius: A Latin Poet among the Vandals, ed. and trans. Morris Rosenblum (New York, 1961), 132, with English translation on p. 133. This was a reversal of the most common pattern of sexual favors in the ancient world: usually the active party paid the passive party.

The Roman custom of forming a union with another male by the legal expedient of declaring him a "brother" appears to have persisted into the early Middle Ages, although it became controversial for a somewhat unexpected reason related to the decline of urban culture and the range of lifestyles around the Mediterranean. Collateral adoption was declared invalid for some outlying provinces in a handbook of Roman law compiled (in Greek) in the fourth or fifth century and translated into Syriac, Armenian, and Arabic for Roman citizens living in regions of the East where Latin and Greek were not understood.[7] The earliest surviving version, a Syriac translation probably from the fifth or sixth century,[8] says,

> If a man wishes to write brotherhood [*achuta*][9] with another man so that they are brothers,[10] and everything they possessed or will possess of their own would be common,[11] the law restrains[12] them and holds what they have written as invalid, for

---

[7.] Karl Georg Bruns and Eduard Sachau edited the code in its then known versions in *Syrisch-Römisches Rechtsbuch aus dem fünften Jahrhundert* (Leipzig, 1880). Their German translations should be viewed cautiously: they are loose to the point of misleading. As their title suggests, they considered the underlying text to be of the fifth century, as does A. Kazhdan, "The Syro-Roman Lawbook," *ODB* 3:2001–2, and Patricia Crone, *Roman, Provincial and Islamic Law: The Origins of the Islamic Patronate* (Cambridge, Mass., 1987), 12. Nallino considered the text an eighth-century translation of a "Greek scholastic manual, redacted in 476–480, expounding norms of the law of Roman citizens [*diritto quiritario*] and of '*ius novum*' " (p. 331). But if Taubenschlag (see following note) is correct that the first Syriac recension is fifth century, the Greek original must be earlier. The Armenian translation is thought to have been effected in the twelfth century from the Syriac (so Nallino, p. 332; cf. Bruns-Sachau, p. 170); the Arabic version is also probably twelfth century, and also probably based on the London Syriac MS (Bruns-Sachau, p. 168). Crone argues that the Arabic was desired by Christians in the Muslim world to show that there was a non-Islamic legal tradition (pp. 12–13). A much later and fuller Syriac version has recently been discovered: Arthur Vööbus, *The Syro-Roman Lawbook: The Syriac Text of the Recently Discovered Manuscripts Accompanied by a Facsimile Edition and Furnished with an Introduction and Translation, II* (Stockholm, 1983) (Papers of the Estonian Theological Society in Exile, 39) (the promised facsimile edition has yet to appear). Estimates of its date range from the thirteenth to the seventeenth century.

[8.] For a persuasive argument in favor of the fifth, see Raphael Taubenschlag, "Il diritto provinciale romano nel libro siro-romano," *Journal of Juristic Papyrology* 6 (1952), 103–19. For opinions favoring a later date, see Kazhdan, ut supra (sixth), Crone (seventh to eighth), Nallino, ut supra (ninth).

[9.] The same word is used among the Sus and other cultures for fraternal adoption, which had been legal and widespread among them: see, e.g., Greengus, "Sisterhood Adoption," ut supra, esp. pp. 12–13 and n. 27.

[10.] ". . . *acha anun*": not "*like* brothers," as Sachau translates (p. 21).

[11.] From the root (*shuā*) used to express the "consubstantiality" of the Trinity in Syriac theological writing.

[12.] Or "forbids": *kla* is also the word used to prohibit consanguineous marriages.

their wives are not common, nor could their children be common.[13]

Scholars have been divided about the practice referred to here. A
few have claimed that it applies to a Semitic custom of fraternal
adoption different in nature and purpose from that seen in Roman
law.[14] But most have related it to the Roman practice of collateral
adoption and the case of Zizonus (treated above, pp. 100ff.), and
concluded that it must be "principally a form of tightly formulated
friendship bond,"[15] or "brotherly friendship" leading to "community
property."[16]

The origins and function of the Syrian lawbook have also been the
subject of some controversy, but there is now general agreement that
the code "represents a didactic and practical work reproducing the
law in effect at the time of its compilation in the Roman province of
Syria . . . including many local elements."[17] It was obviously influenced by Christianity,[18] and Tamassia theorized that it was designed
for use in episcopal courts[19]—a credible hypothesis, given that by the
end of the fifth century in much of the Roman world bishops had
taken over the administrative functions of most civic officials. A similar prohibition occurs in the Greek translation of Roman law used in
Byzantium itself (see below).

The Arabic and Armenian versions of the Roman law are somewhat different, and if, as has been maintained, they were effected
from the Syriac,[20] they do not provide any independent information
about the original text. They do, however, disclose something about
how the practice and its prohibition were understood in other com-

---

[13]. Bruns-Sachau, p. 21, §86, of the Syriac. In the later Syriac MS (Rome) translated by Vööbus
(ut supra) this occurs in §127.

[14]. Nallino disposes well (pp. 337–38) of the idea espoused by some scholars that mention of
"wives and children in common" in the Syrian lawbook means that some form of polyandry
or polygamy was involved. See also n. 86 in Chapter 3.

[15]. Bruns and Sachau: . . . eine Art fest formulierter Feundschaftsbund (p. 256).

[16]. Nallino, p. 342–43.

[17]. Taubenschlag, pp. 103–4: il Libro siro-romano rappresenti un'opera didattica e pratica e riproduca
il diritto vigente al tempo della sua formazione nella provincia romana della Siria . . . intessuto
con molti elementi popolari. This matches closely the opinion of Tamassia (p. 58).

[18]. The Armenian more than the Syriac, and the Arabic more than either.

[19]. P. 57; he also posited 476–77 as the date of its composition (ibid.).

[20]. E.g., by Nallino, p. 341; this has not been a point of contention: nearly all the scholars cited
above have agreed with Nallino about it.

munities. The Arabic reads, "If a man desires[21] a brother [*ikhwān*][22] for himself or for his son, he may not effect a document [*yaktaba*] making his estate common [with the brother]. This is not permitted [*jā'iz*] if they are [heterosexually] married [*mutazawwajain*] because their wives cannot be made common property,[23] nor their children."[24] This rendering seems to acknowledge that the men making such an agreement would not necessarily be married, and it could be interpreted to mean that such a union would be invalid only in the case that they were. Certainly the son mentioned could be unmarried if he was still in the *potestas* of the father, and therefore subject to his authority for obtaining an adoptive brother. (For a case of a mother arranging her son's union with another man, see discussion of the emperor Basil and the widow Danelis, below.)

The Armenian version reads, "If someone wishes to write a document of brotherhood[25] with a friend[26] so that they become one,[27] and in all that they have and will have they are equal[28] owners and heirs, the laws[29] restrain this and hold it void, because their wives and children cannot be common."[30]

Although this provision would scarcely have been apposite by the time that women were no longer considered the "property" of their husbands (i.e., in the High Middle Ages), at least five explanations for it seem worth considering.[31] Only the first has been addressed by previous scholars.

---

21. احبّ (*Ahabba*)—which means "to love [someone romantically]" as well as "to desire [a thing]." The ambiguity of my English translation—whether the man "desires" the brother or simply "desires" to have a brother—is thus present in the original Arabic.

22. R. Dozy, *Supplément aux dictionnaires arabes* (Beirut, 1981), 1:13, gives "beloved" (*bien aimé*) as one of the meanings of this root.

23. Or "public property," or "ownerless property": مباحات (*mubāhāt*).

24. Bruns-Sachau, Arabic, p. 94, §127. Michaelidos-Nouaros (p. 281) sees significant differences between the Syriac/Armenian redactions and the Arabic; I am inclined to agree.

25. Eðbayrout'ean.

26. Or "that friend": ∂nkeroyn. ∂nker could also be translated as "pal," "comrade," or "companion." It is etymologically parallel to the last, being composed of *ker*, "eat," and ∂nd, "with."

27. *Linel noc'a miaban*. *Miabanem* is the verb "to be joined to" and "to unite" (as in, "the Alans united").

28. *Hawasar*: this word also means "friend."

29. *Awrēnk*: which refers to what is "right" [*awrēnk ē*] as well as to what is legal.

30. Bruns-Sachau, Armenian, p. 133, §126.

31. Excluding the theory that some sort of local custom of polyandry or polygamy is involved, which nearly all researchers in this century have rejected for lack of corroborating evidence (for a good summary of arguments against this approach, see Michaelidos-Nouaros, pp. 281–

1. It might be a severely garbled restatement of the decree about Zizonus (which was apparently addressed to a provincial problem).[32] One can imagine that Zizonus' suit might, through misunderstanding and bad translation, result in a law designed to protect the heirs of men desiring to form a fraternal union.[33]

2. It might relate to a procedural irregularity in the formation of such unions. Ordinary adoptions were required by the same code to take place before an official.[34] It is conceivable that it was the private writing of collateral adoption that made it invalid rather than the nature of the union.

3. On the other hand, the stated objection has nothing to do with this. It is assumed in both the Syriac and Armenian versions of the code that both parties entering into such an agreement would necessarily have wives and children—as would most males in premodern societies—and that the agreement would apply to them. This had apparently not been considered a problem in earlier Roman law on collateral adoption for a variety of possible reasons: it might have been that Roman legists never imagined that such an agreement could apply to wives and children,[35] or that Romans accepted—indeed, expected—divorce and a sequence of heterosexual marriages for adult males, whereas the Syriac code, redacted under Christian influence, probably did not. The most likely explanation is that by the time the ruling

---

82). I also exclude Michaelidos-Nouaros' own contention (p. 279) that Roman authorities found collateral adoption a threat to the state because it was associated in their minds with vendetta and other nonapproved modes of organization. This reasoning is predicated on his unquestioned assumption that *adoptio in fratrem* is a primitive form of ἀδελφοποιία, which is too gross an oversimplification to be used in historical analysis. Moreover, Roman law had clearly *allowed* some forms of *adoptio in fratrem*, as is unambiguously shown both by the *Digest* (28.5.59[58]) and by the fact that the edict of 285 specified only one particular type (*apud peregrinos*) as invalid.

32. Michaelidos-Nouaros agrees with Tamassia that this is the most likely explanation (pp. 282–83), although he suggests that the actual source is the poor translation of the code now contained in the *Basilika* 35.13.17, for which see p. 227. A common source for both seems more likely to me.

33. "Imperial rescripts were publicly posted and could create precedents to be used in later legal cases, but they were not intended as general laws with immediate application to all inhabitants of the Empire . . ." Evans-Grubbs, p. 81.

34. A man's giving his son to another man for adoption is valid only if effected before an official: London §52, Arabic §99, Armenian §98.

35. In the case of Zizonus it was an aggrieved son who brought the case to the emperors, but they ruled in his favor.

about brothers was made, most prosperous Romans (who made laws about themselves) had ceased to regard wives as property.[36]

4. Christian influence might also have introduced into the code taboos about marriage to the spouses of siblings, a subject specifically addressed elsewhere in all versions of the lawcode.[37]

5. All things considered, the most likely interpretation would seem to be that the compilers of the law meant to restrain or abolish ceremonies for same-sex unions. Both the Syriac[38] and Arabic[39] versions of the code include a law imposing a death penalty for homosexual behavior ("marriages" in the Arabic)[40]—which is probably traceable to Theodosius' bombastic prohibition of same-sex marriage.[41]

It is, moreover, striking that all versions of the code refer to the relationship of fraternal adoption as a written document rather than a verbal statement (the mode envisioned in the *Digest*). The word for

---

36. On the other hand, Greek Christian law did envision divorce: see pp. 172–73.

37. London §108, Paris §42, Arabic §53, Armenian §54; there is also a prohibition of marrying the children of one's brother: London §109, Paris §43, Arabic §53, Armenian §55.

38. London §78: those who "whore/commit fornication" (Syriac *zana*) with males deserve death "according to the law" (*namus*), along with deceivers/defrauders (from the verb *ramā*, which has many meanings; Bruns translates it as *Betrüger*, "cheat, deceiver, impostor, fake"). The later Syriac version translated by Vööbus omits the second category. Both of these could be taken from the famous lists in 1 Cor. 6:9 and 1 Tim. 1:10, but since the majority of nouns from those lists are missing from this law, it seems more probably related to the *laesa majestatis* concerns of imperial Roman law.

39. Arabic §120: "Those who marry males deserve death, along with kidnappers of either slave or free [children]." Bruns and Sachau comment that "the juxtaposition of sodomy [*sic*] and fraud in this section is quite extraordinary" (p. 244), and cite as precedent for it the Theodosian Code 9.7.3 (about a man marrying as a woman), and 6 (death by burning for forcing men into prostitution).

40. ينكحون (*yankaḥūna*); نكح (*nakaḥa*) is the normal word for "marry" in classical and modern Arabic—the meaning given in all standard lexica (e.g., Lane cites the meaning "marry" for forms 1, 3, 4, 6, and 10, as well as nouns derived therefrom). In the Qur'an نكح occurs twenty-three times (in forms 1, 4, and 10), *only* with the meaning "marry." By contrast حصن occurs less than a dozen times, mostly as a participle, and always ambiguously: its sense as "married" is dependent on and overlaps with the meaning "guarded." زوّج [*zawwaja*] is found only five times, and at least three of them refer to relations (e.g., with *houris*) that could hardly be considered legal matrimony. R. Dozy, *Supplément aux dictionnaires arabes* (Beirut, 1981) cites a single use of نكح, with the meaning "prostitute," but the lexical base for this work was Andalusian and North African, and is not particularly relevent to the Melkite translation of the lawcode. On the other hand, compare nn. 20–24, above, and 45, below.

41. See n. 46 and Ch. 3, pp. 85–86. It is notable that the Armenian version, which is otherwise very close to the Arabic version and includes, in order, Arabic §§ 103–17, 119, 122–23, 121, 124–30, should omit this provision (120), especially since it includes the prohibition of collateral adoption, and is *fuller* than the London Syriac version (by thirty-three paragraphs).

writing is also used in some of the codes for ordinary adoption,[42] but it occurs in *all* of the codes for the formalization of a heterosexual marriage.[43] Nonetheless, the Arabic version, which uses a common Arabic word for "marriage" in prohibiting homosexual unions,[44] employs a different word (*zawwaja*) for heterosexual matrimony, implying that while the two were in some way comparable, they were not *precisely* the same.[45]

That a code compiled under Christian influence included, like the Theodosian Code, an extravagant (and probably unenforced) penalty against same-sex unions is not an indication that Christians were attempting to eradicate what they saw as an immoral pagan practice, especially given that we have no reason to assume that the persons contracting such unions were not also Christians. A more reasonable inference would be that some lawmakers were interested in imposing through legislation a narrower and more ascetic sexual morality than had hitherto prevailed in the region, or were perhaps simply hostile to same-gender sexuality of any sort. (Struggles of this sort among Americans are going on as of this writing in Oregon and Colorado.) It is significant that all versions of the code include what appears to be a mechanism for "divorce" in cases of same-sex union, suggesting that the practice was widespread, persistent, and tolerated in spite of efforts to eliminate it.[46]

---

42. A man who has "written" a son (*k-th-v*, i.e., adopted: the same root used for collateral adoption in §86) cannot reject him afterward, according to the London Syriac version, §58, and the Paris Syriac MS., §72. The Arabic (§102) does not use "write" (كتب in Arabic) in the corresponding location but rather the phrase "adopt as a son" (تبنّى رجل بغلام بين يدي القاضي) [*tabannā . . . bi-ghulām bayna yaday al-qāḍi*]), although the Arabic does use كتب in its section on collateral adoption. (A son "legally adopted" could, however, be *emancipated* before a judge: London §72, Arabic §115, Armenian §114.)

43. In London Syriac §93, Paris Syriac §41b, Arabic §52, and Armenian §52 versions there is also discussion of marriages that are *not* "written," "which is the custom among many peoples"—i.e., apparently in contrast to those employing the lawbook. Those who allow "unwritten" marriage do so with a simple engagement and "with the glorified crown of virginity crown the bride, leading her in peace and joy from the home of her parents to that of her husband" (from London 93). On the requirements for legitimate matrimony among Arabic-speaking Christians, see above, Chapter 5, p. 168, n. 27.

44. الذين ينكحون الذكور. Arabic §127.

45. Despite Qur'anic usage to the contrary (see n. 40, above), *zawwaja* eventually became more common as a term for heterosexual marriage than *nakaha*. It is generally used in Arabic translations of the New Testament (most of which are difficult to date precisely) to render γαμεῖν, and the late medieval Arabic translation of the Byzantine *Eclogues* (*Die arabische Ecloga: Das vierte Buch der Kanones der Könige aus der Sammlung des Makarios*, ed. Stefan Leder [Frankfurt, 1985]), uses it for heterosexual marriage.

46. London Syriac §85, Arabic §126, Armenian §125. N.B. that in all three this provision

It is also quite clear that the parties to such a union were not simply seeking heirs or business partners: each of the codes clearly envisions participants in the unions as possibly having spouses and children, and expresses concern that their status might be affected by the union, which would not be the case in a business partnership. By contrast, in Western Europe during this period it was perfectly legal for a childless person of either gender to adopt anyone as heir to his estate.[47]

The Greek translation of Roman law, designed for use in the Byzantine Empire and called the Basilika[48] (because enacted by monarchs called βασιλεῖς), also took up the ancient question of "adoptive" brotherhood, although it added slightly different elements, since in the urban centers of the Byzantine Empire it could not be assumed by legislators that all males would be married fathers. The case of Zizonus was incorporated into a section on inheritance,[49] which read,

No one shall share a household with a foreigner from outside Rome [or: who is not Roman] by virtue of an arrangement of brotherhood, and if anyone should write something taking an heir "as brother," he [?][50] shall lose the inheritance. 2. And this is because it is not possible for someone to obtain a brother by testament . . .[51]

---

immediately precedes the law about collateral adoption. Cf. London §47, Paris §71, Arabic §97, Armenian §96, none of which is cross-referenced in the otherwise heavily annotated edition of Bruns-Sachau. Cf. also the Theodosian Code 2.9.3: a rule that anyone over twenty-five who promises something of his own free will is not only constrained to fulfill the promise, but can be declared infamis for trying to get out of it. Stempel also discusses (p. 49) means of dissolving collateral adoption.

[47.] Lex ribuaria 50 (48 and 49), Pactus legis Salicae 46, both translated in Laws of the Salian and Ripuarian Franks, trans. Theodore Rivers (New York, 1986).

[48.] Basilicorum Libri LX, ed. Gustave Heimbach (Leipzig, 1843), with scholia, and in H. J. Scheltema, D. Holwerda, and N. van der Wal (Groningen, 1953–88). (Scheltema's edition is more critical, but Heimbach's fuller.) The translation is generally thought to have been effected in the sixth century C.E., although it was not officially promulgated until near the end of the ninth century under Leo VI.

[49.] 35.13: Περὶ δικαίου ἐνστάσεως καὶ δουλοῦ ἐνστάτου, καὶ περὶ ὑποκαταστάτων τελείων καὶ ἀφηλίκων. The preceding chapter is Περὶ αἱρετικῶν ἐνστάσεων; following is Περὶ προσπορισθέας καὶ παραιτητέας καὶ προσελεύσεως καὶ ἐκζητουμένης κληρονομίας καὶ περὶ τῆς πρὸ ἀνοίξεως τῆς διαθήκης κληρονομίας παραπεμπομένης [καὶ περὶ διακατοχῆς] (bracketed words in some sources only).

[50.] It is unclear in the original which party loses the inheritance, but it seems most likely that it is the designated "brother."

[51.] 35.13.17: μηδὲ παρὰ ξένοις τοῖς ἔξω Ῥώμης οἰκοῦσι διὰ θέσεως ἀδελφότης συνιστάσθω. κἂν τις ὡς ἀδελφὸς προσληφθεὶς κληρονόμος γραφῇ, ἐκπιπτέτω τῆς

Two legal innovations surfaced in this version, translated some three centuries after the original rescript, and in quite a different social and legal context: first, it is clear that Byzantine translators of the sixth century understood the original controversy to have been related in some way to the peregrine status of one of the parties in the original case; but, second, they introduce the much-quoted aphorism that it is not, in fact, possible to adopt a brother, although it had clearly been so in the Roman law on which the translation was based.[52] A commentary on the passage says about the inserted words, μηδὲ παρὰ ξένοις ("not with foreigners"), "That is, those who are not relatives. Among relatives fraternal adoption is thus not prohibited. If anyone makes a foreigner [nonrelative?] his heir through adoption as a brother, calling him 'brother,' he does not become heir simply by virtue of the name, because the law prohibits this sort of legal brotherhood."[53] But another commentator, perhaps better versed in the original code, retreated from this position, first repeating in Greek the actual circumstances of the code's ruling in regard to Zizonus, and then reiterating the *Digest* law permitting fraternal affection to occasion joint property arrangements: "I could appoint as heir someone toward whom I have brotherly affection after calling him 'brother' as a public term of affection; however, if [the arrangement] does not arise from this sort of affection, but as the result of an error, the institution is invalid."[54] In the end, the sum of these restatements and reservations appears to have been quite different from the Syrian

---

κληρονομίας. 2: Καὶ ὅτι οὐκ ἔξεστιν τινι εἰς θέσιν λαμβάνειν ἑαυτῷ ἀδελφόν· εἰ δὲ προσληφθῇ κληρονόμος, ἐκπίπτει. N.B. that ἔξω Ῥώμης οἰκοῦσι is a clarification by a later age of something ambiguous in the original, which is cited on p. 100, n. 220.

52. The *Digest* had also stated that even eunuchs could adopt, thus denying the parallel of natural procedures: see Chapter 3, n. 223.

53. Τοῖς μὴ συγγενέσι οὖσι δηλονότι. ὡς οὖν παρὰ τοῖς συγγενέσι οὐ κεκώλυται ἡ κατὰ θέσιν ἀδελφότης. εἰ γάρ τις ξένον τινὰ κατὰ θέσιν ἀδελφὸν ἀντα γράψῃ κληρονόμον, ἀδελφὸν ὀνομάσας, οὐ ποιεῖ κληρονόμον, διὰ τὸ ἀδελφὸν αὐτὸν ὀνομάσαι, ὡς τοῦ νόμου τούτου κωλύοντος τὴν κατὰ θέσιν ἀδελφότητα. Note "m" to this scholia says: *Haec scholia e Syn.* p. 347 *hausit Fabrotus.*

54. κἄν τις ὡς ἀδελφός] Ἐδεήθη τις Βασιλέως, ὅτι ὁ πατὴρ αὐτοῦ ἔλαβεν εἰς θέσιν ἑαυτῷ ἀδελφόν, καὶ τελευτῶν ὡς ἀδελφὸν ἐνεστήσατο κληρονόμον αὐτόν. καὶ λέγει ἡ διάταξις· Οὐκ ἔξεστι τινι λαβεῖν εἰς θέσιν ἑαυτοῦ ἀδελφόν, καὶ δυνατὸν ἀποσπᾶσθαι παρ' αὐτοῦ τὸ μέρος τοῦ κληρονόμου. δύναμαι καὶ γράφειν κληρονόμον τόν, πρὸς ὃν ἔχω σχέσιν ἀδελφικήν, μετὰ τῆς κυρίας προσηγορίας ἀδελφὸν αὐτὸν ὀνομάζων. [Cf. *Digest* 28.5.59(58): *Qui frater non est, si fraterna caritate diligitur, recte cum nomine suo sub appellatione fratris heres instituitur.*] εἰ δὲ μὴ ἀπὸ τοιαύτης σχέσεως, ἀλλὰ κατὰ πλάνην ὡς ἀδελφὸν αὐτὸν ἔγραψα, ἔνστασις ἀκυροῦται. Identified simply as "Sch. b. Fabr. IV. 796."

lawcode: they were designed, ultimately, not to protect offspring or wives, but to limit Roman inheritance arrangements of a subtle nature to Roman citizens, and to protect citizens against impetuous or mistaken testamentary dispositions.

An eleventh-century treatise of Byzantine law, drawn from actual juridical decisions, makes perfectly clear that same-sex unions were well-known and effectively legal by that time, even if still disputed in some technical ways. "Same-sex unions are of persons, and they [the persons joined through the unions] alone incur impediments to marriage, not the other members of their families."[55] The point of this opinion seems to be that the *families* of those joined in same-sex union should not incur any impediment to intermarriage through consanguinity. The ruling makes clear that ἀδελφοποιήσις was completely legitimate in the mind of Eustathius Rhomaios (from whose opinions the πεῖρα was drawn), and did establish some canonical relationship between two parties.

It is, in addition, clear that same-sex unions were commonplace in early medieval Byzantine society, even among the prominent and notable. Strategios, an imperial treasurer, was twice said in the ninth century to have been the same-sex partner (ἀδελφοποιητός) centuries before of the emperor Justinian.[56] No other information about this relationship survives. Procopius in his *History* (2.1.9) mentioned Strategios as a trusted patrician, "a man of good sense and ancestry" (ξυνετῷ καὶ εὐπατρίδῃ), but said nothing about this relationship, which may be apocryphal, although in Procopius, Strategios does seem to have been close to Justinian. In another text[57] Severus, a patrician, is casually mentioned as the same-sex partner of another emperor,[58] but no further details are given.

55. Αἱ ἀδελφοποιήσεις προσώπων εἰσί, καὶ ἐκεῖνα μόνα κωλύονται εἰς γάμον, οὐχὶ δὲ τὰ λοιπὰ τῆς συγγενείας πρόσωπα. Zepos 4:1–260, 49.11, p. 201.

56. Διήγησις περὶ τῆς οἰκοδομῆς τοῦ ναοῦ τῆς μεγάλης τοῦ Θεοῦ ἐκκλησίας τῆς ἐπονομαζομένης Ἁγίας Σοφίας, in *Scriptores originum Constantinopolitanarum*, ed. Theodor Preger, 1 (Leipzig, 1901), 78–79 (§4: Στρατήγιος δὲ μάγιστρος, ὁ τῶν βασιλικῶν χρημάτων φύλαξ, ὁ τοῦ βασιλέως ἀδελφοποιητός) and 1:84–85 (§9: Στρατήγιος ὁ τοῦ βασιλέως ἀδελφοποιητός . . .).

57. Πάτρια Κωνσταντινουπόλεως, in *Scriptores originum Constantinopolitanarum*, as in n. 56, above (Leipzig, 1907), 251–52 (§108). This text is believed to have been composed in the sixth century by Hesychios and revised in the tenth century; for literature on it and the preceding text, see G. Dagron, *Constantinople imaginaire* (Paris, 1984), and E. Vitti, *Die Erzählung über den Bau der Hagia Sophia in Konstantinopel* (Amsterdam, 1986).

58. Κωνστα in the text, but there was no such emperor in the sixth century.

By contrast, details survive about some Byzantine cases of the early Middle Ages. St. Theodore of Sykeon, for example, a contemporary of Justinian (d. 613), was born in Galatia. He was the illegitimate son of a prostitute and an imperial messenger, Kosmas, who had been an acrobat and performed in the imperial circus on camels. Theodore became a hermit, lived for two years in a cave, and then for a time inhabited an iron cage. (This sort of flamboyant asceticism was common in the Christian East.) He became bishop of Anastasioupolis, but ultimately resigned to return to monastic life.

Theodore traveled widely (e.g., to Jerusalem and Constantinople), and was always under the special protection of St. George, whose intervention when he was a child appears to have been largely responsible for his holy life. (The Eastern St. George was invoked in the ceremony of same-sex union: see, e.g., Appendix of Translations, No. 14.) While he was visiting Constantinople the patriarch Thomas became "so attached to him and had such confidence in him that he begged him to enter into ceremonial union with him and to ask God that he would be together with him in the next life."[59]

Although it is hardly credible that such an energetically ascetic man would enter into *any* sort of carnal relationship, it is nonetheless possible that the union was based on passionate feelings, at least on Thomas' part. Indeed, it is difficult to interpret otherwise the latter's desire for them to be together in heaven, since traditionally the chief joy of paradise consisted in the beatific vision of God. This whole incident strongly recalls the story of Serge and Bacchus, one of very few other places in early Christian literature where a personal union in heaven was emphasized. Theodore might have consented to a relationship that ordinarily had sexual possibilities without any intention of partaking in them himself: his near-contemporary St. John the Almsgiver agreed to a heterosexual marriage even though he intended

---

[59.] Literally, "in that life": ἦν γὰρ πολλὴν σχέσιν καὶ πληροφορίαν ἔχων εἰς αὐτόν, ὡς καὶ διὰ πολλῶν δεήσεων πεῖσαι αὐτὸν ἀδελφοποίησιν ποιῆσαι μετ᾽ αὐτοῦ, καὶ αἰτῆσαι αὐτὸν παρὰ τῷ Θεῷ πρὸς τὸ καὶ ἐν ἐκείνῳ τῷ βίῳ σὺν αὐτῷ εὑρεθῆναι, Theophilos Joannou, Μνημεῖα ἁγιολόγικα νῦν πρῶτον ἐκδιδόμενα (Venice, 1884; reprint: Leipzig, 1973, in *Subsidia Byzantina lucis ope iterata*, VIII), §134, p. 481. Theodore's life has been translated in Elizabeth Dawes and Norman Baynes, *Three Byzantine Saints: Contemporary Biographies Translated from the Greek* (New York, 1977), 87–194.

to remain a virgin, and had to be forced by his father-in-law to consummate the relationship.[60]

A few centuries later Basil I (867–886), the founder of the Macedonian dynasty that ruled the Byzantine Empire from 867 to 1156, was reported to have been twice involved in ceremonial unions with other men. Although the most important sources for his life—composed under the rule of his descendants within a century of the events in question—are contradictory on some points and occasionally unreliable,[61] their take on this matter is largely consistent. His biographers (including Western sources: see below) all agreed[62] that when Basil arrived in Constantinople with nothing but a staff and a knapsack—a

[60.] Chapter 3 of his life, edited in Heinrich Gelzer, *Leontios' von Neapolis Leben des Heiligen Johannes des Barmherzigen, Erzbishofs von Alexandrien* (Sammlung ausgewählter kirchen und dogmengeschichtlicher Quellenschriften, 5) (Leipzig, 1893), and in Hippolyte Delehaye, "Une Vie inédite de Saint Jean l'Aumonier," *AB* 45 (1927), 5–74; translated in Dawes and Baynes, pp. 195–206.

[61.] See the somewhat confusing discussion in Gyula Moravcsik, "Sagen und Legenden über Kaiser Basileios I," *Dumbarton Oaks Papers* 15 (1961), 61–126, esp. pp. 110–14, and the more helpful essays of R. J. H. Jenkins, "The Chronological Accuracy of the 'Logothete' for the Years A.D. 867–913," *Dumbarton Oaks Papers* 19 (1965), 91–112, and W. Treadgold, "The Chronological Accuracy of the Chronicle of Symeon the Logothete for the Years 813–845," *Dumbarton Oaks Papers* 33 (1979), 157–97. Neither Moravcsik nor Jenkins knew the modern edition of the chronicle of Genesius, *Iosephi Genesii Regum Libri Quattuor*, ed. A. Lesmueller-Werner and I. Thurn (*Corpus fontium historiae Byzantinae*, 14) (Berlin, 1978). The standard histories of this era are those of J. B. Bury, *A History of the Eastern Roman Empire* (London, 1912) and George Ostrogorsky, *History of the Byzantine State*, trans. Joan Hussey (New Brunswick, N.J., 1957) (revised from the German edition of 1952 and preferable to it). Bury's approach to the sources is less critical than that of more recent authors; he often simply combines their accounts without attempting to assess the superiority of one over another. His discussion of these problems (App. II, pp. 453–61) is useful but outdated. Ostrogorsky was meticulous, but much work has been done in the decades since he published. A new biography of Basil, taking into account sources other than the chronicles (e.g., ecclesiastical and artistic materials) is much needed.

[62.] These include the "Theophanes Continuatus" (ed. I. Bekker in *Corpus scriptorum historiae byzantinae* [Bonn, 1838]), which many scholars, including Moravcsik, consider to be the work of Constantine VII Porphyrogenitus, Basil's grandson. I am less certain. Kazhdan (*ODB* s.v. "Theophanes Continuatus") is also cautious. Moravcsik rightly groups together (pp. 110–11) the texts known as "George the Monk" and Symeon (Magister) Logothete, Χρονογραφία, both published in Bekker, and provides a critical edition of "George's" text bearing on Basil (pp. 115–26). He underrates the significantly different Greek version printed from a Vatican MS by V. M. Istrin (Книгьи временьнія и образньія георгия Мниха. хроника георгія Амартола въ древнемъ славянорусскомъ переводъ. Текстъ, изслъдованіе и словарь [Petersburg, 1920–1922], in Friedrich Scholz, *Die Chronik des Georgios Hamartolos in altslavischer übersetzung* [Munich, 1972]): the Old Church Slavonic translation of this, which Moravcsik admits might be tenth-century, reproduces the Greek text almost word for word where they overlap. By contrast, both Treadgold and Jenkins overvalue the chronicle of Symeon Logothete, which, while doubtless less tendentious, also includes less information. For a general overview of Basil's life as portrayed in the sources, see, in addition to Moravcsik, Bury, pp. 161–79, and M. Adontz, "L'âge et l'origine de Basile Ier," *Byzantion* 8 (1933), 475–500; 9 (1934), 223–60.

young man from the provinces with no connections in the capital—
he was befriended by a certain Nicholas of the church of St. Diomede,
who rescued him from sleeping in the streets, brought him into the
church, bathed and clothed him, and supported him for some time,
until the ambitious Basil was able to attract the attention of a well-
placed courtier related to the imperial family.[63]

In most accounts of their relationship Nicholas and Basil are
united in a church ceremony. According to one tradition, on the
morning after finding him Nicholas "bathed and dressed Basil and was
ceremonially united to him, and kept him as his housemate and companion."[64] Another version is more explicit about the ceremony:
"and on the next day he went with him to the baths and changed [his
clothes] and going into the church established a formal union with
him, and they rejoiced in each other."[65] The odd final phrase would
probably recall to a Christian Greek reader the biblical "Rejoice with
the wife of thy youth."[66]

Given the wording in the chronicles (one uses ἀδελφοποίησις,

---

63. Nicholas had been, according to the chroniclers, alerted mystically to look out for someone
who would one day become emperor. In some sources it is a dream, in others simply a voice.
Nicholas is identified in *Theophanes Continuatus*, 5.9, p. 223, as abbot of the monastery
associated with the chapel (ὁ τῆς μονῆς καθηγούμενος), but Symeon ("De Michaele et
Theodora," 11, ed. Bekker, p. 656) refers to him as προσμονάριος, as does George's chronicle, both in Moravcsik's critical text (p. 120) and as printed in Bekker, p. 819. The Vatican
MS in Istrin (§4, 2:5) describes Nicholas as νεώκορος, "sacristan."

64. τῇ δὲ ἐπαύριον λούσας αὐτὸν καὶ ἱμάτιον περιβαλών, πνευματικὸν ἀδελφὸν
ἐποιήσατο καὶ ὁμώροφον εἶχε καὶ ὁμοδίαιτον, Chronicle of George in Istrin, 2:5.
ὁμοδίαιτον means "sharing a common life." Proclus uses it to characterize the "marriage" of
grace and strength in his encomium to St. Stephen (χάρις καὶ δύναμις, ὁμοδίαιτος
συζυγία: §3, PG 65:812). The Old Church Slavonic translation renders this и наоутре же
измываеть его и в порты ѡблекъ, дховна брата створи себѣ и единохизника и
единотрапезника (Istrin, 1:506). единохизника и единотрапезника means "of one life
and table."

65. τῇ δευτέρᾳ ἡμέρᾳ ἀπελθὼν μετ' αὐτοῦ εἰς τὸ λουτρὸν ἤλλαξεν αὐτὸν καὶ ἐλθὼν ἐν τῇ
ἐκκλησίᾳ ἐποίησεν ἀδελφοποίησιν μετ' αὐτοῦ, καὶ συνηυφραίνοντο ἐν ἀλλήλοις,
George in Moravcsik, p. 120. Cf. the virtually identical version attributed to "Leo Gram-
maticus": *Leonis Grammatici Chronographia*, ed. I. Bekker (Bonn, 1842), 233–34.

66. Prov. 5:18 (καὶ συνευφραίνου μετὰ γυναικὸς τῆς νεότητός σου) is the only place in the
Bible where the verb συνευφραίνομαι occurs. Cf. Symeon (the source most trusted by
recent authors), "De Michaele et Theodora," 11, p. 656: καὶ τῇ ἐπαύριον λούσας
ἤλλαξεν αὐτὸν, καὶ ἀδελφοποιητὸν ποιήσας συνευφραίνετο αὐτῷ, and George, ed.
Bekker, "De Michaele et Theodora," 11, p. 820, where the wording is similar to Moravcsik's
text. The late medieval (fourteenth- or fifteenth-century) Old Slavonic translation of
Symeon has, въ бторыи днь, шде съ нимь въ бана, преѡблъче его и, пришде въ
црковь, побратимиса съ нимь; и веселастаса драгъ съ дргомь, Хроника Симеона
Логоѳета съ дополненіями, ed. V. I. Sreznevskij (St. Petersburg, 1905), in *Die Chronik des
symeon Metaphrastes und Logothetes*, ed. Robert Zett (Munich, 1971), 102.

another ἀδελφοποίητος) and the fact that the union is accomplished in a church, there can be little doubt that the writers have in mind some form of the ceremony published and translated in this text. There is no suggestion of any tribal or family aspect to the relationship, nor of the exchange of blood; it has no military or strategic aspect, nor are any circumstances adduced as requiring or occasioning it (e.g., rescue from danger, a serious illness, which would all be occasions in later Slavic relationships modeled on it). It is clearly a personal relation, undertaken for personal reasons. Both Basil and Nicholas had living biological brothers with whom they were in regular and close contact, so it could hardly have been inspired by a need for a sibling.[67] Indeed, it was Nicholas' own natal brother, a physician, who was responsible for Basil's introduction at court, a fact adduced immediately after the union in all versions. Nor does the mention of rejoicing suggest a coldly calculated relationship. Taken with the statement by Hamartolos that the union led to a sharing of home and hearth, it strongly evokes a wedding, followed by jubilation and a shared life.

It is striking that in a tradition about this relationship in which Nicholas is identified as a monastic, the ceremonial union is not mentioned.[68] By contrast, the chroniclers who do discuss the union characterize Nicholas as a parish cleric in minor orders—hence, not prohibited by ecclesiastical law from entering into same-sex union (see below on this).[69]

From the perspective of Basil, who would otherwise have been sleeping on the streets, formalizing Nicholas' benevolent interest in him could only have been advantageous, at least until he found a means of advancing his career more rapidly with someone more powerful and better connected. It is less clear what Nicholas gained from the impetuous union. Taking the story—including Nicholas' supernatural information about Basil's future greatness—at face value, one could conclude that Nicholas imagined he would ultimately profit from entering into a formal relationship with someone who would

---

[67.] Basil had at least two brothers, Bardas and Marianos; whether there was a third is a subject of dispute: see Adontz, pp. 230–31. His brothers were close enough to him to assist him in assassinating the emperor Michael.

[68.] *Theophanes Continuatus,* 5.9.

[69.] Novel 5.8 prohibits monks from marrying unless they are ψάλτων/*cantores* or ἀναγνώστων/*lectores.*

one day become emperor.[70] But what sort of relationship was it? An explanation is suggested by Basil's subsequent career. He next entered the service of Theophilos,[71] who, in the words of one chronicler, "had a great interest in well-born, good-looking, well-built men who were very masculine and strong,"[72] and when he saw how exceptional Basil was in these respects he appointed him his *protostratorius* (chief equerry). Basil "was loved by him more and more with each passing day."[73] Basil was thus what modern Americans would call a "hunk," and he made the most of the appeal this exercized for some of his contemporaries, both male and female.

While Basil was still in the service of Theophilos, they made a trip together to Greece. A wealthy widow in Achaia showered him with gifts of gold and dozens of slaves.[74] In return for her generosity she asked nothing but that Basil should enter into ceremonial union with her son, John.[75] At first he refused, because he thought it would make him look "cheap" (εὐτελές), but at length she prevailed and he agreed. "I seek and ask nothing from you," she assured him, "except that you love and deal kindly with us."[76] A surviving medieval illustration of this incident shows Basil and John being united before a cleric in church, with the Gospel open before them and John's mother looking on. An accompanying frame depicts Basil, John, and

---

70. According to George's chronicle (ed. Bekker, 10, p. 842), both Nicholas and his brother were honored by Basil when he became emperor, but the major beneficiary was the church of St. Diomede itself.

71. *Theophanes Continuatus* gives the name first as Θεοφιλίτζης Παιδευόμενος, then repeats it as Θεοφιλίδιος and Θεόφιλος (Bekker, 5.9, pp. 224–25); George (Moravcsik, pp. 120–21; Bekker, "De Michaele et Theodora," 7, p. 816; Istrin, 2:5–6) calls him Θεοφιλίτζης.

72. εἰς σπουδὴν ἔχον γενναίους ἄνδρας καὶ εὐειδεῖς καὶ εὐήλικας καὶ ἐπ' ἀνδρίᾳ μάλιστα καὶ ἀρώμῃ σώματος διαφέροντας, *Theophanes Continuatus*, 5.9, p. 225.

73. καὶ ἡμέραν ἐξ ἡμέρας ἐπὶ πλέον ἠγαπᾶτο παρ' αὐτοῦ, ibid.

74. Thirty, to be exact; Adontz oddly misreads as three hundred (p. 487). Steven Runciman, "The Widow Danelis," in *Études dédiées à la mémoire d'André M. Andréadès publiées par un comité d'amis et d'élèves*, ed. K. Varvaressos (Athens, 1940), 425–31, p. 431, describes the widow Danelis somewhat dramatically as "one of the most significant, just as she was one of the wealthiest, figures in Greek economic history."

75. μηδὲν ἕτερον ἐπιζητήσασα τὸ πρότερον παρ' αὐτοῦ ἢ τὸ ποιήσασθαι πνευματικῆς ἀδελφότητος σύνδεσμον πρὸς Ἰωάννην τὸν ταύτης υἱόν, *Theophanes Continuatus*, 5.11, p. 228. A century later, probably drawing on this account, John Skylitzes told the story in largely the same terms: μηδὲν ἕτερον ἐπιζηττήσασα παρ' αὐτοῦ, ἢ πνευματικῆς ἀδελφότητος συνδέσμῳ συνδεθῆται πρὸς Ἰωάννην τὸν ταύτης υἱόν, *Ioannis Scylitzae synopsis historiarum*, ed. I. Thurn (*Corpus Fontium Historiae Byzantinae*, 5) (Berlin, 1973), pp. 122–23.

76. *Theophanes Continuatus*, 5.11, p. 228: οὐδὲν ἕτερον ἐπιζητῶ ἢ ἀπαιτῶ παρὰ σοῦ πλὴν ἵνα ἀγαπᾷς καὶ ἐλεῇς ἡμᾶς.

Danelis (John's mother, mentioned above, p. 223) at a table—doubtless the artist's conception of the feast that would usually follow such a ceremony.[77]

When he subsequently became emperor Basil immediately "sent for the son of the widow Danelis, honored him with the title *protospatarius*, and granted him intimacy[78] with him on account of their earlier shared life in ceremonial union."[79] The widow herself—now too elderly to ride—came to the emperor on a litter, but rather than requesting any munificence from him, she brought more extravagant gifts "than nearly any other foreign ruler had up to that time ever bestowed on a Roman emperor."[80] In addition, she "who was worthy to be called the emperor's mother"[81] made a large gift of her patrimony in the Peloponnese to her son and the emperor *together* (τῷ υἱῷ καὶ βασιλεῖ).[82]

Were it not for the genders involved, this incident would seem quite a familiar feature of the premodern political landscape: a wealthy widow offers her marriageable child to a powerful young man

---

[77.] See Figure 13.

[78.] Or "freedom of access": παρρησία, a word in Roman and Byzantine law relating to unwritten marriage. See, in particular, the Syro-Roman lawbook (discussed on pp. 221ff.), Syriac London MS §93, in which παρρησία is transliterated into Syriac as if it were a technical legal word relating to marriage. For scholarly commentary on this, consult Hans Julius Wolff, *Written and Unwritten Marriages in Hellenistic and Postclassical Roman Law* (Philological Monographs published by the American Philological Association, 9) (Haverford, Penn., 1939), 83–86; C. A. Nallino, "Παρρησία e nozze senza scrittura nel Libro siroromano," *Rivista degli Studi Orientali* 10 (1923), 58–77; and Arnold Ehrhardt, "Παρρησία," *Symbolae Friburgenses in honorem Ottonis Lenel* (Leipzig, 1931), 80–107.

[79.] *Theoph. Cont.*, 5.74, p. 317: τὸν δὲ τῆς Δανηλίδος υἱὸν ἅμα τῷ γενέσθαι τῆς ἀρχῆς ἐγκρατὴς μεταπεμψάμενος τῷ τοῦ πρωτοσπαθαρίου ἐτίμησεν ἀξιώματι καὶ τῆς πρὸς αὐτὸν παρρησίας μετέδωκε διὰ τὴν φθάσασαν κοινωνίαν τῆς πνευματικῆς ἀδελφότατος. Κοινωνία can mean either "common life," "sexual intercourse," or "Communion" (in the technical, liturgical sense). The phrase τὴν φθάσασαν κοινωνίαν τῆς πνευματικῆς ἀδελφότατος is thus richly freighted.

[80.] Ibid., 5.75, p. 318: οἷα τῶν ἐθνικῶν βασιλέων οὐδεὶς σχεδὸν μέχρι καὶ τότε πρὸς βασιλέα Ῥωμαίων εἰσήγαγεν. These included three hundred male slaves, a hundred female servants, great quantities of cloth, and gold and silver vessels. Runciman, "The Widow," pp. 429–30, reasonably concludes from the emphasis on slaves and types of cloth that the Danelis family had made their fortune through the production of cloth. He takes the description of the widow's gifts at face value, noting that the imperial treasury kept very careful records of such matters (p. 427).

[81.] Ibid., 5.75, p. 318: μήτηρ καλεῖσθαι βασιλέως ἀξιωθεῖσα. Runciman (p. 426) notes that the widow "regarded [Basil] as her son—while he treated her as his mother." Adontz unaccountably insists that the relationship between John and Basil is an invention, and that the widow Danelis was in fact Basil's mistress (p. 489).

[82.] Ibid., p. 319. Runciman interprets the phrase as meaning "to the emperor, who [sic] she regarded as her son," but this seems to me to press the text too far.

on the rise, along with a substantial dowry, hoping to ally her fortunes to his. Basil's own father had been married to the daughter of a wealthy widow in a striking parallel.[83] The previous Byzantine dynasty, the Amorian, had been established under similar, though apparently heterosexual circumstances: born of humble parents, uneducated and unconnected, its founder Michael II advanced himself through strength of arms and military skill until he was able to marry Thekla, the daughter of a high-ranking officer, and attracted the attention of the emperor Leo V, who made him *protostratarius*—the same position Basil had held in the service of Theophilos—and became godfather to one of his sons. When Leo attempted to have Michael executed on charges of treason, he was himself assassinated and Michael was crowned emperor.

The widow Danelis was much richer than Basil and, when he became emperor, realized no material gain from the relationship, so it can hardly be viewed as a mercenary arrangement on her part. On the contrary, every year of Basil's life she sent *him* expensive gifts, and years later, when both Basil and her son had died, the widow came again on a litter to see Basil's son Leo, now emperor, and made him her heir, although she had a grandson and other relatives.[84]

The two stories about Basil are similar: in each there is a divine revelation, to a cleric or monk, about Basil's future greatness; in each the relationship established is to Basil's material advantage. It is possible that in imperial circles it was later known that Basil had profited substantially as a young man from a formal relationship with another male, and different chroniclers simply supplied different details. Each of the biographies written within a century of the events contains *one or the other* of the same-sex unions; none contains both.[85] On the other hand, Nicholas does appear in *all* of the most important accounts of Basil's life as his benefactor, even those that mention the union with John, and the wealth of detail about the widow Danelis (including her subsequent relations with Leo) makes it seem unlikely that she was pure invention. Possibly Basil was united to both men. It

---

83. *Theoph. Cont.*, 5.3, pp. 215–16.

84. Ibid., p. 320. Zenobius learns of her death from an ἐκγόνος. Cf. Runciman, p. 426. It is not known whether John was the father of the grandson: she may have had other children as well.

85. Moravcsik, p. 97, n. 163, lists later chronicles referring to this incident.

is not clear that this would have been improper in Basil's day—or that issues of propriety would have constrained his behavior.

After Basil had formed his relationship with John and Danelis, he was taken into the service of the emperor Michael III, a strange young man in his late teens who enjoyed dressing up as a prelate and devoted himself largely to his passion for horses and races.[86] Michael became so attached to Basil that he named him "companion of the bedchamber"—παρακοιμώμενος, a position usually held by a eunuch[87]—and adopted him as his son (υἱοποιησάμενος ἦν τὸν Βασίλειον),[88] though Basil was almost certainly older than the emperor.[89] Ultimately he named Basil co-emperor in a dramatic public scene, announcing that he did so because of Basil's having rescued him from would-be assassins (by which he meant his uncle, Bardas, who had been his closest colleague and adviser before Basil jealously murdered him in the emperor's presence),[90] and on account of "the great love [Basil] bears me."[91]

One of Michael's modern biographers[92] somewhat reluctantly observes of his relations with Basil:

[86.] These details are supplied by chronicles commissioned or written by successors of Basil, who had reason to justify his murder of Michael, and whose portrait of Michael should therefore be viewed with some caution, although most scholars since Bury have seen reason to credit these particular details (Adontz, for example). The ecclesiastical travesty is confirmed by church writers (e.g., Nicetas Paphlagonis, *Vita S. Ignatii* [PG 105:528], on which see R. J. H. Jenkins, "A Note on Nicetas David Paphlago and the *Vita Ignatii*," *Dumbarton Oaks Papers* 19 [1965], 241–47).

[87.] The English "chamberlain" is a comparable title, although the word has different connotations to modern English speakers and was never associated with eunuchs, a significant contextual factor. That eunuchs were used for sexual purposes was axiomatic in antiquity (see, e.g., *Digest* 48.8.3.4: *qui hominem libidinis uel promercii causa castrauerit*) and apparently still widely believed in medieval Byzantium: ὁ διὰ ἡδονὴν ἢ δι᾽ ἐμπορείαν εὐνουχίσας τινά...*Ekloga* 45.34 (Zepos 4:575), probably influenced by but not simply a translation of the *Digest*.

[88.] *Theoph. Cont.*, 5.18, p. 239. Michael II also had an adopted son: εἰσποιητῷ...υἱῷ (ibid., 2.13, p. 56), in addition to his biological heir, Theophilos, this Michael's father.

[89.] On the ages of both, see Adontz, pp. 494–96.

[90.] Ostrogorsky, *History of the Byzantine State*, p. 296, comments, "Michael III had fallen so deeply under the spell of his favourite that he sacrificed his uncle without hesitation."

[91.] καὶ πόθον πολὺν πρός με ἔχοντα, George in Bekker, "De Michaele et Theodora," 30, p. 832. Πόθος, which I have translated conservatively as "love," usually means "longing" or "desire"; it is used in a distinctly sexual sense of Michael's own feelings in *Theoph. Cont.*, 4.37, p. 199, and is the word that Fathers of the Eastern church used specifically of sexual desire between husband and wife (see, e.g., John Chrysostom, *Contra eos qui subintroductas habent virgines*, 1 and passim [PG 47:495–514]; e.g., δι᾽ οὐδὲν γὰρ ἡ συνοίκησις αὕτη νενομοθέτηται, ἢ δι᾽ ἔρωτα καὶ πόθον [col. 502]).

[92.] Cf. n. 86, above.

The intimate friendship between the Emperor Michael and the Armenian groom . . . suggests reflections of a not very pleasing nature. Bad as Michael's character was . . . it seems that we must also credit him with homosexualism [sic]: and this is confirmed, both by his making Basil his bedfellow, and by his choice, when he grew tired of Basil, of a pretty boy to succeed him as favourite.[93]

Liudprand of Cremona, a Western contemporary of Basil's who had been to Constantinople and learned Greek, and whose family had been connected to the court there for generations, simplified the story in his Latin version, but hinted strongly at the same thing:

The Emperor Basil . . . [94] was from a humble Macedonian family, and came to Constantinople . . . under the yoke of poverty to serve a certain abbot. Thus when Michael, who was then emperor, came for prayer to the monastery in which he worked, he saw that he was exceptionally good-looking[95] and approached the abbot and asked if this boy[96] might be given to him (or: that he might be given to this boy).[97] Taking him to the palace, he gave him the office of companion of the bed-chamber.[98]

About a year later Basil orchestrated and took part in Michael's assassination in bed, and thereafter ruled alone.

The singular complexity of imperial sources during this period

---

93. Romilly Jenkins, Byzantium: The Imperial Centuries A.D. 610–1071 (New York, 1966), p. 165. The "pretty boy" to whom Jenkins alludes is presumably Gryllus, whom Michael called his "patriarch."

94. I have omitted several phrases in which Liudprand simply shows off his knowledge of Greek, since these add nothing to the narrative and constitute something of a distraction.

95. Literally, "that he excelled all the others in his exceptional form": hunc forma praeter ceteros egregia.

96. Possibly puer here means "slave," but it seems unlikely in reference to a future emperor.

97. The Latin says unambiguously, "that he might be given to this boy" (ut se donaret hoc puero), and although Liudprand is sometimes clumsy, it would be quite unusual for him to make such a gross grammatical error if he meant to say, "the boy might be given to him." On the other hand, "that he might be given to the boy"—without any explanation—is so peculiar (except as a sexual comment) that I have preferred the alternative.

98. Liudprand of Cremona, Antapodosis, 1.8, in Die Werke Liudprands von Cremona, ed. Joseph Becker (Hannover, 1915) [MGH SSRRGG 41], p. 8; this is repeated word for word at 3.32 (ibid., pp. 88–89).

makes it difficult to decipher the dynastic relations of Michael and Basil before the former's death. Bury summarized the matter thus:

> The confidential intimacy which existed between Michael and his Chamberlain [Basil] was shown by the curious matrimonial arrangement which the Emperor brought to pass. Basil was already married,[99] but Michael caused him to divorce his wife, and married him to his own early love, Eudocia Ingerina. But this was only an official arrangement; Eudocia remained the Emperor's mistress. A mistress, however, was also provided for Basil, of distinguished rank though not of tender years.[100] . . . Thus three ladies, Eudocia Ingerina, Eudocia the Augusta [of Dekapolis—Michael's wife], and Thecla the Augusta, fulfilled between them the four posts of wives and mistresses to the Emperor and his Chamberlain.[101]

This tangle of relationships produced two of the subsequent occupants of the imperial throne, and neither they nor historians since have been altogether certain whose descendants they were,[102] although officially Michael had no children and there is reason to doubt that he sired any.[103] Since it is not known how long either Nicholas or John lived (both had apparently died by the time Leo acceded), and since heterosexual marriage appears to have been simply a means to dynastic ends for both Michael and Basil, little can be inferred with confidence from Basil's life about contemporary views of the relationship between same-sex ceremonial union and heterosexual marriage.

[99.] A youthful marriage: Basil had a son from this union—Constantine, whom he made co-emperor in 869, but who died the following year.

[100.] This was Thecla, Michael's sister, who had been a nun and was now probably forty-three, about two decades older than Basil.

[101.] *History of the Eastern Empire*, p. 169.

[102.] In the *ODB* the entry for Michael III (by Anthony Cutler and Paul Hollingsworth) erroneously asserts (2:1364) that Theodora married Michael to Eudokia Ingerina; it was actually Eudokia of Dekapolis. Kazhdan in his entry for "Macedonian Dynasty" (2:1262) correctly describes Eudokia as the "former mistress" of Michael. He also cites Leo VI as the son of Basil I both in the entry for him (2:1210) and in that for "Macedonian Dynasty" (2:1262), while Cutler and Hollingsworth tantalizingly note in their entry for Michael that Leo VI was "perhaps Michael's son by Eudokia Ingerina" (2:1364).

[103.] ". . . Michael had no children, and in all probability could not have any, either by Eudocia or by anybody else. How far his homosexual tendency and his incurable alcoholism contributed to this state of affairs we need not now enquire, although contemporaries did; but the fact seems to be indisputable," Jenkins, *Byzantium*, pp. 198–99.

It is nonetheless clear that ceremonial same-sex unions were parallel to heterosexual marriage in the ninth century in a number of ways: they were relationships between individuals of a personal nature (rather than tribal, religious, or political); they entailed consequences for the immediate family (John's mother; Nicholas' brother) comparable to the obligations or rights of in-laws; they were recognized by society, and even respected by descendants.

It was most likely for this reason that monks were always and everywhere prohibited from entering into same-sex unions, just as they were forbidden to contract heterosexual marriage in both East and West, by both civil and ecclesiastical law (although in the East other members of the clergy could marry).[104] Basil the Great (in the fourth century) had argued that no sexual relations (which he called πορνείας) of persons in orders (τῶν κανονικῶν) could be regarded as "marriages," and that such unions (συνάφειαν) must by all means be dissolved.[105] Around 580, monks were also forbidden to make "leagues" or "associations."[106] This rule was presumably based on a provision aimed at the laity in the same collection.[107] In the case of the laity the prohibition was certainly not aimed at same-sex unions, but it is conceivable that in the case of monks the same canon was interpreted as a blanket condemnation of all relationships requiring an oath. A more or less contemporary ruling for laypeople makes perfectly evident that same-sex unions were altogether legal.[108]

---

104. E.g., in the East, Novel 5.8 prohibited monks from marrying unless they were ψάλτων/ cantores or ἀναγνώστων/lectores. This could have been the technicality that permitted the cleric Nicholas to contract a same-sex union with Basil (see pp. 231ff.).

105. Letter 188 in Collected Letters of St. Basil, ed. and trans. Roy Deferrari (Cambridge, Mass., 1962), 3, p. 26 [LCL].

106. Περὶ μοναχῶν ποιούντων φρατρίας καὶ συνωμοσίας. Συν·Χαλκηδόνος καν.ιη´ [Συν.ϛ´ καν. λδ]; Nomocanon XIV titulorum, in J. B. Pitra, Iuris ecclesiastici graecorum historia et monumenta, 2 (Rome, 1868), 11.6, p. 596.

107. Περὶ τῶν ποιύντων συνωμοσίας ἢ φρατρίας. Συνόδου Χαλκηδόνος κανὼν ιη´. Συνόδου Καρθαγένης κανὼν νγ´. [Συνόδου ϛ´ κανὼν λδ´]. Ὁ νόμος. Καὶ ὁ πολιτικὸς νόμος τιμωρεῖται τὰς φρατρίας, καὶ τὰς συνωμοσίας, ὡς βιβλίον μη´ τίτ. δ´ διάτ. δ´, καὶ τίτ. ιθ´ διάτ. ια´ καὶ ιϛ´. Ibid., 9.37, p. 576. The sources elliptically cited are the Synod of Chalcedon [451] canon 18; Synod 6, canon 34; the Synod of Carthage, canon 53; Digest 48.4.4 on treason and oaths taken for treason [dolo malo jurejurando], 48.19.11 (robbers who form a band show premeditation: proposito delinquunt latrones, qui factionem habent) and 48.19.16 (coniurationes); Basilika 60.36.4.

108. γαμβρὸς γυναικαδέλφου μὴ βαπτίσει, μήτε νύμφη καὶ τοῦ ἀνδραδέλφου ἢ ἀνδραδέλφης· τὸ δὲ κατὰ ἀδελφοποιητοῦ, ἢ γαμβρὸς καὶ νύμφη βαπτισάτω. ἐν τούτῳ γὰρ στερεώτερόν ἐστιν ἡ συγγένεια, καὶ ἡ συντεκνία, καὶ ἡ φιλία αὐτῷ, ἡ καθαρὴ καὶ ἀγαθή, Nomocanon 277, from J. Cotelière, Ecclesiae graecae monumenta, 1 (Paris, 1677–92), from the early seventh century.

The real context of the prohibition to monks is evident in a re-statement of St. Basil's rule for monks (the equivalent of the Rule of Benedict in the West) by St. Theodore of Studium (759–826), in which the monks were told, "Do not contract same-sex unions with or become spiritual kin [i.e., godparents] to the laity, you who have left behind the world and marriage. For this[109] is not found among the fathers, or if it is, only rarely; it is not legal."[110] This rule was often repeated in later ages (e.g., "It is prohibited for monks to form same-sex unions or be godparents, and the church recommends, by way of admonition, the same [prohibition] for leaders or heads of monasteries. The law does not recognize so-called same-sex unions altogether").[111] Such blanket condemnations inspire skepticism, both because of the historical evidence treated in this chapter and because same-sex union is coupled in such texts with godparenting, which was not only legal but a key element of liturgical life for most Christians in the Middle Ages (see Chapter 5, p. 193, where Blastares is quoted as saying [in the fourteenth century] that it constitutes the *most common* form of relationship).

Harmenopolous, a fourteenth-century jurist, in his commentary on a ruling by the seventh-century council in Trullo that monks may not dine with women, quoted Peter, the *chartophylax* (loosely, "archivist") of the "Great Church" (Hagia Sophia), as adding the comment that monks must also not select boys at baptism and make same-sex unions with them.[112] It is striking that this comment occurs in the context of a prohibition of monks having any sort of intercourse (even social) with women.

A slightly more realistic ruling later in the same century, the *Typikon* of John Tzimiskes (also for the monks on Mount Athos), states that "it is not permitted to any of the brothers to leave the

---

[109.] Sic: but there are two items at issue.

[110.] οὐ σχοίης μετὰ κοσμικῶν ἀδελφοποιίας ἢ συντεκνίας, ὁ φυγὰς τοῦ κόσμου καὶ τοῦ γάμου· οὐ γὰρ εὕρεται ἐν τοῖς Πατράσιν· εἰ δὲ καὶ εὕρεται, σπανιάκις, καὶ τοῦτο οὐ νόμος (PG 99:1820, rule 8; exactly the same wording is found in his *Epistola* 10 [99:941]). This ruling was quoted verbatim in the ninth-century rule (*Typicon*) for the Lavra St. Athanasios on Mt. Athos, published in Philipp Meyer, *Die Haupturkunden für die Geschichte der Athosklöster* (Leipzig, 1894), 101–122.

[111.] Συντεκνίας δὲ, ἢ ἀδελφοποιήσεις ποιεῖν μοναχοὺς, κεκωλυμένον ἐστί· καὶ ἐνταλματικῶς τοῦτο τοῖς ἡγουμένοις, ἢ τοῖς ἐξάρχοις τῶν μοναστηρίων ἡ Ἐκκλησία παρακελεύεται· οὐδὲ γὰρ ὁ νόμος δέχεται τὰς λεγομένας ἀδελφοποιίας ὅλως. RP 5:400.

[112.] For the Greek of this citation, as well as the little known of this Peter, see Ch. 6, n. 59.

mountain to form relationships or unions with laypersons, and *if any should happen to have done something like this* [my emphasis] they may not go to their homes or breakfast with them or dine with them or under any circumstances drink with them."[113] This precise ruling was repeated in 1406 in the *Chrysobull* of Manuel Paleologus II,[114] and about the same time a comparable prohibition was formulated by the patriarch Matthew: "Nor shall the maintenance of the monastery be used as an excuse for forming personal relations with those outside the monastery, especially laypersons, nor shall [the monks] form friendships or same-sex unions or what are called spiritual kinships with laypeople or be involved with loans or secular contracts or [other] worldly matters."[115] On the other hand, of thirty-two known *typika* (loosely, "rules") from Eastern monasteries from the early Middle Ages to the fifteenth century, at most four or five prohibit same-sex unions.[116]

The most obvious interpretation of such prohibitions is that they parallel the rule against monks marrying women. It would, however, be possible to understand them as stemming from a more general Christian antipathy to homosexuality of any sort. This ascetic tendency of Christian Rome—unknown before the advent of the new religion[117]—was certainly plain in such Western legal compilations as

---

113. Μηδενὶ συγχωρείσθω τῶν ἀδελφῶν, τοῦ "Ορους ἐξέρχεσθαι (καὶ) συντεκνίας ἢ ἀδελφοποίησεις ποιεῖν μετὰ κοσμικῶν· (καὶ) εἰ προλαβόντές τινες τοιοῦτόν τι κατεπράξαντο, μηκέτι εἰς τοὺς οἴκους αὐτῶν ἀπίτωσαν ἢ συναριστάτωσαν ἢ συνδειπνίτωσαν ἢ ὅλως μετ' αὐτῶν συμποσιαζέτων. Probably from 972; first published in Meyer, pp. 141–51; a new critical edition appeared in *Archives de l'Athos* 7 (1975), 209–15; this passage occurs on p. 212.

114. Also first published in Meyer, pp. 203–10; new ed. in *Archives de l'Athos* 7 (1975), 257–61.

115. Μηδὲ προφάσει τῆς τοῦ μοναστηρίου συστάσεως τοῖς ἔξω συμφιλιάζειν καὶ μάλιστα τοῖς κοσμικοῖς καὶ ἢ φιλίας ἢ ἀδελφοποιίας ἢ ἃς ὀνομάζουσι συντεκνίας ποιεῖν μετ' αὐτῶν καὶ πρόχρεα καὶ συναλλάγματα κοσμικὰ καὶ πραγματευτικὰς ἐμπορεύεσθαι, in I. M. Konidares and K. Manaphes, «Ἐπιτελεύτιος βούλησις καὶ διδασκαλία» τοῦ οἰκουμενικοῦ πατριάρχου Ματθαίου Α' (1397–1410)," Ἐπετηρὶς. Ἑταιρείας Βυζαντινῶν Σπουδῶν 45 (1981–82), 462–515, p. 496, sec. α'.

116. These are listed in Manaphes, Constantine, Μοναστηριακὰ Τυπικὰ–Διαθῆκαι (Athens, 1970), («ΑΘΗΝΑ» ΣΥΓΓΡΑΜΜΑ ΠΕΡΙΟΔΙΚΟΝ ΤΗΣ ΕΝ ΑΘΕΝΑΙΣ ΕΠΙΣΤΕΜΟΝΙΚΗΣ ΕΤΑΙΡΕΙΑΣ. ΣΕΙΡΑ ΔΙΑΤΡΙΒΩΝ ΚΑΙ ΜΕΛΕΤΗΜΑΤΩΝ, 7), pp. 178–90.

117. See CSTH, pp. 61–90 (in which one passage from Roman law was omitted: *Digest* 48.5.9: *Qui domum suam, ut stuprum adulteriumue cum aliena matre familias uel cum masculo fieret* . . . [Papinian {second or third century}, from his *Adulteries*, Book 2]); and, more recently, S. Troianos, "Kirchliche und weltliche Rechtsquellen zur Homosexualität in Byzanz," *Jahrbuch der Österreichischen Byzantinistik* 39 (1989), 29–48, pp. 30–35; Danilo Dalla, «*Ubi Venus mutatur*» *Omosessualità e diritto nel mondo romano* (Milan, 1987); and Eva Cantarella, "Etica sessuale e diritto: L'omosessualità a Roma," *Rechtshistorisches Journal* 6 (1987), 277–

the Theodosian Code and the Laws of the Visigoths, and in the great legal code of Justinian[118]—all unprecedented efforts to make a Christian theocracy of the traditionally secular Roman state. But in fact sustained and effective oppression of those who engaged in homosexual behavior was not known in Europe until the thirteenth century, and was never common in the Byzantine East. Troianos notes somewhat loosely that in the High and later Middle Ages one finds fewer and fewer penalties for homosexual acts in civil and ecclesiastical sources from Byzantium, although "this circumstance in no way indicates that homosexual relations were not widespread in Byzantium."[119]

The *Eclogues*, a legal handbook issued in 741 by Leo III and Constantine V and constituting the major code of secular law in the East for several centuries, substituted mutilation for the death penalty of late imperial Roman law as a punishment for homosexual behavior.[120] It included the following stipulation, obviously concerning homosexual activity, though no name is applied to the behavior in question: "Those guilty of unchastity—both the active and passive parties—should be punished with the sword.[121] But if the passive party is less than twelve years old[122] he should be forgiven, as his age is clear indication that he did not realize what he was suffering."[123]

---

92. These discussions add little to what was already known: see Chapter 2, n. 1. Troianos discusses the recapitulations of the events of Justinian's day by later Byzantine writers (George the Monk, Kedrenos: p. 35 n. 28), but there is no reason to believe they had better information than Procopius or Malalas. Troianos rightly gives short shrift to P. Pescani's contention that Procopius' account demonstrates further antihomosexual legislation by Justinian ("Tracce di una ignota Novella di Giustiniano in Procopio?" *Iura* 15 [1964], 181–84).

118. *CSTH*, pp. 171–74.

119. *Dieser Umstand bedeutet keineswegs, dass die gleichgeschlechtlichen Beziehungen in Byzanz nicht verbreitet waren, ut supra, p. 47, n. 111.*

120. Not actually common until late imperial times, although the *Institutes* (4.18.4) of Justinian (supposedly a handbook of older Roman jurisprudence) did prescribe it for some forms of incest (parent-child or sibling) and for arson, poisoning, sorcery, murder, and desertion (also for homosexual acts: see n. 118).

121. Presumably the death penalty, as envisioned in the *Institutes* (see n. 118), although it could be a reference to castration, which Justinian's own legislation had required for homosexual behavior, and which was accomplished "with a sword." The *Eclogues* punished most forms of adultery with mutilation of the nose.

122. The *Institutes* had set twelve as the legal age of liability—an innovation, since older Roman law had set the age lower.

123. Οἱ ἀσελγεῖς, ὅ τε ποιῶν καὶ ὁ ὑπομένων, ξίφει τιμωρείσθωσαν· εἰ δὲ ὁ ὑπομένων ἥττων τῶν δώδεκα ἐτῶν εὑρεθῇ, συγχωρείσθω, ὡς τῆς ἡλικίας δηλούσης μὴ εἰδέναι αὐτόν, τί ὑπέμεινεν, ed. L. Burgmann, *Ecloga: Das Gesetzbuch Leons III. und Konstantinos' V* (Forschungen zur byzantinische Rechtsgeschichte, 10) (Frankfurt, 1983) 17:38, pp. 238–39.

This is a mitigation of the *Institutes'* application of the death penalty to sex of any sort between any males.[124] A contemporary canon law collection, however, ruled that boys who had been sexually abused were ineligible for the priesthood or diaconate;[125] even if they were too young to be held responsible, if their "vessel" was "broken"[126] they were "useless" for the priesthood.[127] But the same source decrees if seed was only spilled between his thighs, a boy could be ordained. In another version,[128] the ruling was amplified to stipulate that if it had happened only between the thighs, "especially if it only happened once or twice," the youth was eligible, but not if he was actually inseminated, because then he had been made impure.[129]

Penalties for lesbian activities—though very rare—appear to have been aimed entirely at nuns, and were surprisingly mild: there was a twelve-year canonical penalty for women who had sex *without* men, which was more serious than masturbation (μαλακία), but less than male homosexual acts (or possibly only anal intercourse: ἀρρενοκοιτίας [see note 4, p. 220]). The penance was eighty days for women who practiced μαλακία together; if one nun did it with another, a regimen of penance, bread, and water was prescribed for thirty-eight days. If one nun slept with another, the penance was forty days; if two women slept together and one caressed the other's breasts and "rode her," forty days of penance were prescribed, plus one hundred days of repentance for both, but if there was "flow" the penance was two years.[130]

The *Ecloga aucta*,[131] a revision of the *Eclogues*, mostly eliminated

---

124. 4.18.4: *Item lex Iulia de adulteriis coercendis, quae non solum temeratores alienarum nuptiarum gladio punit, sed etiam eos, qui cum masculis infandam libidinem exercere audent.*

125. According to the "Kanonikon," mistakenly attributed to John the Faster and actually dating from somewhere between the seventh and tenth centuries: *RP* 4:442. See also Suvorov, "Вѣроятный," as cited above, n. 4.

126. This phrasing, as peculiar in the Greek as in my English rendering, probably betrays one of the major underlying causes of prejudice against male-male homosexuality: a phobia about males imitating female behavior.

127. παιδίον δὲ πρός τινος φθαρὲν, εἰς ἱερωσύνην οὐκ ἔρχεται. Εἰ γὰρ κἀκεῖνο διὰ τὸ ἀτελὲς τῆς ἡλικίας οὐχ ἥμαρτεν, ἀλλὰ τὸ αὐτοῦ σκεῦος ἐρράγη, καὶ εἰς ἱερὰν ὑπουργίαν ἄχρηστον γέγονεν, *RP* 4:442.

128. Suvorov, 8:05.

129. εἰ δὲ πλεῖον τούτου, τουτέστιν εἰς ἀφεδῶνα, μηδὲ τὸ σύνολον ἔρχεσθαι εἰς διακόνου ἐμβάθμου ἢ ἱερέως ἀξίαν· εἰ γὰρ κἀκεῖνος οὐχ ἥμαρτεν, ἀλλ'ὅμως τὸ σκεῦος ἐρράγη, καὶ οὐκ ἐνδέχεται αὐτὸν ἱερουργῆσαι, μεμόλυται γάρ.

130. All of these are thoroughly discussed in Troianos, pp. 46–47.

131. Its precise date is somewhat uncertain, but it must postdate the *Eclogues.*

the mutilation the latter had prescribed, although it also reflected a return to the rather more severe provisions of Justinian. But it further raised the age of consent for homosexual relations: "Those guilty of unchastity, both the active and passive parties, should be punished with the sword. But in the case of someone less than fifteen years old, let him be beaten and placed in a monastery, as his age indicates that he suffered this involuntarily."[132] This is a striking mitigation: the age of consent was raised to a new high (particularly striking since the traditional age of puberty among Christians was reckoned from twelve to fourteen).[133] Participation below that age incurred only a beating and confinement in a monastery. It is not obvious whether the youth was actually to become a monk or simply to be confined temporarily, but since homosexual behavior rendered one ineligible for the priesthood or diaconate, it seems unlikely that this stipulation involved more than temporary confinement. In any event, being placed with monks was likely to provide the best environment to locate other men romantically interested in their own gender.

In the *Basilika* (compiled in the sixth century, as discussed in note 48, but probably not actually used as law until the ninth), a ruling from the *Digest* prohibiting a passive male (called ἡταιρηκώς) from pleading anyone else's case in court[134] was translated into Greek. But apart from this there were no criminal sanctions against homosexual activity in the *Basilika*—only indirect rulings from the *Digest*, like the one noted. This absence was regretted by the twelfth-century legal scholar Theodore Balsamon,[135] but he claimed that the penalty of castration prescribed against bestiality in the *Basilika* (60.37.84) and

---

[132] Ὁ ἀσελγὴς ὅ τε ποιῶν καὶ ὁ ὑπομένων ξίφει τιμωρείσθω· ὁ δὲ ἥττων τῶν δεκαπέντε ἐτῶν τυρτέσθω καὶ ἐν μοναστηρίῳ εἰσαφέσθω, ὡς τῆς ἡλικίας δηλούσης τοῦτο ἀκουσίως πεπονθέναι αὐτόν, eds. Dieter Simon and Spyros Troianos, *Eklogadion und Ecloga privata aucta* (*Fontes Minores*, 2, in *Forschungen zur byzantinischen Rechtsgeschichte*, 3) (Frankfurt, 1977), 17.6 (= Troianos' [accurate] citation; the *ODB* gives 17.12b, which is wrong), p. 71.

[133] See discussion of this in John Boswell, *The Kindness of Strangers* (as in Preface, n. 1), pp. 29–36.

[134] 8.1.1.6 [= *Digest* 3.1.1.6]: κωλύεται ὑπὲρ ἄλλων συνηγορεῖν καὶ ὁ ἡταιρηκώς, εἰ μὴ κατὰ βίαν λῃστῶν ἢ πολεμίων πέπονθεν· ὑπὲρ ἑαυτοῦ δὲ οὐ κωλύεται. Scholia, cited in Troianos, "Kirchliche," p. 38, n. 40, shows that ἡταιρηκώς was understood as a passive male generically. Note the curious circumstance that something punished by death (for adults) in a previous lawcode is here cited only as partial disqualification for being a lawyer, suggesting that the death penalty was never enforced.

[135] τὸ μέν τοι κεφαλικῶς τιμωρεῖσθαι τοὺς μοιχούς, ἢ τοὺς ἀρρενοκοίτας, ἢ τοὺς φθορεῖς, οὐκ ἐτέθη εἰς τὰ βασιλικά, RP 1:302.

Prochiron (39.74) applied to homosexuality.[136] This ecclesiastical canon in fact originally had *nothing* to do with homosexuality,[137] which is evident even in the formula Balsamon himself cited.[138] Homosexual relations were often viewed as a subset of other sexual indiscretions, however, so that the same penalty applied to ravishing maidens or young men (νεώτεροι) (Σ 60.22.1; cf. Σ 37.34.3) or to using one's own home for adultery with a female or a male (Σ 60.37.10 = *Digest* 48.5.9).[139] Thus, from Basil's time on, there were few if any penalties against homosexual acts "in force," and most rules about sexual impropriety applied equally across gender or were specifically applicable to monks, called to a higher standard of chastity.

The Sinai Euchologion, a twelfth-century Slavic prayer book that includes one of the most impressive versions of the same-sex union ceremony (and no heterosexual marriage rite), includes a prayer to preserve a man from lustful thoughts or the "looks of fornicatrices,"[140] suggesting that in the mind of the compiler (probably a cleric) sexual danger was represented by the female. This manuscript also includes a penitential in which there is a severe penalty (the same as that for homicide) for "sodomitic fornication" *on the part of an ecclesiastic* (которъі причетьникъ),[141] but then goes on (Sections 11ff.) to prescribe penalties for laymen that are much milder generally and *do not include sodomy*. Observing the "kalends" (колждж еноуаръ) of January, for example, "as the pagans used to do," earns a three-year penance (24), whereas masturbation (presumably of a layman) receives only one year (14). Moreover, the rich can pay to get out of any penance (31). It should be remembered that in the Eastern church at this time ecclesiastics (except for monks) could be married, as is clearly indicated in Sections 12 and 35 (a married ecclesiastic over thirty who has sex with an animal receives a fifteen-year penance; an unmarried one only ten)—all of which suggest that the primary concern about same-sex eroticism would be the extent to

---

136. καὶ ἀνάγνωθι περὶ ἀῤῥενοκοίτων καὶ τὸ τελευταῖον...Οἱ ἀλογευόμενοι... RP 4:220.
137. See discussion in *CSTH*, p. 178 and n. 33, ibid.
138. Οἱ ἀλογευόμενοι, ἤτοι κτηνοβάται, καυλοκοπείσθωσαν, RP 4:220.
139. μοιχείαν μετὰ ἀλλοτρίας γαμετῆς...ἢ μετὰ ἄρρενος στροῦπτον, *Scholia* 9.3690.
140. отъ вьзьрение на ну очецъ люводеицъ, in Jean Frček, "Euchologium Sinaiticum: Texte slave avec sources grecques et traduction française," *PO* 24 (1933), 611–801; 25 (1943), 490–622, pp. 57–58.
141. содомъскъі блждъ, ibid., p. 165, No. 3.

which it constituted adultery. Otherwise, it was simply a form of fornication, technically disapproved, but not viewed as gravely as it would be eventually in the West.[142]

The simultaneous horror of a monk's violating his vow of chastity and general equanimity in the East about what was already considered an "unmentionable sin" in the West is evident in the vivid confession of the abbot Eutropius, who wrote with astonishing candor about his attraction to a boy brought to the monastery by his father.[143]

A certain well-born, prosperous man from Jericho was very fond of me and brought provisions to my monastery and very often visited and ate with me. When he had a son he called on me to act as his godfather, which I did, whereupon the man turned the child over to me altogether, and I received the baby with pleasure and joy and a clean heart in the simplicity of my soul, and I loved him and embraced him as a son given me by God through holy baptism in the Holy Spirit.[144]

When the boy got older and had reached the age of about ten, my reason turned to ill and my will toward evil. I was tortured and overwhelmed by an obscene desire, and the beast of impure lust and a desire for pleasure burned in my soul. . . . I was a changed person and completely in the grip of this unclean passion, and I wanted to have sex with the boy and to be with him [μιγῆναι τῷ παιδὶ καὶ συγγενέσθαι αὐτῷ], to my shame. But I importuned God to hinder me, and I said, "My Lord God, send down fire to consume me rather than [let] me do this awful thing."[145]

[142.] Rules like No. 35 suggest that unmarried men were not held to as high a standard. The origin of all these prescriptions is suggested by No. 44, which prescribes a penance of two years for consciously eating meat intended for sacrifice or blood or strangled. This is a remnant of the list sent out to the early church on the basis of the decision of the Council of Jerusalem recorded in Acts 15, but for the vast majority of Christians the dietary portions had long since become dead letters.

[143.] Although modern Orthodox often pretend that oblation was not known in the East, this is one of many indications that it was. On the general issue of the monastic oblation of children, see John Boswell, The Kindness of Strangers (as in Preface, n. 1), esp. Chapters 5 and 8.

[144.] Or "in a holy spirit": ἐν πνεύματι ἁγίῳ, without the article one would normally expect for "the Holy Spirit."

[145.] Ὑποτυπώσεις καὶ ἑρμενεία περιέχουσα ὡς ἐν συντόμῳ συλλεγεῖσα παρὰ Ἰωάννου τῆς μονῆς τοῦ τιμίου Προδρόμου, in Noctes Petropolitanae: Сорникъ вчзантийскихъ

Finally he ordered the father to come and take the boy away. Though sex with the boy is depicted as something that would be shameful for him, this was obviously because he was a monastic (and the abbot of the monastery, and the father's friend). There is no rhetoric in his account about the "unnaturalness" of this interest, nor any suggestion that the desire itself seemed bizarre to him.[146] On the contrary, the confession provided the occasion for him to comment about how dangerous it was to look on the beauty of *other monks*, and the necessity of looking at the ground when addressing them—as if *any* monk might be similarly tempted—and similarly how likely nuns were to feel desire for each other, all of which were clearly a threat to monastic celibacy.

The boy's father took him away. There is no hint in the text that the father or anyone else was scandalized by the possibility that the abbot might have sexual interest in a young man. But this did not entirely solve the abbot's problems.

> After that I never saw the boy again, but the enemy, knowing this, came after me more fiercely, more hotly, more sharply, and put the boy's form into my mind and glued his likeness and image and appearance into my heart. Overcome, I could not escape or separate myself from this . . . snakelike obsession: even while praying and singing and keeping vigil and reading this vile passion gripped me, the demon of this shameful lust preying on me and torturing me with desire and utterly controlling me.

In spite of equanimity on this subject and a tradition of rather even-handed rulings about sexual indiscretions on the part of the unmarried laity, in 1306, as Western Europe also began to stigmatize homosexual behavior more sharply, the emperor Andronicus re-

---

тедстовъ XII–XIII вковъ (St. Petersburg, 1913; reprint Leipzig, 1976, in [*Subsidia byzantina lucis ope iterata*, xxi]), 1–88, pp. 80–81.

146. Although by this time a profound horror of same-sex attraction had already gripped the West, centuries before this Western monks had treated the matter with similar equanimity —i.e., resolve not to violate their vow of chastity, but a notable lack of concern about the gender that occasioned temptation: see, e.g., the story of Agapitus, a woman who disguised herself as a man and was mistaken by the other monks for a beautiful young man, which caused them all (N.B.) erotic turmoil (*Aelfric's Lives of Saints*, ed. and trans. Walter W. Skeat [London, 1966], 345).

sponded to the request of Patriarch Athanasius and issued a decree which included a reminder that there were prohibitions of fornication and adultery, obsession with males, incest, injustice, and sorcery.[147] This attitude also began to have negative influence on same-sex unions, which were increasingly rejected: "If some wish to enter into ceremonies of same-sex union, we should prohibit them, for they are not recognized by the church."[148] Matthew Blastares, a fourteenth-century canon lawyer, in writing "on the degrees of marriage"[149] divided "relationship" (συγγενεία) into two types: natural and adoptive (τὸ φύσει καὶ τὸ θέσει) (p. 126). "Kinship by marriage is a relationship established through matrimony; it involves the taking into our family of persons who were outside our kingroup. Adoption is the getting of a son without carnal relations."[150] These comments were followed immediately by [§2] a section on same-sex unions, which Blastares said were "not legal," *although adoption was.* "When we are childless we resort to adoption [υἱοθεσίαν] for reasons of inheritance. But no respectable motivation could lead to same-sex union. And what is respectable the law allows; what is not it rejects."[151] The section following dealt with the marriage of an uncle or nephew[152] to an aunt or niece or two first cousins (πρωτεξάδελφοι) to two first cousins, which counted as ἀγχιστεία (relationship), making evident that same-sex union, of which Blastares disapproved (although it was obviously common enough to require discussion), fell in the general category of marriage.

[147.] πορνεία καὶ μοιχεία, ἀρρενομανία, αἱμομιξία, ἀδικία, γοήτεια: Zepos 1:534. This is much like the list of treasonous offenses in Western lawcodes of the time (see CSTH, Chapter 10), but it is difficult to be sure exactly what laws are meant.

[148.] Ἐάν τινες μέλλοντες ποιεῖν ἀδελφοποιΐας, ὀφείλομεν αὐτοῖς ἐπιτρέπειν; Ἀνεπίγνοστοί εἰσιν αὗται τῇ ἐκκλησίᾳ, in Pitra, col. 713, No. 209. Note that Pitra's Latin translation is utterly falsified: *Si nonnulli adoptiones filiorum sint acturi, fas ne est illis id permittere?* There is no *adoptio filiorum* in the original.

[149.] Περὶ τῶν τοῦ γάμου βαθμῶν, *Syntagma* 2.8 (RP 6:125ff).

[150.] καὶ ἔστιν ἀγχιστεία μέν, ἡ ἐξ ἐπιγαμβρίας συγγένεια· ἐγχιστεία δ'ἐστὶν οἰκειότης προσώπων ἐκ γάμων ἡμῖν συνημένων συγγενείας ἐκτός· θέσις δὲ ἡ χωρὶς σαρκικῆς συναφείας υἱοθεσία.

[151.] Ἡ μέντοι ἀδελφοποιΐα οὐ νόμιμον ἐστιν· ἄπαιδες μὲν γὰρ ὄντες, ἐσοφισάμεθα τὴν υἱοθεσίαν εἰς διαδοχὴν τῶν πραγμάτων· τὴν δὲ ἀδελφοποιΐαν οὐδεμία εἰσάγει εὔλογος πρόφασις· τὰ μὲν οὖν τὸ εὔλογον ἔχοντα, καὶ ὁ νόμος ἐδέξατο· τὰ δὲ μὴ τοιαῦτα, οὐ παρεδέξατο, pp. 126–27.

[152.] ἀνέψιος, which meant "cousin" in classical Greek, but clearly by the fourteenth century had come to mean "nephew" or "niece." By this time πρωτεξάδελφος meant "first cousin," as in the following sentence.

Such relations had, despite prohibitions, long been common among monks (as the repeated prohibitions suggest) and were quite licit for other clergy. In the twelfth-century Paterik[153] of the Kievan Caves Monastery the abbot of the monastery, Theodosius, gave advice to Izjaslav M'stislavič, the prince of Kiev, about avoiding contact with Varangian (Latin) Christians. Among other things, he warned that "Christians should not give their daughters to them in marriage [християном же сбоих дщерей не достоит давати за них], nor receive them into their own homes [ни поимати у них за себе], nor form same-sex unions[154] with them, nor have them as godparents, nor exchange kisses with them, nor eat with them, nor drink from any single vessel [with them]."[155] It is striking that a Slavic prince should fear Latin influence in the matter of same-sex unions, but it is most explicable as a subset of his concern about intermarriage.

A tale from the same collection regarding the eleventh century, but recorded by a bishop (Vladimir) about a century later,[156] tells how two powerful laymen (два мужа нѣкая), Serge and John, who were friends (друга себѣ), came to the church of the Dormition of the Caves Monastery in Kiev and there before the icon of the Virgin Mary entered into a same-sex union.[157] Many years later, when John died, he left his estate to the poor, in the care of the superior of the monastery, and to his son, Zaxarija, five years old—in "the care of his friend, as to a faithful brother" (на соблюденіе другу свое му, яко брату вѣрну), instructing him to give the gold and silver he left the boy to him when he attained manhood. When the boy was fifteen, he asked Serge for the money, but Serge lied and said the father gave it all to the poor. Zaxarija offered to split the money with Serge, to take a third, to take a tenth. Serge spurned each offer. Zaxarija then demanded that Serge take an oath in the church of the Kievan monas-

---

153. *Pateryk: Kyjevo-Pečers'kij Pateryk.*, ed. D. I. Abramovich (Kiev, 1930), repr., ed. D. Čyževsk'kyj (Munich, 1964); English translation in *The Paterik of the Kievan Caves Monastery*, trans. Muriel Heppell (Cambridge, Mass.: Harvard Library of Early Ukrainian Literature, English Translations, 1, 1989).

154. *Pateryk*, p. 190: ни брататися с ними. The exact same prohibition in regard to heterosexual matrimony occurs in Simeon of Thessalonika's marital advice, Chapter 287 (PG 155:508).

155. Discourse 37; Heppel, p. 212.

156. *Pateryk*, pp. 12–13; Heppell, pp. 14–15.

157. и въ духовное братство пріидоста.

tery, "where you entered into union with my father" (идѣже и братьство възя сь отцемъ моимъ). After Serge swore in the church in front of the icon of the Virgin Mary that he received no money from John, he was overcome with remorse on leaving the church and spontaneously confessed that the money was hidden at home. Zaxarija took possession of it, gave it to the monastery, and became a monk himself.

In another story[158] two men united by the same-sex union ceremony (два брата бѣста по духу)—the deacon Evagrius and the priest (попъ) Tit—maintained "a great and sincere[159] love between them, so that their closeness [единоумню] and limitless love astonished everyone." They had a falling out and were furious with each other; the monks tried to reunite them but to no avail. When Tit was ill they brought Evagrius to be reconciled with him; he refused, and was struck dead, while Tit recovered.

Discourse 32 (written in the thirteenth century)[160] in the same collection recounts the case of two monks[161] in the community "who had been joined[162] since their youth in heartfelt [сердечиою] love and a shared life [единоуміе имуще] and one devotion to God. They besought the blessed Marko [a gravedigger among the monks] to make a place for them together [обще], so that they might both[163] be in the same place when the Lord called them." The older one (старѣйшій братъ) went away on business and the younger died and was buried. When the elder returned he was upset that the younger had been placed in the upper part of the burial site in spite of their age difference.[164] Marko told the corpse to rise and take the lower[165] spot, which he did.

---

158. Discourse 23 (written in the early thirteenth century by Simon, bishop of Vladimir): *Pateryk*, pp. 122–23; Heppel, pp. 140–42.
159. нелицемѣрну: literally, "unhypocritical"—a phrase that occurs often in the ceremony of same-sex union. Cf. also Romans 9:12 and 1 Pet. 1:22.
160. *Pateryk*, pp. 157–61; Heppell, pp. 177–81.
161. Two fifteenth- and one sixteenth-century redactions give "brothers in spirit" (духовная брата), *Pateryk*, p. 157, n. 56.
162. съпряжена: спрягать means "to conjugate."
163. Reading оба for абіе, as Heppel.
164. It is difficult to be sure whether this is simply owing to a general feeling in the premodern world about being "higher," or is a slightly off-color joke about one "being on top" of the other, which was a sexual concern in the premodern world, and often coupled with age. Cf. following note.
165. нижнем: нижний can mean "under" as well as "lower," as it does in modern Russian нижнее бельё, "underclothes."

In the "Life of the Holy Father Cyril," the thirteenth-century archbishop of Rostov, the life of St. Peter Ordinski, his nephew and khan of the Tatars (1257–66), is also recounted.[166] According to the story, he ran away as a child to serve the bishop because he felt drawn to Christianity, and gave away to the poor the patrimony his father had left him. He was told by SS. Peter and Paul (whom he saw together, radiant with light, in a vision) to found a church in their (joint) names. He was given silver *and* gold to do so (a great point is made in the story that it was both). Peter was then able to persuade Bishop Ignatius and the prince (княз) to build the church.

Peter is described in the account as big and "pretty[167] of face" (возрастомъ великъ [literally, "too big for his age"] и лицемъ красенъ) (p. 244). The bishop and the prince decided that for the glory of the town they should have Peter marry, and they announced this to him, at which point he burst into tears. They chose a girl (unnamed, undescribed in the account) from the local Tatar aristocracy. The prince gave Peter land from his patrimony to be Peter's own family patrimony (p. 244). The wife is never mentioned again in the story; there is no mention of her either surviving Peter or being buried with him, though his death and burial are described in detail, as are those of the bishop and the prince.

And because Peter was sweet of speech [literally, "Peter's answers were sweet"] and of beautiful manners, the prince loved him so much that he ate no meal without him and the bishop

---

166. *Ein Beitrag zur soziologischen Erforschung altrussischer Texte* (Berlin: Freie Universität, Forschungsgruppe ältere slavische Literaturen, 48, 1979). Although the events were thirteenth-century, the texts themselves were composed a century or two later, according to the accompanying study (pp. 15–21). The same volume prints another version of the events, known as the *VIT*, which is clearly a later abbreviation. (Its oldest manuscript is seventeenth-century.) It characterizes Peter (p. 252) as a "nephew of the Khan in brotherly fashion" (or "through his brother"): племянникъ по братъ цара ьерка. In this shorter version, probably composed a century later than the one cited above, there is recognition of a relationship between Peter and the prince, but it is somewhat different: "The prince called Peter his brother, and he and his children also bore him a great love" (а князь нарече Петра себъ братомъ у умаъше къ нему велію лбовъ онъ и дъти его). In this version, the bride (though not named here or elsewhere in the story) is described as "lovely," using the same word the earlier version had used to describe Peter himself and the reason the prince loved him: краснии (и абіе сыска ему князь невъсту отъ вельможъ красну), p. 262.

167. This word occurs in modern Russian mostly for girls.

joined him to the prince in the church, and they said Peter was "brother"[168] to the prince.[169]

Both Peter and the prince had children; after the prince died his children called Peter "uncle" (сего же князя дѣти зваху петра дядею до старости) even when they grew old. The grandchildren of the prince eventually tried to despoil Peter's grandchildren of their property, and a representative of the tsar had to intervene on the latter's behalf. They said "to each other and to their Boyars, 'We have heard that our parents called his father Peter uncle. Our grandfather obtained much silver from him[170] and was united with him in church' [слышахомъ еже родители ваши звацу дядею его отца петра. дѣдъ бо нашь много сребра у него взят и братаця снимъ въ церкви]. But the blood of the Tatars is not our stock [а родъ татарской, костж не наша]. What have we to do with these people? . . . These and similar comments they made, and did not interest themselves in the miracle working [чюдотворениа] of the holy apostle, and forgot the love of their ancestors [а прародитель забыша любовь]."[171]

Roman law survived only fragmentarily in Europe after the collapse of the Roman state, and was usually replaced by Germanic law codes, which were not likely to take cognizance of same-sex relationships. Nonetheless, in Italy and Spain—comparatively urban societies by the standards of the times—the legal fiction of "brotherhood" was not complicated by questions of wife and children, since remaining a bachelor had long been a part of urban Roman life, and was enhanced

168. Ѣрат is used near the beginning of the tale (p. 234) to mean nephew (брата царева), then lower on the same page of the same "lad" (отрокъ) in reference to the death of his father, who is brother to the tsar: тогда отцу его брату цареву умершу. "Brothers" is also used to address readers of the story, e.g., on pp. 236, 238.

169. P. 244: бяху бо Петрови сладцы отвѣти, добрыа обычая во всемъ. и тольми любляше князь Петра, яко и хлба безнего не ясти, яко владыщѣ братати Петра въ церкви съ княземъ. и прозваста Петра брата князю.

170. Only to build a church, which the heirs had apparently forgotten by this point.

171. Some MSS here have "forgot love for their ancestors" (а прародителю любовь забыша) —e.g., the text published in *Die Erzählung über Petr Ordynskij* in *Ein Beitrag zur soziologischen Erforschung*, as cited in n. 166, p. 252, but the author notes that there is another reading, and it is printed as the correct one by both recent editors: in M. O. Skripil', *Русские повести X–XИ веков* (Leningrad, 1958), 98–105, and R. P. Dmitrieva, in Dmitriev and Likhachev, *Памятники Лiитературы Древней Руси: конец XV–первая половина XVI века* (Moscow, 1984), 20–37.

by the social and financial rewards offered by the position of the diocesan clergy (i.e., as opposed to monks), who were pressured throughout the first millennium of Christian history to aspire to complete celibacy, but were not actually required to observe it until a bitter fight over the issue in the eleventh and twelfth century. In many communities, even where the ceremony of same-sex union was not known, informal relationships reminiscent of the Roman legal fiction of "brotherhood" between male lovers served many of the same functions as heterosexual unions—either legal marriages or long-term alternatives like concubinage—in their duration and legal ramifications.

The ambiguity of the few surviving texts precludes categorizing them unequivocally as same-sex marital contracts, but it equally rules out pretending that they were simply business contracts, as previous commentators have tried to do. It is, in fact, possible to interpret them as business documents, but it would also be possible (if utterly mistaken) to interpret most premodern heterosexual marriage agreements (especially prenuptial contracts among the wealthy) as business contracts. (Indeed, Roman law specifically spoke of heterosexual marriage as a "lifelong partnership.")[172] Many aspects of the documents and the arrangements they prescribe argue forcefully against a simple partnership. In most of them there is no quid pro quo: it is not that one party provides capital or labor or land and in return the other invests property or expertise or time. In each case it is simply a division of one person's estate with another, apparently for purely voluntary and personal reasons. In most of them (for example, documents 1 and 2 following) it is specified that the two men will live together, which is hardly an ordinary commercial stipulation. In most there is mention of a personal relationship or emotional quality (e.g., the use of *frater* in No. 1, *adoptivum fratrem* in No. 3, *amiciditate* [sic] in No. 2, and the suggestion in No. 2 that the two must maintain the same friends and enemies).

---

172. Medieval law also took cognizance of partnerships, usually as business arrangements but sometimes as eleemosynary agreements between relatives: see, e.g., Philippe de Beaumanoir, *Coutumes de Beauvaisis*, ed. A. Salmon (Paris, 1899), Chapter 21, which is predominantly about business relations. This code is now conveniently translated into English by F. R. P. Akehurst, *The Coutumes de Beauvaisis of Philippe de Beaumanoir* (Philadelphia, 1992); the section on partnerships occupies pp. 223–36.

1. Document of 776[173]

In the name of God. In the third year of the reign of our lord, Charles, the King of the Franks and Lombards, when he began to rule Lombardy, on the eighth of the kalends of July, in the fourteenth indiction [776 C.E.].

Be it known that I, Rachifrid, a cleric, the son of Fredulo the merchant, do by this document establish, confirm and appoint you, Magniprand, a cleric, the son of Magnipert, to share my dwelling all the days of our lives—that is, the parish house of my church, Saint Dalmatius, and my home within the city near the same church, and my other buildings, and everything belonging to the said church in whatever way, and all the servants attached to it; you should live there and [share] control over the said church and its property, and should have the power of disposing of its servants, except for Magnuculus, a cleric, whom I had previously emancipated.

. . . that as regards the said church of God, and all those things and persons belonging to it, you should be therein my partner [*frater:* see appended discussion of this word and *germanus*] and my heir, so that we should never at any time make division of the said church or the things or persons attached to it, either movable or immovable, but should, as I stated before, live there together, and possess and dispose of whatever belongs there.

And if I should predecease you, I ordain that the said church and all things belonging to it should come under your authority, and you may be able to do with them as you wish. But if I outlive you, everything will revert to my control. Wherefore I, Rachifrid the cleric, promise in your presence, the aforesaid Magniprand the cleric, that if my brother [*germanus meus*] and I

[173.] The editor identifies this text with the rubric "Rachifrid the cleric chooses as his companion for his church of St. Dalmatius in Lucca the cleric Magniprand, ordaining that he should live with him as a brother [*fratello*] and be his heir." The text was first published in *Memorie e documenti per servire all'istoria del ducato di Lucca* 4.1 (Lucca, 1818), 133–34 (No. 83), and ibid. 5.2 (Lucca, 1837), p. 92 (No. 161). It was reprinted with some paraphrasing and commentary by Ulrich Stutz, "Lehen und Pfründe," *Zeitschrift der Savigny-Stiftung für Rechtsgeschichte* 23: *Germanistische Abteilung* 20 (1899), 213–47, pp. 226–27, n. 4, and in a further abridgement by Eduardo de Hinojosa, "La Fraternidad artificial en España," *Revista de archivos, bibliotecas y museos* 3:9, No. 7 (July 1905), 1–18, p. 5 n. 1.

should ever attempt to evict you from the aforesaid church, or the buildings and other things or persons belonging to it, or should ever seek to deprive you of anything belonging to it, except as noted above,[174] or take in another man, including a priest, besides you [super], I bind myself and my brother or our heirs to recompense you, Magniprand the cleric, in the amount of one hundred gold sous, after which penalty the present agreement would remain in force. And as a witness to this document I have asked Philip, the subdeacon, to sign. Executed in Lucca.

Rachifrid had a biological brother, as the document itself makes clear: this was not simply a way to obtain a collateral heir. The biological brother is referred to as *germanus*, a different word from the one (*frater*) applied to Magniprand. In the surviving Luccan documents of the eighth century[175] *germanus* is consistently used for a biological brother,[176] as opposed to *frater*, the traditional Latin term for a male "lover." *Frater* sometimes occurs *in conjunction with germanus*, as in No. 38 (C.E. 731): *fratres germani*. This distinction was widespread and of long standing: in classical Latin both *frater* and *germanus* could mean a biological brother; *frater* was also used for nonbiological emotional relationships (like a homosexual lover), but *germanus* was not. Often they occurred together (*frater germanus*) to mean "brother of the same parents"[177] (e.g., in Cicero, *Pro Caelio* 16.38; *In Verrem* 2, 1.128; cf. *OLD*, s.v., "frater"). In modern Italian the division has become trifold: *frate*, the most direct descendant of *frater*, refers chiefly to religious "brothers" but is also applied either to biological siblings (especially in the south) or to a friend, beloved person (*amico, persona cara*). *Fratello*, derived from it, is the most widely used term for a natal brother, but could also refer to a member of a religious

---

174. Presumably the exception of Magnuculus.
175. All published in *Memorie e documenti*, as cited in n. 173.
176. E.g., in No. 9 [C.E. 770], No. 13 [C.E. 753], No. 37 [C.E. 729], No. 54 [C.E. 761], No. 66 [C.E. 768], No. 106 [C.E. 789]. In the last case the party whose relationship is *germanus* is named *Fratello*.
177. This was because the death of women in childbirth and divorce and remarriage were so common in Roman and even in medieval Italy that many "siblings" were actually only half-brothers or half-sisters, and it was often useful to know—especially for inheritance purposes—that siblings were fully so. In the *Gesta Romanorum*, a high medieval collection of Latin fables, the phrase *fratres carnales* occurs (Tale 188), presumably to distinguish the biological from the emotional bond implied by *frater*.

order, whereas *germano* is used only for biological siblings (and for persons or things from Germany, though *tedesco* is more common for this). By contrast, *soror* is always used in the medieval Luccan vocabulary for sisters, even as the female counterpart of *germanus*.

Two later Spanish documents, though not identical, present a somewhat similar picture of two men arranging a common household based more on affection and understanding than contractual commercial arrangements.

2. Document of 1031 from the Cartulary of Celanova[178]

We, Peter Didaz and Munio Vandilaz, make a pact and agreement mutually between ourselves for the house and church of St. Mary of Ordines, which we jointly own and in which we share the labor, taking care of visitors and in regulating the care of, decorating and governing the premises, planting and building. And we share equally in the work of the garden, and in feeding and clothing ourselves and supporting ourselves. And we agree that neither of us may give to anyone else without the other's consent anything, on account of our friendship, and that we will divide the work on the house evenly, and assign labor equally and support our workers equally and with dignity. And we will remain good friends to each other with faith and sincerity,[179] and with other people [we will remain equally] friends and enemies all days and nights, forever. And if Peter dies before Munio he will leave Munio the property and the documents. And if Munio dies before Peter he will leave him the house and the documents.

3. Document of 1180 from the monastery of Sahagún[180]

I, Garcia de Perales, by virtue of the present document, affirm to those here and not here, that I take you, John of Perales, as I already took you, to be my adoptive brother, for the benefit of the souls of my mother and father, and I grant you half of all my

[178.] Fol. 85v, published in Hinojosa (as cited in n. 173, above), p. 16 n. 2.
[179.] Note that this phrase evokes the ceremony of same-sex union.
[180.] Hinojosa, p. 16 n. 2.

patrimony . . . and generally of the entire inheritance which I
have from my father or mother or family in the town of Berzea-
nos and in Perales.

In some less literate cultures of medieval Europe, where a document of this sort was not really practical, other forms of same-sex
coupling were tried. Two knights in a tale[181] in the Gesta romanorum
"loved each other" (mutuo se dilexerunt) and decided to form a
bond[182] by symbolically drinking small amounts of each other's
blood. The nature of the bond so created was that afterward neither
would "divorce"[183] the other either "in prosperity or adversity,"[184]
and whatever either one earned would be shared equally with the
other. Then they "lived ever after in the same house."[185] One of
them was wise and the other stupid, and the tale turns on their re-
proaching each other for following the "no divorce" rule so fanati-
cally that they ended up facing death together. The wise knight
argued that the foolish one ought to have trusted him when they
faced a difficult choice, and the foolish one replied that, given their
vow, he would have followed the wise one anywhere and the wiser
one ought to have insisted. The moral of the story, as it is passed on,
is that the union of the two knights is a figure for the union of body
and soul, one of which is wiser than the other.

This is precisely the sort of "blood brotherhood" anthropologists
and others anxious to explain away the ceremony of same-sex union
refer to, but it hardly helps their case. Not only is the union in this
case easy to interpret as homosexual in nature, but there is no mention of a church service, nor is the symbolic drinking of blood ever
mentioned in the nearly eighty manuscript versions of the ceremony
consulted for this study.

[181] Tale 67(59); in Oesterley's edition on pp. 378–81; in the translation by Swan, pp. 118–21.
Swan's translation is misleading, as noted below.

[182] Swan translates convencio as "agreement" (p. 118), which seems rather pale, especially
considering other ways in which he misled his readers.

[183] . . . nullus alium dimittet. Dimitto is the word used for "divorce" in the Latin New Testament: e.g., in Matt. 1:19, 5:32, 19:3.

[184] Cf. modern marriage vows about "sickness and health."

[185] . . . in una domo semper remanserunt (Oesterley, p. 378). Swan translates this "After this
they both dwelt in the same mansion" (p. 118), although domus does not usually denote a
"mansion," and there is hardly any reason not to translate semper, except embarrassment
about what it suggests.

Within religious communities, although marriage was not officially permitted, permanent and abiding relationships were nonetheless a familiar part of life. St. Aelred of Rievaulx had several such relationships in his twelfth-century Cistercian abbey, and even appealed to the relationship between Christ and St. John as a "marriage" by way of precedent.[186] Several poems survive from pairs of lesbian nuns of the twelfth century distinctly suggesting permanent relationships between them.[187]

The ceremony itself, on the other hand, was known in the Middle Ages in many areas of the West, including some from which no versions of the ceremony appear to survive (probably as the result of deliberate destruction: see p. 264). Gerald of Wales gives a vivid firsthand description of it in his "Topography of Ireland" (probably written in the late twelfth or early thirteenth century).[188]

A proof of the iniquity [of the Irish] and a novel[189] form of marriage[190]

Among many other examples of their wicked ways, this one is particularly instructive: under the pretext of piety and peace they come together in some holy place with the man they want to join.[191] First they are united in pacts of kinship,[192] then they

---

[186] *CSTH*, p. 226 and n. 57; cf. general discussion on pp. 221–26.

[187] *CSTH*, pp. 220–21, now also translated *Medieval Latin Poems of Male Love and Friendship*, trans. Thomas Stehling (New York, 1984), Nos. 112, 113.

[188] Ed. James Dimock (London, 1867), Chapter 22, p. 167. Because the language of this passage is difficult and extraordinary, I reproduce it here: *De argumento nequitiae, et novo desponsationis genere. Inter alia multa artis iniquae figmenta, hoc unum habent tanquam praecipuum argumentum. Sub religionis et pacis obtentu ad sacrum aliquem locum conveniunt, cum eo quem oppetere cupiunt. Primo compaternitatis foedera jungunt: deinde ter circa ecclesiam se invicem portant: postmodum ecclesiam intrantes, coram altari reliquiis sanctorum appositis, sacramentis multifarie praestitis, demum missae celebratione, et orationibus sacerdotum, tanquam desponsatione quadam indissolubiliter foederantur. Ad ultimum vero, ad majorem amicitiae confirmationem, et quasi negotii consummationem, sanguinem sponte ad hoc fusum uterque alterius bibit. Hoc autem de ritu gentilium adhuc habent, qui sanguine in firmandis foederibus uti solent. O quoties in ipso desponsationis hujus articulo, a viris sanguinum et dolosis tam dolose et inique funditur sanguis, ut alteruter penitus maneat exsanguis! O quoties eadem hora et incontinenti vel sequitur vel praevenit, vel etiam inaudito more sanguinolentum divortium ipsam interrumpit desponsationem!*

[189] Or "new."

[190] Or "betrothal." *Desponsare* is used in medieval Latin for both. Augustine had used it in an important discussion of the theology of matrimony: see Chapter 4, p. 119. For a contemporary instance of its use for marriage, see *Gesta Romanorum* 61.

[191] *Oppetere*: possibly for *appetere*.

[192] This could be the equivalent of negotiations at the beginning of a heterosexual ceremony at the door of the church, or something completely different.

carry each other three times around the church. Then, entering the church, before the altar, in the presence of the relics of saints and with many oaths, and finally with a celebration of the Mass and the prayers of priests, they are permanently united as if in some marriage. At the end, as further confirmation of the friendship and a conclusion to the proceedings, each drinks the other's blood, which is willingly shed for this. [This, however, they retain from the rites of pagans, who customarily use blood in the sealing of oaths.][193]

How often during the very act of this marriage is blood shed by treacherous and violent men so iniquitously and unjustly that one or the other remains all but drained of blood! How often in that very incontinent hour does a bloody divorce either follow, precede, or even, in an unheard-of-way, interrupt the marriage itself!

Although set in the context of Gerald's obvious disapproval both of the "novel form of marriage" and the violent Irish, this description of the ceremony as a wedding, conducted by a priest in church and accompanied by the Eucharist, is unmistakable, although it was apparently combined with the nonreligious rite described in the *Gesta Romanorum*. Its nature has long been obscured both by artful mistranslation[194] and a general unwillingness to recognize something as ostensibly improbable as a same-sex union. Whether there was enough knowledge of Greek in Ireland to support utilization of the Greek original of these ceremonies is the subject of lively debate among specialists; it seems, at the least, overwhelmingly likely that

---

193. This sentence is missing in five of eleven manuscripts, and added to the margin of a sixth, suggesting that it is an explanatory comment added after the first redaction.
194. The sole published English translation of this, by the noted medieval Latinist Thomas Wright (*The Historical Works of Giraldus Cambrensis* [London, 1881], 136–37), titles the chapter "Of a New Mode of Making a League," and of the many occurrences of words relating to marriage in the Latin only renders one in a way remotely approaching honesty (p. 137: "as if it were a solemn affiance"), although even in this case the meaning remains obscure. While it might be argued that Gerald's vehement hostility to the Irish and generally bitter tone justify reading the whole passage as sarcasm, the irony is certainly *weakened* rather than strengthened by failing to translate the central metaphor into English. (On the other hand, having read all of Gerald's works, I find it more likely that he is condemning the Irish here by accurately recounting a practice he found shocking, and assumed his readers would also.) Unless Wright was simply a bad translator (which he was not), it is difficult to postulate any cause for this misreading except prudery, which was particularly virulent in England in the late nineteenth century.

Gerald of Wales would have noted and commented if the ceremony had been conducted in a language unfamiliar to him, as Greek would probably have been.[195] The most likely conclusion is that the ceremony was performed in Latin or Old Irish, and the text has been lost or destroyed.

[195.] The arguments about, and the amount of Greek surviving in, Anglo-Saxon texts (the English at the time still shared an ecclesial culture with Ireland), are ably recounted in Mary Bodden, "Evidence for Knowledge of Greek in Anglo-Saxon England," Anglo-Saxon England 17 (1988), 217–46.

8

*"Those who see and those who do
not . . ."*

SUBSEQUENT
DEVELOPMENTS:

A LOOK FORWARD

ROM THE FOURTEENTH CENTURY on, Western Europe was gripped by a rabid and obsessive negative preoccupation with homosexuality as the most horrible of sins.[1] The reasons for this have never been adequately explained,[2] but the change itself is evident in the fact that Dante (1265–1321), in the most detailed charting of eschatological punishments of his time, placed sodomites in the highest rung of purgatory (*Purgatorio*, Canto 26)— just outside the gates of heaven—along with persons guilty of "too much" heterosexual passion: i.e., near salvation and far above the majority of sinners on the terraces of purgatory and all humans being punished in hell,[3] even though during his lifetime or soon thereafter

---

[1] Discussed and documented in *CSTH*, Chapter 10.

[2] Not that no efforts have been made. I offered suggestions in *CSTH*, which hardly met with widespread support, and which I myself feel less strongly about now. R. I. Moore, *The Formation of a Persecuting Society: Power and Deviance in Western Europe* (Oxford, 1987), offers different explanations, which I admire but also find less than completely persuasive.

[3] Richard Kay, in *Dante's Swift and Strong* (New York, 1978), argued that the "Sodomites" in hell (*Inferno*, 14–16) were not placed there because of homosexual behavior. Although I agree with the argument expounded in a long excursus to this study that Sodom was not traditionally understood as a symbol of homosexuality (my *CSTH* published two years later made the same case), I doubt Kay's central thesis, and think that in such a finely crafted work Dante would not likely have employed the same category for two entirely different categories of sin. Doubtless there are also *other* factors involved in the case of those in hell. Kay ignores

many Italian states enacted legislation savagely punishing homosexual acts.[4] Dante's position was actually theologically correct, although visceral prejudice against same-gender erotic interest was already so pronounced in the general population that Thomas Aquinas, while conceding that homosexual behavior was not more heinous than many other sins, nonetheless felt obliged to recognize popular feelings about its peculiar enormity.[5]

In the Greek-speaking Christian world the change was less extreme, but still evident. In the eleventh century the Greek moralist and writer Kekaumenos criticized the Vlachs (probably residents of the ancient Dacia) for making same-sex unions impetuously and equally impetuously violating their oaths,[6] but within a century a Greek collection of canon law listed homosexuality generically in the same category as bestiality, as did Western canonists of the same epoch.[7]

As a result, in areas where this visceral revulsion took hold, same-sex unions became suspect as in some way legitimizing "the sin that could not be named."[8] In the nineteenth century a "synod of the king of Greece" prohibited it as a "practice against the law, against nature [παρὰ φύσιν], . . . against reason, a soul-corrupting evil and error, a bizarre and irrational union [σύνδεσμον], a practice both irreligious and illicit, an institution outside and wholly foreign to the church."[9] It disappeared from most of Western (as opposed to Central and East-

---

the sodomites in purgatory, who are ultimately more interesting. I will address this whole question in a forthcoming article.

4. See Michael Goodich, *The Unmentionable Vice: Homosexuality in the Later Medieval Period* (Santa Barbara, 1979); Guido Ruggiero, *The Boundaries of Eros* (Oxford, 1985); and Michael Rocke, "Male Homosexuality and Its Regulation in Late Medieval Florence" (Ph.D. diss., SUNY Binghamton, 1990).

5. Discussed at length in CSTH, Chapter 11. See especially p. 328. Richard Trexler (*Public Life in Renaissance Florence* [New York, 1980], 380) cites Bernardino's claim that "sodomites" defend themselves with scriptural references, suggesting a considerable degree of cohesion and defensiveness on the part of the homosexual community.

6. *Cecaumeni strategicon et incerti scriptoris De officiis regiis libellus*, ed. B. Wassiliewsky and V. Jernstedt (Amsterdam, 1965), p. 74: ὀμνύμενον καθεκάστην ὄρκους φρικωδεστάτους πρὸς τοὺς ἑαυτοῦ φίλους καὶ ἀθετοῦν ῥᾳδίως ποιοῦν τε ἀδελφοποιήσεις. Gennadij Litavrin translates ἀδελφοποιήσεις as побратымства in советы и рассказы Кекавмена (Moscow, 1972), p. 269.

7. Paul Gautier, "Moeurs populaires Bulgares au tournant des 12e/13e siècles," *Mélanges Ivan Dujčev* (Paris, 1979), 180–89, p. 187: περὶ κτηνοβασίας καὶ ἀρρενοκοιτήσιας. Both are to be punished as adultery (μοιχείας). For Western attitudes, see CSTH, IV.

8. On the origins of this ringing phrase of condemnation, see Introduction, pp. xxiiiff.

9. K. Rhalle, "Περὶ ἀδελφοποιίας," Ἐπιστημονικὴ Ἐπετηρίς, Γ' (1906–1907) (Athens, 1909), 293–306, p. 301.

ern) Europe altogether, and no Latin versions of the ceremony survive at all, although it must have been performed in Latin in Ireland, and probably sometimes in Italy. Even Greek versions appear to have suffered some depredation by the many clerics who disapproved: folios from the ceremony have been ripped out of at least one Euchologion from the thirteenth century, when it was still permissible to conduct such a ritual,[10] and in two other Greek prayer books the folios immediately *following* the ceremony have been torn out,[11] suggesting either that the censor was not good at reading Greek or that there was some additional text that could not be shared. Even Gerald of Wales' description of the ceremony in Ireland has been defaced in one of its recensions and tampered with in others.[12]

The ceremony remained technically licit from the thirteenth century on, even in the eyes of the Roman Catholic church, which probably failed to recognize its actual significance,[13] although Montaigne seems to describe having seen it in Rome itself in 1578, and suggested that Roman ecclesiastics realized perfectly well what it entailed, even to the point of legitimizing homosexual activity:[14]

. . . the church of Saint John of the Latin Gate, in which some Portuguese[15] some years before had entered into a strange "brotherhood." Two males married each other at Mass, with the same ceremonies we use for our marriages, taking Communion

---

10. Sinai 982: see List of Manuscripts in Appendix 4.

11. Sinai 959 and Grottaferrata Γ.β. VI (see List, as in preceding note).

12. MS Ba of Gerald of Wales has been defaced: the rubric *De argumento nequitiae, et novo desponsationis genere* ("An argument for their wickedness and a new kind of marriage") has been cut out of the page, along with a drawing. This was obviously deliberate: see edition of Dimock, p. 167 n. 1.

13. The papal edict *Sub Catholicae*, issued March 6, 1254, by Innocent IV, one of the most influential of medieval popes, carefully distinguished between rites of Greek-speaking Catholics permitted by the Roman Catholic church and those not allowed (for the text of this edict see J. D. Mansi, *Sacrorum conciliorum nova et amplissima collectio* [Paris, 1901–27; rptd. Graz, 1960–61] 38:304–6). It did not list the ceremony of same-sex union. If the hierarchy were now to prohibit the ceremony it would in doing so implicitly recognize its traditional significance.

14. Very few modern scholars have taken note of this incident, although it was widely reported at the time, as cited below. One exception is Jonathan Spence, *The Memory Palace of Matteo Ricci* (New York, 1983), 226.

15. The Venetian ambassador, Antonio Tiepolo, quoted in note 17, below, reported that they were both Spanish and Portuguese, and that as many as twenty-seven men had been involved (but this number is suspect, as not divisible by two), but that the authorities only burned the eleven they caught on August 2 of 1578. The discrepancy between Montaigne's referring only to Portuguese and Tiepolo's mentioning both Spanish and Portuguese might account for the difference between Montaigne's tally of "eight or nine" burned and Tiepolo's eleven.

together, using the same nuptial Scripture, after which they slept and ate together. Roman experts said that since sex between male and female could be legitimate only within marriage, it had seemed equally fair [juste] to them to authorize [these] ceremonies and mysteries of the church.[16]

The increasing discrepancy between the (largely inexplicable) hostility of the masses and the general equanimity of the church is highlighted in this episode, also relayed in the dispatches of the Venetian ambassador.[17] Montaigne apparently regarded the incident as an amusing oddity, but the Venetian ambassador described it as "horrifying wickedness," and Roman authorities (presumably civic) executed many of those involved by burning, which in the ambassador's opinion "they deserved."[18]

In some regions local authorities might have prohibited the ceremony, but this probably had little effect on an ancient and well-entrenched Christian ritual. The bishop of Ponzoni (in "Middle Dalmatia") forbade the ceremony in 1620,[19] but more than a century later Alberto Fortis witnessed and admired such a ceremony for two women performed *in a church* in Dalmatia.

Friendship, so susceptible among us to change for even the slightest of causes, is very long-lasting among the Morlaks. They

---

[16.] Michel de Montaigne, *Journal de Voyage en Italie par la Suisse et l'Allemagne en 1580 et 1581*, ed. Charles Dédéyan (Paris, 1946), 231: . . . *à Saint Jean Porta Latina, en laquelle Eglise certains Portuguais, quelques années y a, etoint antrés en une étrange confrérie. Ils s'espousoint masle à masle à la messe, aveq mesmes serimonies que nous faisons nos mariages, faisoint leurs pasques ensamble, lisoint ce mesme evangile des nopces, et puis couchoint et habitoint ensamble. Les esperts romeins disoint que parce qu'en l'autre conjoint de masle et femelle, cete sule circonstance la rand legitime, que ce soit en mariage, il avoit samblé à ces fines jans que cet'autre action deviendroit parillemant juste, qui l'auroit authorisée de serimonies et misteres de l'Eglise.*

[17.] *Storia arcana ed aneddotica d'Italia raccontata dai Veneti ambasciatori*, ed. Fabio Mutinelli (Venice, 1855), 1:121 (§7): *Sono stati presi undeci fra Portughesi e Spanuoli, i quali adunatisi in una chiesa, ch'è vicina san Giovanni Laterano, facevano alcune lor cerimonie, et con horrenda sceleraggine bruttando il sacrosanto nome di matrimonio, se maritavano l'un con l'altro, congiongendosi insieme, come marito con moglie. Vintisette si trovavano, et più, insieme il più delle volte, ma questa volta non ne hanno potuto coglier più che quesi undeci, i quali anderanno al fuoco, et come meritano.*

[18.] . . . *come meritano*, as cited in the preceding note. Montaigne (p. 231, as cited in n. 16, above) says that "eight or nine" were burned; Tiepolo gives the figure as eleven, but, again, this figure is suspect as not being divisible by two.

[19.] Milovan Gavazzi, "Das Kulturerbe der Südslaven im Lichte der Völkerkunde," *Die Welt der Slaven: Vierteljahrsschrift für Slavistik* 1 (1956), 63–81, p. 71.

have made it, as it were, a part of their religion, and they form this sacred bond before the altar. The Slavic rite has a special solemn blessing to unite two friends—two men or two women—in the presence of the whole community. I attended the union [*unione*] of two girls who became *posestre* in the church of Perussich. The happiness that shone in their eyes after sealing this sacred bond demonstrated to the onlookers what tenderness of feeling may dwell in souls not influenced—or, to be more precise —not corrupted by the society we call "civilized."

Friends solemnly united in this way are called *pobratimi*, females *posestrime*, which means more or less "half-brothers" or "half-sisters."[20] Friendships between men and women are not marked nowadays with such formalities, but it is possible that in earlier, more innocent days they were.

From these friendships and the semibrotherhood consecrated by the Morlaks and other peoples of the same provenance seem to be derived the "sworn brothers" that are common among our people and also in many places outside Italy. The difference between what takes place among us and the *pobratimi* of the Morlacs lies not only in the absence of the liturgical rite [sc. among us], but in the fact that among the Morlaks every sort of person [takes part] for mutual benefit, whereas among us the troublemakers and bullies are more likely than others to be united [in this way], and to form such unions to the disadvantage and disquiet of the public.

The obligations of the friends so united are to aid each other in any need or danger, to avenge wrongs done the partner [*compagno*], and so on. They are accustomed to carry their passion [*entusiasmo*] for friendship to the point of risking and even losing their lives for *pobratimi*, nor are examples of such sacrifice rare, although there are fewer tales about these ferocious friends than [there were] about the ancient Pilades. If some discord arises between *pobratimi* the whole region speaks of it as scandalous and unprecedented. Yet it does happen occasionally nowadays, to the chagrin of the elder Morlaks, who attribute to interaction

20. This is not in fact what Slavic побратими and посестрими connote: see discussion of this term in Chapter 1, "The Vocabulary of Love and Marriage," pp. 19–25.

with Italians the decadence of their compatriots. Wine and strong drink, which the people are starting to abuse on a daily basis under our influence, do lead to discords and tragedies among them, as among us.[21]

Ceremonies of same-sex union were increasingly performed in Eastern Europe between Christians and non-Christians (especially Muslims, since the Ottomans dominated this area in early modern centuries), which further complicated acceptance of the phenomenon, since even heterosexual matrimony with nonbelievers was viewed dimly by the Christian hierarchy. In 1526 the Ottoman sultan Suleiman I (1520–1566) granted governance of the city of Buda (half of modern Budapest) to John, the count of Siebenbürgen (the childless pretender to the throne of Hungary), who was his same-sex partner.[22]

When the Dominican Jacques Goar (1601–1653) first published the ceremony (it appeared posthumously in 1667) as part of his printed collection of Greek prayer books (*Euchologia*), he felt it necessary to include it because he found it in all the early Greek prayer books he consulted. Nonetheless, he invented an obfuscatory title for it and appended a page of notes about laws he supposed prohibited it, although most of them were of dubious relevance to the actual purpose of the ceremony.[23]

In areas (chiefly Italy, Greece, and Eastern Europe) where the ceremony was still practiced and recognized with its original meaning,[24] however, it was printed without comment and observed as nuptial: "In missals of the sixteenth and seventeenth centuries one usually

---

[21.] *Viaggio in Dalmazia I–II (1774)* (Munich, 1974), 58–59.

[22.] побрат: и даде кралієвиноу оу боудимоу ꙗноушоу воиводи херделсдомоу, побратимоу своемоу. *Svod menších letopisův srbských výčet a poznačení rukopisů*, 2, *sub anno* 7034 [1526], published in Pavel Josef Šafařík, *Památku dřevního písemnictví Jihoslovanu* (Prague, 1873), 83.

[23.] The title is discussed on pp. 26–27. The notes are appended to the ceremony in both editions (Paris, 1667, and Venice, 1730).

[24.] In Romania, however, it seems to have become customary for *heterosexual* couples to employ the ceremony (which had a special name in medieval Romanian, different from that for heterosexual marriage) in the fifteenth century, presumably because it created community property, whereas an ordinary heterosexual marriage usually rendered the wife's property subject to the dominion of the husband. On this, see Gheorghe Cront, *Înfrățirea de moșie: Jurătorii, Instituții medievale românești* (Academia republicii socialiste România, Biblioteca istorica, 18) (Bucharest, 1969) and P. P. Panaitescu and Damaschin Mioc, B. *tara românească* (Documenta rômaniae historica, 1) (Bucharest, 1966), 364–65 and passim, as cited in Cront.

finds one or more prayers read by the priest to the Wahlbrüder[25] at their wedding, as one must rightly call it."[26] German anthropologists from the second half of the nineteenth century, when a strong homosexual rights movement emerged in that country, until near the middle of the twentieth, when the Nazis brutally exterminated it (along with many individual gay people), tended to be frank and realistic about the ceremony and its meaning.[27] Although induced by his age to refer to it as Wahlbrüderschaft, Ciszewski felt comfortable enough to observe that the ceremony "is just like that for marriage, in which the ultimate union of the couple is preceded by a series of introductory rites, an array of symbolic gestures that are supposed to represent the union, and also to introduce the main action of the union."[28] He described such a ceremony in detail, basing his account on eyewitness testimony. It took place on the Feast of St. John, the beloved disciple.[29] The priest and two or three close relatives were invited to the house, ashes from the hearth were sprinkled on two sides of a plank, on which the two men placed their right feet. (In some regions the

25. Wahlbrüder, "elective brothers," is one of the ways anthropologists encoded and disguised the relationship between partners in a same-sex union, but as the influence of West European revulsion spread, it probably came to be more and more accurate. Stanislaus Ciszewski, Künstliche Verwandtschaft bei den Südslaven (Leipzig, 1897), used this term, but interchanged it with Genosse—"companion," "mate," "partner," "comrade," as if they were synonyms.

26. . . . Bei der Trauung—man darf füglich so sagen, Friedrich Krauss, Sitte und Brauch der Südslaven nach heimischen gedruckten und ungedruckten Quellen (Vienna, 1885), 627.

27. In addition to Ciszewski, cited in n. 25, see also Krauss (cited in n. 26), Chapter 29, "Wahlbruderschaft und Wahlschwesterschaft," which is slightly distorted but not unduly reticent. Leopold Kretzenbacher, "Gegenwartsformen der Wahlverwandtschaft 'pobratimstvo' bei den Serben und im übrigen Südosteuropa," Grazer und Münchener Balkanologische Studien. 2: Münchener Studien zu Geschichte und Volkskunde der Balkan-Länder. Beiträge zur Kenntnis Südosteuropas und des Nahen Orients. 2 (1967) and Rituelle Wahlverbrüderung in Südosteuropa. Erlebniswirklichkeit und Erzählmotiv. (Sitzungsberichte der Bayerischen Akademie der Wissenschaften, Philosophisch-Historische Klasse. 1971.) Heft 1 (Munich, 1971), is also cautious, though not overtly deceptive: see discussion following.

28. Stanislaus Ciszewski, p. 53. Earlier (p. 36) he had noted that die Wahlbrüderschaft . . . erinnert uns sehr an die Hochzeitsceremonie and cited Bogošić (Pravni običaji, p. 432) as commenting that such relationships were "indeed amazingly like marriage: the priest asks one, 'Do you take X to be your brother; then the other one the same. Each replies, 'I do.' If one of them dies, the other inherits everything, including spouse and children." Ciszewski was slightly less forthcoming in treating the phenomenon in sixteenth-century Poland: see Künstliche Verwandtschaft, p. 48, and A. Brückner, "Über pobratimstvo bei Polen und Russen im XVI Jahrhundert," Archiv für slavische Philologie unter Mitwirkung, ed V. Jagić (Berlin, 1893), both citing Fabyan Klonowicz's poem Roxolania (Cracow, 1584) about travels in Poland in that century. For a more recent approach, see Marion M. Coleman, Klonowicz and Ukraine: An Introduction to the Poem Roxolania (Marquette University Slavic Institute Papers, 17) (Milwaukee, 1963).

29. According to Ciszewski, persons so joined were often referred to as "young Johns" (p. 42).

men notified all their friends and invited them all to the ceremony, just as in a wedding.)[30] Then the priest asked them if they truly wished to be joined together and if they truly believed in the Trinity, the Gospel, and in fire.[31] The priest read from the Gospel and told them that from this time forward they would be *more than brothers (ja sogar mehr als Brüder)* and must treat each other accordingly. (Folk literature of the region celebrates a case where one partner took the other's place in the army.)[32] Then he called on those present to be witnesses to their new status and wished them good fortune. They bowed to him, kissed the Gospel, the priest's hands, and each other's hands, and then those of the guests older than they. Following the ceremony they gave each other gifts, and in some regions exchanged their baptismal crosses, gave the priest a present, and held a great feast, sometimes one in each of the partner's homes.[33] In some areas the partners legally designated each other as heirs and promised to leave no other descendants.[34]

In the early twentieth century, Näcke, who was himself openly gay and writing in the first journal devoted to the study of homosexuality, was franker still about such unions in Albania, which he discussed specifically in the context of homosexuality:[35] he reported that a native informant assured him that *amor masculus* was common even in the Roman Catholic sections of Albania (as well as among the Muslim population), although he quoted another correspondent as hypothesizing (since he could not know) that Christians tended to practice interfemoral rather than anal or oral intercourse with their partners.[36] Näcke himself drew a direct parallel (pp. 332–34) between such unions in contemporary Albania and those of Greek warriors (especially the Sacred Band of Thebes), which he says were known to

---

30. Ciszewski, p. 66: in Bulgaria, where part of the ceremony also involved binding their hands with the priest's stole.

31. Perhaps a pagan remnant: presumably the reason for the ashes.

32. Ciszewski, p. 90.

33. Pp. 47, 56–57, drawing on the testimony of N. A. Nachov, "за побратимството," *Periodichesko spisanie na bulgarskoto knishnovo druzestvo v Sufia* 49–50 (1895), 32–72, p. 61.

34. Ciszewski, p. 92: *wofern der Betreffende keine erberechtigte Nachkommenshaft hinterlassen sollte.*

35. P. Näcke, "Über Homosexualität in Albanien," *Jahrbuch für sexuelle Zwischenstufen unter besonderer Berücksichtigung der Homosexualität* 10 (1908), 313–37, p. 332: *Brüderschaftsbündnisse sind . . . wahrscheinlich nicht immer nur rein freundschaftliche, sondern gewiss auch bisweilen homosexuell gefärbt.*

36. Pp. 328–29. He refers to the unions as "Brüderschaftsbündnisse," but makes no effort to deceive his audience about their sexual nature.

be "flagrantly sexual" (*stark sexuell*).[37] Indeed, he suggested that many of the men involved in such unions were using them purely for sexual release rather than actually realizing romantic inclinations (pp. 335–37), although he noted that sometimes an educational role (as among the Greeks) was involved *along with* sexuality (pp. 334–35). George Gordon, Lord Byron, was also struck by the powerful homosexual relationships among Albanian men in the early part of the nineteenth century, when he was one of the first Englishmen to visit there.[38]

But even in these areas the influence of Western horror gradually induced the populace to view the ceremony as something else,[39] and by the time anthropologists almost anywhere during the twentieth century made note of it, the vast majority of them preferred to see it as something other than a ceremony of same-sex union, with the attendant and unnerving implication of homosexuality—which was punishable by death in most of Europe at the time and by social and political ruin in areas dominated by the Soviet Union (and not even mentionable in English-speaking nations until the second half of the present century).[40] That anthropologists and even whole societies might turn a blind eye to something as disconcerting as the sexuality of other cultures is well-known. The American Indian *berdache* (an openly homosexual male or female) was ignored, condemned, or even denied by many white anthropologists (and some twentieth-century Native Americans). In 1885 the anthropologist Matilda Coxe Stevenson and her husband brought back to Washington, D. C., We'wha, a male Zuni *berdache* they believed to be a woman; all Washington accepted him as a princess and Stevenson may have thought

---

37. He also compares them (pp. 334–35) to Japanese Samurai relationships of a similar nature. On these, see Paul Schalow, *The Great Mirror of Male Love*, as cited in Introduction, p. xxvi, n. 17.
38. See Louis Crompton, *Byron and Greek Love* (Berkeley, 1985), 133–39.
39. M. E. Durham, *Some Tribal Origins, Laws and Customs of the Balkans* (London, 1928), 156, observes, specifically in relation to this: "People who wished to appear 'civilized' in Montenegro were very apt to deny the existence of customs they thought would be despised. But it was admitted that 'pobratimstvo' had but recently died out." Cf. Ciszewski (as cited above, n. 25), p. 94: *Heute is sie nur einer Titularverbrüderung.* He quotes another observer's similar observation about a different region on p. 97. Krauss, *Sitte und Brauch* (cited above, n. 26), p. 641, also comments on the decline in the practice and meaning of the term in southern Slavic regions.
40. For the distortion even of the classics this occasioned, see *CSTH* pp. 17–22. In general, even Nachov (n. 33, above) is not to be trusted: he falls in the category of those determined to "explain away" the ceremony, although his evidence fails him, as Ciszewski saw.

he was a woman until his death, although, as Will Roscoe shows, it was actually pretty obvious that he was male.[41]

The Italian Giovanni Tamassia was the first author to write a volume about ἀδελφοποιία,[42] but he addressed it solely from the point of view of "artificial kinship" and folk custom, and never considered the possibility that it was a ceremony of same-sex union in some deeper sense.[43] Since his time, discussing the ceremony under rubrics such as "artificial kinship," "blood brotherhood," or "collateral adoption" have become the standard anthropological sleights of hand to obscure its more troubling aspects. Such approaches succeed in sounding nonsexual, impersonal, folkish, and not nearly as electrifying or counterintuitive as "same-sex union," although both "artificial kinship" and "blood brotherhood" are in fact "same-sex unions," if not quite what modern readers might expect from such a term. To a mind inclined to recoil from the possibility of a same-sex equivalent of heterosexual matrimony, discovering that previous scholars discussed varieties of same-sex unions under terms like "artificial relationship" seems to offer a way out, a mechanism for avoiding a disturbing reality.[44]

[41.] *The Zuni Man-Woman* (Albuquerque, 1991), in which other examples of anthropological deception are also documented. On the *berdache* tradition of institutionalized homosexuality among native Americans, see Roscoe's Chapter 8: "The Berdache Tradition." See also the discussion of the efforts of modern informants and anthropologists to disguise Hawaiian homosexuality in Robert Morris, "Aikāne: Accounts of Hawaiian Same-Sex Relationships in the Journals of Captian Cook's Third Voyage (1776–80)," *Journal of Homosexuality* 19, 4 (1990), 21–54, and David Greenberg, *The Construction of Homosexuality* (Chicago, 1988), 74–79. Other problems can also intrude in a society so disturbed by same-sex eroticism: Gilbert Herdt found that his native informants did not trust him enough to disclose widespread homosexual behavior (Greenberg, pp. 78–79), but Herdt himself represented homosexuality among the Sambia as merely a "phase," apparently hoping to placate the dogmatic school of history known as "social constructionism." For a brilliant critique of the last, see Richard Mohr, *Gay Ideas: Outing and Other Controversies* (Boston, 1992), Chapter 7.

[42.] *L'Affratellamento* (ʾΑΔΕΛΦΟΠΟΙΙΑ) *Studio storico-giuridico* (Torino, 1886).

[43.] When the evidence was unmistakable, as in the Greek East, he simply refused to discuss it: *nulla diciamo*, he said about the *spurcissimus gentilium ritus* (even switching into Latin!) of the Byzantines (p. 31 n. 1). He made a similar disclaimer (pp. 7–8) about the subject of the Sacred Band, which he did call *fratellanza militare*, but then demurred to go into further detail (*più in là . . . non possiamo andare*), although in a note he claimed that allegations of homosexuality regarding the Sacred Band "could not be true" (*non può rispondere al vero* [p. 8, n. 2]).

[44.] Examples of such writing include E. Golubinskii, История русской церкви (Moscow, 1904), 1:460–61; the liturgical manual *Novaia skrizhal* (St. Petersburg, 1908), 511–12; S. Bobchev, «О побратимствѣ и посестримствѣ» *Zhivaia starina* 2, 3 (1892), 31–42; Nachov, as cited above, n. 33; T. Volkov, "La fraternisation en Ukraïne," *Melusine* 5.8 (1891), 7.1 (1894), 7.7 (1895); Georgios Michaelidos-Nouaros, "Περὶ τῆς ἀδελφοποιίας ἐν τῇ ἀρχαίᾳ Ἑλλάδι καὶ ἐν τῷ Βυζαντίῳ," *Τόμος Κονσταντίνου Ἁρμενοπούλου ἐπὶ τῇ

But, in fact, as should by now be obvious, the very same terms (e.g., "artificial kinship") could describe heterosexual marriage *just as well* as same-sex unions. An artificial relationship is simply a relationship *created* by two parties rather than inherited genetically from forebears. Many important human relationships are "artificial"—which hardly makes them less emotional, less committed, or even less sexual. Heterosexual marriage is, in fact, the *archetypal* artificial relationship in premodern Europe: it unites two families that were generally *not* previously united by inheritance or biology. Often this is a primary aim of matrimony. (Indeed, if they were related before the marriage, it was generally prohibited.)

The term "artificial brotherhood" gives a misleading impression of both universality and specificity, as if it were a widespread, uniform social institution. In fact, the relationships called "blood brotherhood," "sworn brotherhood," "spiritual brotherhood," and so on, vary enormously from culture to culture (and sometimes within a single society) in their mode of formation, in their social, legal, and religious significance, and in their personal (e.g., affective) aspects. They can be and often are analogized by anthropologists on the basis of shared qualities of one sort or another, but they are not simply variations of a single phenomenon—like, for example, different societies' terms for biological relationships (e.g., brother, sister, aunt), where there is a precise underlying structural similarity overlaid with cultural and linguistic variation. They are not even similar in the way that concepts of friendship entertained by different societies are, since many of the constants associated with variations of friendship (e.g., subsisting between equals, unconstrained, not legally established) cannot be predicated on artificial brotherhood; its attributes vary dramatically on such points. "It" ranges from a mechanical obligation incurred when

---

ἐξακοσιετήριδι τῆς Ἑξαβίβλου αὐτοῦ (1345–1945) (Thessalonika, 1952), 251–313, and entries under ἀδελφοποιία and побратимство in modern Greek and Russian encyclopedias, respectively (including the *ODB*). It does not seem worth critiquing each in detail; the reader will quickly observe that such authors have no wish to consider a possibility as disturbing and socially unacceptable as a same-sex union. Pavel Florenskij, Столп и утвержденіе истины (Moscow, 1914, Berlin, 1929), Italian trans. by Pietro Modesto, *La colonna e il fondamento della verità* (Milan, 1974), did at least discuss the ceremony under the general rubric "love" (pp. 457–63 of the Russian text, pp. 523–28 in Italian translation). Of course, there were doubtless cases where such relationships were *not* same-sex unions, but given the cloud of unknowing that anthropologists have cast over the subject, it is very difficult to be certain: August Vinson's *Voyage à Madagascar au couronnement de Radama II* (Paris, 1865), 281–83, is perfectly ambiguous on this point.

one party is in another's debt, involving no affect whatever, to purely circumstantial status, as when two children are baptized together or two adults bathe at the same time in the Jordan River,[45] to the most intimate and personal bonds in a society, as between Norse warriors, Scythian friends, or homosexual lovers. It is questionable whether applying a single term to such phenomena does not obscure more than it discloses, and throughout this study great care has been taken to keep the use of this abstraction to the barest minimum.

In general it seems fair to suggest that although artificial brotherhood is most commonly practiced between two males, it is not "homosexual" in the sense of carrying publicly recognized erotic overtones or implications. But public acknowledgment of erotic components of relationships is certainly not a reliable indication of what they might mean privately to the individuals involved. The most significant thing about a businessman's relationship with his secretary, both from a personal point of view and from the standpoint of its material consequences, might be that they are in love with each other, even though the public view of such relationships does not involve eroticism. A structural anthropologist might rightly point out that, institutionally speaking, such relationships are not erotic (as marriage or concubinage are, for example), but a historian would want to say something much more nuanced, not only about any particular instance but even about the category. Some forms of structured intimacy and familiarity are much more likely to give rise to sexual or erotic interaction than others, and this must be carefully assessed.

During the first half of the twentieth century, when most of the anthropological work was done on artificial brotherhoods, such severe prejudice attached to the subject of homosexuality in the cultures producing these studies that hardly any researchers would have dared impute an erotic component to the phenomenon unless the evidence was absolutely irresistible. Evidence about emotional states is, however, almost never irresistible. Indeed, it is rarely unambiguous. It would be nearly impossible, for example, to determine whether most nineteenth-century married couples in Africa or even in Europe were "in love" with each other, but the want of the needed data would not

---

45. Ciszewski, pp. 8–9. Even Ciszewski admits that such *Wahlbrüdershaft* does not have the force of its ancient equivalent (p. 35).

be taken, in this case, to indicate the absence of such feelings, simply as a difficulty of research. By contrast, prior to the last decade the absence of any clear evidence of homosexual feelings would have been taken, without challenge, as sufficient evidence that artificial relationships involved no "abnormal sentiments."

Nearing the end of the twentieth century, scholars can no longer predicate serious social research on the moralistic and empirically mistaken assumption that homosexual feelings or behavior are "abnormal," peculiar, or inherently unlikely. The evidence suggests that they occur, and quite commonly, in nearly all cultures; indeed, they have been the predominant public ethos of eroticism in a number of times and places. Claims that certain cultures do not include same-sex eroticism were commonplace in Europe through the opening decades of the twentieth century, dwindled with the scientific advances of the forties and fifties, and would now be entertained by social scientists skeptically and only as evidence of an *unusual* cultural pattern, requiring very substantial proof. Nonetheless, much of the anthropological data accumulated before recent decades bears the heavy stamp of prudery, ignorance, or reticence on this subject, and often gives the impression that homosexuality was unknown in nonindustrial cultures. It must be read with great caution.

There is no reason for a contemporary researcher or reader to assume that homosexuality might not form part of some artificial sibling relationships, and much reason to be suspicious of the absence of any discussion—pro or con—of this subject in the majority of nineteenth- and twentieth-century literature on the subject. It will hardly do to appeal to the mere silence of researchers in whose homelands homosexual acts led to social ruin, incarceration, or even capital punishment.

Artificial sibling relationships occur less commonly between females, and less commonly still between persons of the opposite sex. Many cultures acknowledge the possibility of heterosexual artificial siblings, but far fewer actually produce them. This seems to be related to the potential for sexual interaction involved—i.e., the danger of sexual involvement is too great, and there is therefore pressure against artificial siblinghood between men and women; this fact is exquisitely ambiguous in its relation to the erotic component of *same-sex* artificial brotherhood. On the one hand, it suggests that sexuality is seen as a strong possibility in such relationships; on the other, the prevention of heterosexual couplings presumed at risk for sexuality may indicate that same-sex unions, when they are permitted, are not thought to carry the same risk. It is, however, equally likely that same-sex eroticism was simply less threatening, since it would not produce illegitimate children, complicate bloodlines, or threaten the marital strategies of families, and would most commonly occur between two unmarried females or two men, usually subject to less stringent standards of marital fidelity in any case. There would thus be less reason for a culture to worry about or attempt to preclude it.

Leopold Kretzenbacher, trying like most anthropologists of this century to disguise the nature of the ceremony, first chose a rare heterosexual example of it, which he claimed to have witnessed personally in 1966, and then flatly contradicted himself about the nature of the union, stating first that such a couple could under no circumstances become lovers (p. 168 in "Gegenwartsformen" [n. 27]), but in a later work admitting that the pair, after a ceremony he had acknowledged even in his first study (ibid.) was indistinguishable from a marriage, could indeed become lovers and could never take part in the same ceremony with anyone else as long as they lived.[46]

Another smokescreen deployed by anthropologists is "blood brotherhood." There certainly were forms of blood brotherhood that were not homosexual unions: most readers may feel they know what "blood brotherhood" is, and it is *not* the homosexual equivalent of heterosexual matrimony. It is, for example, Indian and white friends forming lofty (nonerotic) unions, as described by James Fenimore Cooper (in whose native land homosexuality was a capital offense), or school chums becoming "blood brothers" by pricking fingers and running their blood together. This sort of relationship, of course, is not at all what anthropologists are discussing; they are generally describing permanent relationships between adult males, not of different races. It is usually a relationship to unite tribes or kin groups, which involves either the exchange of blood (by drinking it from a chalice rather than pricking fingers) or a religious ceremony, or both. The tribal alliance aspect of such relationships is a good place to contemplate the parallels between such unions and heterosexual marriage, because

---

[46.] *Rituelle Wahlverbrüderung*, as cited above, n. 27.

alliances of tribes or houses or families or even whole peoples was in fact one of the *main functions* of upper-class heterosexual marriage in premodern Europe.

Occasionally anthropologists or historians describe the ceremony as a mode of collateral adoption, but far from disguising its nuptial qualities, this analogy also helps to clarify the ceremony's parallels to opposite-gender marriage, which was often tantamount to collateral adoption (in the senses that the wife was brought into her husband's family, her property became his, she was "given away" by her father or elder brother, she took her husband's family name, the basic ceremony often involved conveying *her* to *his* home). As noted earlier, Aulus Gellius, a Roman writer, observed that "the bride is called 'sister' because she is, as it were, born again and cut out of the family into which she was born and transferred into another household."[47] Sometimes heterosexual marriage was even seen as lineal adoption: the wife became part of the *familia* ruled by husband, who was *paterfamilias*. There was much ancient rhetoric about husbands treating wives as daughters, and it was a great legal issue in Roman law of late antiquity whether a man could marry his ward or *alumna*. In the course of legal discussions of this question, it became apparent that many men adopted foundlings or relatives *precisely* to marry them.[48]

Could the ceremony discussed above constitute a form of collateral adoption or artificial kinship? The answer to this question could be equally yes or no or both, depending on the meaning one assigns the terms "collateral adoption" and "artificial kinship." If they are understood to exclude any emotional or erotic component—which is how most nineteenth-century anthropologists used them—then they also exclude the ceremony, which was unmistakably a personal, emotional commitment, and not simply a tribal or family arrangement.

In addition to German scholars emboldened by their country's incipient homosexual rights movement in the late nineteenth century, only female and gay anthropologists, writers, and historians of nearly any time and place have been able to view the ceremony objectively and without noticeable reticence. The English anthropologist Mary Durham discussed it under the rubric "blood brotherhood," but was

---

47. See p. 41.
48. See Boswell, *Kindness of Strangers*, p. 34, nn. 79, 162.

honest and unabashed enough to quote a native informant with a different opinion: "My old friend, Pope[49] Gjuro of Njegushi, spoke in the strongest terms against this ceremony, which he said the Church should never have permitted. He described it as 'the marriage of two men and against all nature,' and intimated clearly, as did others, that it had been used as the cloak for vice."[50] Similarly, the twentieth-century French historian Evelyne Patlagean not only recognized the homosexual character of what she called *l'affrairement*, but even specifically linked it to the term "brother" in the *Satyricon*, the only historian to do so in this century before the present study.[51]

By contrast, neither Patlagean nor Durham seemed so willing to contemplate the existence of female homosexuality. Although for the most part speculation in this study has been kept to an absolute minimum and attention has been focused entirely on recorded facts and opinions, it may be worthwhile here to venture into some extrapolation from Durham's data in regard to women, whose lives have provided little interest to other scholars except as they relate to male concerns. Although she does not make the connection explicitly, Durham seems to suggest one of the mechanisms by which women in the Balkans in the early twentieth century might have freed themselves from a severely constraining social structure to pursue their own passions and desires.

"The most important object of marriage," she wrote of Albania, "is to obtain sons,"[52] which meant both that cohabitation would take

---

49. An honorific title for an Eastern (Orthodox or Catholic) priest, not to be confused with the bishop of Rome.

50. Durham, ut supra, p. 157. Possibly because he felt a need to cite this passage from Durham, the sociologist Dinko Tomasic observed rather frankly in *Personality and Culture in Eastern European Politics* (New York, 1948), 79, that "Pobratimstvo and posestrimstvo may take on some homosexual aspects. Homosexuality is to be expected in a society in which the relations between men and women are placed in sharp contrast, in which men from their early childhood are almost exclusively in the company of men, and women in the company of women, each group rather secluded from the other. Men are trained to look down upon women as inferior, and are taught to regard all affectionate relationships with them as unheroic."

51. "Christianisation et parentés rituelles: le domaine de Byzance," in "Les rituels de parenté: un dossier," *Annales, Économies, Sociétés, Civilisations* 33,3 (May–June, 1978), 625–36, pp. 628–29: *La réponse patriarcale souligne la présomption d'immoralité qui pèse sur l'affrairement, et on est tenté de rapprocher ce jugement du vocabulaire fraternel qui exprime dans le* Satiricon *une relation homosexuelle,*" citing F. Dupont, *Le plaisir et la loir* (Paris, 1977), 164–69, which does not, however, provide much additional information. Craig Williams also notes the connection in his dissertation (cited in Abbreviations), but it has not yet been published.

52. *Some Tribal Origins*, p. 193.

place to produce a son *before* there was a marriage ceremony, and also that parents would have very little concern about the desires of their children (of either gender) in regard to matrimony. Durham only met one woman who had refused the groom chosen for her, and it caused enormous turbulence in the family.[53]

On the other hand, women did have an option to get out of arranged marriages: a daughter could swear perpetual virginity and "if she pleases, dress as a man. She associates with the men on equal terms, and eats and smokes with them. She may carry arms. . . . One in the Djakova district was said to have served in the Turkish army undetected."[54] A father "could bequeath to her his house and land for her lifetime, after which it reverted to the nearest male heir. Such a virgin had the right to sell her younger sisters."[55]

Although it is not clear whether erotic relations between such women, called *posestra*, would violate an oath of virginity, it is possible that they would not, since they would complicate no bloodlines, and it is also possible that the opportunity to escape from arranged marriage and the risks of childbearing would be worth a life of celibacy, as long as there was companionship with another *posestra*. Durham was as reluctant to address lesbian realities as her male contemporaries were to face male homosexuality, but there is no reason that in the less terrified 1990s thoughtful persons cannot attempt to read between the lines of her descriptions.

Apparently, although it was ignored or disguised by anthropologists, gay men in Europe were well aware of the phenomenon and saw no reason to pretend it was anything else. Hans Christian Andersen, thought to have been gay,[56] immortalized the practice in his novelette *Venskabs-Pagten* in the early nineteenth century, although himself cloaking it somewhat.[57] As Christopher Isherwood steamed down the Danube in 1933 "he kept repeating to himself that they were entering the Balkans—a romantically dangerous region of blood feuds and (so he had been told) male marriages celebrated by priests."[58]

---

53. Ibid., p. 196.
54. Ibid., p. 194.
55. Ibid., p. 195.
56. See Albert Hansen, "H. C. Andersen: Beweis seiner Homosexualität," *Jahrbuch für sexuelle Zwischenstufen unter besonderer Berücksichtigung der Homosexualität* 3 (1901), 203–31, with review of other literature on the subject.
57. In *En Digters Bazar* [A Poet's Bazaar] (Copenhagen, 1842), 206–14.
58. Christopher Isherwood, *Christopher and His Kind 1929–1939* (New York, 1976), 137.

Few observers either then or now have been able to contemplate the possibility that the "blood-brother" relationships among late medieval Scandinavian warriors could have been homosexual, partly because of the mistaken notion that intensely masculine men would have only heterosexual desire—abundantly disproved by reams of evidence from the ancient world. But Thorkil Vanggaard, in a gay-positive but otherwise undistinguished study, does address this possibility: "The more familiar one becomes with the attitudes and way of life of these people, alien to our norms, prejudices and repressions as they were, the more unlikely it seems that the blood-brother relationship should not have included a genital aspect, based on mutuality and equality between the partners."[59]

[59.] *Phallos: A Symbol and Its History in the Male World* (London, 1972), 119. Sex roles among Scandinavian warriors were, however, highly charged with "active/passive" connotations: see, e.g., *Norrön niðdiktning: traditionshistoriska studier i versmagi. I. Nið mot furstar*, Nordiska Texter och Undersökningar 21 (Uppsala, 1965), and Joaquin Martínez Pizarro, "On Nið against Bishops," *Mediaeval Scandinavia* 11 (1978–79), 149–53.

EPILOGUE

LTHOUGH MANY QUESTIONS REMAIN about same-sex unions in premodern Europe, much has also emerged with reasonable clarity. Such unions, in various forms, were widespread in the ancient world, where heterosexual matrimony tended to be viewed as a dynastic or business arrangement, and love in such relationships, where it occurred, arose *following* the coupling. Ordinary men and women were more likely to invest feelings the twentieth century would call "romantic" in same-sex relationships, either passionate friendships or more structured and institutional unions, as exemplified by the recognized couples of Crete or Scythia, the swearing of perpetual love among other Greeks, and the social phenomenon and legal stratagem of "brotherhood" among the Romans.

Since the advent of Christianity only exacerbated doubts about the emotional significance of matrimony, there was little pressure (other than widespread heterosexual desire) to re-evaluate such attitudes. Christianity's main innovation was to privilege and make real widespread voluntary celibacy, implicitly or explicitly suggesting that heterosexual matrimony was a mere compromise with the awful powers of sexual desire, even when it was directed exclusively to the procreation of children, the one rationale Christians found convincing. But passionate friendships, especially among paired saints and holy virgins, continued to exercise a fascination over the early Christians— still residents of the ancient world—and in time were transformed into official relationships of union, performed in churches and blessed by priests.

In many ways from a contemporary point of view, the most pressing question addressed by this work is probably whether the Christian ceremony of same-sex union functioned in the past as a "gay marriage

280

ceremony." It is clear that it did, although, as has been demonstrated at length, the nature and purposes of every sort of marriage have varied widely over time. In almost every age and place the ceremony fulfilled what most people today regard as the essence of marriage: a permanent romantic commitment between two people, witnessed and recognized by the community. Beyond this, it might or might not fulfill specific legal or canonical expectations predicated on the experience of the heterosexual majority (procreative purpose, transfer of property, dowry), but the extent to which particular heterosexual unions matched such niceties did not usually determine whether the neighbors regarded the couple (same-sex or heterosexual) as married. Indeed, in all times and places in its history (including the present) the official teaching of the Roman Catholic church (one of the two bodies in which the ceremony developed) has been that the two parties *marry each other;* the priest merely acts as a witness. If the couple intend to be married, they are. By contrast, in the Eastern Orthodox church the priest *does* perform the ceremony, and in all known cases priests performed the same-sex union.

Such are the historical facts. Their social, moral, and political significance is arguable, but considerable. Even persons who argue that same-sex couples should *now* have the right to contract marriage like anyone else are apt to view such unions as an exotic indulgence of our time, a novel experiment in a liberal society. And many people—both homosexual and heterosexual—argue that same-sex couples should not undertake traditional relationships similar to heterosexual matrimony. While I was preparing this study, I received a visit from a well-known prelate, who remarked to me that heterosexual matrimony had become such a ragged institution in the second half of the twentieth century that it hardly constituted a useful model for same-sex couples, who might better devise something entirely new.

I replied that I had not composed the same-sex union ceremony that seems to parallel heterosexual marriage, but only discovered it, and felt it my duty as a historian to share it. In this connection I offer as a concluding observation that whatever significance the ceremony might (or might not) have for persons living at this juncture of history, its greatest importance lies, along with all the other forms of same-sex union known in premodern Europe, in its role in European history. It is not the province of the historian to direct the actions of future human beings, but only to reflect accurately on those of the past. "Humanity does not pass through phases as a train passes through stations: being alive, it has the privilege of always moving yet never leaving anything behind. Whatever we have been, in some sort we are still," observed C. S. Lewis in a related context.[1] Recognizing that many—probably most—earlier Western societies institutionalized some form of romantic same-sex union gives us a much more accurate view of the immense variety of human romantic relationships and social responses to them than does the prudish pretense that such "unmentionable" things never happened.

---

[1] *The Allegory of Love* (Oxford, 1936), 1.

APPENDIX
of
TRANSLATIONS

ALTHOUGH TRANSLATION of ancient religious texts into premodern rather than contemporary English is likely to strike many readers as precious, I have elected to do so after carefully deliberating the problem—and discussing it with other scholars—for many years. The Greek and Slavic in which these texts were written was not the ordinary vernacular of the persons who composed or subsequently utilized the ceremonies: they were special, learned, liturgical languages rooted consciously in the much older speech patterns of Koine Greek and Old Church Slavonic, used specifically for sacred Scripture and ecclesiastical functions, with characteristic and peculiar cadence, grammar,[1] and vocabulary, imparting force, beauty, and authority.[2] Modern English has no such resonance, which is part of the reason that efforts to turn older English translations of Scripture and prayers into the modern vernacular meet with resistance on the part of many of the faithful.[3] I take no side in this controversy, which pits the advantages of accessibility and relevance against the aesthetics and authority of tradition.[4]

[1] The fact that Jacobean English uses recognizable but discarded inflections for verbs (thou dost) and more complex adverbs ("thereunto," "wherefor") than modern English makes an almost exact parallel to the relationship of older, more elaborately inflected Greek and OCS (Old Church Slavonic) to their less complex vernacular descendants of the Middle Ages.

[2] The foremost authority on Old Church Slavonic asserts that "it is wrong to think of OCS as a semi-intelligible liturgical language like modern C[hurch] S[lavonic]; it was readily comprehensible to all Slavs," (Horace Lunt, *Old Church Slavonic Grammar* [6th ed., The Hague, 1974] p. x). I think it also fair to say that the language of the KJV or of the Anglican/Episcopalian Book of Common Prayer is readily comprehensible to most English speakers, however unfamiliar its inflected verb forms may be: what is at issue here is tone, authority, and connotation, not intelligibility.

[3] Simple conservatism is also a factor.

[4] Examples of such conflicts are the current ferment over the revision of the Episcopalian Book of Common Prayer and disagreement among Roman Catholics about the retention of the Tridentine form of the Mass.

283

In many specific ways—too many and too complex to rehearse here[5]—the English of the King James Version of the Bible and the Book of Common Prayer provides the best historical counterpart for the liturgical and biblical languages of the texts presented here, and I have therefore striven, however clumsily, to render them into the language of the era that produced both the King James translation of the Scriptures—still the standard throughout the English-speaking world—and the Book of Common Prayer, a liturgical manual unrivaled among English nations for its religious and linguistic influence. Both of these texts relied heavily on English translations and texts of the preceding century, so that even in their own time they were archaizing. Nonetheless, except where necessary (and indicated in notes) I have not employed English words postdating the ceremonies in which they occur.

In spite of an archaizing tone in the originals of these documents, the grammar is not always perfect, and I have had to approximate the meaning in many cases. I have, moreover, striven to effect compromises between accuracy and euphony. For example, I have translated "We pray to the Lord" and "Let us pray" more according to the English sense than the Greek grammar. This does no violence to the meaning.

Key to Symbols

< > = speculation on lacunae or reconstruction of abbreviation; these actual letters not in the original

[ ] = words needed to clarify text, supplied by translator

( ) = something in original but not needed or helpful in English

| = actual change of folio in original; folio numbers indicated prior to sentence in which change occurs

5. I cite as one of many the fact that there is little disjunction in the Greek or Old Church Slavonic between the language of the biblical passages and that of the ceremonies; in the later Slavic versions there is more, but it is not comparable to that between modern English and the most common and authoritative versions of the English Bible (e.g., the KJV or RSV). Even employing contemporary translations (NEB, JB) would not solve this problem: since they are translations of an ancient text, even they do not follow the speech or literary patterns of modern English. The Greek Scriptures were not translated for Christians using the Greek versions of the ceremony; for Slavic speakers, the Old Slavonic versions of the liturgy and Scripture were the most ancient texts they knew, and few, if any, of those involved in the ceremony would have known the Scriptures in any other version.

1. HYMN[6] TO SAINTS SERGE AND BACCHUS[7]
[sixth century][8] [Greek]

Elias.

To the tune of Δυνάμει θεϊκῇ.[9]

i.

Of Serge and Bacchus,
the pair[10]
filled with grace,
let us sing, O ye faithful!
Glory to Him who worketh
through his saints
amazing and wonderful deeds!

ii.

Let thy grace overshadow
thy servant, beyond what words can say,
O Christ, creator of all,
cleanser of all my sins
of word and deed,
that I may appear before you
pleasing and humbled,
for I am full of weakness,
. . . .[11]. . . . .
But do thou accept me as thy servant,
that I may call on thee in purity.
Glory to Him who worketh
through his saints
amazing and wonderful deeds!

---

6. Καριοφιλης Μητσακη, *Βυζαντινὴ Ὑμνογραφία ἀπὸ τὴν καίνη διαθήκη ὡς τὴν εἰκονομαχία* (Athens, 1986) classifies this hymn as a *kontakion* (pp. 517–18), which suggests its use in several of the liturgies printed subsequently. It is almost certainly the Greek original of the "hymn of the martyrs" referred to in the Slavic ceremonies.

7. Published in Jean-Baptiste Pitra, *Analecta Sacra: Spicilegio Solesmensi*, 1 (Paris, 1876), 289–91.

8. See discussion in Pitra, pp. xxxiv–xxxv and p. 289, n. 1. There are two possible Eliases who might have been the author: the first lived 494–518, the second 741–767. Pitra favored the first as author, though he was not absolutely certain. I also favor the first, at least as author of this hymn, given its language and content. Cf. comments in Μητσακη, as cited above, n. 6.

9. This word (θεϊκῇ) is postclassical; there are no postclassical words in the hymn itself.

10. Or "dyad"; cf. the hymn to Peter and Paul, ibid., p. 549: ἡ τῶν ἀποστόλων πανσεβάσμιος δυάς.

11. Lacuna.

iii.
Be ye brightened, O people,
by the noble
memory of these warriors!
By God Himself,
as the prophet foretold, were they consumed
in torture:
divine coals,
lighting the world,
verily, in the bright splendor of their miracles,
dazzling their enemies.
Come, let us share
in their virtues as in their joining together [πήγμασιν],
proclaiming again
to the creator,
Glory to Him who worketh
through his saints
amazing and wonderful deeds!

iv.
Strengthen me now,
in imitation of Christ, o ye warriors;
for I am sickened in fear
at the serpent's assault on my soul;
drive ye away
vain thought
as with a mallet;
force ye my steps in the direction
of the good,
as the healing benefactors ye are
to all
them that call on you in joy:
Glory to Him who worketh
through his saints
amazing and wonderful deeds!

Enjoying fame and wealth[12]
forasmuch as the beautiful pair had been found pleasing

12. The indented verses are from another manuscript, possibly by a different author: see Pitra,
p. 664. They clearly belong here to fill out the story of Serge and Bacchus, and the psalm
they quote is not only part of their biography but a traditional part of the ceremony of same-
sex union, in which this hymn was probably sung.

in the sight of the earthly king,
possessing wisdom and courage,
prudence and love for all,
and for Christ,
planted within their hearts.
In Him alone they placed their hopes,
counting as dross the things of the earth,
and eagerly hastening to heaven,
singing out loudly,
Behold, how good and how pleasant it is for brethren to dwell
together in unity.[13]

When, therefore, the evil ones realized that
these two worshipped the Son of God,
and would not sacrifice to idols,
they came privately to denounce them,
and barked such things as,
"Majesty, those who eat thy bread
have dared the worst,
to raise their heels against Thee.
If they do not die,
they will not stop proclaiming
as if they had a single soul,
Behold, how good and how pleasant it is for brethren to dwell
together in unity."

v.
It was not desire for this world
that captivated Serge for Christ,
nor the empty life of worldly affairs
[that captivated] Bacchus;
rather, made one [ἑνωθέντες]
as brethren [ἀδελφοτρόπως]
in the bond of love [συνδέσμῳ τῆς ἀγάπης],
they called out valiantly to the tyrant,
"See in two bodies
one soul and heart,
one will and virtue.

13. Ps. 132:1 (133:1 in the KJV).

Take those that
yearn to please God."
Glory to Him who worketh
through his saints
amazing and wonderful deeds!

vi.
The haughty judge[14]
wickedly denieth
any return for their kindnesses [to him],[15]
and repayeth them with the cloak of dishonor.[16]
O madness!
O thoughtless,
unjust man!
In return for the good done to him
he rusheth unto oblivion,
showing himself an enemy unto his friends
as Judas [was] to the creator.
So the athletes[17]
cry out,
Glory to Him who worketh
through his saints
amazing and wonderful deeds!

---

14. Not the king mentioned earlier: see p. 287.
15. See p. 147.
16. A rich and complex play on words: the "cloak of dishonor" refers to the female attire Serge and Bacchus had been forced to wear, but the Greek also plays on the ἀμοιβάς two lines above. Χλαῖνα ἀμοιβάς is an ancient and common expression for "change of clothes" (see *Odyssey* 14.520–21), and probably recalls the Christian image of putting on the "new man" in Christ as well (Eph. 4:24, Col. 3:10).
17. This term, in the original Greek as well as in the English used here, connoted specifically the heroes of Greek and Roman gymnastic competitions.

2. GELASIAN SACRAMENTARY, HETEROSEXUAL
[seventh–eighth century] [Latin]

Published in H. A. Wilson, *Liber sacramentorum Romanae
Ecclesiae* (Oxford, 1894), pp. 265–68. See discussion on
pp. 166ff.

Here beginneth the nuptial office.[18]

Hearken, O Lord, to our supplications, and assist us kindly with thine institutes, by which thou hast ordained the continuance of the human race, that what is joined together under thine authority may by thine aid be preserved.

We beseech thee, Almighty God, to grace with pious love the institutions of thy providence, and to preserve in lengthy peace those joined together by legal congress, for ever and ever, Amen. Hearken, O Lord, to our entreaties, and accept peacefully and in kindness this offering of thy servants,[19] which they offer to thee for thy handmaid, N., whom thou hast found worthy to reach the age of maturity and attain her wedding day, so that that which accords with thy disposition may be fulfilled according to thy grace, for ever and ever, Amen.

Thou who hast linked the bonds of matrimony in the sweet yoke of concord and the chain of unbreakable peace so that in the multiplication of children of adoption the fecund chastity of the holy married may persist. May thy providence, Lord, and thine ineffable grace dispense to each of them in different ways that what creation accomplished for the peopling of the world, reproduction may achieve in the enhancement of the church.

We beseech thee, Lord, kindly and lovingly to accept therefore this offering from thy servants N. and N., which they bring thee for thine handmaid, N., on behalf of which we implore thy merciful majesty, as thou didst grant her to come unto a meet age for marriage, and provided her in thy generosity union with a nuptial consort in [her] hope to rejoice in offspring, that thou afford her, in thy lovingkindness, the longed-for length of years, and likewise to us, O Lord.

A further prayer on the thirtieth day or the anniversary of the wedding

This offering, therefore, O Lord, which thy servants N. and N. offer thee on the occasion of the thirtieth day [or: first anniversary] of their joining [*con-*

[18.] *Incipit actio nuptialis.* Published in H. A. Wilson, *Liber sacramentorum romanae ecclesiae* (Oxford, 1894), No. 52, pp. 265–68.

[19.] "Thine handmaids" in the *Gelasianum*, thus printed in Wilson, p. 265. Other versions (e.g., Rennes and Gellone, cited by Wilson, p. 267, n. 3) have the inclusive masculine.

iunctionis suae], of the day on which thou didst see fit to join them in matrimonial bonds, we beseech thee kindly to accept. On account of which they return unto thee, living and true God, their vows, for which we make supplication to thy great majesty that they might grow old well and in peace, and that they may see the children of their children unto the third and fourth generation, and might bless thee all the days of their lives. Through Christ our Lord. Which offering Thou, Lord.

The priest completeth the full canon, and sayeth the Lord's Prayer, and blesseth the bride [N.B.] with these words.

God, who didst bless at its beginning the increasing world with the multiplication of offspring, heed our supplications, and pour the effect of thy blessings upon this thine handmaid, that they[20] might be joined in like affection in marital union, in matching of minds, and in mutual holiness. For ever and ever, Amen.

Here beginneth the benediction.

Father, founder of the world, begetter of those born, institutor of the origins of increase, who didst fashion a companion for Adam with thine hands, from whose growing bones in remarkable diversity a similar form appeared, whence for the increase of the whole race the concourse of the marital bed was designed, through which the whole of creation bound itself together, and the ties of the human race were knitted. Thus it hath pleased thee, O Lord, thus it was needful.

Let her marry faithful and chaste in Christ, and remain a follower of holy matrons. May she be amiable to her husband as Rachel, wise as Rebecca, faithful and obedient as Sara. Let the author of deceit usurp nothing of all this, let her remain bound to faithfulness and thy commandments, let her be a devoted servant of the true God, let her strengthen her weakness with the firmness of discipline, joined in a single bed, let her flee the unlawful contacts of life. May she be solemn in modesty, venerable in decency, learned in spiritual doctrine, fecund in offspring, wise and innocent, and may she come to the peace of the blessed and the kingdom of heaven. For ever and ever.

After this he shall say: Peace be with you.

And then he giveth them Communion. After they have received Communion, he pronounceth a benediction over them in these words:

Holy Lord, almighty Father, eternal God, we entreat thee with many prayers on behalf of those for whom Christ is thine intercessor, that thou wouldst look kindly on the unions of thy servants, that they might be worthy of thy blessings, that they might be enriched by succession of children, that thou wouldst deign to confirm their nuptials as those of the first man. May every enemy be averted from them, that they might also imitate the holiness

---

20. Change of subject in original.

of their parents also in this very union, they who, in thy providence Lord, were worthy to be united. For ever and ever.

Hear us, Holy Lord, Almighty Father, eternal God, that what is effected by our service may be more fully realized by thy blessing. For ever and ever, Amen.

3. GROTTAFERRATA Γ.β. VII [tenth century] [Greek]

Office of Same-Sex Union

Published in Gaetano Passarelli, *L'Eucologio Cryptense Γ.β. VII (sec. X)* (Thessalonika, 1982), pp. 130–133.

Prayer for union

O Lord our God, who made humankind in thine image and likeness and gave it power over all flesh everlasting [sic],[21] and who now hast approved thy saints and apostles Philip and Bartholomew becoming partners, not bound together by nature, but in the unity of holy spirit[22] [or: the Holy Spirit] and in the mode of faith, thou who didst consider thy saints and martyrs Serge and Bacchus worthy to be united, bless thy servants, N. and N., joined not by nature . . .[23] But [grant them] to love each other and to remain unhated and without scandal[24] all the days of their lives, with the

---

[21.] Presumably a reference to the resurrection of the human body.

[22.] ἀλλὰ πνεύματος ἁγίου; the editor capitalizes "spirit" and obviously understands the phrase to refer to the third person of the Trinity. While this is one obvious interpretation, it is not necessarily the most accurate reading. The ceremony is often characterized as a "spiritual" (πνευματικός) union (as in the following prayer), and the "spirit" in question is not obviously God; indeed, it seems much more likely that it is the "spirits" or "souls" of the two parties being united. Moreover, elsewhere in this MS, as generally in liturgical Greek, ἅγιος precedes "spirit" when applied to "the Holy Spirit," and usually occurs with the definite article, as in the following prayer, where I have rendered it "Holy Spirit." Here, meeting neither of these conditions, it seems justifiable to entertain the possibility that both "spirit" and "holy" have their more general meanings, and are correlates of "in the manner of faith." ("Spirit" also occurs in Greek liturgies in the familiar "and with thy spirit," where it unquestionably refers to the human soul. "Faith" also has a particular meaning in liturgical Greek (i.e., the Orthodox faith), which is clearly not intended here. Cf. the use of "holy" with "fear" in the following prayer.

[23.] Something is apparently missing between φύσει and ἀλλά: a verb, probably. Cf. this prayer in other comparable ceremonies, e.g., no. 13.

[24.] Although to those inclined to find other interpretations for these ceremonies this may sound like a warning against a carnal component of the relationship, similar comments were standard in heterosexual matrimonial offices, as is evident in the Gelasian (above), Lyre, and

help of the Holy Mother of God and ever virgin Mary. Because to thee belongs all glory, honor and worship.

A further prayer for union

Lord our God, glorified in the council of the saints, great and awesome ruler over all around thee,[25] bless thy servants N. and N., grant them knowledge of thy Holy Spirit. Guide them in thy holy fear, grant them joy, that they may become united more in the spirit than in the flesh. Because it is Thou who dost bless and sanctify those who trust in thee and thine is the everlasting glory.

A further prayer for union

Splendid[26] to us and much sought after is [ἄγει] the sweet smell of love [ἀγάπης], established in the time of the patriarchs, guided by the voices of the prophets, and sanctified by the preaching of the apostles: because of all beautiful things of the earth love is the most excellent. Abraham our forefather brought love to perfection under the oak of Mamre,[27] and accepting the rule of[28] love believed in God and was reckoned among the just;[29] and he obtained for himself an heir of love in blessedness—his firstborn son Isaac, the pledge of faith, the incense[30] of sacrifice, the portent of the Savior, the successor of justice, the father of many peoples and the foundation of the church. Do Thou now, Lord God, grant also to these thy servants, N. and N., the love and peace of thy holy apostles, which Thou hast bestowed on them, saying, "My peace I give you and I leave you my peace."[31] It was love itself that gathered the holy apostles through brotherly love [φιλαδελφίας] into the cheerful haven of the church. It was love that taught thy holy martyrs the patience [to bear] their sufferings during tribulation so they might inherit the unfading crown of eternal glory; love it was that allowed[32] the

---

Edwardian rites (both below), published here as typical heterosexual marriage ceremonies. For a more detailed discussion, see Chapter 6.

[25.] Cf. Ps. 89:8 [LXX/V 88:9]: "O Lord God of hosts, who is a strong Lord like unto thee? or to thy faithfulness round about thee?"

[26.] Literally, ἀνθηρός, "flowerlike."

[27.] Gen. 13:18, 14:13, 18:1, etc.

[28.] Possibly, "taking his beginning from love": λαβὼν ἀρχὴν τῆς ἀγάπης.

[29.] Literally, "it was credited to him as justice."

[30.] θυμιατήν; the normal word is θυμίαμα.

[31.] Paraphrase of John 14:27.

[32.] Possibly "showed them how," which seems to make more sense, but requires taking ὑπεδέξατο as the aorist of ὑποδείκνυμι, a possibility in classical Greek, but not attested in Scripture (which prefers the aorist ὑπέδειξα).

prophets to fulfill their angelic service;[33] love was the forerunner of the Savior, performing its services to all the holy; love offered as a sacrifice before God its own children—those who cherish [ἀγαπήσαντας] brotherly love [φιλαδελφίαν], who for God's sake extend charity [φιλοξενίαν . . . ποήσαντας] to the poor, which they receive back ten thousandfold from Christ.

It is through love that we glorify God, the father of our Lord Jesus Christ, who has called us together from different places to come and see the treasury of love, which all the saints have desired and embraced as an unfading crown, and brought to God as a worthy gift. Yearning for this love Abel brought to God the firstborn of his lambs;[34] yearning for this love Enoch the scribe pleased God with his justice;[35] love strengthened the faith[36] of Abraham so that he could prepare a welcome for the angels;[37] love saved Lot from the Sodomites;[38] yearning for this love, Abraham offered his only son to God as a sacrifice. Yearning for this same love, the most wise[39] Jacob inherited the blessing of Esau; love rescued Daniel from the lions' den; love caused Elijah to be taken up to heaven in a chariot of fire; and love saved Elishah on the mountain. Yearning for this love the three holy children were preserved from the fire in the furnace and offered a hymn of praise[40] to God. And it is through love that we all come to know Thee as the God of all: servants the master, the mortal the immortal, those in time the eternal, those on earth the celestial. We do not enjoin, but implore. We pray to Him and He hears our prayers.[41] Thou hast said, Lord, "Ask, and it shall be given you; seek, and ye shall find;[42] knock, and it shall be opened unto you: For every one that asketh receiveth; and he that seeketh findeth; and to him that knocketh it shall be opened."[43]

We, therefore, kind Lord, mindful of the holy commands of thine awesome and glorious covenant, knock on earth: open to us in heaven. Vouchsafe unto us a share of faith and love with all thy holy angels. Send to us, for us, that angel who guided Abraham, who was Isaac's captain [*sic*:

[33.] The basic meaning of "angel" in Greek is "messenger": both angels and prophets announce.

[34.] Cf. Heb. 11.5–17, which is strikingly similar in rhetorical construction, and lists (among others) the figures Abel, Enoch, Abraham, and Jacob in that order, just as they are listed here. Striking, however, is the fact that in Hebrews all these characters are singled out for their faithfulness (πίστις) rather than love.

[35.] Heb. 11:5; cf. Gen. 5:23.

[36.] ἐπιστώσατο: usually this means "to feel confidence, be convinced," as in 2 Tim. 3:14.

[37.] Gen. 19.

[38.] Ibid. Not understood by Jews or Christians of the Middle Ages as a reference to homosexual love. See Appendix No. 3, "Jewish Perspectives."

[39.] Or: "wily."

[40.] Literally, "of fragrance."

[41.] Although the meaning here is perfectly clear, the text appears to be corrupt: it says literally, "We pray to him and hear [imperative singular] our prayers."

[42.] Passarelli gives εὑρήσειτε; NT has εὑρήσετε.

[43.] Matt. 7:7–8.

στρατηγός], Jacob's companion, the waker of Lazarus, who came to the house of Zacchaeus the tax collector and said to him, "This day is salvation come to this house."[44] For where there is love hatred does not rule, demons have no power, there is not sin. For there are these three things—faith, hope, and the greatest of all, love.[45]

Wonderful and much longed for is the sweet smell of love. On earth it sows the seeds of piety and in heaven it gathers the sheaves of justice. "He hath dispersed abroad; he hath given to the poor: his righteousness remaineth for ever."[46] Turn thy holy ear to the prayer we raise to Thee, for Thou art the provider of all good things and the savior of our souls, and to Thee is endless glory, the Father, the Son and the Holy Spirit.

4. GROTTAFERRATA Γ.Β. II [eleventh century] [Greek]

Text published in Appendix of Documents, No. 1.

Office for Same-Sex Union

i.
The priest shall place the holy Gospel on the Gospel stand and they that are to be joined together place their <right> hands on it, holding lighted candles in their left hands. Then shall the priest cense them and say the following:

ii.
In peace we beseech Thee, O Lord.

For heavenly peace, we beseech Thee, O Lord.

For the peace of the entire world, we beseech Thee, O Lord.

For this holy place, we beseech Thee, O Lord.

That these thy servants, N. and N., be sanctified with thy spiritual bene-diction, we beseech Thee, O Lord.

That their love abide without offense or scandal all the days of their lives, we beseech Thee, O Lord.

That they be granted all things needed for salvation and godly enjoyment of life everlasting, we beseech Thee, O Lord.

That the Lord God grant unto them unashamed[47] faithfulness, <and> sincere love, we beseech Thee, O Lord.

That we be saved, we beseech Thee, O Lord.

---

44. Luke 19:9.
45. Paraphrase of 1 Cor. 13:13.
46. 2 Cor. 9:9, quoting Ps. 112:9.
47. πίστιν ἀκαταίσχυντον: this cliché is usually πίστιν ἀνεπαίσχυντον in these texts, recalling the biblical phrase used in 2 Tim. 2:15.

Have mercy on us, O God.

"Lord, have mercy" shall be said three times.

iii.

The priest <shall say>:[48]

Forasmuch as Thou, O Lord and Ruler, art merciful and loving,[49] who didst establish humankind after thine image and likeness,[50] who didst deem it meet[51] that thy holy[52] apostles[53] Philip and Bartholomew be united,[54] bound one unto the other not by nature but by faith and the spirit.[55] As Thou[56] didst find thy holy martyrs Serge and Bacchus[57] worthy to be united together, bless[58] also these thy servants, N. and N., joined together not by the bond of[59] nature but by faith and in the mode of the spirit,[60] granting unto them peace and love and oneness of mind.[61] Cleanse from their hearts every stain and impurity,[62] and[63] vouchsafe unto them[64] to love one other[65] without hatred and without scandal all the days of their lives,[66] with the aid of[67] the Mother of God and[68] all thy saints,[69] forasmuch as all glory[70] is thine.[71]

---

48. Earlier versions of this prayer are found in Vatican Barberini Grec 336, Sinai 958, and No. 3, in this collection. I have noted here ways in which it diverges significantly from the first, identified as 336, and No. 3, labeled, GF VII.
49. 336 and GF VII omit "Forasmuch as Thou art merciful and loving."
50. 336 adds "and accorded them eternal life"; GF VII adds "and gave them power over all flesh everlasting."
51. GF VII adds "who now have approved."
52. 336 adds "and most blessed."
53. 336 adds "Peter, the foremost of all, and Andrew, and Jacob and John, the sons of Zebedee, and . . ."
54. 336 adds ἀμφοτέρους, with several possible meanings.
55. 336: "of a holy spirit"; see discussion on pp. 26–27.
56. 336: "And who"
57. 336 adds "Cosmas and Damian, and Cyrus and John."
58. 336 adds "now."
59. 336, GF VII omit "the bond of."
60. GF VII omits "but by faith and in the mode of the spirit"; 336 omits "and in the mode of the spirit."
61. Or: "harmony" (ὁμόνοιαν).
62. 336, GF VII omit "granting them peace and love and oneness of mind. Cleanse every stain and impurity from their minds."
63. 336 omits "And."
64. GF VII omits "And grant them"; adds "But."
65. 336 adds "and let their brotherly union be"; GF VII: "and to remain."
66. 336 adds "in the power of your Holy Spirit."
67. 336 adds "our all-holy and sinless Lady."
68. GF VII adds "and ever-virgin Mary"; 336 adds "ever-virgin Mary, and of Saint John the forerunner and the Baptist, of the holy and most blessed apostles and all your holy martyrs, because you are merciful, [trustworthy?], and the Lord of Peace, Christ our God, and yours are the glory and thanks forever."
69. GF VII omits "and all your saints."
70. GF VII adds "honor and worship."
71. 336 omits "all your saints, because all glory is yours."

iv.

Another Prayer for Same-Sex Union[72]

O Lord Our God, who didst grant unto us all those things necessary for salvation and didst bid us to love one another and to forgive each other our failings, bless and consecrate,[73] kind Lord and lover of good, these thy servants who love each other with a love of the spirit and have come into this[74] thy holy church to be blessed and consecrated.[75] Grant unto them unashamed fidelity [and] sincere love, and as Thou didst vouchsafe unto thy holy disciples and apostles[76] thy peace and love,[77] bestow <them> also on these,[78] O Christ our God, affording to them all those things needed for salvation and life eternal. For Thou art the light [and] the truth and thine is the glory.[79]

v.

Then shall they kiss the holy Gospel and the priest and one another, and conclude:[80]

[72.] Earlier versions of this prayer are found in Sinai 957 and 958. Contemporary versions are Paris Coislin 213, Sinai 959, and possibly the Sinai Euchologion. Of these, only Coislin 213 offers significant variations, noted here and identified as 213.

[73.] 213 omits "bless and consecrate, kind"; adds "protect in thy holiness."

[74.] 213 omits "this."

[75.] Sinai 958 omits "and consecrated"; 213 adds "by Thee."

[76.] 213 omits "and apostles."

[77.] 213 omits "and love."

[78.] 213 adds "servants."

[79.] 213 omits "For Thou art the light, the truth, and thine is the glory."

[80.] A line is drawn between the preceding prayer and the following one, but such lines in manuscripts do not reliably indicate the beginning of a new office. It is not really possible that this prayer should constitute part of an office different from what precedes. This would be the grossest scribal error imaginable: the entire prayer would have to have been copied into the manuscript by mistake, and then not crossed out or corrected. Even so, it would be difficult to believe that it was not inserted here *for a reason*. It is surely the more difficult and less likely argument that the scribe copied this prayer into the text from an *unrelated* ceremony. The apparent confusion of priestly dismissal *followed* by a prayer is closely paralleled in many other liturgical collections. In the *Euchologion* of Porphyre Uspenski εὐχὴ ἀντιφώνου δ' τῆς ἀπολύσεως occurs on fol. 57v and 59r, as part of a series in each case, and in each case is followed by other prayers. In Sinai 957 there is a dismissal *before the Communion prayer* in the heterosexual marriage ceremony (καὶ μετὰ τὸ 'Αμὴν μεταδιδοὺς αὐτοῖς ζωοποιοῦ κοινωνίας ἀπολύει); then there is the εὐχὴ τοῦ ποτηρίου (Dmitrievskij, p. 5). In the Barberini Greek 336 εὐχὴ ἤγουν ἀπόλυσις occurs at least *four times* without indicating the end of a ceremony. In Istanbul 615 (757) (Dmitrievskij XCVI, pp. 743–44), the final rubric says "the partners kiss each other and [the priest] gives them Communion and they depart. If they wish to have a liturgy after the reading of the Gospel, the office [of same-sex union] takes place, and those joined together are commemorated again at the blessing, and then there is the dismissal." This is very similar to this office in providing two possible endings. Brightman, in his Greek index, s.v. ἀπόλυσις (p. 595), defines the term as "the conclusion of an office and the formula with which it is concluded." Moreover, the major part of the *beginning* of the liturgy of St. John Chrysostom is called the ἀπολυτίκιον ("conclusion").

Ecclesiastical Canon of Marriage of the Patriarch Methodius[81]

O Lord our God, the designer of love and author of peace and disposer of thine own providence, who didst make two into one and hast given us one to another, who hast [seen fit?][82] to bless all things pure and timeless, send Thou now down from heaven thy right hand full of grace and lovingkindness over these thy servants who have come before Thee and given their right hands as a lawful token of union and the bond of marriage. Sanctify and fill them with thy mercies. And wrapping the pair[83] in every grace and in divine and spiritual radiance, gladden them in the expectation of thy mercies. Per-

---

The *ODB* also observes of "dismissal" (1:639) that it is "a formula pronounced at the end of a liturgical service or sometimes of one of its parts" Cf. Athos Panteleimon 149 [15], in which the rubrics prescribe καὶ γίνεται ἀπόλυσις καὶ ἀσπάζονται τὸ ἅγιον εὐαγγέλιον καὶ ἀλλήλους καὶ ἀπέρχονται, and Athos Panteleimon 780 (No. 13 in this appendix, No. 6 in the next), which is otherwise *almost identical:* the ending is καὶ ἀσπάζονται τὸ ἅγιον εὐαγγέλιον καὶ ἀλλήλους καὶ ἀπόλυσις. In the first, ἀπόλυσις is mentioned, then final acts are prescribed. In the second, derived from it, the final acts are followed by ἀπόλυσις. There is the clear possibility that in either case ἀπόλυσις stands for the final acts themselves, separately mentioned, or is a final blessing not actually given in the text. In any event, these examples show that something important could follow ἀπόλυσις. Other examples of ἀπόλυσις occurring *within* (rather than at the end of) a ceremony, all from Dmitrievskij: XXIII (Sinai 966, thirteenth century), p. 214; LIX (Athos Vatoped. 322 [934], B.C. 1468), p. 422; LXI (Athos Athanas. 88, fifteenth century), p. 442; LXV (Athos Pantocrator 149, fifteenth century), p. 488; LXXI (Athos Panteleimon 364, fifteenth century), p. 569; LXXIV (Sinai 984, fifteenth century), p. 595; LXXXIII (Patmos Ilitari 690, fifteenth century), p. 651; XCIX (Athos Athanasios 21 [91], C.E. 1536), p. 760.

81. On this rubric, cf. the twelfth-century heterosexual marriage ceremonies in Vat. Gr. 1811 (fols. 31v–33: εὐχὴ εἰς εὐλογίαν διγαμίας· ποίημα Μεθοδίου πατριάρχου [Canart, p. 186]), and Vat. Gr. 1872 (unpublished), f. 133r–v: εὐχὴ εἰς τὸ ἐπάραι τὰ σπεφάνια, which includes the strikingly similar phrase Κύριε ὁ Θεὸς ἡμῶν, ὁ τῆς ἀγάπης φητουργὸς [sic], ὁ ποιήσας τὰ ἀφότερα [sic] ἕν [sic] (Canart, p. 425). In Vat. Gr. 1875 (also twelfth century) the heterosexual marriage ceremony both for a first marriage and a second (διγαμία) are characterized as "work of Methodius" (f. 69v ἀκολουθια [sic: no accent] εἰς εὐλογίαν γάμου· ποίημα Μεθοδίου πατριάρχου . . . [Canart, p. 432; Canart compares this to Barb., n. 88, and adds, *Subiungitur* (ff. 78v–79) εὐχὴ τοῦ θαλάμου εἰς τὸ ἐπάρε τὰ στέφη (Goar, p. 326)"]). In Dmitrievskij, a similar rubric is printed for many heterosexual marriage ceremonies (e.g., Sinai 958 [tenth century], No. III pp. 29–30, labeled κανὼν ἐκκλησιαστικὸς εἰς γάμον: this office ends with *two* prayers for removing crowns [p. 31: fol. 84r: εὐχὴ εἰς τὸ ἐπᾶραι στέφανα ἀπὸ τὰς κεφαλὰς τῶν νεονύμφων; and fol. 84v: εὐχὴ εἰς τὸ λῦσαι στέφανα], *neither* of which bears any resemblance to the canon; they are followed by the ceremony of same-sex union]; Sinai 973 [No. VIII] 1153 p. 96 [fol. 59]: κανὼν ἐκκλησιαστικὸς εἰς γάμους). The meaning of the term "canon" as opposed to εὐχή or ἀκολουθία is ably discussed in Baldanza, "Il rito Matrimoniale dell'Eucologio Sinaitico greco 958," pp. 291–93. Passarelli ("Stato della ricerca," pp. 246–47) notes that both Leo Allacci and J. B. Pitra listed some of the marriage ceremonies that call themselves the work (often the "canon") of Methodius among the works of the Patriarch of Constantinople, 842–46. Passarelli lists 13; Pitra, 8. Passarelli also says that such attribution *rimane un problema aperto.* For contemporary prayers closely related to this "canon" (possibly versions of it), see Nos. 6, 14, 15 in this collection and Hilferding.

82. ἐπισχνύμενος: I am unable to identify this word.

83. Literally, "those gathered," which might refer to the whole congregation, but in context seems to apply to the couple.

fect their union by bestowing upon them peace and love and harmony, and deem them worthy of the imposition and consecration of the crowns, through the prayers of her that conceived Thee in power and truth, and those of all thy saints, now and forever.

vi.
And after this prayer the priest shall lift the crowns and dismiss them.

5. PARIS BIBLIOTHÈQUE NATIONALE COISLIN 213 [1027/29 C.E.] [Greek]

Text published in Appendix of Documents, No. 2.[84]

[84.] To help readers appreciate the ambiguity of translating expressions relating to "brother" in these ceremonies, I here append two additional translations of the same Greek text: in the first I have adopted an anachronistically literal mode of translating the words in question; in the second I have tendentiously pushed the ambiguity in the opposite direction. For explanation of these possibilities and why I have elected a more neutral and objective mode of translating the other texts, see Chapter 1: "The Vocabulary of Love and Marriage."

Anachronistically Literal: Prayer for Making Brothers

i. O Lord Our God, who hast granted unto us all things necessary for salvation and didst command us to love one another and to forgive one another our failings, protect in thy holiness, Lord and lover of good, these thy servants who love each other with a love of the spirit and have come into thy holy church to be blessed and consecrated by Thee. Grant them unashamed faithfulness, true love, and as Thou didst vouchsafe unto thy holy disciples thy peace, bestow also on these servants all those things needed for salvation and eternal life.
ii. *(Antiphon)* For Thou art merciful and loving, God, and thine is unending glory, Father and Son and Holy Spirit.
The deacon: [Bow] your heads.
iii. *The priest:* Ruler and Lord, Our God, who hast called the congregation of thy holy apostles to one shepherd, one brotherhood, and sent them out unto all the corners of the world to preach thy commandments, bless now also these thy servants whom Thou hast found worthy to stand before thy glory and to be united in spirit. Keep them in thy name, sanctify them in thy truth, so that living according to thy commandments they may become heirs of thy kingdom, for Thou art the giver of all good things and thine is unending glory, Father, Son and Holy Spirit.

Tendentiously Slanted: Prayer for Homosexual Marriage

i. O Lord Our God, who hast granted unto us all things necessary for salvation and didst command us to love one another and to forgive one another our failings, protect in thy holiness, Lord and lover of good, these thy servants who love each other with a love of the spirit and have come into thy holy church to be blessed and consecrated by Thee. Grant them unashamed faithfulness, true love, and as Thou didst vouchsafe unto thy

Prayer for Same-Sex Union

i.[85]

O Lord Our God, who hast granted unto us all things necessary for salvation and didst command us to love one another and to forgive one another our failings, protect in thy holiness,[86] Lord and lover of good,[87] these thy servants who love each other with a love of the spirit and have come into thy holy church to be blessed and consecrated[88] by Thee. Grant them unashamed faithfulness, true love, and as Thou didst vouchsafe unto thy holy disciples[89] thy peace, bestow also on these servants[90] all those things needed for salvation and eternal life.[91]

ii.

(*Antiphon*) For thou art merciful and loving, God, and thine is unending glory, Father and Son and Holy Spirit.

The deacon: [Bow] your heads.

---

holy disciples thy peace, bestow also on these servants all those things needed for salvation and eternal life.

ii. (*Antiphon*) For Thou art merciful and loving, God, and thine is unending glory, Father and Son and Holy Spirit.

The deacon: [Bow] your heads.

iii. *The priest:* Ruler and Lord, Our God, who hast called the congregation of thy holy apostles to one shepherd, one brotherhood, and sent them out unto all the corners of the world to preach thy commandments, bless now also these thy servants whom Thou hast found worthy to stand before thy glory and to be married. Keep them in thy name, sanctify them in thy truth, so that living according to thy commandments they may become heirs of thy kingdom, for Thou art the giver of all good things and thine is unending glory, Father, Son and Holy Spirit.

85. This prayer is one of the most common components of same-sex union ceremonies, and this is one of the earliest versions of it. The only two earlier copies are Sinai 957, 958; Grottaferrata Γ.β. II (preceding translation) is roughly contemporary. The edition published hereafter collates the prayer with the earlier two versions and Γ.β. II, and with some closely related subsequent versions (Paris Coislin 214, grec 324, 392). Only significant differences in wording are noted in the translation. The Slavic version of the same prayer, from the twelfth century, is translated subsequently.

86. Some versions omit "in your holiness"; Γ.β. II reads "bless and sanctify."

87. Some versions add "ruler" and "lover of mankind."

88. Sinai 958 omits "and consecrated."

89. All other versions add "and apostles."

90. Γ.β. II adds here "Christ our God, affording them . . ."

91. Two versions add "For you are the light, the truth, and yours is the glory."

iii.[92]

The priest: Ruler and Lord, Our God, who hast called the congregation of thy holy[93] apostles to one shepherd, one brotherhood,[94] and sent them out unto all the corners of the world to preach thy commandments, bless now also these thy servants[95] whom Thou hast found worthy to stand before thy glory and to be united in spirit.[96] Keep them in thy name, sanctify them in thy truth, so that living according to thy commandments they may become heirs of thy kingdom, for Thou art the giver of all good things and thine is unending glory, Father, Son and Holy Spirit.

6. SINAI EUCHOLOGION [eleventh–twelfth century] [Old Church Slavonic]

From Macedonia, but written in Old Church Slavonic (with Glagolitic characters). Text published in Rajko Nahtigal, *Euchologium Sinaiticum. Starocerkvenoslovanski Glagolski Spomenik, Slovenska Akademija Znanosti in Umetnosti v Ljubljani. Filosofsko-Filološko-Historični Razred,* 1 (Ljubljana, 1941), 9b–11b, 2 (Ljubljana, 1942) 20–26; and in Jean Frček, "Euchologium Sinaiticum: Texte slave avec sources grecques et traduction française," PO 24 (1933), 611–801, 25 (1943) 490–622. Nahtigal relies on Frček's apparatus, and provides no translation, but his readings are generally more meticulous than Frček's. Frček's translation must be treated with caution; there is, for example, no word "adoptive" in the Slavic or Greek title (see discussion of titles for the ceremony on pp. 22ff. and 182ff.).

---

92. Only four other versions of this prayer are known: Grottaferrata Γ.β. I (eleventh–twelfth century), the Leningrad Antonin. Euch. (thirteenth century; hereafter L), and Istanbul 615 (sixteenth century; hereafter I).
93. One version adds "disciples and."
94. Two versions omit "one brotherhood"; two add "one church."
95. L inserts the names here.
96. I diverges so completely at this point that it is most efficient simply to quote its ending: ". . . joined [anachronistically literal: brothers; tendentious: married], not by the bond of birth, but in the way of faith and holy spirit. Send down, lover of mankind, the grace of thy Holy Spirit so that they may love each other without offense, without hatred, without scandal, and that they may remain in thankfulness all the days of their lives, with the aid of our most holy Queen, the Mother of God and ever-virgin Mary, and all thy saints. For blessed and glorified is thy most honorable and exalted name."

The Order for Uniting Two Men[97]

Placing them before the altar, the deacon shall say these decanal prayers:
In peace,[98] we pray to the Lord.
For heavenly [peace].
For the peace of all.
For their joining together[99] in union[100] of love and life,[101] we pray to the Lord.

For these servants[102] of God, —— and ——,[103] and for their union[104] in Christ, we pray to the Lord.

That the Lord our God unite[105] them in perfect love and inseparable[106] life, we pray to the Lord.

That they be granted discretion[107] and sincere[108] love, we pray to the Lord.

For the presanctified[109] gift of the precious body and blood of our Lord Jesus Christ, that they should receive it without sin[110] and preserve their union[111] without envy, we pray to the Lord.

That they and we be granted all things necessary for salvation, we pray to the Lord.

---

97. Frček prints Roman numerals I–XII for the opening litany, but these are not indicated in the manuscript.
98. Possibly "for peace," as occurs below, but in all the Slavic versions of this litany the first invocation uses peace in the instrumental case.
99. съвькоупльсю са: this verb, used reflexively, usually means "to copulate" in Slavic languages, although its nonreflexive sense is much wider.
100. обьщение: possibly (social) "intercourse," its meaning in modern Russian.
101. Or, "of lifelong love" (любьве житью). Frček confesses uncertainty about this phrase, which he renders as *Pour ceux qui s'unissent pour vivre en communauté d'affection*, and points out that related OCS versions of the ceremony do not seem sure about it either. Cf. Hilferding (see p. 374, n. 16), and, in this collection, Nos. 14 and 15.
102. Here and elsewhere in the ceremony (e.g., "names," directly following) the dual case is used in reference to the parties forming the union.
103. The text has literally, "names."
104. съвькоупленьи: see n. 99, above.
105. съвькоупитъ: see n. 99, above.
106. неразлучьно; неразлучники means "lovebirds" in modern Russian.
107. цѣломждрость: literally, "chaste wisdom." In Russian both целомудренность and целомудрие mean "chastity," but in OCS the meaning was doubtless closer to the Greek σωφροσύνη, from which it was likely borrowed, and which means "discretion," "moderation in bodily matters." Frček translates simply as *sagesse* ("wisdom").
108. неличемрън-, "unhypocritical" in Russian; the Greek has ἀνεπαίσχυντος here.
109. I.e., consecrated on a previous occasion. This term did not enter English until centuries later than that used in these translations, doubtless owing to the fact that the Orthodox were a tiny community in England and generally retained Greek liturgical terminology.
110. Literally, "not badly": ве-скврънѣi.
111. братръство.

That they and we be preserved from all suffering, danger and need.
Protect, save,
Most holy, most pure.

ii.

Prayer for Same-Sex Union

O Lord our God, who grant us what we ask for our salvation, who hath commanded us to love each other and to pardon each other [our] transgressions, bless, Lord, giver of good [things], lover of mankind, these two servants of thine who love each other with a love[112] of the spirit[113] and have come to thy holy temple wishing to receive thy sanctification and benediction; grant them unabashed faithfulness [врж][114] and sincere love,[115] and just as you gave thy holy disciples and apostles thy peace and love, grant [them] also to these, Christ our God, giving them all those things necessary for salvation and eternal life.

(*Exclamation*)[116] For Thou art the light of truth and eternal life, and to Thee we give glory and praise, Father and Son and [Holy Spirit].

iii.

Then prayeth the deacon:
Let us hear the wisdom of the holy Gospel.[117]
The priest[118] readeth[119] from John [17:1, 18–26]:[120]

Jesus lifted up his eyes to his disciples[121] and said, "Father, . . ."
As thou hast sent me into the world, even so have I also sent them into the world.

---

112. възлювлениемь: cf. Russian возлюбленный, "sweetheart"; God's love is simply любвь in the ceremony.
113. Or, "spiritual love." See remarks on the word "spiritual" on pp. 26–27.
114. Or "faith," the usual meaning of the word. I have given "fidelity" because most Greek texts have this meaning at this point, and because the reference to their love immediately following seems to imply that the phrase has to do with their relations with each other, but it is quite possible that it is two separate issues—their faith in God and their love for each other.
115. любьвь.
116. Or "in a loud voice": the MS has вш, traditionally understood as възглашение. Cf. Greek ἐκφώνησις.
117. Nahtigal and Frček read this line differently, but the meaning is clear.
118. The text uses попъ and иерѣи interchangeably.
119. Literally, "prays."
120. For textual commentary, see Nahtigal, 2, pp. 22–23.
121. Paraphrase to this point. The original is "These words spake Jesus, and lifted up his eyes to heaven." Frček (and Nahtigal following him) suggests that the paraphrase is actually a conflation of John 17:1 with Luke 6:20, but it seems to me a simple error of memory.

And for their sakes I sanctify myself, that they also might be sanctified through the truth.

Neither pray I for these alone, but for them also which shall believe on me through their word;

That they all may be one; as thou, Father, art in me, and I in thee, that they also may be one in us: that the world may believe that thou hast sent me.

And the glory which thou gavest me I have given them; that they may be one, even as we are one:

I in them, and thou in me, that they may be made perfect in one; and that the world may know that thou hast sent me, and hast loved[122] them, as thou hast loved me.

Father, I will that they also, whom thou hast given me, be with me where I am; that they may behold my glory, which thou hast given me: for thou lovedst me before the foundation of the world.

O righteous Father, the world hath not known thee: but I have known thee, and these have known that thou hast sent me.

And I have declared unto them thy name, and will declare it: that the love wherewith thou hast loved me may be in them, and I in them."[123]

It is to be found on the seventh Sunday after Easter. And when the priest finisheth the Gospel, the deacon shall recite the decanal prayers.

iv.

The priest shall make this prayer before the table:

Lord God omnipotent, who didst fashion humankind after thine image and likeness and gavest unto them[124] life eternal, whom it hath pleased that thy holy and glorious apostles Peter and Paul, and Philip and Bartholomew, be joined together not by the bond of blood but of fidelity[125] [върож] and love,[126] who didst deem it meet[127] for the holy martyrs Serge and Bacchus to be united together,[128] bless Thou also these thy servants, N. and N., joined together not of birth, but of faith and love. Grant unto them to love one

---

122. ἠγάπησας αὐτοὺς καθὼς ἐμὲ ἠγάπησας; Vulg.: *dilexisti eos, sicut et me dilexisti* (17:23).
123. ἡ ἀγάπη ἣν ἠγάπησάς με ἐν αὐτοῖς ᾖ κἀγὼ ἐν αὐτοῖς; Vulg.: *ut dilectio, qua dilexisti me, in ipsis sit, et ego in ipsis* (17:26).
124. Literally, "it" or "him," referring to mankind.
125. Or "by faith," the usual meaning of върож. I have preferred "fidelity" because the reference to the love of the two immediately following seems to imply that the phrase has to do with their relationship. It is, however, possible that the two are unrelated here, or that some connection between their faith (in God) and their love for each other is presupposed.
126. любъв: Frček's *spirituelle* here does not correspond to the text.
127. Or, "made it proper": съподовлеи.
128. бъіти.

another, let them continue without envy and without temptation[129] all the days of their lives, through the power of thy Holy Spirit and the prayers of the Holy Mother of God and all thy saints who have pleased Thee throughout the ages.

(*Exclamation*) For thine is the power and thine the kingdom, thine the strength [and the glory. In the name of the Father, the Son and the Holy Spirit, now and forever. Amen.]

v.

The priest shall raise his voice and pray: Peace to all.

The deacon: Let us love[130] one another.

Then shall the priest kiss the pair and they one another. Then the deacon shall pray: Let us bow our heads before the Lord.

vi.

And the priest shall make this prayer in a low voice:

O Lord our God, thou art the author[131] of love, the master of peace, and the savior of all, vouchsafe unto us thy love, the fulfilment of the law, and grant unto us to think on[132] that which is of Jesus, thine only Son, our God. Vouchsafe us to receive one another with love [лювъвъ], as thine only son did receive us, and grant unto us to serve one another in love and most heartily[133] to fulfill the law of thy Christ.

(*Exclamation*) For thine is the glory and the power, Father, Son [and Holy Spirit].

vii.

And then shall the priest pray, raising up his arms:

And grant unto us, O Lord, earnestly to serve Thee.[134]

The people: Our father, [who art in heaven, hallowed be thy name. Thy kingdom come. Thy will be done, on earth as it is in heaven. Give us this

---

129. ве-съвлазна; Frček offers as a Greek correspondence (pp. 663–65) a prayer from Goar (p. 707, a conflation of Barberini 336 and Grottaferrata Γ.β. I), in which the equivalent phrase is: Δὸς αὐτοῖς...ἀμίσητον καὶ ἀσκανδάλιστον τὴν ἀδελφοσύνην αὐτῶν εἶναι πάσας τάς ἡμέρας τῆς ζωῆς αὐτῶν, "Let their relationship be unhated and not a source of scandal all the days of their lives." Although the Slavic expression does not match the Greek, it is attested in other Slavic versions; there is no mention of "relationship" in this text.

130. възлювимъ: cf. note 110, above.

131. съвръшитель: perhaps, "perfector." The Greek original (?) is φυτούργος; Frček renders it as *consommé*. Nahtigal cites as a cross-reference Heb. 12.2: τῆς πίστεως ἀρχηγὸν καὶ τελειωτὴν (p. 24), but this seems strained to me.

132. мждръствовати; cf. modern Russian мудрствовать, "philosophize." Frček renders it *pratiquer*, which seems too loose.

133. дръзновениемъ: perhaps, "zeal."

134. съ дръзновениемь: translated above as "might"; no English word seems to render it precisely in all contexts.

day our daily bread, and forgive us our trespasses, as we forgive those who trespass against us. And lead us not into temptation, but deliver us from evil. Amen.] *(To the end.)*

(Exclamation) For thine is the kingdom, the power and [the glory].

viii.

And then [the deacon] shall say:

Behold[135] the holy for the holy.

And the priest, lifting up the ciborium, shall say:

Behold the presanctified holy of holies.

The people: Thou only art holy, O Lord, Jesus Christ.

And he shall give Communion to both.

ix.

And after they have communicated the priest shall take the elder of them that have been joined together and the latter of them in turn takes the younger by the hand, and [the priest] leadeth them both, chanting the eighth tone of David.

Lord, [lead me] in [thy] truth.[136]

Turn thee again, Thou God of hosts, look down from heaven, behold and visit this vine; And the place of the vineyard that thy right hath planted. . . .[137]

(Verse) Blessed is the man that feareth the Lord, that delighteth greatly in his commandments.[138]

Lord, Lord, look down from heaven.

(Verse) Give ear, O Shepherd of Israel, thou that leadest [Joseph like a flock].[139]

x.

(Verse) [Behold,] how good and how pleasant it is [for brethren to dwell together in union.[140]

It is like the precious ointment upon the head, that ran down upon the beard, even Aaron's beard: that went down to the skirts of his garments; As the dew of Hermon, and as the dew that descended

---

135. Literally, "let us behold."

136. Cf. Ps. 25:5: "Lead me in thy truth, and teach me." This is Ps. 24:5 in the LXX and the Sinai Psalter. Subsequent psalm numbers should be one less for their LXX or Sinai equivalent. Nahtigal prints some of the Sinai text.

137. Paraphrase of Ps. 80:14–15 [LXX 79:15–16].

138. Ps. 111:1 in the contemporary *Psalterium Sinaiticum* (112:1 KJV), but also strikingly similar to Ps. 128:1.

139. Ps. 80:1.

140. I have altered the KJV here to reflect its relation to the context. The original is "how good and how pleasant it is for brethren to dwell together in unity."

upon the mountains of Zion: for there the Lord commanded the benediction, even life for evermore.][141]

And thus singing this whole psalm, verse by verse, unto the end, they shall add this verse:
Lord, Lord, look down from heaven. . . .

xi.
Then shall they sing the hymn of the martyrs,[142] following[143] the tone.[144]

xii.
And then: Glory be to the Father, and to the Son: and to the Holy Spirit. As it was in the beginning, is now, and ever shall be: world without end. Amen.

xiii.
And the hymn to the Mother of God.[145]

7. LYRE, HETEROSEXUAL, [twelfth century] [Latin]

The Blessing of Husband and Wife

> Published in Edmond Martène, *De antiquis ecclesiae ritibus libri tres* (Vicenza, 1788), 1.9.5, Ordo III, pp. 2:128–29.[146] Reprinted in Jean-Baptiste Molin and Protais Mutembe, *Le Rituel du mariage en France du XIIe au XVIe siècle* (Paris, 1974), pp. 286–87, with commentary pp. 34–36. Aimé-Georges Martimort, *La Documentation liturgique de Dom Edmond Martène* (Studi e testi, 279) (Vatican City, 1978) No. 693, p. 359, suggests a twelfth-century composition.

Before anything else those who are to be joined in the marriage bed[147] come to the doors of the church with several witnesses, and the consent of each is demanded by

---

141. Ps. 133.1–3.
142. Technically, a troparion or apolytikion (мжченичьно). While it might refer to martyrs in general, it seems likely to me that the prayer refers to Serge and Bacchus, mentioned elsewhere in the rite. See also the "Hymn to Serge and Bacchus," No. 1 in this collection.
143. Literally, "against the tone": противо гласоу; Frček translates *selon le ton* (p. 668).
144. Frček suggests that this should be understood as the prayer given in No. 14 in this collection, but this is not obvious to me. Translation No. 15 offers somewhat different prayers at a comparable juncture.
145. Frček proposes the prayer printed as No. 14 in this collection, but cf. also No. 15.
146. Ritzer's mistaken conclusion (p. 308, note, in the German original of 1962) that this manuscript actually came from the Bibliothèque municipale d'Évreux had already been corrected by the time of the French edition of 1970 (p. 387 n. 609).
147. *thoro maritali conjungendi sunt.*

the priest, and the woman's gift is handed over and some coins are placed in the middle for dividing among the poor, and then finally the woman is given by her father or friends. The man receives her in the faith of God and to preserve her safe and sound as long as he [she?] shall live, and holds[148] her by her right hand, the priest beginning in the following way:

Thy God hath commanded thy strength: strengthen, O God, that which Thou hast wrought for us.

Because of thy temple at Jerusalem shall kings bring presents unto Thee.

Rebuke the company of spearmen, the multitude of the bulls, with the calves of the people, till every one submit himself with pieces of silver: scatter Thou the people that delight in war.[149]

Glory be to the Father and to the Son and to the Holy Ghost, as it was in the beginning, is now, and ever shall be. Amen.

Then the priest blesses the ring, saying:

Creator and preserver of humankind, giver of spiritual grace, who dost grant eternal salvation, send, Lord, thy blessing upon this ring. For ever and ever, Amen.

Let us pray.

Bless, Lord, this ring which we bless ✝ in thy holy name, that she who wears it as a sign of married faithfulness may abide in thy peace and persevere in devoted integrity of faith, and ever live, grow, and age in thy love, and be granted length of days. Through Christ our Lord.

Here let the husband take the ring, and along with the priest place it upon three fingers of the bride's right hand, saying on the first finger, In the name of the Father, and on the second, and of the Son, and on the third, and of the Holy Ghost. And thus let him place the same ring on one finger of her left hand and leave it there, that she might thereafter wear it on the left, to distinguish it from the sign of the bishop, whose ring is worn openly on his right hand as a sign of pure and complete chastity. Then let him say:

The Lord be with you.

The God of Abraham, the God of Isaac, the God of Jacob be with you, and may He Himself join you together, and pour out his benediction who lives in you.

Let us pray.

May God the Father bless ✝[150] you, Jesus Christ keep you ✝, and the Holy Ghost shine ✝ on you; may the Lord turn his face upon you and show you

---

[148.] Martène's text has the plural (*teneant*), but this must be an error.

[149.] Ps. 68:28–30 (Vulg. 67:29–31), an unusual biblical reading.

[150.] These signs are in the published text.

mercy. May He turn his countenance to you and grant you peace, and may He fill you with every spiritual blessing ✝ in forgiveness of all your sins, that you may have life eternal and live eternally. Amen.

After this they are led into the church and prostrate themselves in the middle of the sanctuary, while the priest says:

Blessed are all they that fear the Lord: that walk in his ways.
For thou shalt eat the labors of thy hands: blessed art thou, and it shall be well with thee.
Thy wife as a fruitful vine, on the sides of thy house. Thy children as olive plants, round about thy table.
Behold, thus shall the man be blessed that feareth the Lord.
May the Lord bless thee out of Sion: and mayst thou see the good things of Jerusalem all the days of thy life.
And mayst thou see thy children's children, peace upon Israel.[151]

Glory be to the Father and to the Son and to the Holy Ghost, as it was in the beginning, is now, and ever shall be.
Lord, have mercy.
Christ, have mercy.
Lord, have mercy.
Our father, who art in heaven, hallowed be thy name. Thy kingdom come. Thy will be done, on earth as it is in heaven. Give us this day our daily bread, and forgive us our trespasses, as we forgive those who trespass against us. And lead us not into temptation, but deliver us from evil. Amen.
Preserve thy servant and handmaid.
Send them, Lord, the aid of the Holy [Spirit].
Be to them, Lord, a tower of strength.
O Lord, hear my prayer.
The Lord be with you.
Let us pray.
God of Abraham, God of Isaac, God of Jacob, bless ✝ these young people [*adolescentes*], and sew the seeds of eternal life in their minds, that whatever they learn for their benefit they may seek to do. Through Jesus Christ, thy son, the savior of mankind, who lives with thee.
Let us pray.
Look down, O Lord, from the heavens, and bless ✝ this agreement [*con-*

[151.] Psalm 128, quoted here from the Rheims-Douai version (where it is Ps. 127), because the text indicates that the liturgy used the Gallican psalter, which would make sense in light of the provenance of this ceremony. The King James uses the more accurate Hebrew text, known to the Middle Ages as *Psalmi iuxta Hebraeos*, but generally less utilized in areas influenced by the triumph of the Gallican psalter, Jerome's translation of Origen's *Hexapla* version.

ventionem], and as Thou didst send thy holy angel Raphael to Tobias, and to Sarah the daughter of Raguel, so deign, Lord, to send thy bene✝diction on these young people, that they may abide in thy will and dwell in thy peace, and live and grow old in thy love [*amore*], and become worthy and peaceful and may they be multiplied in length of days. For ever and ever.

Let us pray.

Look down, O Lord, kindly upon this thy servant and this thy handmaid, that in thy name they may receive a celestial blessing ✝, and may safely see the children of their children unto the third and fourth generation, and persevere ever in fidelity to Thee, and in future attain the heavenly kingdom. For ever and ever, Amen. May almighty God, who joined our first parents Adam and Eve by his virtue, hallow and bless ✝ your hearts and bodies, and join [you] as companions [*societate*] and the love of sincere affection. Amen.

May the Lord bless ✝ you with every blessing, may He make you worthy in his sight, and may the richness of his glory be abundant in you. May He teach you with the words of truth, that you be able to please him in body and soul. Amen.

After this they are led into the choir of the church on the right, and with the woman placed on the right of the man, the Mass of the Holy Trinity is begun.

Blessed be the Holy Trinity.

Lord, have mercy.

(*Prayer*) Almighty, eternal God, who has given to thy servants. (*Then the rest.*) Hear us, Almighty and merciful God, that whatever our efforts may attempt may be fulfilled by thy blessing. For ever and ever.

(*The Epistle*) "Know ye not that your bodies are the members of Christ?[152] <Shall I then take the members of Christ, and make *them* the members of an harlot? God forbid.">

(*Gradual*) Blessed art thou, Lord.

(*Blessing*) Alleluia. Blessed art thou, Lord.

(*The Gospel*) "The Pharisees also came unto him, tempting him, and saying unto him, Is it lawful for a man to put away his wife for every cause?"[153]

The creed.

(*Offertory*) Blessed be God the Father.

(*Secret prayer*) Bless, we beseech Thee, Lord God, Triune.

(*Another secret prayer*) Hear, Lord, our supplications, and kindly accept this offering we present Thee for thy servants, whom Thou hast vouchsafed to reach a state of maturity and arrive at their wedding day [*diem nuptiarum*].

(*Preface*) Who with the only-begotten. . . .

[152.] 1 Cor. 6:15. Martène's text does not make clear how much of this is read.

[153.] Matt. 19:3. The text does not indicate how much of this chapter is to be read.

After the Sanctus they prostrate themselves in prayer, with the pallium extended over them, which four men hold at its four corners, and before "Peace be with you" is said, the priest says this prayer over them:

The Lord be with you.

Let us pray.

Receive favorably, Lord, our prayers and assist kindly in thine institutions, through which Thou hast ordained the propagation of the human race, so that what is joined with Thee as author may be preserved through thine aid. Through Christ our Lord, Amen.

Let us pray.

God, who in the power of thy virtue didst create all from nothing, who at the beginning of the universe hast made mankind in the image of God and ordained the inseparable help [*adjutorium*] of woman, that with a feminine body from a male Thou might give flesh its beginning, teaching that what it once pleased [Thee] to establish, can never be split asunder. God, Thou didst consecrate the conjugal union [*conjugalem copulam*] in so excellent a mystery that Thou didst presage it in the nuptial union [*federe nuptiarum*] of Christ and the church. God, through whom woman is joined to man, and society [*societas*] is principally ordained through that blessing, which alone is taken away neither through the penalty of original sin nor by the sentence of the flood, look kindly upon thine handmaid, about to be joined in marital consort, who prays to be safeguarded by thy protection. May she abide in the yoke of affection and peace: let her marry faithful and chaste in Christ and imitate ever saintly women. May she be as kindly to her husband as Rachel, as wise as Rebecca, as long-lived and faithful as Sara. Let the author of falsehood usurp nothing in her or her acts. May she remain bound in faith to [thy] commandments. Joined to one bed let her flee unlawful contact. Strengthen her weakness with the firmness of discipline. May she be solemn in modesty, venerable in decency, learned in spiritual doctrine, fecund in offspring, wise and innocent, and may she come to the wished-for service of seeing the children of her children unto the third and fourth generations, and unto the rest of the blessed, and achieve the heavenly kingdom. For ever and ever, Amen.

After this follows:

The peace of the Lord be always with you.

And the Agnus Dei.

Then they get up from their prayers and the husband receives the peace from the priest and passes it to the wife, kissing her, but neither of them kisses anyone else. But the clergy after this accepting the peace from the priest pass it to others as is the custom.

Communion. Let us bless God.

Postcommunion. May it profit us.

Almighty God, bless us with thy presence at this institution of thy providence, and preserve in long peace those joined through licit connection. For ever and ever, Amen.

After the Mass the bread and wine are blessed in a cup,[154] *and are drunk in the name of the Lord.*

Blessing.

Let us pray.

Bless, Lord, this bread and this drink, and this chalice, as Thou didst bless the five loaves in the desert and the six baskets in Cana in Galilee, that all those tasting of them may be prudent and sober and pure, O Savior of the World. Who live and reign [with God the Father and the Holy Spirit, Amen.]

(Separate prayers at night in the bedroom [ibid., p. 129]).

8. PARIS BIBLIOTHÈQUE NATIONALE GREC 330
[twelfth century] [Greek]

Text published in Appendix of Documents, No. 3.

This prayer is closely related to the most common prayer in same-sex union ceremonies (evident in all those translated here), but is sufficiently different to constitute a separate prayer rather than a variant. It is thus here collated with Sinai 1036, a century later, closely related to Paris 330 but somewhat better. Dmitrievskij gives an opening for Sinai 971 that is very like the opening line of Paris 330, but he equates it with Goar No. 4, which is much closer to other versions of this prayer than to BN grec 330. Istanbul 615 [1522] has a similar but significantly different prayer, translated separately as No. 12.

Prayer for Holy Union

i.

O Lord our God, who madest heaven and earth and humankind after thine image and likeness, and adorned them with thine every grace, bestowing upon them power of life eternal, and didst deem it meet that thy holy apostles Philip and Bartholomew[155] be united together [lacuna in manuscript],[156] not of nature but of a holy spirit and faith. Do Thou now, O loving

---

[154.] Probably the "common cup": see pp. 203–04.

[155.] 1036 adds "as well as your holy martyrs Serge and Bacchus."

[156.] Both manuscripts have, unmistakably, εὐκλινεῖς; I am unable to identify this word, which

Lord, send down the grace of thy Holy Spirit on these thy servants, whom Thou hast found worthy to be united together [lacuna], not bound by nature but by a holy spirit and in the way of faith. And grant unto them thy love, that they abide in safety under thy protection unto their[157] lives' end. And grant unto them thy grace, as Thou gavest [it] unto thy holy apostles with thy lovingkindness and grace.

9. VATICANUS GRAECUS 1811 [1147] [Italo-Greek]

> Text published in Appendix of Documents, No. 4. Italo-Greek; closely related to Grottaferrata Γ.β. II (eleventh century)

Office of Same-Gender Union

The priest[158] shall place the holy Gospel on the Gospel stand and they that are to be joined together place their hands on it, holding lighted candles in their left hands. Then shall the priest cense them and say the following:[159]
Bless us, O Lord.
The priest: Blessed is the reign of the father, and of the Son, and of the Holy Spirit, now and forever.
Then the deacon:
In peace we beseech Thee, O Lord.
For heavenly peace, we beseech Thee, O Lord.
For the peace of the entire world, we beseech Thee, O Lord.[160]
That these thy servants, N. and N., be blessed with thy spiritual benediction, we beseech Thee, O Lord.
That their love abide without offense or scandal all the days of their lives, we beseech Thee, O Lord.
That they be granted all things needed for salvation and enjoyment[161] of life everlasting, we beseech Thee, O Lord.

---

appears to mean "well in bed." The phrase ἀδελφοὺς εὐκλινεῖς γενέσθαι is repeated in Sinai 1036 in reference to Serge and Bacchus.

157. 330 has "our," which makes no sense; 1036 reads "their," which is clearly correct.

158. Throughout the initial portion of this text the priest is indicated by a drawing of a head with eyes—what the twentieth century would call a "happy face." That this means "the priest" is clear both from the context and from comparison with related versions of the ceremony.

159. Cf. Grottaferrata Γ.β. II (No. 4 in this collection) and Hilferding: "The priest [поп] shall prepare the table, and before the service he shall place it before the altar. Then shall he lay their right hands on the Gospel, and into their left hands give a cross."

160. Γ.β. II adds here "For this holy place, we beseech Thee, O Lord."

161. Γ.β. II has "godly enjoyment."

That the Lord God grant unto them unashamed[162] faithfulness, <and> sincere love, we beseech Thee, O Lord.

That they and we ourselves be saved from all affliction,[163] we beseech Thee, O Lord.

Have mercy on us, O God.

Have mercy upon me, O Lord, after thy great goodness; according to the multitude of thy mercies do away with mine offences.[164]

The "Lord, have mercy" shall be said three times.

The priest <shall say>:

Forasmuch as thou art merciful and loving.[165]

(*First prayer*) O Lord our God, Ruler of all, who didst fashion humankind after thine image and likeness,[166] and bestowed upon us[167] power of everlasting life, who didst deem it meet[168] that thy holy[169] apostles[170] Philip and Bartholomew, should be united,[171] not bound unto one other by law of nature but in the manner of a holy spirit[172] and faith,[173] as Thou[174] didst also [bless the joining together of][175] thy holy martyrs Serge and Bacchus[176] in union of spirit. Send down, most kind Lord, the grace of thy Holy Spirit upon these thy servants,[177] whom thou hast found worthy to be united not by[178] nature but by faith and a holy spirit.[179] Grant unto them thy grace[180] to love each other in joy without injury or hatred all the days of their

---

[162.] πίστιν ἀκαταίσχυντον: see n. 47, above.

[163.] Γ.β. II has simply "That we be saved . . ."

[164.] Ps. 51 (50 in the LXX, of which this is verse 3), used at the opening of the Liturgy of the Presanctified (Brightman, p. 345). Omitted in Γ.β. II. Possibly the entire psalm should be said at this point in the service; the directions are unclear for this ceremony. The rubric for the Liturgy of the Presanctified suggests the whole psalm would be chanted. I have quoted the version from the Psalter of the Anglican Book of Common Prayer.

[165.] In Γ.β. II this phrase is inserted into the beginning of the following prayer.

[166.] Barberini 336 adds "and accordedst them eternal life"; Grottaferrata Γ.β. VII (No. 3 in this collection) adds "and gavest them power over all flesh everlasting."

[167.] Literally, "it."

[168.] Γ.β. VII: "who now have approved."

[169.] 336 adds "and most blessed."

[170.] 336 adds "Peter, the foremost of all, and Andrew, and Jacob and John, the sons of Zebedee, and . . ."

[171.] 336 adds ἀμφοτέρους, with several possible meanings.

[172.] Possibly "the Holy Spirit," but the juxtaposition of "faith" makes this unlikely. See also comments above on "holy spirit" (n. 22). "The Holy Spirit" (τοῦ ἁγίου πνεύματος) is unmistakably named further on in the prayer.

[173.] Γ.β. II: "by faith and the spirit"; 336: "of a holy spirit."

[174.] 336: "and who."

[175.] Something seems to be missing here.

[176.] 336 adds "Cosmas and Damian, and Cyrus and John."

[177.] Γ.β. II: "Bless also these thy servants, N. and N."; 336 adds "now."

[178.] Γ.β. II adds "the bond of."

[179.] Γ.β. II: "but by faith and in the mode of the spirit"; Γ.β. VII omits "but by faith and in the mode of the spirit"; 336 omits "and in the mode of the spirit."

[180.] Γ.β. II: "peace and."

lives,[181] with the aid of[182] the all-holy Mother of God and[183] of all thy saints,[184] forasmuch as thou art blessed and glorified everywhere, now and forever.

(*Second prayer*)[185]O Lord Our God, who didst command us to love one another and to forgive each other's failings, do Thou, Ruler and most kind lover of good, [bless and consecrate][186] these thy servants who love each other with a love of the soul and have come into[187] thy holy church to be blessed.[188] Grant unto them unashamed fidelity, sincere love, and as Thou didst vouchsafe unto thy holy disciples and apostles[189] thy peace and love,[190] so also bestow on these servants of thine all things needed for salvation.[191] For to Thee belong all glory, honor and worship. *Then shall they kiss the holy Gospel and the priest and one other, and he shall dismiss them, saying:* The Lord of peace and love be with you. Amen.

10. SINAI 966 [thirteenth century] [Greek]

Dmitrievskij provides a partial transcription [XXIII, p. 215]; full text transcribed in Appendix of Documents, No. 5.

Order for Solemnization of Same-Sex Union

i.[192]

Those intending to be united shall come before the priest, who shall place the Gospel on the center of the altar, and the first of them that are to be joined together

181. Γ.β. II and the others diverge so fully at this point that collation is impractical. They should be consulted in their original.

182. 336 adds "our all-holy and sinless Lady."

183. Γ.β. VII adds "and ever-virgin Mary"; 336 adds "ever-virgin Mary, and of Saint John the forerunner and the Baptist, of the holy and most blessed apostles and all your holy martyrs, because you are merciful, [trustworthy?], and the Lord of Peace, Christ our God, and yours are the glory and thanks forever."

184. Γ.β. VII omits "and all your saints."

185. See comments on a similar prayer in Γ.β. II; collated here (as there) with Paris Coislin 213 (hereafter 213) and Sinai 958.

186. 213 omits "bless and consecrate, kind"; adds "protect in your holiness."

187. Γ.β. II adds "this."

188. Γ.β. II adds "and consecrated"; 213 adds "by you."

189. 213 omits "and apostles."

190. 213 omits "and love."

191. Γ.β. II adds "and life eternal. For Thou art the light [and] the truth and thine is the glory"; 213 omits "For Thou art the light, the truth, and thine is the glory."

192. Although not identical, both this and the following sections resemble Vatican Barberini Greek No. 345 (twelfth century) and Grottaferrata Γ.β. III (fourteenth century).

*shall place his hand on the Gospel, and the second on the hand of the first. And
thus sealing them, the priest sayeth the litany.*

ii.
In peace we beseech Thee, O Lord.
For heavenly peace, we beseech Thee, O Lord.
For the peace of all the world, [we beseech Thee, O Lord].
For these servants of God, N. and N., and their love [ἀγαπήσεως] in Christ,
we beseech Thee, O Lord.
That they be granted love in the spirit and honor each other, we beseech
Thee, O Lord.
That the Lord our God grant them blameless life and pleasing conduct.
That they and we be saved from all [danger, need and tribulation].[193]

iii.[194]
Receive us. Save us. Have mercy upon us.
Mindful of our lady, the all-holy, undefiled, most blessed and glorious ever-
virgin Mary, mother of God, and all the saints, we commend ourselves and
one other and all that liveth unto Christ our God.

iv.
Let us pray.
Lord our God and ruler, who madest humankind after thine image and
likeness and didst bestow upon us power of life eternal, whom it pleased that
thine holy apostles Philip and Bartholomew be joined together, not bound
by the law of nature, but in the mode of faith, who didst commend the union
of thy holy martyrs Serge and Bacchus, not bound by the law of nature, but
in a holy spirit and the mode of faith, do Thou vouchsafe unto these thy
servants grace to love one other and to abide unhated and not a cause of
scandal all the days of their lives, with the help of the Holy Mother of God
and all thy saints. Forasmuch as Thou art our unity and certainty and the
bond of peace, and thine is endless glory, Father, Son, and Holy Spirit.

v.
Peace be with you.
<Bow> *your heads.*
O Lord Our God, who hast favored us with all those things necessary for

---

[193.] Incomplete in MS: cf. comparable entry in, e.g., Grottaferrata Γ.β. III. In the modern liturgy
of Chrysostom this entreaty is "That we might be saved from all tribulation, wrath, danger
and need, we pray to the Lord."

[194.] Standard part of Greek Mass, known since the ninth century and included in present-day
liturgy of St. John Chrysostom.

salvation and hast commanded us to love one another and to forgive one another our failings, [bless], kind Lord and lover of good, these thy servants who love each other and are come into this thy holy church to receive thy benediction. Grant unto them unashamed faithfulness, true love, and as Thou didst bestow upon thy holy disciples and apostles thy peace and love, grant also unto these, O Christ our God, all those things necessary for salvation and eternal life.

For Thou art the light, the truth, and life eternal, and thine is the glory.

vi.

O Lord our God, who in thine ineffable providence didst deem it fit to call brothers the holy apostles and heirs of thy kingdom, accept now these thy servants, N. and N., to be united in spirit and faith,[195] and find them meet to abide unscathed [ἀσκανδαλίστους] by the wiles of the devil and of his evil spirits, to prosper in virtue and justice and sincere love, that through them and through us may be glorified thine all-holy name, the Father, the Son, and the Holy Spirit, now and forever.

vii.[196]

Lord our God, magnified in the congregation of the saints, great and awesome ruler over all that is round about Thee,[197] bless these thy servants <N. and N.>, grant unto them knowledge of thy Holy Spirit. Guide them in thy holy fear, bestow upon them joy in thy power, that they be joined together more in spirit than in flesh.[198] Forasmuch as it is Thou who dost bless and sanctify all things, and <thine> is the glory.

viii.[199]

O Lord our God, who dwellest in the heavens and dost look down upon those things below,[200] who for the salvation of the human race didst send thine only-begotten son, our Lord, Jesus Christ, and didst choose Peter and Paul (Peter from Ceasarea of Philippi, Paul from Tarsus of Cilicia), joining

195. There is an error in the text here; I have substituted comparable wording from closely related ceremonies (e.g., No. 14).
196. This prayer is known in only one other manuscript: Γ.β. VII (tenth century; translated above, No. 3). It varies only in very minor details.
197. Cf. Ps. 89:8 [LXX/V 88:9], "O Lord God of hosts, who is a strong Lord like unto thee? or to thy faithfulness round about thee?"
198. ἵνα γένονται [sic: sc. γένωνται, as in Γ.β. VII] πνευματικοὶ ἀδελφοὶ ὑπὲρ τοὺς σαρκικούς.
199. This prayer exhibits only minor variations from Vatican Barberini Grec 345 and 329, both twelfth-century versions. It is also similar to Γ.β. III, from a century later.
200. Ps. 113:5–6: "who dwelleth on high and looketh down on the low things in heaven and in earth" (Rheims-Douai Version 112:5–6, which is closer to the Greek).

them together in holy spirit,[201] make these thy servants[202] like unto those two apostles. Keep them blameless all the days of their lives, for the sake of thy most venerable and honored name, Father, Son and Holy Spirit, which is <thus> sanctified and glorified, now and forever.

ix.

And they shall kiss the holy Gospel and each other, and it shall be concluded.

11. "OFFICE OF SAME SEX UNION" [first part of the fourteenth century][203] [Serbian Slavonic]

Published in "leaflet" in collection of Learned Society of Serbia, No. 52, by P. Srećković, «чинь братотворению», *Гласник Српскога Ученог Груштва*, 63 (1885), pp. 276–79.

An Order for the Uniting of Two Men [or Two Women]

i.

Those who are to be united[204] shall come into the church, and [the priest] shall place them in front of the holy door,[205] the older one on the right side, and he shall give unto them each a candle. He shall lay their right hands on the holy Gospel, and shall give a cross into their left hands.

ii.

And the priest[206] shall begin:

[201.] Or, "the Holy Spirit," but this is unlikely, both for reasons cited above about "spirit" without the definite article, and because in the three other versions most closely related it is specifically "according to holiness" (κατὰ ἁγιωσύνην).

[202.] All other versions add "N. and N."

[203.] According to Nahtigal (as cited above), note, p. 20. Srećković seemed less certain.

[204.] братимити се: the sole occurrence of this as a verb in the Slavic texts considered here.

[205.] I.e., at the door of the iconostasis, or altar screen, separating the sanctuary from the narthex of Orthodox churches.

[206.] свщеникъ; попь is the OCS word translated as "priest" just following. The two seem to me to be interchangeable, as they are in the Sinai Euchologion, but possibly some distinction is intended. No deacon is mentioned here, and in most versions of the ceremony deacon and priest alternate. свщеникъ, which simply means "holy man," could refer to a deacon, but this seems unlikely in view of the fact that священство means "priesthood." It is also most unlikely that a deacon would administer Communion, as the свщеникъ does in this rite. "Deacon" is indicated in No. 6 by диѣкъ and in No. 15 by дїакцн.

Holy God, [Holy Mighty, Holy and Immortal].[207]
The priest shall say the "Our Father," and the hymn[208] *of the day, according to the liturgy of St. John Chrysostom.*

iii.
Then:
In peace we beseech Thee, O Lord.
For heavenly peace and for the salvation of our souls, we beseech Thee, O Lord.
For the peace of all the world, we beseech Thee, O Lord.
For our Archbishop, we beseech Thee, O Lord.
For those to be joined[209] together in true[210] love, we beseech Thee, O Lord.
For this servant of the Lord N. and [?],[211] we beseech Thee, O Lord.
That he grant them[212] discretion[213] and true love, we beseech Thee, O Lord.
For the sanctified[214] gifts of the most precious body and blood of our Lord God, Jesus Christ, we beseech Thee, O Lord.
That they receive them [i.e., the Body and Blood] without sin[215] and preserve their union[216] without envy, we beseech Thee, O Lord.
That Thou wouldst grant them every prayer for salvation, we beseech Thee, O Lord.
That they be freed from every evil, we beseech Thee, O Lord.
Help, save, have mercy on and protect them.
For all glory is thine.

iv.
Then the priest shall say this first prayer:
O Lord, Our God, grant their prayers for salvation, Thou who gavest the commandment to thy holy apostles to love [любите] one another and forgive one other's faults. O Lord, author of life and friend of mankind,[217] these

---

207. Cf. notes to beginning of Istanbul 8.
208. тропарь.
209. сьвакуплиающих се: see n. 99 on this verb in Sinai Euchologion.
210. неличъмерноую: "unhypocritical" in modern Russian. This same word occurs in the opening litany (i, l. 8) of the Sinai Euchologion. Greek texts use ἀνεπαίσχυντος, "unashamed."
211. Perhaps a copying error: there is a lacuna in this intercession in No. 15 as well.
212. Dual.
213. See note to this word in Sinai Euchologion, I.
214. I.e., consecrated before this occasion: see n. 109.
215. нескврьно: literally, "not badly."
216. братьство.
217. The phrase "friend of mankind" often occurs in reference to God in Eastern and Coptic heterosexual marriage ceremonies from the tenth to twelfth centuries: see, e.g., *Le Grand euchologe du Monastère blanc*, ed. Emmanuel Lanne (PO 28.2) (Paris, 1958), 395.

thy servants, loving each other in a spirit of love from Thee,[218] are now come into thy holy church longing for thy benediction. Grant them un-abashed faithfulness and true love, as Thou didst give to thy disciples and apostles thy peace and holy love. Grant unto them every prayer for salvation and life everlasting. For Thou only art God, and to Thee do we give glory, Father, Son [and Holy Spirit].

v.

(Second prayer) Lord God almighty, who didst fashion humankind after thine image and likeness and give unto them[219] eternal and everlasting[220] life, who didst choose[221] thy holy disciples and glorious apostles Peter and Paul, and Philip and Bartholomew, to be united not in the bond of birth, but in faithfulness [вѣрою] and love, let these love each other without envy and without temptation[222] all the days of their lives. It hath pleased Thee that[223] thy holy martyrs Serge and Bacchus were united[224] not in the bond of birth, but in spiritual faith and love. Grant also that these two servants of thine, N. and N., love each other without jealousy or temptation. Let them abide all the days of their lives under[225] thy Holy Spirit and the prayers of our most pure Queen, the Mother of God, and all thy saints who have pleased Thee through the ages.

For thine is the power and thine the kingdom, thine the strength and the glory, Father and Son.

vi.

And he shall change the crosses to their right hands, and the candles to their left. Then the antiphon in the fourth tone: Wonderful is the Lord among his saints, the Lord of Israel.

(Verse) Bless ye (the Lord) in the congregations.[226]

[218.] Or, possibly, "with a spirit beloved by you."

[219.] Literally, "it" or "him."

[220.] нетлѣньини и вѣчную, with животъ understood for the first and живю for the second.

[221.] Note that this is probably a misunderstanding of the Sinai изволеи.

[222.] ве-съвлазна; Frček offers as a Greek correspondence (pp. 663–65) a prayer from Goar (p. 707, a conflation of Barberini 336 and Grottaferrata Γ.β. I), in which the equivalent phrase is: Δὸς αὐτοῖς...ἀμίσητον καὶ ἀσκανδάλιστον τὴν ἀδελφοσύνην αὐτῶν εἶναι πάσας τὰς ἡμέρας τῆς ζωῆς αὐτῶν ("Let their relationship be unhated and not a source of scandal all the days of their lives"). Other versions of the prayer use related phrases. Although the OCS expression does not match the Greek, it is attested in other Slavic versions; there is no mention of "relationship" (ἀδελφοσύνην) in the Slavic.

[223.] Or, "made it proper": съподовлеи.

[224.] бъити.

[225.] Literally, "through."

[226.] Ps. 68:26: "Bless ye God in the congregations." Cf. 89:5: "And the heavens shall praise thy wonders, O Lord: thy faithfulness also in the congregation of the saints."

vii.

[The First Epistle of] the Apostle Paul to the Corinthians [12:27–31]:[227]

Brothers, Now ye are the body of Christ, and members in particular. And God hath set some in the church, first apostles, secondarily prophets, thirdly teachers, after that miracles, then gifts of healings, helps, governments, diversities of tongues. Are all apostles? are all prophets? are all teachers? are all workers of miracles? Have all the gifts of healing? do all speak with tongues? do all interpret? But covet earnestly the best gifts: and yet shew I unto you a more excellent way.

[13:1–8] Though I speak with the tongues of men and of angels, and have not love,[228] I am become as sounding brass, or a tinkling cymbal.

And though I have the gift of prophecy, and understand all mysteries, and all knowledge, and though I have all faith, so that I could remove mountains, and have not love, I am nothing. And though I bestow all my goods to feed the poor, and though I give my body to be burned, and have not love, it profiteth me nothing.

Love suffereth long, and is kind; love envieth not; love vaunteth not itself, is not puffed up.

Doth not behave itself unseemly, seeketh not its own,[229] is not easily provoked, thinketh no evil;

Rejoiceth not in iniquity, but rejoiceth in the truth;

Beareth all things, believeth all things, hopeth all things, endureth all things.

Love never faileth.

viii.

Alleluia. Blessed is the man that feareth the Lord.[230]

(*Verse*) Give ear, O Shepherd of Israel.[231]

---

227. I have followed the KJV translation of this passage with the sole exception addressed in the following note.

228. I employ the RSV translation of the Greek ἀγάπη as "love," which is both more accurate than the KJV's "charity," and closer to the OCS любъ, cognate with "love" and almost identical in its range of meanings. (All major Slavic translations of this passage use this word or its derivates.) "Charity" may have been more accurate for English readers of King James' day, but even that is debatable; the translators were probably inspired to use "charity" because of Jerome's *caritas*, which is quite different from English "charity." All modern translators use "love."

229. не завить.

230. Ps. 112:1

231. Ps. 80:1.

ix.

Hear the Gospel according to John [17:1, 18–26]:

At that time, Jesus lifted up his eyes to heaven, and prayed, (Father,)
As thou hast sent me into the world, even so have I also sent them into the world.

And for their sakes I sanctify myself, that they also might be sanctified through the truth.

Neither pray I for these alone, but for them also which shall believe on me through their word;

That they all may be one; as thou, Father, art in me, and I in thee, that they also may be one in us: that the world may believe that thou hast sent me.

And the glory which thou gavest me I have given them; they they may be one, even as we are one:

I in them, and thou in me, that they may be made perfect in one; and that the world may know that thou hast sent me, and hast loved[232] them, as thou hast loved me.

Father, I will that they also, whom thou hast given me, be with me where I am; that they may behold my glory, which thou hast given me: for thou lovest me before the foundation of the world.

O righteous Father, the world hath not known thee: but I have known thee, and these have known that thou hast sent me.

And I have declared unto them thy name, and will declare it: that the love wherewith thou hast loved me may be in them, and I in them.

x.

Peace be to all. Let us bow our[233] heads.

Then this prayer:[234] O Lord our God, Thou art the creator[235] of love, the master of peace,[236] and the savior of all, bestow upon us true[237] love to love one another[238] and grant unto us to think on[239] that which is of Jesus,

---

[232] ἠγάπησας αὐτοὺς καθὼς ἐμὲ ἠγάπησας; Vulg.: *dilexisti eos, sicut et me dilexisti* (17:23).

[233] Srećković reads глави ваше, "your heads": either the pronoun or the verb is in error.

[234] Collated here with No. 6, above. Cf. also No. 15 and Hilferding.

[235] съвръшитель: perhaps, "perfector." The Greek is φυτούργος; cf. Sinai Euchologion, where Frček renders it as *consommé*.

[236] Reading Srećković's имерек и наставникь as the Sinai Euchologion's и мироу наставьникъ.

[237] Sinai: "your."

[238] Sinai omits "to love one another"; adds "the fulfillment of the law."

[239] моудрьствовати; cf. Russian мудрствование, "philosophize." Frček renders the corresponding phrase in the Sinai Euchologion *pratiquer*, which seems too loose.

thine only Son, our God. Deem us worthy[240] to receive each other in love [люовъвъ] as thine only son received us, and grant us to serve each other in love and to fulfill the law of thy Christ with our whole hearts. For thine is the power and the kingdom. . . .

xi.

And he shall give them the Gospel to kiss. Then shall they kiss each other.

xii.

Then the priest, raising the Body and Blood in his hands, shall say: Behold, holy things to the holy.
And he shall give them Communion.

xiii.

Then shall the priest take the elder, and he the younger, and shall lead them around the sanctuary thrice to the place whereupon the cross is placed, singing in the first tone:

[Turn thee again, Thou God of hosts,] look down from heaven, [behold and visit this vine]; And the place of the vineyard that thy right hath planted.[241]

Blessed is the man that feareth the Lord, [that delighteth greatly] in his commandments.[242]

(Verse) Give ear, O Shepherd of Israel . . .

xiv.

(Verse) Behold how good [and how pleasant it is for brothers to dwell together in union.][243]

Or: Lord, Lord, look [down from heaven. . . .]
This verse shall be sung in the fourth tone.

xv.

Then the Gloria: [Glory be to the Father, and to the Son: and to the Holy Ghost. As it was in the beginning, is now, and ever shall be: world without end. Amen.]

xvi.

[Then:] Thy martyrs, O Lord, [were] strengthened in faith and encouraged in hope of life, joined in spirit through love of thy cross, shattering the tortures of the enemy, winning crowns with the spirits who[244] pray for our souls.

---

240. Sinai: "Grant us to receive."
241. Paraphrase of Ps. 80:14–15.
242. Ps. 112:1.
243. Ps. 133:1. I have slightly altered the KJV to suit the context. The KJV has "for brethren to dwell together in unity."
244. ?: бспаьтними, according to Srećković and Nahtigal; вспальтними, according to Frček.

xvii.

And then [the Gloria]: [Glory be to the Father, and to the Son and to the Holy Ghost. As it was in the beginning, is now, and ever shall be, world without end. Amen.]

xviii.

And the hymn to the Mother of God: Mother of God, succor of all who pray to thee: in thee do we hope, thee do we praise, in thee is all our trust.[245] Pray to thy son for his [?][246] servants.

xix.

Then shall they leave.

12. EDWARDIAN HETEROSEXUAL MARRIAGE CEREMONY [sixteenth century] [English]

> English heterosexual ceremony of 1549. English text
> published in *The First Book of Common Prayer of Edward VI
> and the Ordinal of 1549* (London, 1869), "The Form of
> Solemnization of Matrimony" (not paginated).

At the day appointed for Solemnization of Matrimony, the persons to be married shall come into the body of the Church with their friends and neighbours: and there the Priest shall thus say: Dearly beloved friends, we are gathered together here in the sight of God, and in the face of his congregation, to join together this Man and this Woman in holy Matrimony; which is an honourable estate, instituted of God in Paradise, in the time of man's innocency, signifying unto us the mystical union that is betwixt Christ and his Church; which holy estate Christ adorned and beautified with his presence, and first miracle that he wrought in Cana of Galilee; and is commended of Saint Paul to be honourable among all men: and therefore is not to be enterprised, nor taken in hand unadvisedly, lightly, or wantonly, to satisfy men's carnal lusts and appetites, like brute beasts that have no understanding; but reverently, discreetly, advisedly, soberly, and in the fear of God; duly considering the causes for the which Matrimony was ordained. One cause was the procreation of children, to be brought up in the fear and nurture of the Lord, and praise of God. Secondly, it was ordained for a remedy against sin, and to avoid fornication; that such persons as be married

---

[245.] упованїе: literally, "hope."
[246.] "Aforementioned"? Srećković prints "запрени (?)"; Frček corrects this to за присни. Nahtigal prints both.

might live chastely in Christ's body. Thirdly, for the mutual society, help and comfort, that the one ought to have of the other, both in prosperity and adversity. Into the which holy estate these two persons present come now to be joined. Therefore if any man can shew any just cause why they may not lawfully be joined so together, let him now speak, or else hereafter for ever hold his peace.

And also speaking to the persons that shall be married, he shall say I require and charge you, (as you will answer at the dreadful day of judgment, when the secrets of all hearts shall be disclosed), that if either of you do know any impediment why ye may not be lawfully joined together in Matrimony, that ye confess it. For be ye well assured, that so many as be coupled together otherwise than God's word doth allow, are not joined of God, neither is their Matrimony lawful.

At which day of Marriage, if any man do allege any impediment why they may not be coupled together in Matrimony; and will be bound, and Sureties with him, to the parties; or else put in a Caution to the full value of such charges as the persons to be married do sustain, to prove his allegation; then the Solemnization must be deferred unto such time as the truth be tried. If no impediment be alleged, then shall the Curate say unto the Man,

N. Wilt thou have this Woman to thy wedded wife, to live together after God's ordinance in the holy estate of Matrimony? Wilt thou love her, comfort her, honour and keep her in sickness and in health; and, forsaking all other, keep thee only to her so long as you both shall live?

The man shall answer,

I will.

Then shall the Priest say to the Woman,

N. Wilt thou have this Man to thy wedded husband, to live together after God's ordinance in the holy estate of Matrimony? Wilt thou obey him, and serve him, love, honour, and keep him in sickness and in health; and, forsaking all other, keep thee only to him, so long as you both shall live?

The Woman shall answer,

I will.

Then shall the Minister say,

Who giveth this Woman to be married to this Man?

And the Minister, receiving the Woman at her father or friend's hands, shall cause the Man to take the Woman by the right hand, and so either to give their troth to other; the Man first saying,

I N. take thee N. to my wedded wife, to have and to hold from this day forward, for better for worse, for richer for poorer, in sickness and in health, to love and to cherish, till death us depart: according to God's holy ordinance: and thereto I plight thee my troth.

Then shall they loose their hands; and the Woman, taking again the Man by the right hand, shall say,

I N. take thee N. to my wedded husband, to have and to hold from this day forward, for better for worse, for richer for poorer, in sickness and in health, to love, cherish, and to obey, till death us depart: according to God's holy ordinance: and thereto I give thee my troth.

Then shall they again loose their hands; and the Man shall give unto the Woman a Ring, and other tokens of Sponsage, as gold or silver, laying the same upon the Book. And the Priest, taking the Ring, shall deliver it unto the Man; to put it upon the fourth finger of the Woman's left hand. And the Man, taught by the Priest, shall say,

With this Ring I thee wed: this gold and silver I thee give: with my body I thee worship: and with all my worldly goods I thee endow. In the Name of the Father, and of the Son, and of the Holy Ghost. Amen.

Then the Man leaving the Ring upon the fourth finger of the Woman's left hand, the Minister shall say,

Let us pray.

O Eternal God, Creator and Preserver of all mankind, Giver of all spiritual grace, the Author of everlasting life: Send they blessing upon these thy servants, this Man and this Woman, whom we bless in thy Name; that as Isaac and Rebecca (after bracellettes and jewels of gold given of th'one to th'other for tokens of their matrimony) lived faithfully together, so these persons may surely perform and keep the vow and covenant betwixt them made, whereof this Ring given and received is a token and pledge. And may ever remain in perfect love and peace together: and live according to thy laws: through Jesus Christ our Lord. Amen.

Then shall the Priest join their right hands together, and say,

Those whom God hath joined together let no man put asunder.

Then shall the Minister speak unto the people.

Forasmuch as N. and N. have consented together in holy wedlock, and have witnessed the same here before God and this company, and thereto have given and pledged their troth either to other, and have declared the same by giving and receiving gold and silver, and by joining hands: I pronounce that they be Man and Wife together. In the Name of the Father, of the Son, and of the Holy Ghost. Amen.

And the Minister shall add this blessing.

God the Father bless you. God the Son keep you: God the Holy Ghost lighten your understanding. The Lord mercifully with his favour look upon you; and so fill you with all spiritual benediction and grace, that you may have remission of your sins in this life, and in the world to come life everlasting. Amen.

Then shall they go into the Quire, and the Ministers or Clerks shall say or sing this Psalm following.

Beati omnes. Ps. 128.

Or else this Psalm following.

Deus misereatur nostri. Ps. 67.

The Psalm ended, and the Man and Woman kneeling afore the Altar, the Priest standing at the Altar, and turning his face toward them, shall say,

Lord, have mercy upon us.

Answer.

Christ, have mercy upon us.

Minister.

Lord, have mercy upon us.

Our Father, which art in heaven, &c.

And lead us not into temptation.

Answer.

But deliver us from evil. Amen.

Minister.

O Lord, save thy servant, and thy handmaid;

Answer.

Which put their trust in thee.

Minister.

O Lord, send them help from thy holy place.

Answer.

And evermore defend them.

Minister.

Be unto them a tower of strength.

Answer.

From the face of their enemy.

Minister.

O Lord, hear my prayer.

Answer.

And let my cry come unto thee.

The Minister.

Let us pray.

O God of Abraham, God of Isaac, God of Jacob, bless these thy servants, and sow the seed of eternal life in their minds; that whatsoever in thy holy Word they shall profitably learn, they may in deed fulfil the same. Look, O Lord, mercifully upon them from heaven, and bless them. And as thou didst send thy angel Raphael to Thobie and Sara, the daughter of Raguel, to their great comfort: so vouchsafe to send they blessing upon these thy servants, that they, obeying thy will, and alway being in safety under thy protection, may abide in thy love unto their lives' end: through Jesus Christ our Lord. Amen.

13. MOUNT ATHOS PANTELEIMON 780
[sixteenth century?] [Greek]

Text published in Appendix of Documents, No. 6. This text is closely related to Mt. Athos Pantocrator 149 (from the fifteenth century), and similar to Istanbul 8 (also fifteenth century), partially transcribed in Dmitrievskij LXIV, pp. 466–67, suggesting its form is at least a century older than the manuscript from which it is taken.

Office for Same-Gender Union

The priest shall recite:

Blessed <be our God now and always and for all ages. Amen.>

Holy <God, holy and mighty, holy and immortal, have mercy on us.> [three times]

Holy Trinity <have mercy on us. Lord, forgive us our sins. Ruler, pardon our wrongdoings.

Holy one, look down and heal our weaknesses for thy name's sake.>

Our father, <who art in heaven, hallowed be thy name. Thy kingdom come; thy will be done, on earth as it is in heaven. Give us this day our daily bread, and forgive us our trespasses as we forgive those who trespass against us. And lead us not into temptation, but deliver us from evil.>

For thine is the kingdom, <the power and the glory, Father, Son, and Holy Spirit, now and forever. Amen.>[247]

[The priest shall recite] the apolytikion[248] *of the day,*[249] *the hymn of holy unity*[250] *and the hymn of the Virgin.*[251]

[247.] These prayers are identified in the text by name only: εὐλογητόν, τρισάγιον, παναγία τριάς, πάτερ ἡμῶν, ὅτι σοῦ ἐστίν.

[248.] The conclusion of a portion (in this case, the entrance) of a liturgy. For the liturgy of St. John Chrysostom (i.e., the ordinary liturgy of contemporary Greek Orthodox) the apolytikion is "Christ our true God, manifested for our salvation in the baptism of John in the Jordan, with the intercession of Thy immaculate mother, of our father St. John Chrysostom, Archbishop of Constantinople, and of all the saints, have mercy on us and save us, as good and loving" (Brightman, p. 361). But the one referred to here is not necessarily the same. Pant. 149 has at this point the troparion of the day. "Troparion" is a more general designation for a hymn; it does not exclude the possibility of an apolytikion, but might refer to the "Hymn of Serge and Bacchus," although this would not necessarily be that of "the day." It was more likely used at the end, as in the Sinai Euchologion.

[249.] Istanbul 8 has simply "the hymn and collect of the day." Pant. 149 has <λέγει> ὁ ἱερεὺς τρισάγιον, παναγία τριάς, πατὲρ ἡμῶν, ὅτι σοῦ ἐστίν, τροπάριον τῆς ἡμέρας καὶ κοντάκιον καὶ ἡ κατὰ α΄ συναπτή.

[250.] In the liturgy of Chyrsostom (Brightman, p. 357): "Bless, O Lord, the holy unity. Blessed be the unity of thy holy saints, now and forever and ever. Amen."

[251.] In the liturgy of Chrysostom (Brightman, p. 357): "For the honor and in memory of our

Then shall he place the holy Gospel on the credence table and those who are to be united shall place their right hands upon it, holding lighted candles.

Then sayeth the priest in a loud voice:

[XLV] Beloved,[252] ye have heard the voice of the Gospel, saying, "we beseech Thee, O Lord,[253]

These things I command you, that ye love one another."[254]

[XLVI] and [ye have heard] the great Paul saying,

"Love is not jealous or boastful; it is not arrogant or rude. Love insisteth not on its own way, . . . rejoiceth not at wrong. Love endeth never."[255]

In Christ our God.

As David announced prophetically:

[XXIII] "Behold how good and how pleasant it is for brethren to dwell together"[256] in the love of God.

Go forth, therefore, unto all the world, now and forever. Amen.[257]

Then he reciteth the litany (συναπτή):

In peace we pray to the Lord.

For heavenly peace and for the salvation of our souls,[258] we pray to the Lord.

For the peace of the entire world, prospering the saints of the church of God and for the unity of all, we pray to the Lord.

For this holy temple and those entering into it with faith, reverence and fear of God, we pray to the Lord.

For our archbishop, and most honorable priesthood in the service of Christ, and for all the clergy and people, we pray to the Lord.[259]

For these servants of God, N. and N., and their love from God,[260] we pray to the Lord.

---

most blessed and glorious Lady, the ever-virgin Mary, Mother of God, by whose intercession do Thou, O Lord, accept this sacrifice at thy heavenly altar."

252. I (see n. 92, above) has "brothers" (ἀδελφοί) or possibly "partners"—i.e., you who are about to be united. In the context either term could refer either to the whole congregation present or just to those being united.

253. Pant. 149 and Ist. 8 omit "we beseech Thee, O Lord."

254. John 15:17. In printing Ist. 8 Dmitrievskij mistakenly takes ταῦτα, "these things," as belonging to the preceding phrase.

255. 1 Cor. 13:4, 5, 8. I have used a modified version of the RSV translation because it translates ἀγάπη as "love." Not only do all modern translations prefer this to the KJV's "charity," but the KJV itself renders the verbal form, ἀγαπάω, as "love"—as, e.g., in the immediately preceding quotation from John. There is no reason to suppose that the noun refers to a different concept.

256. Ps. 133:1.

257. I adds here: ". . . In the kindness and mercies and love for humans of thine only-begotten son, with whom thou art blessed, along with thy most holy and good and life-giving Spirit, now and always and through all ages. Amen."

258. I omits "for the salvation of our souls."

259. Omitted in I.

260. I has "in Christ."

That the Lord our God favor them with sincere love, we pray to the Lord.[261]

That we[262] might be saved from all tribulation, <wrath,[263] and need, we pray to the Lord.>[264]

Receive us. Save us. Have mercy on and preserve[265] us.

God in your kindness. . . .[266]

Mindful of our lady,[267] the all-holy, undefiled, most blessed and glorious mother of God and ever-virgin Mary, and all the saints, we commend ourselves and each other and all life unto Christ our God.

*(Response)*Forasmuch as thine is all glory, honor, and reverence, Father, Son, and Holy Spirit.

Peace be with you all. Bow your heads before the Lord.

Then they reverse their hands upon the holy Gospel, that one having his hand above placing it beneath.[268]

Then prayeth the priest this prayer:

Let us pray to the Lord.

O Lord our God and Ruler, who madest humankind after thine image and likeness, and gavest them power of life[269] everlasting,[270] who approved it when thy holy apostles Philip and Bartholomew were united, bound together not by nature but in the communion of holy spirit,[271] and who didst approve that thy holy martyrs Serge and Bacchus should be united, bless also these thy servants, N. and N., joined not by nature but in the way of faith. Grant unto them, Lord, to love each other without hatred and to abide without scandal all the days of their lives, with the help of the Blessed Mother of God and all thy saints, because Thine is the power and the kingdom and the power and the glory, Father, Son and Holy Spirit.[272]

We pray to the Lord.[273]

O Lord our God, who consideredst not James and John, the sons of

---

[261.] Cf. Vatican Barberini Grec 431, which has "That the Lord God bestow on them unashamed faithfulness, true love, we pray to the Lord."

[262.] I has "they and we."

[263.] I adds "danger."

[264.] From the modern liturgy of Chrysostom.

[265.] I omits "and preserve."

[266.] Omitted in both I and Pant. 149.

[267.] The text simply mentions the name of this prayer (τῆς παναγίας ἀχράντου).

[268.] 1st. 8 omits this rubric here and adds it after the prayer following, though in shorter form; it is given more fully in Pant. 149 (see introduction to No. 13, below).

[269.] Literally, "flesh everlasting": σαρκὸς ἀϊδίου.

[270.] Sinai 958 omits "and gave them power of life everlasting."

[271.] ἀλλὰ πνεύματος ἀγίου κοινωνία: also the wording in Pant. 149. 1st. 8 replaces this with "by faith and in the way of the spirit," which is the earlier wording.

[272.] 1st. 8 ends "Preserve them from every temptation from the devil, so that through them thy most holy name may be glorified, Father, Son, and Holy Spirit." Sinai 958 omits "and Holy Spirit."

[273.] Pant. 149 indicates another switching of hands here.

Zebedee, in thine economy of the flesh, worthy to be united,[274] but [didst call them to be] disciples and apostles, do Thou now, ruler, preserve in peace and union all the days of their lives also these thy servants, N. and N., who love each other with love of the spirit, walking in thy commandments.[275] Guide Thou their way, preserve their light unquenched, count them among the five wise virgins.[276] Save them, have mercy on them, for the sake of thy name, invoked for them, and consider them worthy to find grace in thy sight, not in the things of the the world[277] but those of the spirit.

Forasmuch as Thou art merciful and a lover of humankind, and thine is unending glory, Father, Son, and Holy Spirit. Amen.

Let us pray to the Lord.

O Lord our God, who didst gather together thy holy saints and[278] apostles in the clouds[279] and hast united therein also them that are joined in a holy kiss of peace and union,[280] of sincere love and of the accomplishing of good works and thy commandments,[281] in the grace and mercy and lovingkindness of thine only-begotten son, with whom Thou art forever blessed, together with the Most Holy and Good and Life-Giving [Holy] Spirit. Amen.

Let us pray to the Lord.

O Lord our God, who hast granted us all things necessary for salvation, and didst command us to love one another and to forgive one another our failings, do Thou now, kind and loving ruler,[282] <bless> these thy servants[283] who love each other with a love of the spirit and have come together in thy holy church to be sanctified and blessed by Thee. Grant them unashamed fidelity, true love, and as Thou didst bestow upon thy holy disciples and apostles thy peace and thy love, grant <them> also to these, O Lord

---

274. This is a very strange clause, perhaps playing on the biological sense of ἀδελφοὺς γενέσθαι, which usually has a different meaning in these texts, and suggesting that the union being performed should *not* be understood as parallel to biological brotherhood, or that God reckons biological sibling relations little. The reading is confirmed by that of Pant. 149, which is identical. The negative has disappeared in I, although the contrasting ἀλλά is retained, and the passage is no clearer without the οὐκ. See comments in printed text of 780 at this point.

275. I has "in peace and unity of mind all the days of their lives, fulfilling thy commandments."

276. Note the obvious matrimonial reference to Matt. 25:1–12.

277. Literally, "fleshly."

278. Ist. omits "holy saints and."

279. Mt. Athos Pant. 364 (fifteenth–seventeenth century) reads "in Ephesus"; neither reading seems correct.

280. ἐν φιλήματι ἁγίῳ, εἰς εἰρήνην καὶ σοφροσύνην. Ist. 8 has "in the Holy Spirit," without the following words.

281. Although it would be possible to interpret the entire rest of this prayer as applying to the apostles and saints gathered in heaven, the evidence of I strongly suggests that it was understood by contemporaries to apply to those being joined: its text reads "unite also these partners N. and N., in holy friendship, in peace, and in true love, fulfilling thy commandments."

282. Ist. 8 has "ruler, lord, lover of good and of humans."

283. Ist. 8 has "thy servants N. and N."

our God. Guide them in every good work, forasmuch as Thou art merciful and abidest the God of lovingkindness, and thine is unending glory, with the Father, the Son, and the Holy Ghost.[284] Amen.

Have mercy upon us, Lord, according to the greatness of thy mercy. We beseech Thee. We beseech Thee further, for N. and N., now united, [that Thou wouldst grant] them mercy, well-being, life, salvation, and forgiveness of sins. Because Thou art ever a good and loving God, and thine is the glory, for ever and ever.

The troparion of the day in the second tone plagal.

United and bound together in the bond of love, and submitting themselves to Christ the Ruler of all, they stretch forth their beautiful feet to announce the good news of peace to all.[285]

Then they kiss the holy Gospel and each other and it is concluded.[286]

14. ISTANBUL: HOLY SEPULCHER 615
[1522] [Greek]

Text from Dmitrievskij, No. XCVI, pp. 743–4, supplemented from Brightman.

Office of Same-sex Union

i.

They that are to be joined come to the sanctuary along with the person who speaketh for them,[287] and the priest setteth out the lectionary and placeth the holy Gospel on it, and the first placeth his hand on the holy Gospel, and thereafter the second doth so, and then the person who speaketh[288] for them, and <the priest> bindeth their hands together.[289] They hold lighted candles.

[284.] Ist. 8 concludes this prayer with "bestowing on them all things needed for salvation and eternal life."

[285.] See n. 314, below. This odd prayer is different in Ist. 615, although the two are obviously closely related. Goar, who does not list either manuscript, prints a version of it. I am unable to determine where he got it, although he does not claim to have identified all of his sources. Perhaps he drew it from an earlier printed Euchologion.

[286.] I has "Then the dismissal takes place, and those who have been united kiss the holy Gospel and each other, and they depart, with the priest admonishing them." The "admonition" is a traditional part of the marriage ceremony: see above, p. 205; Ist. 615 also has a more elaborate concluding rhetoric, making provision for a liturgy with a litany for those who have been united.

[287.] ὁ προειπών: presumably the equivalent of the "best man," or παράνυμφος, in a heterosexual ceremony.

[288.] See preceding note.

[289.] Probably with a stole, as in contemporary heterosexual ceremonies.

ii.

The priest sayeth:

Blessed <be our God now and for ever and ever. Amen.>

Holy <God, holy and mighty, holy and immortal, have mercy on us.>

Holy Trinity <have mercy on us. O Lord, forgive us our sins. Pardon our trespasses. Holy one, look down and heal our weaknesses for thy name's sake.>[290]

Our father, <who art in heaven, hallowed be thy name. Thy kingdom come; thy will be done, on earth as it is in heaven. Give us this day our daily bread, and forgive us our trespasses as we forgive those who trespass against us. And lead us not into temptation, but deliver us from evil.

For thine is the kingdom, the power and the glory, Father, Son and Holy Spirit, now and for ever. Amen.>

The apolytikion of the holy trinity[291] and of the day.

iii.

And then the priest: Let us pray to the Lord.[292]

O Lord our God, who didst grant us all things <needed> for salvation, and didst command us to love one another and to forgive one other our failings, do Thou now, Ruler, Lord, Lover of good and of humankind, <bless> these thy servants N. and N., who love each other with a love of the spirit and have come into thy holy church to be blessed by Thee. Grant them unashamed fidelity, true love, and as Thou gavest to thy holy disciples and apostles thy peace and love, grant <them> also to these, Christ our Lord, bestowing on them all things needed for salvation and eternal life.

iv.

Another prayer.[293]

Let us pray to the Lord.

O Lord our God and Ruler,[294] who madest heaven and earth, and who

---

[290]. These prayers are a standard part of the Liturgy of St. John Chrysostom, currently used in the Greek Orthodox church. They are translated here from the text provided by Brightman, p. 353, since the ceremony abbreviates them.

[291]. In the Liturgy of Chrysostom (Brightman, p. 357): "Bless, O Lord, the holy unity. Blessed be the unity of thy holy saints, now and forever and ever. Amen."

[292]. Dmitrievskij prints only the opening lines of this prayer, referring the reader to Goar's text, p. 707. I have instead used the version given in Istanbul 8, which is also fifteenth-century, as opposed to Goar's composite (and undatable) version.

[293]. This prayer is closely related to the first prayer in Translation No. 3, but is sufficiently different to warrant separate translation. It first occurs in Paris grec 330 (No. 8 in this collection), from the twelfth century. It is here collated with both 330 and Sinai 1036, from the thirteenth century. Dmitrievskij gives an opening for Sinai 971 that is very like the opening line of 330, but equates it with Goar No. 4, which is much closer to No. 3 than to 330.

[294]. 330 and 1036 omit "and Ruler."

didst establish and fashion[295] humankind in thine image and likeness,[296] who didst deign to grant unto them authority over life eternal,[297] who didst approve[298] it when thy holy disciples and[299] apostles Philip and Bartholomew[300] were joined together,[301] not by nature but by[302] faith, who didst sanctify the union of thy holy martyrs, Serge and Bacchus,[303] bless[304] these thy servants, N. and N.,[305] not bound by nature but[306] by faith.[307] Vouchsafe unto them that they may love one other and <abide> unhated and blameless, so that all the days of their lives they may glorify thy holy name, with the aid of our most blessed Lady, the Mother of God and ever-virgin Mary, and of thy holy, glorious, and most blessed apostles Philip and Bartholomew, thy holy martyrs Serge and Bacchus, thy holy and glorious great martyrs George and Demetrius, and the two Theodores, and all thy saints. For it is Thou who blessest and makest holy, O Christ our God, and to Thee is all glory, <now and forever. Amen.>

v.

Peace be with you.

<*Bow> your heads.*

[VII][308] O Ruler and Lord, Our God, who hast called the choir of thy holy[309] apostles to one shepherd, and one church,[310] and hast sent them out to all the corners of the world to preach thy commandments, do Thou bless now also these thy servants whom Thou hast deemed worthy to stand before thy glory and to be joined in spirit, not in the bond of nature, but in the way

---

295. 330 and 1036 omit "who established and fashioned."
296. 330 and 1036 add "and adorned them with all thy grace."
297. Literally, "over eternal flesh" (σαρκὸς ἀϊδίου); 330 and 1036 have ζωῆς αἰδίου, which is clearly the meaning.
298. 330 and 1036: "approving."
299. 330 and 1036 omit "disciples and."
300. 1036 adds "as well as thy holy martyrs Serge and Bacchus."
301. 330 and 1036 add εὐκλινεῖς. For the meaning of this, see n. 156 above.
302. 330 and 1036 add "a holy spirit and."
303. 330 omits "and who approved it when thy holy martyrs Serge and Bacchus were united"; 1036 adds εὐκλινεῖς after "brothers" (see n. 156).
304. 330 and 1036 omit "Bless"; add "Do Thou now, loving Lord, send down the grace of thy Holy Spirit on."
305. 330 and 1036 omit "N. and N."; add "whom Thou hast found worthy to become partners . . ."
306. 330 and 1036 add "by a holy spirit and."
307. 330 and 1036 end here with "And grant them thy love, in safety and without injury until their last breath. And grant thy grace to them as Thou didst give [it] to thy holy apostles with goodwill and favor."
308. Only four versions of this prayer are known. It is here collated with the other three, all earlier. For a collation of the earliest text, see No. 5, in this collection.
309. One version adds "disciples and."
310. Two versions add "one brotherhood"; two omit "one church."

of faith and holy spirit.[311] Send down, O lover of mankind, the grace of thy Holy Spirit so that they may love each other without offense, without hatred, without scandal, and that they may continue in thankfulness all the days of their lives, with the aid of our most holy Queen, the Mother of God and ever-virgin Mary, and all thy saints. For blessed and glorified is thy most honored and exalted name <now and forever. Amen.>

vi.

Then we sing the troparion [to be said?][312 in the second tone plagal,[313] twice, or however many times may be desired.

Joined to the Lord of the universe in the bond of love, the apostles consecrated themselves to Christ and extended their beautiful feet, bringing to all the good news of peace.[314]

vii.

Then: Have mercy on us, <O Lord.>

We pray further for mercy, <for health, for life, for salvation of these servants of God, N. and N., who have now been joined together.

Let us pray for them:

The Kyrie eleison is said twelve times.>

viii.

Then the couple kiss each other and <the priest> gives them Communion and they depart.

ix.

If a liturgy is desired, the ceremony takes place after the reading of the Gospel, and for the litany those who have been joined together [οἱ ἀδελφοποιηθέντες] are remembered, and then the dismissal <takes place>.

---

311. 213 and the other versions end here thus: "Keep them in thy name, sanctify them in thy truth, so that conducting themselves in accordance with thy commandments they may become heirs of thy kingdom, for Thou art the giver of all good things and thine is unending glory, Father, Son and Holy Spirit."

312. τροπάριον εἰρημένον, according to Dmitrievskij (p. 744); I suspect this is a misreading of εἱρμός, "sequence."

313. ἦχος πλ. β.' in Western notation *iii plag.*: see Brightman, p. 582, s.v. "music."

314. Paraphrase of Rom. 10:15: "How beautiful are the feet of them that preach the gospel of peace." Cf. Isa. 52:7: "How beautiful upon the mountains are the feet of him that bringeth good tidings, that publisheth peace." Since the Song of Songs seems to be a subtext of the sibling imagery of the ceremony, it is possible that this passage also echoes Song of Songs 7:1 ("How beautiful are thy feet with shoes . . ."), although the Greek is less close than that in Romans.

15. BELGRADE [date uncertain; before the eighteenth century] [Serbian Slavonic]

National Library of Belgrade, MS 10. Published by
P. Srećković, «чинь братотворению», *Гласник Српскога
Ученог Друштва*, 63 (1885), pp. 279–84.

The Order of Celebrating the Union of Two Men

i.

The priest [попь] shall place the right hand of the elder upon the holy Gospel and upon that of the younger.
    Then: Blessed be God, now and for ever and ever. Amen.
    Holy God, holy mighty, holy immortal, have mercy upon us.
    Most Holy Trinity, have mercy upon us.
    O Lord, forgive us our sins.
    O Ruler, pardon our wrongdoings.
    O Holy one, look down and attend to our weakness for thy name's sake.

ii.

Our Father <who art in heaven, hallowed be thy name. Thy kingdom come. Thy will be done, on earth as it is in heaven. Give us this day our daily bread, and forgive us our trespasses, as we forgive those who trespass against us. And lead us not into temptation, but deliver us from evil. Amen.>
    For thine is the kingdom and the power and the glory.

iii.

Hymn [тропар] of the church or of the day, in the first tone.
    O Lord, rescue thy people.

iv.

Then shall the priest [свщеникь][315] take the holy belt and tie it around them. And they that are to be joined shall hold the holy belt in their left hands.

v.

(*First prayer*) Let us pray.
    O Lord, Our God, who hast vouchsafed unto us the promise of salvation, and hast commanded us to love one another and to forgive one another our trespasses, Thou art the Author of grace and Friend of mankind, accept

---

[315.] See n. 206, above.

Thou these thy two servants, N. and N.,[316] who love each other with a love of the spirit, and have desired to come into thy holy church, and grant unto them hope, unashamed faithfulness and true love. As Thou didst bestow upon thy holy disciples and apostles peace and love, grant these also the same, O Christ our Lord, and vouchsafe unto them every promise of salvation and life everlasting. For to Thee do we give glory, [father and son.]

vi.

(*Second prayer*) Lord God almighty, who didst fashion humankind after thine image and likeness and bestow upon us[317] eternal life, Thou thoughtest it right that thy holy and glorious apostles Peter and Paul, and Philip and Bartholomew, should be joined together in perfect love [незазорное братолюбне], [?][318] faith and love of the heart. Thou also didst deem it proper[319] for the holy martyrs Serge[320] and Bacchus to be united.[321] Bless Thou these thy servants. Grant unto them grace and prosperity, and faith and love; let them love each other without envy and without temptation[322] all the days of their lives, through the power of the Holy Spirit and the prayers of our Holy Queen, the Mother of God and ever-virgin Mary, and all thy saints, who worship Thee through the ages.

For thine is the power and thine the kingdom, Father, Son and Holy Spirit, now and for ever and ever.

vii.
The deacon:

In unity[323] we beseech Thee, O Lord.

For heavenly peace.

For the salvation of our souls, we beseech Thee, O Lord.

For the peace of the whole world.

For the prosperity of the holy churches of God and all they that are come together [in them],[324] we beseech Thee, O Lord.

---

316. Srećković erroneously prints и ме.

317. Literally, "it" or "him."

318. A word is apparently omitted here: only the ending ноу is printed in the text. Of the other Slavic versions of this prayer only Hilferding has an adjective modifying вѣрою at this point in the prayer; it is доуховною, "spiritual," "of the spirit," but it follows in Hilferding, so it is not at all clear that it belongs here.

319. Or, "made it proper": съподовлеи.

320. Srećković prints срьпïа, but there is no doubt about what is meant.

321. брата бьіти.

322. See n. 129, above.

323. In Greek it is usually "for peace," as in the intercession immediately following; миром is instrumental, but the grammar of the text is hardly precise.

324. сьвькоуплюних. This phrase could refer either to those who "gather" or "congregate" in the churches, or to the couples that have been "joined" in them. I have retained the

For them that are come together[325] in the pledge of lifelong love [любьви житию], we beseech Thee, O Lord.

For these thy servants [and] for their being joined unto each other, we beseech Thee, O Lord.

That the Lord our God unite them in perfect love and inseparable[326] life, we beseech Thee, O Lord.

That He grant them wisdom and true love, we beseech Thee, O Lord.

For the presanctified[327] gift of the precious Body and Blood of our Lord Jesus Christ, that they receive it without sin[328] and that it preserve their union[329] without envy, we beseech Thee, O Lord.

That he grant them every promise for salvation, we beseech Thee, O Lord.

That he free us from all sorrow, anger and affliction, we beseech Thee, O Lord.

Protect, save, have mercy on and protect [them], O Lord, by thy most holy, perfect and blessed grace.

viii.

(*Troparion in the third tone [ϱ]*) I will tell the names of the brethren.[330]

(*Verse*) Serve the Lord with fear, and rejoice [with trembling].[331]

ix.

[The First Epistle of] the Apostle Paul to the Corinthians [12:27–31]:

Now ye are the body of Christ, and members in particular. And God hath set some in the church, first apostles, secondarily prophets, thirdly teachers, after that miracles, then gifts of healings, helps, governments, diversities of tongues. Are all apostles? are all prophets? are all teachers? are all workers of miracles? Have all the gifts of healing? do all speak with tongues? do all interpret? But covet earnestly the best gifts: and yet shew I unto you a more excellent way. [13:1–8] Though I speak with the tongues of men and of angels, and have not love,[332] I am become as sounding brass, or a tinkling cymbal.

And though I have the gift of prophecy, and understand all mysteries,

---

ambiguity in my translation, although the clear reference in the following prayer to those being joined, using the same verb, inclines me to the former interpretation.

325. See preceding note.

326. неразлучьную; неразлучники means "lovebirds" in Russian.

327. I.e., consecrated on a previous occasion.

328. вьськуплієніе. The Sinai Euchologion and SSS have "not badly" (бе-скврънъі).

329. братство.

330. Cf. 3 John 15: "Greet the friends by name."

331. Psalm 2:11; the text has, literally, "Fearing the Lord, let us rejoice."

332. See n. 228, above.

and all knowledge, and though I have all faith, so that I could remove mountains, and have not love, I am nothing. And though I bestow all my goods to feed the poor, and though I give my body to be burned, and have not love, it profiteth me nothing.

Love suffereth long, and is kind; love envieth not; love vaunteth not itself, is not puffed up.

Doth not behave itself unseemly, seeketh not her own,[333] is not easily provoked, thinketh no evil;

Rejoiceth not in iniquity, but rejoiceth in the truth;

Beareth all things, believeth all things, hopeth all things, endureth all things.

Love never faileth.

x.

Alleluia.

Behold, how good and how pleasant it is for brethren to dwell together in unity.[334]

The Gospel according to John [17:1, 18–26]:

At that time, Jesus lifted up his eyes to his disciples,[335] and prayed,

As thou hast sent me into the world, [Father,] even so have I also sent them into the world.

And for their sakes I sanctify myself, that they also might be sanctified through the truth.

Neither pray I for these alone, but for them also which shall believe on me through their word;

That they all may be one; as thou, Father, art in me, and I in thee, that they also may be one in us: that the world may believe that thou hast sent me.

And the glory which thou gavest me I have given them; they they may be one, even as we are one:

I in them, and thou in me, that they may be made perfect in one; and that the world may know that thou hast sent me, and hast loved[336] them, as thou hast loved me.

Father, I will that they also, whom thou hast given me, be with me where I am; that they may behold my glory, which thou hast given me: for thou lovedst me before the foundation of the world.

---

333. не завить.

334. Ps. 133:1.

335. Paraphrase to this point, apparently influenced by the same passage in the Sinai Euchologion. (No. 6). The biblical text has "lifted up his eyes to heaven."

336. ἠγάπησας αὐτοὺς καθὼς ἐμὲ ἠγάπησας; Vulg.: *dilexisti eos, sicut et me dilexisti* (17.23).

O righteous Father, the world hath not known thee: but I have known thee, and these have known that thou hast sent me.

And I have declared unto them thy name, and will declare it: that the love wherewith thou hast loved me may be in them, and I in them.

xi.

Then: Peace be with you.

Then shall the priest kiss them.

And the two that are to be joined shall kiss each other.

xii.

The priest: Peace be with you.

The people: And with thy spirit.

[The priest:] Let us bow our heads.

The first prayer in a low voice:

O Lord our God, Thou art Author[337] of love, teacher of grace and savior of all, grant unto us thy servants true love[338] to think on[339] Christ Jesus, thine only Son. And vouchsafe unto us to serve Thee and to live according to the laws of thy Christ, with our whole hearts.[340]

Aloud: For thine is all glory and honor.

And then: Grant, O Lord, that we may worthily call upon thee with perfect earnestness,[341] O heavenly God, our Father.

xiii.

The people: Our Father, [who art in heaven, hallowed be thy name. Thy kingdom come. Thy will be done, on earth as it is in heaven. Give us this day our daily bread, and forgive us our trespasses, as we forgive those who trespass against us. And lead us not into temptation, but deliver us from evil.] For thine is the kingdom, the power [and the glory].

xiv.

Then shall the priest elevate the bread, [saying], Behold the holy for the holy.[342]

The people: Thou only art holy, Thou only art Lord, O Jesus Christ, in the glory of God the Father. Amen.

---

[337] съвръшитель: perhaps, "perfector." The Greek in comparable prayers is φυτούργος; cf. Sinai Euchologion, where Frček renders it as *consommé*.

[338] Text No. 14 in this collection has here "to love one another and grant us," which could have been omitted in copying this or inserted in the former. Since the respective dates of the two are not known, and since their relationship is otherwise ambiguous, it is impossible to be sure. The reading of No. 14 is more graceful and coherent.

[339] моудрьствовати; cf. the modern Russian мудрствовать, "philosophize." Frček renders the corresponding phrase in No. 6 *pratiquer*, which seems too loose.

[340] дрьзновениемъ: literally, "courage."

[341] сь дрьзновением неосужденно.

[342] Cf. the Greek phrase τὰ ἅγια τοῖς ἁγίοις.

And he shall give them Communion if they be meet partakers thereof. If not . . . ,[343] he gives them kissel,[344] bread and wine.

xv.
After the Communion, he shall place a cross in the sanctuary and lead them around it. Then they shall bow three times.[345] Then shall the priest sing with them,

Turn thee again, Thou God of hosts, look down from heaven, behold and visit this vine; And the place of the vineyard that thy right hand hath planted.[346]

xvi.
Three times in the sixth tone: Glory to Thee, O Christ, God, praise to Apostles and joy to martyrs and to them that preach the consubstantial Trinity, One in being. Holy martyrs who performed good works and are crowned[347] with heavenly crowns, pray to the Lord that He save our souls.

xvii.[348]
Holy, equally worthy of praise, most holy Virgin, with the prayers of the prophets and martyrs, priests, apostles, pray with the Mother of God for the salvation of our souls.

xviii.
(Verse) Blessed are they that fear God.[349]

(Verse) Behold, how good and how pleasant it is for brethren to dwell together in unity.

(Chant, litany) Have mercy upon us, O God, of thy great kindness. Lord, hear us and have mercy. Lord, have mercy. *(Three times.)*

xix.
We pray further for these servants, N. and N.,[350] for their life, their health, their salvation and forgiveness of their sins. May they continue in union

---

[343.] Ellipsis indicated without clarification by Srećković.

[344.] A starchy paste or jelly of bread and milk or wine: on its significance here—the equivalent in some ways (though not identical to) the "common cup" in heterosexual ceremonies.

[345.] Srećković prints покланияета се г.

[346.] Paraphrase of Ps. 80:14–15. Note that it is not identical to the quotations of this psalm in either No. 6 or No. 14.

[347.] вънчаше: венчать has as a root meaning "to crown," but венчание means "wedding ceremony"—because of the predominantly nuptial connotations of "crowning" among Eastern Christians. That association can hardly have been missed or accidental here.

[348.] This prayer occupies the same position and has essentially the tenor of No. XXXIX, but the wording is rather different. It may be corrupt.

[349.] Probably Ps. 112:1, "Blessed is the man that feareth the Lord," cited at roughly this point in the Sinai Euchologion, but quoted loosely here.

[350.] Srećković prints иже, which I take to be a misreading of име.

without blame and without temptation.[351] Let us all say: Lord have mercy. (*Thirty times.*)

xx.
And the rest.[352]
   And he shall dismiss them.

16. ADOPTION SERVICE[353] FROM SINAI 973 [1153] [Greek]

Published in Dmitrievskij, No. VIII, p. 122. This is the earliest adoption ceremony in Dmitrievskij.

i.

Jesus Christ our Lord and our God, who dost safeguard and preserve infants and who said, as a good man, "Forbid them not, to come unto me: for of such is the kingdom of heaven,"[354] do Thou, Lord, keep also these and what is set aside on account of thy holy name for thy fatherly concern, watching over and guiding them to preserve and fulfill thy commandments, so they may come to thy heavenly kingdom. In the love and mercy and kindness of thine only-begotten son, Jesus Christ.

ii.

[= Goar, p. 562]

At the bowing of heads: Lord, the designer of all creation, who first in Adam established relationship according to the flesh, but in Christ Jesus thy beloved son and our God accepted us also as thy kin through grace, to Thee who knowest all things even before they come to pass, these thy servants bow their heads, and ask blessing from Thee, assigning to each other the bond [συνδέσμῳ] of father and son in Thee. May their hopes and the fitting consequences of this agreement [καταστάσεως] and of adoption in Thee all come to pass, each one behaving as he should, so that in this as in all things thy name may be glorified, Father, Son and Holy Spirit, now and forever. Amen.

[351.] бесьблазни: cf. Sinai Euchologion, v, which Frček renders *sans scandale*, although this seems more appropriate for незавидъно, preceding.
[352.] Possibly the τιμιώτερα; see I, No. x.
[353.] Called in the manuscript εὐχὴ ἐπὶ τεκνοποιουμένων, a very peculiar phrase, especially when compared with the title of the following ceremony.
[354.] Matt. 19:14.

17. SINAI 966 [thirteenth century] [Greek]

Published in Dmitrievskij, No. XXIII, p. 213.

Office of Adoption (υἱοθετοῦντας)

The priest summoneth him that wisheth to adopt, along with him that is to be adopted, and placeth them before the altar, saying:

Blessed be the kingdom . . . [?]

In peace, we pray to the Lord.

For heavenly peace, we pray to the Lord.

For these servants of God, N. and N., and this adoption [διαθέσεως] in Christ and goodly arrangement [ἐπιτηδεύσεως] and spiritual work, and for their peace and harmony, we pray to the Lord.

For their abiding in good works and a worthy life, we pray to the Lord.

That they and we might be saved <from every tribulation and need, we pray to the Lord.>

Receive us. Save us. Have mercy on and preserve[355] us.

Mindful of our lady,[356] the all-holy, undefiled, most blessed and glorious mother of God and ever-virgin Mary, and all the saints, we commend ourselves and each other and all life unto Christ our God.

Let us pray.

O Lord, Our God, who through thy beloved son, our Lord Jesus Christ, hast called us to be sons of God through adoption [υἱοθεσία] and grace of thine almighty and Holy Spirit, who didst say, "I will be to him a father, and he shall be to me a son,"[357] do Thou, merciful Ruler, look down from thy holy dwelling place upon these thy servants, whom Nature hath made separate from each other according to the flesh, and unite them as father and son in thy Holy Spirit.[358] Strengthen them in thy love, bind them with thy blessing, bless them in thy glory, establish them in thy faith, preserving them alway, that what they have promised with their lips may never be denied. Vouchsafe to guard their undertaking, that until the end of their days they may keep unbroken and preserve in integrity the promise they have made before Thee, abiding in Thee our One living and true God. Deem them worthy to become heirs of thy kingdom, for to Thee belongs all glory, honor, and reverence, Father, Son, and Holy Ghost, now and forever and ever. Amen.

---

[355] I, a comparable ceremony, omits "and preserve."

[356] The text simply mentions the name of this prayer (τῆς παναγίας ἀχράντου), which is common in Greek Orthodox liturgies of all sorts.

[357] Heb. 1:5.

[358] τῷ ἁγίῳ σου Πνεύματι (cf. Goar, p. 561).

Peace be with you.

Bow your heads.

Then prayeth the priest:

Lord God and Ruler, creator of all living things, who first in Adam didst establish physical relationship according to the flesh, but in Christ Jesus Thy beloved Son, our God, . . .

18. AGREEMENT OF "BROTHERHOOD" between Louis XI, King of France [1461–83], and Charles, Duke of Bourgogne [Latin]

Published in DuCange [du Fresne], Charles, "Des adoptions d'honneur en frère," in idem, ed., Jean de Joinville, *Histoire de St Louis IX*, 2 (Paris, 1668), pp. 265–66.

Louis, etc.,[359] to all those, etc.:[360] Whereas recently good peace and friendship has been established and negotiated between Us and our very dear and much loved brother and cousin the Duke of Bourgogne, and to the end of affirming it yet further and in such a way that it will remain forever inviolable, and to place and instill therein a more perfect and cordial love, it has been suggested that We contract brotherhood of arms[361] between us. We therefore make it known that We recognize the great benefit that accrues and may in future accrue to the polity of our realm from the union and joining and fraternity of arms between Us and our said brother and cousin, and considering the great courage, skill, honor, loyalty, intelligence, prudence, manners and other lofty and excellent virtues to be found in his person, and the singular and perfect love that We have specifically for him above all others, We in full awareness and with great conviction and mature deliberation have contracted and concluded, and do make, contract and conclude hereby good, true, sure and loyal brotherhood of arms with our aforesaid brother and cousin from Bourgogne, and We have received and accepted, and do receive and accept him as our sole brother in arms, and We establish, decree and declare Ourselves his; and We have promised him and do promise that this brotherhood should continue and flourish without any retraction, and with the provision, aid, support, favor and assistance of Our

---

[359.] *Sic* in text, and probably in the MS: usually this stands for a formula such as "by the Grace of God, King of France," written out fully in the letter sent to the addressee, but abbreviated in the copy retained at court.

[360.] Abbreviated in text, as noted above: probably for ". . . all those who shall see or be made aware of the present letter," or something similar.

[361.] *Fraternité d'armes.*

person and of all Our power in all issues and disputes against any persons, whoever they are or might be, living or dead, excepting no person whatever, and in all his affairs; and (We promise) in all matters to regard his deed as our own, and to fail him in nothing, to the point of death itself. All of the above proposals, and each one of them, We have promised and sworn, and do promise and swear, by the faith and oath of Our body, on the holy Gospels of God, on Our honor, and on the word of the king, to have and to hold firm, settled, and agreed, without any contradiction of any sort whatever, and in this regard We submit, etc.[362]

[362.] A concluding formula is here abbreviated; cf. n. 359.

APPENDIX
of
DOCUMENTS

Key to Symbols

< > = speculation on lacunae or reconstruction of abbreviation; these actual letters not in the original

| = actual change of folio in original; folio numbers indicated prior to sentence in which change occurs

1. GROTTAFERRATA Γ.β. II [eleventh century]

Folio 86v (folio 87v according to modern, stamped numbering; I have retained the older, handwritten numeration visible in the upper right corner). Translated as No. 4 in Appendix of Translations.

Ἀκολουθία εἰς ἀδελφοποίησιν

i.
τίθησιν ὁ ἱερεὺς τὸ ἅγιον εὐαγγέλιον ἐν τῷ ἀναλογείῳ καὶ ἐπιτίθησιν [sic] οἱ ἀδελφοὶ τὰς χεῖρας ἐπάνωθεν, κρατοῦντες ἅπτοντας κηροὺς εἰς τὰς ἀριστερὰς. καὶ θυμιᾷ αὐτοὺς καὶ λέγει ὁ διάκονος:

ii.
Ἐν εἰρήνῃ τοῦ κυρίου δεηθῶμεν.
Ὑπὲρ τῆς ἄνωθεν εἰρήνης.
Ὑπὲρ τῆς εἰρήνης τοῦ σύμπαντος κόσμου.
Ὑπὲρ τοῦ ἁγίου οἴκου τούτου.

Ὑπὲρ τοῦ εὐλογηθῆναι τοὺς δούλους σου ὅ καὶ ὅ εὐλογίᾳ πνευματικῇ, τοῦ κυρίου δεηθῶμεν.

Ὑπὲρ τοῦ διαφυλαχθῆναι τήν τούτων ἀγάπην ἀμίσητον καὶ ἀσκανδάλιστον μέχρι βίου ζωῆς[1] αὐτων, τοῦ κυρίου δεηθῶμεν.

Ὑπὲρ τοῦ δωρηθῆναι αὐτοῖς πάντα τὰ πρὸς σωτηρίαν αἰτήματα καὶ τῶν αἰωνίων ἀγαθὴν ἀπόλαυσιν.

Ὅπως Κύριος ὁ Θεὸς χαρίσαται αὐτοῖς πίστιν ἀκαταίσχυντον, ἀγάπην ἀνυπόκριτον, τοῦ Κυρίου δεηθῶμεν.

Ὑπὲρ τοῦ ῥυσθῆναι ἡμᾶς· ἐλέησον ἡμᾶς ὁ Θεός.

λέγεταϊ τὸ κύριε ἐλέησον γ.

iii.

ὁ ἱερεὺς·

ὅτι ἐλεήμων καὶ φιλῶν δέσποτα κύριε· ὁ ποιήσας τὸν ἄνθρωπον κατ᾽ εἰκόνα σὴν καὶ ὁμοίωσιν, ὁ εὐδοκήσας τοὺς ἁγίους σου ἀποστόλους Φίλιππον καὶ Βαρθολομαῖον ἀδελφοὺς γενέσθαι, οὐ δεσμουμένους φύσεως ἀλλὰ πιστέως καὶ πνεύματος τρόπῳ· ὡσαύτως καὶ τοὺς ἁγίους σου μάρτυρας Σέργιον καὶ Βάκχον ἀδελφοὺς γενέσθαι ἀξίωσας· αὐτός εὐλόγησον τοὺς δούλους σου ὁ δεῖνα καὶ ὁ δεῖνα· οὐ δεσμουμένους δέσμῳ φύσεως ἀλλὰ πιστέως καὶ πνεύματος τρόπῳ, δωρούμενος αὐτοῖς εἰρήνην καὶ ἀγάπην καὶ ὁμόνοιαν. Ἀπόσμηξον πάντα σπίλον καὶ ῥύπον ἀπὸ τῶν διανοιῶν αὐτῶν· καὶ δὸς αὐτοῖς τὸ ἀγαπᾶν ἀλλήλους ἀμισήτως καὶ ἀσκανδαλίστως πάσας τὰς ἡμέρας τῆς ζωῆς αὐτῶν· πρεσβείαις τῆς ἁγίας θεοτόκου καὶ πάντῶν τῶν ἁγίων σου, ὅτι πρέπει σοι πᾶσα δόξα.

iv.

Εὐχὴ ἑτέρα εἰς ἀδελφοποίησιν.

Κύριε ὁ Θεὸς ἡμῶν, ὁ πάντα πρός σωτηρίαν ἡμῖν χαρισάμενος, ὁ καὶ ἐντειλά|μενος ἡμῖν ἀγαπᾶν ἀλλήλους, καὶ συγχωρεῖν ἀλλήλων τὰ πταίσματα, αὐτός δέσποτα φιλάγαθε καὶ φιλάνθρωπε καὶ τούτους τοὺς δούλους σου τοὺς πνευματικῇ ἀγάπῃ ἑαυτοὺς ἀγαπήσαντας καὶ προσελθόντας ἐν τῷ ἁγίῳ ναῷ τούτῳ εὐλογηθῆναι καὶ ἁγιασθῆναι, εὐλόγησον καὶ ἁγίασον· χαρίσαι αὐτοῖς πίστιν ἀκαταίσχυντον, ἀγάπην ἀνυπόκριτον· καὶ ὡς ἐδωρήσω τοῖς ἁγίοις σου μαθηταῖς καὶ ἀποστόλοις τὴν σὴν εἰρήνην καὶ τὴν σὴν ἀγάπην, καὶ τούτοις παράσχου Χριστε ὁ Θεὸς ἡμῶν, χαριζόμενος αὐτοῖς πάντα τὰ πρὸς σωτηρίαν αἰτήματα καὶ ζωὴν αἰώνιον. σοὶ[2] γὰρ εἶ τὸ φῶς, τὸ ἀληθικὸν καὶ σοὶ τὴν δόξαν.

[1] Sic.
[2] Sic: sc. σύ.

Καὶ προσκύνουσι τὸ ἅγιον εὐαγγέλιον καὶ τόν ἱερέα καὶ ἀλλήλους, καὶ ἀπολύεταϊ. [3]

v.

Κανὼν ἐκκλησιαστηκὸς ἐπὶ γάμου, ποίημα Μεθοδίου πατριάρχου.

Κύριε ὁ Θεὸς ἡμῶν ὁ τῆς ἀγάπης φυτουργὸς καὶ τῆς εἰρήνης αὐτουργὸς καὶ τῆς σῆς προνοίας χωρηγὸς, ὁ ποιήσας τὰ ἀμφότερα ἕν καὶ ἀποδοὺς ἡμᾶς ἀλλήλοις· ὁ πάντας τοὺς ἀκραιφνοὺς καὶ ἀκαιρεοφόρους εὐλογεῖν ἐπισχνύμενος·[4] αὐτὸν[5] τὴν ὑπὲρ τουτόν σου δεξίαν, τὴν πλήρις[6] χάριτος καὶ οἰκτιρμῶν οὐρανόθεν ἐξαπόστειλον πρὸς τοὺς παρόντας δούλους σου τούτους, καὶ τὴν δεξίαν ἐπισυνοικεσίαν καὶ σύνδεσμον γάμου ἐννόμως δεδωκότας, εὐλόγησον καὶ πλήρωσον ἐπ᾽ αὐτοὺς τὰ ἐλέη σου. Καὶ ἐπενδύων συναθροίσεις πᾶσι χάρισι καὶ θείαις καὶ πνευματικαῖς ἀμαρύγμασιν, εὔφρανον αὐτοὺς ἐν τῇ προσδοκίᾳ τῶν οἰκτιρμῶν σου. Τελείωσον αὐτῶν τὴν συνάφειαν· εἰρήνην καὶ ἀγάπην καὶ ὁμόνοιαν δώρησαι αὐτοῖς· ἀξίωσον αὐτοὺς καὶ τῆς ἐπιθέσεως τῶν στεφάνων καὶ τῆς ἀνωκλήσεως·[7] ἱκεσίαις τῆς κυρίως καὶ ἀληθῶς σὲ κυησάσης καὶ πάντων τῶν ἁγίων σου, νῦν καὶ ἀεί.

vi.

καὶ μετὰ τὴν εὐχὴν ἐπαίρει τὰ στέφη καὶ ἀπολύει αὐτούς.

[3.] In general in these texts the rubrics describing activity (e.g., "the priest says," "the congregation chants," etc.) precede the prescribed words. If that is the case here as well, as I suppose, then the following prayer is the actual dismissal. If, as is also possible, this is the closing rubric of this ceremony, the following prayer is separate, although not necessarily unrelated to the foregoing. See commentary in the notes to the translation of this ceremony in Appendix of Translations.

[4.] *Sic:* I cannot identify this form.

[5.] *Sic:* sc. αὐτός.

[6.] *Sic:* sc. πλήρης or πλήρη.

[7.] *Sic:* sc. ἀνακλήσεως.

2. PARIS BIBLIOTHÈQUE NATIONALE COISLIN 213
[1027/1029 C.E.]

Folio 41r. Translated as No. 5 in Appendix of Translations.

εὐχὴ εἰς ἀδελφοποίησιν.

i.

Κύριε ὁ Θεὸς ἡμῶν, ὁ πάντα πρὸς σωτηρίαν ἡμῖν χαρισάμενος,[8] ὁ[9] ἐντειλάμενος ἡμῖν ἀγαπᾶν ἀλλήλους, καὶ συγχωρεῖν ἀλλήλων τὰ πταίσματα, αὐτὸς καὶ νῦν[10] φιλάγαθε κύριε[11] καὶ[12] τοὺς δούλους σου τοὺς πνευματικῇ ἀγάπῃ ἑαυτοὺς ἀγαπήσαντας καὶ προσελθόντας ἐν τῷ ἁγίῳ σου ναῷ[13] παρὰ[14] σου εὐλογηθῆναι καὶ ἁγιασθῆναι· φύλαξον <αὐτοὺς> ἐν τῷ σῷ ἁγιασμῷ· χάρισαι αὐτοῖς πίστιν ἀκαταίσχυντον, ἀγάπην ἀνυπόκριτον· καὶ ὡς ἐδωρήσω τοῖς ἁγίοις σου μαθηταῖς[15] τὴν σὴν εἰρήνην καὶ τὴν σὴν ἀγάπην, δώρησαι καὶ τούτοις πάντα τὰ πρὸς σωτηρίαν αἰτήματα καὶ ζωὴν αἰώνιον.
ἐκφώνησις.
ὅτι ἐλεήμων καὶ φιλάνθρωπος Θεὸς ὑπάρχεις, καὶ σοι τὴν δόξαν ἀναπέμπομεν· τῷ πατρὶ καὶ τῷ υἱῷ καὶ τῷ ἁγίῳ πνεύματι.
εἰρήνη πᾶσιν.

ii.
ὁ διάκονος· τὰς κεφαλάς.
ὁ ἱερεύς·

---

8. This prayer is one of the most common two components of same-sex union ceremonies, and this is one of the earliest versions of it. The only two earlier copies are Sinai 957 and 958; Grottaferrata Γ.β. II is roughly contemporary. This edition collates the Paris version with the former, and it is immediately juxtaposed with Grottaferrata Γ.β. II, with which it might also be compared. Paris grec 214, 324, and 392 are also similar. The Slavic version of the same prayer, from the twelfth century, is translated on p. 302.
9. Sinai 957 adds καὶ.
10. Sinai 957 adds δέσποτα.
11. Sinai 957 omits κύριε; adds καὶ φιλάνθρωπε.
12. Sinai 957 adds τούτους.
13. Sinai 957 adds τούτῳ.
14. Sinai 957 has ὑπό.
15. Sinai 957 adds καὶ ἀποστόλοις.

iii.

Δέσπωτα[16] κύριε ὁ θεὸς ἡμῶν, ὁ τὸν χορὸν τῶν ἁγίων σου[17] ἀποστόλων ἐκλεξάμενος[18] εἰς[19] μίαν ποίμνην,[20] μίαν ἀδελφότητα,[21] καὶ[22] ἀποστείλας[23] αὐτοὺς εἰς τὰ πέρατα τῆς οἰκουμένης κηρύξαι τὰ σὰ προστάγματα· αὐτὸς εὐλόγησον[24] καὶ νῦν[25] τοὺς δούλους[26] σου·[27] οὓς εὐδόκησας παραστῆναι κατενώπιον τῆς ἁγίας δόξης σου· καὶ ἀδελφοὺς γενέσθαι πνευματικούς·[28] τήρησον αὐτοὺς ἐν τω σῷ[29] ὀνόματι,[30] ἁγίασον αὐτοὺς ἐν τῇ ἀληθείᾳ σου,[31] ἵνα πολιτευσάμενοι κατὰ τὰς ἐντολάς σου[32] κληρονόμοι γένωνται τῆς σῆς[33]βασιλείας,[34] ὅτι σὺ εἶ ὁ δοτὴρ τῶν ἀγαθῶν καὶ σοὶ τὴν δόξαν ἀναπέμπομεν τῷ πατρὶ καὶ τῷ υἱῷ καὶ τῷ ἁγίῳ πνεύματι.

[16.] This is the earliest occurrence of this prayer; it is collated here with Grottaferrata Γ.β. I [11/12] (hereafter = Grottaferrata I); Leningrad Antonin. Euchologion [C13] [=L]; and Istanbul 615 [16] [=I].

[17.] L adds μαθητῶν καὶ.

[18.] L, I: ἐπιλεξάμενος.

[19.] L adds here μίαν ἐκκλησίαν.

[20.] Grottaferrata I omits μίαν ἀδελφότητα, καὶ ἀποστείλας αὐτούς.

[21.] I omits μίαν ἀδελφότητα; adds καὶ ἐκκλεσίαν μίαν.

[22.] L omits καί.

[23.] L, I: ἐξαποστείλας.

[24.] L, I omit εὐλόγησον.

[25.] L adds ὁ Θεὸς ἡμῶν; I omits νῦν.

[26.] L omits σου· οὓς εὐδόκησας παραστῆναι; adds τούτους ὁ δεῖνα, τοὺς προσελθόντας στῆναι.

[27.] I adds τούτους.

[28.] At this point I diverges so completely that it is more efficient simply to quote its concluding lines: οὐ δεσμῷ φύσεως, ἀλλὰ τρόπῳ πίστεως καὶ Πνεύματος Ἁγίου, αὐτός, φιλάνθρωπε, κατάπεμψον τὴν χάριν τοῦ παναγίου σου Πνεύματος εἰς τὸ ἀγαπᾶν ἀλλήλους ἀφθόνως, ἀμίσως, ἀσκανδαλίστως, καὶ ἐν εὐχαριστίᾳ εἶναι αὐτοὺς πάσας τὰς ἡμέρας τῆς ζωῆς αὐτῶν, πρεσβείαις τῆς πανάγνου Δεσποίνης ἡμῶν Θεοτόκου καὶ ἀειπαρθένου Μαρίας καὶ πάντων τῶν ἁγίων σου. Ὅτι ηὐλόγηται καὶ δεδόξασται τὸ πάντιμον καὶ μεγαλοπρεπὲς ὄνομά σου [from Dmitrievskij, p. 744, *litteratim*, including πανάγνου, although I take this to be a misreading of παναγίου].

[29.] L omits σῷ.

[30.] L adds σου καί.

[31.] L omits σου.

[32.] L: κατὰ τὰς ἐντολάς σου πολιτευσάμενοι.

[33.] All other versions omit σῆς.

[34.] All other versions end at σου.

3. PARIS BIBLIOTHÈQUE NATIONALE GREC 330
[twelfth century]

Folios 173–75. Translated as No. 8 in Appendix of Translations.

Collated here with Sinai 1036, a later and slightly better but very similar version. Sinai 971 is identified by Dmitrievskij as beginning with these words, but he says it is the equivalent of Goar 4, which also begins with these words but is significantly different from PG 330. (Goar says that his No. 4 is from Grottaferrata Bessarion, but this is not correct: Bessarion does not contain this prayer. Dmitrievskij does not print the text, and I have been unable to see it.) Istanbul 615 [1522] (full text in Dmitrievskij) is also closely related to this, but significantly different. For further commentary see English translation.

εὐχὴ εἰς ἀδελφοποίσιν[35]

i.

Κύριε ὁ Θεὸς ἡμῶν, ὁ ποιήσας τὸν οὐρανὸν καὶ τὴν γῆν καὶ τὸν ἄνθρωπον κατ' εἰκόνα σὴν καὶ ὁμοίωσιν, καὶ παντί σου χαρίσματι κατακοσμήσας, καὶ δοὺς αὐτῷ ἐξουσίαν ζωῆς αἰδίου, ὁ καὶ[36] εὐδοκίσας[37] τοὺς ἁγίους σου ἀποστόλους Φίλιππον καὶ Βαρθολομαῖον ἀδελφοὺς εὐκλινεῖς[38] γενέσθαι[39] οὐ δεσμουμένους φύσεως ἀλλὰ πνεύματος ἁγίου καὶ πίστεως τρόπῳ· αὐτὸς καὶ νῦν φιλάνθρωπε κύριε καταπέμψον τὴν χάριν τοῦ ἁγίου σου πνεύματος ἐπὶ τοὺς δούλους σου τούτους, οὓς ἠξίωσας ἀδελφοὺς εὐκλινεῖς[40] γενέσθαι, οὐ δεσμουμένους φύσεως ἀλλὰ πνεύματος ἁγίου καί πίστεως τρόπῳ· καὶ δὼς[41] τὴν ἀγάπην σου ἐν αὐτοῖς ἄσυλον, ἀνεπερέαστον[42] μέχρι τῆς ἐσχάτης ἡμῶν[43] ἀναπνοῆς· καὶ δὼς[44] τὴν χάριν σου ἐν αὐτοῖς ἥν ἐδωρίσω[45] τοῖς ἁγίοις σου ἀποστόλοις εὐδοκία καὶ χάριτι.

35. 1036: ἀδελφοποιησίαν.
36. 1036 adds νῦν.
37. Sic: sc. εὐδοκήσας. Correct in 1036.
38. Sic in 330 and in 1036; cf. below.
39. 1036 adds ὁ καὶ τοὺς ἁγίους σου μάρτυρας Σέργιον καὶ Βάκχον ἀδελφοὺς εὐκλινεῖς γενέσθαι.
40. See n. 4.
41. Sic: sc. δός. Correct in 1036.
42. Sic: sc. ἀνεπηρέαστον. 1036 has ἀνεπαιρέαστον, possibly to be understood as "not proud" (cf. 2 Cor. 11:20), but probably an error.
43. Sic: sc. αὐτῶν, as in 1036.
44. Sic: sc. δός, as in 1036.
45. Sic: sc. ἐδώρησω.

4. VATICANUS GRAECUS 1811 [1147]

Italo-Greek(?).⁴⁶ Folios 52–54. Translated as No. 9 in
Appendix of Translations.

ἀκολουθεία εἰς ἀδελφοποίησιν

i.
τίθησιν <ὁ ἱερεὺς>⁴⁷ τὸ ἅγιον εὐαγγέλλιον ἐν τῷ ἀναλογίῳ καὶ
ἐπιτίθησιν [sic] οἱ ἀδελφοὶ τὰς χεῖρας ἐπ' αὐτῷ κρατοῦντες
ἅπτοντα<ς> κηροὺς εἰς τὰς ἀριστερᾶς χειράς, καὶ θυμιᾶ αὐτοὺς καὶ
λέγει ὁ διάκονος·
εὐλόγησον δέσποτα.

ii.
<ὁ ἱερεὺς>⁴⁸ εὐλογημένη ἡ βασιλεία τοῦ πατρὸς, <καὶ τοῦ υἱοῦ, καὶ
τοῦ ἁγίου πνεύματος, νῦν καὶ ἀεί>.

εἶτα ὁ διάκονος·

Ἐν εἰρήνη <τοῦ Κυρίου δεηθῶμεν>.

Ὑπὲρ τῆς ἄνωθεν εἰρήνης

Ὑπὲρ τῆς εἰρήνης τοῦ σ<ύμπαντος κόσμου>

Ὑπὲρ τοῦ εὐλογηθῆναι τοὺς δούλους σου ὅδε καὶ ὅδε εὐλογήᾳ [sic]
πνευματικῇ, τοῦ Κυρίου δεηθῶμεν.

Ὑπὲρ τοῦ διαφυλαχθῆναι τὴν τούτων ἀγάπην ἀμίσιτον [sic] καὶ
ἀσκανανδάλιστον μέχρι βίον ζωῆς αὐτῶν, τοῦ Κυρίου δεηθῶμεν.

Ὑπὲρ τοῦ δωρεθῆναι αὐτοῖς πάντα τὰ πρὸς σωτηρίαν αἰτήματα καὶ
τῶν αἰωνίων ἀγαθῶν τῆς ἀπολαύσεως, τοῦ Κυρίου δεηθῶμεν.

⁴⁶· The Vatican catalogue of this manuscript compares its version of this ceremony to Goar, pp.
706–9, which is actually his version of Grottaferrata Γ.β. III, but it seems to me to be more
like Γ.β. II, with which it has been compared (though not precisely collated) here. Fols. 31v–
33 in 1811 contain a service called εὐχὴ εἰς εὐλογίαν διγαμίας· ποίημα Μεθοδίου
πατριάρχου, at the end of which the priest joins the couple by their right hands, then adds a
prayer from the ceremony of same-sex union. Cf. Vat. Gr. 1872, fol. 133.

⁴⁷· In the manuscript there is a drawing of a head with eyes.

⁴⁸· See n. 47.

Όπως Κύριος ὁ Θεὸς χαρίσηται αὐτοῖς πίστιν ἀκαταίσχυντον, ἀγάπην ἀνυπόκριτον, τοῦ Κυρίου δεηθῶμεν.

Ὑπὲρ τοῦ ῥυσθῆναι αὐτοὺς καὶ ἡμᾶς ἀπὸ πάσης θλίψεως, τοῦ Κυρίου δεηθῶμεν.

ἐλέησον ἡμᾶς ὁ Θεός.

κατὰ τὸ μέγα ἔλεος σου.[49]

λέγεται τὸ κύριε ἐλέησον γ".

<ὁ ἱερεὺς>·[50] ὅτι ἐλεήμων καὶ φιλάνθρωπος θεὸς ὑπάρχεις.

iii.
Εὐχὴ ᾱ.

Κύριε ὁ Θεός, ὁ παντοκράτωρ, ὁ ποιήσας τὸν ἄνθρωπον κατ᾽ εἰκόνα σὴν καὶ ὁμοίωσιν, καὶ δοὺς αὐτῷ ἐξουσίαν ζωῆς ἀϊδίου, ὁ εὐδοκήσας τοὺς ἁγίους σου ἀποστόλους Φίλιππον καὶ Βαρθολομαῖον ἀδελφοὺς γενέσθαι, οὐ δεσμουμένους φύσεως νόμῳ ἀλλὰ πνεύματος ἁγίου καὶ πίστεως τρόπῳ· ὁ καὶ τοὺς ἁγίους σου μάρτυρας Σέργιον καὶ Βάκχον ἀδελφοὺς γενέσθαι πνευματικούς· αὐτὸς φιλάνθρωπε Κύριε κατάπεμψον τὴν χάριν τοῦ ἁγίου πνεύματός σου ἐπὶ τοὺς δούλους σου τούτους, οὓς καταξιώσας ἀδελφοὺς γενέσθαι, οὐ δεσμομένους φύσεως τρόπῳ ἀλλὰ πίστεως καὶ πνεύματος ἁγίου· δὸς αὐτοῖς τὴν χάριν σου εἰς τὸ ἀγαπᾶν ἀλλήλους ἀφθόνως καὶ ἀμισήτως ἐν εὐχαριστίᾳ πάσας τὰς ἡμέρας τῆς ζωῆς αὐτῶν, πρεσβείαις τῆς ὑπεραγίας θεοτόκου καὶ πάντων τῶν ἁγίων σου, ὅτι εὐλογητὸς εἶ καὶ δεδοξασμένος πάντοτε νῦν καὶ ἀεί.

iv.
Εὐχὴ β̄.

Κύριε ὁ Θεὸς ἡμῶν, ὁ ἐντειλά|μενος ἡμῖν ἀγαπᾶν ἀλλήλους, καὶ συγχωρεῖν ἀλλήλων τὰ πταίσματα, αὐτός δέσποτα φιλάγαθε καὶ πολυέλεε καὶ τοὺς δούλους σου τούτους τοὺς πνευματικῇ ἀγάπῃ ἑαυτοὺς ἀγαπήσαντας καὶ ἐν τῷ ναῷ τούτῳ ὑπὸ σοῦ εὐλογηθῆναι εἰσελθόντας· χάρισαι αὐτοῖς πίστιν ἀκαταίσχυντον, ἀγάπην ἀνυπόκριτον· καὶ ὡς ἐδωρήσω τοῖς ἁγίοις σου μαθηταῖς καὶ

---

[49] Cf. Liturgy of the Presanctified, ed. Brightman, p. 345.
[50] See n. 47.

ἀποστόλοις τὴν σὴν εἰρήνην καὶ τὴν σὴν ἀγάπην, οὕτως καὶ τοῖς δούλοις σου τούτοις χάρισαι πάντα τὰ πρὸς σωτηρίαν αἰτήματα, ὅτι πρέπει σοι πᾶσα δόξα, τιμή, καὶ προσκύνησις.

v.

καὶ εἶθ᾽ ἀσπάζονται τὸ ἅγιον εὐαγγέλιον καὶ τὸν ἱερέα καὶ ἀλλήλους, καὶ ἀπολύει αὐτοὺς λέγων, ὁ Κύριος τῆς εἰρήνης καὶ τῆς ἀγάπης ἔσται[51] μεθ᾽ ὑμῶν. ἀμῖν.

5. SINAI 966 [thirteenth century][52]

Folios 82–85. Translated as No. 10 in Appendix of Translations.

Ἀκολουθία καὶ τάξις εἰς ἀδελφοποίησιν

i.[53]

Προσέρχονται οἱ μέλλοντες ἀδελφοὶ γενέσθαι τῷ ἱερεῖ καὶ αὐτὸς τίθησιν τὸ εὐαγγέλιον εἰς τὸ στῆθος τοῦ θυσιαστηρίου, καὶ ὁ πρῶτος ἀδελφὸς τίθησι τὴν χεῖρα αὐτοῦ ἐπάνω τοῦ εὐαγγελίου καὶ ὁ δεύτερος ἐπάνω τῆς χειρὸς τοῦ πρώτου ἀδελφοῦ, καὶ εἶθ᾽ οὕτως σφραγίσας αὐτοὺς ὁ ἱερεὺς λέγει τὴν συναπτήν·

ii.

Ἐν εἰρήνῃ τοῦ Κυρίου δεηθῶμεν.

Ὑπὲρ τῆς ἄνωθεν εἰρήνης, τοῦ Κυρίου δεηθῶμεν.

Ὑπὲρ τῆς εἰρήνης τοῦ σύμπαντος κόσμου, τοῦ Κυρίου δεηθῶμεν.

Ὑπὲρ τῶν δούλων τοῦ Θεοῦ τόνδε καὶ τόνδε καὶ τῆς ἐν Χριστῷ ἀγαπήσεως, τοῦ Κυρίου δεηθῶμεν.

Ὑπὲρ τοῦ δωρηθῆναι αὐτοῖς πνευματικὴν ἀγάπην καὶ τὴν εἰς ἀλλήλους τιμήν, τοῦ Κυρίου δεηθῶμεν.

51. Sic: for ἔστω.
52. Dmitrievskij publishes a partial text, p. 215.
53. Although not identical, both this and the following section resemble Vatican Barberini Grec 345 (twelfth century) and Grottaferrata Γ.β. III (fourteenth century).

Ὅπως Κύριος ὁ Θεὸς ἡμῶν δωρήσηται αὐτοῖς βίον ἄμεμπτον καὶ πολιτείαν εὐάρεστον, τοῦ Κυρίου δεηθῶμεν.

Ὑπὲρ τοῦ ῥυσθῆναι αὐτούς τε καὶ ἡμᾶς ἀπὸ πάσης θλίψεως, τοῦ Κυρίου δεηθῶμεν.

iii.[54]

Ἀντιλαβοῦ. Σῶσον. Ἐλέησον.

iv.

Τῆς παναγίας ἀχράντου <ὑπερευλογημένης ἐνδόξου δεσποίνης ἡμῶν Θεοτόκου καὶ ἀειπαρθένου Μαρίας μετὰ πάντων τῶν ἁγίων μνημονεύσαντες ἑαυτοὺς καὶ ἀλλήλους καὶ πᾶσαν τήν ζωήν ἡμῶν Χριστῷ τῷ Θεῷ παραθώμεθα.>

v.

Κύριε ὁ Θεὸς ἡμῶν, ὁ παντοκράτωρ, ὁ ποιήσας τὸν ἄνθρωπον κατ᾽ εἰκόνα σὴν καὶ ὁμοίωσιν, καὶ δοὺς αὐτῷ ἐξουσίαν ζωῆς ἀϊδίου, ὁ εὐδοκήσας τοὺς ἁγίους σου ἀποστόλους Φίλιππον καὶ Βαρθολομαῖον ἀδελφοὺς γενέσθαι, οὐ δεσμουμένους φύσεως νόμῳ, ἀλλὰ πίστεως τρόπῳ· ὁ καὶ τοὺς ἁγίους σου μάρτυρας Σέργιον καὶ Βάκχον στηρίξας ἀδελφοὺς γενέσθαι, οὐ δεσμουμένους φύσεως νόμῳ, ἀλλὰ πνεύματος ἁγίου καὶ πιστέως τρόπῳ, δὼς αὐτοῖς χάριν τοῦ ἀγαπᾶν ἀλλήλους, ἀμισήτους καὶ ἀσκανδαλίστους εἶναι πάσας τὰς ἡμέρας τῆς ζωῆς αὐτῶν· πρεσβείαις τῆς ἁγίας θεοτόκου καὶ πάντων ἁγίων σου.

ὅτι σὺ εἶ ἡ ἕνωσις καὶ ἀσφάλεια καὶ ὁ δεσμὸς τῆς εἰρήνης, καὶ σοὶ τὴν δόξαν ἀναπέμπομεν.

Εἰρήνη ὑμῖν.

Τὰς κεφαλὰς ὑμῶν.

vi.

Κύριε ὁ Θεὸς ἡμῶν, ὁ πάντα πρός σωτηρίαν ἡμῖν χαρησάμενος,[55] ὁ καὶ ἐντειλάμενος ἡμῖν ἀγαπᾶν ἀλλήλους, καὶ συγχωρεῖν τὰ παραπτώματα, αὐτός δέσποτα φιλάνθρωπε καὶ φιλάγαθε καὶ τούτους ἀγαπήσαντας καὶ προσελθόντας[56] ἐν τῷ ἁγίῳ ναῷ τούτῳ ὑπὸ σοῦ

[54.] This is a standard part of the Greek Mass, known at least since the ninth century and part of the modern Liturgy of St. John Chrysostom.

[55.] *Sic*; in most texts given as χαρισάμενος.

[56.] *Sic*.

εὐλογηθῆναι, χαρίσαι[57] αὐτοῖς πίστιν ἀκαταίσχυντον, ἀγάπην ἀνυπόκριτον· καὶ ὡς ἐδωρήσω τοῖς ἁγίοις σου ἀποστόλοις καὶ μαθηταῖς τὴν σὴν εἰρήνην καὶ τὴν σὴν ἀγάπην, οὕτοις καὶ τούτοις παράσχου Χριστε ὁ Θεὸς ἡμῶν, πάντα τὰ πρὸς σωτηρίαν αἰτήματα καὶ ζωὴν αἰώνιον.

σὺ γὰρ εἶ τὸ φῶς, τὸ ἀληθινὸν καὶ ζωὴν αἰώνιον, καὶ σοὶ τὴν δόξαν.

vii.[58]

Κύριε ὁ Θεὸς ἡμῶν, ὁ διὰ τῆς ἀφάτου σου οἰκονομίας καταξιώσας ἀδελφοὺς καλέσαι τοὺς ἁγίους ἀποστόλους καὶ κληρονόμους τῆς βασιλείας σου, αὐτοὺς τοὺς δούλους σου τόνδε καὶ τόνδε ἀδελφοὺς πνευματικοὺς[59] ἀνάδειξον καὶ ἐν μέσῳ αὐτῶν γενέσθαι καταξίωσον, ἀσκανδαλίστους αὐτοὺς ἀνάδειξον καὶ ἐν μέσῳ αὐτῶν γενέσθαι καταξίωσον, ἀσκανδαλίστους[60] ἐκ τῶν μεθοδιῶν τοῦ διαβόλου καὶ τῶν πονηρῶν αὐτοῦ πνευμάτων, ὅπως ἐν ἀρετῇ καὶ δικαιοσύνῃ προκόπτοντας καὶ ἀγάπῃ εἰλικρηνῆι, δοξάζηται δι' αὐτῶν καὶ δι' ἡμῶν πάντων τὸ πανάγιον ὄνομα σου τοῦ Πατρὸς καὶ τοῦ Υἱοῦ καὶ τοῦ Ἁγίου Πνεύματος, νῦν καὶ ἀεί.

viii.

Κύριε ὁ Θεὸς ἡμῶν, ὁ ἐνδοξαζόμενος ἐν βουλῇ ἁγίων, ὁ μέγας καὶ φοβερὸς ὑπάρχων ἐπὶ πάντας τοὺς περικύκλῳ σου,[61] εὐλόγησον καὶ[62] τοὺς δούλους σου τούτους,[63] χάρισαι αὐτοῖς τὴν γνῶσιν τοῦ Ἁγίου σου Πνεύματος· ὁδήγησον αὐτοὺς ἐν τῷ ἁγίῳ φόβῳ σου,[64] εὔφρανον αὐτοὺς ἐν τῇ δυνάμει σου,[65] ἵνα γένονται[66] πνευματικοὶ ἀδελφοὶ ὑπὲρ τοὺς σαρκικούς. ὅτι σὺ εἶ ὁ εὐλογῶν καὶ ἁγιάζων τὰ σύμπαντα[67] καὶ σοι τὴν δόξαν.

[57.] Sic; sc. χαρίσαι.
[58.] Unique to this manuscript.
[59.] The text is unclear from here to following note, probably due to a copying error. See next note for details.
[60.] ἀνάδειξον καὶ ἐν μέσῳ αὐτῶν γενέσθαι καταξίωσον, ἀσκανδαλίστους is repeated by mistake in the MS, with αὐτούς substituted for the πνευματικούς in the first occurrence of the phrase.
[61.] Grottaferrata Γ.β. VII: αὐτοῦ.
[62.] Grottaferrata Γ.β. VII omits καί.
[63.] Grottaferrata Γ.β. VII: τοὺς Δ.
[64.] Grottaferrata Γ.β. VII: ἐν τῷ φόβῳ σου τῷ ἁγίῳ.
[65.] Grottaferrata Γ.β. VII omits ἐν τῇ δυνάμει σου.
[66.] Sic: sc. γένωνται, as in Grottaferrata Γ.β. VII.
[67.] Grottaferrata Γ.β. VII omits τὰ σύμπαντα; adds τοὺς ἐπὶ σοὶ πεποιθότας.

ix.

Κύριε[68] ὁ Θεὸς ἡμῶν, ὁ ἐν ὑψιλοῖς[69] κατοικῶν, καὶ τὰ ταπεινὰ ἐφορῶν,[70] ὁ διὰ τὴν σωτηρίαν τοῦ γένους τῶν ἀνθρώπων ἐξαπέστειλας τὸν μονογενῆ σου υἱὸν τὸν Κύριον ἡμῶν, Ἰῆσον Χριστόν, καὶ[71] ὑποδεξάμενος Πέτρον καὶ Παῦλον, Πέτρον μὲν[72] ἀπὸ Καισαρίας τῆς Φιλίππου, Παῦλον δὲ ἀπὸ Ταρσοῦ[73] τῆς Κηλικίας,[74] ποιήσας αὐτοὺς κατὰ πνεῦμα ἅγιον[75] ἀδελφούς· ποίησον καὶ τοὺς δούλους σου τούτους[76] ὡς αὐτοὺς τοὺς δύω ἀποστόλους·[77] ἀμέμπτους αὐτοὺς διατήρησον πάσας τὰς ἡμέρας τῆς ζωῆς αὐτῶν, ὅτι ὑγίασται[78] καὶ δεδόξασται τό πάντιμον καὶ μεγαλοπρεπὲς ὄνομα σου, τοῦ πατρὸς καὶ τοῦ υἱοῦ καὶ τοῦ ἁγίου πνεύματος, νῦν καὶ ἀεί.

Καὶ ἀσπασάμενοι τὸ ἅγιον εὐαγγέλιον καὶ εἶθ᾽ οὕτως ἀλλήλους, καὶ ἀπολύεται.

6. MOUNT ATHOS PANTELEIMON 780
[sixteenth century]

Folios 60–62. Translated as No. 13 in Appendix of Translations.

ἀκολουθία εἰς ἀδελφοποίησιν

i.

ποιεῖ ὁ ἱερεὺς εὐλογητὸν, τρισάγιον, παναγίας τριάς, πατὲρ ἡμῶν, ὅτι σοῦ ἐστιν, ἀπολυτίκιον τῆς ἡμέρας, καὶ κοντάκιον καὶ τοῦ ἁγίου τῆς μονῆς, ὡσαύτως καὶ τὸ κοντάκιον καὶ θεοτοκίον.

[68] Collated here with Vatican Barberini Grec 345, the best earlier (twelfth century) version of this prayer, and with Barberini Grec 329, also twelfth century.
[69] 329: ὑψιστοῖς.
[70] Ps. 112:5–6: ὁ ἐν ὑψηλοῖς κατοικῶν καὶ τὰ ταπεινὰ ἐφορῶν.
[71] 345 and 329: ὁ.
[72] 345 and 329 omit μὲν.
[73] 345 and 329: Τηβέριων.
[74] 345 and 329 omit τῆς Κηλικίας. In the New Testament this name is spelled Κιλικία.
[75] 345 and 329 insert καὶ ἐνέγκας αὐτοὺς καὶ ἐποίησας κατ᾽ ἁγιωσύνην; omit ποιήσας αὐτοὺς κατὰ πνεῦμα ἅγιον.
[76] 345 and 329: τούτους τοὺς δούλους σου; add ὅδε καὶ ὅδε.
[77] 345 omits δύω.
[78] 345 and 329: ἡγίασται.

εἶτα τίθησιν τὸ ἅγιον εὐαγγέλιον ἐν τῷ ἀναλογίῳ καὶ τίθησι τὰς δεξιὰς χεῖρας ἐπάνω αὐτοῦ οἱ μέλλοντες ἀδελφοὶ ποιηθῆναι, κρατοῦσι δὲ κηροὺς ἅπτοντας.

ii.
καὶ ὁ ἱερεὺς λέγει τὰς εὐχὰς μεγαλοφώνως·

'Αγαπητοί[79] ἠκούσατε τὴν εὐαγγελικὴν φωνὴν τὴν λέγουσαν, τοῦ Κυρίου δεήθωμεν,[80]

ταῦτα ἐντέλλομαι ὑμῖν ἵνα ἀγαπᾶτε[81] ἀλλήλους,[82]

iii.
καὶ τοῦ μεγάλου Παύλου λέγοντος,

ἡ ἀγάπη οὐ ζηλοῖ, ἡ ἀγάπη οὐ περπορεύεται,[83] οὐκ ἀσχημονεῖ, ἡ ἀγάπη οὐ ζητεῖ τὰ ἑαυτῆς, οὐ λογίζεται τὸ κακόν,[84] ἡ ἀγάπη οὐδέποτε ἐκπίπτει.[85]

ἐν Χριστῷ[86] τῷ Θεῷ[87] ἡμῶν, ὡς καὶ[88] Δαβὶδ προφητικῶς[89] φάσκει·

ἰδοὺ δὴ τί καλόν, ἢ τί τερπνὸν ἀλλ' ἢ τὸ κατοικεῖν ἀδελφοὺς[90]

ἅμα ἐν ἀγάπῃ Θεοῦ. πορεύεσθε πάντοτε νῦν καὶ ἀεὶ καὶ εἰς τοὺς αἰῶνας τῶν αἰώνων, ἀμην.

iv.
εἶτα λέγει τὴν συναπτήν·

---

[79] From this point until indicated collated with Mt. Athos Panteleimon 149, and through it with Istanbul 8(182) [=Ist.]. Ist. has ' Αδελφοί here.

[80] 149 and Ist. omit τοῦ Κυρίου δεήθωμεν.

[81] MS has ἀγαπαπάτε.

[82] John 15:17.

[83] Sic: sc. περπερεύεται. Ist. adds οὐ φυσιοῦται.

[84] 149 and Ist. omit ἡ ἀγάπη οὐ ζητεῖ τὰ ἑαυτῆς, οὐ λογίζεται τὸ κακόν.

[85] 1 Cor. 13:4,8.

[86] 149 adds Ἰησοῦ.

[87] 149 has Κυρίῳ.

[88] 149 omits καὶ.

[89] 149: προφητηκῶς.

[90] Ps. 132:1 LXX.

Ἐν εἰρήνῃ, τοῦ Κυρίου δεήθωμεν.

Ὑπὲρ τῆς ἄνωθεν εἰρήνης καὶ τῆς σωτηρίας τῶν ψυχῶν ἡμῶν,[91] τοῦ Κυρίου δεήθωμεν.

Ὑπὲρ τῆς εἰρήνης τοῦ σύμπαντος κόσμου, εὐσταθίσας τῶν ἁγίων τοῦ Θεοῦ ἐκκλασιῶν καὶ τῆς τῶν πάντων ἑνώσεως,[92] τοῦ Κυρίου δεήθωμεν.

Ὑπὲρ τοῦ ἁγίου οἴκου τούτου[93] καὶ τῶν μετὰ πίστεως, εὐλαβείας καὶ φόβου Θεοῦ εἰσιόντων ἐν αὐτῷ, τοῦ Κυρίου δεήθωμεν.[94]

Ὑπὲρ τοῦ ἀρχιεπισκόπου ἡμῶν, τοῦ τιμίου πρεσβυτερίου [sic] τῆς ἐν Χριστῷ διακονίας, παντὸς τοῦ κλήρου καὶ τοῦ λαοῦ, τοῦ Κυρίου δεήθωμεν.[95]

Ὑπὲρ τῶν δούλων τοῦ Θεοῦ ὅδεινα καὶ ὅδεινα καὶ τῆς ἐκ Θεοῦ ἀγάπης αὐτῶν,[96] τοῦ Κυρίου δεήθωμεν.[97]

Ὅπως Κύριος ὁ Θεὸς ἡμῶν χαρίσῃ[98] τὴν ἀγάπην αὐτῶν ἀνυπόκριτον, τοῦ Κυρίου δεήθωμεν.

Ὑπὲρ τοῦ ῥυσθῆναι ἡμᾶς ἀπὸ πάσης θλίψεως,[99] ὀργῆς, καὶ ἀνάγκης, τοῦ Κυρίου δεήθωμεν.[100]

v.
Ἀντιλαβοῦ, σῶσον, ἐλέησον καὶ διαφύλαξον ἡμᾶς.[101]

ὁ Θεὸς τῇ σῇ χάριτι.[102]

---

91. 149 omits καὶ τῆς σωτηρίας τῶν ψυχῶν ἡμῶν.
92. 149 omits εὐσταθίσας τῶν ἁγίων τοῦ Θεοῦ ἐκκλασιῶν καὶ τῆς τῶν πάντων ἑνώσεως.
93. 149 adds here καὶ τῆς σωτηρίας τῶν ψυχῶν; omits remainder.
94. Missing in Ist.
95. Missing in Ist.
96. 149: τοῦ δούλου τοῦ Θεοῦ ὅδε καὶ ὅδε.
97. Ist.: ὑπὲρ τῶν δούλων τοῦ Θεοῦ οἱ δεῖνοι καὶ τῆς ἐν Θεῷ ἀγάπης αὐτῶν.
98. 149: χαρίσει.
99. 149 omits remainder.
100. Shortened in Ist., as printed by Dmitrievskij.
101. Shortened in Ist., as printed by Dmitrievskij.
102. 149 and Ist. omit this line.

vi.

Τῆς παναγίας ἀχράντου[103] <ὑπερευλογημένης ἐνδόξου δεσποίνης ἡμῶν Θεοτόκου καὶ ἀειπαρθένου Μαρίας μετὰ πάντων τῶν ἁγίων μνημονεύσαντες ἑαυτοὺς καὶ ἀλλήλους καὶ πᾶσαν τὴν ζωήν ἡμῶν Χριστῷ τῷ Θεῷ παραθώμεθα.>

ἐκφώνησις.[104]

vii.

῞Οτι πρέπει σοι[105] πᾶσα δόξα, τιμὴ καὶ προσκύνησις,[106] τῷ πατρὶ καὶ τῷ υἱῷ καὶ τῷ ἁγίῳ πνεύματι.

εἰρήνη πᾶσιν. τὰς κεφαλὰς ὑμῶν τῷ Κυρίῳ κλίνατε.[107]

viii.

Καὶ[108] ἀλ<λ>άσσουν τὰς χεῖρας αὐτῶν ἐν τῷ ἁγίῳεὐαγγελίῳ. ὁ ἔχων[109] ἄνω τίθησιν[110] ὑποκάτω.

εἶτα ἐπεύχεται ὁ ἱερεὺς λέγων τὴν εὐχὴν ταύτην· τοῦ Κυρίου δεήθωμεν·[111]

ix.

Δέσποτα[112] Κύριε ὁ Θεὸς ἡμῶν, ὁ ποιήσας[113] τὸν ἄνθρωπον κατ' εἰκόνα σὴν καὶ ὁμοίωσιν, καὶ δοὺς[114] αὐτῷ ἐξουσίαν πάσης[115] σαρκὸς ἀϊδίου,[116] ὁ[117] εὐδοκήσας[118] τοὺς ἁγίους σου[119] ἀποστόλους Φίλιππον καὶ Βαρθολομαῖον ἀδελφοὺς γενέσθαι, οὐ δεσμουμένους

---

103. 149 adds ὑπερευλογημένα.
104. Missing in 149 and Ist.
105. Ist. ends here, as printed in Dmitrievskij.
106. 149 and Ist. omit remainder.
107. Missing in 149; Ist.: ᾿Εν εἰρήνη πᾶσι. Τὰς κεφαλὰς ὑμῶν.
108. This sentence missing in Ist. at this point, but a shorter version, specifying the exchange of hands and not mentioning the Gospel, is inserted after the first prayer.
109. 149 adds τὴν χεῖραν.
110. 149 adds αὐτήν.
111. This sentence is missing in Ist., which has in its place ᾿Εν εἰρήνη πᾶσι. Τὰς κεφαλὰς ὑμῶν.
112. Collated with Vatican Barberini Grec 329, the closest earlier version, and with Istanbul 615, a contemporary (1552) variant (translted above in its entirety, pp. 331–34).
113. 615 adds here τὸν οὐρανὸν καὶ τὴν γῆν, καὶ ποιήσας καὶ πλάσας.
114. Mt. Athos Panteleimon 149: δός.
115. Dmitrievskij gives for 615 πᾶσι, but this must be an error.
116. 329 omits ἀϊδίου.
117. 615 adds here καὶ νῦν.
118. Panteleimon 149: εὐλογίσας.
119. 615 adds here μαθητὰς καί.

φύσεως,[120] ἀλλὰ πνεύματος ἁγίου κοινωνία, [121] ὁ καὶ[122] τοὺς ἁγίους σου μάρτυρας Σέργιον καὶ Βάκχον ἀδελφοὺς γενέσθαι ἀξιώσας,[123] αὐτὸς εὐλόγησον[124] καὶ τούς δούλους σου τούτους, ὅδεινα καὶ ὅδεινα,[125] οὐ δεσμουμένους φύσεως ἀλλὰ[126] πιστέως τρόπῳ· δὸς αὐτοῖς, Κύριε, τοῦ[127] ἀγαπᾶν ἀλλήλους[128] ἀμισήτους καὶ ἀσκανδαλίστους εἶναι πάσας τὰς ἡμέρας τῆς ζωῆς αὐτῶν· πρεσβείαις τῆς ἁγίας Θεοτόκου[129] καὶ πάντων τῶν ἁγίων σου.[130] ὅτι σὸν τὸ κράτος καὶ σοῦ ἐστιν ἡ βασιλεία[131] καὶ ἡ δύναμις καὶ ἡ δόξα, τοῦ πατρὸς καὶ τοῦ υἱοῦ καὶ τοῦ ἁγίου πνεύματος.

x.

τοῦ Κυρίου δεήθωμεν·[132]

Κύριε[133] ὁ Θεὸς ἡμῶν,[134] ὁ ἐν τῇ κατὰ σάρκα σου οἰκονομίᾳ Ἰάκωβον καὶ Ἰωάννην,[135] υἱοὺς Ζεβεδαίου,[136] οὐ κατηξίωσας[137] ἀδελφοὺς γενέσθαι,[138] ἀλλὰ[139] μαθητὰς καὶ ἀποστόλους[140] ἀναδείξας· αὐτὸς καὶ νῦν,[141] τοὺς δούλους σου τούτους[142] τοὺς

120. 329 adds δεσμῷ.
121. 329 adds καὶ πίστεως τρόπῳ; 615 omits πνεύματος ἁγίου κοινωνία, adds ἀλλὰ πίστεως τρόπῳ.
122. 329 and 615 omit καί.
123. 149: καταξιώσας; 329 and 615 have καταξιώσας.
124. 615 omits αὐτὸς εὐλόγησον.
125. 329 omits ὅδεινα καὶ ὅδεινα; 615 has τόνδε καὶ ὁ δεῖνα.
126. 329 adds here πνεύματος ἁγίου καί.
127. 329 omits Κύριε, τοῦ; 615 omits Κύριε.
128. Dmitrievskij prints an additional καί here for 615, which makes sense but is wanting in both 329 and 149.
129. 329 ends thus: ἀεὶ παρθένου Μαρίας, ὅτι πρέπει σοι πᾶσα δόξα, τιμὴ καὶ προσκύνησις, τῷ Πατρί, καὶ Υἱῷ, καὶ τῷ Ἁγίῳ Πνεύματι, νῦν καὶ ἀεὶ καὶ εἰς τοὺς αἰῶνας; 615 adds a long final invocation: see Dmitrievskij, p. 743, and translation on p. 333.
130. 149 omits σου.
131. 149 concludes here.
132. 149 adds here καὶ πάλιν ἀλάσσουν τὰς χεῖρας καὶ ὁ ἱερεὺς εὔχεται, τοῦ Κυρίου δεήθωμεν.
133. Collated here with Vatican Greek 1552, the earliest known occurrence of this prayer, and with Istanbul 8 (182) [15] and Mt. Athos Laura Athan. 129 [15].
134. 129 adds φέσποτα; omits ὁ Θεός ἡμῶν.
135. 1552 and 129 add here τούς.
136. Ist. and 129: Ζεβαιδέου.
137. 1552 has καπïξιώσας, possibly οὐκ ἀπïξιώσας, although there is no breathing over the α. Ist. and 129 have κατάξιώσας without a negative, although ἀλλά in both suggests there was one, and the passage is little clearer in them.
138. 1552 reads καλέσαι.
139. 129 adds καί here.
140. τούτους τοῦ has been crossed out here; 149 adds σου here.
141. 1552 adds Δέσποτα Κύριε here.
142. Ist. and 129 add ὅδε καὶ ὅδε (or: ὁ δεῖνα καὶ ὁ δεῖνα).

πνευματικὴν ἀγάπην[143] ἑαυτοὺς ἀγαπήσαντας,[144] ἐν εἰρήνῃ καὶ ὁμονοίᾳ δϊατήρησον[145] πάσας τὰς ἡμέρας[146] τῆς ζωῆς αὐτῶν, ἐργαζομένους τὰς ἐντολάς σου. καὶ[147] κατεύθυνον[148] τὴν ὁδὸν[149] αὐτῶν,[150] τὴν λαμπάδα αὐτῶν ἄσβεστον διατήρησον, συγκαταρίθμων[151] αὐτοὺς μετὰ τῶν πέντε φρονίμων παρθένων.[152] σῶσον,[153] ἐλέησον αὐτοὺς ἕνεκεν τοῦ ὀνόματός σου τὸ ἐπεκεκλημένον[154] ὑπ'[155] αὐτοὺς καὶ[156] καταξίωσαν αὐτούς χάριν εὑρεῖν[157] ἐνώπιόν[158] σου, ὅτι οὐκ ἦν τὰ σαρκικὰ ὡς τὰ πνευματικά.

ὅτι ἐλεήμων καὶ φιλάνθρωπος Θεὸς ὑπάρχεις, καὶ σοι τὴν δόξαν ἀναπέμπομεν τῷ πατρὶ καὶ τῷ υἱῷ καὶ τῷ ἁγίῳ πνεύματι. ἀμήν.[159]

xi.
τοῦ Κυρίου δεήθωμεν.[160]

Κύριε ὁ Θεὸς ἡμῶν, ὁ συναθροίσας τοὺς ἁγίους σου ἀποστόλους ἐν νεφέλαις καὶ ἑνώσας αὐτοὺς ἐνταῦθα ἀδελφοὺς ἐν φιλήματι ἁγίῳ, εἰς εἰρήνην[161] καὶ σοφροσύνην· εἰς ἀγάπην ἀνυπόκριτον καὶ εἰς ἔργα ἀγαθὰ ἐργαζομένους τὰς ἐντολάς σου, χάριτι καὶ οἰκτιρμοῖς καὶ φιλανθρωπίᾳ τοῦ μονογενοῦς σου Υἱοῦ, μεθ' οὗ εὐλογητὸς εἶ, σὺν τῷ παναγίῳ καὶ ἀγαθῷ καὶ ζωοποιῷ σου πνεύματι. ἀμήν.

[143.] In all other versions this is in the dative.
[144.] Other versions read ἀδελφοὺς ὀνομάσαντας.
[145.] Variant spelling in 1552.
[146.] Ist. and 129 omit ἡμέρας τῆς.
[147.] Other versions omit καί.
[148.] Variant spelling in 1552.
[149.] Other versions give τὰς ὁδούς.
[150.] 1552 and 129 add καὶ περϊτείχϊσον τὰς ψυχὰς αὐτῶν here.
[151.] Ist. and 129 have συγκαταρίθμησον.
[152.] 1552 omits παρθένων here.
[153.] 1552 adds καί.
[154.] 1552 and 129 have τοῦ ἐπεκεκλημένου, which is grammatically correct. Istanbul agrees with 149.
[155.] 149 reads ἐπ'; 1552 has εἰς.
[156.] Ist. and 129 have ἐφ' ἡμᾶς· δώρησαι αὐτοῖς.
[157.] 1552 and Ist. have εὑρεῖν χάριν; 129 omits εὑρεῖν.
[158.] 1552 adds τοῦ Χριστοῦ.
[159.] Abbreviated by Dmitrievskij; 1552 ends: ἵνα καὶ ἐν τούτῳ δοξασθῆναι τὸ πανάγιον ὄνομα τοῦ πατρὸς καὶ τοῦ υἱοῦ καὶ τοῦ ἁγίου πνεύματος, νῦν καὶ ἀεὶ καὶ εἰς τὰς αἰῶνας τῶν αἰώνων. αμην. Ist. and 129 add σου after ὄνομα; both omit νῦν καὶ ἀεὶ καὶ εἰς τὰς αἰῶνας τῶν αἰώνων. αμην; add τοῦ Κυρίου δεηθῶμεν. 149 omits τῷ πατρὶ καὶ τῷ υἱῷ καὶ τῷ ἁγίῳ πνεύματι. ἀμήν.
[160.] 149 inserts ὁ ἱερεὺς εὔχεται at the beginning of this line.
[161.] 149 has ἐν εἰρήνῃ.

xii.
τοῦ Κυρίου δεήθωμεν.

Κύριε ὁ Θεὸς ἡμῶν, ὁ πάντα πρὸς σωτηρίαν ἡμῖν χαρισάμενος, ὁ καὶ ἐντειλάμενος ἡμῖν ἀγαπᾶν ἀλλήλους, καὶ συγχωρεῖν ἀλλήλους τὰ πταίσματα, αὐτός[162] δέσποτα[163] φιλάνθρωπε, καὶ τοὺς δούλους τούτους[164] τὴν[165] πνευματικὴν ἀγάπην[166] ἑαυτοὺς ἀγαπήσαντας καὶ προσελθόντας <ἐν> τῷ ἁγίῳ σου θυσιαστηρίῳ[167] ὑπὸ σου ἁγιασθῆναι καὶ εὐλογηθῆναι,[168] χαρίσαι αὐτοῖς πίστιν ἀκαταίσχυντον, ἀγάπην ἀνυπόκριτον· καὶ ὡς ἐδωρήσω τοῖς ἁγίοις σου μαθηταῖς καὶ ἀποστόλοις τὴν σὴν εἰρήνην καὶ τὴν σὴν ἀγάπην, καὶ τούτοις παράσχου Κύριε[169] ὁ Θεὸς ἡμῶν, ὁδήγησον[170] αὐτοὺς ἐν παντὶ ἔργῳ ἀγαθῷ.[171]

ὅτι ἐλέημων καὶ[172] φιλάνθρωπος Θεὸς ὑπάρχεις· καὶ σοὶ τὴν δόξαν[173] ἀναπέμπομεν, τῷ πατρὶ καὶ τῷ υἱῷ καὶ τῷ ἁγίῳ πνεύματι. ἀμήν.

ἐλέησον[174] ἡμᾶς, ὁ Θεὸς, κατὰ τὸ μέγα σου ἔλεος·[175]

δεόμεθα σου·[176]

xiii.
ἔτι δεόμεθα ὑπὲρ τῶν γενομένων ἀδελφῶν ὅδεινα καὶ ὅδεινα ἐλέους, ὑγείας, ζωῆς, καὶ σωτηρίας, καὶ ἀφέσεως τῶν ἁμαρτιῶν[177] εἴπομεν.

ὅτι ἀγαθὸς καὶ φϊλάνθρωπος Θεὸς ὑπάρχεις, καὶ σοὶ[178] τὴν δόξαν ἀναπέμπομεν.

---

162. Other versions add here καὶ νῦν.
163. Other versions add here κύριε φιλάγαθε καί.
164. Other versions add here σου.
165. 149 has here τοὺς.
166. Other versions read πνευματικῇ ἀγάπῃ.
167. Other versions read ναῷ τούτῳ (omitting σου).
168. Other versions omit ἁγιασθῆναι καί.
169. Other versions read Χριστε.
170. 149 has ὁδηγῶν.
171. 1552 ends δωρούμενος αὐτοῖς πάντα τὰ πρὸς σωτηρίαν αἰτήματα καὶ ζωὴν τὴν αἰώνιον.
172. 149 adds here ὁ.
173. 149 omits the καί of this line and omits the words after δόξαν.
174. 149 adds εἶτα ἄρχεται ὁ ἱερεύς· before this line.
175. 149: ἔλεος σου.
176. 149 omits this line.
177. 149 adds αὐτῶν.
178. 149 ends this line here.

xiv.

τροπάριον ἦχος πλ. β '.[179]

xv.

Τῷ συνδέσμῳ ταῖς ἀγάπαις συνδεόμενοι οἱ αὐτάδελφοι τῷ δεσπόζοντι τῶν ὅλων ἑαυτοὺς Χριστῷ ἀναθέμενοι, ὡραίους πόδας ἐξατενίζοντες[180] εὐαγγελιζόμενοι πᾶσιν εἰρήνην.

καὶ ἀσπάζονται τὸ ἅγιον εὐαγγέλιον καὶ ἀλλήλους καὶ ἀπόλυσις.[181]

[179.] These words are in the margin; 149, which places them in the text, adds καὶ ψάλουν; see also Istanbul 615, Dmitrievskij, p. 744.

[180.] 149 has ἐξατενίζοντο.

[181.] 149 ends καὶ γίνεται ἀπόλυσις καὶ ἀσπάζονται τὸ ἅγιον εὐαγγέλιον καὶ ἀλλήλους καὶ ἀπέρχονται.

JEWISH PERSPECTIVES

*B*ECAUSE JEWS HAVE BEEN observers (and often shapers) of nearly every European culture from antiquity to modern times, and have left abundant records of their observations, it seems worth offering a few observations on Jewish remarks about same-sex behavior. I find it inescapable under the circumstances to make some assessment of general Jewish attitudes on the subject, since they are obviously germane to the accuracy of record-keeping about this sometimes controversial subject. For mainstream Judaism the physical posterity of the seed of Abraham has been paramount for millennia, and one might therefore suppose that there would be little room in Jewish thought for same-sex eroticism.[1] But most great Greek and Roman families perpetuated themselves amply while tolerating same-sex eroticism, apparently because most adult males have more than enough semen to spend with their wives for children and with other consorts —male or female—for pleasure.[2] (By contrast, primitive cultures tended to believe that human seed is a fixed and limited commodity.)[3] Of course no ancient families—Jewish or Gentile—lasted forever; no human families do, regardless of their ethical view of homosexual behavior.

[1.] The role of eroticism, even between husband and wife, receives widely varying treatment in the Jewish tradition, sometimes from the same author. Nachmanides opined that "sexual intercourse is held distant and in contempt in the Torah unless it is for the preservation of the human species, and therefore where there can be no offspring, it is forbidden. Similarly, where the child born therefrom will not have a healthy existence, nor succeed from it, the Torah prohibited such a union," *Commentary on the Torah, Leviticus*, trans. Charles Chavel (New York, 1974), 247–48; but cf. ibid., p. 257: "Rabbi Abraham Ibn Ezra commented, 'For there is a threefold purpose to sexual intercourse: one is to beget children, a second is to relieve the body of its fluids, and the third is for passion, which is likened to that of the animals.'" Obviously, this contradicts what went before.

[2.] See Chapter 2 on ancient marriage patterns. The idea that homosexuality or any other extramarital sexuality led to the dying out of the Roman aristocracy is patently false, and is not taken seriously by any modern historians. A cursory glance at Chapter 2 should alert the reader to the fact that, until Augustus, extramarital sex was the *norm* for both Greek and Roman males.

[3.] See, for example, G. Herdt, *Guardians of the Flutes: Idioms of Masculinity* (New York, 1981), *Ritualized Homosexuality* in Melanesia (Berkeley, 1984), and *The Sambia: Ritual and Gender in New Guinea* (New York, 1987).

364

Doubtless more tolerant attitudes were held by members of the dominant cultures among whom Jews lived; some Jews may have chosen this mode to constitute a counterculture and express their divergence from the majority, although in most of the Mediterranean and Europe Jews were by their nature a counterculture, and may have clung more tenaciously to their understanding of ancient tribal values for this very reason.

Unlike the literature of nearly all other ancient peoples, the Jewish Scriptures pay little, if any, attention to same-sex eroticism.[4] Modern fundamentalists often cite passages from what Christians (somewhat simplemindedly) refer to as the "Old Testament" (as if Jews recognized any *other* Testament) as negative sanctions.[5] These isolated references were not usually interpreted by classical Jewish authorities as comments on homosexual behavior or attraction (the second was probably not even a real category to most of them). Of dozens of subsequent biblical and exegetical references to the sin of Sodom, for example, which gave its name to homosexual practices in medieval Europe, the vast majority understood the city's sin to have had to do with the breach of hospitality rather than minority sexual practices.[6] The medieval rabbinical authority Nachmanides composed a long commentary on Genesis 19, which is almost identical to the opinion of most twentieth-century commentators, arguing that the sin of the Sodomites was clearly and unequivocally a sin against hospitality, not sexual purity.

> Their [the Sodomites'] intention was to stop people from coming among them, as our Rabbis have said [N.B.], for they thought that because of the excellence of their land, which was *as the garden of the Eternal*, many will come there, and they despised charity. . . . In the opinion of our Rabbis, all evil practices were rampant among them. Yet their fate was sealed because of this sin [the fact that they 'despised charity'].[7]

Nachmanides recognized, as do many who claim Genesis 19 as a prooftext against homosexual behavior, that the story was related to that of the Benjamites in Judges 19 (". . . they were steeped in immorality and desired sexual relations with the wayfarer"), but considered the Sodomites' sin against charity much more serious: "Know and understand that the matter of the concubine of Gibeah, even though it resembles this affair [i.e., that

---

[4.] Aside from the possible case of David and Jonathan, adduced above, pp. 135–37.

[5.] Gen. 19, Lev. 18:22, 20:13, all discussed (with bibliography and a few other passages) in CSTH, pp. 91–102.

[6.] See CSTH pp. 94–99.

[7.] Ramban (Nachmanides), *Commentary on the Torah: Genesis*, trans. Charles Chavel (New York, 1971), 250–57. Rashi's earlier commentary on both Genesis and Leviticus simply ignored the possible homosexual interpretation of those passages.

of the Sodomites], does not attain the degree of evil of the inhabitants of Sodom [p. 252]."

Learned biblical scholarship has also largely rejected antihomosexual interpretations.[8] This does not, however, demonstrate that Judaic culture did not maintain profound misgivings about and taboos against homosexual behavior: it would hardly be surprising if a code as strict as the Levitical one in regard to matters like eating or dressing or observance of the Sabbath engendered some cultural horror about some forms of extramarital sexuality (but not excluding *heterosexual* concubines: see pp. 30–32).

The word ἀνδρόγυνος, which Plato had used (e.g., in *Symposium* 189D) for a biological hermaphrodite as a mythical symbol of the origins of heterosexuality, occurs in the Septuagint text of the Hebrew Scriptures, but only with the meaning "coward,"[9] although it occurred in *later* Jewish literature with a meaning resembling its original one, which must therefore have been known to some Jews.[10] For example, in the Mishnah (Sabbath, 19:3) a transliteration of ἀνδρόγυνος into Hebrew (אנדרוגינוס)[11] is employed to mean "hermaphrodite" in a biological sense, and in another passage (Bikkurim 1:5) it is contrasted with טומטום, a person of *ambiguous* gender (in the

---

8. Probably beginning with Derrick Sherwin Bailey, *Homosexuality and the Western Christian Tradition* (London, 1955), 29–63 (including discussion of Mishnaic and Talmudic treatments), but it might date further back than this: see n. 7. Bailey's arguments were supported by John McNeill, *The Church and the Homosexual* (Kansas City, 1976), and in *CSTH*, pp. 92–98. Robin Scroggs, *The New Testament and Homosexuality: Contextual Background for Contemporary Debate* (Philadelphia, 1983), especially Chapters 5 ("Palestinian Judaism: Stern Opposition") and 6 ("Hellenistic Judaism: Pederasty Vilified"), distinguished between Jewish cultic objections, which he sees as absolute, and Jewish reaction against Hellenistic sexual exploitation, which must have been situational. On pp. 13–14 he summarized (and apparently agreed with) the positions outlined by Bailey, McNeill, and *CSTH*. *The Torah: A Modern Commentary*, by the Union of American Hebrew Congregations (New York, 1981) notes that "Jewish tradition stresses social rather than sexual aberrations as the reason for the cities' destruction" (p. 133; cf. p. 135). The same commentary concedes that the "ceremonial ordinances" of Leviticus 18 in the time of their composition appear to have had the "same authority as the ethical commandments" (p. 891), but adds that "the Jewish modernist cannot agree with this" (ibid.). More recently, William Basil Zion, *Eros and Transformation: Sexuality and Marriage, An Eastern Orthodox Perspective* (New York, 1992), p. 292, concludes that "it is clear that the Hebrew tradition did not associate Sodom with homosexual sin but, rather, with sin in general. . . . The use of the term 'sodomy' to refer to a specific form of homosexual activity does not originate with the Old Testament but is a later usage."

9. E.g., Prov. 18:8 and 19:15, which do not occur in the Masoretic text, although by comparison with the rest of Proverbs (which does survive in Hebrew) one might conclude that these are clumsy Greek renderings of נפש דמיה. The Vulgate gives *effeminati* for 18:8, but *dissoluta* for 19:15, which is probably closer in meaning to דמיה.

10. See discussion of this in Wayne Meeks, "The Image of the Androgyne: Some Uses of a Symbol in Earliest Christianity," *History of Religions* 13.13 (February, 1974), 165–208, pp. 185–86.

11. Herbert Danby (*The Mishnah* [Oxford, 1933]), p. 117, renders this "androgynous"; Phillip Blackman, משניות (New York, 1963), p. 80, translates it "hermaphrodite."

context of exclusion from temple service). (The meaning of **אנדרוגינוס** is technically defined in Bikkurim 4.)[12]

The Christian authority St. Augustine, living in the same Hellenistic world shortly after the compilation of the Mishnah (354–430 C.E.), also understood ἀνδρόγυνος in this biological sense. "Androgynes," he wrote, "whom they also call Hermaphrodites,[13] although rather rare, nevertheless are hardly ever completely unknown. In them both sexes are evident, so that it is difficult to be certain which name should be applied. However, a custom of speech has prevailed that they be called after the superior sex—that is, the masculine."[14]

A few centuries later the Talmud (Hullin, 92B) credited the Gentiles with three observances of the "commandments of Noah" (the moral laws Jews of the Diaspora expected Gentiles to observe):[15] they do not draw up a marriage document (*kethubhah*) for [two] males; they do not weigh the flesh of the dead in the market; they respect the Torah. Both the first and the third are puzzling: as is evident elsewhere in this study, same-sex unions *were* known both in antiquity and the Middle Ages—how could Jewish culture have been unaware of this? Doubtless these unions took place without the sort of documentation required in Jewish law, but this, of course, was also lacking in Gentile heterosexual marriages. Moreover, no Gentiles (except for Christians, whom this passage may have had in mind)[16] respected the Torah. Conceivably, the meaning of the first law is that *kethubhah* were contracts

---

[12.] Although the tractate is based on Lev. 19:23–25, in which **אנדרוגינוס** does not occur.

[13.] Whereas ἀνδρόγυνος was an ad hoc and imprecise word to express some gender ambiguity, Hermaphroditus was a specific being, whose mythical origins were related by Ovid (*Metamorphoses* 4.285–388) and understood by most Latin writers (e.g., Martial 14:174, 10:4, 6:68).

[14.] *De civitate Dei* 16.8 (CCSL 48:509): *Androgyni, quos etiam Hermaphroditos nuncupant, quamuis ad modum rari sint, difficile est tamen ut temporibus desint, in quibus sic uterque sexus apparet, ut, ex quo potius debeant accipere nomen, incertum sit; a meliore tamen, hoc est a masculino, ut appellarentur, loquendi consuetudo praeualuit.* I am grateful to Matthew Kuefler for reminding me of this passage. Concepts of gender ambiguity, sexual passivity, and unexpected gender behavior are huge and complex in later antiquity and the Middle Ages, and too weighty to be dealt with in passing here. Mr. Kuefler is preparing a dissertation in the Yale History Department on this subject, which should clarify many of the issues.

[15.] The standard list of seven commandments is given in Sanhedrin 56a; Hullin 92a elaborates on this, specifically adding homosexuality as forbidden to Gentiles, although Nachmanides seems to have doubted that homosexual relations were prohibited except in the land of Israel itself (see his *Commentary on the Torah, Leviticus*, trans. Charles Chavel [New York, 1974], 268–75). He claims that the Canaanites (not Gentiles in general) were given to "unchastity with women, beasts and males" (ibid., *Genesis* [New York, 1971], 414), but he also interpreted the story of Sodom as specifically relating to the sin of inhospitality rather than anything sexual (ibid., p. 250: "their fate was sealed because of this sin—i.e., they did not strengthen the hand of the poor and the needy—since this sin represented their usual behavior more than any other), although he recognized the relationship between it and Judges 19:22ff.

[16.] The Talmud was composed during the period Christianity was coming to power in much of the Mediterranean. Jews were aware that Christians regarded the Hebrew Scriptures as "true"

intended for women or for families *about* women, and that Gentiles did not, among their other failings, reverse the gender roles in marriage, but this seems unlikely, because the profound horror of violating a taboo implied by the second item would lead one to expect that a comparable taboo—e.g., revulsion about homosexuality—was at issue in the first. The great rabbinical authority of the twelfth century Moses Maimonides believed that a *kethubhah* was a dowry ("the sum which the husband settles upon his wife [*kethubhah*]"),[17] which probably rarely, if ever, accompanied same-gender unions anywhere.[18]

Maimonides himself nonetheless specifically recognized the familiarity of same-sex unions among the ancients in commenting on Levitical prescriptions regarding forbidden intercourse:

> Our Sages have said, "What did they [the people of the land of Egypt] do? A man would marry a man, or a woman a woman, or a woman would marry two men."[19]

Moreover, the slightly post-Talmudic commentary in *Bereshit Rabbah* 26[20] says, "The generation of the Flood were not blotted out from the world *until* [my emphasis] they composed nuptial songs in honour of pederasty and bestiality."[21] The text uses for the last phrase (which I would render "until they wrote marriage documents for men and animals") גמומסיות, obviously derived from the Greek γάμος, and suggests strongly that this particular early medieval Jewish commentator *did* think Gentiles had drawn up documents for homosexual unions, and he adduced this as a lesson to other Jews, although

---

in some sense, even if the latter thought them to be misunderstood (rather than falsified, as Muslims would claim) by Jews.

17. Chapter 49, Book 3, pp. 113a–19d of دلالة العائرين, ed. S. ben Eleazer Munk (Paris, 1866); the text was written in the Arabic language but in Hebrew characters. The best English translation is that of Michael Friedländer, *The Guide for the Perplexed of Maimonides* (New York, 1881 and subsequent editions); I have quoted the statement above from Friedländer, p. 260.

18. Friedländer disagreed (p. 261, n. 1) with Munk's assertion that Maimonides confounded "the biblical 'dowry' given to the father-in-law with the Talmudic *kethubhah*, given to the wife."

19. *Code of Maimonides, Book of Holiness,* 1:21:8, trans. Louis Rabinowitz and Philip Grossman (New Haven, 1965), 135. Because Maimonides failed to cite his sources (and was bitterly criticized for this), it is impossible to know where he got this information, which is introduced with the phrase "Our Sages have said"—suggesting that he read it somewhere. Note that absolutely no distinction is drawn between sexual impropriety of a heterosexual or homosexual nature, and the offense in the third (ostensibly parallel) case is specifically dependent on the monogamy of heterosexual marriage.

20. Eds. J. Theodor and C. Albeck (Jerusalem, 1965) 1:248. I am grateful to Professor Bernadette Bröoten for this reference.

21. Trans. H. Freedman and M. Simon in *Midrash Rabbah, 1: Genesis* (London, 1983), 213–14.

the observation is followed by remarks about the Sodomites,[22] who were certainly *not* (on the basis of any biblical evidence) involved in permanent homosexual unions, with or without documentation.[23]

The same early and authoritative biblical commentary (*Bereshit Rabbah*—on Genesis) does, however, use the term אנדרוגינוס (ἀνδρόγυνος again) specifically in affirmation of Plato's myth.[24] Oddly, Saadia Gaon, a learned Jew living among Muslims a few centuries later, explicitly denied this, in contradiction to the Midrash tradition well-known to him.[25] Saadia said that the subject was "repulsive" (قبيحا), but no more so than discussion of the opinions of pagans (الكفار),[26] which he had already shown himself willing to discuss. He did not use the word ἀνδρόγυνος (or אנדרוגינוס), but did repeat Plato's myth:

> They maintain that God has created the spirits of His creatures in the form of round spheres, which were thereupon divided by Him into halves, each half being put into a different person. Therefore does it come about that, when a soul finds the part complementing it, it becomes irresistibly drawn to it.[27]

Saadia denied this claim—strangely and inaccurately couched in monotheistic terms—by citing thirteen biblical passages,[28] none originally relating to

---

22. And in 52:10 Esau is identified with Rome as having "made himself free to all like a field"—not precisely an image of "union" (ibid., vol. 2, p. 566). It seems likely that Jewish authorities simply associated homosexual activity with sexual licentiousness, and were not concerned to distinguish between committed relationships and license.

23. This passage recurs in "Leviticus Rabbah," 23.9 (in *Midrash Rabbah, 4: Leviticus*, trans. J. Isrealstam and J. Slotki [New York, 1983], 299). On the story of Sodom and its significance to both Jews and Christians, see *CSTH*, pp. 92–98.

24. For the text, see *Bereschit Rabba mit kritischem Apparat und Kommentar*, ed. J. Theodor (Berlin, 1912), 55; for an English version, consult *Midrash Rabbah: Genesis*, trans. H. Freedman (London, 1983), 54.

25. Saadia, b. Jûsuf al-Fajjûmî, *Kitâb al-Amânât wa'l-Itiqâdât*, ed. Samuel Landauer (Leiden, 1880), 294–96. For a dubious English rendering, not following the order of the original Arabic and often misrepresenting it, see *Saadia Gaon: The Book of Beliefs and Opinions*, trans. Samuel Rosenblatt (New Haven, 1948), 373–78. The discussion does not mention homosexuality by name, or even use the classical Arabic word for it (لواط); instead, the rubric is عشق, which normally refers to passionate love regardless of gender, and occurs more commonly in relation to heterosexual passion (see Lane, *Arabic-English Lexicon*, s.v. عشق). On the other hand, the discussion itself, related here (see especially point No. 3), makes clear that Saadia is criticizing same-gender relationships.

26. A word usually used by Arab writers only to describe pagans, not Christians, who are *dhimmi*. This suggests that Saadia had in fact seen Greek texts or a translation of them (perhaps into Arabic).

27. I have followed Rosenblatt's English here, because the Arabic is difficult to render gracefully in English. Although it is in many other places loose to the point of misleading, it is reasonably accurate here. For a somewhat narrow discussion by a nineteenth-century Jewish author, see J. Guttmann, *Die Religonsphilosophie des Saadia* (Göttingen, 1882), 268–69.

28. Job 24:12, 15, 36:13; Ps. 5:5; Num. 15:39; Hos. 7:6; Prov. 5:19; 7:23, 26, 23:26; Jer. 3:2; Ezek. 23:45; 2 Sam. 13:15.

homosexuality, and he made the following additional arguments: (1) it is inconceivable that God should use such love as a trial for humans (which it had been perceived to be even by pagans)[29] since it was prohibited by him; (2) the doctrine of the spheres, on which such ideas are drawn, is false in any event; (3) if love really arose as they claimed, "it could never happen that Zaid should love Amr [both unambiguously male names in Arabic] without Amr's reciprocation. . . . We do not, however, find the matter to be so";[30] (4) if love arises through the eyes, various biblical injunctions forbid humans from following their eyes;[31] (5–8) passionate love has disadvantages both for social status and bodily health.

Saadia's discussion may be in part designed to persuade Jews to accept the Torah's version of creation rather than Platonic or Qur'anic renderings. He might also have been reacting against the Mutazilites, a highly rationalistic sect within Islam; although they are not known to have favored Platonic myths about creation (and it seems somewhat unlikely they would), they were certainly admirers of Greek philosophy and a potent intellectual force in the environment in which Saadia wrote (in Arabic). They were ultimately repudiated even by other Muslims as too rationalistic.

His intention may also have been to discourage homosexual behavior, although it seems striking that the many biblical passages he cites have to do with improper heterosexual behavior.[32] Jews clinging to their distinctiveness from the majority culture might well have considered the prominence of homosexual behavior among Muslims scandalous and pagan, although Jews in Islamic Spain reacted rather differently, adopting overtly homosexual Arabic literary tropes, if not behavior, in the High Middle Ages.[33]

---

29. The only passages supporting this claim are Job 24:12 and Ps. 5:5, although Saadia must have known the texts of Genesis 19 and Leviticus 18 and 20 cited by modern fundamentalists, Jewish and Christian. The Latin word passio ("suffering"), from which modern English and Romance "passion" is derived, is an indication of the ambivalence even pagans felt about eroticism.

30. Rosenblatt, p. 375, with slight changes. This is a cogent argument against Plato's myth, entirely predicated on male-male eroticism, showing that Saadia was at least familiar with the phenomenon.

31. Especially Prov. 23:26 and Num. 15:39. This is a less telling objection than the preceding.

32. See n. 17.

33. Well discussed in Norman Roth, " 'Deal gently with the young man': Love of Boys in Medieval Hebrew Poetry of Spain," Speculum 57.1 (January 1982), 20–51, replacing the earlier but similar J. Schirmann, "The Ephebe in Medieval Hebrew Poetry," Sefarad 15 (1955), 55–68. More recently, see Roth, " 'Fawn of my Delights': Boy-Love in Hebrew and Arabic Verse," Sex in the Middle Ages: A Book of Essays, ed. Joyce Salisbury (New York, 1991), 157–72, and idem, "The Care and Feeding of Gazelles: Medieval Arabic and Hebrew Love Poetry," Poetics of Love in the Middle Ages, ed. Moshé Lazar and Norris Lacy (Fairfax, Va., 1989), 95–118. Neither Roth nor Schirmann is able to demonstrate whether or not such poetic effusions corresponded to real practice, which may be more related to long-standing literary debates than to this particular issue. Expressions like "boy-love" and "gazelle" might have more to do with such tropes than with actual sexual experience.

But shortly after this, the Jewish community of Europe returned to its erstwhile silence on this subject, punctuated occasionally by hostile Halachic pronouncements. It has not been until the twentieth century that a real variety of opinion about human sexuality and Jewish law has emerged.

MANUSCRIPTS
of
THE SAME-SEX UNION

MANUSCRIPTS CONSULTED CONTAINING CEREMONIES OF SAME-SEX UNION

Date[1]	Current Location	Name and No.	Folios	Published Text or Helpful Reference
8	Vatican	Barb. 336	204v–205r	See above, p. 178, n. 77.
9–10	Sinai	957	20–21	D1,[2] p. 4
10	Sinai	958	85	D3, pp. 31–32
10	Grottaferrata	Γβ VII	87–90	P,[3] pp. 130–33
10	St. Petersburg	Grec 226	114r–v	Jacob[4]
1027	Paris	Cois. 213	41r	D162, p. 998
11	Grottaferrata	Γβ II	87v–88v	- - -
11	Sinai	959	100–101[5]	D5, p. 56
11–12	Sinai	Euch. Sl.	9v–12v	F,[6] pp. 658–68
11–12	Sinai	962	127–28	D6, p. 71

[1.] Single or double-digit numbers refer to the century: e.g., "8" here means "eighth century."

[2.] Alexei Dmitrievskij, Описание литургическихъ рукописей [*Opisanie Liturgicheskix Rukopisei*], 2: *Εὐχολόγια* (Kiev, 1901 [here "D"]). The first number is Dmitrievskij's item number; the second is the page.

[3.] Gaetano Passarelli, *L'Eucologio cryptense Γ.β VII* (Thessalonika, 1982).

[4.] André Jacob, «L'Euchologe de Porphyre Uspenski. Cod. Leningr. gr. 226 (Xe siècle).» *Le Muséon: Revue d'études orientales* 78:1–2 (1965), 173–214.

[5.] Incomplete.

[6.] Rajko Nahtigal, *Euchologium Sinaiticum: Starocerkvenoslovanski Glagolski Spomenik, Slovenska Akademija Znanosti in Umetnosti v Ljubljani. Filosofsko-Filološko-Historični Razred* 1 (Ljubljana, 1941), 9b–11b, 2 (Ljubljana, 1942), 20–26, and Jean Frček, *Euchologium Sinaiticum: Texte slave avec sources grecques et traduction française*, PO 24 (Paris, 1933), 611–802; 25 (Paris, 1943), 490–616.

Date[1]	Current Location	Name and No.	Folios	Published Text or Helpful Reference
11–12	Sinai	961	86	D7, p. 82
11–12	Grottaferrata	Γβ I	128r–128v	- - -
1153	Sinai	973	113–14	D8, pp. 122–23
12	Paris	Grec 392	113v	- - -
12	Paris	Cois. 214	68	- - -
12	Vatican	Barb. 329	116–117	- - -
12	Vatican	Barb. 345	64r–65r	- - -
12	Vatican	Barb. 431	97r–98r	- - -
12	Vatican	Vat. Gr. 1552[7]	30v–31v	Giannelli, p. 132[8]
12	Vatican	Vat. Gr. 1554	111v–112v	Giannelli, p. 139
1147	Vatican	Vat. Gr. 1811	52–54	Canart, p. 186[9]
12	Vatican	Vat. Gr. 1872	141r–142v	Canart, p. 425
12	Vatican	Vat. Gr. 1875	100v–102	Canart, p. 432
12	Paris	Grec. 330	173–75	F, p. 663
12–13	Sinai	1036	57–58	D12, p. 147
13[10]	Grottaferrata	Γβ VI	101	- - -
13	Vatican	Barb. 293	51v–55r	- - -
13[11]	Vatican	Barb. 443	155v	- - -
13	Vatican	Vat. Gr. 1840	3r–v	Canart, p. 294
13	Patmos	104	30–31, 53–54	D14, pp. 156–57
13	Patmos	105	4–5	D17, p. 160
13	Laura[12]	St. Athan. 189	17	D20, pp. 179–80
13	St. Petersburg[13]	Ant. Euch.	26–28	D21, p. 190
13	Sinai	960	39	D22, p. 196
13	Sinai	966	82–85	D23, p. 215
13	Sinai	982	61–?[14]	D25, p. 237
13/14[15]	Grottaferrata	Γβ III	159v–161v	- - -
13–14	Sinai	971	93–96	D28, p. 251

[7]. Olim, 1503.

[8]. *Codices Vaticani graeci: Codices 1485–1683*, ed. Cyrus Giannelli (Vatican City, 1950).

[9]. *Codices Vaticani graeci: Codices 1745–1962*, ed. Paul Canart (Vatican City, 1970).

[10]. Imperfect: only beginning of ceremony; MS ends.

[11]. Ceremony itself more recent than this, according to Jacob, p. 192; but fragmentary.

[12]. Mt. Athos.

[13]. Dmitrievskij says (p. 188) that this MS was owned by the head of the Russian mission to Jerusalem.

[14]. Defective.

[15]. Thirteenth century, according to Goar; fourteenth, according to Antonio Rocchi (*Codices Cryptenses seu Abbatiae Cryptae Ferratae in Tusculano* [Tusculanum, 1883]), a more reliable authority.

Date[1]	Current Location	Name and No.	Folios	Published Text or Helpful Reference
14	St. Petersburg	Hilferding 21	?	M, pp. 108–10[16]
14	Sinai	981	203–4	D39, p. 343
?[17]	Laura	St. Athan. 7	73–74	D47, p. 365
14–15	Paris	Grec 324	108–9	F, p. 661
15	Istanbul[18]	8(182)	57–59	D64, pp. 466–67
?15	Belgrade	10	?	S, pp. 279–84[19]
?15	Serbia	52	?	S, pp. 276–79[20]
15	Mt. Athos	Kost. 19(20)	106	D66, p. 498
15	Mt. Athos	Pantel. 364	15–17	D71, p. 569
15	Sinai	972	420–21	D72, p. 578
15	Mt. Athos	Xiro. 51	79–80	D87, p. 659
15–16[21]	Mt. Athos	Phil. 164	173–74	D88, p. 661
?[22]	Sinai	977	277–78	D94, p. 710
1522	Istanbul	615(757)	293–96	D96, pp. 743–44
1522	Mt. Athos	L. Athan. 129	63–64	D97, p. 747
16[23]	Mt. Athos	Pantocr. 149	97–100	D65, p. 489
1542	Athens University	94	25–26	D103, p. 788
16	Mt. Athos	Pantel. 780	60–62	D120, p. 831
16	Mt. Athos	Kost. 60	71–72	D124, pp. 854–55
16	Sinai	989	311–313	D129, p. 897
16[24]	Patmos	Pat. 703	20–23	D141, p. 920
16	Mt. Athos	Cout. 358	57r–58v	D145, p. 925
16–17	Jerusalem ?	568[25]	224	D152, p. 948
16–17	Mt. Athos	Cout. 341	160–63	D154, p. 953

16. M. Milićević, "Од васкрс адо Петрових Подлада," *Живот Срба сељака, Српски етнографски Зборник*, I (Belgrade, 1894), 108–10. Milićević identified the manuscript as "Hilferding 21." A. F. Gil'ferding was a nineteenth-century historian of the Western and Southern Slavs whose collection of manuscripts was given to the St. Petersburg Public Library (now the Russian National Library). The collection is listed as belonging to Fund 182 in N. F. Bel'chikov, Iu. K. Begunov and N. P. Rozhdestvenskij, Справочник-указатель Печатных Описаний Славяно-русских Рукопицей (Moscow-Leningrad, 1963), 106, with bibliographical reference to Труды Отдела древнерусской литературы Академии наук СССР 15 (1958), 409–17. I have not been able to confirm that this manuscript is part of the collection as listed.

17. 12? 14?

18. Holy Sepulcher Library.

19. P. Srećković, **Чинь братотворению»**, *Гласник Српскога Ученог Друштва*, 63 (1885), 279–84.

20. See preceding note.

21. The Patriarchal Institute of Thessalonika classifies this as sixteenth century.

22. Dmitrievskij: 1516? Murad Kamil, *Catalogue of All Manuscripts in the Monastery of St. Catherine on Mount Sinai* (Wiesbaden, 1970), dates it fifteenth century.

23. The Patriarchal Institute of Thessalonika considers this fifteenth century.

24. But the ceremony itself is fifteenth century, according to Dmitrievskij.

25. Dmitrievskij describes this manuscript as No. 568 in the library of the monastery of Savra Osvyaschenny; in his day part of the Patriarchate of Jerusalem collection (see p. 295).

THE PASSION

of

SS. SERGE AND BACCHUS

The Passion of SS. Serge and Bacchus

Translated from the Greek "Passio antiquior SS. Sergii et
Bacchi Graece nunc primum edita," *AB* 14 (Brussels, 1895),
373–395. This text is apparently the Greek original of the
Latin passion beginning "Imperante Maximiano tyranne,
multus error hominum genus possederat," printed in the *Acta
sanctorum*, October 7, 865–79, and is more ancient than the
more common account of "Metaphrastes." For a more
precise dating, see above, p. 147, n. 172.

(1)[1] Under the rule of the emperor Maximian[2] gross superstition held sway
over the human race,[3] for people worshiped and made sacrifices to stones and

---

[1.] About seventeen of the MS versions of the Bibliothèque Nationale contain Metaphrastes (see
above, p. 154, n. 202) as against three containing the Antiquior; in the Vatican there are
seven of Metaphrastes and only one of the Antiquior. The Latin version departs significantly
from the Greek text at many points. The oldest MS is eleventh century. Manuscripts:
1.B.N..graec. No. 1540 {11–15} [basis of this ed.] fols. 10r–18r; 2.B.N..graec. No. 520 {11} fols.
65b–68b; 3.B.N..graec. No. 1468 {11} [used to suppl. 1540 for defective fols. 14–18] fols. 95r–
104v; 4.Bodl. Laudianus No. 68 {11} fols. 63r–72v.; 5.Bodl. Clarke No. 43 {12} fols. 336–446;
6.Vat. 866 {11/12} fols. 40–45.

[2.] Generally taken to be the emperor Maximian (286–305, 306–8), who was in the East in 296–
297 during the Persian Wars. The editor argues on p. 375, n. 6. that the reference is to
Maximin, [sic], ruler in Syria from 305 to 313, because the widespread persecution of Christians described in the account did not take place until the opening of the fourth century, but
the description does not seem to me to be one of "widespread persecution"—simply normal
late Roman hostility to Christianity.

[3.] This description of persecution in the East is remarkably like that of Eusebius *De martyribus
Palaestinae* 9, 2 (*PG* 20:1491), even in Greek, though this has not been noted by previous
scholars or writers. Eusebius has ". . . everyone, men with their wives and servants and
suckling children, was made responsible for sacrifice and offering to them [sc. the idols] and—
worst of all—for eating the meat offered them." The eating of "polluted" meat is further
emphasized by Severus of Antioch in his Syriac homily (see above, p. 147, n. 172, and p. 155).

wood, the devices of human beings, and they consumed obscene offerings.[4]
Those unwilling to sacrifice were subjected to torture and harsh punishment
and compelled to serve the demons.[5] A decree [to this effect] with severe
threats was posted in the markets of every city. The purity of the air was
defiled with the diabolical smell from the altars and the darkness of idola-
trous error was reckoned a matter of state.[6]

It was then that Serge and Bacchus, like stars shining joyously over the
earth, radiating the light of confession of and faith in our Savior and Lord
Jesus Christ, began to grace the palace, honored by the emperor Maximian.
The blessed Serge was the *primicerius*[7] of the school of the Gentiles, a friend
of the emperor and who had great familiarity with him, so that Maximian
promptly acceded to his requests. (2) Thus the blessed Serge, having a certain friend Antiochus, was able to arrange for him to become the governor[8]
of the province of Augusto-Euphrates.

The blessed Bacchus himself happened to be the *secundarius* of the school
of the Gentiles. Being as one in their love for Christ, they were also undivided from each other in the army of the world, united [συδεσμούμενοι][9]
not by the way of nature, but in the manner of faith, always singing and
saying, "Behold, how good and how pleasant it is for brethren to dwell
together in unity!"[10] They were adept and excellent soldiers of Christ, culti-

---

4. Cf. Acts 15.
5. Greek δαίμονας; the Latin translation has *daemonibus*. The two are not normally the same,
but here it seems likely that δαίμονας has a sense closer to the Latin than to the normal
Greek usage: the human condition.
6. πολιτεῖα τοῖς ἀνθρώποις.
7. The Latin text adds "and chief" (*et princeps*).
8. Greek δοῦκα; Latin *dux*.
9. Σύνδεσμος: a number of terms for "unite" are used in this text, often in rather general senses
(see, e.g., n. 37, below). This instance, however, is quite striking. Σύνδεσμος is not only the
strongest of the possible words for "union," or "uniting," but combines a fascinating range of
associations, all certainly familiar to the author. The most direct of these would be New
Testament phrases, many quoted or echoed in the text, especially Col. 3:14 ("charity, which
is the bond of perfectness" [ἀγάπην, ὅ ἐστιν σύνδεσμος τῆς τελειότητος]) and Eph. 4:3
("to keep the unity of the Spirit in the bond of peace" [although translators since Jerome have
taken πνεῦμα here to refer to the Holy Spirit, the sentence immediately following, in which
it clearly refers to the "spirit" of the community, casts doubt on this]). Less obvious and more
startling is the use of the word in LXX 3 Kings 14:24: καὶ σύνδεσμος ἐγενήθη ἐν τῇ γῇ,
καὶ ἐποίησαν ἀπὸ πάντων τῶν βδελυγμάτων τῶν ἐθνῶν, where the word has been taken
since Jerome to refer to homosexuality (*sed et effeminati fuerunt in terra, feceruntque omnes
abominationes gentium*; KJV [1 Kings] "And there were also Sodomites in the land: and they
did according to all the abominations of the nations"). This is likely a misprision of the
Hebrew (see Boswell, *CSTH*, pp. 98–99), but could hardly have been unknown to the author.
Other biblical passages seem less relevant: in 3 Kings 6:10 (v.l.) it is simply a unit of measure;
in 4 Kings 11:14 and 12:21 and Jeremiah 11:9 it refers to treason; in Job 41:7, Daniel 5:6, and
Col. 2:19 it stands for body parts or joints. In Daniel 5:12 it means "doubts" or "problems,"
and in Isa. 58:6 and 9 and in Acts 8:23 it is applied to the "bonds" of wickedness.
10. Ps. 133:1 (LXX 132:1).

vating assiduously the inspired writings to combat diabolical [δαιμονικῆς] error, and fighting vigorously in battle to defeat the enemy [βαρβάρων].[11]

But the malicious and evil spirit [δαίμονας] afflicted with envy some of those who had been brought to the school of the Gentiles, and they, seeing [the saints] so honorably received in the imperial chambers, so advanced in military rank, and on such familiar terms with the emperor, and being unable to bring any other instrument of malice against them, accused them to the emperor of being Christians.

(3) Waiting for a moment when the saints would not be standing near the emperor, and finding him alone, they said to him, "Such zeal for the cult of the holiest and greatest gods has your immortal majesty that in those holy rescripts of yours which are everywhere disseminated you have commanded that all unwilling to honor and worship them, and in submission to your righteous doctrine, should perish in great torment. How is it then that Serge and Bacchus, the directors of our school,[12] enjoy such familiarity with your eternal power, when they worship Christ, whom those called Jews[13] executed, crucifying him as a criminal; and by persuading many others they draw them away from the worship of the gods?[14]

When he heard this the emperor refused to believe it and said, "I do not think you speak the truth that Serge and Bacchus are not devoted to the veneration and worship of the gods, since I have such a pure affection for them, and they would hardly be worthy of it if they were not truly faithful in their piety toward the gods. (4) But if, as you say, they belong to that unholy religion, they shall now be exposed. Once I have summoned them without their knowing of the charges that have been brought against them, I will go with them into the temple of mighty Zeus, and if they sacrifice and eat of the holy offerings, you yourselves shall bear the risk of the slander of which you are guilty. If they refuse to sacrifice, they shall incur the penalty appropriate for their impiety. For the gods would not have the shield-bearers of my empire be impious and ungrateful."

"We, O Emperor," replied the accusers, "moved by zeal [πόθῳ] and affection for the gods, have brought before your undying majesty what we have

---

11. A deliberate ambiguity, of which there are many in the text: it could refer to either the enemies of the state, whom Serge and Bacchus fought as imperial officers, or to the enemies of Christianity, whom they opposed as Christians.

12. The idea that gay people would "corrupt" the minds or morals of children entrusted to their care as students ultimately became a hallmark of modern Western antigay lore, as evident in such literary works as Lillian Hellman's *The Children's Hour*, and many campaigns to keep gay literature or teachers out of public schools. In Serge and Bacchus' time, however, no such prejudice was known: they were suspect rather as Christians.

13. An odd expression, suggesting the emperor is unfamiliar with Jews, which seems unlikely. Here the λεγόμενοι might in fact refer to what the Jews said about Jesus, but below (s. 8) the meaning is clearly "those called Jews," and I have therefore rendered it so here as well.

14. On "schools" and "recruiting" see n. 12.

heard regarding them. It is for your unfailing wisdom to discover their impiety."

Straightaway the emperor sent for them. They entered with the customary retinue of guards and imperial pomp. The emperor received them and went in their company to the temple of Zeus. Once he had entered, Maximian offered libations with the whole army,[15] partook of the sacrificial offerings, and looked around. He did not see the blessed Serge and Bacchus. (5) They had not gone into the temple, because they thought it impious and unholy to see them offering and consuming unclean sacrifices. They stood outside and prayed as with one mouth, saying, "King of Kings and Lord of lords, who alone possess immortality and inhabit unapproachable light, shed light on the eyes of their minds, because they walk in the darkness of their unknowing; they have exchanged your glory, uncorruptible God, for the likeness of corruptible men and birds and beasts and snakes; and they worship the created rather than you, the creator. Turn them to knowledge of you, that they may know you, the one true God, and your only-begotten Son, our Lord Jesus Christ, who for us and for our salvation suffered and rose from the dead, that he might free us from the bonds [κατάρας] of the law and rescue us from the folly of vain idols. Preserve us, God, pure and spotless in the path of your martyrs, walking in your commandments."

While this prayer was yet in their mouths, the emperor sent some of the guard standing near him and commanded them to be brought into the temple. (6) When they had entered, the emperor said to them, "It appears that, counting on my great friendship and kindness—for which the gods have been your defenders and advocates[16]—you have seen fit to disdain imperial law and to become deserters and enemies of the gods. But I will not spare you if indeed those things spoken of you prove to be true. Go, then, to the altar of mighty Zeus, make sacrifice and consume, like everyone else, the mystical offerings."

In reply the noble soldiers of Christ, the martyrs Serge and Bacchus, answered: "We, O Emperor, are obliged to render to you earthly service of this corporal body; but we have a true and eternal king in heaven, Jesus the Son of God, who is the commander of our souls,[17] our hope and our refuge of salvation. To him every day we offer a holy, living sacrifice, our thoughtful worship. We do not sacrifice to stones or wood, nor do we bow to them. Your gods have ears, but they do not hear the prayers of humans; just as they have

---

15. Probably the imperial guard; but στρατεύματι could refer to the "host" of worshippers.

16. This paragraph, like much of the narrative, relies heavily on military metaphor: "counting on" is τεθαρρηκότες, "taking courage from"; "defender" is ὑπερασπίζοντες, "protecting with a shield"; "advocate" is πρόξενος, a technical word denoting a foreigner with special privileges from the state.

17. Literally, "whom our souls serve," "serve" being the particular verb for military service (στρατεύω).

noses but do not smell the sacrifice brought them, have mouths but do not speak, hands but do not feel, feet but do not walk. 'They that make them,' as the Scripture says, 'are like unto them: so is every one that trusteth in them because Thou are with us.' "[18]

(7) The emperor's countenance was transformed with anger; immediately he ordered their belts cut off, their tunics and all other military garb removed, the gold torcs taken from around their necks, and women's clothing placed on them; thus they were to be paraded through the middle of the city to the palace, bearing heavy chains around their necks. But when they were led into the middle of the marketplace the saints sang and chanted together, "Yea, though we walk through the valley of the shadow of death, we will fear no evil,[19] Lord"; and this apostolic saying: "Denying ungodliness and worldly lusts,[20] and putting off the form of the old man,[21] naked in faith we rejoice in you, Lord, because you have clothed us with the garment of salvation, and have covered us with the robe of righteousness; as brides you have decked us with women's gowns and joined us together for you [or: "joined us to you"] through our confession.[22] You, Lord, commanded us, saying, 'Ye shall be brought before governors and kings for my sake. . . . But when they deliver you up, take no thought how or what ye shall speak: for it shall be given you in that same hour what ye shall speak. For it is not ye that speak, but the Spirit of your Father which speaketh in you.'[23] (8) Rise, Lord, help us and rescue us for your name's sake; strengthen our souls that we may not be separated from you and the impious may not say, 'Where is their God?' "[24]

When they reached the palace Maximian summoned them and said, "Most wicked of all men, so much for the friendship which I had bestowed on you, thinking you to have proper respect for the gods, and which you, confident of my openness and affection, have despised, brazenly offering me in return that which is against the law of obedience and subjection. But why

---

[18.] Ps. 135:18 [LXX 134:18]; reading αὐτοῖς with MSS 4 and 5 instead of printed αὐτῶν.

[19.] Ps. 23:4 [LXX 22.4] with the singular "I" changed to "we."

[20.] Tit. 2:12.

[21.] Cf. Col. 3:9.

[22.] Extremely difficult to translate: ἁρμοσάμενος, "joined together," usually refers to giving in marriage, a sense which can hardly be wanting here, considering the preceding context and the fact that this is the usage of the LXX (Prov. 19:14) and New Testament (2 Cor. 11:2). To whom are Serge and Bacchus to be given in marriage? Either "to each other" or "to you" (i.e., to God) are possible grammatical constructions of the ἑαυτῷ that follows. The occurrence just after of εἰς σέ seems to militate against reading ἑαυτῷ as meaning the same thing; such a pleonasm would be not be consistent with the author's style. On the other hand, in s. 2 ἀλλήλων is used to express "each other." In 2 Cor. 11:2 it is to Christ that Paul has given the church; but here it is Christ who is giving the bride. Either interpretation is striking, given the genders involved. The Latin gives *conjunge nos tibi per confessionem*: "join us to you through confession." This may be a softening of the image, but not necessarily, especially if the writer intended to evoke associations of *conjunx, conjuga*.

[23.] Matt. 10:18–20. The quotation has been shortened, as is indicated by the ellipsis.

[24.] Ps. 79:10 [LXX 78:10]; cf. 115:2 [LXX 113:10]; Joel 2:17.

should you blaspheme the gods as well, through whom the human race enjoys such abundant peace? Do you not realize that the Christ whom you worship was the son of a carpenter, born out of wedlock of an adulterous mother, whom those called Jews executed by crucifixion, because he had become the cause of dissensions and numerous troubles among them, leading them into error with magic and claiming to be a god? The very great race of our gods were all born of legal marriage, of the most high Zeus, who is thought to be the most holy, giving birth through his marriage and union [μίξει] with the blessed Hera.[25] I imagine that you will have also heard that the heroic and twelve greatest labors were worthy of a god, those of heavenly Hercules, born of Zeus."[26]

(9) The noble soldiers of Christ answered, "Your majesty is mistaken. These are myths that ring in the ears of the simpler men and lead them to destruction. He whom you say to have been born of adultery as the son of a carpenter, he is God, the son of the True God, with and through whom was all made. He established the heavens, he made the earth, the abyss and the great sea he bounded with sand, he adorned the heavens with the multitude of stars, the sun he invented for the illumination of the day and as a torch in the night he devised the moon. He divided the darkness from the light, he imposed measure on the day and limits on the night, in wisdom he brought forth all things from nonbeing to being. In these last days he was born upon the earth for the salvation of humankind, not from the desire of a man, nor the desire of the flesh, but from the Holy Spirit[27] and an ever-virgin girl, and living among humans he taught us to turn from the error of vain idols and to know him and his father. (10) He is true God of true God, and in accord with an unknowable plan he died for the salvation of the human race,[28] but he plundered hell and rose on the third day in the power of his divinity, and he established incorruptibility and the resurrection of the dead to eternal life."

Beside himself with rage on hearing these things, the emperor ordered

---

25. The genitive absolute with γεγεννημένου here would normally suggest that Zeus had been born of Hera, but it is hardly likely that even a Christian polemicist of later ages would make such an error, so I have rendered the phrase to accord with the facts rather than the grammar. The manuscripts exhibit considerable variation in these sentences. One Latin text reads, "The greatest race of our gods was born of the legitimate marriage of Jove. The great gods Jupiter and Saturn are honorably named from [his?] union with the blessed Juno." Another manuscript offers a less confused view of the Roman pantheon (AASS [see headnote, p. 375], pp. 865–66).

26. The text appears to be corrupt: Οἶμαι δὲ ὅτι καὶ τοὺς ἡρωικοὺς καὶ μεγίστους δώδεκα ἄθλους θεοπρεπεῖς ὄντας, τοὺς ἐκ τοῦ Διὸς γεγεννημένου θεοῦ Ἡρακλέως . . . Hercules was a demigod, although much venerated in the ancient world.

27. Note the parallel here between the birth of Christ and the love between Serge and Bacchus: neither was occasioned by "nature," in the sense of ordinary human reproduction. Both were brought about by πνεῦμα, in one sense or another. Cf. sec. 2, above.

28. The Latin omits this clause and reads instead, "And if according to the flesh the Jews killed Christ, he nevertheless conquered hell . . ." This is clearly a later anti-Semitic interpolation.

that their accusers be enrolled in their positions in the army and said to them, "I am sending you to Duke Antiochus, thrice-cursed ones—the very man you were able to promote to such rank because of the friendship and familiarity you had with me—so that you will realize how great is the honor you have lost by speaking against the gods and how trivial a court you merit for the worst punishments, since the greatness of the gods has apprehended and brought your blasphemy to the judgment seat for justice."

Immediately he sent them to Duke Antiochus, ordering that their entire bodies be bound[29] with heavy chains, and that they be sent thus to Eastern parts through a succession of officials.[30] (11) He also wrote a letter along these lines: "From Maximian, eternal emperor and triumphant ruler of all, greetings to Duke Antiochus. The wisdom of the greatest gods is unwilling that any men should be impious and hostile to their worship, especially shield and spear-bearers of our empire. Wherefore I commend to your severity the vile Serge and Bacchus, convicted with apposite proof of belonging to the unholy sect of the Christians and plainly deserving of the worst punishment, whom I consider unworthy of the administration of imperial justice. If they should be persuaded by you to change their minds and sacrifice to the gods, then treat them with their own innate humanity, free them from the prescribed torments and punishments, assure them of our forgiving kindness and that they will receive back immediately their appropriate military rank and be better off now than they were before. But if they will not be persuaded and persist in their unholy religion, subject them to the severest penalties of the law and remove from them hope of long life with the penalty of the sword. Farewell."

The same day the officials took them out of the city as far as the twelfth mark, and when evening overtook them they stopped at an inn. (12) About midnight an angel of the Lord appeared and said to [the saints], "Take courage and fight against the devil and his evil spirits,[31] as noble soldiers and athletes of Christ, and once you have thrown[32] the enemy put him under your feet so that when you appear before[33] the king[34] of glory we, the host of the army of angels, may come to greet you singing the hymn of victory, conferring on you the trophies of triumph and the crowns of perfect faith and unity."[35]

[29.] δεθέντας: yet another form for "bound"; cf. nn. 9 and 37.

[30.] Or possibly, "through a succession of way stations": δι' ἀμοιβαίων τῶν τάξεων. Cf. editor's note No. 1, p. 383.

[31.] τῶν πονηρῶν αὐτοῦ πνευμάτων; note yet another use of πνεῦμα.

[32.] καταπλαίω: a wrestling term.

[33.] Literally, "come to be seen by."

[34.] Literally, "emperor": the same word used for Maximian. I have translated it as "king" because "King of Glory" is the standard English equivalent of this phrase.

[35.] ὁμολογίας: referring to their unity with God, with the church, with each other, or perhaps all three.

When morning came they rose and took the road with great joy and alacrity. There were also some of their household servants with them,[36] united with[37] them in longing for the love [ἀγάπης] of Christ, and in true love[38] for their corporal masters, on account of which they would not leave them when they were in such straits. They heard them discussing with each other the appearance of the angel in the night.[39]

Taking the road, the two chanted psalms together and prayed as if with one mouth, thus, "We have rejoiced in the way of martyrdom, as much as in all riches. We will meditate in thy precepts and search out[40] thy ways. We will delight ourselves in thy statutes: we will not forget thy word. Deal bountifully with thy servants, that we may live and keep thy word."[41]

(13) As the emperor had commanded, the soldiers of Christ were sent from city to city through a succession of changing officials [τάξεων] with great security along the road of martyrdom laid down for them, until they were brought to the eparchy of Augusto-Euphrates, which was on the borders next to the people of the Saracens, to a certain fortress called Barbalisus where Duke Antiochus had his seat.

Appearing promptly before him around the ninth hour, their custodians handed over the emperor's letter and also the holy martyrs Serge and Bacchus. Antiochus rose from his dais and accepted the emperor's rescript in his purple general's cloak; when he had read it he summoned privately[42] the official in charge and told him, "Take the prisoners and secure them in the military prison, seeing that apart from the usual constraints they do not suffer anything, and do not place their feet in full manacles of wood. Bring them to the bench of my justice tomorrow, so that I can hear them at the prescribed time, according to the law." The official took them and bound [ἠσφαλίσατο] them as the duke had commanded him. (14) When it was evening, they sang together and prayed, as with one mouth, speaking thus: "Thou, Lord, brakest the heads of the dragons in the waters; thou didst cleave the fountain and the flood; thou hast set all the borders of the earth. Cast thine eye upon us, O Lord, for the enemy hath reproached us, and the foolish people have blasphemed thy holy name. Deliver not the souls of those confessing thee to men more savage than beasts, forget not the congre-

---

36. In Greek as in English the "their" leaves ambiguous whether Serge and Bacchus have one household or two.
37. Συνδεμένοι, from συνδέω: note that this is a different verb, with different connotations, from the one used to describe the "union" of Serge and Bacchus themselves. Cf. n. 9.
38. Literally, "a love potion": φίλτρῳ.
39. This is apparently introduced as a note of realism to explain how the narrator could know about the angelic appearance.
40. ἐκζητήσομεν for LXX κατανοήσω.
41. Ps. 119 [LXX 118]: 14–17, with the singular "I" changed to "we" throughout. Cf. preceding note.
42. The Latin version takes "privately" with "read."

gation of thy poor forever. Have respect unto thy covenant: for the dark places of the earth are full of the habitations of cruelty. Let us not be returned humbled, ashamed: so that we, thy humble servants, may praise thy name.[43] (15) Forget not the voice of thine enemies: the pride of them that hate thee ascendeth continually against us, thy servants,[44] and in vain have the people hated us. But do thou, O Lord, rescue us and free us for thy name's sake."

Then, while they slept for a while, an angel of the Lord appeared to them and said, "Take heart, stand fast and unmovable in your faith and love [ὁμολογίᾳ]. It is God who aids and watches over you."

Rising from their sleep and reporting to their household the apparition of the angel, they were encouraged and began to chant again: "In my distress I cried unto the Lord, and he heard me[45] from his holy mountain. I laid me down and slept; for the Lord sustained me.[46] We will not be afraid of thousands of people, that have set themselves against us round about. Arise, Lord, and save us, O our God: for salvation belongeth unto the Lord: thy blessing is upon thy people."[47]

On the following day, when the duke was seated on the bench of justice in the praetorium, he summoned the *commentarius* and said, "Bring in the prisoners [δεσμίους]." The latter responded, "They are at hand before the righteous [καθαρῷ] bench of your authority." When the saints appeared, he commanded the emperor's letter to be read. Once this was done, Duke Antiochus, prompted by his associate, announced, "It is incumbent on you to obey the orders of the glorious emperor, our lord, and to sacrifice to the gods and become worthy of their benevolence. Since you were unwilling to do this, you have forfeited great glory, and having made yourselves unworthy, were discharged from the military and deprived of all your former wealth. Nonetheless, if you will now obey me and sacrifice to the gods to earn their goodwill, you could earn even greater honor and glory than before, and receive back your military rank and more besides.

"This was prescribed in the letter sent to me, as you yourselves have heard. Being humane, the most holy emperor has disposed that if you repent of those things you have rashly done, and now sacrifice to the gods, you may yet enjoy his favor. Wherefore I, feeling compassion for you, and mindful of your friendship and kindness—especially yours, my Lord Serge, for I myself have benefited from your generosity—advise you that if you will not do this,

---

43. Paraphrase of Ps. 73[Masoretic text: 74]: 13–21.
44. Ibid., 23.
45. Ps. 119 [Masoretic text: 120]:1.
46. Note that this is one of the few quotations from the Psalms where the singular is retained: cf. following note.
47. Paraphrase of Ps. 3:6–9 [Masoretic text: 4–8].

you force me to obey our lord the emperor and to see that his orders concerning you are strictly observed."

(17) In reply the saints declared, "We have left all and followed Christ, so that heedless of earthly and temporal honor, we may become rivals of the angels in heaven, and ignoring terrestrial and corruptible wealth, we may heap up treasure in heaven. What profit would it be if we gained the whole world, but lost our souls?[48] Do not, therefore, so advise us, Antiochus. For your tongue is forked, and the poison of adders is under your lips.[49] You will hardly be able to change our minds while God himself encourages us. Do, therefore, what you will; we will not sacrifice to wood, nor worship stones. We serve Christ, the son of God, the eternal ruler [βασιλεῖ], before whom 'every knee should bow, of things in heaven, and things on earth, and things under the earth,' and whom every tongue should confess.[50] Your gods are man-made idols: if they were divine, they themselves would command humans, and would not [need to] be avenged through human design on those who decline to serve and worship them."

(18) The duke rejoined, "We do not avenge the gods. It is through their disposition that all the powers of our enemies have been subjected to us. But we call you to justice because of your accursed and unholy superstition [ἀσεβείας]."

To which the saints responded, "It is you who are accursed and unholy, and all those persuaded by you to sacrifice to demons [δαίμοσι] and worship insensate stones and wood. All of them will soon be cast eternally into flames, and you also will be punished with them."

In a great rage the duke commanded that the blessed Serge be taken from the praetorium and returned to prison; the blessed Bacchus he ordered held for flogging. The henchmen went at this until they collapsed, exhausted and near dead on the floor. When they could go on no longer, he directed that [Bacchus] be turned over on his stomach to be beaten with four whips of rawhide, saying to him, "Let's see if your Christ will free you from my hands." From the first hour until evening they wore away his flesh; blood flowed everywhere; both his stomach and liver were ruptured.

The blessed Bacchus said to Antiochus: "The devil's servants, your torturers have failed; your impudence is overthrown; the tyrant Maximian is conquered; your father the devil has been put to shame. The more the man without is ravaged by your blows, the more the man within is renewed in preparation for the eternal life to come."

After he said this, there was a great voice from heaven: "Come, rest henceforth in the kingdom prepared for you, my noble athlete and soldier,

---

48. Cf. Matt. 16:26.
49. Paraphrase of Ps. 139:4 [Masoretic text: 140:3].
50. Phil. 2:10, with paraphrase of 2:11.

Bacchus." Those standing by hearing the voice were stupefied and struck dumb. He himself, having borne the blows so long, gave up his spirit to the angels.

The duke, frustrated by his defeat, ordered that his remains not be buried, but thrown out and exposed as meat to the dogs, beasts, and birds outside the camp. Then he rose and left. When the body was tossed some distance from the camp, a crowd of animals gathered around it. The birds flying above would not allow the bloodthirsty beasts to touch it, and kept guard through-out the night.

In the morning, some of the monks [ἀδελφῶν] who lived nearby in caves came and lifted up the body the animals—as if they were rational human beings—had been mourning.[51] They buried him in one of their caves.

Meanwhile the blessed Serge, deeply depressed and heartsick over the loss of Bacchus, wept and cried out, "No longer, brother[52] and fellow soldier, will we chant together, 'Behold, how good and how pleasant it is for brethren to dwell together in unity!'[53] You have been unyoked from me [ἀπεζεύχθης] and gone up to heaven, leaving me alone on earth, bereft [literally, "made single": μεμονωμένον], without comfort." (20) After he uttered these things, the same night the blessed Bacchus suddenly appeared to him with a face as radiant as an angel's, wearing an officer's uniform, and spoke to him. "Why do you grieve and mourn, brother? If I have been taken from you in body, I am still with you in the bond [συνδέσμῳ] of union [ὁμολογίας], chanting and reciting, 'I will run the way of thy commandments, when thou hast enlarged my heart.' Hurry then, yourself, brother, through beautiful and perfect confession[54] to pursue and obtain me, when finishing the course. For the crown of justice for me is with you."[55] At daybreak when he rose he related to those who were with him how he had seen the blessed Bacchus in the night and in what sort of garb.[56]

The next day the duke planned to go out of the fortress of Barbalisus to that of Souros, and commanded that the blessed Serge follow. He enjoined him to sacrifice, but the latter, with noble judgment, refused his blandish-ments. (21) When they reached the castle of Souros, Antiochus took his seat in the praetorium, summoned the blessed Serge, and told him, "The most sacrilegious Bacchus refused to sacrifice to the gods and chose to die vio-

---

51. Literally, "for which they had stood in funeral procession": προπεμπόμενον.

52. On the significance of this term, ἀδελφός, see above, pp. 17ff.

53. Ps. 132 [M:133]:1.

54. ὁμολογίας: also "living together," or "togetherness."

55. Possibly, "my crown of justice is to be with you": σὺν σοὶ γὰρ ἀπόκειταί μοι ὁ τῆς δικαιοσύνης στέφανος.

56. Apparently another note of realism: how the author knows about Bacchus' appearance in the vision.

lently;[57] he got the death he deserved. But you, my lord Serge, why give yourself over to such misery by following that deceptive and impious cult? Mindful of your kindness to me I am disposed to mercy; and it embarrasses me that you were the cause of my having obtained this authority, since now you stand in the dock as the accused, and I sit on the bench as the prosecutor."

To this Christ's witness answered, "Antiochus, this very suffering and present disgrace will stand as a patron for me of great eloquence and eternal glory with the king of heaven and of earth and of every living thing, Jesus Christ, the Son of God. If only you would now heed me and recognize my God and king, Christ, and be as circumspect in regard to the heavenly ruler, Christ, as you are in dealing with earthly kings, you would provide yourself with power unending and perpetual glory. (22) For earthly rulers pass quickly, as the psalm says: 'Ye shall die like men, and fall like one of the princes.'[58] And again, 'I have seen the wicked highly exalted, and lifted up like the cedars of Libanus. And I passed by, and lo, he was not: and I sought him and his place was not found.' "[59]

(23) The duke replied, "Spare us this idiocy and ignorant foolishness; sacrifice to the gods in obedience to the holy command of our ruler, the emperor Maximian. If you will not, know that you force me to forget all that has come to me through you and to subject you to the most rigorous punishment decreed by law."

Serge answered, "Do as you will. I have Christ to preserve me, who said, 'Fear not them which kill the body, but are not able to kill the soul: but rather fear him which is able to destroy both soul and body in hell.'[60] The body is subject to you: torture and punish it if you wish. But bear in mind that even if you kill my body, you can not dominate my soul—neither you nor your father, Satan."

The duke responded angrily: "It appears that my patience has served only to prod you along the path of willfulness." He summoned the official in charge and told him, "Fasten long nails in his boots, sticking straight up, and then put them on him."[61] Once the boots were on, Antiochus sat in his

---

[57.] Literally, "to become βιωθανής," a term often applied by pagans to Christ, and meaning both "one who dies violently," and "one who commits suicide." Antiochus is doubtless suggesting that Bacchus occasioned his own death through his stubbornness. The author, however, may be more concerned to evoke associations with Christ.

[58.] Ps. 81 [M:82]:7.

[59.] Ps. 36 [M:37]:35–36, Rheims-Douai Version, following the LXX; cf. KJV: "I have seen the wicked in great power, and spreading himself like a green bay tree. Yet he passed away, and lo, he was not: yea, I sought him, but he could not be found."

[60.] Matt. 10:28.

[61.] Taking συντόμως as part of Antiochus' speech, as the editor does. It seems to me possible that it was intended to describe the speech itself, in which case the reading would be "He summoned the official in charge and immediately ordered him . . ."

carriage, directed that the animals be driven fiercely all the way to Tetrapyrgium, and ordered the blessed one to run in front of him. Tetrapyrgium
is nine miles from Syrum.[62] While he ran, the blessed one sang, "I waited
patiently for the Lord, and he inclined unto me. He brought me up also out
of a horrible pagan[63] pit, out of the miry clay of idolatry,[64] and set my feet
upon a rock, and establishes[65] my goings."[66]

When they reached the castle of Tetrapyrgium the duke said, "It amazes
me, Serge, that having first been kept in such confinement you can now
sustain these bitter torments." The most holy martyr answered, "These tortures are not bitter to me, but sweeter than honey."[67] The duke got out of
the chariot and went in to breakfast, indicating that [Serge] should be retained in the soldiers' custody.

(24) In the evening [Serge] sang psalms. "Those who did eat of my bread
hath lifted up their heels against me,[68] and with the cords of hideous torture
they have laid a net for my feet,[69] hoping to trip me up. But rise, Lord,
outrun them and cause them to stumble, and rescue my soul from the
wicked." About midnight an angel of the Lord came to him and healed him,
restoring his feet completely.

In the morning, mounting the bench, the duke ordered him brought in,
thinking he would be unable to walk and would have to be carried, on
account of his feet. When he saw him coming, walking a considerable distance and not limping at all, he was astounded, and exclaimed, "The man is
a sorcerer. This must be how he managed to enjoy such familiarity with the
emperor: he accomplished it through sorcery. What I am seeing is the proof
of what they said about him. I would have thought it wholly impossible for
him to walk on his feet after having been disabled by the torture inflicted on
him yesterday. By the gods I am confounded at seeing him now walk as if
nothing had happened!"

(25) When the blessed Serge stood before the bench Antiochus addressed
him. "Come to your senses even now, sacrifice to the gods, and you will
avoid further torture. I will spare you out of respect for your kindness. If you
will not, know that the witchcraft with which you devised to heal yourself
will not avail you."

To which the blessed Serge replied, "If only you could escape the intoxi-
cation of diabolical error. I am in my senses in the Lord who has trampled

---

62. A Roman mile was about eighty yards shorter than its modern counterpart.
63. Literally, "Greek": ἑλληνικῆς. This is not in the psalm.
64. "Of idolatry" is not in the psalm.
65. Sic: imperfect. In the Psalm it is past tense.
66. Ps. 39:2–3 [M:40:1–2], with changes as noted in preceding notes.
67. Literally, "sweeter than honey and honeycomb": μέλι καί κηρίον.
68. Ps. 40:10 [M:41:9], with singular changed to plural.
69. Cf. Ps. 139:6 [M:140:5].

the weapons of your father the devil under the feet of his humble servant, and has given me victory over you, and sent his angel to heal me. It is you who are the magician, and those who worship demons [δαίμοσι]. It is the cult of your nameless idols that invented every sorcery, that is the beginning and cause and conclusion of all evil."

Antiochus sat down on his carriage even angrier, and commanded [Serge] to run before him wearing the same boots as far as the castle of Rosafae, another nine miles from Tetrapyrgium. (26) When they came to the castle of Rosafae, the duke said to the blessed Serge, "Has the agony of the nails untied the knot of your idiocy? Are you prepared now to sacrifice to the gods, or will you persist in this insane obsession?"

The noblest martyr rejoined, "Know this, Antiochus: with this foolishness I will dissolve and undo your malicious and wicked strength. Do what you will: I will not worship demons, nor sacrifice to idols. Blameless in this, I strive to offer sacrifice only to my Lord."[70]

Seeing that he remained steadfast and immovable in his faith and confession of Christ, the duke pronounced sentence against him: "You have rendered yourself unworthy of the favor of the gods, Serge, and become a member of the unholy sect called Christians, injuring the great good [τύχην] of our ruler, the emperor Maximian, by refusing to comply with his holy decree and sacrifice to the gods. For this the law requires that you suffer the penalty of the sword." A number of those present shouted out that the sentence issued against him was just. The guards came immediately and gagged his holy lips, took him out of the courtroom, and led him away to be executed.

(27) A great crowd of men, women, and children followed, to see the blessed one meet his end. Seeing the beauty blooming[71] in his face, and the grandeur and nobility of his youth, they wept bitterly over him and bemoaned him. The beasts of the region left their lairs and gathered together with the people, doing no injury to the humans, and bewailed with inarticulate sounds the passing of the holy martyr.

When they reached the place where the holy martyr of Christ was to meet his end, he called on the guards to allow him a little time to pray. Extending his hands to heaven, he said, "The beasts of the field and the birds of the sky, recognizing your dominion and rule, Lord, have gathered together for the glory of your holy name, so that you will incline and wish of your goodness to turn through their unreason the reason of humans to knowledge of you. For you wish all to be saved and to come to knowledge of the truth. When you lay death upon them, accept their repentance, Lord, and do not

---

70. I have not translated ἐν αὐτῷ, which seems to me pleonastic. Cf. textual apparatus, p. 393.
71. Reading ἐπανθοῦν, with MSS 3, 4, 5, 6. The editor prefers the ἐπαρθοῦν of 1 and 2, but this seems to me an inferior reading.

remember the sin of ignorance which they have perpetrated against us[72] for your sake. (28) Enlighten the eyes of their minds and lead them to the knowledge of you. Receive, Lord, my spirit, and give it rest in the heavenly tents with all the others whom you have found acceptable. To you do I commend my soul, which you have rescued from the snares of the devil."

Saying this and signing himself,[73] he knelt and was beheaded,[74] giving up his spirit to the angels. A voice from heaven said, "Come, also,[75] Serge, soldier and victor, to the kingdom prepared for you. The hosts of angels, the ranks of patriarchs, the choirs of apostles and prophets, the souls of the just all await your coming to share with them the wonderful things in store for you there."

The place that received the holy martyr's blood became a great chasm; God arranged this so that those who wallow like pigs in the mire of paganism [ἑλληνισμῷ], terrified when they saw the abyss, would not dare to approach or trample in this spot the blood of the holy martyr. That was the reason this great chasm came into existence, and the spot has remained so up to the present day, bearing the signs [γνωρίσματα] of great antiquity at the command of God, to establish the miracle visually for unbelievers, so that they may build on it a firm foundation of faith.

(29) Some of those who had come to witness the death of the holy martyr, seeing that they shared a common nature [with him], gathered up his remains and buried them handsomely where the holy one had died. After a great while some religious men from the castle of Souros, prompted by zeal for the service of Christ, but pious in a somewhat piratical way, tried to steal the body from the spot, as if it were some precious treasure. The saint would not suffer his body, which had been dragged around, whipped, and triumphed so publicly in the faith of Christ, to be moved in secret, so he asked of God that a fire be set in the spot, not to seek revenge on those attempting the theft or to burn them, but so that by lightening the gloom of night he would reveal the robbery to those in the castle of Rosafae, which is just what happened. Once the fire was burning in the place where the saint lay, some of the soldiers living there[76] saw the flames reaching to the sky, and thought that the great blaze had been set by some enemy, so they came out armed and pursued those attempting to steal the saint's body. They prevailed[77] on them to remain there a few days and to build from stones and clay a tomb

---

72. Presumably Serge and Bacchus, since Serge does not use the plural as a convention of speech.

73. σφραγίσας ἑαυτόν: making the sign of the cross?

74. ἀπετμήθη τὴν κεφαλήν.

75. δεῦρο καὶ σύ: presumably in addition to Bacchus; cf. n. 72.

76. I.e., in the castle of Rosafae.

77. In the Greek, as in the English, it is not perfectly clear who prevails upon whom. It seems most likely that it is the soldiers who constrain the would-be thieves.

where he lay. Once they had honorably covered the body of the saint, they went away.

(30) After a time, when the religion of our Lord and Savior Jesus Christ had begun to flourish, some very holy bishops—fifteen in number—gathered together and constructed near the castle of Rosafae a shrine worthy of [Serge's] confession, and moved his remains there, installing them in the shrine on the very day he was martyred: the seventh of October.

Many miracles and cures were effected wherever his holy relics were, especially in the tomb where he had first lain. For it is a quality of the place of his death that the saint is able to prevail upon God to heal all those who come there with any sort of disease, and to cure those possessed of unclean spirits [πνευμάτων], and to render savage beasts completely tame. The animals, in fact, observe the day of his death every year as if it were a law, coming in from the surrounding desert and mingling with the humans without doing them any harm, nor do their savage impulses move them to any violence against the humans who come there. Rather, they come to the place in gentleness out of reverence for the holy martyr, at the command of God, to whom be glory, honor, and power, now and for ever. Amen.

INDEX